SENTENCING

Second Edition

Canadian Legal Textbook Series

CARROTHERS: *Collective Bargaining Law in Canada*

WILLISTON AND ROLLS: *The Law of Civil Procedure*

SACK AND LEVINSON: *Ontario Labour Relations Board Practice*

SOPINKA AND LEDERMAN: *The Law of Evidence in Civil Cases*

FEENEY: *The Canadian Law of Wills-Probate*

The Canadian Law of Wills-Construction

CASTEL: *Canadian Conflict of Laws (2 volumes)*

RUBY: *Sentencing (Second Edition)*

WILLIAMS: *The Law of Defamation*

JOHNSTON: *Canadian Securities Regulation*

LINDEN: *Canadian Tort Law*

SCHIFFER: *Mental Disorder and The Criminal Trial Process*

PALMER: *Labour Arbitration in Canada*

REID AND DAVID: *Adminstrative Law and Practice (Second Edition)*

SENTENCING
Second Edition

CLAYTON C. RUBY

B.A., LL.B., LL.M.

of the Ontario Bar

TORONTO

BUTTERWORTHS

CANADA:	BUTTERWORTH & CO. (CANADA) LTD. TORONTO: 2265 Midland Avenue, Scarborough, M1P 4S1
UNITED KINGDOM:	BUTTERWORTH & CO. (PUBLISHERS) LTD. LONDON: 88 Kingsway, WC2B 6AB
AUSTRALIA:	BUTTERWORTH PTY. LTD. SYDNEY: 586 Pacific Highway, Chatswood, NSW 2067 MELBOURNE: 343 Little Collins Street, 3000 BRISBANE: 240 Queen Street, 4000
NEW ZEALAND:	BUTTERWORTHS OF NEW ZEALAND LTD. WELLINGTON: 77-85 Custom House Quay, 1
SOUTH AFRICA:	BUTTERWORTH & CO. (SOUTH AFRICA) (PTY.) LTD. DURBAN: 152/154 Gale Street

Canadian Cataloguing in Publication Data

Ruby, Clayton C., 1942-
  Sentencing

(Canadian legal text series)

Includes index.

ISBN 0-409-86421-8

1. Sentences (Criminal procedure) — Canada.
I. Title. II. Series.

KE9355.R83 1980   345.71′0772   C79-094934-2

To

My Mother
My Father and
Alexander Berkman

Preface and Acknowledgements

The second edition of *Sentencing* not only provides many more cases which elucidate the principles and practice of sentencing in Canada, but it also slightly reorganizes the text of the first edition and tightens up some of the infelicities of that text as well.

Chapters 15 and 16 of the first edition, on Indeterminate Sentences and the Sentence of Death, have been deleted, for obvious reasons, from this edition. The former chapter on the Royal Prerogative of Mercy is now part of the chapter on Discharge. The Range of Sentence chapter has expanded greatly as I continue to collect evidence on the scope and, sometimes, the conflicts, lacunae, irrationalities and archaisms of the practice of sentencing.

Sentencing is more often dealt with inadequately by counsel than any other recurring aspect of a criminal trial. There is little of the excitement that characterizes much of criminal law and much is discretionary. However, the principles controlling the exercise of that discretion are not obscure; they are merely unknown among the profession. Every practitioner keeps a few cases of note tucked away in the back of his mind, but this is hardly an adequate approach to a sentencing problem.

The text attempts to canvass the law of sentencing, but not all cases have been included. The object has been, where possible, to set out and analyze principles, so that more effective submissions can be made with a view to assisting the sentencing judge.

English cases have been relied on, where applicable, for principle and procedures; but so far as quantum of sentence is concerned, it must be remembered that England has a different institutional system from our own and that no real comparison is possible.

The work will be kept up to date and revisions will be made from time to time, as the law of sentencing develops. The author would be grateful if members of the profession would be good enough to write in with criticism or suggestions of any sort; it is only with the help of the profession that this book can remain useful as a guide to sentencing in Canada.

The author would like to mention some of those who were good enough to assist him with argument and suggestions for this book.

Ms. Marlys Edwardh, Ms. Lyn Langford, Paul Copeland, Philip Abramson and Mel Green for doing so much of the preparatory work connected with this or any endeavour; Mr. Brian Jones for helping with the chapter on Range of Sentence; Mr. Sidney B. Linden, Ms. Marlys Edwardh, His

Honour Judge Charles Scullion of Provincial Court (Criminal Division), Province of Ontario, and His Honour Judge Robert Dneiper of the Provincial Court (Criminal Division) for reading the manuscript and making helpful suggestions; Professor Graham Parker and Ms. Harriet Sachs for struggling with the chapter on General Principles; and Statistics Canada for making available the tables of Criminal Statistics.

In addition to my gratitude to those who assisted in the preparation and criticism of the first manuscript of *Sentencing* I would like to add a further note of thanks. Mr. David Cole kindly bent his expertise to the problems with my chapter on parole. Ms. Virginia Field-Smith was good enough to solve difficult editing problems while coping with the inflexibility of my character and my trial and appellate practice.

Responsibility for the work as a whole remains, of course, the author's own.

CLAYTON C. RUBY

Toronto, Canada
January, 1980

JUSTICE

This judge is busy sentencing criminals
Of whose upbringing and environment he is totally ignorant.
His qualifications, however, are the highest —
A B.A. degree,
A technical training in law,
Ten years practice at the bar,
And membership in the right political party.
Who should know better than he
Just how many years in prison
Will reform a slum-product,
Or whether ten or twenty strokes of the lash
Will put an end to assaults on young girls?

F.R. Scott

Yet they (and there were so many of them) did what seemed so astonishing and terrible to him, with such quiet assurance that what they were doing was necessary, and was important and useful work, that it was hard to believe they were mad; nor could he — conscious of the clearness of his thoughts — believe he was mad.

Tolstoi,
Resurrection

Table of Contents

Table of Cases

Cases are listed under the name of the accused whenever the usual method of citation would cause them to be preceded by the abbreviation "R. v." signifying that the prosecution was undertaken by the Crown.

Table of Criminal Code Sections

Chapter 1

General Principles Of Sentencing

Canadian courts have been reluctant to permit philosophical or academic concepts to intrude upon the practical business of sentencing. In one sense this is sensible: the history of the application of our present sentencing concepts discloses that nothing we do has any significant effect on the problem of crime in general; all efforts seem in the long run equally futile. It is evident to all thinking practitioners of law that the causes of crime and their solutions lie not in the legal system but in society itself. But if the hard questions are not asked and the relation of jurisprudence to society is not understood we falter in our first step. At the very least, we should begin by asking: What is this business of sentencing all about?

There is little difficulty in asserting that the principal purpose of the criminal process is the protection of society.[1] One of the fundamental purposes of any sentence is to achieve this end; there is common acceptance in Canadian appellate law of this principle.[2]

But the principle begs two questions: which part of society is being protected and what kind of behaviour is criminal behaviour? Our criminal law, with its emphasis on the protection of property and its abhorrence of physical violence, may well no longer be in step with the most serious kinds of harm prevalent in Canada today. Price fixing, false advertising, income tax evasion and other corporate crimes are lightly penalized and often not prosecuted. Secondly, there is presently a wide diversity of opinion in important areas as to what kinds of behaviour

---

[1] *R. v. Morrissette* (1970), 1 C.C.C. (2d) 307 at p. 309, *per* Culliton C.J.S. (Sask. C.A.).

[2] *R. v. Wilmott,* [1967] 1 C.C.C. 171 at p. 177, *per* McLennan J.A. (Ont. C.A.).

1

warrant invocation of a criminal sanction in order to protect society. Though there may have been times when the interests of the state and the interests of the citizenry did in fact coincide, no such unity can be found today in many areas. Examples of the dislocation of law and social values are highly visible in this society, and one need look no further than at the offences of possession of marijuana and performing an abortion to realize that the problem is both serious and pervasive. If to sentence is to protect we must know whom we protect, from what and how effectively. Neither side of that equation is as self-evident as we pretend.

Two great schools of thought have contended for supremacy on the issue of the purpose of punishment; they may be characterized as the moral and the utilitarian. The moral position is one which assumes retribution is the proper object of punishment, and is best exemplified by the views of Sir James Fitzjames Stephen.[3] Here the infliction of punishment by law is the "solemn ratification and justification to the hatred which is excited by the commission of the offence." Stephen goes on to assert:

> I think it highly desirable that criminals should be hated and that the punishments inflicted upon them should be so contrived as to give expression of that hatred, and to justify it so far as the public provision of means for expressing and gratifying a healthy natural sentiment can justify and encourage it.
>
> These views are regarded by many persons as being wicked, because it is supposed that we never ought to hate, or wish to be revenged upon, anyone. . . . The expression and gratification of these feelings is however only one of the objects for which legal punishments are inflicted.

The utilitarian position on punishment argues that the sentence should deter. After his enthusiastic support of revenge Stephen proceeds to the subject of deterrence:

> Another object is the direct prevention of crime either by fear, or by disabling or even destroying the offender, and this which is I think commonly put forward as the only proper object of legal punishments is beyond all question distinct from the one just mentioned, and of coordinate importance with it. The two objects are in no degree inconsistent with each other, on the contrary, they go hand in hand, and may be regarded respectively as the primary and secondary effects of the administration of criminal justice.

It is quite clear that the two concepts are indeed separate. C. F. Lewis[4]

---

[3] J. F. Stephen, *History of the Criminal Law in England* (1883), vol. 2, pp. 80-83.

[4] C. F. Lewis, *Res Judicatae VI* (1953), p. 224.

argues that only with regard to the moral question of retribution (Stephen's "primary ground") is justice itself involved. The primary ground asks of a sentence: "Is it deserved?" and "Is it just or unjust?". He quite properly points out that asking whether or not the sentence is likely to deter others or to incapacitate, is not a question about justice.

> There is no sense in talking about a "just deterrent" or a "just cure"; we demand of a deterrent not whether it is just, but whether it will deter. . . . just when we cease to consider what the criminal deserves and consider only what will cure him or deter others, we have passively removed him from the sphere of justice altogether; instead of a person, a subject of rights, we now have a mere object, a patient, a "case".

The strength of the moral position should not be minimized but must be examined. Aside from its appeal to traditional and classical thought in criminal law, there appears in the argument a hidden presumption, namely that one of the factors that binds us together as a society is our collective ability to repudiate certain kinds of conduct. Thus society is strengthened and thereby protected when, through the medium of the criminal law, we join together to punish a wrongdoer. What distinguishes a criminal from a civil sanction is just this aspect of community condemnation.

The British Columbia Court of Appeal has said:

> Courts do not impose sentences in response to public clamour, nor in a spirit of revenge. On the other hand justice is not administered in a vacuum. Sentences imposed by Courts for criminal conduct by and large must have the support of concerned and thinking citizens. If they do not have such support the system will fail. There are cases, as Lord Denning has said, where the punishment inflicted for grave crimes should reflect the revulsion felt by the majority of citizens for them. In his view, the objects of punishment are not simply deterrent or reformative. The ultimate justification of punishment is the emphatic denunciation by the community of a crime.[5]

However the moment one goes beyond the position whereby the infliction of suffering on evildoers is justified in itself, as a "moral right", one begins to consider the "utility" of a sentence. The suggestion that punishment is also justifiable as part of the bond which holds society together and provides orderly outlets for emotions that, if denied, would manifest themselves in private vengeance is a justification on the ground of effectiveness or ability. In fact, it is very difficult to separate the two views completely except on a theoretical level.

---

[5] *R. v. Oliver*, [1977] 5 W.W.R. 344.

The classical utilitarian position was emphatically stated by John Stuart Mill in his celebrated essay, *On Liberty:*

> The only purpose for which power can rightfully be exercised over any member of a civilized community against his will is to prevent harm to others.... His own good, either physical or moral is not a sufficient warrant. He cannot rightfully be compelled to do or forbear because it will be better for him to do so, because it will make him happier, or because in the opinions of others to do so would be wise or even right.

This view stresses the effect of the punishment on the offender and others, as opposed to a focus upon the accountability of the offender to his victim and society.

The utilitarian approach measures according to this parameter the economy with which punishment is to be exercised, namely that it should be all that is required to achieve its purpose, but no more than that; if society's notions of just retribution require more, this is an impulse which should not be accepted as a guide to sentencing. A concomitant question therefore in imposing any sentence from the point of view of its utility is: Will the sanctions be effective for the purpose claimed? Further, the object of the sentence should be to take the minimum action which offers an adequate prospect of preventing future offences.[6]

A logical consequence of this position in its pure form is that all custodial sentences should be indeterminate. If the primary object of sentence is to discourage further offences at the cost of minimal interference with liberty, then the moment at which this discouragement is effective enough to justify the offender's release can hardly be forecast in advance: it must depend upon his progress. Therefore, in so far as individual deterrence is concerned, certainly, the indeterminate sentence must be accepted.[7]

The utilitarian position has taken supremacy in modern sentencing practice, but it is not without its difficulties. Deterrence, prevention and reform have achieved pre-eminence because of the conjunction of utilitarianism and a treatment ideology that is current in modern society which views crime as caused by sickness or privation, and concludes that social or *quasi*-medical intervention in the life of the criminal will prevent crime, cure the criminal and thereby protect society.

---

[6] Barbara Wootton, *Crime and Criminal Law* (London: Stevens & Sons, 1963) p. 95.

[7] *Ibid.,* pp. 112-13.

Sentencing in Canada, according to case law, combines a strange liaison of both the moral and the utilitarian positions. Generally speaking, there is agreement that in determining any sentence, regard must be had to deterrence, reformation and retribution.[8] Packer[9] suggests that the two strains of thought can be blended:

> ... I have taken a somewhat skeptical attitude towards the claim that the rehabilitation of offenders is a sufficient justification for imposing punishment. . . . The place for operation of the rehabilitative ideal is not in determining what kinds of conduct should be made criminal. However, once a decision to punish has been made and justified on other grounds, the rehabilitative ideal should be fully used in deciding what kinds of punishment should be imposed. To put it another way, the rehabilitative ideal deserves consideration in evaluating not the propriety of punishment but its severity.

It is evident that the conflicts in the case law may stem in great measure from the fact that these elements in fact cannot be blended, but are in many respects contradictory and inconsistent. Packer's formulation has at least the virtue of intellectual clarity.

A. Retribution

In some appellate jurisdictions, the idea of retribution, though once accepted, has now been rejected as a principle of sentencing. As recently as 1953, the Ontario Court of Appeal attempted to incorporate under this head both the moralistic views of Stephen and the utilitarian philosophy of sentencing:[10]

> The underlying and governing idea in the desire for retribution is in no way an eye for an eye or a tooth for a tooth, but rather that the community is anxious to express its repudiation of the crime committed and to establish and assert the welfare of the community against the evil in its midst. Thus, the infliction of punishment becomes a source of security to all and "is elevated to the first rank of benefits, when it is regarded not as an act of wrath or vengeance against a guilty or unfortunate individual who has given way to

---

[8] *R. v. Willaert* (1953), 105 C.C.C. 172 at p. 175 *per* Mackay J.A. (Ont. C.A.).
[9] H. L. Packer, *Limits of the Criminal Sanction* (Stanford: Stanford University Press, 1968) p. 67.
[10] *R. v. Willaert, supra,* n. 8 at pp. 175-76.

mischievous inclinations, but as an indispensible sacrifice to the common safety": see Bentham, Rationale of Punishment, p. 20 . . .

While the notion of repudiation by society is kept, it is joined by the claim that what justifies the infliction of punishment is not that it is the appropriate and fitting return for a moral evil but that it has beneficial consequences for society.[11] This is a far cry from Stephen:

> The sentence of the law is to the moral sentiment of the public in relation to any offence, what a seal is to hot wax. It converts into a permanent final judgment what might otherwise be a transient sentiment. . . . In short the infliction of punishment by law gives definite expression and solemn ratification and justification to the hatred which is excited by the commission of the offence, and which constitutes the moral or popular, as distinct from the conscientious, sanction of that part of morality which is also sanctioned by the criminal law. . . . The forms in which deliberate anger and righteous disapprobation are expressed, and the execution of criminal justice is the most emphatic of such forms, stand to the one set of passions in the same relation which marriage stands to the other [sexual passions].[12]

This aspect of sentencing may well have its limitations, especially when it is applied to conduct not harmful to others; in such cases it represents the bare expression of moral condemnation as a value which may be pursued at the cost of human suffering, and treats such suffering as a uniquely appropriate "emphatic" mode of expression. This comes uncomfortably close to human sacrifice as an expression of societal cohesion.[13]

No doubt historically one of the origins of criminal law lies in summary community self-help and in off-hand public vengeance by a more or less orderly mob. The regulation of this public vengeance is one of the earliest forms of the criminal law and no doubt that spirit is still alive.[14]

By 1962, MacKay J.A. of the Ontario Court of Appeal[15] concluded:

> At one time punishment was regarded in the light of vengeance or retribution against the wrongdoer and offenders were sentenced to be hanged for comparatively minor offences. This was an outgrowth of the old Biblical

---

[11] H. L. Hart, *Law, Liberty & Morality* (Stanford: Stanford University Press, 1963) p. 59.

[12] J. F. Stephen, at pp. 81-82.

[13] H. L. Hart, at p. 66.

[14] Roscoe Pound and Felix Frankfurter, *Criminal Justice in Cleveland* (Cleveland: Cleveland Foundation, 1922) pp. 559-82.

[15] *R. v. Roberts*, [1963] 1 C.C.C. 27 at p. 45.

concept expressed in the words "eye for eye and tooth for tooth". Retributive justice has faded into comparative insignificance in the present-day administration of criminal justice.

The Court of course confuses the issue by including a reference to hanging for minor offences; excessive quantum of sentence, as compared to the offence, can in no way be laid at the door of retribution, which calls expressly for some just measure between the offence and the punishment. It is simply that values and concepts of justice change. In the same case Schroeder J.A. refused to go even this far, holding that the doctrine of "eye for eye and tooth for tooth" still has influence when punishment is imposed for crimes that are characterized by great viciousness or extreme violence. But he does say:

> Proportionate punishment is no longer to be meted out to the criminal measure for measure, but he is committed to the charge of the officers of the state as a sort of penitential ward to be restrained so far as necessary to protect the public from recurrent manifestations of his criminal tendencies . . .

Again in *R. v. Wilmott*[16] the view is expressed that although a sentence of any kind must of necessity express repudiation by the state of the crime, retribution in the sense of revenge is now of little or no importance in the imposition of a sentence.

The view of the Ontario Court of Appeal has been expressed in *R. v. Warner, Urquhart, Martin and Mullen*[17] *per* Roach J.A. as follows:

> It should be said at once that the purpose of punishment for crime is not that, through the medium of a judge who is authorized by law to impose it, vengeance may be wreaked upon the guilty for their crime, as though crime was private in character. . . .
> Punishment . . . is the expression of the condemnation by the State of the wrong done to society. There must, therefore, always be a right proportion between the punishment imposed and the gravity of the offence. It is in that sense that it is said that certain crimes "deserve" certain punishments, and not on any theory of retribution.

These views were adopted by the Manitoba Court of Appeal.[18] See also *R. v. Wilson*[19] where similar views are accepted.

In Quebec, there is less reticence about invoking the concept of

---

[16] *Supra,* n. 2.
[17] [1946] O.R. 808 at p. 815.
[18] *R. v. Calder* (1956), 114 C.C.C. 155.
[19] (1974), 10 N.S.R. (2d) 629 (C.A.).

retribution.[20] But generally this concept is of small significance across the country in sentencing policy. In those jurisdictions that have not explicitly rejected or limited the concept, it is simply rarely mentioned.

B. Deterrence

There are two positions the court might take when sentencing with deterrence in mind: it may wish to demonstrate to society itself (and, by inclusion, potential offenders) the fearful consequence of committing the offence in question; or, it may wish to teach the offender the unprofitability of repeating his offence or, in extreme cases, prevent him from doing so.

1. GENERAL DETERRENCE

The assumption here is that the threat or example of punishment discourages crime. For Bentham, this was the principal aim of punishment, but there is growing skepticism about the deterrent effect of the example of punishment. The deterrent role of the criminal law is effective mainly with those who are already subject to the dominant socializing influences of the day. Deterrence does not threaten those whose lot in life is already miserable beyond the point of hope. It does not improve the morals of those whose value systems are closed to further modification, either psychologically or culturally; and where the prohibited conduct is the expression of sufficiently compulsive drives or motivations, deterrence is often not possible at all.[21]

In its extreme form, the advocates of deterrence suggest that fear of punishment is the only significant modifier of criminal behaviour. While we do not know the size of that marginal class that exists on the borderline of criminality and is kept in check only by the fear of punishment, it would appear that at least for serious crime the immediate effect of general deterrence on the largest part of the

---

[20] *R. v. Lemire and Gosselin* (1948), 92 C.C.C. 201 (Que. C.A.); *A.-G. Que. v. Charbonneau* (1972), 13 C.C.C. (2d) 226 (Que. C.A.).
[21] H. L. Packer, p. 45.

population is negligible. For the majority, the influence of up-bringing, education and conscience will prevent serious crime.

If a legal prohibition is regarded by the public as silly, unimportant or unconscionable, imports no moral sanction, or conflicts with deeply held moral beliefs, then there is no reason to expect that anything other than general deterrence will give a significant chance of obtaining compliance with the law. Drivers will disregard speed limits generally thought to be unreasonable at the first opportunity; the history of prohibition and of marijuana law enforcement is well known. At the same time the penalties necessary to enforce compliance with sanctions ignored by a large part of society may rise outrageously, giving rise to serious question whether the social cost is affordable in the light of the benefits received.[22]

Despite the serious lack of supporting evidence and the basic intellectual poverty of the idea it seems to be a powerful one and Canadian courts have accepted it uncritically. What evidence there is, suggests that it is the certainty of conviction rather than the severity of sentence which constitutes the deterrent factor in criminal law. The Manitoba Court of Appeal in *R. v. Iwaniw; R. v. Overton*[23] nevertheless has said:

> On the other hand those contemplating potential crimes are not concerned with the question of conviction to anything like the same extent [as the severity of punishment]; for what criminal ever plans a crime thinking *he* will be caught? Consequently the exemplary value of punishment is of necessity related to the severity of sentence for those who are convicted.

One does not know what secret information trial judges may possess unknown to social scientists and laymen alike, but there is a distinct shortage of statistical analysis upon which to base this conclusion. Indeed a contradictory view of the acceptability of deterrence by itself has been taken in Ontario:

> We are of the view that if four years is adequate punishment for their crime it would be wrong to justify a sentence of six years on the basis of deterrence and so to sacrifice the appellants for that purpose. It is our opinion that the object of the principle of deterrence to others like the appellants lies in the fact that for this crime a penitentiary term will be imposed, the length of which depends upon the circumstances.[24]

---

[22] *Struggle for Justice: A Report on Crime and Punishment in America* (New York: Hill & Wang Inc., 1971) p. 57.

[23] (1959), 127 C.C.C. 40 at p. 57, *per* Schultz J.A.

[24] *R. v. Simmons, Allen and Bezzo* (1973), 13 C.C.C. (2d) 65 at pp. 72-73, *per* Brooke J.A. (Ont. C.A.).

Notwithstanding that this statement is somewhat more palatable, it similarly is without any justification whatsoever in terms of evidentiary foundation. We have still not answered the question whether, assuming deterrence works, it is the fact of conviction, the nature of the sentence or its length which is the force behind its efficacy.

The British Columbia Court of Appeal has discussed this problem and applied a somewhat more sophisticated analysis than one usually finds in these cases. In *R. v. Harrison and Garrison*[25] Chief Justice Farris spoke to the question of whether there is a need to order a prison sentence as a general deterrent in a case where imprisonment was apparently not warranted for the specific deterrence of the offender before the Court.

> "It is my view that general deterrence is a by-product of the whole system of justice and not necessarily an aim of any particular sentence.
>
> "It is the moral sense of the community which substantially achieves the objective of the prevention of crime. As far as the law is concerned, prevention is achieved substantially through the educative effect of all parts of the administration of justice — legislation, prosecution, trial and sentence. Prevention follows from awareness of the system and of the efficiency of its operation. This knowledge guides the behaviour of some by appealing to their reason and sympathy. Others it inhibits more through fear, and in this case is properly spoken of as a deterrent. But every sentence need not have as its object the deterrence of others. The effectiveness of the principle of general deterrence (such as it is) is not diminished by refusing to imprison a person who should not be imprisoned."

2. INDIVIDUAL DETERRENCE

The rationale for deterrent sentencing is as weak when applied to the offender as it is when applied to the potential offender. Here the object is to teach the convicted person a lesson in order to deter him from repeating his offence. Yet, for the individual, the punishment implied by the sentence may be gratuitious since the moral obloquy of conviction itself may function as the deterrent. In cases where the offender is a corporation it must be pointed out that, having profited by millions of dollars from its offence, such an offender can hardly be expected to be deterred by a fine in the thousands.

---

[25] [1978] 1 W.W.R. 162 at p. 164.

Let us assume, for the sake of argument, that deterrence actually works on some, as yet undefined, group of offenders. What happens when one finds that, based upon personal and family history or other psychological grounds, individual deterrence is not at all likely to be successful? In such cases, the sentence simply becomes a matter of incapacitation. The undeterrable offender is simply placed in a situation where he can no longer commit offences.

In cases where psychiatric disorders lead to crimes of serious violence courts have been moved recently to impose long sentences simply to protect society from the violence of the offender. These sentences are not seen to be personally deterrent in any way and usually destroy any rehabilitative prospects. So it is that in the cases where the law would seemingly most like to deter, that is, in reference to offences of violence, it often accepts its own impotence and simply incarcerates in order to protect society.

3. CONFLICT BETWEEN INDIVIDUAL AND GENERAL DETERRENCE

The chief problem in dealing with deterrence as matter of practice "is to reconcile what is needed to deter the convict with what is needed to deter others".[26] In a few happy cases these needs coincide; more usually they are in conflict. Some suggestions for the resolution of the problems which arise when individual deterrence is seen to require only a short sentence, but general deterrence a long one, have been given by the Saskatchewan Court of Appeal:

> The problem is different if the purpose of sentence is to deter the offender from repeating the offence from that if the purpose is to deter others who may be inclined to commit the same offence. In neither case does it necessarily follow that a long sentence is required to achieve the purpose. Deterrence should be considered from an objective view if the purpose is to deter others who may be inclined to commit the same offence. In such case, the gravity of the offence, the incidence of the crime in the community, the harm caused by it either to the individual or to the community and the public attitude toward it are some of the matters to be considered. If the purpose is to deter the offender from repeating the offence, then greater consideration must be given to the individual, his record and attitude, his motivation and his reformation and rehabilitation. If both purposes are to be achieved, then

---

[26] *R. v. Fairn* (1973), 12 C.C.C. (2d) 423 (N.S. Co. Ct.).

there must be a weighing of all the factors and a sentence determined that gives a proper balance to each of them.[27]

This proposal, though superficially attractive, ignores the many and recurring cases where there is in fact a conflict which cannot be resolved. The proposal would simply amount to a compromise between the two extremes, which might prove satisfactory to neither purpose.

It is often necessary to determine which sort of deterrence has priority. Courts have attempted to create rules to determine which ought to take precedence in particular circumstances. In *R. v. McKimm*[28] the trial judge had regard to the prevalence of the offence and considered therefore that even first offenders regardless of age should be sent to jail; he accordingly gave priority to the demands of general deterrence based upon, in this case, statistics showing the increase of this particular kind of robbery in the locality. The Ontario Court of Appeal responded:

> If this was intended by the trial Judge as being a general policy that he was about to follow then we think, with great respect, that he was wrong. Each case depends upon its own circumstances and I fail to see how any Judge can prescribe for himself a formula such as the one that was stated here by Judge Martin.

In each case, if the compromise proposed above would result in a solution satisfactory to neither the demands of individual nor general deterrence, a choice must be made. This choice, it appears, must be based not upon general considerations, but on the particular facts of this offence and this offender.

Similarly it is an error for a trial judge to decide that as a general rule the element of general deterrence is more important than individual deterrence.[29]

C. Rehabilitation And Reform

Courts have generally accepted that in considering the fitness of any sentence there are two interests involved: first the interest of the state or the whole community (assuming that they coincide) and secondly, the

---

[27] *R. v. Morrissette* (1970), 1 C.C.C. (2d) 307 at p. 310.
[28] [1970] 1 C.C.C. 340 (Ont. C.A.).
[29] *R. v. Wilson* (1974), 10 N.S.R. (2d) 629 (C.A.).

interest of the accused.[30] Of these two, the interest of the state must be paramount. Rehabilitation and reform come into play not only when considering the interests of the accused, but also and more importantly when considering the interests of the state; if no further crime is committed by the accused, then the state has been protected in the most immediate and tangible way possible.

In the last one hundred years or so, our society has moved increasingly in the direction of this rehabilitative ideal. Much of the impetus for this new direction flows from the failure of retribution and deterrence, together with a rise of public humanitarianism urged on by the siren call of social science. Nevertheless, the promise has been hollow. Often individual liberty is imperiled by claims to knowledge and therapeutic effectiveness that we do not possess and by failure to candidly concede what we do not know. At times it is the practitioners of the behavioural sciences who are guilty of these faults; but more often legislators, lawyers and the public foolishly assume an expertise and an efficacy that simply does not exist.[31]

And yet the temptation has been a real and even a noble one. Barbara Wootton,[32] argues for a redefinition of the function of the criminal law as preventive of social harm broadly conceived, rather than punitive of moral wrong. *Mens rea* then becomes of importance not in relation to criminality but in relation to sentencing. This proposal focuses attention away from the crime and upon the criminal, his nature and his needs. The logical outgrowth of such a position, a conclusion reinforced by the increasing tendency of legislators to make criminal behaviour which extends far beyond the categories of traditional crime, is to view criminality as a problem in behaviour management and social control. Once this is accepted and is placed beside a faith in social scientists to actually effect rehabilitation, indeterminate sentences and the increased use of parole become sensible. This perspective disclaims any intent to use the criminal law for retributive or punishment purposes: the sentence is not punishment because it is not intended as punishment.

The critical assumption made by the courts in this type of sentencing is that whether or not something is punishment is decided by the motive

---

[30] *R. v. Willaert* (1953), 105 C.C.C. 172 (Ont. C.A.); *R. v. Calder* (1956), 114 C.C.C. 155 (Man. C.A.).
[31] Frances A. Allen, "Criminal Justice, Legal Values and the Rehabilitative Ideal" (1959), 50 Journal of Criminal Law, Criminology and Police Science, pp. 226-32.
[32] *Crime and Criminal Law.*

behind its imposition. A better view, albeit an objective one, is that the distinguishing feature of punishment is not any particular motive but its result: the application of force to another person against his or her will. Since criminal law is the sanctioned official use of force, without compulsion it ceases to be law, at least in any formal sense. Violence, direct or implied, is the ultimate sanction reserved for those who disobey. Behind every criminal law, behind every arrest and on every prison wall is the blunt message: your submission or your life. If it is conceded that in some circumstances society must employ coercion against an individual to achieve some compelling social purpose, it nevertheless confuses analysis and obscures the moral nature of our act to pretend that we are not punishing.[33]

The rise of the rehabilitative ideal also implies increasing discretion at every stage of the criminal process. Most notably these are seen in the increasing use of parole and the increasing fashionability of the indeterminate sentence or sentences with indeterminate components. All these measures, and others, provide the necessary "flexibility" whereby decisions crucial to punishment are taken out of the hands of the courts and placed in the domain of the social scientists, the psychiatrists and the administrators.

So long as there remains a retributive aspect to criminal law, there is a vital difference between the situation of a patient who has been committed to a mental hospital, and the situation of an inmate of a penitentiary. This distinction lies precisely in the fact that the patient has not incurred the moral condemnation of his community, whereas the convict has done so. It is therefore unwise, in the interests of a humanitarian perspective, to subsume the latter category to the former merely because a penitentiary now "offers" psychiatric treatment. No matter where he may be, the patient who arrives at his institution as a result of the criminal process is being punished. "The mere deprivation of liberty, however benign the administration of the place of confinement, is undeniably punishment."[34]

Though the idea that imprisonment will rehabilitate is as old as Bentham, there is no statistical evidence whatever to support it. Nevertheless, Canadian courts consistently reiterate the theme that imprisonment provides an opportunity for the reform and rehabilitation

---

[33] *Struggle for Justice,* pp. 22-23.
[34] Garofalo, Criminology, at p. 256 (Miller translation, 1914) found in "Legal Values and the Rehabilitative Ideal", Journal of Criminal Law, Criminology and Police Science.

of the offender.[35] Though there is some support for the view that imprisonment may be necessary for retributive, deterrent or incapacitation purposes, there is no respectable support for the view that imprisonment prevents crime. Rather than reducing the incidence of crime imprisonment simply reduces a prisoner's chance to assume a normal role in society, and may result in the creation of a "social cripple".[36]

A great danger lies in the practice of many appellate courts in imposing lengthy terms of imprisonment in the hope that a cure may be effected during the period of incarceration. Sir Rupert Cross[37] asks whether we should always act on the principle that the maximum of a man's punishment should never be greater than the amount which would be justified by other aims of the criminal justice system than that of reform:

> For my own part, I am content to treat the principle as nothing more than a strong presumption and to reply: "Only if the additional period is not excessively long, and provided there is clear evidence that it will generally have beneficial consequences." As I have already indicated, it seems to me that the evidence is not sufficiently clear to warrant the addition of a day to a prison sentence in the name of reform . . .

Reform and rehabilitation have come to be the goals first sought after in most cases. Only where deterrence has failed or absolute prevention in a sense of incapacitation has become necessary, have courts been willing to abandon, for most offences, that comforting lie, the rehabilitative ideal. As we gain experience, our justification of these ideals becomes more and more subtle.

D. The Road We Are On

It is not suprising that the choice between one sentence and another or one sentencing purpose and another often seems to have remarkably little concrete effect. In an arresting figure, Barbara Wootton[38] assesses

---

[35] *R. v. Wilmott*, [1967] 1 C.C.C. 171 (Ont. C.A.).

[36] *R. v. Johnson* (1971), 4 C.C.C. (2d) 226 (Ont. C.A.).

[37] Rupert Cross, *Punishment, Prison and the Public* (London: Stevens & Sons, 1971) p. 124.

[38] *Crime and Criminal Law,* p. 93.

the statistical evidence to support this thesis and notes that the studies either mask considerable individual differences in the impact of particular sentences upon particular individuals, which are lost in the general totals, or they are evidence that everything we do falls very wide of the mark.

> By analogy, I suppose, if draughts of cold water were prescribed as a treatment for cancer, it would probably not make much difference whether the patient drank large draughts or small ones.

In one sense this is not suprising since the legislator and the public turn instinctively and increasingly to the criminal law whenever a sanction is desired for some new measure. The range of conduct now prohibited by the criminal justice system is immense. If the system has any efficacy at all, it can only operate successfully in a small number of cases and within a narrow field and there has been no attempt to define what sorts of cases these might be.[39]

There is, to use Professor Packer's phrase, an incredible overuse of the criminal sanction.[40] Saddest of all, the rehabilitative ideal, which held out so much promise, has never had an effective chance to operate. A single psychiatrist cannot treat 300 seriously disturbed individuals; yet this is the rule rather than the exception in our penitentiaries. A parole officer cannot effectively supervise or assist in the rehabilitation of a hundred parolees; each gets only fleeting and useless moments of his time. The rehabilitative system has never really been tried. Social workers and professionals who participate in it under present conditions permit their skills and their profession to be abused.

Governments, of course, are politically interested in providing only the semblance of social and psychological facilities. The coercive conditions under which these are offered and the impossibly small amount of time available for any given person make it certain that these measures will be ineffective. But the provision of adequate facilities in an attempt to give this system a reasonable test would be expensive. Not as expensive, it is true, as the cost of crime in our society; but more than we are consciously willing to expend.

There is a serious doubt that the criminal law ought to be in the healing business at all. The illness analogy is beguiling but misleading. It is only in a loose metaphorical sense that crimes which are connected with alcoholism, narcotic addiction or sexual deviation can be termed

---

[39] Roscoe Pound, p. 582.
[40] H. L. Packer, p. 265.

"diseases". Yet there is a tendency to use the metaphor as though it were literally true and to follow it boldly, by invoking a duty upon the offender to submit to being cured, the breach of which duty is then viewed as an adequate basis for invoking the criminal sanction. If particular crimes could in fact be "cured" by therapeutic measures, there would be much to be said for requiring people to submit to them. But when the "illness" turns out to be the individual's total life situation and the "cure" requires drastic changes in that situation, the invocation of the criminal sanction to effect that cure is patently hypocritical.

It is not in sentencing alone but in the criminal law generally where short-term improvements can be made. Short of pervasive and radical societal change there is something that can be done. As a rule of restraint we ought to prohibit something only when the following conditions hold:

1. There is a compelling social need to require compliance with a particular norm. Criminal courts ought not to degenerate into regulatory or collection agencies. A threat merely to "moral sensibilities" is not sufficient reason to impose sanction. Though it is undoubtedly necessary that in order for society to exist, some central moral order must be upheld, the criminal justice system is not the only nor even the the most important basis of this order. Canadian social organizations can tolerate a much wider variety of behaviour than we presently allow.
2. There is no feasible but less costly method of obtaining compliance. There exists a myriad of other agencies which promote compliance with basic social standards. If the criminal law is to retain its force, authority and respect, its scope of activities must be severely restricted to serious objectives commanding widespread public support. The criminal law ought not to be a forum for debate of social issues.
3. There is some substantial basis for assuming that the imposition of the criminal sanction will produce greater benefit for society than simply doing nothing. The imposition of punishment, it would appear, is superior to doing nothing when either there is strong reason to believe that the behaviour in question is capable of being deterred or when the norm is such that non-compliance is generally felt to be so serious that doing nothing would be unacceptable to the overwhelming majority of the population. This is not entirely rational but it is an acknowledgement of the force of social contact theory. Finally, the criminal sanction ought never to be invoked merely in the hope and expectation that through it reform or rehabilitation can be achieved.

The over-all argument for restraint is the notion that the criminal justice system and sentencing, in particular, are to be used as a last resort. A responsible physician does not decide to proceed with a dangerous and costly operation until he has exhausted less risky methods of treatment. To a suprising degree criminal law disregards this sensible stricture.

A more specific manifestation of this argument in the area of sentencing is restraint in the severity of punishment. What evidence there is seems to suggest that increasing the intensity of the criminal sanction fails of and by itself to increase compliance with social norms. If deterrence works then it is in large degree likely that it is the existence and not the intensity of punishment that deters. The permanent damage caused by our prisons is both pervasive and unacceptable.

Chapter 2

Finding An Appropriate Sentence

A. Factors To Be Considered

It is the weight attached to particular aspects of a case which shapes and determines the sentence which is imposed. However, it is first necessary to know what the factors are that are taken into consideration in ordinary sentencing practice. These factors are:

1. the degree of premeditation involved;
2. the circumstances surrounding the actual commission of the offence; *i.e.,* the manner in which it was committed, the amount of violence involved, the employment of an offensive weapon, and, the degree of active participation by each offender;
3. the gravity of the crime committed, in regard to which the maximum punishment provided by statute is an indication;
4. the attitude of the offender after the commission of the crime, as this serves to indicate the degree of criminality involved and throws some light on the character of the participant;
5. the previous criminal record, if any, of the offender;
6. the age, mode of life, character and personality of the offender;
7. any recommendation of the trial Judge, any pre-sentence or probation official's report, or any mitigating or other circumstances properly brought to the attention of this Court;[1]

---

[1] These seven factors were listed by the Manitoba Court of Appeal in *R. v. Iwaniw; R. v. Overton* (1959), 127 C.C.C. 40 at pp. 50-51 *per* Schultz J.A., and approved by the Prince Edward Island Court of Appeal in *R. v. James*

8. incidence of crime in jurisdiction;[2]
9. sentences customarily imposed for the same or similar offences;[3]
10. mercy.[4]

Of all these factors the nature or gravity of the offence is, properly, the most often stressed. It is and must be the "first rule that prompts the magistrate".[5] The concern behind this consideration is that there should be a "just proportion" between the offence committed and the sentence imposed.[6] *A fortiori* the maximum penalty set out in the Criminal Code should be reserved for the worst offence and the worst offender. For example:

> This was a sophisticated, well-planned operation which calls for a substantial sentence. In addition, this man has a very formidable record of previous convictions . . . However, this is not the worst example of theft that one can imagine, and the Court has come to the conclusion that the maximum is not warranted.[7]

An Australian case has pondered how one determines the question of the worst offence and the worst offender. Certainly, the concept does not call upon a judge to indulge in metaphysical speculation in order to conjure up in his mind a worse case. If this were a requirement then human ingenuity would always make it possible to think up a worse case with the result that the maximum penalty would never be appropriate.[8]

The evolution of this concept that there should be a "just proportion" between the crime and the sentence is an interesting one. Its roots are to be found in the principle of retribution. The Biblical definition of retribution as "an eye for an eye and a tooth for a tooth" has often been

---

(1971), 3 C.C.C. (2d) 1; and a similar one taken from 9 *Halsbury* (2d ed.), p. 256, by the New Brunswick Court of Appeal in *R. v. Nash (No. 2)* (1949), 8 C.R. 447.

[2] *R. v. Mikkelson* (1973), 14 C.C.C. (2d) 255 at p. 257 *per* Culliton C.J.S. (Sask. C.A.); *R. v. Wilmott,* [1967] 1 C.C.C. 171 at p. 179 *per* McLennan J.A. (Ont. C.A.).

[3] *R. v. Mikkelson, supra,* n. 2; *Hill v. The Queen (No. 2)* (1975), 25 C.C.C. (2d) 6 *per* Ritchie J. (S.C.C.); *R. v. Barber* (1976), 1 Crim. L.J. 55.

[4] *R. v. Renton* (1975), 11 N.S.R. (2d) 60 (C.A.); *R. v. Clarke,* [1975] Crim. L.R. 595; *R. v. Taylor,* [1977] 3 All E.R. 527.

[5] *R. v. Lemire and Gosselin* (1948), 92 C.C.C. 201 (Que. C.A.).

[6] *R. v. Wilmott, supra,* n. 2, at pp. 178-79 *per* McLennan J.A. (Ont. C.A.).

[7] *R. v. Dawdy* (1973), 12 C.C.C. (2d) 477 at p. 478 *per* Gale C.J.O. (Ont. C.A.); see also *R. v. Willis,* unreported, April 24, 1973 (Ont. C.A.); *R. v. Doughty* (1978), 40 C.C.C. (2d) 224 (P.E.I.C.A.).

[8] *R. v. Manson,* [1974] Qd. R. 191 at p. 202 (C.C.A.).

construed as being a spur to vengeance. This is undoubtedly a misconception. "An eye for an eye" means "*only* an eye for an eye, and not more". Thus we find in Cross:[9] "The retributivist insists that the punishment must not be disproportionate to the offender's deserts". However, because the principle of retribution in sentencing has evolved in such a way as to be inseparable from the notion of vengeance, the development of a separate, clearly articulated concept of "just proportion" is a positive one, and much needed.[10]

Of special interest is the principle involving the "mode of life" of the offender. Expanded this can be taken to encompass the social conditions of the participants in the crime. The reaction of the various courts of appeal to this consideration have been mixed. In *R. v. Nash (No. 2)*[11] a decision of the New Brunswick Court of Appeal, the following statement by the trial judge appears:

> "My understanding of the social conditions in which the participants were living at the time of the incident has enabled me to sufficiently measure the degree of gravity of the crime and the nature of the guilt of the accused as found by the jury."

The Court responded: "I hardly think we should measure the gravity of the crime by the social condition of the participants or that the penalty should be varied by the same scale."

By way of directly contrary authority we have the decision in *R. v. Ayalik,*[12]

> . . . in the present case the learned trial judge had a distinct advantage over the members of the court for with his wide experience in the far-flung areas of the extensive jurisdiction of the trial division of this court he has knowledge of local conditions, ways of life, habits, customs and characteristics of the race of people of which the accused is a member.
>
> . . .
>
> As individual judges we may have imposed a different sentence than the one imposed by the learned trial judge, but as the discretion of a trial judge in imposing a sentence is a wide one we cannot say that the sentence he gave was a wrong one.

---

[9] A.R.N. Cross, *The English Sentencing System,* 2nd ed. (London: Butterworths, 1975) p. 21.

[10] See, *infra,* "Appropriate to Offence".

[11] (1949), 8 C.R. 447 at p. 453 *per* Richards C.J.

[12] (1960), 33 W.W.R. 377 at p. 378 *per* Macdonald J.A. (N.W.T.C.A.); see also *R. v. Evalick and Haniliak,* unreported, March 6, 1978 (N.W.T.).

Reference must be made to a sensible response by the judiciary to a situation where it is clear that our traditional principles do not and cannot work. One such example is the Doukhobour case in British Columbia, *R. v. Switlishoff et al.*[13] In that case the court was attempting to prevent the commission of further crimes by a group of people who had thoroughly rejected the very system that the court represented. The futility of ordinary sentencing principles and the confusion caused by them are clearly evidenced by the following opinion of the trial judge:

> . . . severe sentences imposed on Doukhobours as individuals in the past have failed to achieve results; on the contrary, the sense of grievance or misunderstanding severe sentences seem to have engendered amongst these communal people have led to perpetration of more offences. They have in the past welcomed severe punishment as a form of martyrdom for tenacious adherence to their religious belief.

The appeal court reached the "firm conclusion" that:

> . . . if leniency were now extended there [is] more than a probability not only that these offenders but the great majority of the Sons of Freedom and the Doukhobour colony as a whole would be responsive to that leniency. . . . If we regard the main objects of judicial sentence as protection to the public, deterrence to others and reformation of the individual, then leniency has a real chance of accomplishing now what severity certainly has not in the past.
>
>   . . .
>
> If these respondents could be divorced from their communal philosophy, religious outlook and collective grouping, and treated as other individual offenders that come before the Court, there is no doubt the sentences are wholly inadequate. That the time has not yet arrived when these people can be so divorced is evidenced by the intensity, one might say the fanaticism, with which many of them adhere rigidly and literally to the communal doctrines of the Doukhobour faith which hinders them associating freely with other Canadians, and which seems to beget and continue in each of them a sense of collective personality, entirely foreign to the Anglo-American concept of individual freedom of action under our law.

B. Appropriate To Offence

It follows from the general principles that the sentence, though it be

---

[13] (1950), 9 C.R. 428 at pp. 430-33 (B.C.C.A.).

imposed upon a unique offender, must be one that is primarily and essentially appropriate to the offence. The idea of appropriateness includes both the nature of the crime and the particular circumstances in which it was committed. Upon the question of the gravity of the offence, as well as in the question of guilt or innocence, the accused is entitled to the benefit of any reasonable doubt. From time to time courts have been tempted to excessively "tailor" sentences to deal with what they perceive as problems peculiar to the offender himself and thereby to ignore, or fail to give proper weight, to the offence and its circumstances.

The case law provides many instances where courts of appeal have interfered when the sentencing courts have given inappropriate weight to one aspect of sentencing or taken into account extraneous factors so that, in effect, the sentence becomes inappropriate to the offence committed.

Perhaps the most common misapplication of this principle is found in cases where the offender has committed a relatively minor offence but is in the unfortunate position of possessing a lengthy criminal record. In *Kavanaugh v. The Queen*[14] the accused was convicted of breaking and entering a shack at the rear of the town dump and stealing a small quantity of scrap consisting of copper wire and a coil for a car heater, the value of which was probably less than one dollar. The court in reviewing a three-year sentence approved *R. v. Gumbs*[15] and the principle therein that when a man has committed serious offences and has served long terms for them, it is not required that he should suffer further severe punishment for a later offence which does not intrinsically call for it. Ritchie J.A., finding three years "manifestly excessive", reduced the term to six months.

In *R. v. Scheer,*[16] the Alberta Court of Appeal approved the language of Hewart L.C.J. in *R. v. Durand:*[17] "In considering whether a sentence in such a case as this is proper, one has to beware of treating an offence as serious in itself because it has been committed by a man who previously has committed a series of offences."

Similarly, relying on a series of English cases, the Saskatchewan Court of Appeal in *R. v. Webb*[18] held: "The fact that the appellant has committed other offences is not, in the opinion of the Court, sufficient

---

[14] (1960), 128 C.C.C. 267 (N.B.C.A.).
[15] *R. v. Gumbs* (1926), 19 Cr. App. R. 74.
[16] [1932] 3 W.W.R. 555 at p. 558.
[17] (1924), 18 Cr. App. R. 137.
[18] [1933] 3 W.W.R. 431 at p. 432.

reason for imposing a term in the penitentiary for the comparatively trivial offence in the present case."

In *R. v. Wilson*[19] the British Columbia Court of Appeal acted in a similar manner but noted that it was also clear that the appellant "shows himself unresponsive to leniency and persists in a life of crime".

A variation on this same theme can be seen in *R. v. Luther.*[20] In the course of an altercation in the cells at a police station, the accused attacked another prisoner, doing her no serious physical injury and was convicted of assault causing bodily harm. The evidence indicated that the accused had been a heroin addict for quite some time. The sentencing judge imposed a 12-month sentence, justifying it as not only appropriate to the offence but appropriate for the "safety" and rehabilitation of the accused. Noting that there was nothing in the evidence to suggest that the incident arose because of her use of drugs, the court held that the sentence was in error. Brooke J.A. held that:

> In the absence of express authority to order confinement for the purpose of treatment, it is my view that the processes of the criminal law cannot be used in the manner in which the trial Judge sought to use them here. . . . Nor can such a sentence be justified on the ground of rehabilitation as a principle of sentencing . . .
>
> There is no doubt that this woman was in need of treatment, but surely there must be other means of seeing to it that she is placed in the hands of competent medical people to achieve that purpose rather than to add an additional term to her sentence for a crime quite unrelated to her use of drugs.

The English Court of Appeal has acted in a similar way. In *R. v. Ford*[21] the accused had been sentenced to 27 months' imprisonment for housebreaking and larceny, although his co-accused had only been given 12 months. This difference was due partly to the fact that the accused was an alcoholic and the hope of the sentencing judge was that the additional time in prison would effect a cure. On appeal, the sentence was reduced to 12 months:

> In relation to offences of dishonesty sentences of imprisonment — except where there is an element of protection of the public involved — are normally intended to be the correct sentence for the particular crime, and not to

---

[19] (1944), 82 C.C.C. 65; see to the same effect *R. v. Cross* (1927), 49 C.C.C. 77 (Sask. C.A.).

[20] (1971), 5 C.C.C. (2d) 354 at p. 357 (Ont. C.A.); see also *R. v. Clarke,* [1975] Crim. L.R. 595 and Chapter 5, "E. Imprisonment for Treatment".

[21] [1969] 3 All E.R. 782n at p. 783.

include a curative element. This court wishes to make it clear that what it is now saying has nothing to do with special cases such as those of possessing dangerous drugs or cases of where the protection of the public is involved . . .

Later, in *R. v. Moylan,*[22] the Court explained this judgment by noting that the sentencing court must first determine what are the limits of a proper sentence in respect to the offence charged. Within these limits it may be perfectly proper to increase the sentence in order to enable a cure to be undertaken while the offender is in prison. But, it is clear that it is not correct to increase sentence beyond the appropriate range for the offence "merely in order to provide an opportunity of cure. . . . There might be something to be said for the compulsory cure of alcoholics but it certainly ought not to be introduced by the sidewind of long prison sentences for theft."

In *R. v. Glasse,*[23] the English Court of Appeal upheld a sentence of five years' imprisonment upon a youth of 21 for unlawful possession of heroin and cocaine. He was an addict and there was evidence that voluntary treatment would not be successful for want of co-operation on his part: "This Court has come to the conclusion that for this type of case, a comparatively long sentence of imprisonment is the only course open, not merely as punishment to this man, but as producing the conditions where a cure is the most hopeful."

In the Canadian context it should be noted that this course has not been followed, insofar as Part II of the Narcotic Control Act, which provides for incarceration for treatment, has not been proclaimed as law. In the absence of such proclamation by the federal Government it may be suggested that such an approach to sentencing is not warranted in Canada.

C. Disparity Of Sentence

The notion of equal justice is the source for the principle that there must not be an unjustifiable disparity in sentence between similar offences and offenders. In a sense this is no more than a deduction from the principle that justice in this country is individual, and it follows therefore, that the

---

[22] [1969] 3 All E.R. 783; see also *Coreen v. Josey,* [1970] W.A.R. 70; *Nash v. Whitford,* (1971-72), 25 A.S.R. 333.
[23] (1968), 53 Cr. App. R. 121.

unique and individual factors of each case must be taken into account or reflected in the sentence.[24] This proposition leads to the conclusion that the court ought to interfere so as to rationalize sentences where they are unjustifiably disparate. The rule does not require equal sentences, but only understandable sentences when viewed together.

The rationale for the rule, though often expressed rather vaguely as "in order for justice to be done"[25] has been put in a number of ways. The various statements of the rule will be illustrated below, but it is at the outset perhaps wise to make clear that the rule has not always been recognized, and is in fact of rather recent development.

In *R. v. Connor and Hall,*[26] as recently as 1957, Laidlaw J.A. speaking for the Ontario Court of Appeal said:

> It is difficult, if not impossible, to reconcile the sentence in one case with the sentences in other cases. The Court must strive to its utmost to see that a sentence imposed upon a guilty person is appropriate to the particular circumstances of this case. It serves little useful purpose and affords little assistance to the Court to know what sentences have been imposed in other countries or jurisdictions or by other Courts.

So for example in *R. v. Cornett,*[27] on an application for leave to appeal sentence, the applicant complained that he got the same sentence as his co-accused despite the fact that he had no criminal record and had pleaded guilty. The court seemed to deny any special ground based on this consideration and considered only the question whether the sentence was excessive in itself viewed by itself. Similarly in *R. v. Smith,*[28] in 1962 the British Columbia Court of Appeal, where six years' imprisonment was given to co-accused with a criminal record, refused to interfere with a sentence of four years' imprisonment though acknowledging:

> ... that the difference in the sentences meted out to him and Caldough is not sufficient to mark the great disparity in their culpability.
>
> . . .
>
> The culpability of Caldough does seem to be very much greater than that of the appellant, and the disparity may not be fully reflected in the respective sentences imposed, but that in itself is no reason for allowing this appeal. The

---

[24] *R. v. Emonts,* unreported, June 19, 1973 (Ont. C.A.). See also D.A. Thomas, "Sentencing Co-defendants", [1964] Crim. L.R. 22.

[25] *R. v. Murchie,* unreported, July 12, 1974 (Ont. C.A.).

[26] (1957), 118 C.C.C. 237 at p. 238.

[27] (1949), 96 C.C.C. 316 (N.S.).

[28] (1962), 38 C.R. 217.

appellant's sentence of four years is not too severe when considered in the light of the international scope and the magnitude of the conspirators' fraudulent operations. True, lighter sentences have been imposed in many reported cases just as serious, but each case has its own peculiar circumstances that are reflected in the punishment imposed, and which prevent it being used as an exact measure of the punishment to be meted out in another case.[29]

The problem is illustrated most dramatically in the case of persons jointly accused of the same crime, but it is not by any means restricted to this situation. The principle must, of necessity, apply to other similar crimes.[30]

In other cases one can see the first attempts to grapple seriously with the problem of disparity. In *R. v. Switlishoff et al.*,[31] O'Halloran J.A. said:

> There is no such thing as a uniform sentence for a particular crime. No doubt in somewhat similar circumstances it is desirable to avoid marked disparity in sentences. But the individual himself and his surrounding conditions cannot be ignored. . . . In *Rex v. Stonehouse and Pasquale*, [1928] 1 W.W.R. 161 at 163 . . . this Court said no rule can be laid down defining a uniform punishment for crimes of a particular sort . . .[32]

Indeed, under the traditional rules pursuant to which courts of appeal have interfered with trial sentences, it is hard to find room for a principle authorizing such interference merely because of a disparity in sentence as compared to another save under the notion of a residual jurisdiction remaining in the court to do justice and to see that justice is done. In *R. v. Iwaniw; R. v. Overton*,[33] Schultz J.A. held that in the "unique circumstances" of that case, where the offender least culpable received a heavier sentence than his co-accused, it was both "permissible and necessary" to consider the respective degrees of guilt and alter the sentences accordingly. This was done despite the judge's comments to the effect that comparison of separate cases was not very helpful because the facts in each case and the character and antecedents of the offenders are never completely identical. Uniformity was to be sought not in equality of sentences, nor by direct comparison to other similar cases, but through the notion that ". . . the principles of punishment recognized by this Court should not vary, for in no other way can a uniform pattern

---

[29] *Ibid.*, at p. 218 *per* Davey J.A.
[30] *R. v. Rasper* (1978), 1 C.R. (3d) S-45 (Ont. C.A.).
[31] (1950), 9 C.R. 428 (B.C.C.A.).
[32] *Ibid.*, at pp. 431-32.
[33] (1959), 127 C.C.C. 40 (Man. C.A.).

of punishment be demonstrated or followed nor can the decisions of a Court of appeal be of assistance to trial Courts."

Similarly, in a case where there was no co-accused with whom to compare, *R. v. Baldhead,*[34] the court was faced with an appellant whose sole ground of appeal was that the sentence was not "uniform" with sentences imposed upon other Indians convicted of similar crimes of manslaughter. The court stated the general principle that the adequacy of a sentence depends upon all of the relevant circumstances and that therefore there could be no such thing as a uniform sentence suitable to a particular crime. They went on to declare, however, that this rule was subject to the reservation that where there was "a marked departure" from the sentences customarily imposed in the same jurisdiction for the same or similar crimes, the court, upon being apprised of the circumstances, should be able to rationalize the reason for such a departure. If, after having been made aware of the circumstances, and "after having given full effect to the principles governing an appellate court in reviewing sentence", it was unable to do so, then it became incumbent upon the court to either increase or decrease the sentence in order to achieve a "rational relationship" to sentences imposed for the same or similar crimes. In this case the court examined other manslaughter convictions in the province involving the Indian population and found that they varied between one year and five years according to the circumstances of the crime. In the result a sentence of ten years was reduced to three years in a penitentiary "so as to bring it into reasonable equality" with other similar offences. The language of the court leads to the inference that this was viewed as a matter which was peremptory upon them.

Cross has stated that the principle of justice that like cases should be treated alike is fundamental.[35]

Between the two extremes — that the court is bound to interfere to prevent unreasonable disparity, and the older view that "fitness of sentence", as used in the Criminal Code, involves only an evaluation of the appropriateness of the penalty to the offence and the particular offender — there is a middle ground. The principle has been stated most succinctly in England and meets the needs of a responsible sentencing practice:

> The Court, on many occasions . . . has reduced a sentence to bring it more

---

[34] [1966] 4 C.C.C. 183 (Sask. C.A.).
[35] At p. 167.

in line to the sentence imposed on a co-accused; it is something that this Court tries to do in the general run of cases on the basis that only thereby can a sense of grievance be averted. But there is no principle of law that the sentences must strictly compare . . .

. . . the Court does in general seek to ensure that sentences as far as possible favourably compare one with another, but they are not bound to do so . . .[36]

But this principle has its limits. When the court finds that the sentence of the co-accused is a wholly inadequate one it has refused to sacrifice the principle that the sentence must be appropriate to the offence solely to avert disparity.

The Ontario Court of Appeal has accepted this limitation, and has said it is regrettable "that the other convicts should have escaped with inadequate punishment, but this affords no reason for not inflicting adequate punishment on this man."[37] In *R. v. Hunter,*[38] the Court refused to lower an otherwise proper sentence so as to accord with inadequate sentences imposed by a lower court judge and commented that a trial judge should likewise refuse to do so. The same Court, however, has lowered sentences despite such a circumstance. In *R. v. Dawdy,*[39] the Court said:

We have difficulty understanding why such a lenient sentence was imposed on Bush [the co-accused], particularly in view of his serious criminal record. While we are not bound to sentence Dawdy by reference to Bush's sentence, we do think that the sentence should not be so disparate so as to cause bitterness or resentment on the part of Dawdy.

Though the prime mover in the theft was sentenced to six months' imprisonment plus 18 months' probation, this lesser offender was sentenced to one and a half years' imprisonment by the Court of Appeal. In a similar situation, the Quebec Court of Appeal followed the same course, noting that the Crown had not seen fit to appeal the sentence of the co-accused.[40]

In applying this principle, however it be expressed, it is imperative that

---

[36] *R. v. Coe* (1969), 53 Cr. App. R. 66.
[37] *R. v. Dow* (1938), 70 C.C.C. 318 (Ont. C.A.).
[38] (1970), 16 C.R.N.S. 12 (Ont. C.A.).
[39] (1973), 12 C.C.C. (2d) 477 at pp. 478-79 (Ont. C.A.); see also *R. v. Doughty* (1978), 40 C.C.C. (2d) 224 (P.E.I.C.A.).
[40] *R. v. Carriere* (1952), 14 C.R. 391 at p. 400 *per* Marchand J. and at p. 395 *per* Gailpeault C.J. (Que. C.A.); *R. v. Goldwarg* (1973), 15 Crim. L.Q. 371 (Que. C.A.).

the offence with which the comparison is to take place must (whether it be that of a co-accused or that of someone unrelated) be similar. Only by so doing can the primary principle of appropriateness be maintained. In order to meet this first principle it is important that the sentencing judge not only be informed of the fact of the comparable case and its sentence, but actually be informed of the details of the case.

Secondly, it is important that the principle of avoidance of disparity only be applied after all the ordinary principles of sentencing have been exhausted, and all the factors, whether in mitigation or in aggravation, weighed and assessed.

Accordingly the principle was applied in *R. v. Miller*[41] at the suggestion of the Crown, who pointed out that while the appellant was the greater offender, nevertheless the difference in the offences, as compared to his co-accused, did not justify the great difference in their sentences. On the other hand, in *Antonecchia v. The Queen*[42] the Quebec Court of Appeal said:

> I am not impressed by the argument of appellant's counsel that some of his companions received lighter sentences, despite previous criminal records. Appellant was the instigator of this atrocious attack, and it seems only just that he should receive the heaviest sentence.

In *R. v. Lass*[43] the court approved the English case of *R. v. Vivian*[44] for the proposition that discrimination in sentences imposed on two or more persons for the same offence must be founded on some good reason. In *R. v. LeSarge*[45] the accused appealed a seven-year sentence alleging disparity upon a charge of possession of stolen goods (a tractor trailer and some liquor) with that of a co-accused who pleaded guilty to possession of the liquor only. The accused was sentenced to seven years, his co-accused to only 90 days intermittently, together with probation for three years. The court refused to invoke the principle of disparity because "the conviction was for a different offence", it was "not fully apprised of all the circumstances concerning the sentence that Lunn received, and there is such a tremendous disparity in the sentences that the sentence imposed on Lunn cannot be taken into account."

In accordance with the same approach, the English Court of Appeal

---

[41] *R. v. Miller* (1926), 30 O.W.N. 318 (C.A.).
[42] (1959), 31 C.R. 320 at p. 323.
[43] (1949), 95 C.C.C. 193 (Ont. C.A.).
[44] (1925), 18 Cr. App. R. 37; see also *R. v. Iwaniw; R. v. Overton* (1959), 127 C.C.C. 40 (Man. C.A.).
[45] *R. v. LeSarge* (1975), 26 C.C.C. (2d) 388 at p. 397 (Ont. C.A.).

(Criminal Division) in *R. v. Bocskei*[46] has held that when arguments in relation to disparity are put forward they must have regard to the fact that when consecutive sentences are imposed the final duty of the sentencer is to make sure that the totality of the consecutive sentences is not excessive. In that case the court noted that the fact that a trial judge chose to use the totality principle to reduce the sentence of the co-accused by six months, but would not in any way give the co-accused appellant the kind of grievance which the rule regarding disparity is intended to redress. Similarly in *R. v. Johnston and Tremayne,*[47] the court made adjustments in sentences having regard to the degree of criminality of the accused, but prior to doing so took into account the fact that they pleaded guilty ultimately to different charges and that one of them (importing a narcotic), carried a minimum sentence of seven years. From this act the court inferred that this crime was regarded by Parliament as the more serious of the two offences, notwithstanding the similarity of the acts committed, and thereby justified a harsher penalty. In *R. v. Scheer,*[48] the Alberta Court of Appeal, after taking into account the more serious criminal record of the appellant and slightly greater culpability, still found that the discrepancy in sentence was too great and accordingly reduced the sentence.

In *R. v. Roddick,*[49] the Ontario Court of Appeal invoked the principle of avoidance of disparity in sentences to ensure that the sentence on an appellant who was convicted of possession of a stolen automobile was less than that given a co-accused who was convicted of stealing the same automobile. In *R. v. Potruff*[50] a similar distinction was made, but in a different way. The accused, age 19 was convicted of theft at a time when she was accompanied by her 17-year-old sister, who was granted a conditional discharge. When she was fined, she appealed this disposition submitting that the principle of avoidance of disparity indicated that she too should have an absolute discharge. While of the view that the fine was not appropriate in the light of this principle, the court decided that it must take into account an extra lack of responsibility on her part by setting such an example for her younger sister; but under the circumstances and in accordance with the principle, the court imposed a conditional discharge on the older sister.

---

[46] (1970), 54 Cr. App. R. 519.
[47] [1970] 4 C.C.C. 64 (Ont. C.A.).
[48] [1932] 3 W.W.R. 555 (Alta. C.A.).
[49] Unreported, April 11, 1974 (Ont. C.A.).
[50] Unreported, April 22, 1975 (Ont. C.A.).

In *R. v. Crosby and Hayes*[51] two co-accused who pleaded guilty to fraud were treated differently; Crosby, who had raised £3600 by way of restitution was sentenced to 12 months' imprisonment suspended for two years, whilst co-accused Hayes, who raised only £800, received simply 18 months' imprisonment. The court could see no reason for the difference between the sentences, save that Crosby had raised more money than Hayes which was "not a firm foundation" upon which to base disparity in sentences. In the result he too received a suspended sentence for two years.

In a robbery case, *R. v. Alfs,*[52] the appellant was sentenced to four years while his companion in crime was tried by a different judge and received one year's imprisonment plus two years' probation. The principle regarding disparity of sentence was invoked on the grounds that such a disparity would "justifiably leave Alfs with a sense of injustice" and accordingly the sentence was varied to one of time served, being about ten months, followed by probation for one year.

In *R. v. Murchie*[53] the appellant received a sentence of five years, where his co-conspirators, who had trafficked in a larger amount of marijuana received sentences of two and one half years from a different judge. Another, who was the bookkeeper and who made financial and importing arrangements, received one year. Still another, with lesser involvement, received two months. The Court of Appeal held that in order for justice to be done the sentence should be varied to one of six months in a reformatory.

The reverse was true in *R. v. Gross;*[54] the appellant was treated as one who instigated a scheme for counterfeiting money and his co-accused was given four years, while he received ten. The court characterized the sentences as "rather disproportionate" even in view of the greater relative guilt and imposed instead a sentence of six years.

Sex is not a sustainable ground for inequality of sentence; in *R. v. Williams and Williams,*[55] the court said:

> The sentence on the woman was eighteen months imprisonment and on the man two and a half years. Why it seems so often to be considered, where a man and woman are involved, that the woman should always receive a less sentence than the man, I do not know. Of course there are cases where it is

---

[51] [1975] Crim. L.R. 247.
[52] (1974), 17 Crim. L.Q. 247 (Ont. C.A.).
[53] Unreported, July 12, 1974 (Ont. C.A.).
[54] (1972), 9 C.C.C. (2d) 122 (Ont. C.A.).
[55] (1953), 37 Cr. App. R. 71.

right that she should. If you have a young woman stealing under the influence of a man, it is quite right that she should receive a less sentence than the man.

In the result equal sentences were passed.

Finally, a record of an absolute or conditional discharge is not sustainable ground for disparate sentences. In *R. v. Nickerson*[56] the Prince Edward Island Court of Appeal reduced a sentence of two years to one month because if the trial judge had ignored a conditional discharge, as he should have, there would "not appear to have been any good reason for the wide discrepancy in the sentences imposed."

D. Use In Increasing Sentence

The disparity principle, like all others in sentencing, seems to work two ways. In *R. v. Glowsky*[57] the British Columbia Court of Appeal increased a sentence in a drug case upon the ground that the sentence imposed was not uniform with other sentences passed upon persons convicted of similar offences. Yet at least part of the rationale for the rule is absent in such a case, for it is hard to discern how the Crown can have a "sense of grievance" in the way intended by the rule. Nevertheless, in *R. v. Rudyk*[58] the court raised a sentence from 14 days intermittent with probation and a $250 fine upon a robbery charge in order to reconcile it with the sentence imposed upon his companion (who did not appeal and was sentenced to four years). No major distinction was possible between Rudyk and his companion, but because his companion had a criminal record and a more active part in the crime a two-year penalty was imposed.

E. The Totality Principle

In a number of cases trial judges have been cautioned that they must, in

---

[56] (1975), 7 Nfld. & P.E.I. R. 145 (P.E.I.C.A.).
[57] (1948), 92 C.C.C. 249 (B.C.C.A.).
[58] (1975), 11 N.S.R. (2d) 541 (C.A.).

imposing sentence, have regard not only to the question of whether the sentence is appropriate to the offence in the circumstances, but also to the effect that the totality of sentences then being served will have upon the prisoner. The English Court of Appeal has said in *R. v. Bocskei:* "When consecutive sentences are imposed the final duty of the sentencer is to make sure that the totality of the consecutive sentences is not excessive."[59]

The Ontario Court of Appeal has been following this principle quite regularly in recent years.[60] In *R. v. Conway*[61] three consecutive sentences of three years each following pleas of guilty to counts of armed robbery which occurred during a period of three or four days were appealed. The Court was of the view that the trial judge was correct in imposing consecutive sentences but the result achieved represented an error in principle in that the total sentence of nine years would be a "crushing sentence" on an 18-year-old youth and would remove any hope of reformation. Similarly in *R. v. Culp*[62] the accused appealed an 18-month consecutive sentence following a conviction on the charge of the possession of stolen goods valued at more than $200. The accused had earlier been sentenced to terms amounting in the aggregate to three years for offences committed during a nine-day period. Though of the view that the 18-month sentence was not in itself excessive, the court held that a total sentence of four and a half years was too long under the circumstances and that therefore the sentence for this particular offence would be reduced to six months, so that the aggregate sentence would be three and one half years.

It is not only a sentence that is being served, or a sentence that is imposed at the same time that are subject to the operation of the totality principle, but apparently any sentence from any source. In *R. v. Cathcart,*[63] an extremely large number of charges were each the subject of consecutive sentences, which, when added together, left the appellant with a total of 28 and one-half years' imprisonment. Though there were many aggravating factors, the sentences were reduced to 20 years upon the sole ground that the totality had "the effect of being a sentence of

---

[59] (1970), 54 Cr. App. R. 519.

[60] *R. v. Lukion and Small* (1975), 27 C.C.C. (2d) 11 (Ont. C.A.); see also *R. v. Huskins* (1974), 10 N.S.R. (2d) 553 (C.A.).

[61] Unreported, November 14, 1974 (Ont. C.A.); see also *R. v. Young*, unreported, November 15, 1974 (Ont. C.A.).

[62] Unreported, May 6, 1974 (Ont. C.A.).

[63] Unreported, December 14, 1976 (Ont. C.A.).

preventive detention without the protection afforded by that type of sentence." Accordingly, in *R. v. Black*[64] the court took into account, when the accused committed the kidnapping offence under consideration, that he was on parole, and that the unexpired term which he would have to serve prior to the commencement of the 20-year term would not expire for seven years. Considering therefore the totality of the sentences, the court reduced the sentence from 20 years to 12 years. In *R. v. Evans,*[65] the court said:

> . . . I am of the opinion that a fit and proper sentence, excluding from consideration parole forfeiture, would be imprisonment for one year. I feel, however, that such sentence to be truly fit must to some degree reflect the additional punishment incurred by way of forfeiture of parole. As the forfeiture in this case is no less than approximately 433 days I do not think that a sentence reduction of three months or approximately 91 days, because of such forfeiture, could or should be classified as unwarranted.

Sentence was reduced from 18 months to nine months on assault causing bodily harm. The dissenting judge, Cooper J.A. took the view that the judge may have in mind the provisions of the Parole Act as long as he does not bow to policies of the Parole Board and allow such policies to dictate to him a sentence which he would not otherwise have imposed. Citing with approval *R. v. Heck; R. v. Richardson; R. v. Holden,* and *R. v. Wilmott*[66] he said:

> In my respectful opinion to reduce a sentence to mitigate the effect of forfeiture of parole is to circumvent the provisions of s. 21(1) of the *Parole Act* and, in effect, lessen the sentence which the appellant was serving . . . for the previous offences. I think this is a departure from proper principles of sentencing.

This dissent has been followed, without further analysis or explanation, by the Prince Edward Island Court of Appeal.[67]

---

[64] Unreported, January 8, 1975 (Ont. C.A.); see also *R. v. deVost* (1972), 14 Crim. L.Q. 273 (Ont. C.A.).

[65] (1975), 11 N.S.R. (2d) 91 at pp. 96-97 *per* Macdonald J.A. (C.A.).

[66] *R. v. Heck* (1963), 40 C.R. 142 (B.C.C.A.); *R. v. Richardson* (1963), 40 C.R. 179 (Man. C.A.); *R. v. Holden* (1963), 39 C.R. 228 (B.C.C.A.); *R. v. Wilmott,* [1967] 1 C.C.C. 171 (Ont. C.A.).

[67] *R. v. Keeble* (1977), 37 C.C.C. (2d) 387.

Chapter 3

Procedure

The sentencing process commences with a charge being read to the accused and an inquiry as to how he wishes to plead to it. If the answer is "guilty" then a hearing is held. Counsel for the Crown either calls evidence to substantiate the plea and the charge, or, if the court permits, reads into the record a summary of the facts relied upon by the Crown to support the charge and to assist the trial judge in sentencing. If evidence is called there is a right to cross-examine; if a summary is given, the accused is asked whether or not the facts are substantially correct and if he demurs in any way he is given an opportunity to deny those assertions. If denied, they must be proved in the ordinary way by Crown counsel.

The purpose of an admission of fact to justify one's plea of guilty is not merely a testing of intention but an objective foundation for the plea itself. A mere intention to plead guilty is not in itself sufficient. The trial judge must determine for himself that the plea is justified and the admission factually based.

This general procedure for receiving evidence has been approved by the Supreme Court of Canada by adopting a passage from *Crankshaw's Criminal Code of Canada:*[1]

> After conviction, accurate information should be given as to the general character and other material circumstances of the prisoner even though such information is not available in the form of evidence proper, and such information when given can rightly be taken into consideration by the judge in determining the quantum of punishment, unless it is challenged and

---

[1] Seventh edition, p. 912.

contradicted by or on behalf of the prisoner, in which case the judge should either direct proper proof to be given or should ignore the information.[2]

Thus, though the traditional safeguard constituted by the formal rules of evidence are relaxed after sentence, they are replaced by a different safeguard which is the right of the accused or his counsel to object to the material offered. If the objection be taken then the prosecutor is put to proof and the usual rules of evidence apply.

After considering the summary, the accused will be given an opportunity to offer any factual material he wishes, either by way of calling evidence or by submissions of counsel. The accused himself may testify under oath but "in some cases it might not be to his advantage"; *R. v. Cross.*[3] After this has been concluded through either the accused or through his counsel, counsel for the Crown and the defence have the right to make submissions regarding penalty.

Unfortunately, the procedure, uncomplicated though it is, is often not understood by persons accused of crime. Sometimes the plea is not "guilty", but "guilty with an explanation". Occasionally though, where the plea is one of "guilty", the comments made by the accused in the course of the hearing indicate that this is not the proper plea at all. So, for example, in *R. v. Doiron,*[4] the accused, gave an explanation to the court which "should have prompted the court to enter a plea of not guilty." Elementary consideration of the purpose and nature of a criminal trial indicate that if there is the slightest doubt whether or not the plea of guilty is really intended, then inquiry should be made and, if warranted, the plea should be changed and a different course taken.

If a plea of "guilty" is in fact both justified and intended, a statement put forward in mitigation which in fact negates one of the elements of the crime may be disregarded by the trial judge. The presence or absence of counsel is an important factor in making such a decision.

It is common practice in Canada for pleas of both guilty and not guilty to be made by counsel rather than by the accused. This is extremely unwise, as it leaves open to question the intention of the accused to plead guilty. More significant, it is quite unnecessary, for pleading is simple and can easily be done by the accused personally. It may be that in Canada such a practice is legally permissible, despite such language as that found in s. 534 of the Criminal Code, which speaks of an accused "who is called upon to plead".

---

[2] *R. v. McGrath* (1962), 133 C.C.C. 57 (S.C.C.).
[3] [1975] Crim. L.R. 591.
[4] (1972), 9 C.C.C. (2d) 137 (B.C.).

In summary conviction matters the Criminal Code, s. 735, specifically authorizes an appearance by counsel. However, even in such cases, s. 736 specifically sets out that where the defendant appears he should be asked whether he pleads guilty or not guilty to the information. In matters that proceed by indictment the function of counsel is, in some few respects, set out in s. 578 of the Criminal Code. Nowhere is there any suggestion that pleas should be given by anyone other than the accused. The English Court of Criminal Appeal has taken the view that a plea of guilty tendered by counsel and not by the accused cannot be regarded as an effective and binding one:

> It is a plea which is self-incriminatory and self-incrimination cannot be vicariously accomplished. Any contrary view would be fraught with manifest dangers. Injustice rather than justice would be the likely product of a principle which permitted indirect delegated confessions of guilt.
>
> No qualification of or deviation from the rule that a plea of guilty must come from him who acknowledges guilt is thus permissible. A departure from the rule in a criminal trial [in England] would therefore necessarily be a vitiating factor rendering the whole procedure void and ineffectual. [Though this may not be true in Canada.][5]

The court took a different view of a plea of not guilty upon the ground that it was difficult to understand how any prejudice to an accused person could derive from such a procedure, but it qualified this conclusion by limiting it to situations "where that is the intended plea".

It is not sufficient that the accused should plead guilty, though such a plea was formerly viewed as a complete and effective admission of guilt that rendered any further inquiry unnecessary. The present law requires that in addition to the plea there must be facts read into the record which substantiate the plea of guilty and disclose the guilt of the accused. In *R. v. Voorwinde*[6] the accused was in a car driven by someone else when a suggestion was made that they should siphon some gasoline out of another vehicle. They drove to a truck and one of the accused, who had a five gallon can and a siphon, got out of the car, siphoned a can-full of gasoline from the truck and returned to the car. The appellant remained simply sitting in the car. At some early stage the appellant said, either joking or in earnest, "Well if you are going to get some gas I should get five gallons of it." On arraignment the accused stated: "I was sitting in the car. I knew about it but I was not siphoning the gas." In response to

---

[5] *R. v. Williams,* [1977] 1 All E.R. 874 at pp. 876-77; *cf. R. v. Dietrich,* [1968] 2 O.R. 433 (C.A.).

[6] (1975), 29 C.C.C. (2d) 413 (B.C.C.A.).

his evident confusion as to how he should plead the trial judge explained
to him that, *inter alia:*

> If, on the other hand, you were detached from the matter, you were simply an
> observer and had nothing to do with the planning or the carrying out of it
> then, of course, you should plead not guilty. But it is for you to say. You were
> apparently then charged as a party to the offence but you are the one that best
> knows whether you plead guilty or not guilty. How do you wish to plead?
> [And the appellant said]: I'll plead guilty.

The court noted that, despite the instructions, the facts introduced in
evidence did not support a finding that he was a party to the offence.
Taggart J.A. said:

> Indeed, the facts disclosed by the record may well not be the entire story.
> However, on the basis of those facts as disclosed to the Provincial Court Judge,
> I think he should, upon their disclosure, have reached the conclusion that the
> participation by the appellant, to the extent disclosed by those facts, would not
> make him a party to the offence . . .

> The learned Provincial Court Judge, in my view, erred at that stage by not
> stopping the proceedings and permitting a change of plea so that the trial
> might proceed with the Crown having the opportunity, if it could, to elicit
> the facts which would sustain a conviction of the appellant for the offence of
> theft.

A. The Function Of Counsel In Sentence Matters

Upon a guilty plea and sentence, a prisoner has the right to counsel to the
same extent and for the same good reasons as he would at a contested
trial. In *R. v. Butler,*[7] through no fault of his own counsel (who had been
appointed for the appellant through the legal aid scheme) was not
notified of his retainer until after the trial had concluded; accordingly
the appellant "did not have the assistance of counsel of his choice in his
defence". Although a legal aid duty counsel acted for him on a plea of
guilty, he was not the person who had been selected by the accused to
represent him. For this reason, *inter alia,* a new trial was ordered.

The function of counsel is essentially no different in matters of
sentencing than in any other, for he retains his obligation to protect and

---

[7] (1973), 11 C.C.C. (2d) 381 (Ont. C.A.).

advance his client's interests, while at the same time fulfilling his duties as an officer of the court. It is the duty of counsel both for the prosecution and the defence to know the permissible sentences for the offences with which defendants are charged, and so to be in a position to assist the judge if he makes a mistake, and to avoid the waste of time and money involved in having the Court of Appeal correct such mistakes.[8]

Nevertheless some cases point to particular duties of counsel in this context. Counsel clearly has a duty as an officer of the court to see to it that the plea is a proper one. In *R. v. Johnson,*[9] the appellant had faced a charge of theft of a quantity of tools; on the plea of guilty he stated that it was his intention to bring them back. A finding of guilty was made and the defence counsel submitted to the court pursuant to that plea that the accused was permitted to borrow them for the weekend. The trial judge, quite properly, asked counsel whether or not the accused wished to change his plea in the light of that information. Counsel replied that he had suggested to the accused that the burden of proof would be very heavy on this point if he had pleaded not guilty. The Ontario Court of Appeal took the view that this was "tantamount to saying I am not guilty but I plead guilty because I cannot prove my innocence. Counsel should not have permitted this plea to have been put before the Court." A new trial was ordered in the light of counsel's misconception of both his role and the nature of a plea of guilty.

In *R. v. Foley; R. v. Chandler; R. v. Randle,*[10] before the English Court of Appeal, one accused had a criminal record which appeared to be unrelated to this politically motivated offence, because it was for office-breaking and the possession of housebreaking implements. The Court noted that such a conviction would not have been directly relevant to sentence in a political demonstration case, but commended counsel for the defence for "quite frankly and in compliance with his duty to the Court" disclosing that the offences under consideration were not what they appeared to be, namely, offences of dishonesty, but were "political offences" in that he had broken into the office of a civil defence centre in order to take pamphlets and instructions on civil defense matters with a view to public disclosure. His prior record was viewed as an aggravating factor by the court.

Crown counsel has an obligation to refrain from suppressing relevant

---

[8] *R. v. Kennedy,* [1976] Crim. L.R. 508; *R. v. Newsome; R. v. Browne* (1970), 54 Cr. App. R. 485.

[9] Unreported, January 6, 1977 (Ont. C.A.).

[10] (1967), 52 Cr. App. R. 123.

facts for any oblique motive. Accordingly it was said in *R. v. McKinney*[11] that whenever a prisoner stands at the bar for sentence Crown counsel should advise the trial judge whenever it is the case that the prisoner committed his offence while he was at liberty on bail. It has been held in Australia that to refuse a prosecutor an opportunity of refuting arguments which appear to him to be inconsistent with principle is tantamount to a departure from the fundamental principle of justice of "hearing all evidence, statements, argument and comment made by the other side."[12]

The Court of Appeal (Criminal Division) in England has discussed the duty of counsel where a client instructs him to raise inadmissible or impermissible matters. In *R. v. King; R. v. Simpkins*[13] counsel for the defence made proper representations with regard to sentence and then told the court that he had been asked by his clients to read a "political manifesto" along "classical anarchical lines" to the court; without any dissent from the trial judge he did so. The Court of Appeal said:

> If one can judge from newspaper reports, it would appear that in recent months there have been occasions when young offenders had thought it right to air their political opinions in court. This court wishes to state in the clearest possible terms that courts are not sounding boards for anybody's political views. Anyone attempting to bring political opinions into court is attempting to introduce wholly irrelevant matter. Counsel asked to air an accused's political views should refuse to do so, and if, as in this case, the accused then says "well, I will not accept any advice you give if you do not air my political views," the duty of counsel, so it seems to us, is to say "very well, I will withdraw from the case."

The Court went on to say that if accused persons do dispense with the services of counsel to enable them to air their political views in Court, it is the duty of the judge to stop them from doing so.

The advantage of this case is not its advice regarding political issues, which has not been followed strictly if at all in Canada, but its exemplification of the responsibility of counsel when asked to raise an improper matter by a client. This may arise in sexual offences or cases where the accused has strong feeling against a witness. It is submitted that it is dangerous for counsel to censor his client in this way. If counsel is doubtful of the propriety of raising any particular matter the trial

---

[11] (1963), 40 C.R. 137 (Sask.).
[12] *Kerr v. Matthews* (1977), 1 Crim. L.J. 56 (S.C.S.A.).
[13] (1973), 57 Cr. App. R. 696.

judge can be spoken to, in chambers if necessary, and a decision obtained. Save in the clearest cases, the court, not counsel, should make such decisions.

In *R. v. Lamer,*[14] counsel for the Crown was criticized because he failed to cite any authority or do any research in support of his submissions on appeal which were intended to maintain gaol sentences. The court noted that he was an officer of the court by Quebec statute and emphasized that this factor "does not constitute an empty formula; it is a rule that the persons concerned must translate into acts in the daily exercise of their duties". As a result the court itself had to do the necessary research and uncover the relevant judgments, a function which undoubtedly rests with counsel in any adversary system.

In *R. v. Robinson*[15] the court noted that counsel (in this case counsel for the Crown) permitted a police officer to be called to give evidence which was improper, in that it contained allegations that were likely to be attacked by the prisoner and were of such a general character that they could not be disproved. The court cautioned Crown counsel that he was to "see that a police witness giving evidence after a conviction is kept in hand and not allowed to make allegations which are incapable of proof and which he has reason to think will be denied by the prisoner."

In an unusual case, *R. v. McLean,*[16] the prisoner was convicted of theft of cedar trees and sentenced to six months' imprisonment. The main objection on appeal was that the cross-examination by counsel for the Crown had been prejudicial. The Court of Appeal declined to interfere with the conviction, but on the matter of sentence noted that the cross-examination was improper in that it went to credit but did not contain allegations relating to particular discreditable acts as required by law of evidence. The trial judge stopped counsel for the Crown again and again but counsel persisted in asking his questions. The Court said:

> The learned trial Judge in effect applied this rule in many instances of Mr. Forbes' cross-examination, but he could not prevent the asking of questions, which even though not answered, undoubtedly tended to injure the accused. We cannot say that these questions might not be put and ruled upon. It is largely a matter of whether prosecuting counsel appreciates the ethical considerations which should guide his conduct, and abstain from asking

---

[14] (1973), 17 C.C.C. (2d) 411 (Que. C.A.).
[15] (1969), 53 Cr. App. R. 314; see also *R. v. Wilkins* (1977), 66 Cr. App. R. 49; *R. v. Crabtree* (1952), 36 Cr. App. R. 161.
[16] [1940] 2 D.L.R. 733 at pp. 735-36 (N.B.C.A.).

questions which are suggestive as to the guilt of a person and yet will be ruled out by the trial Judge.

. . .

The Court is of opinion that under the circumstances of the oppressive conduct of the prosecution the sentence should be reduced to five months from the date of the arrest.

It is customary for Crown counsel, often in conjunction with defence counsel, to make representations as to the quantum of sentence. Such a recommendation as to quantum of sentence must be given weight. Failure to do so has been held to be an error. In *R. v. Jones*[17] a recommendation by the Crown attorney for six months' imprisonment was ignored and the magistrate imposed a sentence of two years' imprisonment. On appeal the court, held that the magistrate did not give sufficient weight to, *inter alia,* the recommendation of Crown counsel and reduced the sentence to one of six months.

Although there is no question that the court is not bound by such recommendations, they are customarily given considerable weight. Two interesting cases reflecting this view are *R. v. Minhas*[18] and *R. v. Weber.*[19] In both, the appeal court held different views as to the appropriate sentence to be imposed, but deferred to the recommendations of Crown counsel in the public interest and imposed a more moderate penalty than it had been minded to impose.

The majority in *R. v. Simoneau*[20] held that strictures against any recommendations as to quantum of sentence by Crown counsel were based on English decisions and opinion; the cases cited in this text indicate that in Canada the authority of the Crown in making suggestions concerning sentence is accepted.

One reason for refusing to accept the English practice is the existence of provision in Canada for an appeal by the Crown, with leave, from a sentence imposed by trial court. Obviously Crown counsel in arguing the case on appeal would contend that the sentence was too lenient and that the appellate court should substitute one which was more severe. In *R. v. Wood* the court said: "A position taken by Crown counsel before a trial Judge is a circumstance to be taken into consideration, but we cannot be

---

[17] (1974), 17 C.C.C. (2d) 31 (P.E.I.C.A.); *R. v. Lapointe,* unreported, January 16, 1978 (Ont. C.A.).
[18] (1973), 16 Crim. L.Q. 143 (B.C.C.A.).
[19] (1973), 9 C.C.C. (2d) 49 (B.C.C.A.).
[20] (1978), 2 C.R. (3d) S-17 (Man. C.A.).

bound by any such position taken and are not willing to restrict the appeal of the Crown by such a consideration."[21]

The single judge dissenting was of the view that a joint recommendation as to sentence either fettered or appeared to fetter the discretion of the trial judge; and that the existence of a right to appeal and the different position that might be taken by the Crown on appeal would strike at the fundamental doctrine of the indivisibility of the Crown. His solution to the problem was to create a rule of practice that the Crown counsel should say "nothing or as little as possible" in the matter of the quantum of the sentence.

> Crown counsel is entitled to make a submission to the Judge as to sentence. However, in my opinion, the preferable practice is not to do so unless he is requested by the Judge for a submission. We have found recently that counsel have given us their opinion; this they are not entitled to do; they are only entitled to make submissions. For instance where there is a customary sentence for an offence, Crown counsel is entitled to draw this to the attention of the Judge.

This is clearly not the practice in any other province; nor is it easy to see why a court should be denied the view of the Crown on a matter in issue in an adversary proceeding.

The better view is to be found in *R. v. MacArthur.* The court said:

> It cannot be stated that there is anything wrong in Crown counsel making a submission to the Court as to the sentencing of an accused. In my opinion, where Crown counsel takes the position that it is not their duty to speak to sentence, they are wasting the time of the Court when, not satisfied with the sentence, they immediately appeal sentence. If Crown counsel thinks that a jail sentence is warranted, he should indicate to the Court his feelings.[22]

The failure of counsel for the Crown to make a recommendation for sentence, or to press for a sentence of imprisonment at trial, may later be taken by a court of appeal to bind the Crown.[23] The same view has been taken on occasion by the British Columbia Court of Appeal.[24] Similarly in *R. v. Sutherland,*[25] Crown counsel made submissions at trial that a sentence from 12 to 20 months would be proper. The Crown thereafter

---

[21] (1975), 26 C.C.C. (2d) 100 at p. 110 (Alta. C.A.).
[22] (1978), 39 C.C.C. (2d) 158 at p. 159 (P.E.I.C.A.).
[23] *R. v. James* (1971), 3 C.C.C. (2d) 1 (P.E.I.C.A.).
[24] *R. v. Switlishoff* (1950), 9 C.R. 428 (B.C.C.A.).
[25] (1974), 10 N.B.R. (2d) 221 (C.A.); see also this chapter, "Plea and Sentence Negotiations".

applied for leave to appeal from a sentence of one year. The court, noting the prior position of the Crown, refused to increase the sentence.

B. Inquiries By The Trial Judge

A justice is entitled to take evidence after a plea of guilty in order to determine the nature and quality of the offence as a guide in determining the proper sentence. Since one of the purposes of punishment is the protection of society, it follows that the circumstances of the crime in respect of which sentence is being imposed are not alone a sufficient guide for the judge; the character of the convict is of great importance and this has always been recognized both in law and practice.

> It is important, therefore, that a trial Judge should not be hampered in his efforts to ascertain the character of the convict in the way of securing knowledge of his previous record, beyond what is essential for the protection of the convict.[26]

It is now universal practice, after verdict, to hear evidence of character generally and of any previous convictions not included in the indictment. The case of *R. v. Van Pelz,*[27] cited with approval in *R. v. Carey,*[28] asserts that it is the right of the court "to enquire into any matter on which the Court itself thinks it right to ask for information." This statement is undoubtedly too broad, as the matter inquired into must first be relevant to sentence.

There is an interesting question as to the extent to which, if at all, the trial judge may question the prisoner. If, as Lord Goddard suggests in *R. v. Butterwasser,* there is no longer anything in issue at the sentencing stage at the trial,[29] then adversary proceedings have ceased and one rationale for the right to remain silent no longer exists. On the other hand there is no statutory authority for the suggestion that the sentencing hearing has a different character than any other part of a criminal

---

[26] *R. v. Scheer,* [1932] 3 W.W.R. 555 at p. 557 *per* Harvey, C.J.A. (Alta. C.A.). See also *R. v. Zura; R. v. Ollikkila* (1920), 33 C.C.C. 98 (Ont. C.A.); affg 32 C.C.C. 140. *R. v. Whepdale,* [1927] 3 W.W.R. 704 (Sask. C.A.).

[27] (1943), 29 Cr. App. R. 10; *R. v. Wilkins* (1977), 66 Cr. App. R. 49; *R. v. Crabtree* (1952), 36 Cr. App. R. 161.

[28] (1952), 13 C.R. 333 (Ont. C.A.).

[29] See also this chapter "Establishing a Factual Basis for Sentencing".

process. It is perhaps surprising to find a diversity of views on this important question.

In *R. v. Edwards,*[30] it was said:

> It appears to me improper for a judge or magistrate to ask a prisoner questions with a view of obtaining an answer which may justify the judge or magistrate in passing a more severe sentence than he would upon a first offender. Under our criminal laws, as it is well known, an accused person cannot be called upon to answer any question which would incriminate him unless he voluntarily makes himself a witness in his own behalf. I think it is wrong for a magistrate who is about to pass sentence on a prisoner to ask him a question with a view of extorting a confession that he has been previously convicted, so that the prisoner might thereby receive several years additional punishment.

Phippen J.A. noted that the interest of the public demanded a just conclusion, which could not be reached in ignorance of the prisoner's past and stated that it was impossible to lay down any hard and fast rule on the subject. Richards J.A. did not deal with the matter.

In *R. v. Donovan,*[31] the majority noted that the learned trial judge questioned the accused as to previous convictions after the verdict of the jury and held questioning of that kind to be improper. Richards J.A., in dissent, refused to accept the ruling of the majority as a complete bar to such questioning, saying that "ought rarely to be done, but the door should not be closed entirely. Some discretion should be left to the trial Judge. Circumstances may exist which would justify such a course."

1. RECEIVING INFORMATION

The court will hear evidence from the Crown or the prisoner, either *viva voce* or by affidavit. But no matter how the information is obtained, the circumstances must be such that the accused has the right to contradict the material which is put forward. In *R. v. Carey,*[32] Laidlaw J.A. speaking for the majority, said:

> . . . consent of counsel for the prosecution and for the prisoner cannot confer upon the Court the right to make private inquiries or receive information for the purpose of assisting in determining the appropriate sentence to impose on

---

[30] (1907), 17 Man. R. 288 at p. 292 *per* Perdue J.A. (C.A.).
[31] (1947), 4 C.R. 212 (N.B.C.A.).
[32] *Supra,* n. 28 at p. 338. See also *Webb v. The Queen* (1975), 39 C.R.N.S. 341 (P.E.I.C.A.).

a prisoner in any way other than in accordance with the settled practice of the Court.

All information should be given in open court in the presence of the prisoner, who must be given an opportunity to challenge or contradict any of the statements.

But does there have to be any enquiry at all, should the judge choose not to make one? Lord Goddard was of the view that there was no such obligation; in *R. v. Butterwasser*[33] he said:

> What happens after verdict is very different from what happens before verdict. After verdict, there is no longer an issue between the Crown and the prisoner. The issue has been determined by the verdict of the jury and there is no more room for evidence, except to inform the mind of the Court as to what the prisoner's previous history has been for the purpose of enabling the Court, if the Court desires to hear it, to assess the proper sentence. There are occasions where the Court does not want to hear evidence of the prisoner's character, because, whatever it may be, the Court thinks the offence itself demands either a very small sentence, or even in some cases a very long sentence. There is no obligation on a Court to hear evidence after verdict.

This case was cited with apparent approval in *R. v. Benson and Stevenson.*[34] It is doubtful whether, in a Canadian context, it could be accurately said that the question of sentence was not "in issue" between the Crown and the defence. This view is hardly sustainable in modern conditions. In *R. v. Wallace,*[35] no evidence was called by either the Crown or the appellant on the issue of sentence. There was, however, a lengthy submission made by counsel for the appellant, in which he emphasized the appellant's psychiatric disorder and drug addiction and his need for treatment. These submissions brought to light the existence of documents relating to treatment already received at a psychiatric hospital and a "pre-sentence report to be used in the event of conviction". Counsel for the accused urged the court to consider the documents but this was not done. The Ontario Court of Appeal held that to sentence the accused without regard to the hospital documents or the pre-sentence report was in error. Similarly in *R. v. Samaras,*[36] there was a guilty plea to one count of armed robbery and to another of attempted armed robbery. The accused who was represented by duty counsel, was asked whether the facts stated by the Crown concerning the events of the

---

[33] [1948] 1 K.B. 4 at p. 8.
[34] (1951), 13 C.R. 1 (B.C.C.A.).
[35] (1973), 11 C.C.C. (2d) 95 (Ont. C.A.).
[36] (1971), 16 C.R.N.S. 1 at p. 2 *per* Brooke J.A. (Ont. C.A.).

robberies were correct, to which he answered they were and as to whether or not he had a criminal record, at which time the Crown indicated that he had not. No further information was requested by the court and the appellant was sentenced to a term of eight years. The majority of the court took the view that this was not a sufficient enquiry upon which to base a sentence, particularly one of such gravity:

> In our opinion, serious efforts must be made to provide the Court with the fullest information about any individual who is to be incarcerated and certainly this is so where a lengthy sentence is considered. If such information is not readily offered to the Court, then it should be called for. There may be circumstances where information is not available, or alternatively is refused, but that is not the case here.

Apparently, such circumstances will be exceedingly rare.

The general rule is that justice should not only be done but should manifestly and undoubtedly be seen to be done, and this includes the fair conduct of the criminal trial through all its stages, from arraignment to and including sentence. In *R. v. Martin*[37] it was said: "It is essential for the protection of the convict that any statements made as to his past record should be made in his presence, so that he and his counsel might have the opportunity of contradicting such statements."

Thus whether information is placed before the court orally through counsel, or through a pre-sentence report, or by any other means, if the report contains prejudicial observations which the court considers relevant and likely to influence the sentence and this material is denied by the prisoner, then proof of it, if required, should be given in open court where its accuracy may be tested by cross-examination. The onus of proving the accuracy of disputed statements, even if they came before the court as part of a pre-sentence report order by the trial judge, lies upon the Crown.[38] Alternatively, if the court does not consider it of sufficient importance to justify formal proof, then such matters should be ignored as factors influencing sentence.[39]

There is a suggestion in *R. v. Benson and Stevenson*[40] that one exception to this general rule might arise when the convicted person is suffering from some mental disorder or unusual mental condition. The rationale for this departure is that such information is "not a factor

---

[37] (1947), 3 C.R. 64 at p. 68 (N.B.C.A.).
[38] *R. v. Morelli* (1977), 37 C.C.C. (2d) 392 (Ont.Prov.Ct.).
[39] *R. v. Benson and Stevenson, supra,* n. 34; *R. v. Wood* (1975), 26 C.C.C. (2d) 100 (Alta. C.A.); *R. v. Campbell* (1911), 6 Cr. App. R. 131.
[40] *Supra,* n. 34.

which should in ordinary cases influence the court to impose a higher sentence". However, the recent increasing willingness of courts to impose heavier sentences upon just such grounds, up to and including life imprisonment, certainly militates against such a conclusion. The court went on to say that the rule was a general one and "within that framework and according to the circumstances of each case a certain discretion must be left to the trial court" provided that the principles of natural justice are kept in mind.

In *R. v. Bezeau*[41] the trial judge had a conference after the trial with a psychiatrist, in apparent contravention of the rules set down in *R. v. Carey.*[42] Schroeder J.A. speaking for the majority, accepted this "salutory rule" but took the view that the information was not sought for the purpose of sentence, but rather as the basis for an administrative recommendation to the proper authorities that the prisoner, who was apparently suffering from some mental abnormality, should be placed in an institution where he could receive the appropriate care and treatment. The rule is, however, usually followed.

In *R. v. Smullin*[43] evidence taken by the magistrate when the information was sworn out was relied upon in imposing sentence and the court held that it was improper for him to do so because the evidence should have been taken in the presence of the accused. So also in *R. v. Gauvin,*[44] the trial judge prior to sentencing the appellant requested and read the confidential instructions of the Crown and apparently bore them in mind in sentencing. The procedure was held to be in error and the sentence drastically reduced.

Though the accused must be present for all enquiries that relate to sentence, he need not be present while everything is done. In *R. v. Tomlinson,*[45] the accused was in court while he was sentenced to a fine of $500 and placed on probation for one year. After he left the courtroom the trial judge imposed a term of three months in default of payment of the fine. It was argued that s. 557(1) of the Criminal Code was not complied with, since the applicant was not present in court during the whole of this "trial", and it was sought to quash the conviction and sentence. Agreeing that sentence formed part of the trial, Smith J. held that the sentence was the fine itself, and that the term of imprisonment

---

[41] (1958), 28 C.R. 301 (Ont. C.A.).
[42] *Supra,* n. 28.
[43] [1948] 3 D.L.R. 561 (N.B.C.A.).
[44] Unreported, October 15, 1974 (Ont. C.A.).
[45] (1971), 2 C.C.C. (2d) 97 (B.C.).

was in default thereof, one of several means open to the Crown of enforcing payment. The prison term, the argument continues, formed no part of the sentence itself and hence no part of the trial within the meaning of s. 557(1) of the Criminal Code. In the result, that part of the "sentence" was quashed, but the fine remained valid.

There is nothing in law or practice requiring the presence of the informant or a representative of the Crown upon sentencing of an accused, and the absence of an informant does not justify the dismissal of an information after a guilty plea and conviction upon an earlier date: *R. v. Born.*[46]

C. Sentencing Hearing

Criminal Code:

> 595. Where a jury finds an accused guilty, or where an accused pleads guilty, the judge who presides at the trial shall ask the accused whether he has anything to say before sentence is passed upon him, but an omission to comply with this section does not affect the validity of the proceedings.

It is not clear whether this section is a codification of the common law allocutus. If this is so, the purpose is to give the prisoner an opportunity of moving in arrest of judgment on a point of law to show some reason why he ought not to be sentenced. However, in the light of other Criminal Code provisions which demand that argument contesting jurisdiction be raised at earlier stages, s. 595 may only provide an opportunity to present any information in mitigation that the accused wishes to have before the court.[47]

It would be sensible to suppose, however, that an omission to comply with this section would give grounds for the introduction of further (not fresh) evidence.

The sentencing hearing need be neither lengthy nor formal. Information given in open court can be taken into consideration in determining the quantum of punishment unless it is challenged or contradicted by or on behalf of the prisoner.

---

[46] (1972), 6 C.C.C. (2d) 70 (Man. C.A.).
[47] *R. v. Gombos,* [1965] 1 All E.R. 229; *R. v. Rear,* [1965] 2 All E.R. 268.

"It is important that there should be precision and accuracy in any such information. . . ."

. . . if challenged by the accused, proper proof should be required or the information so obtained should be ignored by the Court in passing sentence. Care on the part of the Court in determining what is fact and what is rumour in the information thus obtained and in seeing that the accused, if he so desires, exercises his right to controvert any of the statements so made will always prevent any injustice being done. . . .[48]

It appears that an express admission is not necessary so long as there is an opportunity to question or contravert the facts offered.[49]

There is a danger in neglecting to call evidence under oath and subject to cross-examination of the circumstances or the character and antecedents of the prisoner. If there should be a contradiction between the statements of Crown counsel and those of the defence, there will not be any reason on the record in most cases, which indicate why one set of statements should be accepted rather than the other.[50]

The best course is to call sworn evidence; but if not, there must be at least a statement from counsel in the record to justify a conclusion reached by the trial judge. Sentences have been reduced where there was no evidence to justify the trial judge's conclusion that the accused was carrying on as a "fence" and that he had been engaged in a life of undetected crime;[51] or a statement as to the incidence of a particular type of crime in Canada;[52] that drug distribution was for gain, or that the prisoner was "a man of means".[53] Indeed it has been held that in the absence of proof, it was an error for a trial judge to take into account the admittedly "natural inference" that the offence was not an isolated one but rather an incident in series.[54]

On the other hand if evidence is offered, it is equally in error for the trial judge to ignore it. Accordingly, in *R. v. Doherty*[55] upon an

---

[48] *R. v. Markoff,* [1937] 1 D.L.R. 77 at pp. 78-79 (Sask. C.A.).

[49] *R. v. Scheer,* [1932] 3 W.W.R. 555 (Alta. C.A.).

[50] *R. v. Hinch and Salanski,* [1968] 3 C.C.C. 39 (B.C.C.A.); *R. v. Pinder* (1923), 40 C.C.C. 272 (Alta. C.A.); *Tremeear's Criminal Code,* pp. 1356-57.

[51] *R. v. Seguin* (1953), 105 C.C.C. 293 (B.C.C.A.).

[52] *R. v. Jones* (1974), 17 C.C.C. (2d) 31 (P.E.I.C.A.).

[53] *R v. Beresford* (1972), 2 S.A.S.R. 446; *R. v. Johnson* (1971), 5 C.C.C. (2d) 541 (N.S.C.A.).

[54] *R. v. Spence* (1961), 132 C.C.C. 234 (P.E.I.).

[55] (1972), 9 C.C.C. (2d) 115 (Ont. C.A.).

examination of the record, the appeal court determined that the trial judge was wrong in reaching the conclusion that there was no evidence of commercial enterprise in a drug trafficking scheme.

In determining the facts of the offence it is, in addition, proper for the trial judge to look at the transcript of the preliminary hearing in cases where it is available. After doing so he must give counsel for the defence a chance to make any reply or contradiction that he wishes. In any event, before a trial judge can permit a plea to a lesser and included offence, he has a duty to acquaint himself with the facts as far as possible and for this purpose the reading of the transcript of evidence on the preliminary enquiry is permissible.[56]

In any event, the purpose of evidence adduced after a plea of guilty is two-fold: first, to substantiate the plea of guilty; secondly, to assist the judge in imposing sentence.[57]

Some controversy exists as to whether or not the trial judge may take judicial notice of such factors as the incidence of crime of a particular sort in a jurisdiction. In *R v. Hemsworth,*[58] the Nova Scotia Court of Appeal declared that judicial notice may be taken of the fact that Nova Scotia is in a similar position to other provinces and the increase in use of drugs there had become a matter of grave concern to the whole community. The widespread incidence of shop-lifting was termed "a matter of public notoriety" in *R. v. Sanchez-Pino.*[59] But that case is distinguishable in that this fact was mentioned by the Crown attorney and apparently not contradicted by the defence. It is submitted that the better position is that expressed by the Nova Scotia Court of Appeal in *R. v. Wilson:*[60]

> In my opinion judges cannot and should not be oblivious to what is reported by the news media, be it by radio, television, newspaper or news magazine. Such media, certainly of late, have been indicating an increase in certain types of criminal activity. Thus, although a judge must of necessity be aware of such reports, I am of the opinion that without further and better proof of their accuracy, such reports should not influence the judicial sentencing process.

---

[56] *R. v. Wilson* (1974), 10 N.S.R. (2d) 629 (C.A.).
[57] *R. v. Doherty, supra,* n. 55.
[58] (1971), 2 C.C.C. (2d) 301 (N.S.C.A.).
[59] (1973), 11 C.C.C. (2d) 53 (Ont. C.A.).
[60] *Supra,* n. 56 at p. 635 *per* MacDonald J.A.

1. THE NATURE OF THE EVIDENCE

Opinions have varied widely on the question of the strictness with which information must be proved when it is placed before the court on sentence. In *R. v. Marquis,*[61] the English Court of Criminal Appeal decided that the trial judge could accept hearsay evidence of character after conviction. The Court noted that the police officer who gives the information but who cannot speak of his own knowledge about criminal convictions of the prisoner, can produce the prisoner's record,

> . . . and it is always perfectly proper to take into account any information which can be given for or against the prisoner, although the matter is not proved with the strictness which would be necessary to prove an issue during a trial. It would be a very unfortunate thing if evidence of that kind could not be given, because it would prevent evidence from being given in favour of the prisoner, and would prevent a police officer from saying: 'I have made enquiries of the prisoner's employer, he works well and his character is good'. After conviction any information which can be put before the court can be put before it in any manner which the court will accept.

However, some 18 years later, the same court took what appears to be a directly opposite view.

In *R. v. Robinson*[62] a police officer gave evidence that the appellant

> is the largest chap in the Midlands engaged on the sale of cannabis and he sells it to other coloured pushers. We have kept observations during the night and have seen other drug pushers go to his house over periods of one or two hours at a time . . . this man is one of the main distributors of drugs in the Midlands.

Relying upon *R. v. Van Pelz*[63] the court affirmed that the police officer who is called to give evidence of character and antecedents should in general confine his evidence to the previous convictions and antecedents of the prisoner, including evidence of the prisoner's home life if his age makes this information material. He should also inform the court of any matters which he believes are not disputed by the prisoner and ought to be known by the court. He should further inform the court of anything known in the prisoner's favour, such as periods of employment or good conduct.

---

[61] (1951), 35 Cr. App. R. 33.
[62] (1969), 53 Cr. App. R. 314; see also *R. v. Sargeant* (1974), 60 Cr. App. R. 74; *R. v. Wilkins* (1977), 66 Cr. App. R. 49.
[63] (1943), 29 Cr. App. R. 10; *R. v. Crabtree* (1952), Cr. App. R. 101.

Noting that the allegations in the present case were likely to be attacked and were of a general character such as was condemned by *Van Pelz,* the court determined that such evidence should not have been given; but that admissible evidence directed to the issue of whether this man was a mere possesser or a trafficker would have been relevant.

> However in the view of this court, such evidence should not be admitted unless the officer giving the evidence can speak from first-hand knowledge without relying on hearsay or records, and unless the evidence is sufficiently particularized to make it possible for the accused to challenge it. The vice in the present case of the allegations made was that in their general terms it was quite impossible for them to be effectively challenged, and the admission of such evidence is a clear and obvious injustice.

The Court went on to state that where evidence of aggravation (here trafficking), which was not led at the trial, is to be given, notice should be given to the defence of that evidence, thus giving them an opportunity to consider it and prepare to challenge it if they wish. If such notice is not given the result will clearly be to give the trial judge discretion as to whether he will admit or reject the evidence when tendered. (Such a discretion may well not exist in Canada.)

Regarding hearsay, the English court has said: "Nothing gives a bigger sense of injustice to a convicted man than false statements being made about him after the verdict. We hope that it will not be necessary for some time now to remind anybody of the importance of this matter."[64] Hearsay evidence has been deprecated in at least one circumstance in Canada. In *R. v. Short*[65] the learned trial judge erred in considering, upon sentence, a hearsay report that the accused was a drug user. This report was unsubstantiated and was denied by the prisoner. Clearly the learned trial judge ought to have disregarded the evidence or called for proper proof, but it is questionable whether the material was admissible at all.

Even greater strictness was seen in *R. v. Leggo*[66] where Norris J.A. for the majority, in a case involving criminal sexual psychopath proceedings, dealt with the proceedings as though they were merely a matter of sentence and determined that even on this footing, such matters must be properly proved. A *voir dire* was held to be necessary regarding statements of the prisoner made to persons who might be

---

[64] *R. v. Sargeant* (1974), 60 Cr. App. Rep. 74 at p. 79; *R. v. Wilkins, supra,* n. 62; *R. v. Crabtree, supra,* n. 63.
[65] Unreported, September 5, 1974 (Ont. C.A.).
[66] (1962), 133 C.C.C. 149 (B.C.C.A.).

persons in authority and the statements should be shown to be voluntary within the ordinary meaning of the rules on confessions before they could be considered by the court. The dissent on this issue did not go so far as to suggest that the rule as to confessions did not apply on a sentencing hearing, but only took the point that, in this context, an admission made to a psychiatrist could not be an admission or a confession to a person in authority within the meaning of the rule.

It is, of course, clear that the trial judge is restricted to the evidence. In *R. v. Snorrason*[67] the accused came before the court on charges of breaking and entering, extortion and attempting to obstruct the course of justice. He pleaded guilty to all charges. The trial judge openly speculated on the possibility that the accused may have participated in similar kinds of activity which had not come to the attention of the police authorities; there was no such evidence before the court. The Manitoba Court of Appeal was unanimous in finding that the court erred in considering matters which went outside the record.

The standard of proof to be applied in a sentencing hearing has recently come into question. Arnup J.A. spoke for the Ontario Court of Appeal[68] in a case where the accused had pleaded guilty to unlawful sexual intercourse with a female under the age of 14 years. The Crown had offered hearsay information as to the circumstances of the offence which was not accepted by the accused, who offered (not under oath) a totally different version. The dispute concerned whether or not the offence was a "near rape" or one where a 14-year-old girl had stated she was 16 and led the accused on towards intercourse. As the Crown chose not to call any evidence, the Court dealt with the matter "on the basis that the appellant was undoubtedly guilty of the offence but that the precise circumstances under which it occurred are not proved." They then reduced to 12 months a sentence of two years less one day.

It is impossible to understand that a Court could reach such a conclusion without any evidence before it whatsoever. It should be noted that the Court was minded to dispose of the matter quickly because, as they noted in oral reasons for judgment, "in view of the fact that we are on the eve of the summer vacation a disposition ought to be made of this case now, rather than send it back to the Provincial Court." Expedience does tend to make bad law; the Court asserted *obiter dicta* that the party offering evidence on sentence had to prove it only on a balance of probabilities.

---

[67] Unreported, June 23, 1977 (Man. C.A.).
[68] *R. v. Cieslak* (1977), 37 C.C.C. (2d) 7.

Some difficulty for Arnup J.A.'s comment can be found in *R. v. MacDonald*[69] where in dissent Martland J. said:

> Proof beyond reasonable doubt is the well-recognized standard applied in the criminal law in respect of the establishing of guilt of an accused person. In my opinion it has no application to the matter of the imposition of sentence. . . . In my view, a standard which is applied in weighing proof of a fact, i.e., guilt of the accused, has no application to the formulation of opinion as to what is expedient to protect the public.

The better view is that the sentencing hearing is indeed part of the trial;[70] that the issue involved is one of fact, namely, proof of facts that will aggravate the eventual sentence; and that the principle in *Woolmington's* case continues to operate throughout. Other cases to the contrary include *Alberton Fisheries Ltd. v. The King*[71] where Campbell C.J.P.E.I. said: ". . . on the question of the gravity of the offence, as well as on the question of guilt or innocence, the accused is entitled to the benefit of any reasonable doubt." It can further be seen that the proposed change in the standard between that of trial and that of sentencing hearing could hardly work in practice.

The Ontario Court of Appeal, when called upon to re-examine the *obiter dicta* in *Cieslak* has expressly overruled it. The standard of proof of facts in aggravation of sentence is re-affirmed as proof beyond a reasonable doubt.[72] Evidence may be offered as part of the proof at trial; but often it will only arise on sentence in determining the nature and gravity of the offence. It may well be that the Crown, in the appropriate case, could choose whether to call such evidence on sentence or at trial.

If Arnup J.A. were correct then on sentence the standard of proof would be much lower and a decided advantage conferred on the Crown. Accordingly, in a given case, depending upon the course chosen by the prosecution, some facts adverse to the accused which were relevant to the sentence would have to be proved beyond a reasonable doubt and others only to the standard of a balance of probability.

---

[69] (1965), 46 C.R. 399 at p. 404 (S.C.C.); see also *R. v. Butterwasser,* [1948] 1 K.B. 4.

[70] *R. v. Tomlinson* (1971), 2 C.C.C. (2d) 97 (B.C.).

[71] (1944), 17 M.P.R. 457 at p. 460 (P.E.I.).

[72] *R. v. Gardiner,* unreported, October 11, 1979 (Ont. C.A.), leave to appeal to S.C.C. granted December 3, 1979; see also *R. v. Sayer,* unreported February 27, 1976 (Ont. C.A.).

The question has been canvassed in Australia.[73]

This case raises in a novel form the question which is increasingly troubling appellate courts, namely, what version of the facts should the trial court accept for the purpose of imposing a sentence after a plea of guilty? It is clear that the plea admits no more than the essential ingredients of the offence. . . . The plea does not in itself permit any circumstances of aggravation which may be alleged by the prosecution; nor conversely does it in itself negative any circumstances of mitigation not amounting to exculpation which may be within the knowledge of the defendant alone . . . if a defendant disputes circumstances of aggravation alleged in sworn evidence from the prosecution, he must do so by sworn evidence from himself or someone else: if on the other hand the aggravating matter is not sworn to and is only alleged on the one hand, and not on the other, in unsworn form, then "it is the duty of the trial Judge to act upon the version of the facts which, within the bounds of reasonable possibility, is most favourable to the accused": *Maitland's Case* (1963) S.A.S.R. 332 at page 335 . . .

In the present case the accused had pleaded guilty to a charge of driving whilst disqualified. This was an offence where *mens rea* was not an ingredient at all, and as counsel put forward accordingly in mitigation, he had honestly but mistakenly obtained a driving licence from another jurisdiction and thought he was entitled to drive under that authority. The magistrate rejected this excuse, which was given orally by counsel, pointing to a disparity in the application for the second licence and the history of the accused regarding such offences. The court felt that if the explanation had been accepted the penalty actually imposed would have been manifestly excessive.

The Court said:

Normally that version is put forward by the defendant's counsel if he is represented or, if he is not, by himself without his being sworn. The court can reject the explanation if it passes the bounds of reasonable possibility, but I do not think it ought to take this course without giving the defendant an opportunity to support his story by his oath and that of any other witnesses he desires to call. Some stories which might appear incredible when related in *oratio obliqua* by counsel, or for that matter by the defendant himself, become believable, or at least appear as if there is a reasonable possibility that they might be true, when related on oath in the box after surviving the test of cross-examination.

That was not done in this case and I think the appellant should be given an opportunity to do it if he so desires. It is true that no request was made by the

---

[73] *Law v. Deed*, [1970] S.A.S.R. 374 *per* Bray C.J.

appellant's counsel; but he could not be expected to anticipate the learned Special Magistrate's rejection of the story and I think that, before the learned Special Magistrate finally rejected it, he should have given the defendant an opportunity to enter the witness box.

. . . What if the court is willing to accept it as being within those bounds but the prosecution desires to challenge it? I do not think the prosecution can force the defendant into the box. But of course if the prosecution thinks that it can disprove the defendant's account by other witnesses, it should be given an opportunity to call such witnesses, and if this is done and the defendant has not entered the box the case will be one of sworn testimony against unsworn statement and the ordinary principles laid down in *Maitland's Case* will apply.

2. MATTERS UPON WHICH NO EVIDENCE MAY BE CALLED

The rule in Canada is that so far as the nature of the case permits the court must exclude consideration of one untried charge or other potential charges from adjudication upon sentence for a particular offence.[74] The exception to this rule occurs when the accused requests that other offences be taken into consideration.

> But a Judge following this procedure must avoid the danger of giving consideration, in passing sentence, to aggravating circumstances disclosed by such evidence which may change the character of the offence charged against the prisoner. He must avoid the error of sentencing the prisoner in reality for the commission of a greater offence than the one with which he has been charged.[75]

In *R. v. Huchison,*[76] the prisoner pleaded guilty to a single act of incest with his daughter and took the position that one act of incest only had taken place. The daughter had made an allegation of continual intercourse. The trial judge, in difficulty as to how to treat the matter, heard evidence from both the prisoner and his daughter, satisfied himself that continuing intercourse had taken place and passed sentence upon that basis. The Court of Appeal (Criminal Division) held that this course was wrong in that the prisoner was in effect deprived of his right to trial by jury with regard to the additional offences suggested by the daughter.

---

[74] *R. v. Spence* (1961), 132 C.C.C. 234 (P.E.I.); *Lees v. The Queen* (1979), 46 C.C.C. (2d) 385 (S.C.C.).
[75] *R. v. Whepdale,* [1927] 3 W.W.R. 704 at p. 705 (Sask. C.A.).
[76] (1972), 56 Cr. App. R. 307.

The Crown, if it was dissatisfied with the single count, ought to have preferred an indictment charging the other incidents or have amended the indictment so as to cover them and thus permit sentence for other alleged incidents.

A similar case was *R. v. Burton,*[77] where the prisoner was convicted on charges of receiving stolen property, originally the property of the railway company which had employed him. A police officer employed by the railway company was called to give evidence and said "The police enquiries have proved definitely that the prisoner has been responsible for the losses which have taken place. . .". The court said:

> In our opinion that was a most improper statement to make. Either the police could prove that statement, in which case they ought to have prosecuted the appellant, or at least have given him an opportunity of asking for those offences to be taken into consideration, or they could not, in which case they ought not to have invited the presiding judge to increase the appellant's sentence in respect to felonies for which he had never been charged, and therefore had never had an opportunity of disproving.

In the result the sentence was reduced substantially.[78]

In *R. v. James,*[79] upon a charge of assault causing bodily harm, the Crown appealed because the trial judge refused to take into account the fact that the victim was a police officer. The court acknowledged that the maximum punishment for assaulting a police officer is the same as for assault causing bodily harm, but noted that nevertheless they were distinct offences:

> It is my opinion that the offence against s. 232(2)(*a*) is a more serious offence than an offence against s. 231(2) and a more serious punishment should be provided in the case of an assault on a peace officer. . . . The sentences, however, within the limit set by Parliament, are a matter in the discretion of the trial Court and in exercising its discretion the trial Court should consider only the offence with which the person has been charged or some included offence.

3. ESTABLISHING A FACTUAL BASIS FOR SENTENCING

Since a first principle is that the sentence must be appropriate to the

---

[77] (1941), 28 Cr. App. R. 89.
[78] See Chapter 8, "Other Offences Disclosed by the Evidence".
[79] (1971), 3 C.C.C. (2d) 1 at pp. 4-5 (P.E.I.C.A.).

offence, it is of cardinal importance to determine the nature and gravity of the offence beyond the typological specification in the information or indictment. On a trial by judge alone a problem will not usually arise, because the judge as he hears the evidence forms his own view of the facts beyond a reasonable doubt.

A number of Australian cases have approved the view that: ". . . the principle by which a defendant has the benefit of any reasonable doubt applies all through the criminal law and to matters of penalties as well as to matters of guilt or innocence except in the case of the defence of insanity or in the case of any special statutory provision to the contrary." [80]

It is important that the trial judge should restrict himself to the charge in finding the facts for a sentence. In *R. v. Ingram and Denniston* [81] the accused pleaded guilty to two counts of conducting a mock auction, contrary to the Mock Auctions Act — an offence which did not contain dishonesty as an essential ingredient of the charge. He had a lengthy record which counted violence and dishonesty within it, had conducted two other auctions and received a warning from the police. The trial judge sentenced him to twelve months' imprisonment on each count on the basis that his conduct was dishonest. On appeal, however, the court noted that the charges contained no allegation of dishonesty, and that other specific counts that did allege dishonesty had not been pressed by the Crown. Accordingly, the court reduced the penalty to a fine of £50. The principle is clear; a sentencer must adopt, for the purposes of a sentence, a view of the facts that is consistent with the plea which has been accepted. Where an adverse inference is to be drawn against the accused, at the very least the issue should be raised in time for argument and evidence to be called upon that issue. [82] A sentencer may not adopt a view of the facts which would have justified a conviction for a more serious offence than the one for which the accused has been convicted. [83]

Where a trial is by jury, however, the problem may become acute. Where the jury verdict is unambiguous, as for example where only one defence is offered which would reduce the original charge and this is accepted; or where all of the various defences are rejected, the jury verdict will ordinarily indicate their view of the facts. The trial judge

---

[80] *Law v. Deed, supra,* n. 73 at p. 378; *R. v. Maitland,* [1963] S.A.S.R. 332; *Samuels v. Festa,* [1968] S.A.S.R. 118.

[81] (1976), 64 Cr. App. R. 119.

[82] *R. v. Lester,* [1976] Crim. L.R. 389.

[83] *R. v. Foo,* [1976] Crim. L.R. 456.

must in such cases be guided by the jury verdict and not by his own view of the evidence.[84] However there are cases where the verdict is ambiguous, as for example when on a charge of murder where a verdict of manslaughter is received, the defences offered may be various. One cannot know which state of facts the jury accepted, or even if all of the jurors accepted a single state of facts, yet this distinction may be crucial for sentencing. For example, provocation as a defence has much more weight in reducing the sentence than a defence of drunkenness.

The view of the Australian courts on this matter was set out in *R. v. Harris:*[85]

> The responsibility of awarding punishment once a jury has convicted a prisoner lies solely upon the judge. He has to form his own view of the facts and to decide how serious the crime is that has been committed, and how severely or how leniently he should deal with the offender. The learned judge in forming his view of the facts must not, of course, form a view which conflicts with the verdict of the jury, but so long as he keeps within those limits, it is for him and him alone to form his judgment of the facts.

A parallel problem arises where a fact not directly in issue becomes crucial to the question of sentence. It may be clear from the verdict of guilty on a charge of rape, for example, that some violence was used against the victim, but the claims of the defence and the prosecution regarding the extent of the violence may vary immensely; the jury may not have accepted the Crown's position, but at the same time may well have accepted that there was some force used. Or, the prosecutrix in the rape trial may have alleged that she was a virgin, while the defence in addition to denying this proposition alleged that on previous occasions she permitted intimacies of a lesser nature with the prisoner. These matters are not directly in issue at all in the rape verdict, yet they will be crucial in determining the quantum of sentence.

In England, there is a practice of resolving ambiguous verdicts by putting questions to the foreman of the jury after the verdict has been returned.[86] This practice was disapproved by the English Court of Appeal in 1943[87] subsequently approved in 1958[88] and mentioned

---

[84] *R. v. Jama* (1968), 52 Cr. App. R. 498.
[85] [1961] V.R. 236.
[86] *Cf.* D.A. Thomas, "Establishing a Factual Basis for Sentencing", [1970] Crim. L.R. 80.
[87] *R. v. Larkin,* [1943] K.B. 174.
[88] *R. v. Matheson,* [1958] 1 W.L.R. 474.

noncommitally in 1967,[89] but in any event the practice is not followed in Canada. It is easy to see that asking questions of a jury after verdict may cause confusion and could in some instances cast doubt upon a jury verdict unless great care is taken with the questioning — a result that should be avoided where possible.

The Canadian practice seems to leave it to the judge to form his own view of the evidence when the jury verdict is either ambiguous or does not speak to issues which are important for sentence. This procedure is really quite inconsistent with the general principles of sentencing. The safest and best solution would be for the prosecution to state the view of the facts that it puts before the trial judge for the purposes of sentence and for these to be either admitted or contested by the defence. If necessary, evidence could be called before the trial judge alone on these peripheral issues in a sentencing hearing following the jury verdict.

A similar problem may arise on a guilty plea. In *R. v. Wilson,*[90] the Nova Scotia Court of Appeal approved the use of a preliminary hearing transcript as a basis for establishing the facts for sentence, provided that the defence was given an opportunity to challenge or reply to any of them.

4. COMMENCEMENT AND POSTPONEMENT OF SENTENCE

Section 649(1) of the Criminal Code provides that: "A sentence commences when it is imposed, except where a relevant enactment otherwise provides."

There are a few "relevant enactments" which permit a sentence to commence other than when it is imposed. The section prior to amendment left a general discretion in the court to order otherwise, but this discretion has been removed.

One such enactment is the Parole Act, which provides in certain circumstances for sentences to commence at a different time than when they are imposed. Another is the provision in the Criminal Code for consecutive sentences.

By virtue of s. 649(3), notwithstanding s-s. (1), a term of imprisonment, whether imposed by a trial court or the court appealed to,

---

[89] *R. v. Warner* (1967), 51 Cr. App. R. 437.
[90] (1974), 10 N.S.R. (2d) 629 (C.A.).

commences or shall be deemed to be resumed, as the case requires, on the day on which the convicted person is arrested and taken into custody under the sentence. There is no longer any authority in the statute for the judge to make any other direction.

Time spent in custody after conviction but before sentence therefore is not part of the sentence.[91] The proper course is to give such imprisonment consideration by abbreviating the term to be imposed in the sentence.[92]

In the ordinary course, prisoners who plead guilty are sentenced immediately, or after proper inquiry, but this course ought not to apply where several persons are indicted together and one pleads guilty and the others plead not guilty. In such a case sentence ought to be postponed on the prisoner who has pleaded guilty until the others have been tried and then all who have been convicted can be dealt with together, because by that time the court will be in possession of the facts relating to all of them and will be able to assess properly the degree of guilt between them. This is not possible where one accused elects to be tried in the General Sessions of the Peace and another before a magistrate, but it is a reason for a magistrate to exercise his discretion to strike the election and to insist upon all persons being tried in the same forum. This would, of course, not be necessary where a magistrate makes inquiries of counsel for the Crown and counsel for the defence and is informed that with their assistance it will not be difficult to assess relative responsibility so far as the facts are concerned.

However, where a prisoner who pleads guilty is intended to be called as a Crown witness, the rule is reversed, and he must as a matter of good practice be sentenced there and then, prior to giving his evidence, so that there should be no suspicion that what he says may be coloured by the fact that he hopes to get a lighter sentence because of the evidence which he has given.[93]

A recurring improper practice is that shown by *R. v. Fuller,*[94] where the magistrate sentenced the respondent, on a charge of possession of a narcotic to a term of nine months' imprisonment and at the time of sentencing directed that the warrant of committal be withheld for a period of seven days saying: "I assume Mr. Fuller that you are planning to leave the city."

---

[91] *R. v. Patterson* (1947), 87 C.C.C. 86 (Ont. C.A.).
[92] Criminal Code, s. 649(2.1).
[93] *R. v. Payne* (1950), 34 Cr. App. R. 43.
[94] [1969] 3 C.C.C. 348 (Man. C.A.).

The prisoner left Winnipeg and took up residence in Vancouver where he continued to reside. The Manitoba Court of Appeal held that the judicial function of the magistrate ended when he caused a conviction to be drawn up and when he sentenced the accused to nine months' imprisonment. Although issuance of the warrant of committal was a "mere ministerial act" and did not effect the sentence there is no authority whatever for withholding the warrant of committal. The sentence was attacked on the grounds that, viewed as a whole, it amounted to a sentence of banishment — and which would be contrary to the Canadian Bill of Rights: The Court distinguished this argument by noting that the fellow was not obliged to leave Winnipeg, but was rather given the option of doing so, though no doubt it was hoped that he would do so.

> In Canada communities are interdependent and relations between them should be marked by mutual respect and understanding. A practice whereby one community seeks to rid itself of undesirables by foisting them off on other communities violates this basic concept of consideration for the rights of others and should not be tolerated.

Dickson J.A. (as he then was) commented on postponement of sentencing as follows:

> This Court recognizes that it may be necessary to postpone sentencing for the purpose of obtaining a pre-sentence report or additional information concerning the offence or the offender. This Court is firmly of the opinion, however, that sentencing should not be postponed for a lengthy period simply for the purpose of determining whether an accused will behave himself during the period of postponement. No such course of conduct is authorized by any provision of the *Criminal Code.*

In *R. v. Brookes,*[95] the Ontario Court of Appeal adopted that view and commented as well that there was no justification for postponement of sentence for "any length of time" in the belief that the Criminal Code would be amended in the meantime. Similarly, the same Court disapproved of a postponement of sentence so that an appeal against the conviction could be taken.[96]

However in *R. v. Nunner,*[97] the Ontario Court of Appeal approved an adjournment for sentencing of approximately five months to see if the

---

[95] [1970] 4 C.C.C. 377 (Ont. C.A.).
[96] *R. v. D'Eri* (1972), 10 C.C.C. (2d) 252 (Ont. C.A.).
[97] (1976), 30 C.C.C. (2d) 199 (Ont. C.A.); see also *R. v. Griffiths* (1977), 15 A.L.R.I. 1.

accused's efforts at rehabilitation would in fact continue, with a view to eventually imposing a suspended sentence and probation on a pending charge of robbery. The Court stated that it is neither a collection nor investigative agency and should not exercise the inherent power to postpone sentence to determine whether the accused makes restitution, or cooperates with the police to recover goods, or aids in the investigation of others. A lawful postponement should not run beyond a month or two except in the most unusual circumstances.

5. THE DOCTRINE OF FUNCTUS OFFICIO

The expression *functus officio* means "having discharged a duty". When used in relation to a court it may also mean "whose duty or authority has come to an end". In general it seems that once a court has passed a valid sentence after a lawful hearing it is *functus officio* and cannot reopen the case for any reason whatever.[97a] This doctrine applies to a magistrate's court, but probably does not apply to the common law criminal courts which may alter a sentence so long as the court itself is in session. In *R. v. Uxbridge Justices, Ex p. Clarke,*[98] the justices realized they had given an illegal sentence and thought to change it to conform to the law, but the Divisional Court determined that the justices were *functus officio.* The distinction made was that in this case there had been a perfectly proper legal hearing and the court distinguished cases where the hearing itself had been a nullity. It has been suggested that a proper distinction to be made would be one between an invalid or unlawful sentence (which ought to be amendable) and an otherwise valid sentence which the court wishes to alter because it has changed its mind or because fresh facts have come to its attention.[99] In the latter case the present law seems to be that the magistrates are unable to alter their order.

A general distinction has been made between matters of judicial adjudication, where the doctrine of *functus officio* applies, and administrative acts which are not part of the judicial function reposing upon a court by virtue of the Criminal Code for the purposes of a judicial disposition of a case. In the case of an order of dismissal drawn

---

[97a] *R. v. Riddle* (1977), 4 A.R. 205 (C.A.).

[98] (1968), 52 Cr. App. R. 578.

[99] *R. v. Wilson, Ex p. Neil* (1953), 117 J.P. 273; see also C. T. Latham and A. R. Rickard, *The Doctrine of Functus Officio* (London: Justice of the Peace Ltd., 1971).

up pursuant to s. 43 of the Criminal Code, it can be made (subject to any specific statutory language) at any time, as it records but is not part of the judicial disposition of the case: *R. v. Riddle.*

In *R. v. Grice,*[100] the English court noted that prior to codification a Judge of Assize passed sentences in court, and at the end of the Assize he signed the calendar authenticating the sentences which he had passed. Recorders in Sessions Courts did the same thing. This system existed for hundreds of years prior to 1972. From time to time judges have passed sentences in court and thought better of it in the course of the next few days, and when signing the calendar reduced it: "But certainly no judge, in our experience, ever used that provision to increase the sentence. It may technically have been possible to do so, and there may be some exceptional circumstances in which the sentence could be increased." Even when it can be done, it most certainly could not be done because of some event that had taken place after the original sentence had been passed. The English codification of the common law provision that permitted changes in sentence was viewed by the judges to "include slips of the tongue or slips of memory." It is quite wrong to use such a power for a fundamental change of mind about the sentence that was earlier imposed.

Where a sentence is to be altered, it is desirable, whenever possible, that the alteration be stated publicly in open court when the accused is present.[101]

In *R. v. Lee Park,*[102] a magistrate completed a lawful sentence and signed the conviction, being authorized by the then statute "at the time of conviction and sentence" to make an order preventing the deportation of the prisoner, but failed to do so. Some days later he so endorsed the order and it was held he was *functus officio* and the order was not part of the sentence.

R. v. Gallicano and *Re Skied and The Queen*[103] can usefully be compared. In *Gallicano* the accused pleaded guilty to a charge of possessing a narcotic. The trial judge neglected to ask Crown counsel if he had any submissions to make concerning penalty before imposing a fine of $100. Thereafter Crown counsel stated that there were two

---

[100] (1978), 66 Cr. App. R. 167; see also *R. v. Sodhi* (1978), 66 Cr. App. R. 260.
[101] *R. v. Tomar* (1949), 33 Cr. App. R. 91.
[102] (1924), 43 C.C.C. 66 (B.C.C.A.).
[103] [1978] 2 W.W.R. 93; reversed on further appeal on jurisdictional grounds, [1978] 3 W.W.R. 453 (B.C.C.A.); *Re Skied and The Queen* (1975), 24 C.C.C. (2d) 93 (B.C.).

previous convictions. On appeal, a subsequent sentence of 30 days was held to be improperly imposed and a nullity as the trial judge was *functus* at the time of the "resentencing", and the second "corrected" sentence was therefore a nullity.

In *Skied,* the Provincial Court Judge in British Columbia had imposed on a man aged 32 a combination of definite and indeterminate sentences which is illegal. Some five days later the accused was called before the court and the trial judge purported to alter the sentence by substituting a sentence of imprisonment for 12 months. It was argued unsuccessfully that the sentence with respect to the definite term was not separable from the indeterminate term and that thus the whole sentence was invalid. Therefore, it was argued, the court, on *habeas corpus,* could impose another sentence or refer the matter back for sentencing. A warrant of committal was quashed and *habeas corpus* was granted upon the grounds that at the close of the first sentence the judge was *functus officio.*

In *R. v. Smith*[104] the trial judge, noting that he had committed an error in the formalities of the warrant, made an alteration in them. The court held that he could do so while they were still under his control. A broader principle was stated in *Ex parte Stokes,*[105] noting that upon imposing sentence and signing the conviction in the form provided by the Criminal Code, the magistrate completed his judicial function. The court went on to say that the administrative acts that followed must necessarily be in the terms of the judicial disposition of the case. The warrant of committal, as an administrative process, may not interfere with the sentence of the court. McRuer C.J.H.C. said "In any case the court has always jurisdiction to control its own orders so that the formal order may express the true meaning and judgment of the court."

In any event, motions based on this sort of technicality are often brought up by *certiorari* or *habeas corpus,* where the court has the discretion to refuse or a right to adjourn the application. This discretion is frequently exercised to prevent success on merely technical grounds.[106]

Another case worth noting is *Re R. and Mroch.*[107] In this case the accused was convicted of impaired driving. The endorsement on the information indicated that he was prohibited from driving anywhere in

---

[104] (1912), 19 C.C.C. 253 (N.S.C.A.).

[105] (1951), 100 C.C.C. 238 (Ont.); *R. v. Yamelst* (1975), 22 C.C.C. (2d) 502 (B.C.).

[106] *R. v. Horsefall* (1971), 19 C.R.N.S. 79 (Sask. C.A.); *Ex p. Stokes, supra,* n. 105; *Re Skied and The Queen, supra,* n. 103.

[107] (1973), 11 C.C.C. (2d) 528 (Alta.).

Canada for six months, but had a further notation on it that the accused might re-apply for a restricted license anytime during the six-month prohibition period. Such application was made successfully and an appeal was taken. The appeal court held that the trial judge became *functus officio* when he made the initial prohibition order. Had he made an order granting intermittent driving at the time of sentence he would have been within his authority, but having imposed a complete sentence he could not, by his endorsement, for permission to reapply for a restricted licence, have retained jurisdiction to revise, amend or reimpose another and less severe sentence.

In *R. v. Hislop*[108] the trial judge sentenced Hislop to a term of 12 months' imprisonment plus probation for three years upon a charge of break enter and theft, a term of three months consecutive upon a charge of escaping from lawful custody and a term of 12 months concurrent on a charge of possession of stolen goods valued at less than $200. It was then made a condition of the sentence that Hislop sign the probation order to indicate his acceptance of those terms. Hislop refused, whereupon he was brought back to court some six days later, and the sentence for breaking entering and theft was substantially increased. The Ontario Court of Appeal termed the increased sentence a nullity because the trial judge had already imposed sentence and was therefore *functus officio*. The earlier sentence however remained valid, and was affirmed.

Where sentence has not been passed, however, a trial judge may in proper circumstances change a finding of guilt and hear further evidence; in effect, he may re-open the case.[109]

6. FORMALITIES OF WARRANTS

Section 716 of the Criminal Code provides that no warrant of committal shall on *certiorari* or *habeas corpus* be held to be void by reason only of any defect therein, where (a) it is alleged in the warrant that the defendant was convicted and (b) there is a valid conviction to sustain the warrant. Similar provisions even wider in scope are found in s. 711 of the Criminal Code. Nevertheless, in making a warrant of committal a judge has no authority to stipulate the time that was to be served prior to release on parole; this is a matter governed by the Parole Act. Such a

---

[108] Unreported, February 4, 1975 (Ont. C.A.).
[109] *R. v. Lessard* (1976), 30 C.C.C. (2d) 70 (Ont. C.A.).

portion of a warrant was declared to be surplusage in *R. v. Gardner; Ex p. Hamilton.*[110]

The general rule is that the sentence governs and if it is at variance with the warrant of committal, it is the sentence pronounced by the judge that must be taken as being correct. Accordingly in *R. v. Woodard,*[111] the appeal was allowed to make a ten-year sentence concurrent rather than consecutive and thus to conform to the order of the trial judge in open court. If real ambiguities are found in the construction or application of a warrant of committal it should be applied in such a manner as to favour the person against whom it is sought to be enforced. Thus, where a sentence is stated to be consecutive but it is not clear whether it is consecutive to yet another sentence, the construction most favourable to the applicant must be taken.[112]

The general rule regarding persons jointly convicted is that it depends upon the wording of the particular statute applicable to each case and the quality of the offence whether each person is liable to a distinct penalty, or all persons collectively subject to but one penalty. Convictions are individual under our Criminal Code. Accordingly in *R. v. James,*[113] the court held that a joint penalty of $400 was unlawful. Similarly in *R. v. Pretty*[114] where there were two separate informations charging separate offences, it was an error for the magistrate to draw up a single conviction imposing a single penalty with regard to both offences. Separate convictions and separate penalties ought to have been passed with respect to each offence.

Similarly, an endorsement upon an indictment or an information represents the sentence of the court; where the order of committal is at variance with that endorsement, it is the endorsement on the indictment that must take precedence over the committal order.[115] What happens when the trial judge is too incompetent to read correctly aloud his own endorsement of sentence on the indictment is a question that must be left to the speculation of future scholars of the law.

---

[110] [1970] 2 C.C.C. 165 (Ont.); *Ex p. Risby* (1975), 24 C.C.C. (2d) 211 (B.C.).
[111] Unreported, October 24, 1972 (Ont. C.A.).
[112] *R. v. Foster,* [1976] 4 W.W.R. 681; revd [1976] 5 W.W.R. 566 (B.C.C.A.).
[113] (1917), 29 C.C.C. 204 (N.S.C.A.).
[114] (1971), 5 C.C.C. (2d) 332 (P.E.I.C.A.).
[115] *R. v. Mitchell,* [1977] 2 All E.R. 168.

7. TAKING INTO CONSIDERATION

Upon conviction, whether following a plea of guilty or not guilty, the prisoner may ask the court in passing sentence to take into consideration other offences committed by him. He understands by this that the sentence imposed upon the conviction will be greater in order to reflect those other offences, but he expects and hopes that the total sentence will be less than he would have received had he been charged and convicted separately of each one. An offence taken into consideration is not a conviction and the plea of *autrefois convict* will not lie as a result. In cases where special orders are available, such as disqualification from holding or possessing a weapon, restitution orders and perhaps others, they cannot flow from an offence taken into consideration. The procedure developed is a means of protecting the accused from re-arrest upon his release from prison for an offence committed before he was sent to prison. It is designed to produce a clean slate upon release. No doubt it saves a great deal of time because separate trials are not necessary for each offence. Undoubtedly, also, it helps the police clear up their occurrence sheets. The total sentence imposed after offences have been taken into consideration may not exceed the maximum permissible on the offence for which the conviction is registered, regardless of the seriousness of the offences. Ordinarily the offences taken into consideration should be similar, but in England this practice is not strictly followed. A judge may in his discretion refuse to take an offence into consideration, even though there is consent by the Crown and by the defence.

This practice is common in England but is rare in Canada. Nevertheless it has received judicial approval here. In *R. v. Garcia and Silva*,[116] three young men were charged with three offences but were arraigned and convicted only upon a charge of breaking and entering. The Crown indicated that if all the offences were reflected in the penalty, it would be satisfied and the remaining charges would be withdrawn. The Ontario Court of Appeal agreed that it was frequently a sensible and proper thing for a judge to take into consideration, under proper safeguards, other charges laid against a convicted person. The safeguards ought at least to include the condition that they are charges with respect to which the accused would plead guilty or would otherwise

---

[116] [1970] 3 C.C.C. 124 (Ont. C.A.); see also *R. v. Oliver* (1977), 20 Crim. L.Q. 25 (B.C.C.A.).

be proved guilty and that the Crown commits itself not to proceed with these other charges in the event that they are taken into consideration in sentencing upon the conviction before the court.

The danger the court wished to guard against was illustrated by *R. v. Forbes,*[117] a reference to the Court of Appeal (Criminal Division), where upon a plea of guilty to two offences some 142 outstanding offences were taken into consideration; subsequent investigation disclosed that Forbes could not possibly have committed 88 of them and that he had in fact fabricated his own guilt.

Insofar as procedure is concerned, the English Court of Criminal Appeal has ruled that it is not necessary in every case to put to the prisoner the details of each offence which it is sought to take into consideration; instead, a list may be given to him for which he signs a receipt and he is then asked: "Do you admit those offences and wish them to be taken into consideration?"[118] The questions put must be without any suggestion of pressure put upon the applicant. Such pressure may be inferred by the court from a statement to the effect that if he does not wish to have the offence taken into consideration "the prosecution may well want to try them."[119]

Aside from this procedure, other untried charges or potential charges must not be reflected in any way in the sentence for a particular offence.[120]

There is another case in Canada in which the procedure was applied and approved by an appellate court. In *R. v. Lauzon,*[121] after conviction upon one charge, the complainant in a related charge refrained from laying any information, but reserved to himself the right to do so if he did not approve of the sentence which was imposed for the other offence. Counsel for the Crown and counsel for the defence offered this complainant a postponement of sentence to allow him to lay an information so that all sentences could be imposed at the same time, but this was refused. The court felt that this method of proceeding involved a "threatening attitude" to the court itself. With the consent of both counsel, the trial judge rendered sentence and in it reflected the complaint that the other informant had refused to bring forward. Upon the charge of theft involving a stock speculation the accused was

---

[117] (1968), 52 Cr. App. R. 585.
[118] *R. v. Marquis* (1951), 35 Cr. App. R. 33.
[119] *R. v. Nelson* (1967), 51 Cr. App. R. 98.
[120] *R. v. Spence* (1961), 132 C.C.C. 234 (P.E.I.).
[121] (1940), 74 C.C.C. 37 (Que. C.A.).

sentenced to six months' imprisonment. Several months after he had served his sentence the complainant did proceed to lay a new information, and the same trial judge imposed no additional penalty. The Crown, having previously indicated that it would not ask for any further punishment on this charge, reneged and appealed. The court unanimously dismissed the appeal and approved the procedure taken by the trial judge in taking the outstanding similar charge into account and reflecting it in the sentence, approving the principle that pending charges ought, if possible, to be dealt with at the time of conviction or failing that as soon as may be before sentence expires.

8. OFFENCES COMMITTED IN ANOTHER LOCALITY

Criminal Code:

434(1) Subject to section 6, subsections (2) and (3) of this section and sections 665 and 666, nothing in this Act authorizes a court in a province to try an offence committed entirely in another province.

. . .

(3) Where an accused is charged with an offence that is alleged to have been committed in Canada outside the province in which he is, he may, if the offence is not an offence mentioned in section 427 and
  (a) in the case of proceedings instituted at the instance of the Government of Canada and conducted by or on behalf of that Government, the Attorney General of Canada consents, or
  (b) in any other case, the Attorney General of the province where the offence is alleged to have been committed consents,
appear before a court or person that would have had jurisdiction to try that offence if it had been committed in the province where the accused is, and where he signifies his consent to plead guilty and pleads guilty to that offence the court or person shall convict the accused and impose the punishment warranted by law, but where he does not signify his consent to plead guilty and plead guilty, he shall, if he was in custody prior to his appearance, be returned to custody and shall be dealt with according to law.

(4) Notwithstanding that an accused described in subsection (3) has been committed to stand trial or that an indictment has been preferred against him in respect of the offence to which he desires to plead guilty, he shall be deemed simply to stand charged of that offence without a preliminary inquiry having been conducted or an indictment having been preferred with respect thereto.

. . .

435. Where an accused is charged with an offence that is alleged to have

been committed in the province in which he is, he may, if the offence is not an offence mentioned in section 427, and

> (*a*) in the case of proceedings instituted at the instance of the Government of Canada and conducted by or on behalf of that Government, the Attorney General of Canada consents, or
>
> (*b*) in any other case, the Attorney General of the province where the offence is alleged to have been committed consents,

appear before a court or person that would not otherwise have jurisdiction to try that offence, but that would have had jurisdiction to try it if it had been committed in the place where he is, and where he signifies his consent to plead guilty and pleads guilty to that offence, the court or person shall convict the accused and impose the punishment warranted by law, but where he does not signify his consent to plead guilty and plead guilty, he shall, if he was in custody prior to his appearance, be returned to custody and shall be dealt with according to law.[122]

The general rule set out herein is that with consent and upon a plea of guilty, the court where the accused is found has jurisdiction to deal with offences committed out of the province or jurisdiction. It appears that, perhaps by omission, when the amendments providing for discharges were set out in the Criminal Code, these sections were not considered; it is doubtful, given the wording, whether the full range of sentence (including a discharge) is available because of the phrase "convict" in the section. Though it is true by reason of *R. v. McInnis,*[123] that a judge who says "I convict" is not thereby precluded from imposing a discharge, it is submitted that there is a legal difference between the wording of a statute and the utterances of a judge and that in fact there is no jurisdiction to grant a discharge upon transfer. This is regrettable and should be corrected. The statutory instruction to the court to "impose the punishment warranted by law" serves to reinforce the idea that this result is intentional, as the essence of a discharge is that the appearance in court and the finding of guilt is sufficient punishment; the discharge provisions do not operate as punishment.

It was held in *R. v. Johnsen*[124] that when a person is an adult in the province in which the case originally arose and is transferred into a jurisdiction which treats a person of that age as a juvenile, that only the juvenile court has jurisdiction over the offences and that the criminal courts can not proceed. It appears that the minority reasons of Branca J.A. suggesting that the convicting court under s. 434(3) has jurisdiction

---

[122] R.S.C. 1970, c. C-34, as amended.
[123] (1973), 13 C.C.C. (2d) 471 (Ont. C.A.).
[124] (1972), 4 C.C.C. (2d) 526 (B.C.C.A.).

only over the offence and not the offender, may well be the better position. The matter is certainly not free from doubt.

It has been held that where the authorities make no efforts to bring a person back to a province for trial when they know that he is in another province serving a sentence, nor notify him of the outstanding charges so that he can invoke the provisions of s. 434(3), this will be a ground for reducing sentence drastically when it is imposed at a later date.[125]

9. PLEA AND SENTENCE NEGOTIATIONS

Criminal Code:

> 534(4) Notwithstanding any other provision of this Act, where an accused pleads not guilty to the offence charged but guilty of an included or other offence, the court may in its discretion with the consent of the prosecutor accept such plea of guilty and, if such plea is accepted, shall find the accused not guilty of the offence charged.

It has been held that the expression "other offence" in s. 534(4) includes offences not found in the Criminal Code, whether summary or indictable, as, for example, contributing to the delinquency of a juvenile, a summary offence pursuant to the Juvenile Delinquents Act.[126] But this case must be taken to have been overruled in *R. v. Hogarth,*[127] where upon an indictment charging theft of a motor vehicle of a value exceeding $200, a conviction was accepted to a charge of taking a motor vehicle without the consent of the owner. The court held there was no jurisdiction to permit such a plea where the theft indictment was not worded so as to include the lesser offence. The phrase "other offence" is restricted to "any other offence of which the accused could, by law, be convicted on the indictment before the Court." The court stated, *obiter dicta,* that this category includes summary offences.

Plea negotiations are an attempt by counsel to minimize the effect of rigid categorization of criminal offences and multiple charging of offences by police. It must be remembered that in Canada, unlike many countries, the selection of the appropriate charge or charges is made by the police officers, not by law officers of the Crown. The process involves a frank exchange of information between Crown counsel and defence

---

[125] *R. v. Parisien* (1971), 3 C.C.C. (2d) 433 (B.C.C.A.).
[126] *R. v. Mills* (1974), 16 Crim. L.Q. 381 (Ont.).
[127] (1976), 31 C.C.C. (2d) 232 (Ont. C.A.); *R. v. Filiault,* unreported, November 26, 1976 (Ont. C.A.).

counsel about the strengths and weaknesses of their respective cases and the circumstances of the offence and of the offender. Experienced Crown and defence counsel use this opportunity to ensure that individual justice is done. The strength of the process lies in the fact that these informal negotiations are not inhibited by the formal rules of evidence and result from more personal and extensive involvement with the offender, the victim, and the police investigators.

Nevertheless, it is a process which can be subject to abuse when it is not revealed in open court. Unless what went on in the informal pre-trial negotiations is placed accurately on the record before the trial judge, and the operative considerations are there explained, though justice may be done, it may not have the appearance of being done; and the public may suspect, rightly or wrongly, that an impropriety has occurred.

The occasions when an accurate account of plea negotiations cannot be put on the record will be few. These may involve the protection of police informers or the release to the public of information which might do harm to innocent persons or information of a personal nature which if revealed might cause unnecessary harm to the accused. In such circumstances, it is both appropriate and a practice of long standing for counsel to see the trial judge in chambers and acquaint him with such facts. Subject to this limitation, it is submitted that the essence of the plea or sentence negotiation should be placed on the record by both counsel. Any bargain which is incapable of being justified in open court, apart from the rare exceptions above, is a bargain which ought not to have been struck.

The English Court of Appeal (Criminal Division) in *R. v. Turner*[128] has discussed this process. In that case the trial on a charge of theft was going badly for the defence. Counsel told his client that if he persisted in his line of defence (which involved an attack upon police veracity) he might well go to jail, but if he changed his plea to guilty there might well be a non-custodial sentence. Counsel then left and spoke with the trial judge and came back and gave his opinion of the judge's views on the question: if the accused persisted in his trial he might receive a sentence of imprisonment, but if at this stage he pleaded guilty he would receive a non-custodial sentence. A short time later a plea of guilty was entered and the allegation upon appeal was that the plea did not result from the exercise of a free choice. The Court of Appeal accepted the right and

---

[128] (1970), 54 Cr. App. R. 352; *R. v. Grice* (1978), 66 Cr. App. R. 167; *R. v. Ryan,* [1978] Crim. L.R. 306.

duty of counsel to advise his client in strong terms, "provided always that it is made clear that the ultimate choice and the free choice is in the accused person". But the court took the view that counsel had given the impression that it was the judge's views of the matter that were being conveyed and not his own, and the appellant was never disabused of this impression. Accordingly the court treated the plea as a nullity and ordered a new trial. Then the court proceeded to "make observations":

> 1. Counsel must be completely free to do what is his duty, namely to give the accused the best advice he can and if need be, advice in strong terms. This will often include advice that a plea of guilty, showing an element of remorse, is a mitigating factor which may well enable the court to give a lesser sentence than would otherwise be the case. Counsel, of course, will emphasize that the accused must not plead guilty unless he had committed the acts constituting the offence charged.
> 2. The accused, having considered counsel's advice, must have a complete freedom of choice, whether to plead guilty or not guilty.
> 3. There must be freedom of access between counsel and judge. Any discussion, however, which takes place must be between the judge and both counsel for the defence and counsel for the prosecution. . . . This freedom of access is important because there may be matters calling for communication or discussion, which are of such a nature that counsel cannot in the interests of his client mention them in open court. . . .
> 4. The judge should, subject to the one exception referred to hereafter, never indicate the sentence which he is minded to impose. . . . The only exception to this rule is that it should be permissible for a judge to say, if it be the case, that whatever happens, whether the accused pleads guilty or not guilty, the sentence will or will not take a particular form, *e.g.* a probation order, a fine or a custodial sentence. Finally, where any such discussion on sentence has taken place between judge and counsel, counsel for the defence should disclose this to the accused and inform him of what took place.

It is often the case that such discussions and negotiations occur not after the trial has begun, but before trial or plea. However, the Alberta Court of Appeal has taken the view that such negotiations are impermissible, subject to the exceptions such as those in *R. v. Turner.* Not even the form of sentence is to be discussed with the trial judge.[129]

> There is no place in the sentencing procedure for hole-and-corner bargaining. . . .
> However, in my opinion, a Judge should take no part in any discussion as to sentencing before a plea has been taken, and all the circumstances in regard

---

[129] *R. v. Wood* (1975), 26 C.C.C. (2d) 100 at p. 108 (Alta. C.A.).

to the particular case have been placed before him, then having listened to the submission of counsel he should give his decision. To take part in a discussion of sentencing prior to a plea being taken would constitute a grave dereliction of duty. . . . For a Judge in Alberta to take any part in what has been called "plea bargaining" is, in my opinion, quite improper.

In *R. v. Bird*,[130] improper plea bargaining had taken place between counsel and the judge. The judge improperly indicated that a plea would result in a suspended sentence but that a conviction by the end of trial would result in immediate imprisonment. Counsel referred to the case law on the subject and then asked to see the judge again, having sent a note explaining why they wanted to see him to ask him whether their earlier conversation had been confidential. The judge asked, "Is that a warning to me?" and said that indeed the conversation had been confidential. Upon appeal from the sentence of imprisonment, the court said that counsel had properly made public what ought not to have been said privately in the judge's room.

In *R. v. Fleury*,[131] Montgomery J.A. set out his views on the proper procedure to be followed; the other judges did not seem to disagree:

> Where, after a plea of Guilty, the Crown recommends a light sentence, I do not suggest that this recommendation is binding on the trial judge. He may quite properly state that he intends to impose a heavy sentence and ask the accused whether he wishes to withdraw his plea of guilty.

In an earlier Quebec case, Hugessen J.[132] of the Quebec Court of Queen's Bench said:

> Where there has been a plea of guilty and Crown counsel recommends a sentence, a court, before accepting the plea, should satisfy itself that the accused fully understands that his fate is, within the limits set by law, in the discretion of the judge, and that the latter is not bound by the suggestions or opinions of Crown counsel. If the accused does not understand this, the guilty plea ought not to be accepted.

This function, ascribed above to the trial judge, is really within the duty of defence counsel, but a trial judge can do no harm by such inquiries.

The courts are unanimous that they are not bound to accept any recommendation offered by counsel.[133] Nevertheless, there have been

---

[130] [1978] Crim. L.R. 237.
[131] (1971), 23 C.R.N.S. 164 at p. 175 (Que. C.A.).
[132] *A.-G. Can. v. Roy* (1972), 18 C.R.N.S. 89 at pp. 92-93 (Que).
[133] *R. v. Johnston and Tremayne*, [1970] 4 C.C.C. 64 (Ont. C.A.).

several expressions of the reasons why a trial judge generally accepts such recommendations. Turgeon J.A. of the Quebec Court of Appeal accepted the following statement by the trial judge in *Fleury:*

> The trial judge is inclined, particularly when faced with a plea of guilty, to adopt the suggestions put forward by counsel for the Crown, since the latter has received the confidential report of the investigating officer and is as a result familiar with certain information and certain extenuating circumstances of which the judge may be totally ignorant.

One might well ask why it is that "information" and "extenuating circumstances" should be kept from the court if they are indeed "relevant".[134]

Thus in *R. v. Clarke,*[135] though the appellate court could not accept in full the recommendations of Crown and defence counsel that a suspended sentence was appropriate, "realizing that they have been in close personal touch with the appellant and all the parties involved, I feel their opinions are worthy of the attention of this court." Accordingly, it reduced the sentence of one year to six months' imprisonment with time served to count.

The general position is that once a sentence suggested by counsel for the Crown has been acted upon by the trial judge, the Crown, like any other litigant, ought not to be heard to repudiate before an appellate court the position taken by its counsel in the trial court, except for the gravest possible reasons.[136]

Such reasons may well exist if the Crown can demonstrate that its counsel had in some way been misled, or if it could be shown that the public interest in the orderly administration of justice is outweighed by the relative gravity of the crime and the gross insufficiency of the sentence, or when the sentence is illegal.[137]

In refusing leave to the Crown to repudiate its position on appeal the Canadian courts have relied on other factors as well.[138] The court may rely on the fact that at the time of appeal it is too late for the accused to appeal conviction and ask leave to change his plea; or the reasons used to justify an increase of sentence may be insufficient:

---

[134] *R. v. Simoneau* (1978), 2 C.R. (3d) S-17 (Man. C.A.).

[135] (1959), 124 C.C.C. 284 (Man. C.A.).

[136] *R. v. Christie* (1956), 115 C.C.C. 55 (Sask. C.A.); *R. v. MacArthur* (1978), 39 C.C.C. (2d) 158 (P.E.I.C.A.).

[137] *R. v. Hogarth* (1976), 31 C.C.C. (2d) 232 (Ont. C.A.).

[138] *Ibid.*

I might add, that if I were shocked by a fine of $150 for this offence, my outrage would not be much appeased by the fine of $500 which the Crown now suggests. Despite all this, the Crown now asks that I should set aside the bargain that it has made. The Crown may feel that it has made a bad bargain, but the solution to that must surely be for the Crown to make no bargains at all.

Similar reasoning is found in the judgment of Montgomery J.A. in *Fleury:*

> . . . I am of the opinion that it is only in the most exceptional circumstances that a court of appeal should intervene. Apart from the possibility that the accused might wish to withdraw his plea, he might wish to make further evidence in mitigation of sentence.

An additional reason is found in the majority judgment in *R. v. Wood.* There, after pleading guilty, the accused, through his counsel, disclosed to the court that he had been seen by two psychiatrists. A minority view in the case would have ordered a new trial and directed the Crown not to produce in evidence the fact of the previous guilty plea. The majority pointed out that the Crown was now aware of the visits to the psychiatrists and the incriminating evidence given to them. The court noted:

> The Crown may now call both of these psychiatrists as witnesses. Their evidence is both competent and compellable. The Court cannot prevent such evidence from being called. This would surely prejudice the accused. . . .
>
> . . . because we cannot put the accused back into the position he was in before the first plea . . . I would refuse leave to appeal.

One further instance in which the court would intervene was illustrated by the Quebec Court of Appeal, *R. v. Mouffe,*[139] discussed in *Fleury:*

> In the *Mouffe* case, where the majority of the Court felt that we should intervene, the accused had pleaded guilty to charges of armed robbery and assault, and the trial Judge in his report stated that in showing clemency he had relied entirely on the recommendations of counsel for the Crown. In the present case . . . It appears from the trial Judge's report that he weighed the various extenuating circumstances and felt that the recommendations of counsel were fitting.

The court by a majority therefore refused to interfere.

Generally it has been felt to be unfair, not only to the trial judge but to

---

[139] (1971), 16 C.R.N.S. 257 (Que. C.A.).

the accused, for the Crown by means of an appeal to repudiate a position taken at trial. Further, it appears that where counsel for the Crown at trial repudiates even a pre-trial agreement, the appeal court will enforce it. In *R. v. Brown,*[140] prior to the commencement of trial, counsel agreed that if the Crown withdrew all other charges and would make representations to the trial judge that he was not asking that any sentence imposed be consecutive to time then being served, the appellant would plead guilty to the two charges of theft and possession of a stolen motorcycle. "Crown counsel then vacillated" and a consecutive term was imposed. The Court of Appeal varied the term to make it concurrent in accordance with the agreement.

The same strictness is not enforced vis-à-vis the defence. In *R. v. Soucie,*[141] upon a plea to manslaughter, counsel for the defence suggested a range of eight to ten years; counsel for the Crown, on the other hand, submitted that an appropriate range of sentence would be between ten to 15 years. The trial judge imposed a sentence of ten years and the accused appealed. Though reiterating that the trial judge was entitled, in determining the appropriate sentence, to give weight in the submissions of the "experienced counsel" in this case, the court noted that he was not bound by either counsel's submissions. Taking all the facts into account, the appeal court determined that the sentence did not give adequate weight to the mitigating circumstances which were before the trial judge. The sentence was reduced to one of eight years.

Selected Readings: Plea Negotiations

G. A. Ferguson, "The Role of the Judge in Plea Bargaining" (1972), 15 Crim. L.Q. pp. 26-51.

G. A. Ferguson and D. W. Roberts, "Plea Bargaining: Directions for Canadian Reform" (1974), 52 Can. Bar Rev. 497.

B. A. Grosman, *The Prosecutor* (1969), pp. 29-43.

T. H. Hartnagel, "Plea Negotiations in Canada" (1975), 17 Can. J. of Corrections pp. 45-46.

R. Hyman, "Legal Bargaining" (1970), Chitty's L.J. 266.

D. J. Newman, "Pleading Guilty for Considerations: A Study of Bargain Justice" (1956), 47 J. Crim. L.C. and P.S. 780.

G. Parker, "Copping a Plea" (1972), 20 Chitty's L.J. pp. 310-311.

---

[140] (1972), 8 C.C.C. (2d) 227 (Ont. C.A.).
[141] Unreported, June 16, 1977 (Ont. C.A.).

E. I. Ratushny, "Plea Bargaining and the Public" (1972), 20 Chitty's L.J. pp. 228-241.

"Judicial Plea Bargaining", 19 Stan. L. Rev. 1082.

P. Thomas, "The Judicial Approach to Plea Bargaining" (1972), 5 Man. L.J. pp. 201-204.

P. Thomas, "Plea Bargaining and the Turner case" (*R. v. Turner* [1970] 2 All E.R. 281), [1970] Crim. L.R. 559.

P. Thomas, "Exploration of Plea Bargaining", [1969] Crim. L.R. 69.

R. C. Underwood, "Let's Put Plea Discussions and Agreements — On Record", I Loyola U.L.F. (Chicago).

Chapter 4

Criminal Record

The one fact that is uniformly relied upon to assist the court in sentencing is the criminal record of the prisoner. In *Doiron v. The Queen*[1] the language of the decision indicates that it is the Crown's choice whether or not they wish to prove prior convictions and implies that the Crown may properly in some cases not so wish: "Where after a conviction, on a plea of guilty or after a trial, the Crown desires prior convictions to be taken into consideration in the imposition of the sentence . . .". This is consistent with the fundamental assumptions of an adversary system. The rationale for relying upon a criminal record is rarely given, but one statement of it is as follows:

> Wilful persistence in the deliberately-acquired habit of crime marks the offender as an enemy of society in proportion to the extent of such persistence. An individual's actions may indicate his permanent tendencies, or, on the other hand, they may merely be the result of transient moods or momentary impulses. Where we find an individual, over a period of time, pursuing a course of conduct, it is thereby possible reasonably to determine his character or mental attitude. That is why judges consider the previous record of a delinquent in determining the penalty to be imposed upon him. The older and more mature the individual is, the easier it is to determine his character and attitude from his conduct. In a youth the testing-time is short; in the mature man it has been longer.[2]

This rationale suffers from premises which have little currency today. Few people view crime as a habit "deliberately acquired" but instead

---

[1] (1958), 124 C.C.C. 156 at p. 158 (N.B.C.A.).
[2] *R. v. Warner, Urquhart, Martin and Mullen,* [1946] O.R. 808 at p. 816 *per* Roach J.A. (Ont. C.A.).

83

refer to the social, economic and environmental aspects of its origin. We are also, today, alive to the fact that only certain kinds of crime result in detection, charge and conviction, with the result that criminal records tend to be acquired by those who commit only certain kinds of offences. Other crimes like income tax evasion, large scale fraud and combines offences often escape the net. This is hardly accidental and could be said to result from a policy decision: we focus on the poor, on those who commit crimes that are easy and cheap to detect and prosecute and ignore many more harmful crimes committed by the wealthy and the corporate offender.

In addition, the 1946 decision is dated by the concept of an "enemy of society". It is doubtful whether the notion of a criminal class marked as an "enemy of society" as used above, is in any way a useful concept. For example, the English Court of Appeal has said:

> The learned judge increased the sentences . . . because of his view, for which there was ample evidence, that these young men were enemies of society. But the Court has to bear in mind that in our system of jurisprudence there is no offence known as being an enemy of society. . . . It may well be that at a trial the evidence establishes that those who have committed the offence as charged are dangerous men. When the evidence establishes that, the Court has no reason for mitigating the penalties in any way. If the evidence does establish that the accused are dangerous men, then it is no good, their saying that they have no previous convictions . . .[3]

Nevertheless, the acquisition of such a record does mark someone as a danger and since the basic purpose of sentencing is the protection of society, a criminal record is often relevant in determining the measures that will be needed to protect society from this particular individual.

Therefore, courts often state that "a second offence is always considered more serious than a first." It has long been the case that in some instances an increased penalty is provided by statute for second offences of a similar type. Unless Parliament so legislates the purported universality of the rule can not be justified on rational grounds. Although the courts generally avoid critical appraisal of the "danger to society" notion, they do place limits on the incarcerations which are imposed as a result of the notion. Some courts have concluded that a lengthy criminal record disentitles an accused to their leniency. Nonetheless, these courts have noted that they cannot justify sentences

---

[3] *R. v. King; R. v. Simpkins* (1973), 57 Cr. App. R. 696.

disproportionate to the gravity of the offence, despite their disinclination toward leniency in these cases.[4]

A. First Offenders

If the criminal record is relevant because it indicates the extent to which society needs protection, the lack of a criminal record may be relevant as well, and may be used as a mitigating factor that ought to be reflected in sentence.

There are circumstances where the lack of criminal record in and of itself does not benefit a prisoner. In *R. v. Smith*,[5] a four-year sentence for conspiracy to defraud the public was upheld by a trial judge who acknowledged giving only "minor consideration" to a previous good character. The court said "the good reputation of a person engaged in fraud assists in deceiving his victims", and accordingly refused to give significant weight to this factor.

The principle is usually confined to fraud cases, but there is no reason why it should not be extended where appropriate, though the number of instances will be limited. In *R. v. Devlin and Marentette*,[6] the court analyzed the various roles or functions in a large-scale heroin syndicate and noted that there was a person known in the trade as the "backend". This person is responsible for holding the drugs so that the principle never actually takes possession. He receives the drugs in bulk powder form and distributes it to designated locations for customers to pick up. Accordingly he must be a person who does "not have a criminal record or be known to the police and in most instances, should be gainfully employed. The reason for these characteristics is that it is unlikely for such a person to be observed by the police." The court determined that it was by reason of his lack of criminal record that he was acceptable for the part that he was to play in the conspiracy and upheld a heavy sentence, refusing to give the usual weight to the lack of a criminal record. Brooke J.A. dissented on this point, noting that the lack of a criminal record was relevant not merely as a matter of sympathy, but as part of the attempt to

---

[4] *R. v. Cosgrove,* unreported, February 9, 1976 (Ont. C.A.).
[5] (1962), 38 C.R. 217 (B.C.C.A.)
[6] (1971), 3 C.C.C. (2d) 20 (Ont. C.A.).

judge the need for someone's imprisonment, having regard to his rights and those of the community.

It is not possible to treat all first offenders in the same manner. Some crimes are more serious than others and some offences, viewed as examples of their type, are more grave than others. Yet our courts have shown a marked inclination to avoid or minimize, wherever possible, imprisonment for first offenders, relying on the lesson experience has taught: imprisonment leads to more imprisonment.

It is the factor of association with confirmed criminals that the courts seem to view as the principal danger. In *R. v. Kosh*[7] the court upheld a suspended sentence with two years' probation for two charges of trafficking in narcotics:

> It appears to me . . . that leniency at this time may be the factor that will save this young man from following in the footsteps of his father [who had a lengthy criminal record]. Incarceration will no doubt bring him into contact with criminals who in the past have been associated with his father and this could have only detrimental results. The conduct of the respondent since being released on probation is such as to warrant the belief that the purpose for which the lenient sentence was imposed may be achieved. Such a result is in the best interest both of the public and of the respondent. . . .
>
> . . . I do not want to be understood as suggesting that in the case of a first offence a suspended sentence is necessarily the appropriate sentence. Like all other offences, the sentence imposed must be considered in the light of all the known facts and circumstances of each particular case.

The Alberta Court of Appeal in *R. v. Wood*[8] has said: "The offences which require a prison sentence for first offenders grow fewer as more humane and varied types of punishment are developed." However, there are some offences for which a prison sentence is nevertheless required to "adequately express and support society's execration" of the offence; here, an act of gross indecency with a nine-year-old step-daughter.

Two decisions of the Ontario Court of Appeal make explicit the approach that a sentencing judge ought to take to a first offender. There exists a presumption of fact that one who has not offended previously is capable of reform and ought to be dealt with accordingly. In *R. v. Samaras,*[9] Brooke J.A. speaking for the majority said: "In the case of a first offender there should be evidence which reveals that it is unlikely

---

[7] (1970), 1 C.C.C. (2d) 290 at p. 292 (Sask. C.A.).

[8] (1975), 26 C.C.C. (2d) 100 at p. 107.

[9] (1971), 16 C.R.N.S. 1 at p. 3 (Ont. C.A.); see also *R. v. Francis* (1970), 13 Crim. L.Q. 12 (Ont. C.A.), for a reformatory sentence on a serious armed robbery.

that there is a probability of his reformation, and in the absence of such evidence his reformation must be given serious consideration in the determination of the quantum of the sentence."

In a later case, *R. v. Stein,*[10] Martin J.A. for the court sets down a rule of approach to the sentencing of first offenders:

> In our view, before imposing a custodial sentence upon a first offender the sentencing Court should explore the other dispositions which are open to him and only impose a custodial sentence where the circumstances are such, or the offence is of such gravity that no other sentence is appropriate.

Accordingly, a sentence to an indefinite term not to exceed six months concurrent on each of 13 charges of obtaining property by false pretenses through the use of N.S.F. cheques over a period of one month was reduced to a suspended sentence and one year's probation, with an added condition for payment by way of restitution during that period. The court noted: "In our view, this offence does not fall within the category of offences where a custodial sentence is the only appropriate sentence to be imposed upon a first offender, nor are there other circumstances which require the imposition of a custodial sentence."

Such "other circumstances" may be found in cases such as *R. v. Dorkings,*[11] where 30 days' imprisonment was imposed for the theft of three air-conditioners, the property of a former employer. The element of breach of trust was an important consideration and the court felt that it would uphold a short custodial sentence. However, in an attempt to minimize the impact of imprisonment on a first offender, the sentence was varied to be served intermittently on weekends. In *R. v. Trask*[12] the court said:

> It is a principle of sentencing often acted upon by this Court that in ordinary circumstances a custodial sentence should be avoided when practicable in the case of a first offender. In the case of a serious offence involving violence to the person, however, that principle must yield to the

---

[10] (1974), 15 C.C.C. (2d) 376 at p. 377 (Ont. C.A.); see also *R. v. McLafferty* (1973), 15 Crim. L.Q. 371 (Ont. C.A.); *R. v. Beacon; R. v. Modney* (1976), 31 C.C.C. (2d) 56 (Alta. C.A.); *R. v. Casey and Smith,* [1974] Qd. R. 132. The principle outlined in *Stein* has been extended: one may be treated as if one were a first offender if one has received a pardon: *R. v. Spring* (1977), 35 C.C.C. (2d) 308 (Ont. C.A.), if one has never served a custodial sentence: *R. v. Alfs* (1974), 17 Crim. L.Q. 247 (Ont. C.A.), or has served a very minor term of imprisonment: *R. v. Trask* (1974), 28 C.R.N.S. 321 (Ont. C.A.).

[11] Unreported, October 15, 1974 (Ont. C.A.).

[12] (1974), 28 C.R.N.S. 321 at p. 323 (Ont. C.A.).

necessity of a sentence which gives emphasis to the factor of general deterrence to like-minded persons.

This was a case where two years less one day was imposed on a charge of indecently assaulting a female. In this case the woman was kidnapped and repeated threats of death were made.

These cautions are also applied to another common aggravating factor in sentence, the prevalence of a particular crime in the community (amounting to "an alarming increase").

In *R. v. Erdlyn,*[13] the Ontario Court of Appeal in reviewing a sentence of three months on a first offender for keeping a common betting-house said:

> Counsel urges, because this is the first occasion on which the accused has been convicted of an offence, that it would be appropriate to sentence the accused to a fine. We cannot accede to that argument. We think that the learned Magistrate, with great experience and knowledge of conditions in the particular locality (and that is a matter which properly may be taken into consideration), and with full knowledge of the seriousness of this kind of offence, was quite warranted in the exercise of his discretion in imposing a term of imprisonment.

If one may generalize on the basis of these cases it would appear that only rarely will factors unconnected with the nature and severity of the crime itself be sufficient to justify a custodial term for a first offender if, based on the crime, a non-custodial term would have been appropriate.

Nevertheless, there are serious crimes for which avoidance of imprisonment on first conviction is not possible (such as the drug trafficking and fraud cases mentioned earlier). But even in these cases, moderation in the length of the sentence is intended to minimize the effect of imprisonment upon the individual. For a first offender, return to society after serving a short sentence may be a wise, useful and humanitarian act, whereas such clemency for an inveterate offender may be only "weakness and error".[14] In lowering sentences of 15 years and ten lashes to three years and five lashes for armed robbery Bissonnette J.A. said:

> Is it not wiser, more logical, more humane, to view the accused at the bar and, with the aid of all his senses, to distinguish him from the mass of criminals, to separate him from an anonymous crowd and punish him according to the

---

[13] (1956), 117 C.C.C. 207 at p. 213.
[14] *R. v. Lemire and Gosselin* (1948), 92 C.C.C. 201 at p. 210 (Que. C.A.); see also *R. v. Willaert* (1953), 105 C.C.C. 172 (Ont. C.A.).

circumstances of his crime, in the light of his inexperience in crime and according to the weaknesses and unfortunate temptations of his age or perhaps his inherited ignorance or his defects? To act otherwise is *summum jus, summa injuria!*

When he pronounces sentence, the Magistrate does not punish, for example, theft with violence, he punishes the author of the theft. The sentence, I repeat, must be individual. It is a culprit that one punishes, not the crime. If it were the offence, all would be punished uniformly. Hence the sentence would be no longer subjective, no longer individual . . .

Note however the concurring comments of Mackinnon, J.A.:

The appeal on the sentence has caused me considerable difficulty in view of the fact there has been the general trend towards leniency in dealing with first offenders or those whose first offence has been comparatively a minor one, when the accused are in their late teens or early twenties. One cannot overlook the fact that today most of the serious crimes of theft and robbery by violence and other kindred offences are being perpetrated by youths and that the Courts in dealing with these offenders should be given more latitude in dealing with youthful offenders more severely than they have been in the past.[15]

This is clearly a minority view.

The New Brunswick Court of Appeal in *R. v. McDonald and Reynolds,*[16] a case of robbery, sustained a sentence of two years in a penitentiary for a first offender: "The element of violence involved puts it in an entirely different category from ordinary theft where Courts are inclined to be lenient with first offenders." In sustaining the sentence, the court said: "While it is true Reynolds had no previous record it is no reason that he should not be sent to the penitentiary when his first offense is of so serious a nature."[17] The Ontario Court of Appeal has taken a different view as a matter of policy in cases involving youthful first offenders. Rehabilitation for the youthful offender is unlikely if imprisonment is served in a penitentiary rather than a reformatory. Eight years for violent armed robberies was reduced to two years less one day.[18]

Though it is clear that for the most serious crimes there is no alternative to a jail sentence, there exists "a middle range" of criminality where either a suspended sentence and probation or a short jail term is

---

[15] At p. 217.
[16] (1958), 28 C.R. 197 at p. 198 (N.B.C.A.).
[17] *Ibid.*
[18] *R. v. Dunkley* (1976), 3 C.R. (3d) S-51 (Ont. C.A.).

possible and other factors will determine the result. In *R. v. Garcia and Silva,*[19] the two accused appealed sentences of 18 months definite and 12 months indeterminate for a breaking and entering offence. A third man had pleaded guilty to this offence and the Court of Appeal ordered his sentence to be suspended and he be placed on probation for two years. They refused, however, to follow this pattern for the two appellants because they had a greater involvement and "their circumstances and reputation" were not quite as favourable. Nevertheless, the chances of rehabilitation were not reflected sufficiently in the sentence, in that 18 months' imprisonment for a young first offender would "tend to destroy whatever hope he had of rehabilitation" and the court varied the sentence to one of three months definite and 12 months indeterminate.[20]

The case of *R. v. Willaert*[21] also shows that being a first offender and being of previous good character are not at all the same thing, though often found together. There is no reason why they should not be viewed separately as different circumstances to which regard can be had in determining the appropriate sentence.

As a general rule it is undesirable that a first sentence of immediate imprisonment should be very long, disproportionate to the gravity of the offence or imposed for reasons of general deterrence as a warning to others.

B. The Use Of A Criminal Record

To sentence a prisoner solely on account of his past crimes would be unjust. At the same time, though it would not be proper to increase a sentence by reason of a criminal record, such a record is a ground for refusing to extend leniency. Though these principles are no more than corollaries of the central proposition that the sentence must be appropriate to the offence, they have not always been followed with the scrupulousness that one might wish.[22]

---

[19] [1970] 3 C.C.C. 124 (Ont. C.A.).

[20] *Ibid.* This case is also one of the rare Canadian examples of "taking other offences into consideration" and the sentence of imprisonment here may reflect that factor as well.

[21] (1953), 105 C.C.C. 172 (Ont. C.A.).

[22] See Glanville Williams, "The Courts and Persistent Offenders", [1963] Crim. L.R. 730.

In *R. v. Wilson,*[23] the British Columbia Court of Appeal approved the English case of *R. v. Betteridge*[24] as follows:

> We think it is not right to hold over a man's past offences which have been dealt with by appropriate sentences, as we must assume past offences have been dealt with, and add them up and increase accordingly the severity of the sentence for a later offence. That is dangerously like punishing a man twice over for one offence. If a man who has been convicted shows himself unresponsive to leniency and persists in a life of crime, that is a reason for giving him the proper and deserved sentence in the particular case. If, on the other hand, there are some merits, it may be that the Court will treat him more leniently because he has shown himself in some way responsive to the warnings which he has had.

The Ontario Court of Appeal has not gone quite so far as to say that a sentence may not be raised from what is appropriate by reason of the criminal record but it has gone part way. In *R. v. Lass,*[25] Roach J.A. said:

> It has been said that a man should not be punished for his past bad record. I agree. But in determining the sentence which should be imposed for a given offence, the previous record of the prisoner must be taken into consideration. It provides perhaps the best test as to the character of the prisoner and the extent and nature of his evil inclinations. He is not, of course, to be sentenced entirely on the basis of his previous record. The facts of the offence for which he has been last convicted and is about to be sentenced have been said to be more important in determining the extent of the sentence than is his previous record: *Rex v. Woodward* (1929), 21 Cr. App. R. 137.

Similarly in *R. v. Woods and Langthorne,*[26] the Court of Appeal examined records and concluded that the accused had shown themselves "unresponsive to the leniency extended to them in the past" and accordingly refused to interfere with heavy sentences.

The statements on this matter are not inconsistent and it is submitted that the true principle is that the appropriate range of sentence for the offence should first be determined and that although the higher part of that range might well be appropriate for someone with a lengthy criminal record, the range should not be exceeded by reason of the criminal record or for that matter by reason of any factor peculiar to the offender as distinct from the offence.[27]

---

[23] [1944] 3 D.L.R. 671 at pp. 672-73.
[24] (1942), 28 Cr. App. R. 171.
[25] (1949), 95 C.C.C. 193 at p. 197 (Ont. C.A.).
[26] (1944), 82 C.C.C. 218 (B.C.).
[27] Glanville Williams, at p. 733.

The English position with regard to the effect of a criminal record in general has been stated in *R. v. Griffiths:*[28]

> This Court has said again and again, and I repeat it now, that a man is not to be twice punished for the same offence and it does not in the least follow that a subsequent sentence must be heavier than the sentence which preceded it.

With regard to this principle, which really does no more than preserve the discretion given by a statute to a trial judge, the Alberta Court of Appeal has dissented:

> If the proper implication of this last pronouncement is that a sentence should not be made heavier because of the convict's bad record, shown by previous convictions, then I think it is not in accord with the law and practice in this country.[29]

Surely this is indeed not the proper implication. The appropriate sentence is determinable primarily by the offence itself, and there is no need for a subsequent conviction for a relatively minor offence to have a penalty which is greater than that earlier imposed for a more serious offence. Similarly it may be appropriate, having regard to all the circumstances, to extend leniency, even at a late time because of positive supportive factors in the environment of the prisoner.

This does not mean that even a lengthy record may not be examined and explained by extrinsic evidence. In *Cavanaugh v. The Queen,*[30] the Nova Scotia Court of Appeal permitted counsel to call medical evidence to explain why a prisoner with a lengthy record "has persisted in a life of crime and has not shown himself responsive to the warnings which he has had". The evidence, however, also indicated

> . . . that he is a person dangerous to society, most likely to continue to be so, and unlikely to respond to leniency or to reform. It is on this basis and not on the basis of punishment for offences, for the commission of which has already undergone punishment, that the previous record of the appellant must be considered.

In the result the sentence was lowered from a total of 35 years to a total of eight years.

Sentences for subsequent offences may be reduced where it is shown that in the earlier conviction the offender did not have the benefit of

---

[28] (1932), 23 Cr. App. R. 153 at p. 156.
[29] *R. v. Scheer,* [1932] 3 W.W.R. 555 at p. 558 *per* Harvey C.J.A.
[30] (1953), 106 C.C.C. 190.

"proper probation services".[31] So, too, where the offence was committed only two days after the release from prison, and while under the influence of alcohol, the court will take into account that the prisoner had not had time to adjust to freedom.[32]

C. Procedure

The procedure for proving a criminal record has been a subject of much discussion. In *R. v. Scheer*[33] the prosecutor orally read out in court a statement of the prisoner's record. Relying on English precedent, the court declared that the trial judge was justified in considering the record for the purpose of determining the appropriate sentence, as neither the prisoner nor his counsel had questioned the correctness of the statements made. The majority noted, in upholding the practice, that "It is important . . . that a trial Judge should not be hampered in his efforts to ascertain the character of the convict in the way of securing knowledge of his previous record, beyond what is essential for the protection of the convict." The minority would have disregarded the record thus tendered, demanding that "Every opportunity should be given to the accused to deny such material and the party supplying it, should . . . be subject to cross-examination by the accused."

It is nevertheless clear that by some method or other the record must be placed in evidence and must be proved.[34] The usual practice in Canada is for the prisoner to be asked whether or not he admits it. In *R. v. Blackburn*[35] the prisoner declined to make such admission and questioned on appeal the propriety of the trial judge taking that into account on sentence. The convictions were ultimately proved properly and put into evidence, but evidence of identity between the record and the prisoner seemed to be lacking. The Nova Scotia Court of Appeal held that the fact that the name on the conviction was the same as that which

---

[31] *R. v. McMullen,* unreported, March 2, 1978 (Ont. C.A.); *R. v. Blacklar,* unreported, January 16, 1978 (Ont. C.A.).

[32] *R. v. Wallace,* [1977] Crim. L.R. 685.

[33] *Supra,* n. 29.

[34] *R. v. Kennedy* (1956), 23 C.R. 185 (B.C.C.A.).

[35] (1929), 32 C.C.C. 119 (N.S.C.A.).

the prisoner bore, was evidence of identity upon which the judge could act.

In *R. v. Lalonde,*[36] no evidence of previous convictions had been put in prior to sentence; because of an error in the fingerprint section of the RCMP, the prisoner was dealt with as a first offender. Subsequently the prisoner was advised in writing that he did not have to make any statement whatsoever in connection with his alleged criminal record, but that if he did see fit to admit it, that admission would be used as evidence in the prosecution of an appeal. He acknowledged the record and it was held that the admission of the respondent "in the circumstances" constituted clear and unequivocal proof of the accuracy of the record alleged against him and of his identity as the offender in each of the previous convictions. In the course of the judgment the Ontario Court of Appeal makes it clear that there is no single method of proof of convictions which is mandated by the legislation. One alternative is s. 500(4) of the Criminal Code.

It is unclear whether this section, which is found in Part XVI of the Criminal Code and entitled "Indictable Offences — Trial without Jury" applies to indictable offences with a jury or to summary conviction offences. The Criminal Code, in s. 594, incorporated by s. 740 for summary conviction matters, provides for a relatively easy method of proving criminal records in all cases.

A third method of proving a criminal record is found in s. 23 (1) of the Canada Evidence Act.

In *R. v. Graves,*[37] the Ontario Court of Appeal held that a prior summary conviction could not be proved by the oral testimony of witnesses present at the trial of the first offence in purporting to prove what conviction was then made.

In Canada there has never been any difficulty, as a matter of professional courtesy and of fairness to the accused, obtaining from the Crown or the police a copy of the criminal record of the accused. In England the question has been the subject of a practice direction from the Court of Criminal Appeal.[38]

---

[36] (1951), 11 C.R. 71 (Ont. C.A.).
[37] (1910), 16 C.C.C. 318. This decision was approved in *R. v. Scammel* (1949), 95 C.C.C. 370 (Ont. C.A.).
[38] "Practice Direction", [1966] 2 All E.R. 929; *R. v. Crabtree* (1952), 36 Cr. App. R. 161.

D. Prior And Subsequent Convictions

In view of the practice whereby a first offence is dealt with as lightly as possible but any subsequent offence may be viewed more seriously, it is a matter of some importance to determine whether or not a conviction was prior or subsequent to the offence in question. A misapprehension of this fact may result in a prisoner being treated more harshly than his record warrants. So, in *R. v. Johnston,*[39] a 15-month definite and one year less one day indeterminate sentence was imposed upon conviction for breaking and entering a summer cottage. The trial judge misapprehended the facts, apparently believing that the instant offence occurred following the appellant's conviction and sentence on another charge. In fact, the two charges arose at the same time, but the other case was tried first and the learned trial judge erroneously treated the other convictions as a prior criminal offence. The court held that, because of this misapprehension, *inter alia,* the sentence should be varied to nine months definite and three months indeterminate.

It is only sensible that a repetition of a serious offence after one has been, so to speak, warned and "put on notice" by the imposition of a prior sentence, may, absent some explanation or a reason for leniency, be more serious than a first offence *simpliciter.* It follows from this that any such misapprehension regarding the order of convictions must be corrected on appeal. In *R. v. Pritchard,*[40] the accused appeared before a provincial judge in March of 1973 and requested that all outstanding charges against him in other provinces be forwarded to be dealt with upon guilty plea at the same time. This was done, and terms totalling 33 months were imposed. The accused while serving that sentence escaped custody and was convicted and sentenced for this offence. It appears that not all the offences outstanding against him in other provinces had been forwarded to the original hearing; another charge of escaping custody had been omitted, so once again the accused came before the provincial judge to be dealt with on this old charge of escaping custody, but this time there was included in his record the charge of escaping custody which, as noted above, had occurred after the offence for which he was to be sentenced. The majority of the Ontario Court of Appeal was of the view that in taking this escape custody conviction into consideration the

---

[39] Unreported, June 9, 1972 (Ont. C.A.).
[40] Unreported, October 30, 1973 (Ont. C.A.).

provincial judge erred. The appeal was allowed and the sentence reduced.

Gale C.J.O. dissented, arguing, *inter alia,* that had the judge who imposed the earlier sentence known of this offence he would probably have imposed a greater sentence than he did. This is, however, hardly the accused's fault and there is no precedent for sustaining a harsh sentence because one should have received a harsher sentence on an earlier occasion.

Nonetheless, oblique support for this dissent can be found in *R. v. Rogers (No. 2)*[41] where the Prince Edward Island Court of Appeal noted that the appellant claimed upon sentencing at trial a previous good character which the trial judge took into account. As it turned out one and one half months after the conviction and sentence on the fraud charge before the court, the appellant had been convicted of arson which was committed prior to the fraud. Bearing this in mind "this Court is in a better position now than was the learned trial Judge to assess properly the weight which should be given to the factor of the previous good reputation of the respondent. While that crime carries its own punishment, it also partially, if not entirely, removes from consideration the mitigating factor of an otherwise good reputation in the community."

Gale C.J.O. in *R. v. Pritchard,* also asserted, with considerable force, that if the principle accepted by the majority were right, an accused would be permitted to "take advantage of the sequence in which he was convicted and say, in effect, that in both cases he is a first offender." It is submitted that this anomaly remains, but that it is in all the circumstances, proper and inevitable. Cases of error or negligence apart, it is simple enough for the Crown to move to have trials brought on promptly; they will then usually be in sequence. Failing that, the court can be advised of other outstanding charges and if the present offence is committed while an accused is on bail, any violation of the specific terms in a release order breached though the offence may be taken into consideration in sentencing. It would be better to deal with any such breach in a separate prosecution. But the central principle is that in Canada we sentence people for particular offences and not for whatever criminal activity they may have engaged in at a later date.

A further variation upon this difficult theme occurred in *R. v. Hutchins.*[42] The offence was committed in 1954 at which time the

---

[41] (1972), 6 C.C.C. (2d) 107 at p. 119.
[42] (1958), 75 N.S.W.W.N. 75 at p. 76.

offender was a boy aged 17 years. He fled and was not apprehended for his crime until 1957. Between these two dates, however, he was sentenced for other offences of a serious nature in another jurisdiction. The trial judge felt that if he had been dealing with the case in 1954 when the offence was committed a proper sentence bearing in mind the age of the offender would have been 12 months' imprisonment. The Court of Appeal said the trial judge was entitled to take into account as matters for his consideration the convictions which had occurred between the date of commission of the offence and the date of sentencing but only for

> the purpose of considering whether he should reduce what he would otherwise have regarded as the proper sentence because some leniency should be extended to the applicant in the light of his youth.
>
> ... the applicant's behaviour since he committed the offence has certainly not justified any leniency on that ground. That still leaves the difficulty of whether it would still be proper to have regard to the fact that the sentence which would have been a proper one in 1954, namely, a sentence which I assume might have been twelve months because of his youth, should now be the sentence that should be imposed. I think that the real relevance of the subsequent conviction is to whether that sentence ought to suffer any further reduction because of the applicant's own personal rectitude in other matters. The applicant has forfeited any claim to leniency in that regard, but in all the circumstances, although it is difficult to be logical in these matters and perhaps to state the position logically, I think that the proper sentence to impose at the present time would be the sentence which, in my opinion, his Honour intended to indicate he might have imposed in 1954. . . .

Accordingly, one can look at such convictions not for the purpose of imposing a sentence on the present charge heavier than would otherwise have been imposed, but for the purpose of considering whether the applicant was deserving of more lenient treatment now than he would have been at the time when the offence was committed.

1. GRAVITY OF THE RECORD

As we have seen, it is the practice of criminal courts, absent some explanation, to punish persistent offenders more severely than those who have not been previously convicted or have not committed other crimes. Where the criminal record discloses that the accused is a "professional" in a particular crime he is committing this will justify a severe sentence.[43]

---

[43] *R. v. Belegratis,* unreported, November 5, 1975 (B.C.C.A.).

Nevertheless, in *R. v. Murray*,[44] the Saskatchewan Court of Appeal cited with approval a passage from *Halsbury,* to the effect that, if the offence for which punishment is awarded does not indicate a deliberate return to crime and there are circumstances which do not show that the offence was planned beforehand, less weight is to be given to previous offences. This is a sensible approach because the principle purpose of a criminal record is to show character with a view to indicating whether and to what extent society needs protection from this accused. The primary indicator in the determination of this question must be the offence itself, and such circumstances surrounding it as planning, deliberation, and the grieviousness of this particular count.

Ordinarily, a minor criminal record can be expected to carry less weight. It is rarely the practice to give much or any weight to "juvenile convictions" but this has been done: see *R. v. Connor and Hall*,[45] where it was noted that, though the record was a juvenile record, nevertheless it disclosed repeated acts of misconduct, not one act in violation of the law but numerous acts. It must be kept in mind that such records reveal not crimes but delinquencies. However, this general rule does not seem to be operative in British Columbia where the Court of Appeal upheld a heavy sentence on a first offender after describing and noting in detail an "appalling" juvenile record which disclosed an anti-social personality.[46]

The court is generally keenly aware of the nature of the offences under consideration. In *R. v. Sardo*,[47] the Ontario Court of Appeal noted that though there was a long record of prior convictions, most, if not all, of them could be characterized as "nuisance offences". Accordingly the court took the view that the length of the record was not really as significant as it might be in other cases. In determining the seriousness of the record the court may have resort to the penalty actually imposed as an indication of whether or not it was a serious crime of its sort.[48]

Evidence of a prior discharge cannot be presented to the court as a circumstance of aggravation, but only to indicate that a further

---

[44] (1960), 32 W.W.R. 312.
[45] (1957), 118 C.C.C. 237 (Ont. C.A.); see also *R. v. Andrejeczuk* (1976), 19 Crim. L.Q. 152 (Man. C.A.); *R. v. Beacon; R. v. Modney* (1976), 31 C.C.C. (2d) 56 (Alta. C.A.).
[46] *R. v. Bouzane,* unreported, January 31, 1977.
[47] Unreported, October 28, 1974 (Ont. C.A.); see also *R. v. McKenzie* (1952), 6 W.W.R. 192 (Sask. C.A.).
[48] *R. v. Eaton* (1968), 53 Cr. App. R. 118.

discharge would not be in the best interests of either the accused or the public.[49]

2. THE SAME OR SIMILAR OFFENCES

It has been suggested that where offences are related in kind to the offence for which sentencing is to be performed, "the circumstances would be most unusual and extenuating" for the court to order a period of imprisonment for a related crime of less duration than one previously imposed. These comments were made by a District Court Judge and the result was approved by the Saskatchewan Court of Appeal only as disclosing "no basis upon which the court would be justified in interfering." This falls short of an express appellate approval of the rule, and indeed, it is submitted the principle is unsupportable. In an earlier case the same court, differently constituted, did impose a lower sentence upon a recidivist for related crimes saying "surely a previous record cannot condemn an accused for all time and prevent a court from exercising leniency where the circumstances warrant it": *R. v. Kennedy.*[50]

In *R. v. Zedd,*[51] the court had to deal with an accused whose record consisted of 12 convictions for either being an inmate in or keeping a common gaming-house, each of which resulted in a fine. The court, viewing this record, determined that the accused had "defied and flouted the law. It is the clear duty of the courts to stop this contemptuous attitude to the law. The fact that the accused (and possibly others) does not agree [with the law] is immaterial." Accordingly a jail sentence was imposed instead of still another fine. In *R. v. Murray*[52] the Saskatchewan Court of Appeal rejected the application of the *Zedd* case where the criminal record of an accused consisted, not of a series of the same offences, but of a number of different offences. Such a record did not amount to bringing the law itself into disrepute.

Nevertheless, where the courts are faced with an offender who has frequently been involved in offences of the same nature, the protection of the public, absent an explanation that discloses reason to expect an end to

---

[49] *R. v. Tan* (1974), 22 C.C.C. (2d) 184 (B.C.C.A.).
[50] (1972), 5 C.C.C. (2d) 373 (Sask. C.A.).
[51] (1959), 30 W.W.R. 330 (Man. C.A.).
[52] (1960), 32 W.W.R. 312.

the behaviour, demands a heavier sentence.[53] In *R. v. Brookes,*[54] one reason for increasing sentence was the fact that the accused had a previous record of six similar offences.

Similarly in *R. v. Pezzo,*[55] the Ontario Court of Appeal refused to interfere with a one-year sentence, in view of the fact that the appellant had previous convictions including one for joyriding. The conviction there was on a charge of theft of a motor vehicle.

However, there are limits to which the previous convictions can be put. In *R. v. Newman,*[56] sentences totalling seven years were reduced on appeal to three years on charges of break and enter, theft over, and possession of a restricted weapon. The 24-year-old accused had a record going back six years involving 16 convictions, most for theft-related offences. Viewed in its totality the total of seven years was too high even with such a criminal record.

In *R. v. Trask,*[57] the accused, charged with indecent assault upon a female, had a record that disclosed that he had been convicted of theft under for which he received ten days' imprisonment, and an attempted theft, for which he was fined $200. The court said "these previous offences were obviously petty, and are totally unrelated to the matter under appeal . . . ". Therefore, the question of sentencing could "be approached as if the appellant had no previous record in view of his otherwise exemplary past."

There is no rule that only previous convictions of the same type should be considered as aggravation, but consideration in mitigation may be given to the fact that the offence was out of character with and was not part of the accused's ordinary criminal activity.[58] Conversely, more weight should be given to offences of the same character.

One problem that the courts have had to face is that of deciding whether or not an offence is "related" or "similar". In at least one case, *R. v. Harnett,*[59] the category to which the court had resort was whether or not there had been any other "offence involving dishonesty" — it disregarded convictions for disorderly conduct. Conversely, in a case

---

[53] *R. v. Pasternak; R. v. McNeil; R. v. Andrews* (1961), 36 W.W.R. 423 (B.C. C.A.).
[54] [1970] 4 C.C.C. 377 (Ont. C.A.).
[55] (1972), 9 C.C.C. (2d) 530.
[56] (1977), 22 N.S.R. (2d) 488 (C.A.).
[57] (1974), 28 C.R.N.S. 321 (Ont. C.A.).
[58] *R. v. Woods,* [1962] Crim. L.R. 646.
[59] Unreported, September 23, 1974 (Ont. C.A.).

involving political demonstrations, *R. v. King; R. v. Simpkins,*[60] the English Court of Appeal was of the view that offences of dishonesty would not be "directly relevant when one is considering a sentence in this type of case". However, in that case, counsel disclosed to the court that though the offences in the record seemed on their face to be dishonesty offences (office breaking and possessing housebreaking instruments by night) in fact these offences were political in nature in that the break-in was to the office of a civil defense centre with a view to taking pamphlets and instructions which had not been issued to the public. "These were not therefore offences of dishonesty in the ordinary sense, but demonstration offences." Accordingly they could be taken into account on the charge of unlawful assembly arising out of a demonstration against the late Greek dictatorship.

The same case discloses the way in which the court treated a record of "similar" offences arising from taking part in demonstrations. A series of 14 offences involving obstructions and breaches of the peace arising out of the accused's political beliefs was used only to show that the accused persisted in a course of conduct which he knew brought himself in conflict with the law.

In *R. v. Munday,*[61] the court confined itself to "the sort of dishonesty that is involved in charges of larceny and shopbreaking". The offences which were not taken into account were those such as indecent assault and motoring offences, save and except one that was taking and driving away a car.

In *R. v. Simmons, Allen and Bezzo,*[62] Brooke J.A. for the majority, in discussing the criminal record of the appellants, noted that although they did have criminal records they were not in reference to "morals offences"; this was the categorization he used to evaluate criminal records on a charge of rape.

E. Crimes of Violence

It is clear that when the propriety of the sentence for a crime of violence is under consideration, an examination of the record is appropriate to

---

[60] (1973), 57 Cr. App. R. 696.
[61] (1971), 56 Cr. App. R. 220.
[62] (1973), 13 C.C.C. (2d) 65 (Ont. C.A.).

determine whether or not there have been previous crimes of violence.[63] The absence of such a record is a mitigating factor; the presence, an aggravating one, for it discloses with greater certainty that the prisoner is a serious danger to society.

> This record does not reveal any crimes of violence and thus weighs less heavily against him than it would if he had a previous conviction or convictions involving violent crime. In so saying I do not mean to suggest that the previous criminal record of the appellant is not a factor to be considered in assessing what a fit and proper sentence should be. It is rather a question of the weight to be attached to such previous record.[64]

On a charge of assault causing bodily harm, for this reason, among others, the sentence was reduced from 18 months to nine months.

F. The Jump Effect

Though not by any means a principle in Canada at the present time, one of the features often disclosed by an examination of a criminal record is the fact that the sentence imposed or to be imposed in the instant case is considerably longer than any to which the accused has been subjected previously. There seems to be a rule of thumb that, except where there is a marked increase in the seriousness of the crime committed, there should not be too great a "jump" in the length of the sentence imposed. This is really no more than the principle that if less will do, then more is superfluous. Accordingly in *Re Morand; Re Simpson,*[65] the Saskatchewan Court of Appeal noted as one of the reasons for reducing a sentence from four years to three years, the fact that the longest sentence previously imposed was two years. Similarly in *R. v. Alfs,*[66] the Ontario Court of Appeal noted that the appellant had never received a custodial term before and for that, among other reasons, the court varied a four-year sentence for armed robbery to one of time served being about ten months followed by one year's probation. That a principle is

---

[63] *R. v. Jourdain and Kudyba* (1957), 25 W.W.R. 160 (Man. C.A.); see also *R. v. Young,* unreported, November 15, 1974 (Ont. C.A.).

[64] *R. v. Evans* (1975),11 N. S. R. (2d) 91 at p. 96 *per* MacDonald J.A. (C.A.).

[65] (1959), 30 C.R. 298 (Sask. C.A.).

[66] (1974), 17 Crim. L.Q. 247.

emerging for this question is evident in *R. v. Sloane,*[67] where a jump from a non-custodial sentence to one of eight years' imprisonment "offends in principle".

G. The Gap Principle

Since both sentencing and crime are human endeavours, it is natural for the courts to give credit to someone who has made an honest effort to avoid conflict with the criminal law. In the nature of things, an effort such as this will often not be completely successful, but if a substantial period of time passes without convictions this is often a matter which will be taken into consideration. As put by Cross:[68] "Assuming that it is not merely the outcome of lucky non-detection, the trouble-free period shows in these cases that the offender is not a professional criminal, and therefore the public needs less protection from him."

It surprises no one to learn that the ordinary practice is to treat harshly an offence committed shortly after a release from custody.[69] The principle discussed here is no more than the converse of that notion.

In *R. v. Kennedy,*[70] the accused was convicted of manslaughter and sentenced to two years less one day. The Crown appealed, bringing forward a record involving jail sentences over a period of years for such crimes as assault, breaking and entering, escape custody, mischief, wilful damage and another breaking and entering. All criminal involvement had ceased for a five-year period prior to the manslaughter conviction. In these circumstances the Court of Appeal determined that: "after having gone five years without involvement in the law, the past record should not be a too material factor in determining an appropriate sentence."

In *R. v. Hudson,*[71] the court had to evaluate a lengthy record, but noted that, though there had been more recent convictions, there had earlier been an eight-year period without convictions and indeed "some

---

[67] [1973] 1 N.S.W.L.R. 202.
[68] R. Cross, *The English Sentencing System,* 2nd ed. (London: Butterworths, 1975) p. 168.
[69] *R. v. Denholm* (1970), 11 C.R.N.S. 380 (Sask. C.A.). But *cf. R. v. Wallace,* [1977] Crim. L.R. 685.
[70] (1972), 5 C.C.C. (2d) 373 (Sask. C.A.).
[71] (1928), 20 Cr. App. R. 11.

intervals in which he is known to have got an honest living". The court regarded this interval as "a new start" and was disposed to show leniency. Accordingly a term of five years was reduced to 12 months' imprisonment. This case was approved by the Ontario Court of Appeal in *R. v. Harrell,*[72] where an accused with a record for similar offences was sentenced to five years' imprisonment. There was a gap of 11 years where he was not convicted of "any serious offence" followed by further convictions for breaking and entering and uttering two forged cheques — uttering being the very offence of which he had been convicted and for which he now stood sentenced. The Court, noting this 11-year gap which did not immediatly precede the conviction at bar, came to the conclusion that this "long interval, free from serious convictions is entitled to due weight" and noting other factors as well, reduced the sentence to three years. In *Re Morand; Re Simpson,*[73] the accused had a nine-year gap between the present offence and his only previous offence. In the result the three-year sentence for breaking and entering was reduced to two years less one day. Similarly in *R. v. Murray,*[74] the court noted the accused "deserves credit" for a one and a half year period free from crime following his marriage, a period which had been interrupted only by the crime under consideration.

In *R. v. Clements,*[75] a sentence of eight months on charges of trafficking in marijuana and hashish oil was reduced to 90 days intermittent. The court noted that the 31-year-old accused had a serious record but since his release from prison in 1971 he had obtained a job and could work if given an intermittent sentence. This "change in lifestyle" had to be reflected in the sentence.

Not all periods of abstention from crime operate in mitigation of the penalty that might otherwise be imposed. In *R. v. McKenna,*[76] the appellant appealed a sentence of ten years for a conviction of armed robbery. He stole a car and, armed with a sub-machine gun, robbed a merchant. The court found that McKenna's "deliberate return to crime in this fashion made his abstention from crime for a period of years of questionable value" and the nature of the crime supported the

---

[72] (1973), 12 C.C.C. (2d) 480; see also *R. v. Riordan* (1974), 15 C.C.C. (2d) 219 (N.S.C.A.).

[73] *Supra,* n. 65; see also *R. v. McKeachnie* (1975), 26 C.C.C. (2d) 317 (Ont. C.A.).

[74] (1960), 32 W.W.R. 312 (Sask. C.A.).

[75] Unreported, April 28, 1978 (Ont. C.A.).

[76] Unreported, April 25, 1973 (Ont. C.A.); see also *Grayson v. The King* (1920), 22 W.A.R. 37.

conclusion that this was his way of life. The court seemed to be going behind the period of abstention and inferring that this was a man who had simply not been caught in the interval. Similarly in *R. v. Devlin and Marentette,*[77] the court refused to give effect to the principle in a case of conspiracy to traffic heroin on a very large scale where, after a release from penitentiary, the appellant Devlin kept out of trouble for a ten-year period. The court, noting that for those ten years he managed to make a good living and that he "deliberately" returned to trafficking in heroin for no apparent reason at all, refused to give any credit for this period. The court increased the sentence to one of life imprisonment. Possibly the nature of the crime affected the result here, as well.

For the gap principle to come into effect the period under consideration need not be totally crime free. A nine-year period marred only by minor offences, such as causing a disturbance and driving a motor vehicle while disqualified, merited consideration in *R. v. Graveline, Bezaire and Cassidy.*[78] The court concluded "it would appear that since then he has been making some effort to stay out of trouble or at least he has not been in as much trouble since then." Accordingly a one-year period was reduced, for this reason among others, to six months. Similarly in *R. v. Harnett,*[79] the court gave effect, upon a charge of possession of stolen copper wire, to the gap of 14 years marred only by offences of disorderly conduct that were attributable to an alcohol problem, but dishonesty had not been a part of them. In the result a sentence of two years with three years' probation was reduced to one year followed by two years' probation.

---

[77] (1971), 3 C.C.C. (2d) 20 (Ont. C.A.).
[78] (1958), 27 C.R. 287 (Ont. C.A.).
[79] Unreported, September 23, 1974 (Ont. C.A.).

Chapter 5

Psychiatric Aspect Of Sentencing

The use of material giving evidence of psychiatric disorders in sentencing requires sensitivity and caution on the part of the trial judge and diligence on the part of counsel to bring forward every fact that may be of assistance to his client or to the court.

A. Procedure

Usually counsel will make relevant psychiatric material available to the trial judge. A trial judge should be aware that pursuant to s. 543(2) he may, at any time before sentence, when of the opinion, supported by the evidence of at least one duly qualified medical practitioner, or by his report in writing where Crown and accused consent that there is reason to believe that an accused is mentally ill, remand him by order in writing to such custody as the court directs for observation for a period not exceeding 30 days. Where compelling circumstances exist for so doing and when a medical practitioner is not readily available to examine the accused and give evidence, a court may still make that order. Further, a judge may extend it to a period of more than 30 days, but not exceeding 60 days, when he is satisfied that observation for such a period is required in all the circumstances of the case and his opinion is supported by the evidence of at least one duly qualified medical practitioner or by his report in writing where Crown and accused consent.

Pursuant to s. 543(3) where it appears that there is sufficient reason to doubt that the accused is, on account of insanity, capable of conducting his defence, the court shall, if he the accused is not represented by counsel, assign counsel to act on his behalf. One purpose of these sections of the Criminal Code is to prevent the possibility that anyone shall be tried or sentenced when he is not fit to stand trial. In *R. v. Harvey*,[1] at the time of sentencing, evidence of a general practitioner who examined Harvey while in custody was given to the effect that the appellant needed psychiatric assessment. The general diagnosis given was that Harvey was suffering from either manic or potential schizophrenia. The Ontario Court of Appeal held that it was incumbent upon the trial judge, with the evidence of the medical practitioner on record, to address himself to the issue of whether or not the appellant, at the time of entry by him or on his behalf of a plea of guilty, was medically speaking in a position to enter or instruct such a plea. The court held that justice could not be done nor have the appearance of being done until that matter had been explored. Accordingly a new trial was directed.

In *R. v. Wallace*,[2] no evidence was called at trial either by the Crown or the prisoner on the issue of sentence. The trial court was, however, urged to consider documents that were in existence at the time of trial, which related to the prisoner's attendance at a psychiatric hospital and a "presentence report to be used in the event of conviction", apparently prepared by the same hospital. The appellant had never seen these documents personally, nor did the court call for them after having been informed of their existence. The trial judge sentenced the accused without regard to this material. The Ontario Court of Appeal held this was error by the trial judge and proceeded to consider the material afresh on sentence. Where psychiatric material exists, it will inevitably be relevant to sentencing.

There is a comment in *R. v. Benson and Stevenson*[3] to the effect that in ordinary cases where material indicates that the accused person is suffering from a mental disorder, this is not a factor which should influence a court to impose a higher sentence than would ordinarily be imposed. Therefore, it follows that there need be no absolute rule to the effect that the contents of a psychiatric report should be disclosed to the prisoner, even if it is part of the material upon which sentence is to be based. Sloan C.J.B.C. speaking for the British Columbia Court of Appeal, *obiter dicta*, said that the "examining doctor would be the best judge as to whether or not the result of his examination should be fully

---

[1] Unreported, September 21, 1971 (Ont. C.A.).
[2] (1973), 11 C.C.C. (2d) 95 (Ont. C.A.).
[3] (1951), 13 C.R. 1 (B.C.C.A.).

disclosed to the convict". It is submitted that this is incorrect in principle and contrary to the established practice throughout Canada. If there were ever a rule that sentence was not increased for this reason such a situation no longer exists.

It is clear that psychiatric evidence cannot be brushed aside by the court. In *R. v. Taylor,*[4] a police officer was convicted of theft of goods valued at less than $50 and sentenced to six months determinate and six months indeterminate. Psychiatric evidence indicated that he was in a mentally depressed state which would give him a feeling of guilt and unworthiness and lead him to commit a crime so he would be punished. The trial judge said, in dismissing this unchallenged evidence, that if he had felt in a bad way mentally he ought to have reported to his chief and had himself examined by a psychiatrist. The Court of Appeal felt it "not necessary" to comment on those reasons. The magistrate appeared to have imputed to the accused the capacity to decide that he ought to consult a mental specialist and criticized him for not doing so. This was improper and an error. Accordingly sentence was varied to one of time served.

There is a divergence of opinion upon the question as to whether, before the psychiatric condition can be reflected in the sentence, it is necessary to show that it has somehow contributed to the commission of the offence for which he is being sentenced. In *R. v. Bartlett; R. v. Cameron,*[5] the court dealt with a complaint that the trial judge did not give sufficient weight to the report of a psychiatrist, which indicated that the prisoner was of low normal intelligence but without any evidence of insanity or major psychiatric illness, although he displayed evidence of anxiety, emotional disturbance and instability. The Manitoba Court of Appeal said:

> The circumstances of the crime show no evidence of emotional reaction on his part or impulsive action. Indeed it appears that he had his emotions well under control and his actions bear no relation to his clinical epileptic disorder. . . . Barlett's condition of mental health may be such that he requires medical treatment, but it is obvious that it played no part in the offences to which he pleaded guilty; if it deserves attention on other grounds, that is not the responsibility of this Court.

On the other hand, though the facts are distinguishable in that the

---

[4] [1959] O.W.N. 1 (C.A.).
[5] (1961), 131 C.C.C. 119 (Man. C.A.).

psychiatric disorder did play a part in causing the crime, in *R. v. Wallace*[6] the Ontario Court of Appeal noted evidence that Wallace was a disturbed person who, when depressed was given to self-destruction and had previously attempted to take his own life. It appeared that imprisonment was likely to produce such a depression and thus create a danger to him. The Court dealt with his disturbance not simply as part of the causation of the commission of the offence, but also that:

> It is plain that a sentence the length of that imposed was very much more severe punishment for this man than for a normal person, because of the terror that he experiences, the danger of self-destruction and the loss of amenability to treatment [which was in this case unavailable in prison] as well as the fact it is unlikely he can achieve an early release because that treatment which he is in need of must be deferred . . .

It is submitted that the two cases of *R. v. Bartlett* and *R. v. Wallace* are not necessarily in conflict. A sentence can be reduced on psychiatric grounds because it shows, in some cases, that the accused is not a confirmed criminal and that with certain changed environmental or psychiatric factors, he will not be a danger to the community. This rationale, however, is not available if the psychiatric problems did not in fact lend themselves causatively to the crime. On the other hand, totally separate from this consideration, is the idea that in determining the quantum of punishment (whether as individual deterrence or as punishment *per se*) and also out of a sense of mercy, the subjective impact of imprisonment or any other penalty should be considered in assessing its fitness and propriety.

B. Increase Of Sentence

We have seen that "in ordinary cases" the fact that someone is suffering from mental disorder should not influence the court to impose a higher sentence except insofar as the mental instability should render the prisoner a menace to society.[7] (In that early case an exception was noted for sexual crimes.) A judgment of the English Court of Appeal (Criminal Division) in *R. v. Ford*[8] contains a comment expanding on this notion.

---

[6] *Supra,* n. 2 at p. 100.
[7] *R. v. Benson and Stevenson, supra,* n. 3.
[8] [1969] 3 All E.R. 782*n.*

The court said that in relation to offences of dishonesty, sentences of imprisonment are normally intended to be the correct sentence for the particular crime and not to include a curative element. The court specifically excepted such "special cases" as those of possessing dangerous drugs or cases where the protection of the public was involved. The same Court in a later case[9] referred to *Ford* and explained it further:

> In our judgment, in cases of dishonesty where there is, as it were, a background of alcoholism in respect to the accused the court must first determine what are the limits of a proper sentence in respect of the offences charged. Within those limits it may be perfectly proper to increase the sentence in order to enable a cure to be undertaken whilst the accused is in prison. But . . . it is clear that it is not correct to increase the sentence above . . . the appropriate range for the offence itself merely in order to provide an opportunity to cure.

The Ontario Court of Appeal, in *R. v. Luther,*[10] expressed a similar view. The appellant was convicted on a charge of assault causing bodily harm arising out of a fight in the common cell of the jail at Toronto during which she assaulted the complainant, a fellow prisoner, banged her head against the wall and scratched her neck. Another person who had assisted her in this endeavour was fined $50. It appeared that Ms. Luther, however, was addicted to drugs and the learned trial judge sentenced her to 12 months' imprisonment in order that she would receive treatment for her drug addiction. The court enunciated the principle that it is not the function of a criminal court to order confinement solely for the purpose of treatment of a physical or mental disorder.

The Ontario Court of Appeal has apparently acted upon the same principles as the English Court of Appeal (Criminal Division) with regard to raising a sentence, within the proper limits for the offence and the offender, in order to assure treatment. In *R. v. Robinson,*[11] the Crown appealed sentences imposed upon Robinson on two counts of rape and one count of attempted rape, all of which occurred within an 11-day period and were similar in pattern. The total sentence imposed amounted to two years less a day definite and two years less a day indeterminate. The psychiatric report noted a poor potential for control,

---

[9] *R. v. Moylan,* [1969] 3 All E.R. 783 at pp. 785-86.
[10] (1971), 5 C.C.C. (2d) 354 (Ont. C.A.).
[11] (1974), 19 C.C.C. (2d) 193 at p. 197 (Ont. C.A.); see also *R. v. Craig* (1975), 28 C.C.C. (2d) 311 (Alta. C.A.).

but asserted that Robinson could be treated within the reformatory system although it would take at least two years during which he would require intensive therapy; thereafter a further period of at least five years would be required as a "follow up". In order to give Robinson the treatment that was available in the reformatory system this sentence was imposed. The court said:

> This is a case where it is not really accurate to say that the sentence should be a deterrent because others like him lose touch with reality and as such the deterrence of this sentence is of course meaningless to them. Further, the sentence should not proceed on the basis of punishment because the Court should not punish people who commit crimes because of mental illness. The important purposes of the sentence are the protection of the public so long as this man remains in this dangerous state and his early return to the community when he is cured or, to put it another way, rehabilitated. The emphasis must be on the protection of the public, and of course this may be first achieved by his cure, and so the sentence must be of sufficient length to ensure full treatment but of course conversely, if that is not successful, that the public must be protected as best as can be accomplished.

Taking the view that the treatment which was needed was available in the penitentiary system, the court, having regard to all the circumstances, including the fact that the sentence must not exceed that which would otherwise be fit for the offence, imposed total sentences amounting to eight years placing reliance upon the National Parole Board to effect Robinson's release as soon as it was safe for the public that this be done and perhaps to require of him that he continue treatment or observation, while on parole.

C. The Dangerous Offender: A Status Offence

All of the above is a sensible approach to imprisonment for treatment, but it must be kept quite separate from the notion, *infra,* that a dangerous offender (especially one who is dangerous by reason of a psychiatric disorder) can in some circumstances have a lengthy sentence imposed — not as treatment but purely to prevent him from causing further harm. This idea of psychiatric imprisonment is not new but it is today gaining some increased popularity. Of late there has been a practice in several courts and particularly the Ontario Court of Appeal, in the case of serious crimes where psychiatric problems complicate the sentencing problem, to impose very lengthy terms or life imprisonment. In an *obiter* comment in *R. v. Pion; R. v. McClemens,*[12] the Court explained this practice as no more than the specific application of a more general principle.

> Nevertheless, all members of the Court wish to go on record with respect to their view of the appropriateness of life sentences where it is demonstrated, without anything further, that the record and evidence before the Court discloses a continuing danger to the public from a convicted person. Where that is demonstrated and in appropriate circumstances surrounding the particular case the members of the Court, as presently constituted, hold the view that nothing else need be shown to justify a life sentence and, specifically, that mental disease or other abnormalities need not be shown.

The English rationale for this practice has been set out in *R. v. Picker:*[13]

> There is no doubt that a life sentence can properly be imposed in mercy. Thus in a case where the nature of the offence and the make-up of the offender are of such a nature that the public require protection for a considerable time unless there is a change in his condition, maybe a mental condition at present unknown, it is right for the judge to impose a life sentence. This will enable some other authority to ascertain from time to time whether the condition has changed and it is safe for the offender to be released.

But a theory, albeit an attractive one, that does not contain within it any hint of the limitations that ought to be imposed on its use is a very dangerous theory indeed.

In terms of the English practice, it has been stated that if this were not done, the judge might have to impose a long definite term. But the life sentence in England permits an early review by the parole authorities or a grant of clemency through the Home Secretary — a condition which does not apply in Canada. Thus the sentence is viewed there, rightly, as an act "in mercy". However, "where no such condition exists, it is quite clear, in the opinion of this Court, that a judge should not pass the difficult matter of sentencing and the length of detention to others."[13a]

There are now many cases where, due to psychiatric problems which tend towards serious criminality, the court has come to the conclusion, that "the safety of the public must be first considered"[14] and therefore the accused must be kept in an institution for as long as he might be

---

[12] (1971), 4 C.C.C. (2d) 224 at p. 224 (Ont. C.A.).
[13] (1970), 54 Cr. App. R. 330 at pp. 332-33.
[13a] *Ibid.,* at p. 333.
[14] *R. v. Leech,* [1973] 1 W.W.R. 744 (Alta.).

dangerous. The most grave examples occur when there is no likelihood of successful medical treatment.

In *R. v. Jones,*[15] upon a charge of rape, where the psychiatric report indicated "considerable underlying aggressiveness", it was concluded that the prisoner was "potentially dangerous to others" and the possibility of treatment was poor. The Ontario Court of Appeal imposed a life sentence noting that if and when it became safe for the prisoner to be at large, the Parole Board had ample powers to release him. In *R. v. Hill,*[16] the court, upon a charge of rape and causing bodily harm with intent to wound a 14-year-old virgin, noted that Hill's condition could be treated by psychotherapy but that the outcome of such treatment was uncertain. His diagnosis indicated that his aggressive tendencies would probably begin to abate at about age 35 but that he could continue to be affected until age 60. The court concluded that where

> . . . an accused has been convicted of a serious crime in itself calling for a substantial sentence and when he suffers from some mental or personality disorder rendering him a danger to the community but not subjecting him to confinement in a mental institution and when it is uncertain when, if ever, he will be cured of his affliction, in my opinion the appropriate sentence is one of life. Such a sentence, in such circumstances, amounts to an indefinite sentence under which the parole board can release him to the community when it is satisfied, upon adequate psychiatric examination, it is in the interest of the accused and of the community for him to return to society.

Accordingly the court increased the 12-year sentence to one of life imprisonment. Nevertheless, in order to bring this principle into operation, there must be evidence that the mental disorder bears a causal relationship to the offence committed.

In *R. v. Head,*[17] upon a charge of rape upon a six-year-old girl, where there was a previous conviction for a similar offence and the psychiatric evidence showed that he was likely to repeat the offence, particularly if he consumed any alcohol, the court concluded that the prime factor to be considered was the protection of the public. As this could only be accomplished by keeping him in custody until such time that it could be reasonably certain that it was safe for him to be at large, the court upheld a sentence of life imprisonment. In such cases, the courts are really

---

[15] (1971), 3 C.C.C. (2d) 153 (Ont. C.A.).

[16] (1974), 15 C.C.C. (2d) 145 at pp. 147-48 (Ont. C.A.); affd *sub nom. Hill v. The Queen (No. 2)* 25 C.C.C. (2d) 6 (S.C.C.); see also *R. v. Haig* (1974), 26 C.R.N.S. 247 (Ont. C.A.).

[17] (1970), 1 C.C.C. (2d) 436 (Sask. C.A.).

legislating a change in the dangerous offender provisions. Their authority to do so is not apparent.

Indeed, some judicial reticence has crept into the doctrine established by *R. v. Hill.* In *R. v. Oliver,*[18] the court had before it a 17-year-old appellant who had been sentenced to 12 years for rape. The court noted that "the circumstances of the rape itself might not merit a sentence of the severity imposed, but a psychiatrist's report indicated that the appellant is a dangerous psychopath who is very apt to cause harm, if not death, to other persons in the future and it was this consideration that led the learned trial judge to impose the sentence that he did."

In the course of the judgment the court said:

> . . . we wish to point out with some emphasis to the Crown that a case of this kind is an appropriate one to proceed under s. 689 of the Criminal Code, R.S.C. 1970, c. C-34, and have the appellant declared a dangerous sexual offender. If it were not for the fact that the time within which the Crown might apply to have him so declared has expired in this case, we would allow the appeal and urge the Crown to proceed accordingly. We hope that these words will be taken into account by the Crown in future cases and that in the appropriate circumstances it will rely on s. 689 rather than the adjudication of this court in *Regina v. Hill* . . .
>
> The obvious protection to an appellant by the Crown proceeding under s. 689 is, of course, that there is an annual review of the desirability of keeping the accused in custody.

What is quite amazing about *R. v. Oliver* is that the court in effect sanctioned an increased sentence beyond what would be appropriate for the offence upon the grounds the offender was dangerous. To increase a sentence beyond that which would be justified by the offence upon the ground that the offender needs treatment has long been held to be improper, and quite justifiably so as it infringes upon fundamental ideas of equal justice.

Since the assessment of future dangerousness and the possibility of achieving a positive result and thereby successful treatment is hopelessly speculative, there can be little justification for raising a sentence beyond what the appropriate punishment for the offence would be, merely by magical incantation of the phrase "protection of the public".

Similarly, upon a charge of wounding, the Ontario Court of Appeal[19] had the benefit of psychiatric evidence indicating that the appellant

---

[18] (1977), 39 C.R.N.S. 345 at p. 345 (Ont. C.A.); see also *R. v. Luther* (1971), 5 C.C.C. (2d) 354 (Ont. C.A.); *R. v. Moylan,* [1969] 3 All E.R. 783.

[19] *R. v. Bradbury* (1973), 14 C.C.C. (2d) 139.

suffered from a character disorder of such severity that he was capable of further aggressive and dangerous behaviour both to himself and others; that his emotions were not controlled to the extent that a normal person's would be controlled; and that in addition he had very few social values that would assist in this control. The psychiatrist expressed the opinion that a lengthy period of treatment was required and that probably five years would be necessary before he would start to show any improvement; it might take much longer. He further stated that the treatment should be given where there was some security and discipline and recommended a penitentiary hospital. Accordingly the maximum sentence of 14 years was upheld bearing in mind the nature of the offence — unprovoked assault on a young girl with the use of a knife.

In *R. v. Fisher*,[20] the majority increased a sentence for a charge of the stabbing of a guard in a reformatory to the maximum sentence of 14 years. The offence of wounding was considered a grave one, involving of necessity a "substantial sentence". The court learned that the accused had been institutionalized on and off since he was about eight years of age, that he had spent almost 20 years at a psychiatric hospital for the criminally insane, and that he had three times attempted murder. He was a dangerous person; there was no indication that he would ever be cured. Houlden J.A. dissented, saying that when such a sentence was imposed the court was in effect passing a sentence of preventive detention without affording an accused man any of the protections afforded by the Criminal Code to a person who is subject to that type of sentence.

The court has of course no authority to order mental treatment. They can only recommend it or bring it to the attention of the penitentiary authorities by noting it on the court order or by relying upon counsel to inform the authorities of their view. Unfortunately few of these cases reach prison psychiatric hospitals and facilities for treatment in penitentiaries generally are simply laughable.

Though no limit can be put on the type of offence which is sufficiently grave to warrant this kind of negation of all our sentencing principles, the English Court of Appeal (Criminal Division) has described these offences as those where "the consequences to others may be specially injurious, as in the case of sexual offences or crimes of violence."[21]

The Ontario Court of Appeal has begun to clarify and limit the use of increased sentences to the maximum penalty such as those discussed

---

[20] (1975), 23 C.C.C. (2d) 449 (Ont. C.A.).
[21] *R. v. Hodgson* (1967), 52 Cr. App. R. 113.

here. In *R. v. Skedden,*[22] *R. v. Hill* was distinguished as being "clearly examples of the worst type of rape". Further, where there is no proof before the trial judge that the accused represents a continuing danger to the public or part of it, there is no ground for increasing sentence to the maximum permitted by law.

The doctrine in *R. v. Hill* is capable of great abuse, as the courts have begun to recognize. The court has emphasized that the imposition of a maximum sentence is not to be used as an alternative to invoking the provisions of the Criminal Code dealing with preventive detention with its attendant safeguards.

First, the nature of the crime itself must be such as to justify the maximum penalty by reference to ordinary sentencing principles; the case should fit reasonably within the description of Mr. Justice Ritchie in *R. v. Hill* as a crime of "stark horror". An added factor in such cases is that the offender suffers from a mental defect or disorder which makes it likely that he would, if at large, commit further offences involving serious acts of violence. Where any of these tests are not met, sentences will be altered, and a sentence appropriate to the offence imposed.[23]

D. Decrease Of Sentence

In some cases it appears from the psychiatric evidence that the chances of improvement or cure through treatment are favourable. Where there is a history of psychiatric difficulty, any term imposed should take into consideration where the accused might best receive assistance.[24] One such case is *R. v. D.*[25] D., a school-teacher, was convicted and sentenced to a total of 12 months definite and six months indeterminate upon charges of assaulting young girls. He was a pedophile who shortly before the offence recognized his problem and voluntarily commenced treatment with a psychiatrist. While undertaking this treatment he committed these offences. The psychiatric evidence disclosed that if he

---

[22] Unreported, March 5, 1976 (Ont. C.A.).

[23] *R. v. Haig* (1974), 26 C.R.N.S. 247 (Ont. C.A.); *R. v. Hatton* (1977), 39 C.C.C. (2d) 38 (Ont. C.A.); *R. v. Pontello* (1977), 38 C.C.C. (2d) 262 (Ont. C.A.); *R. v. Keefe,* unreported, October 24, 1978 (Ont. C.A.).

[24] *R. v. Dumesnil,* unreported, February 15, 1977 (Ont. C.A.).

[25] (1971), 5 C.C.C. (2d) 366 (Ont. C.A.).

were permitted to continue treatment in a noncustodial setting the chances for a cure were favourable: "If such treatment outside the prison is likely to effect such a cure and his imprisonment may not, we think that it is in the general interest of society to have him treated rather than imprisoned." It was accepted that he could undergo similar treatment in one of the correctional institutions while serving his sentence. Noting that his present psychiatrist had had some success with him and, "psychiatric treatment being of a personal nature", the court determined that it would be in the best interests of the community to continue the cure at the earliest possible occasion.

> Deterrence in this case is of small moment because the Court is of the view the appellant suffers from an illness, as do all pedophiles; they are not deterred by punishment to others. If the appellant is allowed out of custody, undertakes the treatment and repeats this sort of offence, then he should expect to be dealt with in a quite different way because it will then be demonstrated that the public welfare would best be served by isolating him from society.

The court varied the sentence to one of time served, together with a probationary term for two years on condition that he submit to treatment at a private psychiatric hospital.

In *R. v. D.* the court made no reference to its earlier decision *R. v. Doucet,*[26] where it was dealing with a prisoner who had been convicted of indecently assaulting a young boy and sentenced to two years less one day definite and two years less one day indeterminate. In the period between the conviction and the imposition of sentence this pedophile received private psychiatric treatment and the prognosis was extremely favourable with a "minimal" likelihood that he would repeat the offence provided he continued in treatment. On the other hand, two other doctors presented opinions to the trial judge which indicated that a term of imprisonment would act as a deterrent to this man, as well as a deterrent to other unfortunate men afflicted with the same abberration. The court noted that the trial judge had to make a very difficult decision

> . . . since our penal system does not make provision for the cure of persons afflicted in the same way as the appellant, but rather simply provides a place of incarceration. Had I been in the Judge's position, I might very well have come to the conclusion that the interests of society in the end analysis would be better served by a term of probation in which treatment could be administered and that incarceration would be unnecessary. However, I

---

[26] (1970), 2 C.C.C. (2d) 433 (Ont. C.A.).

cannot say that the Judge was wrong in doing what he did, or that he erred in principle in his decision.

Brooke J.A. dissenting, took the view that:

> If through probation and continued psychiatric treatment this appellant achieved a cure, surely this is of greater value to society rather than to send him away and have him restored to society still suffering from his illness with the probability that he would give way to the old compulsion.

Schroeder J.A. while agreeing with the majority judgment, expressed the view that he had no such reservations about the sentence imposed by the trial judge. This is no doubt indicative of an older view such as that in *R. v. Jones*[27] where Pickup C.J.O. for the majority, in dealing with three charges of indecent assault involving young girls aged six, seven and eight years respectively, determined that a fine and costs was an inadequate sentence:

> It is said that the prison term will not have any deterrent effect upon other persons who are truly sex perverts. That may be so, but I do not think it justifies disregarding the deterrent effect upon those persons whom sentence will deter and who might be disposed to commit an assault of this character.

The court imposed a term of six months definite and 12 months indeterminate. It is respectfully submitted that this older view has now been rejected by the Ontario Court of Appeal in *R. v. Robinson.*[28]

> This is a case where it is not really accurate to say that the sentence should be a deterrent because others like him lose touch with reality and as such the deterrence of this sentence is of course meaningless to them. Further, the sentence should not proceed on the basis of punishment because the Court should not punish people who commit crimes because of mental illness.

There are many cases in which one can see that effect has been given to psychiatric opinion by way of a reduction of sentence. In a number of cases, the court has given effect to the principle that, where possible, the type of sentence will be varied so as to be conducive to a cure if the crime flows to some extent from mental illness. In *R. v. Allen*[29] the prisoner was convicted of assaults on a number of young girls and was sentenced to a total of two years in a penitentiary. This sentence was the maximum for

---

[27] (1956), 23 C.R. 364 at p. 365 (Ont. C.A.).
[28] (1974), 19 C.C.C. (2d) 193 at p. 197; see also *R. v. Marceau* (1978), 4 C.R. (3d) S-53 (Ont. Prov. Ct.) (manslaughter); *R. v. Gionet* (1977), 22 N.S.R. (2d) 316 (C.A.).
[29] (1954), 20 C.R. 301 at p. 305 (B.C.C.A.).

the offence of indecent assault, imposed specifically because the trial judge was informed (presumably correctly), that there was no treatment available at the reformatory. A later psychiatric report gave the opinion that further institutional care would be of no particular benefit, whether it be in a mental hospital or penal institution, but that this care could best be given on an out-patient basis and that thereby a recurrence would be "extremely unlikely". The court noted that there was no report produced by the Crown to throw any doubt upon these conclusions, and further that if he continued to serve his sentence in prison ". . . then the likelihood is he will emerge from prison uncured, embittered, and more likely to be a greater (and certainly no less) danger to young girls and to the community at large than he was when convicted." Accordingly the sentence was varied to one of time served so that treatment could be commenced.

It would be misleading to think that these principles apply only to cases such as rape and sexual offences.

In *R. v. Roberts*[30] the court reviewed sentences totalling 24 years' imprisonment, following conviction on nine counts of arson committed by a compulsive pyromanic. The information before the court from psychiatrists indicated that since the totality of sentences was so great, it operated as a deterrent to the prisoner's desire to help himself — a matter which was of vital importance in successful treatment. The psychiatric evidence further indicated that the possibility of release at some indefinite time in the future by the Parole Board was not adequate to overcome this effect. Accordingly the court reduced the total term of imprisonment to 12 years, taking the view that this was sufficient for the protection of society and at the same time removed an important obstacle to the prisoner's recovery.

In *R. v. Connors*[31] the accused was sentenced to two years less one day for offences of attempted breaking and entering and a theft, one of which was committed while on bail for the other. The accused had previous convictions for mischief, three charges of breaking and entering, and one assault causing bodily harm. The appellant had been placed with the Children's Aid Society at a very early age and had lived in several foster homes. He suffered from mental retardation due to his emotional problems and gross learning disabilities. On appeal further information was put before the court which indicated that he had accepted placement in a rehabilitation centre where he had been residing while on bail

---

[30] [1963] 1 C.C.C. 27 (Ont. C.A.).
[31] (1976), 18 Crim. L.Q. 290 (Ont. C.A.).

pending appeal. The opinion of those in charge of the rehabilitation centre was that, though his capacity to adapt to society would be gradual and slow, he was an excellent candidate for rehabilitation.

The court held that although probation had not been effective with Connors in the past, it was premature to abandon the hope of rehabilitating him in the community. In view of his intellectual and motivational problems, he would be particularly vulnerable to the negative influence of the prison sub-culture. The social and mental health services available to him appeared to be the best means of providing him with the capacity and motivation to become a useful and productive member of the community. Accordingly, the sentence was reduced to time served together with two years' probation.

In *R. v. Bikker,*[32] the appellant unlawfully, with intent to mislead, caused a peace officer to enter upon an investigation by reporting an offence that had not been committed. Sentence was suspended and he was placed on probation for three years. The accused, who was 17 years of age had telephoned the police warning them against the presence of explosives in a public building; these were figments of his imagination. The court noted that he had a history of psychological disturbance, but appeared to be making progress in a rehabilitation programme. The psychiatric report expressed the view that the granting of a discharge would be conducive to the success of the treatment being offered him. Accordingly the court set aside the sentence and imposed a conditional discharge with three years' probation.

In *R. v. Wallace*[33] the accused was sentenced to a total of ten years' imprisonment following charges of robbery and assault. The psychiatric report indicated that the conduct which brought the accused before the court was attributable to a depressed and disturbed state and suggested that minimum imprisonment would be appropriate, so that he might be treated for his disorder. There was no suggestion that a lengthy term was needed in order to provide such treatment. The court said:

> The best future protection for society lies in imposing a sentence which will make the appellant's rehabilitation probable through the provision of medical treatment that can be made available to him. It seems then that if a moderate term of imprisonment had been imposed, the medical treatment which he needed would have been available during such term and the sentence must be altered so that we can accomplish his cure and protect the community.

---

[32] Unreported, May 22, 1975 (Ont. C.A.).
[33] (1973), 11 C.C.C. (2d) 95 (Ont. C.A.).

Accordingly, a sentence of four years was substituted for the ten-year period of imprisonment. Quite often the psychiatric problems the accused has, tend to make other inmates, particularly in penitentiaries, violent towards him and put him in personal danger. A reformatory term has been substituted in some cases both to provide treatment and to give less exposure to those who might abuse the prisoner.[34]

It is important to remember that psychiatric opinion is only opinion; and that it is very often wrong. In *R. v. Luknowsky,*[35] the only mitigating factor on a charge of manslaughter was that the causative force in the killing was a disturbed psychiatric state. A few days before the death of his wife the accused had voluntarily entered a hospital for psychiatric treatment where he remained four days. The death occurred less than two days after his release. At trial, the psychiatrists were of the opinion that he was amenable to treatment and that he was neither a danger to public nor likely to commit any further offence. The court noted:

> It does not appear that the medical authorities treating prior to the killing foresaw any danger in his condition, otherwise they would not have released him. Their present opinion, because of this, must have less weight than it would ordinarily be accorded. The court must have a high degree of assurance that the mental problem has been corrected or eliminated where the crime was the result of a disturbed mental condition or a personality disorder.

It is quite amazing that the courts accord these opinions weight in the ordinary case. The failure of psychiatric and psychological predictive skills is notorious. Indeed, responsible psychiatrists rarely claim a high degree of accuracy in predicting future human conduct. The court, in asking for a "high degree of assurance" that the mental problem has been "corrected or eliminated" is asking for both the unobtainable and the impossible.

It is not always the prospects of treatment for psychiatric disorder that lead to a reduction in sentence. Often it is simply an acknowledgement by the court that had it not been for the difficulties the accused had he would not have become involved in the crime in the first place. So, in *R. v. Antone and Antone,*[36] upon a charge of manslaughter involving the death by starvation of a six-year-old daughter, the court gave mitigating effect to the personality defects of the parents. Mrs. Antone believed the

---

[34] *R. v. Menkes* (1977), 19 Crim. L.Q. 278 (Ont. C.A.).
[35] (1976), 19 Crim. L.Q. 18 (B.C.C.A.); see also *R. v. Usher,* unreported, June 12, 1978 (B.C.C.A).
[36] (1977), 20 Crim. L.Q. 143 (Ont. C.A.).

girl was favoured by the grandparents and so she took out her hostilities on her. Mr. Antone was described as passive, seeking to avoid the realization of what was happening. Thus there was a "unique combination of personality characteristics in the parents" which in effect caused the offence.

E. Imprisonment For Treatment

In *R. v. Petrov*,[37] a trial judge imposed a sentence of "one year indeterminate directed to be served" at a public mental hospital. The Ontario Court of Appeal, upon the concession of the Crown that the sentence was illegal, allowed the appeal, set aside the sentence and imposed a suspended sentence with probation for one year with a condition that the accused undergo treatment throughout the term of probation as deemed necessary in the hospital's discretion. There is no power in the Criminal Code to make such an order unless it be found in the terms of s. 663(2)(h) empowering a court to enforce "such other reasonable condition as the court considers desirable". This interpretation was obviously adopted in the *Petrov* case.

The place of confinement and the length of sentence may be varied to permit the accused to take advantage of unusual treatment facilities in a particular institution. In *R. v. Mulhall*,[38] a penitentiary term of five years' imprisonment was imposed upon two counts of robbery and two counts of indecent assault. The court, because of the accused's emotional state aggravated by his addiction to alcohol, was of opinion that he should not be sent to the penitentiary but should be imprisoned in a reformatory because there were "unusual facilities for giving him such medical treatment as may be advisable having regard to his condition" at that place. Accordingly the court set aside the penitentiary term and imposed the term of two years less one day.

---

[37] Unreported, January 25, 1973 (Ont. C.A.); see also *R. v. Luther* (1971), 5 C.C.C. (2d) 354 (Ont. C.A.) and chapter 2 "Appropriate to Offence".

[38] (1952), 103 C.C.C. 211 (Ont. C.A.).

Chapter 6

Aggravating Factors

No hard and fast rule is possible for determining the appropriate penalty for any offence, but since few crimes are truly original, their characteristic features repeat themselves with appalling regularity. It is therefore useful to examine some recurring factors which increase the gravity of an offence and decrease the consideration which can be given the offender. The list is not by any means exhaustive and no factor will operate in aggravation of the offence at all times; depending upon the context and the circumstances, it may be a factor which ought to be ignored, or given little weight.

A. Method

The court almost always has recourse to an examination of the method whereby the offence was committed. If the method is sophisticated and involves premeditation, planning or the evolution of a system, this generally indicates a more serious offence of its type. Some types of offence, however, by their nature require these characteristics. The theory seems to be that persons capable of such sophistication are also capable of doing more harm as criminals by reason of their greater abilities. Presumably these individuals constitute a greater danger to society because they have made a deliberate choice for criminality.

Drug trafficking is a crime which often requires elements of planning, deliberation and system.[1] Nevertheless, even within the framework of this type of crime, an unusually sophisticated scheme has been noted as justifying, in part, an unusually heavy sentence.[2] In *R. v. Pearce,*[3] the court noted that, with a view to increasing profits, the appellants' scheme eliminated the usual layers of middlemen.

In some crimes the element of planning necessary shows premeditation (as opposed to impulsive behaviour), and this is a factor that has been considered.[4] An example is *R. v. Novlan.*[5] In this case, avoiding payment of sales tax involved not merely a failure to pay, but assent given to the filing of false returns and omitting material particulars from the books of the company. Similarly, in a case of armed robbery, the facts disclosed that the appellants had had to steal a car, steal licence plates from another car, and equip themselves with weapons. These were factors that led the court to the conclusion that what "stands out is the cool, callous, deliberate preparation which all the accused made to execute the robbery which they planned."[6] Similarly, in rape cases the court often has recourse to an examination of the facts to determine whether the crime was an impulsive act or whether there was a measure of premeditation and planning.[7]

Even in offences which require, of necessity, premeditation and planning the court will take into consideration that the "premeditation was short-lived" and that the motive arose out of a sudden impulse.[8] In *R. v. Gorman,*[9] the Ontario Court of Appeal by a majority increased a sentence, noting, *inter alia:* "Earlier detection of these defalcations was prevented by the manner in which the respondent conducted his operations and the provision by him, during the course of a protracted period, of forged statements of audit."

Similarly, upon conviction for the operation of an illegal combine,

---

[1] *R. v. DeJong,* (1970), 1 C.C.C. (2d) 235 (Sask. C.A.); *R. v. Hemsworth* (1971), 2 C.C.C. (2d) 301 (N.S.C.A.).

[2] *R. v. Brookes,* [1970] 4 C.C.C. 377 (Ont. C.A.); *R. v. Johnston and Tremayne,* [1970] 4 C.C.C. 64 (Ont. C.A.).

[3] (1974), 16 C.C.C. (2d) 369 (Ont. C.A.).

[4] *R. v. Iwaniw; R. v. Overton* (1959), 127 C.C.C. 40 (Man. C.A.); *R. v. Thompson* (1974), 20 C.C.C. (2d) 100 (Ont. C.A.).

[5] (1971), 9 C.C.C. (2d) 85 (Ont. Co. Ct.).

[6] *R. v. Warner, Urquhart, Martin and Mullen,* [1946] O.R. 808 (C.A.).

[7] *R. v. Wilmott,* [1967] 1 C.C.C. 171 (Ont. C.A.).

[8] *R. v. Lauzon* (1977), 19 Crim. L. Q. 285 (Que. C.A.).

[9] (1971), 4 C.C.C. (2d) 300 at p. 331 *per* Kelly J.A.

McRuer C.J.H.C. analyzed the method used by the companies and concluded that:

> . . . the parties involved were making it as difficult as possible for the proper authorities to ascertain exactly what was done and who was responsible for doing it, so that it would be very difficult eventually to succeed in a prosecution. . . .
>
> Having all that in mind, I cannot bring myself to have the same sympathy for these convicted companies as I have for the Queen's subject who is charged with an ordinary criminal offence and is brought to the Court for justice.[10]

The principle is as old as Coke: *"omnia delicata in aperto levioria sunt"*[11] (all crimes are less grave when done openly).

In *R. v. Kehoe*[12] the Ontario Court of Appeal decided that a longer sentence was dictated by, *inter alia,* the fact that upon a plea of guilty to a charge of possession of a stolen pistol and ammunition, it was apparent that the stolen goods in question could be used for criminal activity and that the prisoner admitted that the weapon was intended for an unlawful purpose.

The setting wherein the offence takes place may be an aggravating factor as well: "This offence involves the invasion of a private home, a place of security, for the purpose of an attack on the person of this woman. In these days of large population, high density living, the people are vulnerable and the law must protect them. . . . the sentence must reflect the need for protection and the complete repudiation by the public of such conduct."[13]

The Court will also consider viciousness in commission of the offence as an aggravating factor. For example, the fact that an assault is unprovoked or methodical is a factor which can be considered.[14]

B. Continuation Over A Period

The fact that criminal activity has continued over a lengthy period of

---

[10] *R. v. Northern Electric Co. Ltd.* (1956), 24 C.R. 201 at p. 204 (Ont. C.A.).
[11] 8 Rep. 127.
[12] Unreported, June 24, 1971.
[13] *R. v. Thompson* (1974), 20 C.C.C. (2d) 100 at p. 103 (Ont. C.A.).
[14] *R. v. Bradbury* (1973), 14 C.C.C. (2d) 139 (Ont. C.A.).

time will, in many cases, indicate that there has been a conscious and deliberate decision to engage in criminality. Courts are not inclined to show leniency to such persons, even when they are first offenders. *A fortiori*, the harm that has been done by continuing crime will be greater, and this of course must be borne in mind in making the sentence appropriate to the offence. Accordingly, in *R. v. Pearce*,[15] the court noted that the evidence disclosed that the appellant had been in the business of distributing "speed" for some two years. Upon a charge of conspiracy to defraud, the evidence disclosed that the offence was planned and carried out over a long period and this was a ground for increasing sentence.[16] In *R. v. Foran*,[17] the court noted that the operations which gave rise to the charge of defrauding a public company started some five years earlier; and in *R. v. Johnston and Tremayne*,[18] the court noted that the offence of possession of marijuana for the purpose of trafficking and conspiracy to import was carried out "not on one occasion but deliberately as a continuing business."

C. The Magnitude And Impact Of The Crime

The application of this factor is wide, for it is essentially an assessment of the scale and effect of a crime. In *R. v. Wells*,[19] the magistrate, in assessing a penalty upon a scheme to induce persons to enter Canada illegally, ostensibly to attend a school regarding which the accused made false representations, noted that "I cannot overlook the magnitude of the accused's unlawful operations in Hong Kong and the number of students whom they adversely affected." In another case there was evidence that the seizure of drugs was the largest made in Toronto up to that time and that after the appellant's arrest "the East End dried up for quite some time".[20] This was of some importance in assessing sentence.

---

[15] (1974), 16 C.C.C. (2d) 369 (Ont. C.A.).

[16] *R. v. Major* (1966), 48 C.R. 296 (Ont. C.A.); *R. v. Oliver* (1977), 20 Crim. L.Q. 25 (B.C.C.A.).

[17] [1970] 1 C.C.C. 336 (Ont. C.A.); *R. v. Soble* (1978), 3 C.R. (3d) S-1 (Man. C.A.).

[18] [1970] 4 C.C.C. 64 (Ont. C.A.).

[19] (1972), 7 C.C.C. (2d) 480 (Ont. Prov. Ct.).

[20] *R. v. Pearce* (1974), 16 C.C.C. (2d) 369 (Ont. C.A.); *R. v. McAllister* (1976), 1 C. R. (3d) S-46 (Ont. C.A.).

The number of victims may also be important. In *Curley v. The Queen,*[21] a charge of conspiracy to defraud, the court noted that the offences which were committed were of a "far more serious nature than those involving fraud directed against a single individual, because they affect the whole of society". The conspiracy was one to defraud the provincial Department of Revenue.

An interesting approach to the question of how much a sentence ought to be increased by virtue of the magnitude of the crime or the consequences to the victim can be seen in *R. v. Mellstrom.*[22] The accused was found guilty of criminal negligence in the operation of a motor vehicle which caused death to three persons. A three-and-one-half-year sentence was left undisturbed on appeal, the court saying:

> While the enormity of the tragic consequences of an offence is a factor to be taken into consideration it must not be permitted unduly to distort the consideration of the Court as to the appropriate sentence for the offence committed. In other words, applying this line of reasoning to the case under consideration the fact that three people were killed should not be permitted to magnify the offence in the minds of the Judges over its sufficiently serious nature if only one person had been the victim.

This focus upon the issue of what the accused either intended or contemplated rather than the consequences is new and undoubtably correct.

D. Profits Available From The Crime

In *R. v. Robert; R. v. Shacher,*[23] the Ontario Court of Appeal cited with approval a passage from a judgment delivered by Lord Justice Cairns in an English case:

> "What must be taken into consideration is that the profits available from this kind of traffic are so substantial that the courts will not be doing their duty if they fail to impose such sentences as will make it clear to these young men and to others who might think of following their example, that this kind of crime will not be allowed to pay."

---

[21] (1969), 7 C.R.N.S. 108 (Que. C.A.).
[22] (1975), 22 C.C.C. (2d) 472 (Alta. C.A.); see also *R. v. Sayer,* unreported, February 27, 1976 (Ont. C.A.).
[23] (1971), 3 C.C.C. (2d) 149 at p. 151.

The Court noted that in cases of drug trafficking, unlike other crimes, this was not merely a consideration but the paramount consideration. There, the existence of a substantial commercial aspect may make a difference between a custodial and a non-custodial sentence.[24] The general rule can be applied to any crime which has a commercial aspect to it.

E. Characteristics Of The Victim

Not all crimes have victims, but where there is a victim his or her relative vulnerability will be considered an aggravating factor. The general principle has been stated by the Ontario Court of Appeal in *R. v. Major:*[25]

> Society has a special responsibility for those who are unable fully to look after themselves: children, infirm, aged and the blind, and those who took advantage of persons unable to protect themselves are particularly vicious.

Similar remarks were made by the trial judge with regard to those who preyed upon persons suffering from a hearing loss in a fraudulent scheme to sell hearing aids.[26] In *R. v. Rogers (No. 2),*[27] the Prince Edward Island Court of Appeal increased sentence upon a charge of defrauding the public, where the members of the public defrauded were persons on welfare; and in *R. v. Rooney and Rooney,*[28] the court noted as an aggravating factor that the assault had taken place upon a man who was lying on the ground at the time. In *R. v. Roy*[29] on a charge of manslaughter, the court noted that there was something "particularly repugnant" about the killing of a sleeping victim.

The fact that an assault exemplifies and flows from prejudice is an aggravating factor; such violence must always be dealt with severely, and the idea of deterrent sentencing is strong in such cases.[30]

---

[24] *R. v. McLay* (1976), 17 N.S.R. (2d) 135 (C.A.).

[25] (1966), 48 C.R. 296 at p. 297.

[26] *R. v. Riordan* (1974), 15 C.C.C. (2d) 219 (N.S.C.A.).

[27] (1972), 6 C.C.C. (2d) 107.

[28] (1967), 51 Cr. App. R. 62.

[29] (1975), 18 Crim. L. Q. 17

[30] *R. v. McKay,* [1975] Crim. L. R. 591; *R. v. Atkinson, Ing and Roberts* (1978), 43 C.C.C. (2d) 342 (Ont. C.A.).

In *R. v. Ingram and Grimsdale*,[31] two accused had engaged in a racially motivated attack upon a non-white immigrant to Canada. The Court of Appeal stated firmly that the racial motivation for the cowardly attack was an aggravating factor to be taken into consideration:

> ... just as it would be an aggravating factor if the victim were elderly, feeble or retarded.
>
> It is a fundamental principle of our society that every member must respect the dignity, privacy and person of the other. Crimes of violence increase when respect for the rights of others decreases, and, in that manner, assaults such as occurred in this case attack the very fabric of our society. ... An assault which is racially motivated renders the offence more heinous. Such assaults, unfortunately, invite imitation and repetition by others and incite retaliation. The danger is even greater in a multicultural, pluralistic urban society.[32]

Where the victim of the crime is one who by virtue of his employment is especially vulnerable to this sort of crime, or who is not entirely a free agent in the company he keeps or where he goes, this will be an aggravating factor. Accordingly, in *R. v. Iwaniw; R. v. Overton*,[33] where a robbery was committed upon a taxi driver, he was an "easy victim", because if he was to retain his employment he must go where he was directed and upon the facts here he was directed to a secluded place. Similarly, an assault upon a waiter in a bar led to the comment:

> I recognize that the factor of deterrence is of great importance in cases of this kind where the victim of the assault is by the very nature of his employment exposed to the dangers of violence. Such people must be protected.[34]

A recurring factor in rape cases is the age of the victim, and the fact, if it is the case, that she is a virgin. These aspects tend to direct severe and deterrent sentences.[35]

The fact that the victim of a crime is a police officer or prison guard acting in the execution of his duty will ordinarily tend to increase sentence because of the necessity of protecting the police and the importance of upholding respect for law.[36] Where the crime is an assault

---

[31] (1977), 35 C.C.C. (2d) 376 (Ont. C.A.).

[32] *Ibid., per* Dubin J. at p. 379.

[33] (1959), 127 C.C.C. 40 (Man. C.A.).

[34] *R. v. Evans* (1975), 11 N.S.R. (2d) 91 at p. 96 *per* MacDonald J.A.

[35] *R. v. Wilmott*, [1967] 1 C.C.C. 171 (Ont. C.A.).

[36] *R. v. Sherwood* (1958), 122 C.C.C. 103 (B.C.C.A.); *R. v. Barrette*, unreported, July 11, 1978 (B.C.C.A.).

upon police in the execution of their duty and the accused is under the influence of alcohol, this is not always the case.[37]

However, where the charge is assault causing bodily harm, the fact that the victim is a police officer should be ignored in sentencing. If the Crown wished to urge upon the court the circumstance that the victim was a peace officer engaged in the execution of his duty when the assault took place as a reason for more serious punishment, the appropriate charge could have been laid under the section of the Criminal Code involving those factors. To take such a factor into account would be in fact to sentence the offender for an offence for which he has been neither tried nor convicted.[38] This rationale fails when the facts do not permit the laying of a charge that contains the special ingredient of the victim's identity as a peace officer. An opposite view was taken, without argument on the point, in *R. v. Hodgins; R. v. Wedge.*[39]

F. Breach Of Trust

Where a person has voluntarily assumed a position of trust, the courts see as aggravating the fact that he or she commits a crime upon the beneficiary of the trust. The nature of the trust and its circumstances may vary widely. For example, a system of defrauding the welfare authorities and the public who received welfare by one employed by the welfare department provides an example of breach of trust as an employee,[40] as is theft from a former employer,[41] such as that of Treasurer of the Sick Benefit Fund of the Fire Department and who stole from the moneys entrusted;[42] or the officer of a private company who steals from that company;[43] and even an officer of a public company who defrauded the public.[44]

---

[37] *R. v. Chingee,* unreported, May 18, 1977 (B.C.C.A.); *R. v. Smith,* unreported, November 15, 1977 (B.C.C.A.).

[38] *R. v. James* (1971), 3 C.C.C. (2d) 1 (P.E.I.C.A.).

[39] (1962), 132 C.C.C. 223 (N.B.C.A.). See also *R. v. Luciens* (1975), 18 Crim. L. Q. 18 (Ont. C.A.).

[40] *R. v. Rogers (No. 2)* (1972), 6 C.C.C. (2d) 107 (P.E.I.C.A.).

[41] *R. v. Dorkings,* unreported, October 15, 1974 (Ont. C.A.).

[42] *R. v. Gorman* (1971), 4 C.C.C. (2d) 330 (Ont. C.A.).

[43] *R. v. Novlan* (1971), 9 C.C.C. (2d) 85 (Ont. Co. Ct.).

[44] *R. v. Foran,* [1970] 1 C.C.C. 336 (Ont. C.A.).

Despite this factor, extenuating circumstances may intervene to decrease the sentence. In *R. v. Lachance*[45] a postal employee stole a $100 gold bracelet from the mail. She was 24 years of age and had been of previously good character, but had developed psychiatric difficulties when her marriage broke down. At the time of the appeal she was expecting a child. Though the offence was extremely serious because of the breach of trust involved, the court reduced the sentence to one of time served (one month).

Offences committed by police officers are of particular significance because the police are in a position of trust in that "the administration of justice depends upon the fidelity and honesty of the police".[46] In much the same way offences by lawyers take on a added seriousness because they are committed by an officer of the court.[47]

In *R. v. Hunt*[48] the Crown appealed an absolute discharge given to a corporal with 16 years' service in the R.C.M.P. who had illegally converted to his own use some $11,000 which was in safekeeping in connection with drug cases. He used the money in a speculative stock exchange venture. One year later his superiors recovered the whole sum from him but it was not in fact the same money. He was dismissed from the force. The Court of Appeal said that the absolute discharge was contrary to the public interest "if one includes in the public interest the interest of the R.C.M.P.". A sentence of one year was imposed.

Similarly, in *R. v. Oliver*[49] the court took the view, upon a charge of fraud from a client, that it was not wrong to sentence a person more severely just because he was a lawyer. The court noted that lawyers are integral to the business community and are often entrusted with large funds. As well, lawyers are officers of the court and it is from the ranks of lawyers that judges are chosen. The public's confidence in the judiciary must not be impaired. In this case the lawyer was a person of excellent reputation in the community who, as is usual, used his reputation to perpetrate the fraud.

Parents who commit crimes with regard to their children similarly are

---

[45] Unreported, June 29, 1976 (Ont. C.A.).

[46] *R. v. McClure* (1957), 26 C.R. 230 (Man. C.A.); *R. v. Cusack* (1978), 41 C.C.C. (2d) 289 (N.S.C.A.).

[47] *R. v. Tober* (1977), 39 C.R.N.S. 133 (Man. C.A.).

[48] Unreported, January 10, 1978 (B.C.C.A.).

[49] (1977), 20 Crim. L.Q. 25 (B.C.C.A.).

in a position of trust; so also if they are not in fact the parents, but merely stand *in loco parentis.*[50]

It was suggested in an older case that one rationale for the severe treatment of persons of mature years who have abused their trust is that:

> Such persons are not those whom it is expected to be reformed by imprisonment. Their imprisonment is simply by way of punishment for their wrongs committed. [Other measures are reserved for] the case of younger men or women whose character are not definitely moulded and who may be saved from a life of crime.[51]

This is perhaps outdated today. The true rationale seems to be that it is important for society as a whole that one who acknowledges a trust should be held to it, and that deterrent penalties therefore become the means whereby the criminal law asserts the importance of that trust.

The rule treating breach of trust as a serious aggravating factor is not inflexible. In *R. v. Humes,*[52] the accused was a store manager who, through the falsification of invoices and cheques, obtained excess commissions. He had an excellent background and complete restitution was made before the laying of the charge. A serious alcohol problem had now been overcome. The court noting that because of the position of trust and because the offence extended over a long period of time a custodial sentence was usually imposed, but in view of the "exceptional circumstances" the accused was given a suspended sentence and two years' probation. In minor cases, the fact that a breach of trust is involved will not be sufficient to impose a severe penalty. In *R. v. MacEwan,*[53] a 39-year-old employee stole from his employer. He had no criminal record and all goods were recovered; the thefts were separated by only a few days. The Court of Appeal imposed an absolute discharge.

---

[50] *R. v. Cudmore* (1972), 5 C.C.C. (2d) 536 (Ont. C.A.); *R. v. Coolen,* unreported, June 14, 1973 (Ont. C.A.); *R. v. Wood* (1975), 26 C.C.C.(2d) 100 (Alta. C.A.).

[51] *R. v. Bond,* [1937] 3 D.L.R. 479 at pp. 483-84 (Ont. C.A.).

[52] Unreported, March 13, 1978 (Ont. C.A.); see also *R. v. McEachern* (1978), 42 C.C.C. (2d) 189 (Ont. C.A.).

[53] (1978), 39 C.C.C. (2d) 523 (P.E.I.C.A.).

G. Involving Others In Crime

The fact that the prisoner has involved others in criminal activities is a further aggravating factor. In *R. v. Pearce*,[54] the Ontario Court of Appeal noted that the prisoner had employed as "runners" recently released convicts who were in need of money or were drug users or both.

In *R. v. Seguin*,[55] the court said:

> . . . there is heavy indication in the evidence that the appellant encouraged Worobec to bring stolen goods to him for sale. This would influence Worobec, a boy of about 16 years, to follow a life of crime and is a factor which, under the circumstances, I think the Court is justified in weighing in an effort to determine the proper sentence to be imposed.

No doubt the youth of the person involved bore an especially heavy weight.

The questions of which of a number of persons involved in a crime was the instigator or who influenced the others is a factor which often has justified a heavier sentence for that person.[56] The fact that the prisoner involved others in the crime is invariably viewed as an aggravating factor.[57]

For some offences, the fact that two or more persons together commit the offence render it in and of itself more serious. This is especially so in rape.[58] The rationale seems in some cases to be that such a crime is more cowardly; in others, it renders resistance by the victim impossible or more difficult; and in still others it indicates planning and deliberation.

H. Conduct At Trial

Appellate courts have often referred to the advantage possessed by a trial

---

[54] (1974), 16 C.C.C. (2d) 369 (Ont. C.A.).

[55] (1953), 105 C.C.C. 293 at pp. 293-94 (B.C.C.A.). See also *R. v. Soble* (1978), 3 C.R. (3d) S-1 (Man. C.A.).

[56] *R. v. Iwaniw; R. v. Overton* (1959), 127 C.C.C. 40 (Man. C.A.); *Antonecchia v. The Queen* (1959), 31 C.R. 320 (Que. C.A.).

[57] *R. v. Morrissette* (1970), 1 C.C.C. (2d) 307 (Sask. C.A.); *R. v. Rogers (No. 2)* (1972), 6 C.C.C. (2d) 107 (P.E.I.C.A.).

[58] *Ibid.*

judge in assessing sentence — this advantage lies in the ability of the judge to observe the prisoner and his demeanour at trial. Thus observation may indicate what the bare words of the transcript do not: the sort of character that implies a danger to the public and thus demands protection. In *R. v. Costelloe*[59] the manner in which the prisoner gave evidence in the course of a defence to the charge of wounding was important: "I wanted to put him in hospital for life, killing would be too good for him." He was sentenced to life imprisonment for the protection of the victim and the Court of Appeal upheld this sentence. Usually however, it is the protection of the public as a whole which the court has in mind when drawing inferences from the demeanour of the prisoner at trial. In *R. v. Matrai,*[60] the prisoner had assaulted the premier of a foreign country who was visiting Canada, and with regard to his conduct at trial, the appeal court noted:

> He [the accused] there [in the Court below] sought, unsuccessfully, to persuade the Provincial Court Judge that the whole incident was merely accidental and occurred merely as a result of his having been jostled in the crowd which, of course, is utterly ridiculous and untrue according to the evidence before the Court. Nor does his attitude in this Court impress the Court. It is not here one of realization of the seriousness of his action for his country but, rather, one of attempted minimization of the whole affair as merely another common assault.

There are occasions where the attitude of the accused appears from his conduct during the offense itself to be a serious aggravating factor. In *R. v. Johnston*[61] the court stressed as an aggravating factor the "defiant attitude" of a prisoner who refused to testify against other inmates at a murder trial and was convicted of contempt of court. A severe sentence was considered necessary to bring home to the accused and to those others like him serving prison terms that the "legal standards by which free men live applied with equal force to those temporarily deprived of their freedom."

There is serious question as to what weight should be attached to this factor. The accused is, after all, being sentenced for his offence only. If his conduct is sufficiently inappropriate to warrant a separate conviction for contempt of court during his trial, then no doubt an additional penalty would be justified. But to increase sentence on this ground is to

---

[59] (1969), 54 Cr. App. R. 172.
[60] (1972), 6 C.C.C. (2d) 574 at p. 575 (Ont. C.A.).
[61] (1976), 18 Crim. L.Q. 286 (Ont. C.A.).

encourage false shows of humility, deference and repentence, which do nothing for the administration of justice.

In *R. v. Simmons, Allen and Bezzo,*[62] the dissenting judge relied upon the trial judge's observation that the three accused found their proceedings "humorous and boring" and he characterized their attitude as cynical and a little short of contemptuous and indicating a complete lack of contrition. The majority, apparently also taking these factors into account, nevertheless lowered the sentence.

I. Behaviour After The Offence

It has been said that the attitude of the offender after the commission of the crime tells us a good deal about the character of the offender.[63] This aggravating factor has been set out most explicitly in *R. v. Warner, Urquhart, Martin and Mullen:*[64]

> The next circumstance which impresses me is the utter callousness of each of the accused from the time of the commission of the crime to the date of their arrest, two or three days later. That they all knew as they drove away from the scene of the crime that Tobias had been shot there can be no doubt.... One would have thought that in these circumstances the accused would have been overwhelmed with remorse and fear. Mullen alone hid. The others carried on almost as though nothing had happened, frequenting their usual haunts, including the pool-rooms. On the night of the tragedy Warner even went to the moving-picture show, not apparently for the purpose of secreting himself from observation, but merely to satiate his desire for entertainment. The next night he went again. . . .

> Without further reviewing their conduct subsequent to the shooting, it will suffice to say that it was entirely inconsistent with the theory that this was a crime committed by four youths in an interval when they were subject to impulses which were foreign to their ordinary moods, and that it does not reflect their tendencies and dispositions towards society.

The failure to show remorse (in statements made to police after the event, or the pre-sentence report, or as observed by the Court of Appeal where the prisoner appears in person) is indicative of an attitude which

---

[62] (1973), 13 C.C.C. (2d) 65 (Ont. C.A.).
[63] *R. v. Iwaniw; R. v. Overton* (1959), 127 C.C.C. 40 (Man. C.A.).
[64] [1946] O.R. 808 at pp. 814-15 (C.A.).

shows that no reform is really possible.[65] So in *R. v. Kehoe,*[66] upon a charge of possession of a stolen pistol and ammunition, the court noted as an aggravating factor that the prisoner had offered no explanation as to where the gun was obtained.

In *R. v. Rogers (No. 2),*[67] the court noted the attitude of the accused after the crime was discovered, in that he burned vast numbers of cancelled welfare cheques which would have been evidence against him. This indicated "a high degree of criminality on [his] part". Although co-operation with the police may be a factor in mitigation of sentence, mere failure to co-operate cannot be an aggravating factor.[68]

J. Lack Of Response To Previous Orders

Gaol is intended to have a deterent effect upon the prisoner himself. Therefore the court will take into consideration the fact that an offence has been committed just shortly after a release from imprisonment upon a prior conviction.

Although no court has indicated that it is a factor to be taken into consideration in aggravation, there has often been comment in the text of judgments to the effect that the accused was released from prison only shortly before the offense was committed. *R. v. Jackson*[69] comments dryly on this eventuality: "This is hardly surprising given the utterly hopeless record of our penal institutions in the matter of rehabilitation."

Accordingly in *R. v. Salamon,*[70] the Ontario Court of Appeal noted that the prisoner had been released only a matter of months before he was detected attempting to sell morphine, the subject of the instant charge. Similarly, if an offence is committed while the offender is already under a suspended sentence and on probation "there is little justification to ask for or expect favourable consideration".[71] The Ontario Court of Appeal,

---

[65] *R. v. Bezeau* (1958), 28 C.R. 301 (Ont. C.A.).

[66] Unreported, June 24, 1971 (Ont. C.A.).

[67] (1972), 6 C.C.C. (2d) 107 (P.E.I.C.A.).

[68] *R. v. Rosen* (1976), 30 C.C.C. (2d) 565 (Ont.); *R. v. McLenaghan,* unreported, November 14, 1975 (Ont. C.A.).

[69] (1975), 23 C.C.C. (2d) 147 (N.S.C.A.).

[70] (1972), 6 C.C.C. (2d) 165.

[71] *R. v. Collins* (1959), 124 C.C.C. 173 (Man. C.A.); *R. v. Markl,* unreported, October 20, 1975 (B.C.C.A.).

in *R. v. Kehoe,*[72] indicated as a circumstance dictating a longer sentence, *inter alia,* the fact that the offence was committed while the respondent was on parole. On the other hand, a sentence has been reduced because insufficient allowance was made for the fact that parole would be cancelled as a result of the conviction.[73]

There is no authority for the proposition that committing an offence while on bail for another offence is justification for the imposing of a harsher sentence, but it hardly can dispose a court towards leniency.[74] Where there is imprisonment in both cases there is abundant authority for the proposition that sentences are ordinarily to be consecutive.[75] As part of the examination of the circumstances of the offence, where the offence was committed while on probation, the English Court of Appeal (Criminal Division) has said:

> This is a typical example of the kind of case where we think it right to decline the invitation to make a fresh probation order. . . . How can we say that the West Riding Quarter Sessions, in saying that the appellant had shown his contempt for the probation order made in his favour in June 1967, were wrong in principle in sending him to detention? We cannot. We think on the contrary that Quarter Sessions took the only possible course in the interest both of this appellant and the public . . .[76]

In *R. v. Coolin and Losch,*[77] the fact that an offence was committed while the accused was at large on the terms of a conditional discharge was a factor in sustaining a relatively heavy sentence.

It has been said that the mere fact of a previous discharge having been given does not "form the basis of a request for greater punishment" but, rather, may satisfy the court that a further discharge should not be given. This proposition is undoubtedly necessary in order to give effect to the fact that a discharge is deemed to be an acquittal by statute, but it constitutes an exception to the principle discussed in this section.[78]

The fact that an accused has not paid the fines imposed on previous

---

[72] *Supra,* n. 66.

[73] *R. v. Evans* (1975), 11 N.S.R. (2d) 91 (C.A.), not followed in *R. v. Keeble* (1977), 37 C.C.C. (2d) 387 (P.E.I.C.A.).

[74] *R. v. Pelletier* (1974), 18 C.C.C. (2d) 516 (Ont. C.A.).

[75] *R. v. McKinney* (1963), 40 C.R. 137 (Sask.).

[76] *R. v. Thompson* (1968), 52 Cr. App. R. 670.

[77] Unreported, July 2, 1975 (Ont. C.A.).

[78] *R. v. Tan* (1974), 22 C.C.C. (2d) 184 (B.C.C.A.); *R. v. Murray* (1976), 19 Crim. L.Q. 26 (Ont. C.A.).

occasions can be taken into account as an aggravating factor on subsequent occasions.[79]

An order, to be taken into consideration as an aggravating factor, need not be one made by a court. For example, a lawyer converted his client's money to his own use while he was under investigation by the Law Society in connection with his accounts and was under an order of the Society prohibiting the issuance of trust account cheques (such as that in this case) without the signature of a Law Society official. The sentence was raised upon appeal.[80]

K. The Use Of Weapons

Though the possession and use of weapons in the commission of a crime is itself a separate offence, there are situations where it has been considered as an aggravating circumstance, *i.e.,* where it for some unfathomable reason does not fall into the prohibition against sentencing the prisoner for a crime upon which he has not been tried and thereby depriving him of the right to a fair trial with regard to that charge. For example, on a charge of robbery, which may be committed with or without a weapon, the fact that one chooses to go armed is clearly an aggravating factor. "A man who goes out to engage in an armed robbery destroys the balance of equality between himself and his victim by putting in his own hands a weapon which the victim cannot resist."[81]

In *R. v. Pigeon,*[82] in lowering a sentence for armed robbery, the court noted that the weapon was an air pistol: "not a very deadly weapon". It thus appears that the nature of the weapon and the consequent danger to the public is a factor to be considered. The court here canvassed cases where heavier sentences had been given with loaded pistols of a more serious nature and seemed to equate, through the analysis of cases, the use of a toy pistol with that of an air pistol in seriousness.

In *R. v. Iwaniw; R. v. Overton,*[83] one of the factors to be considered

---

[79] *R. v. Mellstrom* (1975), 22 C.C.C. (2d) 472 (Alta. C.A.).

[80] *R. v. Tober* (1977), 39 C.R.N.S. 133 (Man. C.A.).

[81] *R. v. Major* (1966), 48 C.R. 296 at p. 297 (Ont. C.A.).

[82] [1970] 2 C.C.C. 177 (Que. C.A.), see also *R. v. Johnston* (1976), 18 Crim. L.Q. 286 (Ont. C.A.).

[83] (1959), 127 C.C.C. 40 (Man. C.A.).

according to Schultz J.A. was the amount of violence involved in the employment of an offensive weapon as an aggravating circumstance. In that case, where a loaded revolver had been used as a club to effect the robbery Schultz J.A. said:

> Surely the true assessment of the situation is that the use of the revolver as a club did not deprive the weapon of its potentially deadly nature. . . . Admittedly their offence is not as serious as if the revolver had been used with a threat to shoot; but the fact that it was taken with them is an important one for which they offered no explanation.

Similar considerations are applied to a charge of wounding, as in *R. v. Bradbury*,[84] where the fact that a knife was used was considered to be an aggravating factor; and to assault causing bodily harm.[85]

Generally speaking the use of a weapon indicates a disregard for the safety of the public which should be reflected in a harsher sentence upon the ground that the public needs more protection from such an offender, and must repudiate such conduct.[86]

This view is not by any means universally held. An accused broke and entered school premises while armed with a semi-automatic pistol which was loaded with seven rounds and in clip.[87] He was sentenced to two years' imprisonment for breaking and entering, one year consecutive for possession of a weapon for a purpose dangerous to the public peace, and one year concurrent for the possession of an unregistered firearm. The court was of the view that the sentence imposed for breaking and entering was light, and noted that they would have sustained a longer sentence. The Crown had not sought to have the sentence increased. Despite these views the consecutive sentence in the weapon charge was made concurrent. It is not clear whether the court is saying that the use of a weapon is not an aggravating factor, or rather, that any increase in penalty by reason of this aggravation ought to be reflected in the principal offence. The latter interpretation is unlikely, as on its face it would seem that the principal punishment ought to relate to the offence that caused the actual harm.

---

[84] (1973), 14 C.C.C. (2d) 139 (Ont. C.A.).
[85] *R. v. Squires* (1975), 25 C.C.C. (2d) 202 (Nfld. Prov. Ct.); vard 35 C.C.C. (2d) 325 (C.A.).
[86] *Ibid.*
[87] *R. v. McGregor,* unreported, June 28, 1975 (B.C.C.A.).

L. An Affront To The Law Itself

Some crimes by their nature strike more deeply than others at the fabric of law itself. For example, in *R. v. Phillips*,[88] the prisoner appealed from sentence upon a charge of having his face masked by night without a lawful excuse. One of a group of some 50 to 75 men, disguised with hoods extending from the top of their heads to their knees, took a woman from her house by intimidation. Of this crime the court said:

> The accused and his companions took it into their own hands to interfere with her rights. In doing so they not only committed an illegal offence as regards her, but also a crime against the majesty of the law. Every person in Canada is entitled to the protection of the law and is subject to the law. . . . The attack . . . was an attempt to overthrow the law of the land, and in its place to set up mob law, lynch law, to substitute lawlessness for law enforcement which obtains in civilised countries. The greatest calamity that can befall a country is the overthrow of the law. Without it there is no security for life or property. Mob law such as is disclosed in this case is a step in that direction, and, like a venomous serpent, whenever its horrid head appears, must be killed, not merely scotched. It is the duty of the Court to protect the authority of the law . . .

Accordingly the court set aside the fine and imposed a period of imprisonment.

The evidence in support of a crime may disclose that the prisoner does not accept one particular law, and in fact repudiates its authority. "Such an attitude is not one that forms a sound base for leniency. On the other hand, it indicates what a potential danger he may be [to young people] until he changes his attitude and outlook."[89]

Offences committed by police not only involve the element of breach of trust, but also strike at the nature of law itself. They are treated particularly severely because "the administration of justice depends upon the fidelity and honesty of the police."[90]

Where the object of the crime is an attempt to defeat the ends of administration of justice, this is a most serious aggravating factor. For example, in *R. v. Mountain*[91] a Crown appeal was allowed and a sentence

---

[88] (1930), 38 O.W.N. 323 (C.A.); see also *R. v. Ingram and Grimsdale* (1977), 35 C.C.C. (2d) 376 (Ont. C.A.).
[89] *R. v. DeJong* (1970), 1 C.C.C. (2d) 235 (Sask. C.A.).
[90] *R. v. McClure* (1957), 26 C.R. 230 (Man. C.A.).
[91] Unreported, January 6, 1978 (B.C.C.A.).

raised from eight years to 15 years upon a man with an extensive record who was convicted of attempted murder. He severely beat a female acquaintance with a chain in an alley following a drinking session in a Skid Row hotel. She had earlier witnessed the injuring of a man who subsequently died; that death was then the subject of a police investigation. The respondent was present at the earlier offence and the court inferred that the reason for the attempt to murder her was that she should be unable to testify or give information to the police concerning the earlier crime.

M. Prevalence Or Increasing Prevalence Of A Crime In A Particular Locality

The idea of deterrence gives reason for the court to consider the prevalence of the particular crime of which the accused is convicted as an aggravating factor.[92] Indeed, sentences which otherwise would have been excessive have been approved because of this factor — its presence justifies a harsher sentence than either the offence or the offender would warrant.[93] It has also been stated that such considerations should not be so applied as to result in a convicted man being made the scapegoat for other persons who have committed similar crimes, but have not been caught and convicted.[94] In *R. v. Erdlyn,*[95] the court said:

> We think that the learned Magistrate, with great experience and knowledge of conditions in that particular locality (and that is a matter which properly may be taken into consideration), and with full knowledge of the seriousness of this kind of offence, was quite warranted in the exercise of his discretion in imposing a term of imprisonment.

This course of action is often taken in the hope that through the use of deterrent sentences, a particular type of crime may be brought under control. The theory has little, if any, statistical base upon which to stand and is not self-proving. It is nevertheless popular. In *R. v. Kissick*[96] the

---

[92] *R. v. McGrath* (1945), 1 C.R. 23 (Sask. C.A.).
[93] *R. v. Marshall* (1977), 23 N.S.R. (2d) 234 (C.A.).
[94] *R. v. Withers* (1935), 25 Cr. App. R. 53.
[95] (1956), 117 C.C.C. 207 at p. 213 (Ont. C.A.).
[96] (1969), 70 W.W.R. 365 at p. 371 (Sask. C.A.). See also *R. v. Porta,* [1945] 1 W.W.R. 351 (B.C.C.A.); *R. v. O'Brien,* [1948] 1 W.W.R. 591 (Man. C.A.).

court noted ". . . with the increasing incidences of armed robberies, the learned magistrate rightly concluded that sentences should be imposed that would be an effective deterrent, not only to the appellant, but to others who might be inclined to engage in similar activities."
The appeal court will carefully scrutinize a sentence based on such "personal" assessments.[97]

In *R. v. LeBlanc; R. v. Long*,[98] upon charges of conspiracy to commit the indictable offence of rum-running, the court specifically took into account the prevalence of rum-running in the province and the extreme audacity which characterized it. The evidence, at least in part, upon which this was based was judicial notice taken of the number of cases before the court dealing with the same subject.

In *R. v. Joslin*,[99] Campbell C.J. of the Prince Edward Island Court of Appeal said:

> I express no opinion as to whether severe punishment of minor first offenders is likely to act as a deterrent to others. Nor do I find it necessary to decide whether a general law of Canada should be more rigidly applied in localities where offences are on the rapid increase; this question does not arise here, where no offences have been disclosed until the current year.

This was a case of possession of marijuana. The opposite view has been taken by the British Columbia Court of Appeal in *R. v. Hartley and McCallum (No. 2)*:[100]

> It was our hope then, although I was not party to that decision, that substantial gaol sentences imposed upon people convicted of having possession of marijuana for their own use would reduce the number of users, and consequently the trafficking necessary to supply the market. We also feared that if we did not treat this offence seriously that the traffic would continue to develop and users would increase. Our fears have been borne out by the experience over the past few years.

The learned Chief Justice attributed the failure of this experiment to magistrates who failed to understand this principle and were too lenient in their treatment of this crime. Such a theory of causation is utterly simplistic and undoubtably incorrect.

Occasionally a heavy sentence will be imposed simply because the offence itself is a serious one, and the particular locality has been free of

---

[97] *R. v. Trecartin* (1955), 114 C.C.C. 376 (N.B.C.A.).
[98] [1939] 2 D.L.R. 154 (N.B.C.A.).
[99] [1970] 3 C.C.C. 50 at p. 52.
[100] [1968] 2 C.C.C. 187 at p. 188.

it: the theory seems to be that the deterrent effect of a heavy sentence will continue to keep the incidence of the offence low.[101]

N. The Effect Upon The Victim

Though no Canadian case refers to the subject directly, the full Court of Appeal of Victoria, Australia, has set out views on the effect of the crime upon the victim which are consistent with the policies of our criminal law, at least in crimes with a full *mens rea*.[102]

> It is always open to a judge to have regard to the fact that no evil effect resulted from the crime to a victim. That is a common occurrence and a fact properly taken into account. But conversely, a learned judge is equally entitled, in our view, to have regard to any detrimental, prejudicial, or deleterious effect that may have been produced on the victim by the commission of the crime.

This was a case where the accused had pleaded guilty to rape; the victim gave birth to a child born a little over eight months after the rape. The trial judge did not proceed on the basis that the accused was the father of the child but did take into account the emotional effect of the uncertainty as to parentage prior to birth. The woman testified: "I am not sure who the father of that baby is until I have it . . . The last few months have just about drove [me] mental."

---

[101] *R. v. Pitcher* (1976), 19 Crim. L.Q. 158 (B.C.C.A.).
[102] *R. v. Webb* (1971), V.R. 147 *per* Winneke C.J. at pp. 150-51.

Chapter 7

The Plea In Mitigation

This chapter does not purport either to exhaust the range of pleas in mitigation (any more than the previous chapter purported to exhaust the varieties of aggravating factors) or to substitute any test other than the central one, that the sentence be appropriate to the offence and the offender. It is instead an analysis of the important recurring factors of mitigation. As with aggravating factors it is the circumstance of each case which gives greater weight to some mitigating factors and less weight to others.

A. Role In The Offence

The role played in the commission of the offence is usually a relevant factor in sentencing. An aider and abetter may, upon the facts, deserve a lesser sentence than a principal.

In the case of an accessory after the fact the punishment provided by law may itself be significantly less than the punishment which the principal offender could receive. An interesting discussion regarding whether or not in such circumstances the penalty imposed upon an accessory after the fact should be less than that of the principal as a matter of course or whether it should be looked at on its own took place in *R. v. White and White.*[1] Two brothers who had helped strip and dump a car, knowing that it had been stolen, were sentenced to the same period

---

[1] (1977), 1 Crim. L.J. 320; see also *R. v. Vickers* (1975), 61 Cr. App. R. 48.

of imprisonment as the principal offender who stole the vehicle. Speaking for the majority Jacobs J. took from the words of the Australian statute an inference that "an accessory is to be dealt with according to his involvement as an accessory, irrespective of the principal felony, or the fate of the principal felon." The fact that the principal offence carried a higher penalty was of no relevance. "If Parliament had intended that the punishment of an accessory after the fact must be in some way related either to the seriousness of the principal offence or the punishment of the principal offender, it might have been expected to say so in language very different . . . ".

It might reasonably be said that our statute does relate the punishment of the accessory after the fact to the seriousness of the principal offence albeit not to the punishment of the principal offender. There is sufficient latitude in the range provided to give a great deal of emphasis to the particular role of the accessory after the fact and the particular nature of the offence. In his dissent, Bray C.J. took from the structure of the statute an "implied command of Parliament" to impose a lesser punishment to an accessory after the fact than to the principal felon.

The court may ask whether the accused was a "follower" or a "leader". Additionally counsel may show that the actual part the accused played in the offence was less significant than that played by others. It would seem that one who enters into crime because he is influenced by another is more capable of reform and rehabilitation than one who enters into it uninfluenced.[2] For example, in *R. v. LeSarge*[3] the court said: "If the appellant were the person who engineered and planned this crime, I would have thought the seven-year sentence to be appropriate, but the evidence convinces me that he is merely one of the underlings in the scheme."

In *A.-G. Que. v. Charbonneau,*[4] upon a charge of contempt of court, it was noted in mitigation that the evidence disclosed that the accused "were under external pressure from union superiors which is probably quite difficult to withstand."

In *R. v. Southam Press (Ontario) Ltd.*[5] a finding by the court that the

---

[2] *R. v. Kosh* (1970), 1 C.C.C. (2d) 290 (Sask. C.A.); *R. v. Andreau,* [1977] Crim. L.R. 366; *R. v. Johnston,* unreported, June 22, 1976 (Ont. C.A.); *R. v. Iwaniw; R. v. Overton* (1959), 127 C.C.C. 40 (Man. C.A.); *R. v. McAllister* (1976), 1 C.R. (3d) S-46 (Ont. C.A.).
[3] (1975), 26 C.C.C. (2d) 388 at p. 397 (Ont. C.A.).
[4] (1972), 13 C.C.C. (2d) 226 (Que. C.A.).
[5] (1976), 31 C.C.C. (2d) 205 (Ont. C.A.).

editor and publisher who had just been found guilty of contempt of court were only "vicariously responsible", in that neither had been sufficiently diligent in carrying out their duties, led the court to conclude that their role in the offence was not a "deliberate" one and led the court to set aside their sentence.

Marriage can also be a relevant factor in sentencing. When a wife commits an offence "out of loyalty to her husband", and without giving the matter sufficient thought, this can be taken into account in mitigation.[6]

B. Situational Exigencies

The court is always willing to listen to the reasons which impelled a prisoner to commit a crime in the hope that the circumstances may disclose that the prisoner is not one who is committed to crime as a way of life, but rather that pressures of the immediate human situation led to the criminal activity. This factor has more weight, of course, when it can be shown that the situational exigencies have ceased or have some likelihood of abating.

Since much crime is property crime, it is not unusual that a recurring motivation is a temporary financial difficulty. The more extreme such difficulty and the greater the extent to which it is not attributable to irresponsibility or vice, the less necessary will punishment be.

Cases are abundant which show that difficult personal circumstances are honoured as mitigating the sentence. Financial difficulties (*R. v. Stein*[7]), marital and family problems (*R. v. Stein; R. v. Zehr*[8]), emotional problems (*R. v. Young*[9]), medical problems (*Cavanaugh v. The Queen*[10]), and youth (*R. v. McGregor*[11]) all have been accepted in mitigation of sentence. That the court recognizes the insidious effects of these

---

[6] *R. v. Lee*, [1975] Crim. L.R. 589.
[7] (1974), 15 C.C.C. (2d) 376 (Ont. C.A.); see also *R. v. Johnston and Tremayne*, [1970] 4 C.C.C. 64 (Ont. C.A.); *R. v. Bates* (1977), 32 C.C.C. (2d) 493 (Ont. C.A.).
[8] Unreported, June 26, 1975 (Ont. C.A.).
[9] Unreported, November 15, 1974 (Ont. C.A.).
[10] (1953), 106 C.C.C. 190 (N.S.C.A.).
[11] Unreported, February 7, 1975 (Ont. C.A.); and *R. v. Paquet* (1977), 20 Crim. L.Q. 25 (P.E.I.C.A.).

conditions of lawful behaviour is seen in *R. v. Gunnell*,[12] where the court makes reference to the "twin plagues" of domestic misfortune and economic conditions.

C. Future Prospects: Potential For Rehabilitation

The hope of counsel, in asking for a pre-sentence report and in calling evidence, is to disclose material which supports a submission that there exists some rehabilitative potential. It is the duty of the court, where rehabilitative potential is apparent, to respond to it in some fashion, be it a lesser prison sentence, or a different type of individualized measure. Frequently relied upon, as in *R. v. Smith*,[13] are such facts as that the prisoner is married, supports two children, is steadily employed and has no previous record. In *R. v. McGregor*,[14] it was not only a favourable pre-sentence report, but the information that since the date of the charge, McGregor had been accepted as a student at a community college and was prepared to accept responsibility for restitution to the victim. "A 'sincere and permanent reform' will justify a reduction in sentence."[15] In the case of a young offender charged with break and enter offences, *R. v. Belfry*,[16] the court noted evidence that the prisoner was a good student, had an excellent record and strong support from his family. In *R. v. Bagnullo*,[17] regard was had to the prisoner's desire to return to school and prepare himself for a trade. In *R. v. Haig*,[18] evidence of a probation officer that the chances of rehabilitation were good was used as a factor in lowering a sentence upon charges of rape and robbery.

---

[12] (1951), 14 C.R. 120 (Que. C.A.); and *R. v. Johnston* (1976), 18 Crim. L.Q. 286 (Ont. C.A.).

[13] Unreported, March 7, 1974 (Ont. C.A.); but see *R. v. McLaughlan* (1976), 20 Crim. L.Q. 149 (N.S.C.A.).

[14] *Supra*, n. 11.

[15] *R. v. Pottie and Keating* (1978), 26 N.S.R. (2d) 646 (C.A.); *R. v. Justason*, unreported, April 24, 1973 (Ont. C.A.).

[16] Unreported, May 24, 1973 (Ont. C.A.).

[17] Unreported, May 29, 1973 (Ont. C.A.).

[18] (1970), 1 C.C.C. (2d) 299 (Ont. C.A.).

D. Age

Youth is generally conceded to be a mitigating factor, probably because it discloses the greatest possibilities for reform and because we do not expect so much from youthful judgment. Occasionally a crime may reflect nothing more than "a lack of maturity", or a lack of parental supervision and guidance.[19] In *R. v. Turner,*[20] upon a charge of rape and robbery, the court noted that there was an error by the trial judge in that, in dealing with a person who was 16 at the time of his offences and with reasonably good antecedents, the court did not pay sufficient regard to his age or the prospects of his rehabilitation; accordingly the court reduced the sentence. In *R. v. Wells*[21] the court noted that the fact that the accused was 71 years old and presently bankrupt operated in mitigation. The court came to the conclusion that no useful purpose would be served by a jail sentence. This proposition, however, cannot be recorded without noting one dissent, which stands alone in the cases.

In *R. v. Nutter, Collishaw & Dulong,*[22] the British Columbia Court of Appeal, considering charges of armed robbery of a trust company said:

> I do not think the ages of persons makes much difference when they are committing these violent crimes. Young men who persist in committing crimes of this sort cannot expect that their ages will be regarded as mitigating circumstances. We are in a period now where, as I have already said, there is a rash of crimes of violence. This is no time for softness and sentimentality to govern in the imposition of sentences for offences of this sort.

This court is probably saying (or ought to be saying), that for the most serious offences the mitigating effect of youth or reformative prospects has strict limitations.

For the most serious offences courts have been increasingly sensitive to the hopelessness of the reformative possibility in a penitentiary. In two similar cases the Ontario Court of Appeal[23] has said:

---

[19] *R. v. McFee* (1970), 13 Crim. L.Q. 151 (Ont. C.A.); *R. v. Cheung and Chow* (1976), 19 Crim. L.Q. 281 (Ont. C.A.); *R. v. Caja and Billings* (1977), 36 C.C.C. (2d) 401 (Ont. C.A.).

[20] (1970), 1 C.C.C. (2d) 293 (Ont. C.A.).

[21] (1972), 7 C.C.C. (2d) 480 (Ont. Prov. Ct.); see also *R. v. Kalsta* (1977), 20 Crim. L.Q. 21 (Ont. C.A.).

[22] (1970), 7 C.C.C. (2d) 224 at pp. 228-29.

[23] *R. v. Elliot* (1976), 19 Crim. L.Q. 25 and *R. v. Demeter and Whitmore* (1976), 3 C.R. (3d) S-55 at p. S-57. See also *R. v. Dunkley* (1976), 19 Crim. L.Q. 277 (Ont. C.A.); *R. v. Chamberlain* (1974), 22 C.C.C. (2d) 361 (Ont. C.A.).

> In the case of youthful offenders, [deterrence] must yield to the long-term benefit to, and protection of, society resulting in the real possibility of rehabilitation of the youthful offender. Such rehabilitation is unlikely if imprisonment is served in a penitentiary rather than a reformatory.

and

> In considering what is an appropriate sentence for the very young, the paramount consideration must be their immediate rehabilitation. Speedy apprehension, arrest, public trial and a criminal record, with its consequences, should be the best deterrent for those young persons who may be tempted to commit an offence such as this.
> In the instant case there is no reason to believe that these two youths had set upon a course of criminal activity as a pattern for their future.

In *R. v. Casey*[24] the 17-year-old appellant was convicted of several criminal charges in the space of several months and with failure to comply with a probation order. The day after he was brought back before the court which had originally convicted him on a charge of robbery his probation was revoked and he was sentenced to 18 months' imprisonment. The court noted that it was "obvious that . . . since he did not respond to probation, a custodial term now seems the best alternative. A sentence should not be imposed on a youthful offender for the purpose of general deterrence but rather be directed at rehabilitation. [Casey's] sentence should be such that it teaches him the lesson he should have learned from the lighter sentences." The sentence was held to be excessive and was reduced.

A difference of approach between the courts of British Columbia and those in Ontario can be seen in *Nutter*[25] and in *Casey*.[26] In the absence of any evidence to suggest that lengthy prison terms provide more safety for the public in the long run, the Ontario approach is to be preferred.

The special principles to be considered when sentencing a juvenile who is tried as an adult under the provisions of the Juvenile Delinquents Act are canvassed in *R. v. Chamberlain*.[27] These principles probably apply to some extent to all youthful offenders.

Extreme old age leads to the same conclusion. On a charge of assault causing bodily harm, a 77-year-old accused, without provocation, broke a glass in a beer hall and slashed another man across the face,

---

[24] (1977), 20 Crim. L.Q. 145 (Ont. C.A.).
[25] *Supra*, n. 22.
[26] *Supra*, n. 24.
[27] (1974), 22 C.C.C. (2d) 361 (Ont. C.A.).

permanently scarring him. A conditional discharge was imposed instead of a sentence of six months which would "under usual circumstances" not be inappropriate. There was no "useful purpose" in putting the appellant at that age in jail for six months.[28]

E. Conduct After Offence

Of course, prospective matters must inevitably carry less weight than steps already taken by the prisoner. In *R. v. Cunningham*,[29] the accused was a barrister who was convicted of theft and disbarred. Following his disbarment he showed "a willingness to take work for which he was not trained or accustomed" such as cutting grass and helping in the erection of a barn. Eventually he was able to pay to the Law Society a substantial sum on account to reimburse the society for moneys paid out to compensate the victims of the theft and had arranged to pay the balance by monthly installments. Accordingly the court sustained, for these reasons, *inter alia*, a suspended sentence. In *R. v. Ansley*,[30] the prisoner was sentenced to three years upon a charge of theft of tapes and records of a value over $200 from a parked automobile. The prisoner, who had a lengthy record, committed the offence while on parole and while drunk. However, since the offence, he had "shown some signs of rehabilitation" in that he had been employed and had contributed to his family's financial well-being. The court, "in order to give proper weight to Ansley's efforts to rehabilitate himself" varied the sentence to one year's imprisonment. Factors such as these are of the first importance, because in extending leniency to such a prisoner, the court realizes it is taking a risk; such evidence tends to indicate that if leniency is given, the appropriate response will be made. In *R. v. Alfs*,[31] before the appellant was arrested upon a robbery offence, he had gone to the police with information involving other persons on a charge of non-capital murder and subsequently had testified at their trial. As a result of this co-operation with the authorities Alfs was harassed by inmates in the penitentiary, beaten on one occasion, and as a result placed in solitary

---

[28] *R. v. Nezic,* unreported, December 2, 1976 (B.C.C.A.).
[29] (1960), 34 C.R. 40 (Ont. C.A.).
[30] (1974), 22 C.C.C. (2d) 113 (Ont. C.A.).
[31] (1974), 17 Crim. L.Q. 247 (Ont. C.A.).

confinement for his own protection for a four-month period. The court took this into account in reducing the sentence upon appeal to one of time served, being about ten months, followed by probation for one year. It seems clear in principle, that a reasonable expectation of similar treatment, or merely the taking into account of the kind of character indicated by this sort of co-operation would warrant a response by a trial judge in an appropriate case. In *R. v. Bartlett; R. v. Cameron*,[32] the court noted that the appellants gave themselves up and surrendered to the police without resistance, although at that time they had lethal weapons in their possession and plenty of ammunition. "This circumstance in no way excuses the offences that preceded their surrender but it does indicate a degree of recognition of their wrongdoing and therefore is a mitigating circumstance." The facts disclosed that the accused agreed to surrender at the insistence of the victim, but only when repeated plans to escape had failed.

Co-operation with the police or prosecution may well justify mitigation of sentence.[33] However, though co-operation with the police may be a factor in mitigation of sentence failure to cooperate cannot be an aggravating factor.[34] A confession is a "relevant factor" as indicating that the hope of rehabilitation ought not to be disregarded.[35] In *R. v. McKimm*,[36] there was a conviction of a breaking, entering and theft of a truck. Upon learning that the police were looking for him, the accused telephoned them and surrendered himself and co-operated with them. He was, in the court's view, "genuinely remorseful and disgusted with his performance".

In *R. v. Ng and Dhalai*[37] a sentence was reduced when the Crown was assisted by each of the accused giving evidence for the Crown, with the statement that there should be a "visible difference" between the appellant's sentence and those passed on others involved in the offence.

This reasoning is not without its problems. In *R. v. Davies*,[38] the accused pleaded guilty to a number of robberies. When arrested he helped the

---

[32] (1961), 131 C.C.C. 119 at p. 125 (Man. C.A.); see also *R. v. McMurrich*, [1977] Crim. L.R. 491.
[33] *R. v. James; R. v. Sharman* (1913), 9 Cr. App. R. 142; *R. v. Green* (1918), 13 Cr. App. R. 200; *R. v. Syres* (1908), 1 Cr. App. R. 172.
[34] *R. v. Bosen*, unreported, March 29, 1976 (Ont. C.A.).
[35] *R. v. Yorke and Keays* (1970), 12 Crim. L.Q. 345 (Ont. C.A.); *R. v. Blythe*, [1977] Crim. L.R. 686.
[36] [1970] 1 C.C.C 340 (Ont. C.A.).
[37] [1978] Crim. L.R. 176.
[38] [1975] Crim. L.R. 596.

police. He was sentenced immediately after his plea, and gave evidence for the prosecution, and had given them further assistance since the trial. The court dealing with the appeal from sentence, said:

> There could have been only one reason why the prosecution asked the judge to pass sentence at the outset, namely the possibility that [the appellant] might give evidence for the Crown. It would be an unfortunate development if after a proper sentence had been passed an accused could come back to the judge and say, "Didn't I do well in the witness box? Will you show your appreciation by reducing my sentence?" It would be equally unfortunate if he could come to the Court of Appeal and say the same. . . . Occasionally new facts would justify an alteration [in sentence] but further help to the authorities should not be used as the basis of an appeal.

The most useful case, perhaps, of conduct after the offence being taken into account occurs when there is a lengthy period intervening between the offence and apprehension.

In *R. v. Duguid*,[39] the appellant participated in a bank robbery in Toronto in 1942. He was not then arrested, and in 1947, he engaged in a second bank robbery and was charged but escaped while awaiting trial. After his escape the appellant went to British Columbia where, as a married man with children growing up, he lived and worked without resorting to crime until 1953. At that time he committed a housebreaking offence and proceeded to clear up his past record through the imposition of several lengthy consecutive sentences. The court said:

> . . . where a man seeks deliverance from past crimes which he has committed and admits past guilt — and particularly where he has been living a respectable life for a period of years — it is desirable, if practicable, for one Court to review the whole situation and decide what the total punishment should be in order to permit the accused to resume his life freed from fear of the past.

In the result the sentence was substantially reduced.

But the opposite view has also been taken. In *R. v. Miller and Couvreur*,[40] the accused were sentenced to lengthy terms for a robbery involving great violence in the form of beating a store proprietor with a crowbar until he suffered permanent brain damage and some six years after the event was nothing more than a living vegetable. The accused were not apprehended until some six years after the robbery occurred; in the interim each lived a life of relative good character and were able to

---

[39] (1954), 17 C.R. 370 (Ont. C.A.).
[40] (1972), 8 C.C.C. (2d) 97 at p. 98 (Man. C.A.).

produce letters of recommendation and character references. The court said:

> To argue or suggest that their lives have been relatively law-abiding since the offence and that no purpose could be served by incarcerating them now, appears to me to be giving them good marks for not being caught immediately, and pleading guilty after the lengthy time it took to catch them.

In *R. v. Murray*[41] the court took into consideration, *inter alia,* that after an attempt to break into a drug store, the accused, without the intervention of anyone, stopped the attempt; the court stated that this should "weigh heavily in his favour." Similarly in *R. v. Bates,*[42] on a charge of welfare fraud, the fact that before detection the accused ceased committing the offence was the reason for imposing a suspended sentence in lieu of a term of imprisonment.

In *R. v. Spiller,*[43] it was noted that the prisoner, who had stolen a very large amount of money from the bank where she was employed, had co-operated with the bank and the police in tracing where the stolen moneys had gone and had signed over to the bank all her real and personal property other than some clothing. The court said: "This may deserve some consideration, but I do not think that a convict can claim the right to buy a year or two off his or her sentence in this way. Nor is an attempt to do so consistent with the submission also made that the respondent feels intense remorse."

It has been said in *R. v. Hatfield,*[44] that if an accused person after his apprehension, has been of assistance to the police and has assisted them to recover stolen property, this fact is often taken into consideration in imposing sentence. But the mere fact that some of the property has been recovered, the court said, does not in itself mitigate the offence. There is, however, really no justification for the notion that co-operation with the police and a repentant attitude and actions cannot be viewed from two aspects: first, as indications of remorse, and secondly, as an attempt to mitigate the harm to the victim which deserves consideration on sentence.

---

[41] (1960), 32 W.W.R. 312 (Sask. C.A.).
[42] (1972), 9 C.C.C. (2d) 74 (Ont. Co. Ct.).
[43] [1969] 4 C.C.C. 211 at p. 215 (B.C.C.A.).
[44] [1937] O.W.N. 559 (C.A.); see also *R. v. Djemal and Djemal,* [1978] Crim. L.R. 54; *R. v. Vickers* (1975), 61 Cr. App. R. 48.

F. Alcohol

The considerations involved here may to some extent apply to the use of drugs; the phenomena are similar except that use of drugs is illegal in some cases. Both are problems of increasing severity in our society, but there are as yet no cases specifically commenting on drug use.

The cases in which alcohol is a mitigating factor do not suggest that drink is an excuse for a crime, but it is a circumstance to be taken into account — sometimes in aggravation, sometimes in mitigation — in assessing responsibility.[45]

Courts tend to view pleas that the appellant was intoxicated, with some skepticism; it is not unusual for the evidence to be carefully analyzed to determine whether the facts support the allegation. In *R. v. Calder,*[46] the court rejected the suggestion; evidence from the officers who took the appellant into custody indicated that, though there was an odour of liquor upon him, he was not drunk; moreover his method of committing the crime showed the existence of a considered plan and premeditation to an extent quite inconsistent with a level of intoxication that the court would accept as mitigation. In some circumstances, the level of intoxication need not be extreme. In *R. v. Morrissette*[47] the court said:

> There is no doubt that on the night in question liquor had been consumed by those at the party. There is no suggestion that they were intoxicated, but it may be that the alcohol consumed by James Morrissette aroused his passions and clouded his judgment. This, of course, would be no justification for his actions, but may be an explanation.

Upon a charge of rape, for this reason and others, the sentence was reduced.

In another case, an analysis of the evidence relative to alcohol use was rejected by a single judge because of the large degree of premeditation, the evidence of a witness that the accused did not appear to be under the influence of liquor, and, most important, that immediately after the offence he engaged in an elaborate scheme in order to avoid detection

---

[45] *R. v. Iwaniw; R. v. Overton* (1959), 127 C.C.C. 40 *per* Tritschler J.A. dissenting (Man. C.A.).

[46] (1956), 114 C.C.C. 155 (Man. C.A.).

[47] (1970), 1 C.C.C. (2d) 307 at p. 315 (Sask. C.A.); see also *R. v. Madill,* unreported, May 12, 1976 (Ont. C.A.).

and produced a false alibi.[48] Courts have shown some reluctance to give major effect to alcohol as a plea in mitigation in the more serious offences: "The appellant said that he had been drinking and acted foolishly. Unfortunately there are many who drink and act foolishly. They must be told that drunkenness is not a defence to robbery and that if they engage in such criminal attempts their punishment will be substantial."[49]

There are significant exceptions to this proposition. Evidence of incurable alcoholism which is part of a pattern of violence when drunk may operate to increase sentence in order to protect society from a continuing danger. In *R. v. Kalsta,*[50] the accused was sentenced to six months' imprisonment together with probation on a charge of manslaughter. The evidence indicated that the accused had arteriosclerosis and rigid personality structures, and that when these features were combined with alcohol they tended to produce violence. The psychiatric evidence also indicated that if the accused were living alone and drinking to excess he might react with deadly violence when confronted with a similar situation. The accused, however, said that on the evening of the killing he had consumed alcohol for the first time in 20 years and that he had not had a drink since. The sentence was upheld.

In *R. v. Smith*[51] the British Columbia Court of Appeal upheld a suspended sentence together with probation for three years for an assault upon a police officer where the accused had three previous convictions for the same offence. The Court stated that normally an assault on a police officer called for a jail sentence because the officers were entitled to the protection of the courts. The Court permitted the suspended sentence to stand, noting that if rehabilitation did not materialize the probation order would permit the appellant to be brought back and sentenced. This particular case should not be treated as a precedent.

In another case of assault on two police officers arising out of a liquor violation, the Court said:

> The court is not condoning the accused's conduct. It was, presumably, necessary that she be locked up; however necessarily connected with this particular offence is the general conduct of a drunken person, obstinacy, unco-operative behaviour, and other things that one associates with

---

[48] *R. v. Iwaniw; R. v. Overton, supra,* n. 45, *per* Schultz J.A.
[49] *R. v. Calder, supra,* n. 46 at p. 157.
[50] (1977), 20 Crim. L.Q. 21 (Ont. C.A.); see also *R. v. Empey* (1978), 4 C.R. (3d) S-59 (Ont. C.A.).
[51] Unreported, November 15, 1977.

drunkenness. This behaviour, unfortunately, must be accepted by the police when they are taking actions pursuant to the *Government Liquor Act.*

An absolute discharge was imposed.[52]

In any event, to the extent that intoxication mitigates criminal conduct, it can properly rest upon the assumption that under the excessive influence of alcohol, a condition which hopefully can be remedied or prevented in the future, the accused acted in a manner which was out of character; and that ordinarily he showed a character that would justify a lenient treatment.[53] Where past behaviour shows little likelihood of this, the mitigating effect is still present, but is not as important in sentencing because some danger from the accused will still be present. In *R. v. Bezeau,*[54] Porter C.J.O. speaking for himself alone, was of the view that where the probation report indicated that the accused showed no signs of remorse, but rather an attitude of callous indifference, the excuse of intoxication disappeared.

Particularly in less serious offences, problems with alcohol and alcoholism have been among the factors which suggested lenient treatment possibilities. In *R. v. Fox,*[55] a sentence of 18 months definite and six months indeterminate upon a charge of resisting a peace officer levelled against a prisoner whose record showed a propensity to engage in assaults, was varied to 18 months definite. The appellant attributed his problems to alcohol and alcoholism, the court accepted that he was sincere in this admission and coupled the reduction with a recommendation to the correctional authorities that the appellant, if he requested, be given an opportunity of taking treatment at an alcoholic treatment centre. In *R. v. Wilson,*[56] the court reduced a sentence of five years' imprisonment on a charge of armed robbery on a taxi driver to one of two years less a day definite and two years less a day indefinite. The court noted that the prisoner had become an alcoholic and was on a drinking spree at the time of the offence; but looking at the evidence as a whole, came to the view that this conduct was, by reason of the alcohol, entirely out of character and was unlikely to be repeated. In *R. v. Smith,*[57]

---

[52] *R. v. Chingee,* unreported, May 18, 1977 (B.C.C.A.).

[53] *R. v. Simmons, Allen and Bezzo* (1973), 13 C.C.C. (2d) 65 (Ont. C.A.); *R. v. McKimm,* [1970] 1 C.C.C. 340 (Ont. C.A.).

[54] (1958), 28 C.R. 301 (Ont. C.A.).

[55] Unreported, January 30, 1973 (Ont. C.A.).

[56] Unreported, May 8, 1974 (Ont. C.A.).

[57] Unreported, March 7, 1974 (Ont. C.A.); see also *R. v. Wallace,* [1977] Crim. L.R. 685.

the rationale was slightly different; the sentence was reduced upon a charge of robbery, because the evidence disclosed that it was a "spur of the moment decision by an inebriated man". This statement stresses the underlying reasons why alcohol use is taken into account: the evidence showed that the offence was unlikely to be repeated and did not flow from a truly criminal character.

Finally, there are judgments where the fact of intoxication, without any further explanation is noticed as a factor in mitigation.[58]

G. Previous Good Character

In *R. v. Spiller,*[59] the accused pleaded guilty to offences of theft amounting to $492,000 and falsification of accounts, the victim being her employer, a chartered bank. The court, having been referred to her general good character, said:

> Good character may be a mitigating circumstance in some kinds of crimes, *e.g.,* an isolated case of criminal negligence or an unpremeditated assault in a fit of anger. But, in my opinion, this is not so, where the offence is a series of acts, planned and carried out over a lengthy period. The person of good character, who can appreciate to the full how wrong what he is doing is, seems to me to be just as culpable as a person of poor character who appreciates less clearly the wrongness of his acts. . . .
>
> . . .
>
> She used her apparent good character to enable her to perpetrate her crime; now her counsel wants to use it in mitigation of penalty!

This case was approved and applied in *R. v. Rogers (No. 2),*[60] a case where an employee of the welfare department defrauded his employer in the amount of $25,000. The Court of Appeal, while acknowledging that general previous good character is normally a mitigating factor in sentence, noted that the evidence showed that the appellant, while refusing to forge cheques himself, would use others to do criminal acts of this sort not readily traceable to him. "Consequently, there is nothing to indicate that much consideration should be given to the fact that the

---

[58] *R. v. McKenzie* (1952), 6 W.W.R. 192 (Sask. C.A.).
[59] [1969] 4 C.C.C. 211 at p. 214 (B.C.C.A.).
[60] (1972), 6 C.C.C. (2d) 107 (P.E.I.C.A.).

respondent was well regarded in the community or that he had no previous criminal record."

On the other hand, in *R. v. Gunnell,*[61] the Quebec Court of Appeal had before it a charge of embezzling, over a period of four months, from the employer, the Royal Bank of Canada, by means of several forgeries the sum of $6,802.35. A sentence of six months' imprisonment was upheld, upon Crown appeal; the Court of Appeal held that it was no exaggerated clemency or abuse of discretion for the trial judge to give the prisoner the benefit of his "stainless antecedents, of his mature age, of his character". This is the more usual response to this factor.

H. The Victim

There is some hesitancy disclosed by the case law about how the court should regard the conduct of the victim or the wishes of the victim regarding sentence. On the one hand there are statements such as that by Walsh J.A. in *R. v. Lauzon,*[62] one of several judges in the majority in dismissing a Crown appeal:

> . . . there is also another principle which recognizes that Courts are not to be constrained to meet the views and wishes of complainants. It is not a question of maintaining a Judge's prestige; Judges are indifferent as to that, I am sure. It is however a question of discarding all considerations of retaliation, vengeance and indemnities in the application of the criminal law, when judgments and sentences are in order, and that of following the dicates of justice solely. The only interests are those of society and of the criminal.

That was a case where the complainant attempted to have the court impose a heavier sentence than justice would otherwise have demanded. The court understandably refused.

In England, in *R. v. Hampton,*[63] upon a charge of rape, the court said "the girl's remorse could not affect the propriety of the sentence". The victim had subsequently expressed her distress at the three-year sentence and said she had resisted the accused because she was frightened. He had been associating with her on familiar terms for some three weeks and there was some evidence that the girl had acted in a way "which might

---

[61] (1951), 14 C.R. 120.

[62] [1940] 3 D.L.R. 606 at p. 619 (Que. C.A.).

[63] [1965] Crim. L.R. 564; see also *R. v. Pritchard* (1973), 57 Cr. App. R. 492.

have led him to suppose she would be willing to have sexual intercourse".

On the other hand, Coyne J.A. speaking for himself alone, but concurring with the majority in the result, took the view that upon a charge of bigamy the sentence ought to be reduced, and that one factor to be considered was "the benevolent change of attitude of the complainant" who regretted laying the charge of bigamy and wished to resume living with the prisoner.[64] Similarly, in *R. v. MacArthur*[65] the accused pleaded guilty to a charge of criminal negligence causing bodily harm in shooting his common-law wife. It was noted that the victim had in some degree instigated the incident and that cohabitation had since resumed between them. A suspended sentence and three years' probation was imposed.

In *R. v. Hardy*[66] the court accepted and acted upon a petition from the family of the deceased stating that they were aware of extenuating circumstances in the case and asking for a minimum sentence.

The conduct of the victim may become relevant both at trial and upon appeal where there have been delays which are not explained. In *R. v. Cunningham,*[67] a case of theft by a solicitor, the court noted that the "unusual circumstance" in that the charges were not laid for more than a year after the accused was disbarred and that some charge of a similar nature had been laid and withdrawn earlier. In the meantime the accused had achieved significant rehabilitation; a Crown appeal from a lenient sentence was dismissed. The rationale must simply be that the conduct of the victim in delaying the bringing of the charge puts the accused at a special disadvantage which ought to be taken account of at sentence. It may amount to a "Sword of Damocles"[68] hanging over his head.

In assessing the gravity of the prisoner's misconduct in a determination of an appropriate sentence, the court may look in mitigation to acts of the victim which in one way or another contributed causally to the commission of the offence.[69] Yet this submission has been rejected on occasion, for example in *R. v. Spiller,*[70] a case of large-scale theft from a bank, where it was suggested that if the bank had been more

---

[64] *R. v. Clarke* (1959), 124 C.C.C. 284 (Man. C.A.). See also *R. v. Jover* (1977), 41 C.C.C. (2d) 24 (Ont. Prov. Ct.).

[65] (1978), 39 C.C.C. (2d) 158 (P.E.I.C.A.).

[66] (1976), 33 C.R.N.S. 76 (Que.).

[67] (1960), 34 C.R. 40 (Ont. C.A.).

[68] *R. v. Fireman* (1971), 4 C.C.C. (2d) 82 (Ont. C.A.).

[69] *R. v. Dash* (1948), 91 C.C.C. 187 (N.S.C.A.); *R. v. Hardy* (1976), 33 C.R.N.S. 76 (Que.); *R. v. Linda* (1924), 24 C.C.C. 110 (Alta.).

[70] *Supra,* n. 59.

alert the respondent would have been caught sooner and so she should be sentenced as though she had been caught before the moneys stolen had reached any large amount. The court referred to this as "sophistry" and rejected the suggestion.

I. Inapplicable Defences

Matters, which either did not or could not go to the question of guilt or innocence may nevertheless operate in mitigation, on sentence, in an extremely forceful way. Generally speaking, any matter which would have been a defence, if effective in law or fact, even if it is not fully accepted operates in this fashion.

The application of such considerations seem to fall under the general head of such "extenuating circumstances as may appear from the evidence", and among these has been mentioned such provocation as was received by the prisoner, if the crime is one of violence.[71]

So in *R. v. Dash,*[72] upon a charge of unlawfully inflicting grievous bodily harm upon his brother by shooting him with a loaded rifle, the court upheld an extremely lenient sentence by assessing the degree of misconduct on the part of the prisoner and noting with respect to it that

... it should not be overlooked that the negligent act of the injured brother in going in a direction contrary to the one in which it had been previously agreed between himself and the accused that he would go, caused the accused to make a negligent mistake that he would not otherwise have made. While contributory negligence is not a defence, it is on the facts here a matter for consideration in determining sentence.

Another example is *R. v. O'Neill,*[73] where the appellant pleaded guilty to a charge of manslaughter of one man and inflicting grievous bodily harm upon another. The sentences were reduced from a total of eighteen months to time served, the court noting that:

Although it may be that technically this man could not rely on the defence of self-defence, yet to all intents and purposes he was a man who was in fear of being set upon, if not actually set upon, by Hans and his friends. . . . There are

---

[71] *R. v. Nash (No. 2)* (1949), 8 C.R. 447 (N.B.C.A.).
[72] *Supra,* n. 69.
[73] (1966), 51 Cr. App. R. 241. See also *R. v. Muttart* (1971), 1 Nfld. & P.E.I. R. 404 (P.E.I.C.A.).

strong grounds for thinking throughout this episode that Hans was the aggressor . . . and had a shocking history of violence. . .

In *R. v. Cormier*[74] the evidence on a charge of manslaughter by a battered wife showed that she had been abused physically on the very evening that her husband's death occurred. The court upheld a suspended sentence and probation for this reason, *inter alia,* noting "exceptional circumstances".

Though necessity as a defence is difficult to establish and rarely seen in the cases, necessity as mitigation has often been taken into account. In *R. v. Hennessey; R. v. Bowers,*[75] two young men absconded from a prison and committed offences of a nature that "would enable them as absconders to live, stealing foodstuffs, a rucksack, blankets, thermos flask and matters of that sort". The court came to the conclusion that "absconders who inevitably commit a certain number of offences, albeit not very serious, in order to live", find themselves in a situation where it is "not right to impose a heavy sentence" in respect of such offences.

A failed defence of duress has also been given some weight as where some pressure had been put on the accused to get him to take part in a crime; such a case is not an appropriate one to use for general deterrence purposes.[76]

Where a treaty Indian was convicted of violation of game laws by hunting out of season the court took into account his belief that he had a right to commit the act in question and that his motives were good, *i.e.,* that he was hunting to give the meat to a needy Indian family.[77]

J. Other "Penalties"

The court demands a view of the circumstances of the offender as a whole in assessing the impact of the particular penalty to be imposed. In consideration of the perspective of deterrence to others, the sentence of the court includes recognition, as Brooke J.A. put it,

> . . . of the other consequences to such a person upon his conviction of such an

---

[74] (1974), 22 C.C.C. (2d) 235 (N.S.C.A.).
[75] (1970), 55 Cr. App. R. 148.
[76] *R. v. Mackey,* unreported, February 19, 1976 (Ont. C.A.); *R. v. Vickers* (1975), 61 Cr. App. R. 48; *R. v. Taonis* (1974), 59 Cr. App. R. 160.
[77] *R. v. Wesley* (1975), 9 O.R. (2d) 524 (Dist. Ct.).

offence and the imposition of any term of imprisonment. These events probably assure the destruction of that individual's position in society as he will be publicly and privately shunned by his former acquaintances, will bring disgrace upon his family, future opportunities for employment will be substantially restricted, and probably his family's financial security is destroyed.[78]

In *R. v. Gorman*[79] the court noted that as a result of the conviction, Gorman had lost his employment with the fire department (from which he embezzled some $16,000) where he had some 12 years' seniority, had lost his standing amongst his associates and had put himself in a position where employment was difficult to find. The court conceded that the losses, financial and otherwise, which the respondent had suffered did in themselves constitute punishment.

Examples abound. In *R. v. Taylor,*[80] the court noted that the accused would not be restored to his position as a police officer, "a great punishment in itself." In *R. v. D.,*[81] the court noted that, quite apart from the court proceedings, the appellant had been subjected to severe punishment as he had lost his position as a school teacher.

In *R. v. Fraser*[82] the court noted that the normal sentence for a charge of possession for the purpose of trafficking and a charge of simple possession of marijuana would be 45 days. However, the accused had already served this term as a result of an earlier dangerous driving conviction which arose out of the same incident, as the accused was involved in a police chase while the officers were attempting to apprehend him. The court noted that this sentence had already satisfied the aspect of deterrence and therefore imposed a fine.

The principle has not been universally accepted. In *R. v. Soble*[83] the fact that the accused, who committed fraud in the course of the operation of his pharmacy, lost his licence as a pharmacist, was not taken into consideration.

In *R. v. Poynton,*[84] the court refrained from imposing a fine noting, *inter alia,* that a penalty of some $4,200 was already imposed upon the

---

[78] *R. v. Gorman* (1971), 4 C.C.C. (2d) 330 at p. 332 (Ont. C.A.).

[79] *Ibid.*

[80] [1959] O.W.N. 1 (C.A.).

[81] (1971), 5 C.C.C. (2d) 366 (Ont. C.A.). Similarly in *R. v. Cunningham* (1960), 34 C.R. 40 (Ont. C.A.) the accused was disbarred following thefts from his trust account.

[82] Unreported, July 11, 1978 (Ont. C.A.).

[83] (1978), 3 C.R. (3d) S-1 (Man. C.A.).

[84] (1972), 9 C.C.C. (2d) 32 (Ont. C.A.).

prisoner under the provisions of the Income Tax Act. In *R. v. Fraser,*[85] in fixing the amount of a fine in a relatively low amount, the court stated that they were "taking into account the fact that his offence had already involved the respondent in another form of pecuniary penalty, namely, the payment of his own costs of defending the appeal". This rationale would have strange implications in a province where legal aid was available.

Nor need the prisoner, in order for this principle to operate, be a person of standing and status in the community. In *R. v. Hogan; R. v. Tompkins,*[86] the court stated that, in sentencing for an escape, the trial judge in deciding upon sentence "would have to take into consideration" administrative penalties already imposed upon the appellants as a matter of prison discipline. The forfeiture of privileges which they suffered as a result of a hearing inside the prison upon a related administrative charge (escape and prison breach), were matters that were to be taken into account.

In *R. v. Smith,*[87] upon conviction of a breach of the Narcotic Control Act, the Provincial Court Judge ordered a motor vehicle which was involved in the offence forfeited pursuant to the provisions of that Act. In addition, the accused was sentenced to 45 days' imprisonment and two years' probation thereafter. The trial judge specifically stated that the order for forfeiture was considered by him as part of the sentence. Though this characterization of the order was incorrect, the magistrate was correct in taking into consideration the fact of a prior forfeiture order. Similarly, if such an order was requested after sentencing, he could, in exercising his discretion whether to grant the forfeiture, take into consideration the sentence already imposed. It is obviously preferable that any such application should be made prior to sentencing.

In *R. v. Gregory, Choquette and Hebert (No. 2),*[88] the accused were convicted of misleading advertising. The trial judge imposed a fine as punishment and disregarded the request of Crown counsel for a period of imprisonment. In arriving at this conclusion the trial judge took into consideration pending charges of fraud against the same accused arising out of the same transaction. The Crown alleged that the trial judge really reduced sentence upon the ground "that the accused will perhaps one day be punished for this other pending charge". The Quebec Court of

---

[85] [1944] 2 D.L.R. 461 (P.E.I.).
[86] (1960), 44 Cr. App. R. 255.
[87] (1978), 2 C.R. (3d) S-35 (Nfld. C.A.).
[88] (1974), 20 C.C.C. (2d) 509 (Que. C.A.).

Appeal said that the trial judge had not taken it into account in this sense at all, but rather, quite correctly and properly, took it into account in considering the "anguish that the respondents will surely suffer as a result of this Sword of Damocles hanging over their heads". This is a fine distinction and one might perhaps doubt whether the operation of law itself, absent any suggestion of abuse by the Crown through "overcharging", should be accepted as a factor in mitigation.

K. The Avoidance Of Unnecessary Hardship

This subject-matter could really be headed "mercy": it is the operation of the principle, not always followed, that wherever possible the court should sentence in a way that will avoid unnecessary hardship to the accused or those dependent upon him or close to him. Examples are legion. In *R. v. Donovan*,[89] the court substituted a conditional discharge for a sentence of imprisonment, because such a sentence would mean that the prisoner could not continue his career in the Royal Air Force. In *R. v. Larre*,[90] the court upheld a prison term specifically designed to be short and to take place during the Christmas break in a university term, taking the view that it would not be in the public interest to impose a term of imprisonment which would have meant the complete loss of the prisoner's university year. More generally, in *Geraldes v. The Queen*,[91] the court, in assessing sentence, took into consideration "the danger that a period of imprisonment might involve the disintegration of the family to the great prejudice of the child". Again in *R. v. Simmonds*,[92] the court, in reducing a sentence of imprisonment, said: "He has got responsibilities at home, his wife, an aged mother and children in those circumstances, the court does feel that there is something in this case to be said by way of mitigation."

Similarly, in *R. v. Grandmond*[93] the court reduced a sentence in the light of the fact that the accused had a seriously handicapped

---

[89] [1960] Crim. L. R. 441.

[90] [1970] 1 C.C.C. 382 (Sask. C.A.).

[91] (1965), 46 C.R. 365 (Que. C.A.). See also *R. v. Lubitz* (1972), 14 Crim. L.Q. 395 (Ont. Co. Ct.).

[92] (1969), 53 Cr. App. R. 488. See also *R. v. Cormier* (1974), 22 C.C.C. (2d) 235 (N.S.C.A.).

[93] Unreported, November 29, 1976 (Ont. C.A.).

four-year-old daughter and was the only person who could look after her and in view of the fact that, unknown to the sentencing judge, her sentence was not being served in a modern jail but rather another older jail (since torn down) "which resulted in a custodial sentence of greater severity."

In *R. v. Tanguay*[94] one of the factors considered by the court on a charge of accepting benefit as a public servant was that if a discharge were not imposed the appellant would lose his position with the Government and the employee benefits which accrued to him over the last 25 years on the job.

Where the health of the prisoner indicates that there might be a danger in imprisoning him, as where there is a history of heart attacks, the court should consider the imposition of a non-custodial sentence.[95]

In *R. v. Arellano and Sanchez*[96] the effect of a sentence of imprisonment was considered:

> A further factor which I think it is proper to bear in mind is the fact that the accused are Bolivian nationals and speak little or no English or French. This necessarily means that detention for them in a Canadian penitentiary will be very much more difficult than it would be for a Canadian or even for a foreigner who had a working knowledge of one of the official languages. Also because of the great distances involved, the possibility of either accused receiving visits from or maintaining contacts with family and friends must be regarded as extremely remote. While these facts, of course, do nothing to excuse the accused, I think they do justify some measure of clemency when it comes to pronouncing sentence.

Perhaps the clearest statement of the principle involved in the avoidance of further and unnecessary harm to the prisoner and those about him was made in *R. v. Clarke,*[97] by Schultz J.A.: "The personal character of the offender and the desirability of giving him an opportunity of redeeming himself and protecting, as far as he can, those who have suffered as a result of his offence, are matters which require consideration."

It should be stressed that these principles operate only where there are not other or more important aspects requiring severe or deterrent sentences. The submission cannot affect the nature of the offence. In *R. v.*

---

[94] (1975), 24 C.C.C. (2d) 77 (Que. C.A.).
[95] *R. v. Herasymenko,* unreported, December 2, 1975 (Eng. C.A.); see also *R. v. Boudreau* (1978), 25 N.S.R. (2d) 63 (C.A.).
[96] (1975), 30 C.R.N.S. 367 at p. 371 (Que.).
[97] (1959), 124 C.C.C. 284 at p. 287 (Man. C.A.).

Pritchard,[98] after conviction and sentence, the appellant's wife and mother-in-law wrote letters to the court begging for mercy while the appeal was pending. The court observed that

> . . . distress to the wife and disaster to the family frequently comes to this Court as an argument for reduction of sentence. It can rarely, if ever, be a relevant consideration. The Court has paid the closest attention and understands the feelings of the relatives in this case, but the point has to be stressed that appeals subsequent to the commission of an offence can rarely affect the seriousness and gravamen of the offence itself at the time it is committed.

Nevertheless as an act of mercy "in the interests of the public, and not by reason of the distress to the family," the court substituted a sentence of three years for one of four years.

In the *Doiron* case,[99] the court was informed that the appellant's family might suffer through the incarceration of the accused. The court stated that this was a matter for consideration on a remission application rather than through the court and refused to consider it.

In *R. v. Carr,*[100] it was held that it is necessary to consider and give effect to a jury's recommendation for mercy.

The British Columbia Court of Appeal, *obiter dicta,* has held that even if a medical problem personal to the accused was such that prison would have a very harmful effect on his physical health, it would, nonetheless, be improper for a court to act on such factors. Such matters should be left to the parole authorities.[101]

This is not always the case, nor logically should it be. In *R. v. Forsyth*[102] the accused pleaded guilty to stealing $10,000 from her employer. On appeal, further evidence indicated that her 14-year-old daughter was under medication, having been subject to epileptic seizures and required her care and attention. She was separated from her husband, but there was some evidence that they were being reconciled. The court decided that the accused's presence at home with her daughter as soon as reasonably appropriate was most important and varied the sentence

---

[98] (1973), 57 Cr. App. R. 492 at pp. 494-95.

[99] *Doiron v. The Queen* (1958), 124 C.C.C. 156 (N.B.C.A.). See also *R. v. Lauzon* (1977), 19 Crim. L.Q. 285 (Que. C.A.).

[100] [1937] 3 D.L.R. 537 (Ont. C.A.). See also *R. v. Muttart* (1971), 1 Nfld. & P.E.I. R. 404 (P.E.I.C.A.).

[101] *R. v. Moncini* (1975), 23 C.C.C. (2d) 452 (B.C.C.A.).

[102] (1976), 19 Crim. L.Q. 280 (Ont. C.A.).

from an indefinite term not to exceed two years to an indefinite term not to exceed six months, together with 18 months' probation.

L. Deportation

Deportation may be viewed as an administrative penalty which, when likely to be imposed, may be taken into account in sentencing as a specific example of the principle that a sentence should be structured to avoid unnecessary harm; or as a sentence that, because of its imposition, would be disproportionate in its effect in relation to the offence itself. The likelihood of deportation is often regarded as a fact in mitigation of sentence. In *R. v. Hunter,*[103] in the course of discussing the problem of disparity in sentencing between the co-accused, the court said:

> Harmer's sentence may be explained by the fact that he is a United States citizen, and, presumably, upon his serving the sentence or being granted parole, he will be quickly deported. That may be the reason why the Provincial Court Judge decided to make parole available to him as soon as could reasonably be done.

In *R. v. Sullivan,*[104] a sentence of ten years for armed robbery was reduced, *inter alia,* by the mitigating fact that "undoubtedly upon the expiration of his sentence he will be deported from Canada". Similarly, in *R. v. Johnston and Tremayne,*[105] the court explicitly stated that the fact that the appellants would be deported when they were released from penitentiary was a fact in mitigation.

All of the above are Ontario cases. The only other appellate court that has discussed the issue is the Quebec Court of Appeal. The prisoner,[106] being accused of organizing and leading a band of armed ruffians numbering from 15 to 30 persons to the home of a notary, broke down the door, caused considerable damage, stole various objects, and manhandled and terrorized the notary and his family. The Court said:

> Nor do I think that, in a crime of this gravity, we should be swayed by the probability that the accused will be deported. If the Government of Canada

---

[103] (1970), 16 C.R.N.S. 12 at p. 13 (Ont. C.A.).
[104] (1972), 9 C.C.C. (2d) 70 (Ont. C.A.).
[105] [1970] 4 C.C.C. 64 (Ont. C.A.).
[106] *Antonecchia v. The Queen* (1959), 31 C.R. 320 at p. 323.

sees fit to deport appellant before he has served the whole of his sentence, I see no objection.

The appeal against sentence was dismissed. It may well be that in the most heinous of crimes this particular factor has little or no weight. That seems to be the view of the Quebec Court of Appeal. Nevertheless, the Ontario cases show that in quite serious crimes, such as conspiracy to import narcotics and robbery, the principle does operate. There appears to be a conflict that can only be resolved with time. One of the arguments in favor of the principle, from a practical point of view, is the suggestion that there is really very little point in the Government of Canada paying upwards of $25,000 each year for the maintenance of a prisoner who will ultimately be deported.

No such problem arises with the practice of altering a non-custodial penalty so as to avoid the consequence of deportation. Simple considerations of equality between persons convicted of similar offences dictate that no one should suffer a disproportionate penalty merely because he is an immigrant. It is not a matter of circumventing the operation of the Immigration Act, but since the conditional discharge legislation is there and courts have a discretion as to when to impose it, they have an obligation to consider all relevant factors in exercising that discretion. In *R. v. Papadopoulos and Kalafatis,*[107] the Ontario court did substitute a conditional discharge for a conviction and a fine on charges of theft under $200. The court accepted that by reason of the fact that they were immigrants, the consequences of a conviction would be very grave, and held that the gravity of those consequences were so disproportionate to the offence committed that this was one of the rare occasions where a conditional discharge should be granted.

M. Marginal Criminality

Occasionally the court examines the facts of a case and takes the view that though a conviction was proper, otherwise lawful conduct involved just "slips over the line" into the criminal. An example of such a "borderline" case is *R. v. Lafontaine,*[108] where the prisoner was

---

[107] Unreported, May 7, 1974 (Ont. C.A.).
[108] Unreported, June 9, 1975 (Ont. C.A.); see also *R. v. Southam Press (Ontario) Ltd.* (1976), 31 C.C.C. (2d) 205 (Ont. C.A.).

sentenced to 30 days' imprisonment and a prohibition from driving for two years following his conviction on a charge of dangerous driving. The court took the view that the case, on the facts, was at best only marginally one of dangerous driving and possibly only a case of speeding. In all the circumstances, including the youth of the prisoner and his lack of criminal record, the court varied the sentence to a conditional discharge with probation for six months.

Where the offence is stopped early enough by the police that the offender's goal was not fully realized this will be a factor in mitigation. In this light the deterrent goal of sentencing ought not be unduly emphasized, particularly when the offence is "more in the nature of an attempt . . . or was something preparatory. . .".[109] In *R. v. White*[110] the appellant was committing an act of *fellatio* with a passenger in his automobile while parked in a parking lot at approximately 11:30 in the evening. The court determined that a conditional discharge was appropriate because "having regard to the setting and the time of night, the circumstances were as private as they could be, and yet lead to the commission of this offence."

And, finally, in *R. v. Blake*[111] the accused was the Chief of Police who was convicted of perjury in giving evidence. The court noted that had the evidence been properly called, the result would not have been any different and being "satisfied that the commission of this offence did not stem from any real criminal intent" the court imposed a nominal sentence.

Such a submission is really no more than one that the penalty must be appropriate to the offence, though when put in extreme form, as above, it takes on the appearance of a new principle.

N. Test Case

Occasionally, cases are brought forward in order to determine a principle of law or fact. This is rare in the criminal field, but when it happens, it is a mitigating factor which may be taken into account. In *R.*

---

[109] *R. v. Haire* (1976), 19 Crim. L.Q. 282 (Ont. C.A.); *R. v. Lee,* [1975] Crim. L.R. 589.
[110] (1975), 25 C.C.C. (2d) 173 (Ont. C.A.).
[111] (1978), 39 C.C.C. (2d) 138 (P.E.I.C.A.).

v. Watts and Gaunt, [112] it was decided to test a legal question arising out of a practice whereby loggers paid a certain sum for logs recovered from beachcombers, rather than acknowledging a supposed obligation to give such timber up to the owner. The court noted: "Crown counsel has advised us that this is a test case and he consents to sentence being suspended."

In *R. v. Newsome; R. v. Browne*[113] a court had to decide a point of sentencing law on appeal and determined it in a way that was adverse to the appellants. In doing so they overruled a previous decision. The court said:

> . . . it is of particular importance . . . to see that the individual appellant who is the subject of the present appeal suffers no injustice . . . we are highly conscious of the fact that these two appellants should not be allowed to be prejudiced in the result merely because these lawyers' battles have taken place over the cases in which they were concerned.

Accordingly the court gave the most lenient sentence possible under the law.

By analogy, the rarity of prosecution for a particular offence operates in the same way. In *R. v. Keystone Enterprises Ltd.,* [114] the charge was one of publishing an advertisement of an article intended or represented as a method of preventing conception. Upon the finding of guilt, the court noted that prosecutions under this section are rarely, if ever commenced, using the reported decisions as a "yardstick". In view of this fact, the court imposed a nominal fine.

O. Guilty Plea

In *R. v. deHaan,* [115] the appellant, during the course of his trial, changed his plea from not guilty to guilty at a point in the trial before an opportunity came for him to testify. The mitigating elements found by the trial judge were twofold: first, that the appellant had changed his plea to guilty and secondly, that he had not tried to lie his way out of the

---

[112] [1953] 1 D.L.R. 610 (B.C.C.A.); revd on other grounds [1953] 3 D.L.R. 152 (S.C.C.).
[113] (1970), 54 Cr. App. R. 485 at p. 493.
[114] (1931), 133 C.C.C. 338 (Man. Mag. Ct.). This is no longer an offence.
[115] (1967), 52 Cr. App. R. 25.

offences. The court stated that it was "undoubtedly right" that a confession of guilt should tell in favor of an accused person as being "clearly in the public interest". It was held that a four and a half-year sentence did not reflect an adequate consideration of that mitigating element and the sentence was reduced to one of three years.

In Canada the guilty plea has been acknowledged as a factor that must be taken into consideration to mitigate the penalty as early as 1952.[116] In another case, it was considered together with the fact that the appellant surrendered and made frank and honest confessions to the police.[117]

The case of *R. v. deHann* was explicitly accepted and adopted by the Ontario Court of Appeal in *R. v. Johnston and Tremayne*[118] with a practical rationale:

> Believing as we do that 14 years might very well be regarded as a maximum sentence for the offences involved, it is obvious that little, if any, consideration was given by the trial Judge to the fact that these two men pleaded guilty and thus saved the community a great deal of expense.

A different rationale was expressed in *R. v. T.,*[119] where the court noted that, by pleading guilty upon a charge of having sexual intercourse with a girl of 14, the accused by his plea had saved the girl the ordeal of appearing in court. This factor of saving embarassment to the victim of a crime is one that obviously should be viewed favourably.

In *R. v. Spiller,*[120] the British Columbia Court of Appeal, having been referred to *R. v. deHaan,* decided that the principle was not one of universal application ". . . though it may well be appropriate to apply it in some cases, and I do not think any significant weight should be given to the plea of guilty here: the respondent knew that she was inescapably caught." It seems reasonable that less weight should be given to a plea of guilty where there is really no other choice, but it should nevertheless be of some significance in any case because of the saving in time and money of a trial.

Nevertheless, a serious problem remains in permitting a reduction of sentence upon a guilty plea because of the essential principle that a person shall not be penalized for insisting upon his right to a jury trial and a plea of not guilty. There is some logical difficulty in understanding

---

[116] *R. v. Carriere* (1952), 14 C.R. 391 (Que. C.A.).

[117] *R. v. Bartlett; R. v. Cameron* (1961), 131 C.C.C. 119 (Man. C.A.).

[118] [1970] 4 C.C.C. 64 at p. 67. See also *R. v. Tanguay-Dupere* (1971), 13 Crim. L.Q. 436 (Que. C.A.).

[119] [1965] Crim. L.R. 252; *R. v. Shanower* (1972), 8 C.C.C. (2d) 527 (Ont. C.A.).

[120] [1969] 4 C.C.C. 211 at p. 215.

how it is that, at least from the perspective of a co-accused, it can be said that one is not being punished for pleading not guilty, when he notes that his co-accused received a lower sentence in return for a plea of guilty. There is also a serious question whether this principle encourages unduly pleas of guilty in cases where they are not otherwise warranted.

Any suggestion of oppression around this question is met by frequent assertions by trial judges that they are not increasing the penalty upon the one who pleads not guilty, but merely giving an unusually lenient sentence to the fellow who has been persuaded that his best interests lie in a guilty plea. Since there is such a wide range of sentence available for most crimes, this rule must from time to time be abused. It may thereby lead to a real sense of grievance. Nevertheless, there must be some fitting acknowledgement of the expense saved by a guilty plea and the evidence of remorse indicated thereby in the case of a sincere defendant. The problem perhaps remains insoluble.

P. Time Spent In Custody

Criminal Code s. 649(2.1) reads as follows:

> (2.1) In determining the sentence to be imposed on a person convicted of an offence, a justice, magistrate or judge may take into account any time spent in custody by the person as a result of the offence.

This section is new and there have been no cases on its meaning. A strict reading of the section would infer that it narrows the previously available discretion, permitting account to be taken of time spent in custody for any reason, to a discretion only to take or not to take into account time spent in custody as a result of "the offence". Problems may arise as follows: suppose a person has spent time in custody on a very nominal offence, but has been at large on bail on a more serious offence. If a non-custodial sentence was in any event to be imposed on the less serious offence (the one which resulted in time spent in custody) it would not appear to be proper, upon a strict reading, to use that time in custody to mitigate the penalty on the more serious offence for which imprisonment will in fact be imposed. Alternatively, what is to happen when a man has spent three months in custody on a charge that results in an acquittal and is convicted upon a charge regarding which he had been granted conditional release? The better view is that though the section sets out a power which was not explicit before, it was not intended to limit the discretion in the judge to take into account any matter that seems relevant in accordance with established principles.

One alternative view of the meaning and impact of the new section is shown by *R. v. Shecter.*[121] Using s. 649(2.1) the trial judge sentenced an accused convicted of importing a narcotic, where the minimum penalty is seven years' imprisonment, to a term of six and one-half years. The section was employed to give authority to take time spent in custody into account in sentence in a situation where, prior to its enactment, such consideration would have been impossible.

The authority of this section to authorize such a sentence has been disputed. In *R. v. Brown,*[122] the trial judge, after conferring with another member of his court, decided not to follow *R. v. Shecter*[123] because he "could not determine the rationale for this decision." It had been argued, unsuccessfully, that the law, when interpreted contrary to *R. v. Shecter,* contravened s. 1(b) of the Canadian Bill of Rights in that a person for whom a fit sentence was thought to be nine years could have the time spent in custody taken into account, but one for whom the mandatory minimum penalty of seven years was the appropriate sentence could not. As a result, so the rejected argument went, the latter accused was denied equality before the law. Though rejected, the force of this argument seems compelling, and it awaits appellate determination.

In any event it is usual to take into account time spent in jail pending trial and as well time spent in custody after trial but pending sentence.[124]

In *R. v. Rowan,*[125] the court noted that nine months that were spent in the Don Jail in Toronto in connection with the offence for which sentence was being considered and for another offence for which the accused was discharged after a preliminary hearing. The court, noting that incarceration in the Don Jail for any but a brief period is "severe punishment", took this into account and adjusted the sentence accordingly.

A recurring problem is that of determining what quantum of reduction in sentence would appropriately reflect time spent in custody.

---

[121] (1973), 15 Crim. L.Q. 263 (Ont. Co. Ct.).

[122] (1975), 19 Crim. L.Q. 156 (Ont. Co. Ct.).

[123] *Supra,* n. 121.

[124] *R. v. Wooff* (1973), 14 C.C.C. (2d) 396 (Ont. C.A.); *R. v. Goodale* (1974), 21 C.C.C. (2d) 471 (Ont. C.A.); *R. v. O'Connell,* [1970] 4 C.C.C. 162 (P.E.I.C.A.).

[125] Unreported, June 7, 1976 (Ont. C.A.).

Often, pre-trial custody takes place in abysmal, overcrowded conditions, where no facilities for recreation or rehabilitation are available. Moreover, statutory remission and parole do not operate on such periods of custody. Accordingly, it is useful to note that in *R. v. Gravino,*[126] Montgomery J.A. of the Quebec Court of Appeal stated that it is a recognized "rule of thumb" that imprisonment while awaiting trial is the equivalent of a sentence of twice that length.

The Alberta Court of Appeal, demurred:

> In our view, no such rule of thumb has ever been recognized by the Courts of this Province, and, furthermore, such a rule ought not to be recognized in the future. Each instance of sentencing has to be considered on its own merits, and, no doubt, in proper cases time already spent in custody, and the circumstances thereof, may be taken into account as provided by the *Criminal Code*. Beyond that, we do not believe any rule in this regard can be laid down.[127]

It is worth noting that the Court does not say that a period of custody can never be equivalent to a sentence twice that length; it simply says that the circumstances of the custody must be looked at in each case.

In *R. v. Arellano and Sanchez,*[128] the court said:

> Another factor which must, of course, be taken into account is the fact that the accused have already spent nearly eight months in preventive detention awaiting trial. Since time thus spent cannot be reduced by statutory or earned remission to which a convicted person would otherwise be entitled, and without wishing to lay down any hard and fast rule in this regard, I would view this time as being approximately the equivalent of one year's sentence time.

However in *R. v. Hatfield,*[129] it was urged that the trial judge failed to make any allowance to the prisoner for the time he was in custody in the United States resisting extradition upon the charge for which he was convicted:

> The extradition proceedings were long drawn out, the accused appealing from the order and thus securing considerable delay, during which time he had to remain in custody. This was his own action. This affords no reason for

---

[126] (1971), 13 Crim. L.Q. 434.

[127] *R. v. Regan, Huntley, Hasey and Blenkinsop* (1975), 24 C.C.C. (2d) 225 at p. 226, *per* Sinclair J.A. (Alta. C.A.).

[128] (1975), 30 C.R.N.S. 367 at p. 371 (Que.). See also *R. v. Langillo,* unreported, March 1, 1976 (Ont. C.A.).

[129] [1937] O.W.N. 559 at p. 560 (Ont. C.A.).

reducing the proper sentence to be imposed when he comes to be punished under our law for his crime.

In *R. v. Wooff*,[130] after conviction but prior to sentence, the appellant had spent 30 days in custody and it was argued that the time spent in custody prior to sentence would be regarded as the "custodial sentence" which all judges agreed was required in this case. Speaking for the majority Gale C.J.O. said:

> I do not so regard it. It must be taken into consideration . . . that is as far as I am prepared to go with respect to the pre-sentence time in custody. If countenance were given to that argument, pre-sentence custody abuse would soon occur. By counting that as part of the sentence, any person who receives that treatment might very well be prejudiced.

Dubin J.A., dissenting, preferred to consider the substance of the sentence rather than its form and considered that 30 days' imprisonment had been imposed by way of sentence and that therefore the requisite custody had been in fact imposed.

It is difficult to see the difference between 30 days spent in custody prior to sentence and 30 days spent in custody afterwards. Surely it is to be regretted that any judge should impose a period of imprisonment prior to sentence, when he is not certain that imprisonment is the only course available; but this course of action can be discouraged by appropriate comment from the appeal court. Why there should be an absolute rule that time spent in custody pursuant to a judicial order, though prior to sentence, is not a "custodial term", is hard to understand. It is also difficult to see how this can be taken into consideration in cases where the appropriate sentence would have been 30 days.

Q. Ignorance And Mistake Of Law

A popular belief has it that "ignorance of the law is no excuse". It is probably true that it is no defence, but it has upon occasion operated as an excuse. This is commonly the case for technical breaches of law. It is customary to take ignorance of the law into consideration on the

---

[130] (1973), 14 C.C.C. (2d) 396 at p. 398 (Ont. C.A.).

question of penalty. In *R. v. T.,*[131] one of the factors taken into consideration by the Court of Appeal on a charge of sexual intercourse with a girl of 14 was the claim by the accused that he did not know that the conduct was criminal.

In *R. v. Campbell and Mlynarschuk,*[132] the accused had committed the offence of taking part in an immoral or obscene performance as a "go-go dancer" and stripper. There had been an earlier case in the City of Edmonton where a judge had acquitted someone in a similar situation, and, though she did not completely understand the judgment and misconstrued it, the court held that this mistake of law could be taken as mitigation. The court said:

> It perhaps can also be argued that no reasonable person could find, in the judgment of Riley, J., justification for some of the things that this lady is alleged to have done. But to argue that would be to argue that she would have to have a rather sophisticated knowledge of what he said, and the significance of what he said, and that is unreal. She understood, as she said, that some Judge had said dancing bottomless is now okay, and I cannot reasonably test her understanding on that too closely.

In *R. v. Potter,*[133] where the accused had been led by custom officials, to whom he had made reasonable enquiries, to believe that a game he was importing was not a game of chance, the trial judge applied the passage from *Kenny, Outlines of Criminal Law,* first edition, p. 69: ". . . although mistakes of law, unreasonable or even reasonable thus leave the offender punishable for the crime for which he has blundered into, they may of course afford good grounds for inflicting on him a milder punishment."

R. Informers

It is the policy of the law to encourage wrongdoers not only to repent and desist, but to assist law enforcement agencies in the apprehension of other offenders. In *R. v. James; R. v. Sharman,*[134] the court said:

> He deserves the term of seven years imposed, but the court reduces it to

---

[131] [1965] Crim. L.R. 252; see also *R. v. McNaughton* (1976), 43 C.C.C. (2d) 293 (Que. C.A.).
[132] (1973), 10 C.C.C. (2d) 26 at p. 36 (Alta. Dist. Ct.).
[133] (1978), 3 C.R. (3d) 154 (P.E.I.).
[134] (1913), 9 Cr. App. R. 142.

three, for he betrayed the thieves; it is expedient that they should be persuaded not to trust one another, that there should not be 'honour among thieves'. He is now rewarded for informing against his accomplices, especially for denouncing Stephen Sharman and for refusing a bribe not to give evidence.

It is interesting that the court considers this as a matter of expediency, and not one of principle. This policy is often reflected in a more lenient sentence for persons who inform on others.[135] Because of the danger to informers and the necessity for respecting their understandable desire for secrecy, these factors are rarely mentioned in judgments. Nevertheless it is a common practice.

In *R. v. Lowe*,[136] the accused pleaded guilty to a "massive" number of very serious offences involving robbery, burglary and weapons charges. He was sentenced to a total of eleven and a half years' imprisonment. After sentence was passed the accused co-operated with the police by informing on other persons; as a result a "vast amount" (£400,000) was recovered by the police. He was convicted on the basis of his own confessions for the most part, which were voluntarily given. The police therefore had made progress in "the process of clearing up most of the serious gangs of criminals throughout the East End of London." The court noted that in offences committed by a criminal gang there was virtually no other way to get substantial information except by an informer who had previously been closely involved with them. "Unless credit is given in such cases there is no encouragement for others to come forward and give information of invaluable assistance to society and the police which enables these criminals . . . to be brought to book." The court took into account that the imposition of such a long sentence on this appellant, "might well have the effect of deterring other informers from coming forward with the information and enabling the gangs of this kind to be broken up." The accused had to be kept in solitary confinement for his own safety while in prison and, as a result, the sentence was reduced to one of five years.

Even when the accused himself is not co-operative in this way, the fact that others close to him have been so, is taken into account as a mitigating factor. Where the father of the accused turned in his son on a charge of possession of marijuana for the purpose of trafficking, in the hope that this action would get his son away from evil companions, the Court of Appeal took this into consideration and reduced his sentence of

---

[135] *R. v. Switlishoff* (1950), 9 C.R. 428 *per* Robertson J.A. dissenting (B.C.C.A.).
[136] (1978), 66 Cr. App. R. 122.

two years less one day definite and two years less one day indeterminate to one year's imprisonment.[137]

In *R. v. Twaddell,*[138] at the request of the Crown, a four-year sentence was made concurrent to a ten-year sentence rather than consecutive to it. The court noted that the accused was at some risk to himself at the time for giving evidence for the Crown on a drug conspiracy case. It viewed this action as "sure signs of not only remorse but rehabilitation." The court inferred from the Crown's request that this change would be "in the interests of justice." It is difficult to see how assurance from the Crown on a matter exclusively within the jurisdiction of the court itself (at that stage) could relieve the court from enquiring into the justice of such a move itself. Further, the court might have considered in its decision whether such a policy would encourage persons to testify falsely for the Crown in return for leniency.

S. Delay In Proceeding With Charges

Though it is the police and not the trial court who have *de facto* control in the laying of most criminal charges, that does not mean that the court is powerless to deal with abuse. A recurring matter is delay by the police or by the complainant in laying a charge. In *R. v. Bower,*[139] the court reduced sentence on a charge of theft by fraudulent means from six months to three months solely upon the ground that the complainant delayed for an unreasonable time in laying the information. The offence was committed in December 1951 but proceedings were not commenced until April 1955. "While the accused appears to have misled the complainant by promises and by statements that he had or would look after the claim of the corporation, the complainant was sufficiently aware of the facts at least at the end of 1952 to enable him to proceed with the information."

In *R. v. Burke,*[140] the appellant was arrested and sentenced to a term which, after appeals, amounted to six months' imprisonment. On the day before the appellant was due to be released from the Ontario

---

[137] *R. v. Akerman,* unreported, November 4, 1975 (B.C.C.A.).
[138] Unreported, February 18, 1976 (B.C.C.A.).
[139] (1955), 23 C.R. 186 at p. 187 *per* Martin C.J.S. (Sask. C.A.).
[140] [1968] 2 C C.C. 124 (Ont. C.A.).

Reformatory at Guelph, he was arrested once again and charged with a similar offence alleged to have been committed four days prior to the offence for which he was about to have finished serving his time. The court noted that in the circumstances, the alleged commission of the earlier offence must have been known to the police at the time of the first arrest. "The procedure followed here, to use as neutral word as possible, was most unfortunate. There arises a possible inference of unfairness which we believe should not be allowed to prevail." The court reduced the sentence to one of time served.

In *R. v. Busby,*[141] Busby was fined $25,000 on a charge of keeping a common betting-house. The court noted that the charge in question dealt with an offence that took place in June and that the charge was not laid until October, during which interval Busby was prosecuted for other offences of a similar nature. The court reduced the fine to $15,000. In *R. v. Fairn,*[142] a "strong suggestion" was made that the police had delayed service of the summons on the possession of marijuana offence in order to make sure that consecutive sentences were imposed. The court said:

> I do not attribute any wrong motive to the police in withholding service in this case, but it is a situation where the maxim, that justice must very clearly be seen to be done, is appropriate. . . . Any suggestion the police are using Court procedures to ensure that sentences are served consecutively by withholding service of process, ought to be repudiated not only by the police but by the Courts, if their fight against the drug traffic is to obtain the necessary public support. I do not attach undue importance to this factor but I think it must be considered.

Accordingly, the sentence was reduced from five months to 21 days.

In *R. v. Parisien,*[143] the charges were not at all similar, and in fact the appellant was serving time in Alberta while the British Columbia authorities failed to act on or notify him of the existence of a warrant in British Columbia. The court noted that had he known about the offence in British Columbia he might have asked that it be transferred to Alberta for a guilty plea. The court affirmed that "it is in the interests of the public that justice be speedily administered and that all known charges against an accused be disposed of as early as possible." Accordingly the court reduced the sentence of two and one-half years to one of one year.

The British Columbia Court of Appeal has attempted to elucidate the

---

[141] Unreported, June 25, 1973 (Ont. C.A.).

[142] (1973), 12 C.C.C. (2d) 423 at pp. 440-41 (N.S. Co. Ct.). See also *R. v. Costelloe* (1969), 54 Cr. App. R. 172.

[143] (1971), 3 C.C.C. (2d) 433 (B.C.C.A.).

rationale why delay in bringing the matter on to trial should operate as a mitigating factor. Even an offence which would usually call for a jail term as a matter of general deterrence, if it has been subject to long delays, will give rise to such mitigation: "Undoubtedly deterrence is the main feature involved in sentencing for offences of this kind [trafficking in hashish] but it is not very much of a deterrent when the public become aware of the history of a case of this kind — all influence of deterrence is then lost." The Court held the accused was not entitled to a lesser sentence because of delays which he had caused in the course of allowing himself to be brought to trial; but where the delays were caused by both sides, a suspended sentence and probation was upheld.[144]

In *R. v. Simon*,[145] the accused was sentenced to three years' imprisonment for a break and enter offence that had occurred some two-and-a-half years earlier. The accused was not arrested or brought to trial though he remained in the vicinity where the offence occurred. No explanation for the delay was offered. The court said: "We think that it was wrong to bring him back and impose a very severe sentence for these offences after so much time had elapsed." The sentence was reduced to one year's imprisonment.

In *R. v. Reilly*,[146] the police delayed bringing forward charges which were outstanding during a period wherein the appellant served his entire sentence, and indeed for a further two months following his release from prison. In this case the appellant, while he was in prison serving the sentence referred to, had written to the Crown asking that outstanding charges against him be disposed of at that time. The court accordingly reduced the sentence.

T. Interference By Police Officers With The Choice Of Plea

Though one can only suspect that it is a common practice, police officers have no right whatsoever to give advice to an accused as to how he ought to plead or what the consequences thereof might be. In *R. v. Butler*,[147] the

---

[144] *R. v. Gardiner*, unreported, May 2, 1975 (B.C.C.A.); see also *R. v. Harvey* (1978), 6 C.R. (3d) S-26 (Ont. C.A.).
[145] (1975), 25 C.C.C. (2d) 159 (Ont. C.A.).
[146] (1974), 18 C.C.C. (2d) 511 (Ont. C.A.).
[147] (1973), 11 C.C.C. (2d) 381 (Ont. C.A.).

accused appealed from a conviction for possession of stolen automobiles, following pleas of guilty on three charges. He was sentenced to three and one-half years on each charge, the sentences to run concurrently. The accused, who was defended by duty counsel provided by the legal aid plan rather than by counsel of his choice, alleged that pending trial a police officer suggested to him that a guilty plea would assure him of clemency before the court and that he would be sentenced to a minimum security institution for a period not to exceed 18 months. The court took the position that the assertion might be quite untrue, but as long as it stood there was left a possible impression that this man did not receive a fair and impartial trial, and in the circumstances a new trial was directed. In *R. v. Lemire and Gosselin,* [148] allegations that the police officers told the accused to plead guilty were examined carefully, and it appears that had these allegations been sustained the court would have directed a change of plea and a new trial. On the facts, the court found that the allegations were not substantiable.

In *R. v. Stone,* [149] the accused made a bargain with the police that she would give them information that they wanted concerning her offence; in return the minimum fine of $50 was to be imposed upon her. She gave the information, but the officers considered it valueless. They therefore considered themselves absolved from the bargain, but they never told her so. There was some dispute on the facts as to whether or not she relied on that promise in pleading guilty, but certainly the promise was made and was broken. Accordingly, the Nova Scotia Supreme Court upheld the earlier appeal decision that had quashed the conviction, thereby dismissing the Crown appeal.

In *R. v. Bond,* [150] the court noted that Bond said in his affidavits on appeal that he was in fact not guilty of either of the charges of shopbreaking, and that he pleaded guilty to the said charges at the suggestion of a police constable on the understanding that he would receive a light sentence, and that the female accused would be released. The court said: "The accused at his trial was represented by an experienced criminal lawyer, one of His Majesty's counsel and cannot be heard to allege that he was not guilty in view of the plea entered."

---

[148] (1948), 92 C.C.C. 201 (Que. C.A.).
[149] (1932), 58 C.C.C. 262 (N.S.C.A.).
[150] [1937] 3 D.L.R. 479 (Ont. C.A.).

U. Improprieties By The Police During The Course Of Their Investigation

That this is a matter which is frequently taken into consideration by trial judges in lower courts cannot be disputed, but similarly, it is a matter which rarely becomes the subject of judicial comment, and even more rarely finds its way to the appeal courts. The reasons are obvious. In *R. v. Steinberg,* [151] the police, while executing a search warrant, took advantage of their visit to the premises to "plant an electronic device" in a room in the accused's premises; this tape recording resulted in a conviction. The court held that the method of obtaining evidence did not affect its admissibility, and sustained the conviction. When it came to sentence the court said:

> ...we are not satisfied that that which occurred has the appearance of justice, and we feel that the appearance of justice is an important element to be considered in criminal matters. Bearing that in mind, we will allow the appeal against sentence so as to reduce the amount of the fine on count 1 from $10,000 to $5,000.

A three-month jail sentence was not disturbed. It is suggested that this principle has wider application than the single case exemplifies.

In *R. v. Pelletier,* [152] the learned trial judge was satisfied that the Crown had proved an assault upon the police in the execution of their duty. However, the evidence disclosed that the police, subsequent to the assault, had assaulted the accused using unnecessary force. Cullen J. of the Alberta Supreme Court said:

> A crime is an offence against society deserving of punishment. The law reserves the punishment ordinarily to the Court; it doesn't hand it over to the police. . . . if [the constable] chose to award the punishment himself at that time, certainly the Court is not moved to add to that punishment nor to go along with this type of prosecution.

In the circumstances, the trial judge imposed an absolute discharge.

---

[151] [1967] 3 C.C.C. 48 at p. 51 (Ont. C.A.).
[152] Unreported, June 13, 1974 (Alta.).

V. Entrapment And Misuse Of Police Informers

Courts recognize that, disagreeable as it may seem to some, the police must be able in certain cases to make use of informers and, as a corollary, that within certain limits such informers should be protected. At the same time, unless the use made of informers is kept within strict limits, grave injustice may result.

In *R. v. Price,*[153] a drug trafficking case, the court noted that when a charge arises as a result of an activity of an undercover agent that should be considered when determining the sentence that should be imposed. Repeated requests on the part of the agent may indicate an unwillingness to commit crime, and show hope of reform. In *R. v. Araki,*[154] an absolute discharge was imposed following a finding of guilt on a charge of trafficking of two capsules of heroin in exchange for a leather coat to an undercover officer. The officer had gone to the accused's house on a previous occasion to complete a similar transaction and had been told to go away. He persisted and told the accused that he was desperately ill from withdrawal symptoms. After an initial refusal the accused eventually completed the transaction. The argument of entrapment was accepted after an initial refusal, but the court said:

> after lengthy consideration of what control techniques are open to the Court where entrapment, as in this case, is found — be it by way of stay of proceedings as an abuse of process or an acquittal on an outright defence — I have decided that in the particular circumstances of the charge at bar, that I should adopt the possibility or possible control technique in the *dicta* of the learned Chief Justice of Canada in *Kirzner.*

Accordingly an absolute discharge was imposed.

In *R. v. Opyc,*[155] a sentence of four years on five charges of fraud and three counts of false pretences was reduced to two years less one day, thereby taking the accused out of the penitentiary and into the reformatory on the ground that the accused gave valuable assistance to the police in connection with the prosecution of others on extortion charges. The court said that if the accused were compelled to serve his sentence in a penitentiary his life would be in danger. The court said that notwithstanding the accused's previous record his assistance to the

---

[153] (1970), 12 C.R.N.S. 131 (Ont. C.A.).
[154] Unreported, May 30, 1978 (B.C. Co. Ct.).
[155] Unreported, November 19, 1976 (Ont. C.A.).

police at some risk to his own safety was a relevant factor to be considered in mitigation of sentence.

In *R. v. Birtles,*[156] after examining the facts upon a charge of burglary and carrying a firearm with intent to commit burglary, whereon the prisoner had been sentenced to five years' imprisonment, the court came to the conclusion that:

> there is a real possibility here, that the appellant was encouraged by the informer and indeed by the police officer concerned to carry out this raid on the post office. Whether or not he would have done it without that, again no one can say, but there is, as it seems to this court, a real likelihood that he was encouraged to commit an offence which otherwise he would not have committed.

The court, bearing in mind not only the possible encouragement but at the same time the fact that the appellant had been minded to use a real firearm, made the sentences concurrent so that the total time was three years' imprisonment. The court set out certain rules in dealing with informers. In the first place, it is important that the court of trial should not be misled.

This case was the subject of later comment in *R. v. McCann.*[157] In that case a police informer had been involved in the planning of a theft which resulted in four years' imprisonment. The court noted that, well before the offence was committed, the police had abundant evidence of conspiracy and ought at that point to have arrested the accused upon that charge. The court said that it was the duty of the police to take all proper steps to detect crime and to prevent crime happening, and found that there was at least "some possibility" that the accused might not have carried through this theft had the opportunity to do so not been provided by the police. The court rejected the proposed test of asking whether the crime had been "laid on" once the conspiracy charge became substantial and real as "somewhat legalistic". Nevertheless, the court took this matter into account by dealing with sentence on the basis of a conspiracy to steal rather than an actual theft. Accordingly the court lowered the sentence to two years' imprisonment.

In *R. v. Marco,*[158] the accused was charged with robbery together with a man "unknown". In fact the man "unknown" was an informer who, together with the police, warned the victim of what was going to take

---

[156] (1969), 53 Cr. App. R. 369.
[157] (1971), 56 Cr. App. R. 359.
[158] [1969] Crim. L.R. 205.

place, and had in fact gone through the pretense of tying up the victim while the police were concealed upon the premises. The fact, therefore, was that the appellant had pleaded guilty to an offence which had never been committed as there had never been any robbery at all. The court concluded that there was no harm in not revealing the fact that there was an informer, but it is quite another thing to conceal facts which go to the quality of the offence. And secondly it is "vitally important" to insure that the informer does not create an offence, that is to say,

> incite others to commit an offence which those others would not otherwise have committed. It is one thing for the police to make use of information concerning an offence that is already laid on. In such a case the police are clearly entitled, indeed it is their duty, to mitigate the consequences of the proposed offence, for example, to protect the proposed victim, and to that end it may be perfectly proper for them to encourage the informer to take part in the offence or indeed for a police officer himself to do so. But it is quite another thing, and something of which this Court thoroughly disapproves to use an informer to encourage another to commit an offence or indeed an offence of a more serious character, which he would not otherwise commit, still more so if the police themselves take part in carrying it out.

Chapter 8

Matters That Are Not Taken Into Consideration On Sentencing

Although generally the trial judge is entitled to make such enquiries as he sees fit and to act upon the material disclosed if it is properly before him, there is general agreement that some subject-matters ought not to be taken into consideration in any manner whatsoever as regards sentence. The reasons differ according to the subject-matter. In some cases it is a question of accepted practice; in others it is the conclusion that unless such a course be followed, proper principles of sentencing would be frustrated.

A. Other Offences Disclosed By The Evidence

Insofar as the nature of the case permits, the court must exclude consideration of one untried charge or potential charge from adjudication upon another tried one.[1] An exception to this general rule is commonly made in England and very occasionally in Canada through the procedure of taking other offences into account upon sentencing; but this cannot be done without the consent of the accused, his admission of guilt on the facts, and upon an understanding that the sentence imposed for the instant offence will reflect the harm done upon another occasion.

The basic premise for the rule is that if the prisoner is in fact guilty of

---

[1] *R. v. Spence* (1961), 132 C.C.C. 234 (P.E.I.).

other crimes which have not been made the subject of the particular charge in question he might in the future be separately tried and punished for them. Under our adversary system, it would appear to be the obligation of Crown counsel, if he wishes to urge upon the court a particular fact which discloses another offence in an attempt to justify increased punishment, to see that the appropriate charge be laid. However, in sentencing, the court may consider not only the offence for which the person has been charged, but also any included offence.[2] In *R. v. Spence,*[3] the court held that though the inference was a "natural" one, the court could not sentence upon the assumption that the offence for which sentence was being imposed was not an isolated act, but rather one incident in a series. In *R. v. Jimmo,*[4] the accused was charged with possession of a restricted drug. The court said:

> . . . it is of the utmost importance that no notice be taken of the fact that the appellant's companion was a young girl of 14 years of age. Revolting as this conduct on the part of the appellant may be it was the subject of another charge of contributing to juvenile delinquency for which another sentence has been imposed.

In *R. v. Whepdale,*[5] the court cited the danger of giving consideration, in passing sentence, to aggravating circumstances disclosed by the evidence which might change the character of the offence charged against the prisoner. This danger is particularly present where sworn evidence from a victim is given on sentence in preference to the procedure whereby the Crown, by agreement, relates only the relevant facts. In *R. v. Campbell and Mlynarchuk,*[6] the court, upon a count charging that the accused appeared in an indecent or obscene performance, refused to take into consideration that she had also committed the crime of being nude in a public place. Similarly, in *R. v. Harris,*[7] the prisoner was convicted of having intoxicating liquor in a place other than a residence and the maximum penalty was imposed because of evidence given on sentence to the effect that the prisoner had admitted having sold liquor and realized therefrom the sum of $1,500. The court said:

---

[2] *R. v. James* (1971), 3 C.C.C. (2d) 1 (P.E.I.C.A.).
[3] *Supra,* n. 1.
[4] (1973), 16 C.C.C. (2d) 396 at p. 398 *per* Owen, J.A. (Que. C.A.).
[5] [1927] 3 W.W.R. 704 (Sask. C.A.).
[6] (1973), 10 C.C.C. (2d) 26 (Alta. Dist. Ct.).
[7] (1917), 40 D.L.R. 684 at p. 685 (Ont.).

In effect, the learned magistrate, without an information, has found the defendant guilty of the offence of illegal sale; and, in consequence, has added the sum of $800 therefore to the penalty of $200, which he regarded as the appropriate penalty for the offence of having liquor in an unauthorised place. If, after such sentence, an information had been laid against the prisoner for the illegal sale in question, he would, if found guilty, have been punishable therefor; that is, he would have been punished twice for the same offence; if acquitted, he would stand fined, to the extent of $800, for an offence of which he had been found innocent.

. . .

. . . the defendant is entitled to be relieved from the injustice done him by the disregard of this rule.

In *R. v. Fogarty,*[8] upon a charge of unlawfully printing pool tickets and selling information on Canadian Football League games, the trial judge was informed that the prisoner had earned between five and seven thousand dollars from his operations over a period of six and one-half years prior to the date of the offence mentioned in the indictment: on that basis the trial judge determined that the fine should be $5,000. The Ontario Court of Appeal held that this was not a valid approach to the problem: "In effect, [he] was punished for offences he had never been charged with or convicted of." In the result the sentence was varied to a fine of $1,000.

Similarly, in *R. v. Johnston,*[9] a ten-year sentence for contempt of court was lowered to two years. The accused had testified at a murder trial and had given evidence that the jury had not believed; when asked to name other persons who were relevant to the story he was narrating he refused to answer. In his reasons the trial judge referred to the accused as a "killer, a psychopath and an executioner" indicating that he would have sentenced him to life imprisonment for contempt had the jury believed his evidence. The court held that the trial judge erred by taking into account a number of factors not relevant to the offence of which the accused was convicted, noting that he was not convicted of perjury, murder or conspiracy to defeat justice.

In *R. v. Morelli,*[10] the probation and parole officer in the pre-sentence report stated, upon the charge of theft from Dominion Stores by transferring groceries to a relative at a cash register without receiving payment: " 'It was revealed that she had been suspected of similar

---

[8] Unreported, September 20, 1974 (Ont. C.A.).
[9] (1976), 18 Crim. L.Q. 286 (Ont. C.A.).
[10] (1977), 37 C.C.C. (2d) 392 (Ont. Prov. Ct.).

incidents previously at the Dominion Store involving family members. The Manager stated he felt the offender was a leader and organizer of the illegal scheme.'" The court refused to consider this statement in evidence because it disclosed untried criminal offences: " . . . the Crown can prosecute the accused giving her a full opportunity to a fair trial in relation to any new criminal charges she has to face."

On a charge of possession of unregistered firearms, police produced evidence that they had found in the accused's home, in addition to the firearms, Nazi and racist literature. The accused testified under oath that he had the guns for use as a member of a gun club but the judge disbelieved his explanation, as he was entitled to do. However, having disbelieved him, he was then left with no evidence as to any aggravating factor. Nevertheless, he imposed sentence as though the accused had been convicted of possession of the guns for a purpose dangerous to the public peace — an offence with which he had not been charged. The sentence was substantially reduced.[11]

Occasionally, the other offence in question is not one that arises from the facts of the offence itself, but rather from the conduct immediately following the offence (absconding bail is an obvious example).[12] The same rule applies. In *R. v. Balcerczyk*,[13] the court, *obiter dicta*, said: "It is a little unfortunate that the learned trial judge did, in pronouncing sentence, refer to the fact that the offence was made more serious by the accused running away and leaving the poor boy to die in the street and the girl to suffer." In that case, upon a charge of causing death by criminal negligence, the court came to the conclusion that whether or not the learned trial judge committed this error, in the result the sentence was a fit and proper one and the appeal court should not interfere. However, they did allow time served pending the appeal, to count against sentence in accordance with discretion formerly vested in the appeal courts.

Similarly in *R. v. Carr*,[14] upon another charge of causing death by criminal negligence, the court said:

> . . . however much the conduct of the accused after the accident is open to censure, it is clear that the offence was committed when the unfortunate man was struck down by the motor car, and what happened subsequently was not receivable in evidence to prove the commission of the offence, nor . . . should

---

[11] *R. v. Auerswald* (1976), 28 C.C.C. (2d) 177 (Ont. C.A.).
[12] *R. v. Hansen*, [1961] N.S.W.R. 929 (C.A.).
[13] (1956), 114 C.C.C. 391 (Ont. C.A.); affd 117 C.C.C. 71 (S.C.C.).
[14] [1937] 3 D.L.R. 537 at pp. 540-41 (Ont. C.A.).

it be looked at in order to determine the measure of punishment. His failure to return to the scene of the accident was a violation of the law . . . for which he might have been prosecuted and have suffered the penalty for that offence, but . . . there is no justification for increasing the sentence for one offence because the accused has committed a subsequent offence for which the statute provides a penalty.

Nevertheless the principle may have its limitations. In *R. v. Collier,*[15] the charge was one of leaving the scene of an accident. O Hearn Co.Ct.J. said that, in considering retribution, all the circumstances of the case had to be taken into account, and this included the fact that the boy involved died, "as indicating how serious the injury was, although of course, it is clear that the defendant cannot be punished for causing the death in this proceeding and that that factor must be excluded." The death of the boy was involved as a factor in sentencing only as "tending to show that it was very wrong for the defendant to leave the scene of the collision in the circumstances." The case may simply be in conflict with others.

There are some charges however in which the nature of the crime itself is broad enough to include conduct which might well have been charged separately as other offences. For example, in *R. v. Janeway,*[16] a sentence of three months for criminal negligence in the operation of a motor vehicle was raised upon a Crown appeal to nine months in prison. The accused had been on a drinking spree and went through a radar trap. To escape apprehension for this offence he led a high-speed police chase which reached speeds of over 100 miles per hour. The accused made several U-turns, struck the side of the police car on one occasion, and was finally halted — when he again struck a police car that pulled in front of him. The court held that the accused's acts in attempting to escape and in deliberately placing the lives of the police officers in jeopardy called for a substantial term of imprisonment.

However, if the accused in sentencing puts his character in issue by leading evidence of good character the Crown may lead evidence of unproved offences to show the accused's true character and conduct. Similarly, if the accused leads medical evidence to show he is not a danger to the community, such evidence may then become relevant and admissible.[17]

An exception seems generally to be made for the question of weapons.

---

[15] (1971), 6 C.C.C. (2d) 438 (N.S. Co. Ct.).
[16] Unreported, March 3, 1978 (Ont. C.A.).
[17] *R. v. Lees* (1979), 46 C.C.C. (2d) 385 (S.C.C.). *R. v. Taylor,* [1959] O.W.N. 1 (C.A.) must be taken to be wrongly decided.

It is an offence in most circumstances to carry a weapon, certainly while involved in crime, but it is often treated as an aggravating factor to the offence itself. So, in *R. v. Morrison,*[18] the Ontario Court of Appeal took particular regard to the fact that the accused, convicted of possession of LSD for the purpose of trafficking, had committed the offence while he was armed, as showing that the offence was a serious one of its kind.

B. Conduct Of Defence

There is a general rule that whatever may be the conduct of the defence, it is improper to base any consideration of sentencing upon it in such a way that the sentence is thereby increased. It would undoubtedly be an unwise policy that penalized persons in any way for taking a course of action which they or their advisors considered necessary in their own defence; it would tend to bring the system of justice as a whole into disrepute. There is a further and more practical reason for inadmissibility of this factor and that is that it is very hard to decide who has chosen a particular line of defence. Though theoretically it is the responsibility of the client to instruct counsel, as a matter of practice these decisions are very often mixed and in some cases the contribution of the client may be minimal. Whether this is proper or not is quite beside the point; it undoubtedly occurs.

The principle as put by David Thomas[19] is that a defendant is not to be penalized in terms of his sentence for exercising his rights, although he may lose some of the mitigation which would otherwise be attributable to remorse. This is nevertheless a difficult principle to understand. If the sentence is to be longer because of lack of remorse (as indicated by the conduct of the defence), then there is very little difference between that indirect course of action and increasing sentence directly because of the conduct of the defence. It is submitted that the supposed distinction is illusory. Either a man is penalized for the conduct of his defence, or he is not; and the above formulation looks suspiciously like an attempt to ride two horses at the same time.

In *R. v. Jamieson,*[20] the accused was convicted of stealing a half bottle

---

[18] [1970] 2 C.C.C. 190; *contra, R. v. Hansen, supra,* n. 12.
[19] *Principles of Sentencing* at p. 196.
[20] [1975] Crim. L.R. 248.

of whiskey from a supermarket. He was fined £300. The court enunciated the principle that a man should not be sentenced more heavily if he exercised his right of trial by jury. The situation becomes slightly more complicated when the ground for increasing sentence is the fact that in the conduct of his defence the prisoner had made allegations against the police. In *R. v. Skone,*[21] the court flatly stated that the fact that the appellant had attacked the police officers in the course of his defence should not have added one day to his sentence but, looking at the sentence as a whole, the court was of the view that it was lenient in any event and that even had he pleaded guilty, for example, it would have been impossible to pronounce a lesser sentence. Presumably, in such a case there is a finding of fact by the judge, or (by implication) by the jury, that the allegations were unfounded. Nevertheless, it is difficult to show how this could ever be clearly known, save in exceptional cases. Some of the allegations might have been accepted in almost any case. Similarly in *R. v. Harper,*[22] in the course of sentencing, the learned Recorder said:

> The defence which you instructed your learned counsel to run involved allegations of perjury by prosecuting witnesses, intimidation, threats and improper behavior by senior police officers, and allegations that two boys who pleaded guilty and had been punished for breaking into Mrs. Parkes' house were telling lies.

The Recorder went on to say that this behaviour showed that the appellant had no remorse. But the Court of Appeal nevertheless came to the conclusion that despite the alleged causal connection between the conduct of the defence and a lack of remorse: "There is a real danger . . . that this appellant was being given what was undoubtedly a serious sentence because he had pleaded not guilty and had run his defence in the way indicated by the Recorder."

Unfortunately, this clear position was blurred by the same court, almost in passing, in a comment made some six years later when the court was differently constituted. In *R. v. Pritchard,*[23] it was noted that the trial judge in sentencing the prisoner observed that, by reason of the conduct of the defence upon a charge of rape and the allegations put to the unfortunate victim, all mitigation had been destroyed. The appellate judgment says: "In the course of the trial the complainant was, by reason of the appellant's conduct as far as the defence was concerned, compelled

---

[21] (1966), 51 Cr. App. R. 165.
[22] (1967), 52 Cr. App. R. 21.
[23] (1973), 57 Cr. App. R. 492.

to go into the witness-box and describe this revolting occurrence." This of course is nothing unusual in a rape case, and it is hard to see that this by itself could justify any increase of sentence. In the course of judgment the court said: "He perpetrated a bad case of rape and made matters worse by criticizing the complainant in the course of the trial and showed no remorse."

Clearly one of the two cases must be wrong and it is submitted that there is considerable fault to be found with the reasoning that suggests that choosing a trial and criticizing witnesses in the course thereof is justification for increasing the sentence upon the ground of lack of remorse. It is one thing to say such an accused gets no special credit for pleading guilty, or otherwise showing remorse, but it is submitted that the defence chosen should never be grounds for increasing sentence or justifying an otherwise excessive sentence.

A second common suggestion is that the sentence might be increased because the trial judge finds, either by himself or through his interpretation of the jury's verdict, that the appellant has lied under oath. It is difficult to understand how one decides when someone has perjured himself. It is the common experience of the law that witnesses may quite honestly believe matters that have no foundation in fact whatever; the difficulty in deciding whether there is perjury is emphasized in our law by the requirement of corroboration. This is, it is submitted, a dangerous ground upon which to act. Further, it amounts to an allegation of a separate offence for which the accused could be punished if charged.

In *R. v. Dunbar,*[24] the Court of Appeal had before them a case where the trial judge noted that a man called Davidson, who had been with Dunbar on the shopbreaking offence, had just been sentenced to 18 months, and then proceeded in the case of Dunbar to impose a more severe sentence, saying:

> You were prepared to go further . . . to persuade others to change their evidence whilst you pleaded not guilty and told lies to the justices; that makes your part in the breaking and larceny more serious than those who pleaded guilty and told the truth from the word go.

The Court of Appeal took the view that it appeared that the one year was being added merely for an offence or conduct amounting to an offence

---

[24] (1966), 51 Cr. App. R. 57.

with which he was not charged, and secondly, for telling lies, and in those circumstances the Court removed the extra 12 months' imprisonment.

In Canada, a single judge of the Supreme Court of Nova Scotia has taken the opposite view. In *R. v. Cornett,*[25] upon an application for leave to appeal against sentence, the justice noted that the trial judge considered the general character of the appellant,

> ... as evidenced of what the Judge considered the willingness of the appellant to commit perjury, and there is abundant authority for his so doing, so long as it is clear that the sentence is not a punishment for the crime of perjury, but for the offence for which the appellant stood convicted on his plea of guilty.

There is hardly abundant authority for considering general character in aggravation of an offence; but rather, in Canada, a total absence of it. Secondly, it is impossible to understand how an increased sentence for this reason would not be in fact a punishment for the crime of perjury, even if the total sentence did not exceed the proper range for the particular offence and the particular offender.

Lies by an accused are not rare, but the reflection of them in punishment is and should be. It is suggested that where it is absolutely clear that an accused has lied, this factor, at the most, simply disentitles him from the consideration that would have been given him had he pleaded guilty at the outset. It cannot justify increased punishment under any pretext.

An extension of the principle here contended for can be seen in *R. v. Burton.*[26] There the trial judge made reference to the fact that the appellant's wife had given evidence that some of the property which was the subject-matter of a charge of receiving stolen property had been bought by her in various places. This evidence appeared to be untrue. Nothing was said upon sentencing the appellant with regard to this matter, but in sentencing his co-defendant, the trial judge observed that it was very much in his favour that he did not put his wife into the box to commit perjury. The Court of Appeal said: "If that meant that the Deputy Chairman assumed, without evidence, that the false evidence given by the appellant's wife had been suggested to her by her husband, the observation was unfortunate." Taking the whole of the

---

[25] (1949), 96 C.C.C. 316.
[26] (1941), 28 Cr. App. R. 89.

circumstances into consideration the Court reduced the sentence by halving it.

C. Other Charges

In *R. v. Fairn,*[27] O Hearn Co.Ct.J. noted that he was advised by counsel for the Crown that another charge against the defendant was withdrawn and said, quite correctly on principle, that he did not see how he could take it properly into account one way or the other.

In *R. v. Arellano and Sanchez,*[28] upon a charge of importing cocaine, there was evidence brought forward that upon the release of the accused from prison in Canada, they would be deported to Bolivia where they would have to face a further trial in connection with the same incident. The court said:

> After reflection, however, I have decided that this is not a matter which I could properly put into the scales even if the evidence on it were more satisfactory than it is. My concern is and must be only with the administration of the laws of Canada and if the laws of another country may result in their being punished twice for the same offence that is a matter for the courts of that country to take into account.

D. Civil Remedies

In *R. v. Anderson & Friends Ltd.,*[29] Doyle Co.Ct.J. had to deal with a charge of misleading advertising concerning a statement attributed to the complainant in an advertisement for the "Doctor's 10-Day Quit Smoking Plan" that she definitely looked and felt ten years younger. The court noted: "It is true that Mrs. Heading may have recourse to civil damages; we need not be concerned with that."

---

[27] (1973), 12 C.C.C. (2d) 423 (N.S. Co. Ct.); *R. v. Denniston,* [1977] Crim. L.R. 46.

[28] (1975), 30 C.R.N.S. 367 at p. 371 (Que.).

[29] (1973), 11 C.C.C. (2d) 398 at p. 401 (Ont. Co. Ct.).

E. Petitions And Public Response

In *R. v. Lim Gim,*[30] the court noted that the trial judge on sentencing was handed a petition asking for leniency, signed by a number of businessmen in Vancouver, which was "well-described as wonderfully worded". The court determined that the trial judge was in error in receiving it, either because it was not legal evidence or because it was not in accordance with past practice. (On sentencing procedure the better position is that it is not past practice; it really falls into the category of consent submissions by counsel.) The court said ". . . we have felt impelled to disapprove of this novel innovation at its inception . . .".

In *Re Gamester*[31] an application for prohibition was granted against a trial judge who, following accused's plea of guilty on a charge of dangerous driving, adjourned the case to hear submissions from the public on "alcohol-related offences". In *R. v. Porter*[32] the court considered it inappropriate for the judge to have regard to "the reaction of the public" and "the general satisfaction of the public" to his sentence. Where petitions come from those who have some involvement with the offence, they have been received and acted upon.[33]

F. The Sex Of The Accused

In *R. v. Williams and Williams,*[34] the court said:

> The sentence on the woman was eighteen months imprisonment and on the man two and a half years. Why it seems so often to be considered, where a man and woman are involved, that the woman should always receive a less sentence than the man, I do not know. Of course, there are cases where it is right that she should. If you have a young woman stealing under the influence of a man it is quite right that she should receive a less sentence than the man. In this case one would have supposed that it was the woman who was by far the more to blame; she was the post-mistress, she was helping herself to the money and she was using it for the business in which she was

---

[30] [1928] 1 D.L.R. 1038 (B.C.C.A.).
[31] Unreported, January 5, 1978 (P.E.I.).
[32] (1976), 15 O.R. (2d) 103 (C.A.).
[33] *R. v. Hardy* (1976), 33 C.R.N.S. 76 (Que.).
[34] (1953), 37 Cr. App. R. 71.

interested along with her husband. The husband seems to have been a weak sort of person who did not protest, and yet he gets a year more than the woman gets.

The sentences were in the result reduced so that they were equal between the man and woman.

G. Station In Life

The Canadian Bill of Rights, enacted in 1960, affirms in regard to Canadian criminal law "the right of the individual to equality before the law and the protection of the law." The idea, however, predates the Canadian Bill of Rights by some time. In *R. v. Carr,*[35] the court annunciated the principle, certainly of wider application than the particular case in which it was stated, that the station in life of a person who is convicted of criminal negligence when driving a motor car should not affect the sentence imposed upon him. Taking the view that the trial judge had been influenced by this factor, the Court of Appeal altered the sentence. In *R. v. Johnson,*[36] the accused appealed his sentence upon a charge of having care or control of a motor vehicle while his ability was impaired. In sentencing the appellant, the trial judge said that he approached the question with the impression that Johnson was a man of means to whom the imposition of a fine would mean virtually nothing. Taking the view that a fine even of $500 (the maximum) would probably be ineffective to deter this defendant and others in like station in life from repeating or committing this offence, the trial judge imposed a sentence of seven days' imprisonment. The Court of Appeal said:

> What concerns the Court deeply is the cardinal principle upon which our criminal judicial system, with which we are concerned here, is based, namely, that all persons stand equal before the Court. It matters not what the race, creed, colour, status in society, whether pauper or rich man, an accused must receive equality of treatment before the law.
>
> Should it be otherwise, the principle cornerstone of our criminal judicial system would be seriously impaired, if not destroyed.
>
> . . .
>
> If the Court can discriminate according to class in imposing sentence, then

---

[35] [1937] 3 D.L.R. 537 (Ont. C.A.).
[36] (1971), 5 C.C.C. (2d) 541 at p. 543 (N.S.C.A.).

there is nothing to prevent it from imposing punishment based on race, creed, colour or society status of the accused.

The Court imposed a fine of $200.

Such cases are simple because the error is glaring. More subtle was the reference of the trial judge in *R. v. Nash (No. 2)*[37] where it was said: " 'My understanding of the social conditions in which the participants were living at the time of the incident has enabled me to sufficiently measure the degree of gravity of the crime and the nature of the guilt of the accused as found by the jury.' " To which the Court of Appeal replied: "I hardly think we should measure the gravity of the crime [manslaughter] by the social condition of the participants or that the penalty should be varied by the same scale."

Accordingly, a sentence of three years was declared inadequate and was increased to seven years' imprisonment.

Exactly the opposite perspective was taken by the Nova Scotia Court of Appeal in *R. v. Cormier*.[38] During the course of a domestic dispute the accused killed her husband and was convicted of manslaughter. A suspended sentence was imposed; and the judge said " '. . . I have to keep in mind what I know and have learned about the kind of community in which you live. There may be different standards. Standards may be looser, lower and I hope that nobody gets the idea that this kind of conduct can be condoned.' " This comment was specifically approved by the Court of Appeal as it showed the advantage the trial judge had in seeing and observing the witnesses and "forming an impression not only of them but of the circumstances surrounding this whole tragic affair."

Conversely, in *R. v. Legere*[39] the court came to the conclusion that sentences of nine months definite and six months indeterminate upon two charges of possession of stolen property were harsh in the circumstances: "Although the trial judge may have been irked by Legere's lifestyle and his apparent lack of ambition, such matters should not weigh against the accused in the sentencing process." The appeal was therefore allowed and the definite term of the sentence reduced to six months.

Occasionally, the plea is made, ostensibly in mitigation, that because of his or her social position punishment of imprisonment would fall

---

[37] (1948), 8 C.R. 447 at p. 453 (N.B.C.A.).
[38] (1974), 22 C.C.C. (2d) 235 (N.S.C.A.); see also Chapter 2, "Factors to be Considered".
[39] Unreported, June 22, 1973 (Ont. C.A.).

much more heavily on him than others. In *R. v. Cargill*,[40] cited with approval in *R. v. Bottomley*,[41] the court said:

> This case revealed a very unfortunate state of things at Hull; the place was infested with a plague of very juvenile prostitutes. That being so, and a clear case found of a man assisting in that stage of things, and breaking the law, it was necessary to inflict a substantial punishment. In addition to this it is very desirable, if possible, to pass a sentence on a man in a good position exactly the same as on a man in a different position; it is true the sentence is harder, but the offence is correspondingly greater; the man ought to know better, and the way of meeting that is to give exactly the same sentence; the sentence is worse, but by reason of the prisoner's position, the offence is worse.

Though closely reasoned, it is possible that a different view may be taken. For some offences, position (for example, in breach of trust) in fact makes the offence worse; but for many offences, especially those of a minor sort, the basic premise for the rule cannot obtain. A poor man may not have a penny for his fine, while to a rich man, no reasonable sum can be too great. Nevertheless equality must be maintained, for it would certainly leave a sense of grievance in the mind of a poor man to know that he is serving a longer sentence than one who is not so unfortunate simply on the grounds of an apparent excessive hardship for the man of means. Further, the factual premise has not yet been explored. There is no evidence to suggest that a lengthy term in prison is any more difficult in and of itself for a rich man than a poor one.

H. Character Of The Victim

In *R. v. Winters, Knox and Palmer*,[42] the three accused persuaded a party to take them to the rooms of a drug trafficker ostensibly to purchase hashish, but on the way it was learned that they intended not to purchase hashish but rather to rob the trafficker. The trial judge in passing sentence took into consideration the fact that the Crown's case "was tainted by the fact that its principle witnesses were engaged in an illegal activity, namely, the trafficking and sale of hashish. The only victim of this crime was himself a criminal . . .". The Court of Appeal said:

---

[40] (1913), 8 Cr. App. R. 224.
[41] (1922), 16 Cr. App. R. 184.
[42] (1974), 16 C.C.C. (2d) 551 at pp. 554-55 (N.S.C.A.).

If the learned trial Judge meant to suggest that the sentence was properly less than it otherwise would have been because the victim himself was a criminal, I must, with the greatest respect, suggest that this is not a matter which should be taken into account. The character of a victim of a crime does not affect his right to be protected from robbery and possible violence.

Unfortunately this principle has not always been thoroughly accepted, especially in cases of rape. In *R. v. Skone,*[43] there was a conviction on three charges of having sexual intercourse with a single girl between the ages of 13 and 14. It was shown at the trial that the complainant was a "thoroughly immoral girl, who, in spite of her age, had had a good deal of sexual experience with other men . . .". The Court of Appeal upheld a sentence of six months, but did so "in spite of the girl's character".

I. Unsatisfactory Conduct As A Crown Witness

In *Phillips v. The Queen,*[44] the prisoner was sentenced to three years' imprisonment upon a charge of breaking and entering. While in custody awaiting sentence (a situation which should never occur) the accused was called as a Crown witness against Warren MacArthur, who was an accomplice in the crime with him. In his evidence he denied any knowledge of another person being involved in the break-in, although he himself in his earlier statement to police had indicated that there were others involved. The trial judge said:

> "There is no question that you were far from a satisfactory witness. You gave statements oral and written and then denied each and every one of them. For purposes of rehabilitation one must be basically honest or have a desire to better himself. I haven't a question in my mind that you, if not actually perjured yourself, came very close thereto."

The Court of Appeal noted that a review of the record left the distinct impression that if the appellant had given evidence at the trial of MacArthur which would have supported a conviction, the sentence would have been less than three years' imprisonment. The Court said:

> The suggestion that a convicted person might receive a less severe punishment if he gives evidence implicating another accused person is

---

[43] (1966), 51 Cr. App. R. 165.
[44] (1973), 24 C.R.N.S. 305 (P.E.I.C.A.).

repugnant to all the guiding principles to be followed in sentencing a convicted person. The suggestion that a more severe punishment has been given because his evidence has failed to implicate another accused person is equally repugnant. . . . this was an improper consideration.

In the result the Court reduced the sentence of imprisonment to one of two years.

J. Offers Of Surgical Operations

In *R. v. Belt*,[45] the accused appealed from a sentence of life imprisonment upon the plea of guilty to a charge of buggery; he had a history of long and continued unnatural offences involving small boys and there was every indication that there would be no change in this pattern of behaviour. On appeal the prisoner suggested (and the suggestion emanated from him), that he was willing to undergo a surgical operation so that his "unnatural propensities" might thereby be cured. The court indicated that:

> . . . the suggestion is one which we cannot take into account in reaching our decision upon the question of reduction of sentence. . . . Should we now in turn express our willingness to reduce the sentence in the light of the proposed physical change in the appellant we would be placed in the position of attempting to strike a bargain with him in that regard. We consider such a position highly improper and one in which the court must in consequence refuse to be placed. There are other authorities who may, if the occasion arises, review the sentence on that basis with propriety, but we cannot do so.

The court dismissed the appeal and thereby placed the matter in the hands of the Parole Board. It should be noted that several American jurisdictions have recently been accepting such proposals and the matter is about to be tested in the Supreme Court of the United States in the light of the American constitutional requirements for criminal process.

---

[45] (1944), 84 C.C.C. 403 (B.C.C.A.).

K. Submissions Inconsistent With Guilty Plea

In *R. v. Sumarah et al.,*[46] the accused pleaded guilty to charges of wilfully evading the payment of taxes and making false and deceptive statements in his income tax returns. It was held that thereafter he could not rely on the explanation that the moneys taken were viewed as promotional gifts, because such an explanation would be negated by the state of mind shown by his plea. It is submitted that this is a correct position, but if the accused persists in his explanation, the proper course is not to reject it out of hand, but to consider whether or not he ought to be permitted to change his plea.

L. Future Changes In The Law

It has generally been recognized that the court has a duty to administer the law as it presently exists and that it would be improper to take into account changes in legislation that might occur in the future. This position was upheld in Ontario and adopted in Alberta in the context of proposed changes in the law as regards to drugs, where it was said "for us to give weight to such a contention would be to encroach on the proper field of the Parliament of Canada".[47]

M. The Law In Other Jurisdictions

In *R. v. Thomas*[48] the accused were convicted of assisting in the commission outside the United Kingdom of an offence corresponding to the import and export of a narcotic. She and her fiancé went to Pakistan and ran hashish into Denmark. During the course of his judgment the learned trial judge noted that the maximum penalty in Denmark for smuggling drugs was six years and commented that that was a useful

---

[46] [1970] 5 C.C.C. 317 (N.S. Co. Ct.).
[47] *R. v. Bosley and Duarte,* [1970] 1 C.C.C. 328 (Ont. C.A.); *R. v. Doyle and 10 others* (1970), 2 C.C.C. (2d) 82 (Alta. C.A.).
[48] [1977] Crim. L.R. 47.

guide in determining sentence. The English Court of Criminal Appeal said that the maximum sentence under the law of another country was irrelevant.

N. Refusal To Inform On Others

In *R. v. Dunne*[49] the accused elected to testify on his own behalf at a sentencing hearing to the effect that he was in need of money and that a friend of his whom he had approached for a loan refused but suggested that he would supply $500 worth of marijuana which could be sold so that the accused could make a profit. The Crown attorney asked him to name that person; the accused refused. The trial judge refused the request to cite him for contempt of court though he held that the question was a proper question and relevant to credibility. However, he held that once the accused had acknowledged his guilt, the court's concern was credibility only as it might reflect on his personality and character for the purpose of sentencing.

Though this decision insofar as the exercise of discretion is concerned cannot be faulted, it does not appear that the decision is correct on principle. By taking the stand the accused exposes himself to full cross-examination. One of the crucial issues is whether or not the story he has told, which minimizes his own guilt at the expense of another, is true. Crown counsel should have the right to suggest through cross-examination that the "friend" and his role in the offence are fictitious. The accused who refuses to answer may reflect adversely on the credibility of the story he has told as well as on his general credibility. But, at worst, the evidence he has given ought to be ignored; he cannot be penalized for his silence on this subject.

---

[49] (1977), 35 C.C.C. (2d) 147 (Nfld. Dist. Ct.).

Chapter 9

Discharge And Mercy

The provisions enabling a court to impose an absolute or a conditional discharge for certain offences were enacted by the Criminal Law Amendment Act, 1972.[1] The purpose of the legislation is to enable a court, before which an accused pleads guilty to an offence or which finds an accused guilty of an offence, to make a disposition of the case, in appropriate circumstances, which will avoid ascribing a criminal conviction to the accused.[2] Implicit in this is the recognition by Parliament that a criminal conviction as such may be a form of punishment and that punishment is neither appropriate nor necessary in some instances. On occasion, very harsh effects upon an accused person's life can result from the acquisition of a criminal record and this legislation is one way of relieving this consequence in appropriate cases.[3] A person who has been granted a discharge may truthfully state that he has never been convicted of a criminal offence.[4]

Criminal Code:

662.1 (1) Where an accused, other than a corporation, pleads guilty to or is found guilty of an offence, other than an offence for which a minimum punishment is prescribed by law or an offence punishable, in the proceedings

---

[1] 1972 (Can.), c. 13, s. 57.

[2] *R. v. McInnis* (1973), 13 C.C.C. (2d) 471 (Ont. C.A.).

[3] "Absolute and Conditional Discharges Under the Criminal Code", by His Honour Judge T. R. Swabey, 20 C.R.N.S. 132. See also "Absolute and Conditional Discharge" by F. G. Bobias (1974), 6 Ottawa L. Rev. 608 and "Absolute and Conditional Discharge" by E. L. Greenspan in *Studies in Criminal Law and Procedure* (Canada Law Book Ltd.: Toronto, 1973). Also refer, *infra,* to Section H.

[4] *R. v. Kitt,* [1977] Crim. L.R. 220 (Mag. Ct.).

commenced against him, by imprisonment for fourteen years or for life, the court before which he appears may, if it considers it to be in the best interests of the accused and not contrary to the public interest, instead of convicting the accused, by order direct that the accused be discharged absolutely or upon the conditions prescribed in a probation order.

(2) Subject to the provisions of Part XIV, where an accused who has not been taken into custody or who has been released from custody under or by virtue of any provision of Part XIV pleads guilty to or is found guilty of an offence but is not convicted, the appearance notice, promise to appear, summons, undertaking or recognizance issued to or given or entered into by him continues in force, subject to its terms, until a disposition in respect of him is made under subsection (1) unless, at the time he pleads guilty or is found guilty, the court, judge or justice orders that he be taken into custody pending such a disposition.

(3) Where a court directs under subsection (1) that an accused be discharged, the accused shall be deemed not to have been convicted of the offence to which he pleaded guilty or of which he was found guilty and to which the discharge relates except that

(*a*) the accused may appeal from the direction that the accused be discharged as if that direction were a conviction in respect of the offence to which the discharge relates;

(*a*.1) the Attorney General may appeal from the direction that the accused be discharged, as if that direction were a judgment or verdict of acquittal referred to in paragraph 605(1)(*a*); and

(*b*) the accused may plead *autrefois convict* in respect of any subsequent charge relating to the offence to which the discharge relates.

(4) Where an accused who is bound by the conditions of a probation order made at a time when he was directed to be discharged under this section is convicted of an offence, including an offence under section 666, the court that made the probation order may, in addition to or in lieu of exercising its authority under subsection 664(4), at any time when it may take action under that section, revoke the discharge, convict the accused of the offence to which the discharge relates and impose any sentence that could have been imposed if the accused had been convicted at the time he was discharged, and no appeal lies from a conviction under this subsection where an appeal was taken from the order directing that the accused be discharged.

A. The Use Of The Discharge Provisions

There is a wide, albeit judicial, discretion vested in the trial court when considering a discharge. In applying the statutory criteria the court must consider all the circumstances of the accused and the nature and circumstances of the offence, against the background of proper law enforcement in the community.[5]

In *R. v. Fallofield*,[6] the accused, a furniture mover in his spare time, was convicted of theft for taking, from the premises where he was making a delivery, five pieces of left-over carpeting valued at $33.07. He stated at the time that he thought they were scraps. The trial judge, referring to standards derived from British legislation both similar to and different from our own, took the view that he could not grant a discharge because he did not believe that "this was a case of strict liability or that it is a case where the offence being committed was entirely completely unintentional or unavoidable". The British Columbia Court of Appeal took the view that the trial judge proceeded on a wrong principle and that there was nothing in the language of the discharge provisions of the Criminal Code to so limit its application. The Court held that the section may be used in respect of any offence, other than an offence for which a minimum punishment is prescribed by law or one punishable by imprisonment for 14 years or for life or by death. Secondly, the Court made clear that the section contemplates the commission of any offence, and that there is nothing in the language of the statute that limits its operation to a breach of a technical or trivial nature.

These provisions cannot be used where there is a minimum penalty.

The meaning of the phrase "punishable, in the proceedings commenced against him, by imprisonment for fourteen years," has been canvassed by the Ontario Court of Appeal in *R. v. Sampson*.[7] The accused was charged with possession for the purpose of trafficking which carried a maximum penalty of life imprisonment. He was not found guilty of the full charge but convicted of possession of marijuana as an included offence. The penalty for possession of marijuana upon indictment is seven years. The Crown argued that since Sampson was liable to life imprisonment if guilty of the charge laid against him, a discharge was precluded by the phrase "in the proceedings commenced against him". The Ontario Court of Appeal held that the phrase relates only to the proceedings with respect to which he was found guilty and therefore allowed the appeal, set aside the conviction and imposed a conditional discharge.

---

[5] *R. v. Sanchez-Pino* (1973), 11 C.C.C. (2d) 53 (Ont. C.A.).
[6] (1973), 13 C.C.C. (2d) 450 (B.C.C.A.).
[7] (1975), 23 C.C.C. (2d) 65.

R. v. Fallofield also sets out the principle that these sections should not be applied routinely to any particular offence. Any resultant lack of uniformity will be more apparent than real if it flows from the differences in the circumstances of the cases. Nevertheless, in *R. v. Taylor*,[8] the Ontario Court of Appeal held that where the circumstances are such that conditional discharges have been granted in similar cases (there, shoplifting of a pair of sunglasses), the trial judge is obliged to give consideration to the question of whether one should be granted under the circumstances of the particular case. It is apparent that these two decisions are not at all inconsistent.

One of the two conditions precedent to the exercise of the jurisdiction to impose a conditional or absolute discharge is that the discharge must be "in the best interests of the accused". The Ontario Court of Appeal has said that this means

> ... that deterrence of the offender himself is not a relevant consideration, in the circumstances, except to the extent required by conditions in a probation order. Nor is his rehabilitation through correctional or treatment centres, except to the same extent. Normally he will be a person of good character, or at least of such character that the entry of a conviction against him may have significant repercussions.[9]

If it is not in the best interests of the accused, then that is the end of the matter so far as the discharge is concerned. If however, the first condition is fulfilled, the court must proceed to consider whether or not the giving of a discharge would be "contrary to the public interest". The Ontario Court of Appeal has said:

> One element thereby brought in will be the necessity or otherwise of a sentence which will be a deterrent to others who may be minded to commit a like offence — a standard part of the criteria for sentencing.
>
> Obviously the section is not confined to "simple cases of possession of marijuana". It is not confined to *any* class of offences except to the extent I have noted. On the other hand, it is only common sense that the more serious the offence, the less likely that it would appear that an absolute discharge, or even a conditional one is "not contrary to the public interest". In some cases, the trivial nature of the offence will be an important consideration; in others, unusual circumstances peculiar to the offender in question may lead to an order that would not be made in the case of another offender.

---

[8] (1975), 24 C.C.C. (2d) 551.
[9] *R. v. Sanchez-Pino, supra,* n. 5 at p. 59.

Discharges are not restricted to "trivial matters."[10]

However, the Prince Edward Island Court of Appeal seems to have confused these issues. In *R. v. Griffin*[11] a young police officer who was escorting a drunken prisoner to the cells struck the prisoner in the face and injured his eye to such an extent that it had to be removed. The trial court, accepting that it was not a "premeditated act" (though it had to be intentional as a matter of law) refused to grant a discharge largely because of the serious result of the assault upon the prisoner. He imposed a suspended sentence and probation. The Court of Appeal found that the trial judge gave undue weight to the actual result of the assault as opposed to the probable results: ". . . from the nature of the act and the circumstances the probability of the drastic results would not have been in the mind of the appellant when the assault took place."

Of equal interest in this surprising conclusion was the method used by the Court of Appeal to determine whether or not the grant of a discharge would be contrary to the public interest. The Court of Appeal had before it letters from the Chief of Police and the Chairman of the Police Committee supporting the police officer and stating that they would recommmend that he be rehired in his former capacity if he was granted an absolute discharge. The Court accepted the material, and commented that both persons were "competent to assist the Court in reaching a proper conclusion" on the question of whether or not a discharge would be contrary to the public interest. As it is hard to imagine that the hiring or rehiring of any particular police officer is a matter which involves the public interest, one can only conclude that the Court has confused the two statutory conditions pertinent to the granting of a discharge. One would hope that the fact that the accused was a police officer did not in itself influence the judgment towards leniency.

There seems, so far, to be very little indication as to when an absolute as opposed to a conditional discharge ought to be granted. On its face, it would appear that an absolute discharge should be imposed in the more trivial case, or when there is a perception that official interference with the life of the accused is not necessary. But there is no guidance in the statute itself. One relies simply on the general principle that the lesser "penalty" should be for the lesser case and the lesser offender.

In *R. v. Ramolla*[12] the court granted a discharge because a criminal conviction would make it improbable that the accused could go with her

---

[10] *R. v. Vincente* (1975), 18 Crim. L.Q. 292 (Ont. C.A.).
[11] (1975), 23 C.C.C. (2d) 11.
[12] (1975), 18 Crim. L.Q. 18 (Ont. C.A.).

husband, who was being transferred by his employers to a foreign country.

In *R. v. Tschirhart,*[13] an 18-year-old youth appealed a fine of $150 which had been imposed upon the charge of theft of two cassette tape decks with a value of $64.95. The tape decks were recovered later and in a saleable condition. The other youth, with whom he committed the crime, was granted an absolute discharge by another judge. Tschirhart had no prior criminal record, had contributed somewhat to the family's finances and had saved sufficient funds for his school tuition. The court refused to impose an absolute discharge saying that it was not appropriate "since there was insufficient mitigating circumstances surrounding the commission of the offence to warrant an absolute discharge." Accordingly, a conditional discharge with probation for one year was imposed. In *R. v. Martin,*[14] the court imposed a conditional rather than an absolute discharge to "insure that the appellant is kept aware that he committed a criminal offence and must behave himself", *i.e.,* for considerations of personal deterrence.

In *R. v. Cheung and Chow*[15] the Provincial Court judge erred in failing to grant a discharge on a shoplifting offence merely because more than one item of goods were stolen. In its reasons for judgment the court said: "A suspended sentence is not a greater deterrent to youths tempted to steal than a discharge, certainly not a conditional discharge. Speedy apprehension, arrest and trial with the public disgrace and jeopardy which is occasioned should be sufficient deterrent."

The difficulty of deciding whether to disallow a discharge because of the need for general deterrence would be easier to solve if courts would first decide whether or not they in fact believe in general deterrence, and whether there is any evidence to substantiate the notion that it is efficacious.

B. Procedure

Because of the passage of these sections of the Criminal Code, it is now appropriate for a trial judge to first determine the issue of guilt or

---

[13] Unreported, January 14, 1975 (Ont. C.A.).
[14] (1974), 17 C.C.C. (2d) 66 (N.S.C.A.).
[15] (1976), 19 Crim. L.Q. 281 (Ont. C.A.).

innocence and make a finding. If there is a finding of guilt, then the trial judge proceeds to consider whether or not a discharge ought to be granted. If it is not to be granted then and only then can he convict the accused. Nevertheless the use by the trial judge of the words "I convict" do not preclude him from imposing a discharge.[16] Where a trial judge, upon making his finding of guilt, purports to grant a discharge, but nevertheless sentences the accused to pay a fine, the sentence is illegal. Without convicting the accused he cannot impose a fine, and if he convicts he cannot grant a discharge. Where the judge purported to do both, as in *R. v. Leonard*,[17] the court replaced this illegal sentence with a conditional discharge and set aside the imposition of a fine.

C. Deemed Not To Have Been Convicted

Because of the provisions of s. 662.1(3), an accused is deemed not to have been convicted of the offence of which he has been found guilty except for certain limited purposes. In *R. v. Nickerson*,[18] the accused was sentenced to two years' imprisonment, but the principal offender in the crime of theft of money valued at more than $200 was sentenced to six months' imprisonment. The offence was committed after the accused had been sentenced on other charges which resulted in a conditional discharge. The trial judge took that discharge into account in imposing sentence. The Prince Edward Island Court of Appeal said:

> The "previous record" referred to by the Magistrate in sentencing the Appellant to two years in a Federal Penitentiary must relate to the offences to which I have just referred . . . In such circumstances it is our opinion that such pleas of guilty, or a finding of guilt on such pleas do not constitute a previous record because the *Code* specifically provides that such an accused is deemed not to have been convicted.

Accordingly, the Court was unable to find any "good reason" for the wide discrepancy in the sentences imposed; taking into account that he had served five months' imprisonment pending appeal, the Court imposed a term of imprisonment for one month.

---

[16] *R. v. McInnis* (1973), 13 C.C.C. (2d) 471 (Ont. C.A.); *R. v. Sampson* (1975), 23 C.C.C. (2d) 65 (Ont. C.A.).

[17] (1973), 11 C.C.C. (2d) 527 (Ont. C.A.).

[18] (1975), 7 Nfld. & P.E.I. R. 145 (P.E.I.C.A.).

There is as yet no other case on the question of whether or not a discharge can be taken into account on a subsequent sentence and to what extent it can if at all be considered, but in *R. v. Coolin and Losch,* [19] the Ontario Court of Appeal, in sustaining a sentence of imprisonment for one accused despite lowering it for others, justified this disparity by noting that he was "at large on the terms of a conditional discharge". This, it would seem, avoids the problem of taking into account conditional discharge as a conviction, but necessitates penalizing someone instead for breaching the probation with which it is associated. Not only does this involve punishment without trial for breach of a probation order, but it does seem to be a whittling down of the notion that a discharge is quite unlike a conviction. On the other hand, the court is entitled to know and consider as a factor in sentencing whether or not the accused has been responsive to supervision in the past and his potential for reform. A discharge may be deemed not a conviction, but it is not deemed to be secret. There would seem to be no problem, therefore, with informing a court of a previous discharge, if the purpose is not to increase penalty (*i.e.,* treat it like a conviction) but merely to suggest that the case is an inappropriate one for the granting of still another discharge, *i.e.,* is contrary to the public interest.

D. Factors Considered In Assessing "The Best Interests Of The Accused"

Generally speaking, if it appears that the conviction will have an effect on the future of the accused that is disproportionate to the crime itself and all the other statutory requirements are met, the court will grant a discharge.[20] Such future considerations have included possible jeopardy to a career,[21] or difficulty in obtaining or keeping future employment.[22] Accordingly, in *R. v. Meneses,* [23] the accused was fined $100 following a theft of a bottle of vitamins from a drugstore. She was a widow who supported five children and had come from the Phillipines where she had

---

[19] Unreported, July 2, 1975 (Ont. C.A.).
[20] *R. v. Shanab,* unreported, November 22, 1973 (Ont. C.A.).
[21] *R. v. Fallofield* (1973), 13 C.C.C. (2d) 450 (B.C.C.A.).
[22] *R. v. Bateson,* unreported, October 8, 1974 (Ont. C.A.).
[23] (1974), 25 C.C.C. (2d) 115 (Ont. C.A.).

been a practicing dentist. She was intent on resuming the practice of dentistry and qualifying in the Province of Ontario to do so, but it became clear that a conviction for theft might disqualify her in that endeavor. The court held that it was not only in her interest but also in the public interest "for this woman to be given every opportunity to become a useful person in the community and earn a livelihood for herself and her family." Thus a single factor disclosed that the discharge was both in the interest of the accused and not contrary to the public interest.

Similarly, in *R. v. Fallofield*,[24] the fact that the accused was cooperative and friendly and was characterized by a police officer as "rather than being a thief, . . . was more simply a foolish individual" was considered. The age of the accused (16 years), that she was a student, that the crime was committed while she was under emotional stress and possibly undesirable influences and that she had left the family home because of a dispute with her parents were all personal factors that tended towards the grant of a discharge.[25] The discharge provisions cannot be said to be restricted to or even primarily applicable to youthful offenders as distinct from mature offenders.[26]

In *R. v. Taylor*,[27] upon a theft of a pair of sunglasses from a store, it was disclosed that at the time of the offence, Taylor was in the midst of a separation from his wife and under psychiatric care. The court noted that the offence was out of character for him and occurred while he was in the midst of an unusual disturbance in his life's routine. Accordingly a conditional discharge was granted.

In *R. v. Bikker*,[28] the accused was convicted on a charge of unlawfully, with intent to mislead, causing a peace officer to enter upon an investigation by reporting an offence that had not been committed. The accused was 17 years of age and had telephoned the police warning them against the presence of explosives in a public building. The matters reported were figments of his imagination. He had a history of psychological disturbance but appeared to be making progress in a rehabilitation program. The psychiatric report expressed the view that the granting of a discharge would be conducive to the success of the

---

[24] *Supra*, n. 21.
[25] *R. v. McInnis* (1973), 13 C.C.C. (2d) 471 (Ont. C.A.).
[26] *R. v. Culley* (1977), 36 C.C.C. (2d) 433 (Ont. C.A.).
[27] (1975), 24 C.C.C. (2d) 551 (Ont. C.A.).
[28] Unreported, May 22, 1975 (Ont. C.A.).

treatment being offered him. Accordingly a conviction was set aside and a discharge with probationary terms for three years imposed.

E. Factors "Contrary To The Public Interest"

When the court comes to the question of whether or not it is contrary to the public interest to impose a discharge, the factors are equally varied. The seriousness of the crime will be important. In theft cases, the small value of the goods has been noted as a reason for granting a discharge,[29] especially when it is coupled together with an assessment that the theft was the result of a "mental lapse".[30] In *R. v. Sanchez-Pino,*[31] in rejecting the suggestion of a discharge, the court found that the theft

> . . . was not the result of a sudden momentary impulse. She stole a number of articles, from several different places in the store, stuffing them in a shopping bag obviously brought along for the purpose. It was not a matter of momentary forgetfulness, for she did pay for two trivial items, and stole the rest.

The Ontario Court of Appeal has said that, in the case of shoplifting at least, the fact that the theft was an act of impulse and a single isolated incident indicated a discharge was appropriate.[32] Similarly, the fact that the accused admitted responsibility for the theft upon being arrested was one indication that there was no reason to expect a recurrence of such behaviour.[33]

Another factor the court looks to seems to be whether or not to refuse to enter a conviction would encourage an ongoing programme of rehabilitation. In *R. v. McRae*[34] the accused, after having a substantial amount to drink, stole a taxicab in which the driver had left the motor running. In the resulting chase the accused hit four other cars, causing a total of $4,000 damage. He pleaded guilty to a charge of theft over $200 and was sentenced to nine months definite and six months

---

[29] *R. v. Shanab,* unreported, November 22, 1973 (Ont. C.A.); *R. v. Brymer,* unreported, December 18, 1975 (Ont. C.A.).
[30] *R. v. Marcon* (1974), 18 C.C.C. (2d) 575 (Ont. C.A.).
[31] (1973), 11 C.C.C. (2d) 53 at p. 59 (Ont. C.A.).
[32] *R. v. Mann* (1975), 18 Crim. L.Q. 291 (Ont. C.A.).
[33] *R. v. Pace* (1975), 18 Crim. L.Q. 291 (Ont. C.A.).
[34] (1975), 18 Crim. L.Q. 291 (Ont. C.A.).

indeterminate. Though he had no previous convictions he had an unstable family life and had been brought up in 13 foster homes. Since his release on bail the appellant had led an exemplary life, having been steadily employed as an attendant in a gasoline station. The court held that in all the circumstances, society would probably be best served and protected by the granting of a discharge.

The need for deterrence of others is a factor which the court can take into account. In *Sanchez-Pino* the widespread incidence of shoplifting in the community was a factor considered.

That same court, in *R. v. Wood*,[35] allowed a Crown appeal against a conditional discharge together with three years' probation imposed following a plea of guilty to a charge of assault causing bodily harm. The assault was committed without provocation upon a much smaller man and resulted in serious injuries to his face and eyes. Despite an excellent background, and aspirations to be a professional hockey player which would be jeopardized by a conviction, the court took the view that in cases of violence resulting in injury, the requirement of general deterrence to the public militates, in almost every case, against the grant of a conditional discharge, notwithstanding considerations personal to the accused.

This case was distinguished in *R. v. Jover*[36] where "violence" was limited to cases involving hostility between parties. Where in the course of a friendly joke a weapon was pointed unlawfully and as a result a death occurred a conditional discharge was nevertheless granted.

The British Columbia Court of Appeal however, in *R. v. Fallofield*,[37] has said that the public interest in the deterrence of others, while it must be given due weight, does not preclude the judicious use of the discharge provisions. Again, it is submitted that these principles are not necessarily inconsistent.

As an aid in determining whether the second condition exists, courts have on occasion asked themselves whether or not they could believe "that deterrence of others would be in any way diminished by failure to impose a formal conviction."[38]

The fact that the offence can be characterized as being in the nature of a "prank", though not going so far as to be a complete defence, has been

---

[35] (1975), 24 C.C.C. (2d) 79 (Ont. C.A.); *R. v. Gilpin* (1975), 36 C.R.N.S. 363 (Ont. C.A.), *contra R. v. Watson* (1975), 26 C.C.C. (2d) 150 (Ont. Prov. Ct.).
[36] (1977), 41 C.C.C. (2d) 24 (Ont. Prov. Ct.).
[37] (1973), 13 C.C.C. (2d) 450.
[38] *R. v. Martin* (1974), 17 C.C.C. (2d) 66 (N.S.C.A.).

one factor considered in granting a discharge. So has the fact that criminality has been "marginal".[39] Similarly in *R. v. Campbell and Mlynarchuk*,[40] upon a conviction for taking part as a performer in an immoral performance the court took into consideration a reasonable "mistake of law" to the effect that a judge had earlier said, as reported in the newspapers, that "dancing bottomless was permitted in Edmonton".

A minor role in the offence, together with a lack of personal benefit from the fraud committed, are also indicators that a discharge is appropriate.[41] Likewise, an act of vandalism that was "impulsive and childish" was considered appropriate for a discharge.[42]

The fact that there are two charges is not a factor which militates necessarily against the granting of a discharge. In *R. v. McInnis*,[43] a discharge was granted by a court that noted that both offences were committed on the same day and involved a theft of two sweaters from one store and another sweater from another store. On the other hand, in *R. v. Cano*,[44] a discharge was not considered because though there was one charge of fraud, it involved 49 instances of fraudulent acts.

F. Conditional Discharges And Deportation

The possibility or likelihood of deportation in the case of non-citizens has been a factor frequently considered. The present Immigration Act (Immigration Act 1976) permits deportation of landed immigrants if they are convicted of an offence under any Act of Parliament for which a term of imprisonment of more than six months has been imposed or which carries a maximum penalty of five years of more. Non-residents (students, visitors) may be deported if convicted of an offence under the Criminal Code or of an offence that may be punishable by way of indictment under any Act of Parliament.

It is important to note that provisions for deportation are dependent upon a "conviction". Accordingly, if an absolute or conditional discharge is granted, deportation cannot follow.

---

[39] *R. v. White* (1975), 25 C.C.C. (2d) 173 (Ont. C.A.).
[40] (1973), 10 C.C.C. (2d) 26 (Alta. Dist. Ct.).
[41] *R. v. Cvitko*, unreported, May 28, 1976 (Ont. C.A.).
[42] *R. v. Martin, supra,* n. 38.
[43] (1973), 13 C.C.C. (2d) 471 (Ont. C.A.).
[44] Unreported, June 23, 1975 (Ont. C.A.).

In *R. v. Melo*,[45] the accused and a friend went into three stores and stole several items of very little value. The court held that the fact that a convicted shoplifter may be in jeopardy under the Immigration Act is not in itself sufficient ground for the granting of a discharge, but is only one of the factors which may be considered by the trial judge; the Immigration Appeal Board has the power to alleviate any undue hardship.

In *R. v. Melo,* the court considered *R. v. Fung*[46] and its own previous decisions in *Shanab* and in *Papadopoulos and Kalafatis.* The latter case, unreported, involved two Greek nationals who had been drinking heavily when they stole a number of items from a supermarket in a clumsy manner. In that case again the court took the view that the gravity of the consequences was so disproportionate to the offence committed that the case was "one of the rare occasions where a conditional discharge should be granted". The court said: "In a case where clearly on the facts disclosed a discharge would not be granted, the fact that the convicted person may be subject to deportation is not sufficient to 'tip the scales' the other way and lead to the granting of a discharge". It concluded: "On the other hand, this offence was not a single isolated act, nor committed on impulse, nor at a time when the appellant was emotionally upset or under the influence of either drugs or alcohol (I use these illustrations having in mind some other cases that have come before the Court)."

The Ontario Court of Appeal seems to take the view that deportation is a factor related primarily to the question of whether a discharge is "in the best interests of the accused". The Alberta Court of Appeal, in *R. v. Fung,* had before it an appeal from sentence to a fine of $75 for shoplifting. The appellant was on a student visa from Hong Kong and if the conviction stood he might have had difficulties remaining in Canada. The Court said:

> The appellant is in Canada not as of right but as a privilege. We do not think the section should be applied in order to influence the immigration authorities; in fact to the contrary, we think the immigration authorities are entitled to know that the appellant has committed the offence and to take such into consideration in coming to a decision whether the appellant should be allowed to remain in Canada.[47]

---

[45] (1975), 30 C.R.N.S. 328 (Ont. C.A.).
[46] (1973), 11 C.C.C. (2d) 195 (Alta. C.A.).
[47] At p. 196.

It is respectfully submitted that this is wrong. There is no judicial authority for a court on sentence to refuse to exhaust its jurisdiction by acting in such a way as to refer the matter to the Immigration Department. Courts are to impose the proper sentence having regard to all the facts, including a consideration of the possibility of deportation for whatever weight it might have. If Parliament wished all immigrants who were found guilty of offences and given discharges to be subject to deportation, it would be simple enough to amend the Immigration Act to achieve that result. The fact that Parliament has not done so, leads to the conclusion that courts have freedom to consider and give appropriate weight to any unjust hardship that might result from a conviction, and there is no warrant whatever at common law or by statute for excepting the possibility of deportation from this broad statutory mandate.

However, the Ontario Court of Appeal in a more recent decision seems to have retreated from the doctrine in *R. v. Melo* so far as they can without overruling it. In *R. v. Cheung and Chow,*[48] *obiter dicta,* the Court said that if a case were indeed borderline, deportation would then be a factor to consider on the issue whether or not the granting of a discharge was contrary to the public interest.

In any event, the Alberta Court of Appeal, after considering and distinguishing its own previous decision in *R. v. Fung* seemed to make a distinction without a difference. In *R. v. Wing Shee Au Yeung,*[49] the accused stole a necklace worth $8 from a department store. She was a student from Hong Kong who was enrolled at the University of Alberta. She married a Canadian citizen and the Court noted that if she had a criminal conviction in this matter she would be ineligible to become a landed immigrant. The general policy, they noted, of the Immigration Department was to deport such persons. The Court said that the *Fung* case was distinguishable as in this case the discharge was not being sought to influence the immigration authorities. Here, a strain would be imposed on her marriage because her husband's occupation required him to travel frequently to other countries. Such a result would be out of all proportion to the seriousness of the offence. Accordingly, they ordered a discharge.

It would appear that if one is merely being deported (even if deportation is to a country where one will be killed or will starve to death) deportation is not relevant; however, the sanctity of marriage is such that if as a result of the deportation the marriage would be

---

[48] (1976), 19 Crim. L.Q. 281.
[49] (1976), 19 Crim. L.Q. 22.

disrupted, then by all means a discharge may be given. Thus the courts do indirectly what they will not do directly. A similar approach was taken by the Ontario Court of Appeal in *R. v. Ramolla.*[50]

G. Appeal

It is now clear that upon an appeal from sentence, and probably upon appeal from conviction as well, a Court of Appeal may exercise jurisdiction to remove the conviction and substitute a discharge.[51]

Despite the awkward wording of s. 662.1(3)(a), an appeal against the discharge order is an appeal against sentence, thus requiring leave from the Court of Appeal for either party, but not requiring the Crown to show an error in law as it must in the case of an appeal against a conviction.[52]

H. Expunging Of A Discharge Record

The Criminal Records Act:

2(2) This Act applies to a person who has been granted an absolute or conditional discharge under section 662.1 of the *Criminal Code* as if he had been convicted of the offence in respect of which the discharge was granted except that where the discharge was granted in respect of an offence punishable on summary conviction in proceedings under Part XXIV of the *Criminal Code,* the inquiries referred to in subsection 4(2) may be made if one year has elapsed from

    (a) the date on which the discharge was granted, in the case of an absolute discharge, and

    (b) the date of termination of the period of probation in the case of a conditional discharge,

---

[50] (1975), 18 Crim. L.Q. 18.

[51] *R. v. Sanchez-Pino* (1973), 11 C.C.C. (2d) 53 (Ont. C.A.), distinguishing *R. v. Stafrace* (1972), 10 C.C.C. (2d) 181 (Ont. C.A.); *R. v. Christman* (1973), 22 C.R.N.S. 338 (Alta. C.A.); *R. v. Fallofield* (1973), 13 C.C.C. (2d) 450 (B.C.C.A.).

[52] *Miles v. The Queen* (1976), 33 C.R.N.S. 265 (S.C.C.).

and where the discharge was granted in respect of any other offence or in proceedings other than proceedings under Part XXIV of the *Criminal Code*, the inquiries referred to in subsection 4(2) may be made if three years have elapsed from whichever of the dates referred to in paragraphs (*a*) and (*b*) is appropriate.

(3) The terms "conviction" and "convicted", where they appear throughout this Act, shall be read so as to give effect to subsection (2).

The unfortunate implication of this legislation is that records may be kept of discharges in the same way as they are kept for criminal records, so that the much heralded difference and divergence between the two becomes less significant. As His Honour Judge Swabey argues, in a sensitive annotation,[53] this to some extent defeats the whole purpose of the concept of conditional and absolute discharges in lieu of conviction. One resulting anomaly is that a person sentenced to a fine of $25 for possession of marijuana on summary conviction can apply for a pardon to "lock up" his conviction pursuant to the Criminal Records Act after two years; an offender who is treated more "leniently" and given a conditional discharge for a period of two years, will not be eligible for the same procedure until three years after the date of his court hearing. This raises the very serious question of who in fact is treated more leniently and who is suffering as a result of the court disposition. Accordingly, as Judge Swabey suggests, this legislation "is bound to be misleading to many and sure to hold out false promise to some."

Discharges have been given where the offence is "trivial",[54] committed on the spur of the moment,[55] "childish" and "not premeditated",[56] the result of a "mental lapse" or of borderline criminality.[57] Previous criminal conviction is not a bar to the granting of a discharge.[58]

I. Impaired Driving

Amendments which received Royal Assent on March 30, 1976 (not yet

---

[53] "Absolute and Conditional Discharges under the Criminal Code", 20 C.R.N.S. 132.
[54] *R. v. Stafrace* (1972), 10 C.C.C. (2d) 181 (Ont. C.A.).
[55] *R. v. Bennett,* unreported, November 5, 1973 (Ont. C.A.).
[56] *R. v. Martin* (1974), 17 C.C.C. (2d) 66 (N.S.C.A.).
[57] *R. v. White* (1975), 25 C.C.C. (2d) 173 (Ont. C.A.).
[58] *R. v. Charles,* unreported, December 15, 1976 (B.C.C.A.).

proclaimed in force in all provinces) to s. 234 of the Criminal Code relate to impaired driving. They provide that notwithstanding s. 662.1(1), a person found guilty of impaired driving may be discharged rather than convicted upon conditions in a probation order. These may include a condition respecting his attendance for "curative treatment in relation to his consumption of alcohol or drugs" if, after hearing medical or other evidence, the court considers that the accused is in need of such curative treatment and that it would not be contrary to the public interest to make such an order. Similar provision is made for the offence of driving with more than 80 mg of alcohol in 100 ml blood.

J. Provincial Offences

It has been decided by two county court judges that the discharge provisions do not apply to provincial offences.[59] Most provincial summary conviction acts for example, the Summary Conviction Act of Ontario,[60] incorporate by reference the parts of the Criminal Code which include s. 720(1). There seems to be no reason in principle why this provision would be inconsistent with the existing provincial sentencing options. Indeed, in *R. v. Trow*[61] a single judge of the British Columbia Supreme Court decided that pursuant to the terms of the British Columbia summary conviction statute, discharges were available in summary conviction offences where no minimum penalty was provided.

K. Royal Prerogative Of Mercy

The Criminal Records Act:

> 2(1) In this Act
> "Board" means the National Parole Board;

---

[59] *R. v. Gower* (1973), 10 C.C.C. (2d) 543 (N.S. Co. Ct.); *R. v. Rendall* (1974), 21 C.C.C. (2d) 253 (Ont. Dist. Ct.).
[60] R.S.O. 1970, c. 450, s. 3.
[61] (1977), 38 C.C.C. (2d) 229.

"Commissioner" means the Commissioner of the Royal Canadian Mounted Police;

"Minister" means the Solicitor General of Canada;

"pardon" means a pardon granted by the Governor in Council under subsection 4(5);

"period of probation" means a period during which a person convicted of an offence was directed by the court that convicted him to be released upon his own recognizance to keep the peace and be of good behaviour, or to be released upon or comply with the conditions prescribed in a probation order, which period shall be deemed to have terminated at the time the recognizance or the probation order, as the case may be, ceased to be in force.

(2) This Act applies to a person who has been granted an absolute or conditional discharge under section 662.1 of the *Criminal Code* as if he had been convicted of the offence in respect of which the discharge was granted except that where the discharge was granted in respect of an offence punishable on summary conviction in proceedings under Part XXIV of the *Criminal Code*, the inquiries referred to in subsection 4(2) may be made if one year has elapsed from

(a) the date on which the discharge was granted, in the case of an absolute discharge, and

(b) the date of termination of the the period of probation in the case of a conditional discharge,

and where the discharge was granted in respect of any other offence or in proceedings other than proceedings under Part XXIV of the *Criminal Code*, the inquiries referred to in subsection 4(2) may be made if three years have elapsed from whichever of the dates referred to in paragraphs (a) and (b) is appropriate.

(3) The terms "conviction" and "convicted", where they appear throughout this Act, shall be read so as to give effect to subsection (2).

3. *Application for pardon* — A person who has been convicted of an offence under an Act of the Parliament of Canada or a regulation made thereunder may make application for a pardon in respect of that offence.

4. *Procedure* — (1) An application for a pardon shall be made to the Minister, who shall refer it to the Board.

(2) The Board shall cause proper inquiries to be made in order to ascertain the behaviour of the applicant since the date of his conviction, but such inquiries shall not be made

(a) where the applicant was convicted of an offence punishable on summary conviction in proceedings under Part XXIV of the *Criminal Code*, until, in the case of the imposition on the applicant of

   (i)   a sentence of imprisonment,

   (ii) a period of probation, or

   (iii) a fine,

two years have elapsed since the termination of the sentence of imprisonment, the termination of the period of probation or the payment of the fine, as the case may be, or in the case of the imposition on the applicant of

(iv) a period of probation in addition to a sentence of imprisonment,

(v) a period of probation in addition to a fine, or

(vi) a fine in addition to a sentence of imprisonment,

two years have elapsed since the later of the termination of the sentence of imprisonment, the termination of the period of probation or the payment of the fine, as the case may be; or

(b) in any other case, until five years have elapsed since the date from which the two year period provided in paragraph (a) would have been computed, if that paragraph had been applicable to the applicant.

(3) For the purposes of this section, in calculating the period of any sentence of imprisonment imposed on an applicant there shall be included, in addition to any time spent by him in custody pursuant to that sentence, any period of statutory remission granted to him in respect thereof.

(4) Upon completion of its inquiries, the Board shall report the result thereof to the Minister with its recommendation as to whether a pardon should be granted but, if the Board proposes to recommend that a pardon should not be granted, it shall, before making such a recommendation, forthwith so notify the applicant and advise him that he is entitled to make any representations to the Board that he believes relevant; and the Board shall consider any oral or written representations made to it by or on behalf of the applicant within a reasonable time after any such notice is given and before making a report under this subsection.

(5) Upon receipt of a recommendation from the Board that a pardon should be granted, the Minister shall refer the recommendation to the Governor in Council who may grant the pardon which shall be in the form set out in the schedule.

5. *Effect of grant of pardon* — The grant of a pardon

(a) is evidence of the fact that the Board, after making proper inquiries, was satisfied that an applicant was of good behaviour and that the conviction in respect of which the pardon is granted should no longer reflect adversely on his character; and

(b) unless the pardon is subsequently revoked, vacates the conviction in respect of which it is granted and, without restricting the generality of the foregoing, removes any disqualification to which the person so convicted is, by reason of such conviction, subject by virtue of any Act of the Parliament of Canada or a regulation made thereunder.

6. *Custody of records* — (1) The Minister may by order in writing addressed to any person having the custody or control of any judicial record of a conviction in respect of which a pardon has been granted, require that person to deliver such record into the custody of the Commissioner.

(2) Any record of a conviction in respect of which a pardon has been granted that is in the custody of the Commissioner or of any department or agency of the Government of Canada shall be kept separate and apart from other criminal records, and no such record shall be disclosed to any person, nor shall the existence of the record or the fact of the conviction be disclosed to any person, without the prior approval of the Minister who shall, before granting such approval, satisfy himself that the disclosure is desirable in the interests of the administration of justice or for any purpose related to the safety or security of Canada or any state allied or associated with Canada.

7. *Revocation* — A pardon may be revoked by the Governor in Council

(a) if the person to whom it is granted is subsequently convicted of a further offence under an Act of the Parliament of Canada or a regulation made thereunder; or

(b) upon evidence establishing to the satisfaction of the Governor in Council

   (i)   that the person to whom it was granted is no longer of good conduct, or

   (ii)   that such person knowingly made a false or deceptive statement in relation to his application for the pardon, or knowingly concealed some material particular in relation to such application.

8. *General* — No application form for or relating to

(a) employment in any department as defined in section 2 of the *Financial Administration Act,*

(b) employment by any Crown corporation as defined in Part VIII of the *Financial Administration Act,*

(c) enrolment in the Canadian Forces, or

(d) employment upon or in connection with the operation of any work, undertaking or business that is within the legislative authority of the Parliament of Canada,

shall contain any question that by its terms requires the applicant to disclose a conviction in respect of which he has been granted a pardon that has not been revoked.

9. Nothing in this Act in any manner limits or affects the provisions of the *Criminal Code,* or of the Letters Patent Constituting the Office of Governor General of Canada, relating to pardons, except that sections 6 and 8 apply in respect of any pardon granted either before or after the commencement of this Act pursuant to any authority conferred by those provisions.

10. *Offences* — Any person who violates any provision of this Act is guilty of an offence punishable on summary conviction.

The Criminal Code provides:

683(1) Her Majesty may extend the royal mercy to a person who is sentenced to imprisonment under the authority of an Act of the Parliament of Canada, even if the person is imprisoned for failure to pay money to another person.

(2) The Governor in Council may grant a free pardon or a conditional pardon to any person who has been convicted of an offence.

(3) Where the Governor in Council grants a free pardon to a person, that person shall be deemed thereafter never to have committed the offence in respect of which the pardon is granted.

(4) No free pardon or conditional pardon prevents or mitigates the punishment to which the person might otherwise be lawfully sentenced on a subsequent conviction for an offence other than that for which the pardon was granted.

685(1) The Governor in Council may order the remission, in whole or in part, of a pecuniary penalty, fine or forfeiture imposed under an Act of the Parliament of Canada, whoever the person may be to whom it is payable or however it may be recoverable.

(2) An order for remission under subsection (1) may include the remission of costs incurred in the proceedings, but no costs to which a private prosecutor is entitled shall be remitted.

686. Nothing in this Act in any manner limits or affects Her Majesty's royal prerogative of mercy.

In *R. v. Lord*[62] the English Court of Appeal, interpreting a section identical to our own setting out powers of the Court of Appeal to deal with an appeal from sentence, noted that once a sentence of death had been commuted to one of life imprisonment no appeal lay from that sentence. The reasoning is that the sentence of death originally pronounced is one "fixed by law" and there was therefore no appeal to the Court of Appeal; the royal prerogative of mercy having operated so as to reduce this sentence, any subsequent proceedings were merely the machinery for carrying into effect the commuted sentence. There is of course no appeal against a decision granting the royal prerogative of mercy or any order made in consequence of that decision.

In *Reference re Effect of Exercise of Royal Prerogative of Mercy Upon Deportation Proceedings,*[63] the Supreme Court of Canada approved a passage from Dicey:[64]

"The 'prerogative' appears to be historically and as a matter of actual fact nothing else than the residue of discretionary or arbitrary authority, which at any given time is legally left in the hands of the Crown. The King was originally in truth what he still is in name, 'the sovereign,' or, if not strictly

---

[62] (1908), 1 Cr. App. R. 110.
[63] [1933] S.C.R. 269 at pp. 272-73.
[64] *Law of Constitution,* 8th ed. at p. 420.

the 'sovereign' in the sense in which jurists use that word, at any rate by far the most powerful part of the sovereign power."

The Court held that an unconditional pardon of an offence can take effect whether or not there is acceptance by the person to whom the pardon is granted. Accordingly, a convict under sentence of death could not, in point of law, insist on his right to be hanged.

A free pardon, or a pardon under the Great Seal:

> if general in its purport and sufficient in other respects, obliterates every stain which the law attached to the offender. Generally speaking, it puts him in the same situation as that in which he stood before he committed the pardoned offence; and frees him from the penalties and forfeitures to which the law subjected his person and property.[65]

In *R. v. Spring*[66] the Ontario Court of Appeal had before it an accused who had been pardoned for an earlier offence; they treated him as a first offender, "because we think the statute gives us this discretion in these circumstances". It is hard to imagine how the discretion could be exercised otherwise, in view of the clear language of s. 5, which provides that previous convictions "should no longer reflect adversely on . . . character". Indeed, it is strange that the Court was even informed of the earlier offence.

---

[65] *Reference re Effect of Exercise of Royal Prerogative, supra*, n. 63 at p. 278. A short but excellent discussion of the Royal Prerogative of Mercy can be found in *Tremeear's Annotated Criminal Code*, 6th ed., L. J. Ryan, ed., at pp. 1219 *et seq.*

[66] (1977), 35 C.C.C. (2d) 308.

Chapter 10

Suspended Sentence And Probation

A. The Suspended Sentence

The history of the suspended sentence has been discussed in an annotation by Eric Armour, K.C.,[1] as he then was, in some detail and there is little point in repeating it here. It is important to note that it is not the sentence itself, but its passing, that is suspended. Therefore a court cannot set a fixed term and thereafter suspend it, as the English statute and practice permits. Indeed a court should not even mention any fixed term of proposed imprisonment for to do so might place the court in the position of binding itself should the accused subsequently be brought before that court for sentence.[2]

Consequently it is improper to impose a fine and then release an accused on "suspended sentence". Sentence can be suspended only if the sentencing court decides not to impose a fine or imprisonment at that time.[3] If it is desired to either fine or imprison the accused and have him on probation as well, then s. 663(1)(b) of the Criminal Code must be invoked and not 663(1)(a).

It is doubtful whether there is any power in a criminal court to merely

---

[1] 46 C.C.C. 98.

[2] *R. v. Sangster* (1973), 21 C.R.N.S. 339 (Que. C.A.); *R. v. Tippett, Ex p. Morris* (1955), 112 C.C.C. 47 (N.B.C.A.); *R. v. Blain* (1950), 99 C.C.C. 152 (Sask. C.A.); *R. v. Giffen* (1959), 125 C.C.C. 113 (Ont. C.A.); *R. v. Switzki* (1930), 54 C.C.C. 332 (Sask. C.A.).

[3] *R. v. Beam* (1954), 19 C.R. 367 (Ont. C.A.); *R. v. Stokkeland* (1960), 33 C.R. 265 (B.C. Co. Ct.).

suspend the passing of sentence, without at the same time directing that an order of probation be entered into.[4] Certainly no such power is given expressly in the Criminal Code.

In any event, in the case of a criminal offence sentence cannot be suspended until there has been an adjudication of guilt.[5]

The Criminal Code states:

> 663(1) Where an accused is convicted of an offence the court may, having regard to the age and character of the accused, the nature of the offence and the circumstances surrounding its commission,
>
> (*a*) in the case of an offence other than one for which a minimum punishment is prescribed by law, suspend the passing of sentence and direct that the accused be released upon the conditions prescribed in a probation order;
>
> (*b*) in addition to fining the accused or sentencing him to imprisonment, whether in default of payment of a fine or otherwise, for a term not exceeding two years, direct that the accused comply with the conditions prescribed in a probation order; or
>
> (*c*) where it imposes a sentence of imprisonment on the accused, whether in default of payment of a fine or otherwise, that does not exceed ninety days, order that the sentence be served intermittently at such times as are specified in the order and direct that the accused, at all times when he is not in confinement pursuant to such order, comply with the conditions prescribed in a probation order.
>
> (2) The following conditions shall be deemed to be prescribed in a probation order, namely, that the accused shall keep the peace and be of good behaviour and shall appear before the court when required to do so by the court, and, in addition, the court may prescribe as conditions in a probation order that the accused shall do any one or more of the following things as specified in the order, namely,
>
> (*a*) report to and be under the supervision of a probation officer or other person designated by the court;
>
> (*b*) provide for the support of his spouse or any other dependents whom he is liable to support;
>
> (*c*) abstain from the consumption of alcohol either absolutely or on such terms as the court may specify;
>
> (*d*) abstain from owning, possessing or carrying a weapon;
>
> (*e*) make restitution or reparation to any person aggrieved or injured by the commission of the offence for the actual loss or damage sustained by that person as a result thereof;

---

[4] *R. v. Silverstone* (1925), 44 C.C.C. 335 (Que. C.A.); *Laplante v. Court of Sessions of the Peace,* [1938] 1 D.L.R. 364 (Que.).
[5] *R. v. White* (1915), 34 O.L.R. 370.

(*f*) remain within the jurisdiction of the court and notify the court or the probation officer or other person designated under paragraph (*a*) of any change in his address or his employment or occupation;

(*g*) make reasonable efforts to find and maintain suitable employment; and

(*h*) comply with such other reasonable conditions as the court considers desirable for securing the good conduct of the accused and for preventing a repetition by him of the same offence or the commission of other offences.

(3) A probation order may be in Form 44, and the court that makes the probation order shall specify therein the period for which it is to remain in force.

(4) Where the court makes a probation order, it shall

(*a*) cause the order to be read by or to the accused;

(*b*) cause a copy of the order to be given to the accused; and

(*c*) inform the accused of the provisions of subsection 664(4) and the provisions of section 666.

664(1) A probation order comes into force

(*a*) on the date on which the order is made, or

(*b*) where the accused is sentenced to imprisonment under paragraph 663(1)(*b*) otherwise than in default of payment of a fine, upon the expiration of that sentence.

(2) Subject to subsection (4),

(*a*) where an accused who is bound by a probation order is convicted of an offence, including an offence under section 666, or is imprisoned under paragraph 663(1)(*b*) in default of payment of a fine, the order continues in force except in so far as the sentence renders it impossible for the accused for the time being to comply with the order; and

(*b*) no probation order shall continue in force for more than three years from the date on which the order came into force.

(3) Where a court has made a probation order, the court may at any time, upon application by the accused or the prosecutor, require the accused to appear before it and, after hearing the accused and the prosecutor,

(*a*) make any changes in or additions to the conditions prescribed in the order that in the opinion of the court are rendered desirable by a change in the circumstances since the conditions were prescribed,

(*b*) relieve the accused, either absolutely or upon such terms or for such period as the court deems desirable, of compliance with any condition described in any of paragraphs 663(2)(*a*) to (*h*) that is prescribed in the order, or

(*c*) decrease the period for which the probation order is to remain in force,

and the court shall thereupon endorse the probation order accordingly and, if it changes or adds to the conditions prescribed in the order, inform the accused of its action and give him a copy of the order so endorsed.

(4) Where an accused who is bound by a probation order is convicted of an offence, including an offence under section 666, and

> (*a*) the time within which an appeal may be taken against that conviction has expired and he has not taken an appeal,
>
> (*b*) he has taken an appeal against that conviction and the appeal has been dismissed, or
>
> (*c*) he has given written notice to the court that convicted him that he elects not to appeal his conviction or has abandoned his appeal, as the case may be,

in addition to any punishment that may be imposed for that offence the court that made the probation order may, upon application by the prosecutor, require the accused to appear before it and, after hearing the prosecutor and the accused,

> (*d*) where the probation order was made under paragraph 663(1)(*a*), revoke the order and impose any sentence that could have been imposed if the passing of sentence had not been suspended, or
>
> (*e*) make such changes in or additions to the conditions prescribed in the order as the court deems desirable or extend the period for which the order is to remain in force for such period, not exceeding one year, as the court deems desirable,

and the court shall thereupon endorse the probation order accordingly and, if it changes or adds to the conditions prescribed in the order or extends the period for which the order is to remain in force, inform the accused of its action and give him a copy of the order so endorsed.

(5) The provisions of Parts XIV and XV with respect to compelling the appearance of an accused before a justice apply *mutatis mutandis* to proceedings under subsections (3) and (4).

665(1) Where an accused who is bound by a probation order becomes a resident of, or is convicted of an offence including an offence under section 666 in a territorial division, other than the territorial division where the order was made, the court that made the order may, upon the application of the prosecutor, and, if both such territorial divisions are not in the same province, with the consent of

> (*a*) the Attorney General of Canada, in the case of proceedings in relation to an offence that were instituted at the instance of the Government of Canada and conducted by or on behalf of that Government, or
>
> (*b*) in any other case, the Attorney General of the province in which the order was made,

transfer the order to a court in that other territorial division that would, having regard to the mode of trial of the accused, have had jurisdiction to make the order in that other territorial division if the accused had been tried and convicted there of the offence in respect of which the order was made, and the order may thereafter be dealt with and enforced by the court to which it is so transferred in all respects as if that court had made the order.

(2) Where a court that has made a probation order or to which a probation order has been transferred pursuant to subsection (1) is for any reason unable to act, the powers of that court in relation to the probation order may be exercised by any other court that has equivalent jurisdiction in the same province.

666(1) An accused who is bound by a probation order and who wilfully fails or refuses to comply with that order is guilty of an offence punishable on summary conviction.

(2) An accused who is charged with an offence under subsection (1) may be tried and punished by any court having jurisdiction to try that offence in the place where the offence is alleged to have been committed or in the place where the accused is found, is arrested or is in custody, but where the place where the accused is found, is arrested or is in custody is outside the province in which the offence is alleged to have been committed, no proceedings in respect of that offence shall be instituted in that place without the consent of the Attorney General of such province.

667. For the purposes of sections 662 to 666, "court" means

(*a*) a superior court of criminal jurisdiction,

(*b*) a court of criminal jurisdiction,

(*c*) a justice or magistrate acting as a summary conviction court under Part XXIV, or

(*d*) a court that hears an appeal.

There are three situations whereby, pursuant to the present Criminal Code, a person may be directed to comply with the conditions of a probation order: when the passing of sentence is suspended; when the sentence is either a fine or a term of imprisonment not exceeding two years; and as part of a conditional discharge.

B. When Probation Is Appropriate

Whether consequent upon a suspended sentence, a conditional discharge, or upon a fine or imprisonment, it is the probation order which in fact provides the period of control and supervision which is the essence of this form of sentence.

In deciding whether or not to impose a probation order the court is required to have regard to a number of factors, among them the nature of the offence and the circumstances surrounding its commission. Some offences by their nature are unlikely to be suitable for a probation order; they are too serious. Almost identical language has been used with regard to such charges as robbery, rape and manslaughter:

> While there may be exceptional circumstances when the suspending of sentence on a conviction for manslaughter may be justified, these exceptional circumstances do not exist in the present case. . . .
>
> . . .
>
> . . . the suspending of the passing of sentence is likely to be construed by the public as an indication that the courts do not take a serious view of a manslaughter conviction.[6]

The circumstances of the offence are most relevant. In *R. v. Linda,*[7] the accused was convicted of contributing to the delinquency of a minor girl by having sexual relations with her. The court examined the circumstances in detail and found that though her age was 15 years she was thoroughly sexually experienced and had been the aggressor "in a most bold manner". Accordingly, the court replaced a period of imprisonment with a probation order.

Similarly, the court must have regard to the age and character of the accused. In *R. v. Brookes,*[8] the court disapproved the probation order upon this ground. The accused had earlier been convicted of six previous offences and the court noted that he had received a suspended sentence on five occasions, and had been committed to jail for only 15 days in total: "This experience seems to us to be an abuse of the practice of awarding a suspended sentence in proper circumstances."

In one older case, the fact that the accused had earlier been released on probation on a single occasion was sufficient to militate against a further order of that nature.[9] However, if the previous probation has not had conditions that were helpful then this may be itself a reason for imposing a further term of probation at a later date which will contain such conditions.[10]

---

[6] *R. v. Smith* (1973), 25 C.R.N.S. 350 at p. 353 (Sask. C.A.); see also *R. v. Shanower* (1972), 8 C.C.C. (2d) 527 (Ont. C.A.); *R. v. Calder* (1956), 114 C.C.C. 155 (Man. C.A.).

[7] (1924), 24 C.C.C. 110 (Alta.).

[8] [1970] 4 C.C.C. 377 (Ont. C.A.).

[9] *R. v. Backshall* (1956), 115 C.C.C. 221 (Ont. C.A.), a case of indecent assault on a young girl.

[10] *R. v. McMullen,* unreported, March 2, 1978 (Ont. C.A.).

In *R. v. Dawdy*,[11] a sophisticated theft was committed by a man who had a very formidable record of previous convictions: "The question of probation for this man is, of course, quite immaterial; he is not the proper type for probation."

In *R. v. McCormick*,[12] the court took the view that the probation services would not be able to deal with a man such as McCormick, who had an extensive record of prior convictions and was 54 years of age. Accordingly, that part of the sentence which provided for probation was struck from the imprisonment imposed. However, quite often there is simply no need for probation at all. In *R. v. Taylor*[13] the court noted that the accused was of dull normal intelligence, working part-time and that therefore a term of probation was "neither necessary nor appropriate".

C. The Purpose And Effect Of A Probation Order

The most obvious use of a probation order is in the case of young first offenders who have committed crimes that are not too serious. In *R. v. Stein*,[14] the court stated that before imposing a custodial sentence upon a first offender the sentencing court should explore the other dispositions which are open to it and only impose a custodial sentence where the circumstances are such, or the offence is of such gravity that no other sentence can be appropriate. In that case, upon a plea of guilty to 13 charges of obtaining property by false pretenses, namely cash and merchandise, by means of cheques which were dishonoured for want of sufficient funds, the Court of Appeal quashed a period of imprisonment imposed upon a 29-year-old married woman with two children, and imposed a term of probation for one year with provision for restitution.

Similarly, in *R. v. Denholm*,[15] the County Court Judge said:

> To my mind the balance should shift heavily to the welfare of the offender at the time of his first appearance in open Court and there is considerable to be said for it remaining on that side of the scale on a second or perhaps even a

---

[11] (1973), 12 C.C.C. (2d) 477 (Ont. C.A.); *R. v. Doughty* (1978), 40 C.C.C. (2d) 224 (P.E.I.C.A.).

[12] Unreported, October 29, 1974 (Ont. C.A.).

[13] (1977), 19 Crim. L.Q. 279 (Ont. C.A.).

[14] (1974), 15 C.C.C. (2d) 376 (Ont. C.A.); *R. v. Bates* (1977), 32 C.C.C. (2d) 493 (Ont. C.A.).

[15] (1970), 11 C.R.N.S. at p. 380, affirmed 11 C.R.N.S. 380 (Sask. C.A.).

third occasion. For at such early stages of detection of criminal ways what can be more important than endèavouring to show the individual that it is in his best interests to change his methods and lead a useful and meaningful life.

The object of the sections dealing with probation is to ensure that appropriate persons convicted of criminal offences be given an opportunity to rehabilitate themselves, without being sent to prison, through the supervision of probation officers and the convicting court.[16] The value of probation lies in the fact that it is a restraint upon the freedom of the accused through supervised control and the realization that the breach of probation would likely lead to a term of imprisonment.[17]

It is submitted that the principal virtue of probation lies not in probation itself, but in the contrast which it provides to the inflexibility of imprisonment, and the impersonal nature of the fine. For example, in *R. v. Doucet,*[18] upon a charge of indecent assault upon a young boy a psychiatric opinion to the effect that the accused was a pedophile with a favourable prognosis provided he continued in therapy for a year was given. The majority of the court noted that the sentencing judge was required to make a very difficult decision, and declined to interfere with a jail sentence:

> . . . since our penal system does not make provision for the cure of persons afflicted in the same way as the appellant, but rather simply provides a place of incarceration. Had I been in the Judge's position, I might very well have come to the conclusion that the interests of society in the end analysis would be better served by a term of probation in which treatment could be administered and that incarceration would be unnecessary.

Accordingly, the accused was sentenced to imprisonment for two years less a day definite and two years less a day indeterminate. Brooke J.A., dissenting, came to the conclusion that under the circumstances of this case there was error in that the sentence unduly emphasized the possible deterrence of other unfortunate persons like the appellant. He concluded: "If a sentence to jail is a deterrent, then surely the threat of jail by reason of breach of probation is equally a deterrent and would ensure in this case fulfilment of the terms of the order suggested."

It would seem that where a great deterrent (supposing for the purpose

---

[16] *R. v. McGowan* (1970), 75 W.W.R. 481 (B.C.); affirmed [1971] 5 W.W.R. 279 (C.A.).

[17] *R. v. Marcello* (1973), 11 C.C.C. (2d) 302 (Ont. C.A.).

[18] (1970), 2 C.C.C. (2d) 433 at p. 434 *per* Gale C.J.O.

of argument, that jail in fact deters) is needed, the probation order will not serve; but it would be better to avoid discussing deterrence and speak, instead, directly in terms of the protection of the public. There are offenders from whom the public cannot be protected except through imprisonment. Conversely, where community supervision may offer that protection, the probation order is a suitable and much less expensive device.

D. Unlawful Delegation

Because of the express language in the Criminal Code fixing the trial court with the responsibility for imposing sentence, this power cannot be delegated to a probation officer. Accordingly, in *R. v. Beam,*[19] a term of the probation order "that during the period of probation he will from time to time promptly and faithfully obey the directions of the Probation Officer as to his habits of life and mode of living . . ." was held to constitute an unlawful delegation. Since the power to decide these questions rests with the magistrate, he must exercise that power himself.

Nevertheless, it is clear that from time to time that same Ontario Court of Appeal, differently constituted, has either not followed its own precept, or has permitted a more limited delegation under different circumstances. The Court is not often referred to the *Beam* case. For example, in *R. v. Stein,*[20] the Court of Appeal itself imposed a condition "that during the period of her probation she will make such payments by way of restitution from time to time as her probation officer considers that she is reasonably capable of making".

In *R. v. Stennes*[21] the trial judge imposed a condition that the appellant stay within the province unless permission to leave was granted by a probation officer. The court found this to be an improper delegation and suggested that if the appellant wanted to leave the province he should apply to the court for permission to do so. And in *R. v. Siple,*[22] the court imposed the most incredible delegation to be found in the cases. An order

---

[19] (1954), 19 C.R. 367 (Ont. C.A.).
[20] (1974), 15 C.C.C. (2d) 376 (Ont. C.A.); *R. v. Bates* (1977), 32 C.C.C. (2d) 493 (Ont. C.A.).
[21] (1975), 35 C.R.N.S. 123 (B.C.C.A.).
[22] Unreported, February 9, 1973 (Ont. C.A.).

of probation was imposed which was to contain "the conditions in s. 663 and such other provisions as fixed from time to time by the probation officer". It is respectfully submitted that this is clearly unlawful.

E. The Certainty Requirement

Common sense alone indicates that a probation order, like any other court order must be reasonably certain in order to be valid or enforceable. In *R. v. Doiron,*[23] the probation order contained conditions, *inter alia,* as follows:

(1) That he must notify John William Shea promptly of any change of address or occupation;

(2) That he must ask permission of John William Shea if he wishes for any reason to leave the town where he resides;

(3) That he must work under the supervision of John William Shea;

. . .

(5) That he must reside within the jurisdiction of this Court with the exception of employment out of town.

The court said:

The conditions of this particular probation order must be read together. When so read together, they are open to more than one interpretation. On the one hand, it appears from condition (3) that it was ordered that the appellant must work under the supervision of Mr. Shea, presumably at the times and places chosen by Mr. Shea. On the other hand from condition (1) that he could live and work at places of his own choosing if he notified Mr. Shea promptly of any change of his address or occupation. Condition (5) is open to the interpretation that he could change his residence from British Columbia to anywhere in the world if such change was made for the purpose of his employment. Condition (2) appears to say he must always be physically present in the town where he resides unless he had asked (but not necessarily received permission) of Mr. Shea to leave the town even for a few minutes.

The court held that the conditions of the probation order, read together, were so vague, uncertain and contradictory as to be incapable of rational interpretation or enforcement and were therefore void.

---

[23] (1972), 9 C.C.C. (2d) 137 at pp. 138-39 (B.C.). See also *R. v. Boland,* unreported, December 5, 1974 (Ont. C.A.).

Accordingly a conviction of breach of probation based upon the allegation that he left town without asking Mr. Shea's permission was quashed.

F. Conditions In Probation Orders

It is, of course, clear that there is no need to impose any optional conditions, even reporting to a probation officer, in any order of probation. There are many cases where the absence of such conditions is normal and appropriate. However, if it appears that the accused is in need of assistance, proper conditions are called for. It is the supervisory aspect of probation which provides the principal benefit in cases of offenders whose breaches with the law are really the outcome of difficulties in coping with life in society. Accordingly, in *R. v. McMullen*[24] the accused was convicted of five counts of forgery and sentenced to 12 months' imprisonment. The accused had previously been convicted of uttering forged documents and had been on that occasion given a suspended sentence without any special terms as part of the probation order. The Ontario Court of Appeal reduced the sentence to one of six months together with 12 months' probation upon the ground that as the accused had not had the benefit of "proper probation services" on a prior occasion it would be appropriate to give him such benefit now.

It is useful to provide some examples which cover certain of these conditions. In *R. v. Beam:*[25]

> ... the appellant will report at least once a month to the probation officer; that he will be home every evening not later than 10 o'clock unless accompanied by a parent or legal guardian or unless he has the permission of the probation officer ...

R. v. Vandale and Maciejewski:[26]

> ... that he should report once each month to his probation officer during the first year and thereafter at such intervals as the probation officer may require; that he will seek and endeavour to maintain gainful employment; that he will live in such place as may be approved by his probation officer;

---

[24] Unreported, March 2, 1978 (Ont. C.A.).
[25] (1954), 19 C.R. 367 at p. 371 (Ont. C.A.).
[26] (1974), 21 C.C.C. (2d) 250 at p. 252 (Ont. C.A.).

that he will during the period of two years during which he is on probation pay the sum of $250 by way of restoration at such times and in such amounts as his probation officer considers that he can reasonably make.

R. v. Matrai:[27]

During the period of probation the accused will remain within the Province of Ontario and notify the Court or the Probation Officer or other person designated by the Court of any change of address, employment or occupation.

. . .

During the period of probation the accused shall not for any purpose leave the Municipality of Metropolitan Toronto without first notifying his Probation Officer of where he intends to go and the purpose of such departure whenever reasonably possible.

The last term mentioned above was specifically included by the court to provide for an unusual event or a circumstance of an emergency nature where it would not be practicable for the accused to notify his probation officer.

Many courts across the country have been using "community service orders". In *R. v. Shaw and Brehn*[28] the Ontario Court of Appeal approved community service orders pursuant to s. 663(2)(h) of the Criminal Code and urged that "in appropriate cases [they] should be more extensively used."

G. Conditions Not Properly Included In A Probation Order

In *R. v. DeKleric,*[29] a trial judge imposed a term that the accused should pay, through the clerk of the Magistrates' Court, in favour of the Vancouver Superannuated Police Officer's Association, the sum of $500 at the rate of $100 per month upon conviction on a charge of possession of marijuana. The court said:

If the circumstances required a fine, it should have been imposed as a fine. If the circumstances required as a condition of suspended sentence, restitution or reparation to the injured parties within the meaning of the provisions of

---

[27] (1972), 6 C.C.C. (2d) 574 at pp. 575-76 (Ont. C.A.).
[28] (1977), 36 C.R.N.S. 358.
[29] [1969] 2 C.C.C. 367 (B.C.C.A.).

the *Code* which allow such a condition to be imposed as a term of suspended sentence, then it should have been done that way. This innovation is a most dangerous one. It can lead to the greatest abuses, and for myself I hope it is the last time we see such a condition imposed as a term of any suspended sentence.

A term requiring a donation to the Society for the Prevention of Cruelty to Animals by an accused who was convicted of cruelty to animals has similarly been held to be improper.[30]

In *R. v. Beam,*[31] the trial court imposed a condition that the accused pay the costs of the prosecution for obtaining by false pretenses goods to the value of $200. The court held that this condition was in fact a fine cast in the form of a condition of probation and as such it was inconsistent with a suspended sentence. In *R. v. Pawlowski,*[32] a provision forming part of a probation order compelling the accused to pay costs of $1,000 was held to be unlawful. The sum bore no possible relation to the costs of the Crown in the proceedings and it was nothing more nor less than a substantial fine. The court went on to decide that s. 663(2)(h) does not have so wide an ambit as to empower a sentencing magistrate to require payment of costs in indictable offences.

Occasionally it appears from the facts of the case that a term of probation is being imposed as additional punishment, not, as authorized by the general residual powers in the section, as a reasonable condition considered desirable for securing the good conduct of the accused and for preventing the repetition by him of the same offence or the commission of other offences. One such case was *R. v. Ziatas.*[33] Counsel argued that the term which prevented the accused from operating a motor vehicle for a period of one year could not be inserted in the probation order, since s. 238 of the Criminal Code expressly empowered a court that convicted an offender of any of the offences enumerated therein to make such an order, and since the offence for which the appellant was convicted was an assault with intent to resist arrest (not mentioned in that section), the court declined to decide that question. It took the view that the trial judge proceeded upon a wrong principle inasmuch as he imposed this term of the probation order as an additional punishment rather than for the statutory purpose.

The same conclusion was reached with regard to a term of probation

---

[30] *R. v. Bewley, Ex p. A.-G. B.C.,* [1969] 2 C.C.C. 167 (B.C.).
[31] *Supra,* n. 25.
[32] (1972), 5 C.C.C. (2d) 87 (Man. C.A.).
[33] (1973), 13 C.C.C. (2d) 287 (Ont. C.A.).

order that followed conviction of a native Indian who had breached the British Columbia Fisheries Act regulations applicable to Indians who were permitted wide rights to fish for food but whose fish must in such cases be marked so that they can be identified and so that any sale to non-Indians could be prevented.[34] As a term of his probation order the accused was wrongly required to surrender his permit to fish for one month.

In *R. v. Caja and Billings*[35] probation orders originally imposed were varied to delete a condition preventing the operation of a motor vehicle upon charges of break and enter where $3,200 worth of auto parts were stolen from a garage. This term was not required to secure the good conduct of the accused. Terms prohibiting the non-medical use of drugs were also deleted in the absence of any evidence of a drug problem. Finally, a condition that the accused was not to apply for unemployment insurance was deleted upon the simple ground that it was not authorized by s. 663(2), presumably because such a condition could never be said to be "required to secure the good conduct of the appellants and for preventing a repetition of other offences".

It has been held in England[36] that a probation order having as one of its terms a requirement that the offender return to Ireland and stay there during the period of probation was unlawful. Pursuant to the English statute, the subject of a probation order must be "under the supervision of a probation officer" for the period of probation. The court reasoned that such a term would be unlawful because he could not in Ireland be under the supervision of an English probation officer. In Canada, a probation order can be made without the addition of this term and therefore the reasoning would seem to be inapplicable. Nevertheless s. 2(a) of the Canadian Bill of Rights demands that no law of Canada shall be applied so as to authorize or effect the arbitrary exile of any person and such an order might well run counter to this provision.

In *R. v. Knight,*[37] the magistrate suspended sentence upon condition that the accused dispose of his property and move out of the community and also undertook to deliver his children to one John Dodge for care. The Court of Appeal held that the magistrate had no power to enter into such an arrangement or stipulation with the defendant. There were numerous other errors and irregularities and the report does not make

---

[34] *R. v. Gladstone,* [1978] 2 W.W.R. 751 (B.C.C.A.).
[35] (1977), 36 C.C.C. (2d) 401 (Ont. C.A.) .
[36] *R. v. McCartan* (1958), 42 Cr. App. R. 262.
[37] (1916), 27 C.C.C. 111 (Ont. C.A.).

clear whether the condition would have been improper had the order otherwise been lawful.

But it is hard to imagine that so far-reaching an order could be proper. A term ordering an accused to provide support to his wife and child is also beyond the powers of the court under these provisions.[38]

In *R. v. Stennes*[39] conditions were imposed in a probation order that the appellant should not partake of any restricted or prohibited drugs and should subject himself to a urinalysis test at the direction of a police officer, probation officer or social worker. The court reviewed the evidence in this case and found that there was no evidence to suggest that this appellant had at the time of this offence or ever before used drugs. Accordingly, the condition was struck. In the same case there was a condition imposed that a curfew should be observed between twelve midnight and seven o'clock in the morning. The court, noting that the appellant was 32 years of age, found that though such a condition might well be applicable "in the case of a young man who was inclined to lean towards a criminal life", it would not be an appropriate condition for a man of the appellant's age. The court noted that though it might well be helpful to have such a condition for the protection of the public, because it was not "a necessary condition" in the circumstances it became by virtue of his age "unreasonable".

The appellant in this case was a member of a motorcycle gang known as the "101 Knights". The trial judge forbade him to associate with persons who were members of that club or any other motorcycle "gang". In particular, there was a list of 11-named persons with whom the appellant was not to associate. The court said:

> . . . I do not think that there is any suggestion, although this man was a member of the 101 Knights, that being a member of that club makes him a criminal or inclined to criminal activities. It may well be that some members of that club have in the past been in trouble, as well as members of other clubs have, whether motorcycle clubs or otherwise; but it does seem to me that in the particular circumstances of this case, when we are dealing with a motorcycle mechanic, it would be unreasonable to expect that he should not associate with any motorcycle club or "gang", as the learned Judge referred to it. I see nothing that was before the learned sentencing Judge upon which he could properly pick out any persons with whom the appellant should not associate, with the possible exception of Brimacombe who was with him in connection with this particular offence. However, I do not think it requisite

---

[38] *R. v. Graves,* unreported, October 30, 1975 (B.C.C.A.).
[39] (1975), 35 C.R.N.S. 123 (B.C.C.A.).

that all the names should have been listed as being people with whom this man was not to associate. In my view there was not sufficient evidence upon which the learned Judge could impose such a restrictive condition on the habits of this man. I mention only that one of the names was the landlord at the home in which this appellant lived, and it seems to me that the effect of an order of this kind goes too far and would make a complete change in this man's whole standard of living, without any suggestion that his association with these people has been to his detriment in the past.

The court commented that the sentencing judge's intentions were "of the highest" but they went beyond what was reasonable under the circumstances.

H. Community Service Orders

Modelled after the English experience, and later justified by legislation, the courts have been invoking s. 663(2)(h) to justify probation orders that contain terms requiring a period of services to the community. In some provinces the provincial governments have set up programmes designed to use such a scheme. In other cases enterprising and imaginative judges have been doing their own investigation of suitable work projects that could benefit the community and, in select cases, including terms for such work in probation orders. It is clear that it is not every accused who will benefit from such an order. Nevertheless, the order has the advantage of demonstrating clearly that it is the community that has been wronged and that it is to the community the accused must be responsible in terms of his punishment. In addition, it may well be that the satisfaction of a job well done for a worthy purpose would awake better instincts and responses than a purely penal measure. So for example, in *R. v. Myles*[40] there was an order for 400 hours of community service in an old-age home.

Strangely enough, in another case, a condition of probation which required the accused to "leave British Columbia within forty-eight hours and not physically enter British Columbia" for a two-year period has been upheld. The matter arose over a family dispute where the accused was convicted of possession of a weapon for a purpose dangerous to the public peace. He had unlawfully pointed the weapon at his estranged

---

[40] (1977), 20 Crim. L.Q. 147 (B.C. Prov. Ct.).

wife and her boyfriend. The court upheld the condition because the term was "concerned principally with the necessity of preventing an explosive situation resulting in tragedy".

Generally, a Canadian citizen or a resident of Canada is entitled to reside in any part of Canada that he chooses; therefore, there must be a valid reason before an order is made prohibiting a person from residing in any particular part of Canada. It is neither possible nor desirable to lay down any general rules. It would seem that such an order ought rarely to be made as a matter of general principle. It may be contrary to the Canadian Bill of Rights; in any event, if the accused keeps the peace and is of good behaviour, as required by the balance of the order, there is then no reason to keep him out of a particular province.[41]

That same court has deleted a similar condition, in a case which shows the inadvisability of this sort of order. In *R. v. Ross,*[42] the accused was involved with a man who was a bank robber. The terms of her probation on a minor criminal charge included orders that she remain outside the Province of British Columbia and that she reside with her parents in Winnipeg, Manitoba. She found it difficult to live with her parents and difficult to live in Winnipeg; in the end result she was admitted to the psychiatric wards of two hospitals as a result of depression caused by this situation. The court deleted the two terms.

I. Statutory Limitations On The Imposition Of Suspended Sentences And Probation Orders

Criminal Code:

> 646(2) An accused who is convicted of an indictable offence punishable with imprisonment for more than five years may be fined in addition to, but not in lieu of, any other punishment that is authorized.

There is no doubt that by acting under s. 663(1)(a), where no fine is imposed, sentence can be suspended and probation ordered for any indictable offence. A problem only arises when it is desired to both fine and put an accused on probation for an indictable offence carrying a penalty of more than five years. The entire question turns upon whether

---

[41] *R. v. Herbert,* unreported, May 6, 1976 (B.C.C.A.).
[42] Unreported, October 26, 1976 (B.C.C.A.).

probation is "other punishment", within the meaning of the section.

Several courts which have considered this matter directly have taken the view that the probation order is "other punishment".[43] On the other hand, the Prince Edward Island Court of Appeal, in *R. v. Pretty*,[44] took the opposite view, saying that a sentence of a fine together with probation for an indictable offence with a maximum penalty greater than five years was illegal. The *Pretty* case is rendered *per incuriam* of all the other cases, and the case of *R. v. Johnson* is *per incuriam R. v. Pretty.*

If one analyzes the various reasons for arriving at either position, some of them are strong and some of them make little sense. In favour of the "first position" — that probation is other punishment — these reasons have been given:

(1) Section 663 which authorizes probation is found in Part XX which is headed "Punishment, Fines, Forfeitures".[45]

(2) The accused is always liable to be brought back to court to be punished.[46]

(3) The probation order is burdensome because it requires reporting.[47]

(4) Any contravention of the probation order may result in imprisonment.[48]

(5) The definition of punishment in the Shorter Oxford English Dictionary is "a penalty imposed to ensure the application and enforcement of a law."[49]

(6) Section 663 overrides s. 646.[50]

(7) If one contrasts s. 663(1)(a) with s. 663(1)(b), one can clearly determine that the former paragraph is not punishment but a suspension of punishment and therefore, because one may presume that the complete field is intended to be covered by

---

[43] *R. v. Johnson* (1972), 6 C.C.C. (2d) 380 (B.C.C.A.); *R. v. Desmarais* (1971), 3 C.C.C. (2d) 523 (Que. C.A.); *R. v. Zezima* (1970), 13 Crim. L.Q. 153 (Que. C.A.); *R. v. Roy* (1971), 13 Crim. L.Q. 439 (Que. C.A.).

[44] (1971), 5 C.C.C. (2d) 332.

[45] *R. v. Demarais* (1971), 3 C.C.C. (2d) 523 *per* Lajoie J.A.; *R. v. Johnson* (1972), 6 C.C.C. (2d) 380 (B.C.C.A.).

[46] *R. v. Demarais* (1971), 3 C.C.C. (2d) 523 (Que. C.A.).

[47] *Ibid.,* a probation order necessarily involves some element of deterrence to the offender who is subject to it: *R. v. Sanchez-Pino* (1973), 11 C.C.C. (2d) 53 (Ont. C.A.).

[48] *R. v. Desmaris, ibid.*

[49] *Ibid.*

[50] *Ibid.*

Parliament, it logically follows that the latter paragraph is in fact punishment by way of contrast.[51]

(8) It is argued that there is no difference in principle between an accused being ordered to pay a sum of money as a fine and an accused being ordered to perform certain actions or abide by certain conditions of conduct.

However, it should be noted that the Criminal Code does not in fact require that any condition whatsoever shall be inserted in a probation report, other than that the accused should keep the peace, be of good behaviour and appear before the court when required to do so by the court — conditions which could hardly be described as onerous and more properly do not place upon the probationer any obligation beyond that arising by operation of law upon the ordinary citizen. But the true significance of this point may be to indicate that the entire issue is primarily one of fact as noted in points (4) and (5).

However, if one is seeking to determine whether or not something is a "punishment", it does not enlighten us very much to change the form of the question to an inquiry whether or not something is a "penalty" as noted in point (5).

This argument, however, can carry but little weight. It relies upon the unreported case of *R. v. Foisy*,[52] but ignores the ordinary rule of statutory construction that the specific overrides the general. It is not an argument, but a conclusion.

The eighth reason, though sensible, is perhaps subjective and one wonders whether this is the approach one ought to take when interpreting this section. Alternatively, if it is an objective statement, it amounts to no more than the assertion that an order is an order; which begs the question, since one is trying to determine whether or not some orders constitute punishment.

It is significant in connection with this argument that in *R. v. Marcello*,[53] the court recognized that probation is a restraint on freedom. A person under a probation order is bound to return to court without the intervention of any independent court process or the laying of any new information. His is a continuing obligation to the court, whereas everyone else's is a contingent one dependent upon the separate initiation of a charge or proceeding. Cross,[54] in his book on sentencing

---

[51] *R. v. Johnson* (1972), 6 C.C.C. (2d) 380 (B.C.C.A.).
[52] Unreported, January 15, 1971 (Que. C.A.).
[53] *R. v. Marcello* (1973), 11 C.C.C. (2d) 302 (Ont. C.A.).
[54] *The English Sentencing System*, at p. 18.

notes with regard to the English Act that there is a provision which prevents the court from making a probation order unless the accused expresses his willingness to comply with its requirements.

> This emphasizes the theoretically non-punitive nature of probation, for it is at least doubtful whether any pain, to the infliction of which upon himself a person can consent, should be described as punishment in anything other than an extended or metaphorical sense.

By way of contrast then, noting that the present Canadian legislation requires no consent from an accused, one might infer that consent is the element which distinguishes punishment from non-punishment.

In favour of the "second position" — that probation is not "other punishment": stand: *R. v. Pretty; R. v. Zezima* and *R. v. Pawlowski.*

In *R. v. Pawlowski,*[55] the Manitoba Court of Appeal, relying upon *Foisy,* the decision in *R. v. Zezima* and an earlier case, *A.-G. Can. v. Wong,* held that a probation order did not constitute "any other punishment" within the meaning of the Code. The judgment was given by Dickson J.A. (as he then was) and except *Foisy* other cases were not mentioned.

The argument in *R. v. Pretty* is not developed at all, but simply asserts the conclusion that probation is not the type of punishment which is meant by s. 646 of the Criminal Code. This conclusion is supported by a comment of the Ontario Court of Appeal in *R. v. Ziatas,*[56] where a provision prohibiting the offender from driving a motor vehicle was set aside upon a determination that the trial judge imposed this term "as an additional punishment to be imposed upon the accused" and therefore proceeded upon a wrong principle. Whether this comment accurately characterizes s. 663 of the Criminal Code generally is doubtful, since in that case the court was construing not the section as a whole but only s. 663(2)(h), which permits "such other reasonable conditions as the court considers desirable for securing the good conduct of the accused and for preventing a repetition by him of the same offence or the commission of other offences." It has not yet been determined whether the philosophy expressed in that subsection governs the section as a whole.

On balance, the weight of authority and reasoning would appear to be in favour of the position that probation in Canada does constitute "other

---

[55] (1972), 5 C.C.C. (2d) 87; *R. v. Zezima* (1970), 13 Crim. L.Q. 153 (Que. C.A.); *A.-G. Can. v. Wong,* [1961] Que. Q.B. 907 (C.A.).

[56] (1973), 13 C.C.C. (2d) 287 (Ont. C.A.); but see *contra R. v. Wardley,* unreported, October 10, 1978 (Ont. C.A.).

punishment" and that therefore a fine can be imposed together with probation, for indictable offences where the maximum penalty is more than five years.

When a court acts pursuant to s. 663(1)(b) of the Criminal Code, it may either fine the accused or sentence him to imprisonment and thereafter impose a probation order; but it may not do both. This conclusion was reached by Morrow J. in *R. v. Smith,*[57] who found that the phrasing of the section, which uses the word "or", was deliberate and invoked Maxwell's *Interpretation of Statutes* for the proposition that where an enactment may entail penal consequences, no violence must be done to its language to bring people within it, but rather care must be taken that no one is brought within it who is not within its express language. This result was also reached by the Ontario Court of Appeal in *R. v. Blacquiere.*[58]

There is jurisdiction to impose a probation order only when the period of imprisonment that is imposed "whether in default of payment of a fine or otherwise" does not exceed two years.[59] A penitentiary sentence of two years can legally be imposed together with a term of probation.

J. Varying A Probation Order

In *R. v. Siple,*[60] the prisoner appealed a sentence of 14 days plus 15 months of probation and sought a reduction in the severity of the terms of probation, which were quite strict. The Ontario Court of Appeal noted that the proper forum to vary those terms was the convicting judge, pursuant to s. 664 of the Criminal Code. However, because there had been a great delay in hearing the appeal and because further delay would have been a hardship to the accused, the Court allowed the appeal and varied the probation order. It is clear that only in unusual circumstances would the Court of Appeal undertake a task which could more practically be carried out by the trial judge. It is the convicting judge who has knowledge of the accused and local circumstances from his first

---

[57] (1972), 7 C.C.C. (2d) 468 (N.W.T.).
[58] (1975), 24 C.C.C. (2d) 168.
[59] *R. v. Brookes,* unreported, January 28, 1974 (Ont. C.A.); see also *R. v. Marlott,* unreported, March 26, 1973 (Ont. C.A.).
[60] Unreported, February 9, 1973 (Ont. C.A.).

hand impression and trial experience and who is in the best position to decide such questions.

In *R. v. Wehner,*[61] the English Court of Appeal held that despite language in an enactment which made it mandatory for the Court to explain to the offender that if he was convicted of another offence during a certain period he would be liable to be sentenced for the original offence, it was permissible for the judge to delegate that obligation to another — for example, the offender's solicitor — provided that the Court did satisfy itself that the order had been fully explained to the defendant in accordance with the statute. A direct explanation is sound practice but in that case the responsibility was primarily delegated to counsel.

K. Section 663(4) Of The Criminal Code

In *R. v. Cottrelle,*[62] Judge Marin, upon a charge of breach of probation, had to deal with the argument that there was no evidence adduced by the Crown that the probation order was read to the accused or that he received a copy of it, nor that he was informed of the provisions of ss. 663(4) and 666 of the Criminal Code. He held that the provisions of s. 663(4) were not judicial but administrative in character. If at a trial for a breach of probation, an accused wished to avail himself of the defence of lack of knowledge of the terms of the order, he must lead evidence to satisfy the court of non-compliance with the provisions of s. 663(4).

The opposite approach was taken by Bence C.J. in *R. v. Piche.*[63] He disagreed with the decision in *R. v. Cottrelle* and ruled that putting the onus on the accused to establish that he was unaware of the conditions in the order was entirely contrary to fundamental principles inherent in our criminal law; he found it difficult to conclude that the requirements of the statute could be disregarded on the basis that they are purely administrative. He also held that the making of a probation order is not predicated on compliance with these conditions, but that in a prosecution, proof of such compliance was necessary for its enforcement.

---

[61] (1977), 65 Cr. App. R. 1.
[62] (1972), 7 C.C.C. (2d) 30 (Ont. Prov. Ct.).
[63] (1976), 31 C.C.C. (2d) 150 (Sask.).

L. Section 664(4) Of The Criminal Code

In *R. v. Graham,*[64] the accused was not brought back before the judge who had originally placed him on probation but was brought before a judge in another judicial district. The court held that unless there has been a transfer of jurisdiction to another judge by virtue of s. 665(1) of the Criminal Code the accused must be brought back before the original trial judge. Where such a transfer is made the prosecutor must produce for the new judge all the background material and information (such as a presentence report if there were one) which were in the hands of the original court out of fairness to the individual upon whom the sentence was to be imposed.

M. Commencement And Duration

A probation order worded to begin after "the expiration of a term of imprisonment" commences upon the release of the accused from custody, even on mandatory supervision; there is no hiatus when an accused is neither incarcerated nor bound by a probation order. Two judges, dissenting, held that the statutory language was equivocal, and that the probation did not come into effect until the term of imprisonment was completed, though the accused was not incarcerated during the latter portion of his term.[65]

In *R. v. Noble,*[66] probation was ordered for a period of two years with a condition that restitution should be made to Steinberg's Ltd. in the sum of $4,000 during that period. After the two-year period had elapsed, the money not having been paid, an information was laid for breach of the recognizance. The court held that the relevant date was the date of hearing of the charge of breach of recognizance. This did not occur until after the two years had elapsed and the probation order was then no longer in force. Accordingly the trial judge had no power to deal with the matter and could not impose a sentence for the breach.

---

[64] (1975), 27 C.C.C. (2d) 475 (Ont. C.A.).
[65] *R. v. Constant* (1978), 40 C.C.C. (2d) 329 (Man. C.A.).
[66] [1966] 3 C.C.C. 66 (N.B.C.A.).

A recognizance or an order of probation for a term in excess of the prescribed statutory period of two years is a nullity.[67]

The Ontario Court of Appeal has taken the view that where probation is indicated but a sentence of some incarceration is necessary as well, the two should be properly balanced. A sentence of probation is most effective if it follows a shorter sentence. Accordingly, the court in *R. v. Reading*[68] reduced a sentence upon a 17-year-old first offender for robbery from 23 months coupled with two years' probation to one year's imprisonment with two years of probation.

N. Breach Of Probation Order

Some comments about breach of recognizance are perhaps useful because of the implications it has for lawful sentence practices. Where a defendant who has appealed his conviction by way of trial *de novo* is awaiting appeal and then breaches his recognizance, a magistrate has no jurisdiction to impose a sentence for the breach while the conviction from which it flows is under appeal.[69]

The essence of the offence set out in s. 666 of the Criminal Code is wilful disobedience of a probation order, and accordingly the plea of *autrefois convict* will not lie where the defendant has already been convicted for drinking under age, before being charged with breach of a recognizance containing a term that he was not to consume alcohol.[70] In *R. v. McGowan*,[71] a juvenile who was tried in an ordinary criminal court pursuant to the provisions of the Juvenile Delinquents Act, convicted there and placed on probation, was thereafter charged with wilfully failing to comply with one of its terms. The court decided that he was, though still a juvenile, liable to prosecution in the provincial court without any further order, because it was inconceivable that Parliament should have intended that a juvenile should be able to breach such an order with impunity.

---

[67] *R. v. Fisher,* [1964] 3 C.C.C. 37 (Man. C.A.).
[68] Unreported, March 7, 1978 (Ont. C.A.).
[69] *R. ex rel. McKnight v. Cross* (1968), 4 C.R.N.S. 301 (Ont.).
[70] *R. v. Firth* (1970), 12 C.R.N.S. 184 (N.W.T.). But recent decisions in the Supreme Court of Canada, such as *R. v. Keinapple* make the correctness of this decision doubtful.
[71] (1970), 75 W.W.R. 481 (B.C.); affirmed [1971] 5 W.W.R. 279 (C.A.).

It has been held that failure to comply with a term of a probation ordering restitution of moneys which were stolen, does not constitute a continuing offence; and therefore failure to prosecute within six months was a bar to the prosecutor pursuant to the time limitation contained in s. 721(2) of the Criminal Code.[72]

In *R. v. Oakes*[73] the court considered s. 664(4) of the Criminal Code which authorizes the court that made the probationary order to revoke the order and impose any sentence that could have been imposed originally; and this punishment can be "in addition" to any punishment that may be imposed for an offence committed while on probation. The court held, however, that this would not authorize the imposition of a consecutive sentence to a term which did not exist at the time of the original sentencing. The power to direct that terms of imprisonment shall be served consecutively is set out exclusively in s. 645 of the Criminal Code.

O. Provincial Probation Acts

Some of the provinces have Probation Acts whose terms and conditions are much different than those in the Criminal Code. For example, The Probation Act (Ontario)[74] provides that a person charged with having committed any offence against any statute of Ontario may be released on probation. This wording indicates that the section is applicable after a person has been charged but before he has been convicted.[75]

P. Presentence Reports

Criminal Code:

662(1) Where an accused, other than a corporation, pleads guilty to or is found guilty of an offence, a probation officer shall, if required to do so by a

---

[72] *Butkans v. The Queen,* [1972] 4 W.W.R. 262 (Man. Co. Ct.).
[73] (1977), 37 C.C.C. (2d) 84 (Ont. C.A.).
[74] R.S.O. 1970, c. 364.
[75] *R. v. Weir* (1973), 13 C.C.C. (2d) 572 (Ont.).

court, prepare and file with the court a report in writing relating to the accused for the purpose of assisting the court in imposing sentence or in determining whether the accused should be discharged pursuant to section 662.1.

(2) Where a report is filed with the court under subsection (1), the clerk of the court shall forthwith cause a copy of the report to be provided to the accused or his counsel and to the prosecutor.

It is quite often the case, especially when probation is a possible part of a sentence, that the trial judge will call for a presentence report in order to assist him in assessing the proper sentence. In *R. v. Rudyk,*[76] the probation officer prepared a report which elicited from the accused his version of the facts of the case. As it turned out that version contradicted the guilty plea. The Court of Appeal said:

> I would here urge that a presentence report be confined to its very necessary and salutary role of portraying the background, character and circumstances of the person convicted. It should not, however, contain the investigator's impressions of the facts relating to the offence charged, whether based on information received from the accused, the police, or other witnesses, and whether favourable or unfavourable to the accused. And if the report contains such information the trial judge should disregard it in considering sentence.

The reasoning involved was that any story given to the probation officer may well be self-serving, and in any event was not subject to cross-examination by counsel for the Crown. The proper place for the facts of the offence to be investigated is in open court. Caution is to be exercised by anyone who is to present such information to a court. In *R. v. Elley,*[77] allegations were made that the accused was dismissed for stealing from two former employers and that he was an associate of thieves. The Court of Appeal made inquiry and satisfied themselves that the information given was inaccurate. The Court stated that it was ". . . the bounden duty of all . . . to exercise the most scrupulous care in presenting to any Court the record of an accused person. Police reports are not based strictly in law upon evidence which can be tested fully by judges or counsel . . .".

In *R. v. Bartkow*[78] the court commented on the undesirability of including in the presentence report allegations of other crimes of which

---

[76] (1975), 11 N.S.R. (2d) 541 at p. 544 (C.A.); *R. v. Craig* (1975), 11 N.S.R. (2d) 695 (C.A.).
[77] (1921), 15 Cr. App. R. 143.
[78] (1978), 24 N.S.R. (2d) 518 (C.A.); *R. v. Giler Rose,* [1978] Qd. R. 61.

the accused has not been convicted; nor should it supply the criminal record. Such references should be ignored by a trial judge. The presentence report ought not to describe nor detail the evidence of the offence then before the court: *R. v. Cleveland.*[79]

Probation officers have an important role to play in assisting the administration of justice but it is necessary to recognize that when dealing with individual cases there are limits which must be placed upon their activities. In *Webb v. The Queen*[80] the trial judge in his report to the Court of Appeal stated, in justification of his imposition of a fine on a charge of shoplifting: "I have even considered, after discussion with the Chief Probation Officer, the imposition of a short term of imprisonment, say a weekend as appropriate." No presentence report was ordered in the case. The Court held that section (s. 662):

> . . . makes it clear that if the court requires the assistance of a probation officer, such assistance must be obtained in the manner provided for by the section. . . . It is only a written report "relating to the accused" which the court is entitled to receive and act upon. In the case at bar the Provincial Court Judge improperly took into consideration informal discussions with a probation officer to which the appellant was not a party and the exact nature of which is unknown to all interested parties.

It cannot be doubted that a judge has the right to consult in general terms with officers of the probation service in order to keep himself informed about trends and matters of concern to him, but he may not do so about a particular case.

Whenever there is a denial by the accused, the court should disregard such material unless properly proved. If there is anything in the report which is contradicted by the accused, the court ought to either hear evidence on the matter or disregard it.[81] In *R. v. Benson and Stevenson,*[82] the court held that in certain cases, particularly where there are psychiatric problems, it was better not to inform the accused of the contents of his presentence report to the extent that it related to that subject. It would appear that by statutory amendment this is no longer possible, if it was ever advisable.

In *R. v. Smith,*[83] the English Court of Appeal (Criminal Division), said

---

[79] (1978), 25 N.S.R. (2d) 372 (C.A.).

[80] (1975), 39 C.R.N.S. 314 at p. 322 (P.E.I.C.A.).

[81] Chapter 3, "Receiving Information"; see also *R. v. Lucky* (1974), 12 S.A.S.R. 136 *per* Bray C.J.; *R. v. Carlstrom,* [1977] V.R. 366.

[82] (1951), 13 C.R. 1 (B.C.C.A.); *R. v. Dolbec,* [1963] 2 C.C.C. 87 (B.C.C.A.).

[83] [1968] Crim. L.R. 33.

that in normal circumstances it was preferable not to read out a probation report in full in open court. Such a reading is in any event not done in Canada.

In *R. v. Descoteaux,*[84] the accused appealed the sentence of a fine of $200 following conviction on a charge of theft under $200. She had no criminal record, she cared for her young child, she was separated from her husband and she was unemployed and supported by mother's allowance. After the trial judge determined that this was a proper case for a presentence report, he remanded her in custody until the report was prepared. The Ontario Court of Appeal took the view that the trial judge erred in refusing to remand her out of custody pending the receipt of the presentence report. The sentence was varied to a conditional discharge with probation for one year.

It would seem that the proper principle is that unless the court has determined that a period of imprisonment longer than the time necessary to prepare a presentence report is in any event inevitable because of the seriousness of the crime, it is the better practice to remand the accused out of custody pending the presentence report. Custody cases will of course be confined only to the most serious crimes, and where there is any doubt about the matter only to those where counsel is in a position to assure the court that there are not such extraordinary circumstances that probation could be considered.

---

[84] Unreported, March 5, 1975 (Ont. C.A.); *R. v. Nicholson,* unreported, December 13, 1976 (Ont. C.A.).

Chapter 11

The Fine

It has been said that the fine is simple, uncomplicated, adaptable, and popular, because it involves no expense to the public, no burden on the prison system, no social dislocation and less stigma than most other criminal sanctions.[1] Though this is perhaps somewhat of an overstatement, the fine is one of the most prevalent means of dealing with crime. It is extremely useful where the object is to prevent the criminal from making a financial profit from his crime,[2] and especially so in victimless crimes where restitution is not an alternative. On the other hand, where guidance and control are necessary, the fine is a poor substitute for probation. In many cases the crime itself is too serious to permit the imposition of a fine.

If one accepts the premise that no measure presently in use is effective in reforming criminals or deterring crime, it can be said that the fine, though equally ineffective, involves less expense and disruption than any other penal measure in use.

Criminal Code:

645(3) Where an accused is convicted of an offence punishable with both fine and imprisonment and a term of imprisonment in default of payment of the fine is not specified in the enactment that prescribed the punishment to be imposed, the imprisonment that may be imposed in default of payment shall not exceed the term of imprisonment that is prescribed in respect of the offence.

646(1) An accused who is convicted of an indictable offence punishable

---

[1] Alec Samuels, "The Fine: The Principles", [1970] Crim. L.R. 201.
[2] *R. v. Lewis,* [1965] Crim. L.R. 121; *R. v. Morris,* [1954] Crim. L.R. 65; *R. v. Markwick* (1953), 37 Cr. App. R. 125.

with imprisonment for five years or less may be fined in addition to or in lieu of any other punishment that is authorized, but an accused shall not be fined in lieu of imprisonment where the offence of which he is convicted is punishable by a minimum term of imprisonment.

(2) An accused who is convicted of an indictable offence punishable with imprisonment for more than five years may be fined in addition to, but not in lieu of, any other punishment that is authorized.

(3) Where a fine is imposed under this section, a term of imprisonment may be imposed in default of payment of the fine, but no such term shall exceed

(*a*) two years, where the term of imprisonment that may be imposed for the offence is less than five years, or

(*b*) five years, where the term of imprisonment that may be imposed for the offence is five years or more.

(4) Subject to the provisions of this section, where an accused is convicted of an indictable offence and is fined, the court that convicts the accused may direct that the fine

(*a*) be paid forthwith, or

(*b*) be paid at such time and on such terms as the court may fix.

(5) Where a court imposes a fine, the court shall not, at the time the sentence is imposed, direct that the fine be paid forthwith unless

(*a*) the court is satisfied that the convicted person is possessed of sufficient means to enable him to pay the fine forthwith,

(*b*) upon being asked by the court whether he desires time for payment, the convicted person does not request such time, or

(*c*) for any other special reason, the court deems it expedient that no time should be allowed.

(6) The court, in considering whether time should be allowed for payment and, if so, for what period, shall consider any representation made by the accused but any time allowed shall be not less than fourteen clear days from the date sentence is imposed.

(7) Where time has been allowed for payment the court shall not issue a warrant of committal in default of payment of the fine until the expiration of the time allowed for payment.

(8) Where no time has been allowed for payment and a warrant of committal in default of payment of a fine of the accused is issued the court shall state in the warrant the reason for immediate committal.

(9) Notwithstanding subsection (7), where, before the expiration of the time allowed for payment, the accused appears before a court as defined in section 644, and signifies in writing that he prefers to be committed immediately rather than to await the expiration of the time allowed, the court may forthwith issue a warrant committing the accused to prison.

(10) Where a person who has been allowed time for payment appears to the court to be not less than sixteen nor more than twenty-one years of age,

the court shall, before issuing a warrant committing the person to prison for default of payment of the fine, obtain and consider a report concerning the conduct and means to pay of the accused.

(11) Where time has been allowed for payment under subsection (4) the court that imposed the sentence may, upon an application by or on behalf of the accused, allow further time for payment, subject to any rules made by the court under section 438.

(12) In this section "fine" includes a pecuniary penalty or other sum of money.

647. Notwithstanding subsection 646(2), a corporation that is convicted of an offence is liable, in lieu of any imprisonment that is prescribed as punishment for that offence,

    (*a*) to be fined in an amount that is in the discretion of the court, where the offence is an indictable offence, or

    (*b*) to be fined in an amount not exceeding one thousand dollars, where the offence is a summary conviction offence.

648. Where a fine that is imposed on a corporation is not paid forthwith the prosecutor may, by filing the conviction, enter as a judgment the amount of the fine and costs, if any, in the superior court of the province in which the trial was held, and that judgment is enforceable against the corporation in the same manner as if it were a judgment rendered against the corporation in that court in civil proceedings.

650(1) Where a term of imprisonment is imposed in default of payment of a penalty, the term shall, upon payment of a part of the penalty, whether the payment was made before or after the issue of a warrant of committal, be reduced by the number of days that bears the same proportion to the number of days in the term as the part paid bears to the total penalty.

(2) No amount offered in part payment of a penalty shall be accepted unless it is sufficient to secure reduction of sentence of one day, or some multiple thereof, and where a warrant of committal has been issued, no part payment shall be accepted until any fee that is payable in respect of the warrant or its execution has been paid.

(3) Payment may be made under this section to the person who has lawful custody of the prisoner or to such other person as the Attorney General directs.

(4) A payment under this section shall, unless the order imposing the penalty otherwise provides, be applied to the payment in full of costs and charges, and thereafter to payment in full of compensation or damages that are included in the penalty, and finally to payment in full of any part of the penalty that remains unpaid.

(5) In this section, "penalty" means all the sums of money, including fines, in default of payment of which a term of imprisonment is imposed and includes the costs and charges of committing the defaulter and of conveying him to prison.

651(1) Where a fine, penalty or forfeiture is imposed or a recognizance is forfeited and no provision, other than this section, is made by law for the application of the proceeds thereof, the proceeds belong to Her Majesty in right of the province in which the fine, penalty or forfeiture was imposed or the recognizance was forfeited, and shall be paid by the person who receives them to the treasurer of that province.

(2) Where

(*a*) a fine, penalty or forfeiture is imposed

    (i) in respect of a violation of a revenue law of Canada,

    (ii) in respect of a breach of duty or malfeasance in office by an officer or employee of the Government of Canada, or

    (iii) in respect of any proceedings instituted at the instance of the Government of Canada in which that government bears the costs of prosecution; or

(*b*) a recognizance in connection with proceedings mentioned in paragraph (*a*) is forfeited,

the proceeds of the fine, penalty, forfeiture or recognizance belong to Her Majesty in right of Canada and shall be paid by the person who receives them to the Receiver General.

(3) Where a provincial, municipal or local authority bears, in whole or in part, the expense of administering the law under which a fine, penalty or forfeiture is imposed or under which proceedings are taken in which a recognizance is forfeited,

(*a*) the lieutenant governor in council may, from time to time, direct that the proceeds of a fine, penalty, forfeiture or recognizance that belongs to Her Majesty in right of the province shall be paid to that authority, and

(*b*) the Governor in Council may, from time to time, direct that the proceeds of a fine, penalty, forfeiture or recognizance that belongs to Her Majesty in right of Canada shall be paid to that authority.

652(1) Where a fine, pecuniary penalty or forfeiture is imposed by law and no other mode is prescribed for the recovery thereof, the fine, pecuniary penalty or forfeiture is recoverable or enforceable in civil proceedings by Her Majesty, but by no other person.

(2) No proceedings under subsection (1) shall be instituted more than two years after the time when the cause of action arose or the offence was committed in respect of which the fine, pecuniary penalty or forfeiture was imposed.

722(1) Except where otherwise expressly provided by law, every one who is convicted of an offence punishable on summary conviction is liable to a fine of not more than five hundred dollars or to imprisonment for six months or to both.

(2) Where the imposition of a fine or the making of an order for the payment of money is authorized by law, but the law does not provide that

imprisonment may be imposed in default of payment of the fine or compliance with the order, the court may order that in default of payment of the fine or compliance with the order, as the case may be, the defendant shall be imprisoned for a period of not more than six months.

(3) A summary conviction court may direct, subject to the provisions of this section, that any fine adjudged to be paid shall

(*a*) be paid forthwith, or

(*b*) be paid at such time and on such terms as the summary conviction court may fix.

(4) Where a summary conviction court directs that an accused pay a fine, the court shall not, at the time the sentence is imposed, direct that the fine be paid forthwith unless

(*a*) the court is satisfied that the convicted person is possessed of sufficient means to enable him to pay the fine forthwith,

(*b*) upon being asked by the court whether he desires time for payment, the convicted person does not request such time, or

(*c*) for any other special reason, the court deems it expedient that no time should be allowed.

(5) The court in considering whether time should be allowed for payment and, if so, for what period, shall consider any representation made by the accused but any time allowed shall be not less than fourteen clear days from the date sentence is imposed.

(6) Where time has been allowed for payment the court shall not issue a warrant of committal in default of payment of the fine until the expiration of the time allowed for payment.

(7) Where no time has been allowed for payment and a warrant of committal in default of payment of a fine of the accused is issued the court shall state in the warrant the reason for immediate committal.

(8) Notwithstanding subsection (6), where, before the expiration of the time allowed for payment, the accused appears before a summary conviction court and signifies in writing that he prefers to be committed immediately rather than to await the expiration of the time allowed, the court may forthwith issue a warrant committing the accused to prison.

(9) Where a person who has been allowed time for payment appears to the court to be not less than sixteen nor more than twenty-one years of age, the court shall, before issuing a warrant committing the person to prison for default of payment of the fine, obtain and consider a report concerning the conduct and means to pay of the accused.

(10) Where time has been allowed for payment under subsection (3) the court that imposed the sentence may, upon application by or on behalf of the accused, allow further time for payment.

(11) In this section "fine" includes a pecuniary penalty or other sum of money.

753(1) A person does not waive his right of appeal under section 748 by reason only that he pays the fine imposed upon conviction, without in any way indicating an intention to appeal or reserving the right to appeal.

A. General Principles

There are several principles which provide the foundation for fines. They can be summarized briefly: the offender must not gain from his or her wrongdoing; the amount fined must not be excessive; the amount fined should reflect the offence only and not extraneous factors; the amount fined must be applied without reference to the wealth of the offender; and the imposition of a fine must not be seen as licence to commit the offence.

It is likely that the principle that the amount of the fine must not be excessive was part of the common law even before it was enunciated in the English Bill of Rights. There is mention of it as far back as Magna Carta, 1215: "for a trivial offence, a freeman shall be fined only in proportion to the degree of his offence, and for a serious offence correspondingly, but not so heavily as to deprive him of his livelihood."

In *R. v. Busby et al.,*[3] upon charges of keeping a common betting house, Busby was fined $25,000. Noting that the charge dealt with an offence which took place in June and that the charge was not laid until October, during which interval Busby was prosecuted for other offences of a similar nature, the court, taking into account the nature of his operations, lowered the fine to $15,000.

In *R. v. Lewis,*[4] the prisoner was convicted of taking part in a conspiracy to smuggle watches on a large scale. He did not take part in the actual smuggling but helped to run a business which operated as a cover and concerned itself with the distribution of the goods. He joined the conspiracy after it began and left before it was uncovered and started an honest business. He did not appear to have made a large personal profit. A £10,000 fine was imposed. It was clear that the accused could not pay the whole fine himself. The court held:

> A fine should be within the defendant's own capacity (though not necessarily his present capacity) to pay, otherwise he may be saddled with a fine he

---

[3] Unreported, June 25, 1973 (Ont. C.A.).
[4] D. A. Thomas, at p. 221 note 1. This is an extract from the judgment of the Court of Criminal Appeal in *R. v. Lewis, supra,* n. 2.

cannot pay and have to go to prison and the impression may be given that he has been saved from a prison sentence by the wealth of his friends.

In the result the fine was varied to £5,000. In so doing the court held that it was wrong to impose a fine utterly beyond the means of the accused. Yet, on the other hand, a court should not assume that a present inability to pay will be permanent.[5]

The conclusion that one of the purposes of a fine is to see that the offender does not gain from his wrong-doing can be seen in *R. v. Poynton:*[6] "It is not the intention of the Court to impose a fine in addition to a gaol term in view of the fact that the money illegally appropriated has been repaid and that a penalty of some $4,200 has been imposed upon the respondent under the provisions of the *Income Tax Act.*"

The amount of a fine should reflect the offence actually committed, and not extraneous factors. In *R. v. Fogarty,*[7] the trial judge imposed a fine of $5,900 upon learning that approximately this amount had been earned from pool-selling operations on the Canadian Football League games during a period of six and one-half years prior to the date of the offence in the indictment. The court held that in the circumstances the fine was grossly excessive because it reflected other offences for which the prisoner had never been charged or convicted, and reduced the fine to $1,000.

In *R. v. Dunton,*[8] the trial judge imposed a sentence of 30 days' imprisonment on a charge of theft of a sum of money under $50 from the T. Eaton Co. Because this was a first offender, aged 47 years, the court determined that neither imprisonment nor probation would be appropriate: "It was suggested that a fine might be imposed. This Court is not sympathetic to the idea of ordering fines to be paid in cases of theft unless the circumstances are very unusual. To do so might appear to be tantamount to the ordering of a licence for committing a theft."

On the other hand, in *R. v. Covell,*[9] the accused was convicted of taking a vessel without the owner's consent and sentenced to two months definite and one month indeterminate. The accused was 38, a respected citizen and a successful businessman; the act was a first offence wherein he yielded foolishly to an impulse. The court determined that a fine

---

[5] *R. v. LeBlanc; R. v. Long,* [1939] 2 D.L.R. 154 (N.B.C.A.); *R. v. Churchill (No. 2),* [1966] 2 All E.R. 215; *R. v. Dodd,* [1957] Crim. L.R. 159.
[6] (1972), 9 C.C.C. (2d) 32 at pp. 45-46 (Ont. C.A.).
[7] Unreported, September 20, 1974 (Ont. C.A.).
[8] (1973), 24 C.R.N.S. 116 at p. 117 (Ont. C.A.).
[9] Unreported, June 22, 1973 (Ont. C.A.).

"would serve the ends of justice more effectively that any other form of punishment." Clearly there is no consistency in dealing with the problem of theft.

It is not permissible to impose a jail sentence merely because someone is "a man of means" to whom a fine would mean "virtually nothing". In *R. v. Johnson,*[10] the court said:

> What concerns the Court deeply is the cardinal principle upon which our criminal judicial system . . . is based, namely, that all persons stand equal before the Court. It matters not what the race, creed, colour, status in society, whether pauper or rich man, an accused must receive equality of treatment before the law.

The court varied the prison sentence and imposed a fine instead.

It appears that the opposite is the case where the accused is a corporate body, where a fine is in fact the only penalty which can be imposed.

> To fine a large, faceless corporation can hardly be said to be punishment or a deterrent unless the fine is substantial.
>
> Realistically it cannot be said that the stigma of conviction and penalty to a large corporation, or even some smaller corporations, will reflect unfavourably on their corporate images in the business world or with the consumer public which, in the final analysis, this whole process is designed to protect. However, on occasion, unfortunately, relatively unimportant personal offenders or small businessmen operating as one shareholder corporations may suffer consequences out of all proportion to those suffered by the large impersonal corporations whose executive offices and guiding personalities are relatively anonymous.[11]

The lack of any realistic alternative in cases of corporate offences and the demands of the criminal law seem to require a different perspective on the use of fine than applies to individual offenders.

In *Childs v. The Queen,*[12] the sentencing judge said, in the process of imposing three months' imprisonment plus a fine of $200 or a further month in jail, that the fine was for the purpose of placing the accused "in a position that you might get out in three months." The appeal court varied the sentence to delete the fine as the sentence really amounted to four months' imprisonment with the right of the accused to be released in three months if he was able and willing to pay the fine. "I think it entirely

---

[10] (1971), 5 C.C.C. (2d) 541 at p. 543 (N.S.C.A.).
[11] *R. v. Armco Canada Ltd. and Nine other Corporations (No. 2)* (1975), 24 C.C.C. (2d) 147 at pp. 149-50 (Ont.); vard 30 C.C.C. (2d) 183 (C.A.).
[12] (1958), 122 C.C.C. 126 (N.B.C.A.).

wrong, in a case of this nature, for the length of the imprisonment to depend on the ability of the accused to pay a fine."

Once the court has decided that a fine is proper, then there are many factors to be considered: amongst them, the amount involved in the crime, the amount obtained from the crime by the accused, if this is known, and the accused's capacity to pay.

A fine rather than imprisonment might well be indicated where the offender's state of health, such as a history of heart attacks, indicates that it would be dangerous to imprison him.[13]

Certain procedural rules are followed upon the imposition of a fine. A fine ought not to be assessed on the expectation that a third party will pay. Where two persons are jointly charged and convicted, a separate penalty should be imposed on each of them, even if the offence is a joint one. It is improper to impose a joint and several fine, and to provide for imprisonment of both accused until payment by either of them.[14] A fine may be imposed with a term of imprisonment in default of payment even if the maximum term of imprisonment has already been given.[15]

B. Means[16]

In *Curley v. The Queen,*[17] in the course of discussing a particular fine, the court analyzed the purpose behind s-ss. (3) to (11) of s. 646, regarding means and making available time to pay. The court quoted the comments of the then Minister of Justice upon introducing these provisions in Parliament, as follows:

> The objective of these amendments is to eliminate, so far as our criminal law is concerned, to the greatest extent possible any remnant of imprisonment for debt. We hope that the result of the amendment will be that imprisonment for a failure to pay a fine will only occur where there has been a contempt of court, that is a failure by the convicted person to pay a fine ordered by the court even though he has the means to pay it!

---

[13] *R. v. Wallace,* [1969] Crim. L.R. 211.
[14] *R. v. Jarvis; R. v. Smith* (1925), 44 C.C.C. 97 (Ont. C.A.).
[15] *R. v. Chiovitti* (1950), 96 C.C.C. 177 (B.C.C.A.).
[16] See also Chapter 19, "Ability to Pay".
[17] (1969), 7 C.R.N.S. 108 (Que. C.A.); *R. v. Rasper* (1978), 1 C.R. (3d) S-45 (Ont. C.A.).

The court concluded that it was logical to assume that Parliament never intended these provisions to be used to disguise a more severe sentence by the use of a fine with provision for imprisonment in default.

Contingencies such as promotion or salary increase or legacy should be largely discounted in assessing means.[18] Care must be taken in assessing such resources:

> This is much too high a fine for this kind of offence by an undergraduate in the circumstances in which this young man was living in Cambridge with the undergraduate income that he had. It is true that he comes from a well off family and had been sent to a very well-known English public school before he went to Cambridge. But the sins of the children in this connection must not be visited on the parents, and it would be unreal to expect this young man to pay a total sum of £500 — £250 fine and £250 costs — out of an income of some £60 a month which we were told he was allowed by his father apart from having his university fees paid.[19]

The principal problem with a fine has been the difficulty of dealing with the fact that for some persons the same fine causes more hardship and suffering than for others. In *R. v. Natrall,*[20] it was argued that the routine imposition of a fine with imprisonment in default, places rich and poor on an unequal footing before the law, in that the one class has the means to pay and the ability to purchase liberty, whereas the other class is not in that position. It was said that this was contrary to the Canadian Bill of Rights. The court rejected this argument:

> I agree that no one should be imprisoned for non-payment of a fine if in truth he is so devoid of means that he is quite unable to pay it. But *Criminal Code,* s. 722 does not provide for *routine* imprisonment. It places upon the tribunal which proposes to act under it, and which contemplates imposing punishment by a fine instead of, or in addition to, imprisonment, a duty to have regard to the ability or lack of ability of the particular accused to pay whatever fine is proposed to be imposed. The power . . . is permissive and discretionary, not mandatory.
>
> . . .
>
> The spirit and intent of the section is that, when it comes to imposing a fine and imprisonment in default of payment thereof, consideration shall be given to the means of the particular accused and the amount of the fine and the terms of payment shall not be such that they are beyond his ability to meet.

---

[18] *R. v. Davidson* (1917), 28 C.C.C. 44 (Alta. C.A.).
[19] *R. v. Tao,* [1976] 3 All E.R. 65 at p. 70.
[20] (1973), 9 C.C.C. (2d) 390 at pp. 397-98 (B.C.C.A.).

Indeed, in some cases the Judge may leave the matter in the position that imprisonment is not to follow default in payment but recovery of the fine is to be left to civil proceedings by the Crown: see *Criminal Code,* s. 652.

The court acknowledged that a poor man who is fined inevitably suffers more than a rich man; but concluded that "equality before the law" within the meaning of the Canadian Bill of Rights somehow had no application in such matters.

Similar views have been expressed in England. In *R. v. Reeves,*[21] the trial judge refused to order a fine because the prisoner was unable to pay, and accordingly sent the man to prison because he saw no other alternative. The court held that the language used must have indicated to anyone who might be listening in court that the prisoner was being sent to prison not because the offence itself merited a sentence of immediate custodial imprisonment, but because he had not the financial wherewithal to pay a substantial fine. This comment was wrong, and the sentence was lowered because of the appellant's possible sense of grievance arising from the impression that he had been sent to prison solely because of his lack of means.

On the other hand, in *R. v. Rowe,*[22] the court upheld a heavy fine of £ 250 and justified it by noting that the accused "was a man of means". Tallis J. of the Northwest Territories Supreme Court has imposed fines that were different for similar offences upon the ground that the accused who was able to pay a larger amount should do so.[23]

Alec Samuels,[24] in an excellent article, sums up the somewhat unclear position in England as permitting a reduction of a fine upon the less affluent offender, so as to bring it within his ability to pay, but rejecting an increase upon the more affluent so as to bring it up to ability to pay. But even the English cases do not by any means entirely support this general principle. Cross[25] in *The English Sentencing System* argues that at least in the case of acquisitive offences, the wealth of the offender aggravates the crime just as his poverty mitigates it. It follows then that a heavier fine would be justified upon the man of means because his offence is graver. This is a useful categorization.

---

[21] (1972), 56 Cr. App. R. 366.
[22] [1975] Crim. L.R. 245.
[23] *R. v. Evalik; R. v. Haniliak,* unreported, March 6, 1978.
[24] "The Fine: The Principles", [1970] Crim. L.R. 201; *R. v. Cargill* (1913), 8 Cr. App. R. 224.
[25] At p. 24.

C. Imprisonment In Default

Where imprisonment is ordered in default of payment of a fine, it is clear that if the accused finds it impossible to pay the sentence is inevitably a sentence of imprisonment.[26]

In *R. v. Hall,*[27] the court said:

> If a fine is to be imposed with an alternative of imprisonment, there must be a true alternative and not an illusory one. Here there was really no alternative for a bankrupt facing such a sentence but to serve the supposedly alternative term of imprisonment.

The court held that a fine was not appropriate and substituted a period of imprisonment based on the seriousness of the offence itself. Fines have often been rejected as a sentencing alternative because the lack of means coupled with the imposition of imprisonment in default of payment would in effect mean a heavier punishment.[28] In *R. v. Tessier,*[29] the court said: "It is my opinion that resort should be had to the sanction of imprisonment to enforce payment of a debt only where there is no doubt of ability to pay, and clear evidence that the debtor wilfully refuses to discharge his obligation."

There is increasing disquiet about the number of persons who are forced to serve jail terms in default of payment of fines. In *R. v. Yamelst,*[30] Toy J. noted a practice of provincial court judges, at least in Vancouver, to invariably provide for a jail sentence in default of payment of fines. He said:

> In my respectful view, before applying s. 722(2) and ordering a jail term in default, Courts should give appropriate consideration to what, if any, reformation will occur, what deterrent effect will occur, or how society will be protected if a person serves 14 or 30 days in the Lower Mainland Correctional Centre if [he] fails to meet the deadline to pay a fine . . . I have concluded that the real reason that the "in default" adjudication is made in the majority of cases is because the threat of jail in lieu of non-payment of a fine is a practical method for the Crown to force the collection of its financial penalties. The Crown has its civil remedies for the collection of its penalties pursuant to s. 652 of the *Criminal Code* of Canada and I, for one, am not

---

[26] *Architects Registration Council v. Breeze* (1973), 57 Cr. App. R. 654.

[27] (1968), 52 Cr. App. R. 736.

[28] *R. v. Sommers et al. (No. 11)* (1958), 29 W.W.R. 350 (B.C.).

[29] (1957), 21 W.W.R. 331 at p. 333 (Man. Co. Ct.).

[30] (1975), 22 C.C.C (2d) 502 at pp. 507-08 (B.C.).

convinced that it was Parliament's intention that s. 722(2) be utilized to give the Crown such a right, privilege or preference over other obligations that the convicted person may have.

It is hoped that this judicial expression of opinion will result in a decrease of such orders which are often made without thought or consideration.

It is a clear principle that any term of imprisonment imposed as an alternative to payment of a fine should not be out of proportion to the fine itself. Where this is not the case, the sentence will be varied.[31]

Considerable dispute exists as to whether or not imprisonment imposed in default of payment of a fine is punishment, or simply a means of enforcing payment of the fine and not in itself a punishment. In *R. v. Chong Chow,*[32] a statute which provided that upon imprisonment the offender shall be deported was held not to extend to a case in which the imprisonment was imposed merely in default of payment of a fine; such imprisonment is not imposed as punishment.

The question came up again, in a different context, in *R. v. Tomlinson.*[33] Tomlinson pleaded guilty to a charge of assaulting a peace officer and was sentenced to a fine of $500 payable in instalments, and placed on probation for one year. He thereupon left the courtroom. The judge immediately realized that he had not imposed a term of imprisonment in default of payment of the fine and made such an order in the absence of the accused. An application was brought to quash the conviction and sentence by way of *certiorari* on the basis of the accused's absence during part of his trial. The court held that though sentence is part of the trial, neither sentence nor conviction were vitiated because the sentence was the fine itself and the term of imprisonment in default of payment thereof was simply the fixing of one of several means open to the Crown of enforcing payment of the fine. Accordingly the trial judge's "afterthought" formed no part of the sentence and therefore was not part of the trial. An order went quashing that part of the sentence but the balance of the sentence and the conviction were permitted to stand. Supporting this view is *R. v. Chiovitti,*[34] to the effect that where both imprisonment and a fine are imposed, even if the imprisonment is for the maximum period permitted by statute, the fine may nevertheless have further imprisonment ordered in default of payment.

---

[31] *R. v. Sydorik and Zowatski,* [1926] 3 W.W.R. 458 (Sask. C.A.).
[32] (1925), 38 Que. K.B. 440 (C.A.).
[33] (1971), 2 C.C.C. (2d) 97 (B.C.).
[34] (1950), 96 C.C.C. 177 (B.C.C.A.).

On the other hand, in *R. v Davidson,*[35] the court came to the contrary view, saying: "If the offender chooses not to pay the fine and prefers to go to gaol surely he is suffering punishment for his offence and not merely for non-payment of the fine."

It is respectfully submitted that the *Chong Chow* and *Tomlinson* cases are analytically correct. It is the nature of imprisonment *qua* punishment that it be certain; if the imprisonment is contingent, then, though it may be served in expiation of the offence, it is not what we ordinarily mean by a "sentence" of imprisonment. However, this conclusion offers little solace to the impecunious imprisoned debtor, and makes little human sense. That imprisonment is in human terms a qualitatively more severe sanction than a fine seems self-evident, despite the fact that it is not discussed in case law.

D. Time To Pay

In the case of any fine the court may, in accordance with the statute, allow time in which to pay it. Implied in this is undoubtedly the ability to order that it should be paid in particular periodic instalments. It has been said that the periodic payment provides a continuing and useful reminder of the offence and the need for atonement.[36]

It is generally undesirable to impose a fine so large that, given the means of the accused, it would be necessary for him to pay it over a very long period of time. In England it has been said that living under the threat of imprisonment for defaulting on payments over a period of four years was too heavy a penalty to impose despite grave wrong-doing.[37] In *R. v. Tessier,*[38] the court said: "Any such order must provide for instalments large enough to discharge the penalty . . . within a reasonable time."

In *R. v. Berger,*[39] the trial judge ordered "the accused to remain in custody until the monies are paid. These sums are to be paid within one

---

[35] (1917), 28 C.C.C. 44 (Alta. C.A.).
[36] Alec Samuels, "The Fine: The Principles", [1970] Crim. L.R. 201; *R. v. Blake* (1978), 39 C.C.C. (2d) 138 (P.E.I.C.A.).
[37] *R. v. Hewitt* (1971), 55 Cr. App. R. 433.
[38] *R. v. Tessier* (1957), 21 W.W.R. 331 at p. 332 (Man. Co. Ct.).
[39] [1971] 1 O.R. 765 (C.A.).

month, or the Reformatory sentence goes in." The Ontario Court of Appeal struck the sentence stating that there is no provision in the criminal law for incarceration pending payment of a fine as was ordered above.

On the other hand it is undoubtedly within the discretion of a trial judge to refuse to permit time to pay the fine if he complies with statutory conditions. Trial judges often do not so comply.

In *Ex parte Andrews,*[40] an application for *habeas corpus* was made upon the ground that a warrant of committal in a summary conviction matter was defective in that it did not state the reasons for the order that the fine be paid forthwith as required by the Criminal Code. Meredith J. found that the purpose of these sections generally is to ensure that an accused person will not be deprived of his liberty simply because he has no immediate access to means to pay a fine. They confer on the accused the right that reasons be assigned by the court for payment of the fine forthwith, and that such reasons be specifically set forth in the warrant of committal. The requirement for reasons in the warrant of committal constitutes the principal safeguard the accused has that the provisions of the law have been in fact observed. Meredith J. rejected the argument that the statement of reasons was a matter of procedure only, directory and not mandatory. He held that s. 716 of the Criminal Code applied only to defects in form and not, as here, to a prerequisite to jurisdiction to sentence and imprison.

In the case of indictable offences there is no need to make such a notation in the committal warrant, but the Criminal Code does provide that the trial judge shall not direct that the fine be paid forthwith unless he is satisfied that there is sufficient means; or the accused person, upon being asked by the court whether he desires time, does not request such time; or if for any other special reason the court deems it expedient that no time should be allowed. In *Curley v. The Queen,*[41] the court noted that no portion of the record, transcript, or judgment imposing sentence indicated that these provisions had been complied with. For this reason, *inter alia,* the fine was struck from the sentence. Similarly in *R. v. Doucette,*[42] the court said:

> Upon a perusal of the record of the trial in the Court below it does not

---

[40] (1973), 15 C.C.C. (2d) 43 (B.C.); *R. v. Rosen,* unreported, March 29, 1976 (Ont. C.A.).

[41] (1969), 7 C.R.N.S. 108 (Que. C.A.).

[42] (1974), 6 Nfld. & P.E.I. R. 100 at p. 103 (P.E.I.).

appear that the above directions were invoked either by Counsel or the trial Magistrate. Neither did the accused give evidence before the trial Magistrate as to his future intentions or his inability to pay the fine forthwith.

The court gave time to pay, and, bearing in mind the occupation of the accused, that time was stipulated to be "on or before the close of the Lobster Fishery Season" in the area.

In *R. v. Yamelst,*[43] the accused had been given time to pay by the convicting Provincial Court Judge and, further, when he was unable to pay within that time an extension was allowed him. He still did not pay and was committed to prison. An application was made for a further extension of time to pay the fine, and the trial judge refused on the ground that he had no jurisdiction to do so because the warrant of committal had been executed. Toy J. noted that the language of s. 722(10) contained neither hint nor inference that the power to extend time for payment, once granted, exhausted that power or that any time limitation whatsoever existed within which such an application must be brought. These sections disclose, as their primary objective, the early and orderly collection of financial penalties due to the Crown. But they do not disclose an intention to limit time within which an application for an extension could be made and there is no substance to an argument that the court was *functus officio* once the accused had been arrested pursuant to a warrant of committal, since the signing of such warrants is merely a ministerial function of the court.

E. Other Punishment

In cases where the offence is punishable by more than five years' imprisonment (for indictable offences) a court has no jurisdiction to impose a fine only.[44] Similarly the imposition of a fine following the suspension of sentence is illegal.[45]

What would otherwise be a technical fault in the sentence because of a maximum penalty in excess of five years can be corrected by the

---

[43] (1975), 22 C.C.C. (2d) 502 (B.C.).
[44] *R. v. England* (1925), 43 C.C.C. 11 (Sask. C.A.).
[45] *R. v. Agozzino,* [1970] 1 C.C.C. 380 (Ont. C.A.); *R. v. Pawlowski* (1972), 5 C.C.C. (2d) 87 (Man. C.A.).

imposition of a nominal period of imprisonment, such as one day; and this is often done.

A fine with imprisonment in default can be imposed in cases where the maximum penalty has also been imposed.[46]

F. The Payment Of The Fine

It is not possible to order payment of fines on two different charges to be concurrent. In *R. v. Derdarian, Reycraft and Derdarian,*[47] Moorhouse J. stated that he was not aware of any authority which permitted an order that the fines for two separate offences should be paid at the same time. If a trial judge intends that payment of one fine should cover punishment imposed for two offences, he is in error.

The fine must be paid to the Crown in accordance with the provisions of the Criminal Code. There is no authority whatever to impose a fine and try to make it serve the function of restitution or compensation. In *R. v. Sperdakes,*[48] the court ordered that half of the $1,000 fine was to be paid to the railway company from whom the accused fraudulently stole electricity. The court held that the sentence was illegal. Similarly in *R. v. England,*[49] a direction that the fine should be paid to the victim "as restitution" was held to be unlawful.

There is an interesting conflict as to whether or not the acceptance of payment by the Crown operates to prevent a Crown appeal from the sentence. In *R. v. Bernier,*[50] the accused was convicted of an offence under the Excise Act and was fined $100. In accordance with that statute the cheque was sent to the Minister of Finance and was accepted; later the complainant gave notice of appeal. Though it is clear that the Criminal Code provisions now permit an accused to appeal after he pays his fine (in derogation of the common law notion of acquiescence), the court held that the provision of the Criminal Code providing for such an exemption to the accused but not to the complainant or informant was

---

[46] *R. v. Chiovitti* (1950), 96 C.C.C. 177 (B.C.C.A.).
[47] [1965] 2 O.R. 724. For a discussion of whether or not probation is "other punishment" see Section I in Chapter 10 dealing with statutory limitations.
[48] (1911), 24 C.C.C. 210 (N.B.C.A.).
[49] (1925), 43 C.C.C. 11 (Sask. C.A.).
[50] (1939), 71 C.C.C 380 (Que.).

deliberate and that therefore the acceptance of the fine constituted acquiescence and the Crown appeal was dismissed. In *R. v. Fraser,*[51] Campbell C.J., in what appears to be a *per incuriam* decision, came to the opposite conclusion by holding that there exists such a thing as a common law principle of reciprocity which governed and made it unjust to apply the section in favour of the accused and not to the Crown. The entire position needs to be examined by a modern court in the light of the present provisions of the Criminal Code governing appeals.

---

[51] [1944] 2 D.L.R. 461 (P.E.I.).

Chapter 12

Costs

Criminal Code:

656. The person in whose favour judgment is given in proceedings by indictment for defamatory libel is entitled to recover from the opposite party costs in a reasonable amount to be fixed by order of the court.

657. Where costs that are fixed under section 656 are not paid forthwith the party in whose favour judgment is given may enter judgment for the amount of the costs by filing the order in the superior court of the province in which the trial was held, and that judgment is enforceable against the opposite party in the same manner as if it were a judgment rendered against him in that court in civil proceedings.

742. Where several persons join in committing the same offence and upon conviction each is adjudged to pay an amount to a person aggrieved, no more shall be paid to that person than an amount equal to the value of the property destroyed or injured or the amount of the injury done, together with costs, if any, and the residue of the amount adjudged to be paid shall be applied in the manner in which other penalties imposed by law are directed to be applied.

744(1) The summary conviction court may in its discretion award and order such costs as it considers reasonable and not inconsistent with such of the fees established by section 772 as may be taken or allowed in proceedings before that summary conviction court, to be paid

    (a) to the informant by the defendant, where the summary conviction court convicts or makes an order against the defendant, or

    (b) to the defendant by the informant, where the summary conviction court dismisses an information.

(2) An order under subsection (1) shall be set out in the conviction order or order of dismissal, as the case may be.

(3) Where a fine or sum of money or both are adjudged to be paid by a defendant, and a term of imprisonment in default of payment is imposed, the defendant is, in default of payment, liable to serve the term of imprisonment

imposed, and for the purposes of this subsection, any costs that are awarded against the defendant shall be deemed to be part of the fine or sum of money adjudged to be paid.

(4) Where no fine or sum of money is adjudged to be paid by a defendant, but costs are awarded against the defendant or informant, the person who is liable to pay them is, in default of payment, liable to imprisonment for one month.

(5) In this section, "costs" includes the costs and charges, after they have been ascertained, of committing and conveying to prison the person against whom costs have been awarded.

758. Where an appeal [from summary conviction or sentence] is heard and determined or is abandoned or is dismissed for want of prosecution, the appeal court may make any order with respect to costs that it considers just and reasonable.

759(1) Where the appeal court orders the appellant or respondent to pay costs, the order shall direct that the costs be paid to the clerk of the court, to be paid by him to the person entitled to them, and shall fix the period within which the costs shall be paid.

(2) Where costs are not paid in full within the period fixed for payment and the person who has been ordered to pay them has not been bound by a recognizance to pay them, the clerk of the court shall, upon application by the person entitled to the costs, or by any person on his behalf, and upon payment of any fee to which the clerk of the court is entitled, issue a certificate in Form 38 certifying that the costs or a part thereof, as the case may be, have not been paid.

(3) A justice having jurisdiction in the territorial division in which a certificate has been issued under subsection (2) may, upon production of the certificate, by warrant in Form 23, commit the defaulter to imprisonment for a term not exceeding one month, unless the amount of the costs and, where the justice thinks fit so to order, the costs of the committal and of conveying the defaulter to prison are sooner paid.

760(1) A conviction or order made by the appeal court may be enforced

(a) in the same manner as if it had been made by the summary conviction court, or

(b) by process of the appeal court.

(2) Where an appeal taken against a conviction or order adjudging payment of a sum of money is dismissed, the summary conviction court that made the conviction or order or a justice for the same territorial division may issue a warrant of committal as if no appeal had been taken.

(3) Where a conviction or order that has been made by an appeal court is to be enforced by a justice, the clerk of the appeal court shall send to the justice the conviction or order and all writings relating thereto, except the notice of intention to appeal and any recognizance.

610(3) A court of appeal [for a province or a territory] may exercise in relation to proceedings in the court any powers not mentioned in subsection (1) that may be exercised by the court on appeals in civil matters, and may issue any process that is necessary to enforce the orders or sentences of the court but no costs shall be allowed to the appellant or respondent on the hearing and determination of an appeal or on any proceedings preliminary or incidental thereto.

650(1) Where a term of imprisonment is imposed in default of payment of a penalty, the term shall, upon payment of a part of the penalty, whether the payment was made before or after the issue of a warrant of committal, be reduced by the number of days that bears the same proportion to the number of days in the term as the part paid bears to the total penalty.

(2) No amount offered in part payment of a penalty shall be accepted unless it is sufficient to secure reduction of sentence of one day, or some multiple thereof, and where a warrant of committal has been issued, no part payment shall be accepted until any fee that is payable in respect of the warrant or its execution has been paid.

(3) Payment may be made under this section to the person who has lawful custody of the prisoner or to such other person as the Attorney General directs.

(4) A payment under this section shall, unless the order imposing the penalty otherwise provides, be applied to the payment in full of costs and charges, and thereafter to payment in full of compensation or damages that are included in the penalty, and finally to payment in full of any part of the penalty that remains unpaid.

(5) In this section, "penalty" means all the sums of money, including fines, in default of payment of which a term of imprisonment is imposed and includes the costs and charges of committing the defaulter and of conveying him to prison.

In general, unless specifically authorized by statute, costs are not to be imposed. Thus, subject to the exception in s. 656 of the Criminal Code on the trial on appeal of indictable offences there is no authority to impose payment of costs. Costs can be imposed in summary conviction matters, in accordance with the tariff set out in the Criminal Code, and on appeals from summary conviction offences.[1]

Since every criminal prosecution is carried on in the name of the Crown, any order for costs must be read as being applicable to the person at whose instance the procedure of the Crown was set in motion.[2]

In England it has been decided that it is wrong to make an order for costs leaving the sum or any portion thereof unspecified. "To make an

---

[1] *R. v. Pawlowski* (1972), 5 C.C.C. (2d) 87 (Man. C.A.); *Re R. and Sheldon* (1972), 8 C.C.C. (2d) 355 (Ont.).
[2] *R. v. Blackley* (1904), 8 C.C.C. 405 (Que.).

order for the payment of the quarter of the costs of the prosecution does not help one to know to what that quarter will amount and whether there is any possibility of a defendant complying with the order."[3]

In the same case the court struck out the order because in the circumstances it would be wrong: "It could be implemented, if ever, only when these two men are released, which is just the time that they will need such money as they earn to get started in life again." Accordingly it would appear to be wrong to impose costs together with a lengthy period of imprisonment (here three years), at least where it appears at trial that the accused would be unable to pay the costs from moneys then available. Costs may never be imposed routinely, as their imposition may well run counter to more important purposes of the criminal law.

Similarly, it has been held that it is wrong not to set the amount of costs or at least to estimate them beforehand. In *R. v. Rowe,*[4] the order at trial was simply to pay the prosecution costs. It later turned out that these amounted to about £1,000 and the accused's own costs were about £1,500. Taking this total financial penalty into consideration, the court determined that if the trial judge had considered this matter he would have been unlikely to have set the amount as high as £1,000, and in the circumstances the order was quashed.

Aside from jurisdictional questions, an order for the payment of costs is one based on mixed fact and law and therefore the quantum thereof cannot be a question of law alone, such as would enable the question of costs to be appealed in a summary conviction matter to a court of appeal for a province.[5]

One of the justifications in criminal, as in civil, matters is success; costs ordinarily follow the party who has succeeded.[6] In exercising a discretion as to whether or not to impose costs, the court is entitled to take all the circumstances into account, including the strength of the case against the accused, and his knowledge of its strength at the time he pleaded not guilty. The accused has, of course, a right to plead not guilty, however strong the case against him and however conscious he may be of his guilt, and take his chances with the jury. But if he fights and loses a case in which the evidence against him is very strong, then he cannot reasonably complain if he is ordered to pay part of the costs consistent

---

[3] *R. v. Judd* (1971), 55 Cr. App. R. 14.
[4] [1975] Crim. L.R. 245.
[5] *R. v. Masurak* (1961), 37 C.R. 5 (Sask. C.A.).
[6] *R. v. Fairn* (1973), 12 C.C.C. (2d) 423 (N.S. Co. Ct.).

with his own means.[7] In awarding costs the appeal court should consider whether the appeal had merit or was frivolous; in the latter situation the respondent should be compensated as fully as possible for actual expenses incurred. However, costs should not be so high in any event that legitimate appeals would not be taken due to a fear of the financial burden. The court has noted that this had become a problem with respect to civil matters and ought not to be allowed to happen in the area of criminal law.[8]

In Canada, under the old Criminal Code (which permitted costs in indictable prosecutions) McRuer C.J.H.C. imposed costs in *R. v. Northern Electric Co. Ltd.*[9] because the accused persons "were making it as difficult as possible for the proper authorities to ascertain exactly what was done and who was responsible for doing it, so that it would be very difficult eventually to succeed in a prosecution."

---

[7] *R. v. Yoxall* (1973), 57 Cr. App. R. 263.
[8] *R. v. Higgins* (1977), 1 C.R. (3d) 382 (N.S. Co. Ct.).
[9] (1956), 24 C.R. 201 (Ont.).

Chapter 13

Imprisonment

Criminal Code:

645(1) Where an enactment prescribes different degrees or kinds of punishment in respect of an offence, the punishment to be imposed is, subject to the limitations prescribed in the enactment, in the discretion of the court that convicts a person who commits the offence.

(2) Where an enactment prescribes a punishment in respect of an offence, the punishment to be imposed is, subject to the limitations prescribed in the enactment, in the discretion of the court that convicts a person who commits the offence, but no punishment is a minimum punishment unless it is declared to be a minimum punishment.

658. Every one who is convicted of an indictable offence for which no punishment is specially provided is liable to imprisonment for five years.

659(1) Except where otherwise provided, a person who is sentenced to imprisonment for

(a) life,

(b) a term of two years or more, or

(c) two or more terms of less than two years each that are to be served one after the other and that, in the aggregate, amount to two years or more,

shall be sentenced to imprisonment in a penitentiary.

(2) Where a person who is sentenced to imprisonment in a penitentiary is, before the expiration of that sentence, sentenced to imprisonment for a term of less than two years, he shall be sentenced to and shall serve that term in a penitentiary, but if the previous sentence of imprisonment in a penitentiary is set aside, he shall serve that term in accordance with subsection (3).

(3) A person who is sentenced to imprisonment and who is not required to be sentenced as provided in subsection (1) or (2) shall, unless a special prison is prescribed by law, be sentenced to imprisonment in a prison or other place of confinement within the province in which he is convicted, other than a

penitentiary, in which the sentence of imprisonment may be lawfully executed.

(4) Where a person is sentenced to imprisonment in a penitentiary while he is lawfully imprisoned in a place other than a penitentiary he shall, except where otherwise provided, be sent immediately to the penitentiary and shall serve in the penitentiary the unexpired portion of the term of imprisonment that he was serving when he was sentenced to the penitentiary as well as the term of imprisonment for which he was sentenced to the penitentiary.

(5) Where, at any time, a person who is imprisoned in a prison or place of confinement other than a penitentiary is subject to two or more terms of imprisonment, each of which is for less than two years, that are to be served one after the other, and the aggregate of the unexpired portions of those terms at that time amounts to two years or more, he shall be transferred to a penitentiary to serve those terms; but if any one or more of such terms is set aside and the unexpired portions of the remaining term or terms on the day on which he was transferred under this section amounted to less than two years, he shall serve that term or terms in accordance with subsection (3).

(6) For the purposes of this section, where a person is sentenced to imprisonment for a definite term and an indeterminate period thereafter, such sentence shall be deemed to be for a term of less than two years and only the definite term thereof shall be taken into account in determining whether he is required to be sentenced to imprisonment in a penitentiary or to be committed or transferred to a penitentiary under subsection (5).

(6.1) Where, either before or after the coming into force of this subsection, a person has been sentenced, committed or transferred to a penitentiary, otherwise than pursuant to an agreement made under subsection 15(1) of the *Penitentiary Act,* any indeterminate portion of his sentence shall, for all purposes, be deemed not to have been imposed.

(7) For the purposes of subsection (3) "penitentiary" does not, until a day to be fixed by proclamation of the Governor in Council, include the penitentiary mentioned in section 82 of the *Penitentiary Act,* chapter 206 of the Revised Statutes of Canada, 1952.

660(1) A sentence of imprisonment shall be served in accordance with the enactments and rules that govern the institution to which the prisoner is sentenced, and a reference to hard labour in a conviction or sentence shall be deemed to be a reference to the employment of prisoners that is provided for in the enactment or rules.

(2) A conviction or sentence that imposes hard labour shall not be quashed or set aside on the ground only that the enactment that creates the offence does not authorize the imposition of hard labour, but shall be amended accordingly.

In Canada imprisonment for a fixed term has been a standard and much used form of sentence.

The Criminal Code sets out that "except where otherwise provided, a person who is sentenced to imprisonment for life [or] a term of two years or more, or two or more terms of less than two years each that are to be served one after the other and that, in the aggregate, amount to two years or more, shall be sentenced to imprisonment in a penitentiary".[1] Once sentenced to imprisonment in a penitentiary, any sentence for a term of less than two years which is thereafter incurred shall be served in a penitentiary.[2] All other persons are to serve their sentences in a place of confinement where a sentence of imprisonment may be lawfully executed in accordance with the laws of the province in which the conviction took place, or in a "common gaol, public or reformatory prison, lock-up, guard-room or other place in which persons who are charged with or convicted of offences are usually kept in custody."[3]

A sentence of imprisonment "at hard labour" means no more than that the prisoner shall be employed in the manner provided by the relevant enactment.[4]

In *R. v. Bradshaw,*[5] the question before the Supreme Court of Canada was whether or not the provisions of s. 234(a) of the Criminal Code, which require upon a finding of guilt for impaired driving "a fine of not more than $500 and not less than $50 or . . . imprisonment for three months or to both" was "other than an offence for which a minimum punishment is prescribed by law" so as to enable the Court, pursuant to s. 662.1(1) of the Code, to impose a conditional discharge. Spence J., speaking for the Supreme Court of Canada, noted that s. 234(a) did prescribe a "minimum penalty" ". . . that is, a fine of $50. It might prescribe an alternative form of penalty and fail to prescribe a minimum for that other kind but it has none the less prescribed a minimum penalty."

Clearly, when a sentence is one of imprisonment the protection of society is accomplished in an absolute sense by preventing an offender from repeating his unlawful acts upon society during the term of his imprisonment. But that is not the only purpose of imprisonment, for we assume the sentence will deter the offender from committing other offences on his release and also deter others from committing the same or different offences. Courts insist "imprisonment also provides an

---

[1] Criminal Code, s. 659(1).
[2] Criminal Code, s. 659(2).
[3] Criminal Code, s. 659(3); Criminal Code, s. 2: "prison" defined.
[4] Criminal Code, s. 660.
[5] (1975), 21 C.C.C. (2d) 69.

opportunity for the reform and rehabilitation of the offender." The evidence to support this theory is virtually non-existent. Confessing to scepticism on this point, Cross asserts "It *is* impossible to train men for freedom in a condition of captivity",[6] and suggests that the belief that people can be reformed by being sent to prison has had a baneful influence on the courts by encouraging them to impose prison sentences more frequently and to lengthen them in the name of rehabilitation. In any event, the possibility of reform is at best incidental in the case of imprisonment. Even if imprisonment does not permanently crush an imprisoned offender, it means loss of employment, temporary (if not permanent) loss of family, risk of harmful influences from other prisoners and few chances of future employment.[7] A lasting stigma attaches to those people who have been imprisoned that does not seem to exist with those who have had other penal measures imposed on them.

As Cross also says, "Small wonder then that prison has come to be regarded as the sentencer's last resort."[8] Experience teaches us that there is a real danger that someone who is already a bad man when he goes into prison will come out considerably worse. Hughes D.C.J.[9] affirms that penitentiary "has often been described as a college offering a post-graduate course in crime."

A. The Practice Of Imprisonment

Nevertheless there are offences and offenders for whom there is no other alternative consistent with the judicial responsibility to protect the public. Thus, when one examines the factors determining the imposition of imprisonment, one should bear in mind that imprisonment acts almost entirely as punishment and contains little if any reformative aspect.

There is a general conviction, perceivable over the years and increasing in strength, that custodial sentences ought to be imposed only as a last resort and where all other measures either have failed or cannot

---

[6] R. Cross, *Punishment, Prison and the Public* (1971) at p. 85.
[7] *R. v. Kosh* (1971), 1 C.C.C. (2d) 290 (Sask. C.A.).
[8] At p. 109.
[9] *R. v. Denholm* (1970), 11 C.R.N.S. 380 (Sask. C.A.).

reasonably be expected to succeed.[10] In addition, custodial sentences are necessary where the offence itself is so serious that no other measure will adequately express the condemnation which society directs at the crime, or where the element of deterrence to others demands a sentence of imprisonment.

Even for minor offences, imprisonment may be necessary in some cases. For example, imprisonment in shoplifting cases is rare, but "when, as in this case, there is repetition time and time again over a period of years, then . . . the sentencing court ought to consider and impose a custodial sentence unless there are unusually compelling circumstances against such a course."[11]

This element of persistent criminality is one of the factors that may lead the court towards the imposition of a custodial term in cases where otherwise it would not be warranted. For example, in *R. v. Vandale and Maciejewski,*[12] in dealing with a number of breaking and entering and theft offences in respect of a tourist camp where serious damage was caused as a result, the court relied upon "the repeated and deliberate nature of the appellants' conduct" as justifying a custodial term.

The older practise of imposing a term of imprisonment in order to assist and help an offender has fallen out of favour. In *R. v. Allen,*[13] the British Columbia Court of Appeal noted that the trial judge had imposed a penitentiary term because of his belief that the prisoner had a mental problem and could be treated by a full-time psychiatrist at the penitentiary. The appeal court, being in receipt of information that suitable facilities for treatment were in fact available in the community, reduced the sentence to time served with a view to taking him out of the penitentiary; the evidence indicated that further institutional care would have been of no particular benefit to him whether in a mental hospital or in a penal institution.

---

[10] See also Chapter 4, "First Offenders".
[11] *R. v. Anderson* (1972), 56 Cr. App. R. 863; *R. v. Pasternak; R. v. McNeil; R. v. Andrews* (1961), 36 W.W.R. 423 (B.C.C.A.); *R. v. Gibbings,* [1936] S.R. 36.
[12] (1974), 21 C.C.C. (2d) 250 (Ont. C.A.).
[13] (1954), 20 C.R. 301.

B. The First Custodial Term

It is only common sense to acknowledge that one's first custodial term should be as short as possible. The Ontario Court of Appeal, in *R. v. Vandale and Maciejewski*[14] cited with approval the following comments from *R. v. Curran:*[15]

> As a general rule it is undesirable that a first sentence of immediate imprisonment should be very long, disproportionate to the gravity of the offence, and imposed as this sentence was, for reasons of general deterrence, that is as a warning to others. The length of a first sentence is more reasonably determined by considerations of individual deterrence; and what sentence is needed to teach this particular offender a lesson which he has not learnt from the lighter sentences which he has previously received.

The court noted that these observations were of particular applicability in the case of a youthful first offender and altered sentences of 150 days and 120 days respectively to a term of 30 days, to be followed by two years' probation with conditions for reparation and restitution. Upon a charge of robbery, the court of appeal reduced sentence to one of six months.[16] The court said:

> There is no question that this is a serious offence and if the appellant had a record of any kind the sentence would be clearly appropriate. However, the court is concerned that a sentence of two years less one day to a twenty-one year old boy who has never had any previous trouble may end up in destroying him and indeed it is going to make sure that he is into the ways of crime.

Similarly, a sentence of five years imposed upon a conviction for armed robbery, where there was a minor previous record, was reduced to two years less one day definite together with two years less a day indeterminate.[17] The principle does not mean that there are not crimes the gravity of which demand a lengthy penitentiary term; but such instances by their nature will be rare.

In *R. v. Ferguson,*[18] the Ontario Court of Appeal, by a majority, altered a three-year sentence upon a charge of robbery to one of two years less

---

[14] *Supra,* n. 12 at p. 251; *R. v. Casey* (1977), 20 Crim. L.Q. 145 (Ont. C.A.).
[15] (1973), 57 Cr. App. R. 945 at pp. 947-48.
[16] *R. v. O'Brien,* unreported, November 21, 1977 (Y.T.C.A.).
[17] *R. v. Wilson,* unreported, May 8, 1974 (Ont. C.A.).
[18] (1971), 14 Crim. L.Q. 271.

one day definite and one year indeterminate. Noting that the offence was serious, the court stated that it was not so grave "as to negative the principle that in the case of a first prison sentence, in the absence of unusual circumstances it should be confinement to a reformatory" and commented that the judge ought to have given effect to this principle because the presentence report indicated good prospects of rehabilitation. The fact that there were previous convictions which did not result in custodial terms did not alter the application of the principle. The total period of imprisonment remained the same. Similarly in *R. v. Latulippe*[19] the Ontario Court of Appeal reduced sentences totalling three years in penitentiary to a total of 18 months definite and 18 months indeterminate, saying that there was error in sending to the penitentiary a young man only 18 years of age who had a prior record but had never been in custody before.

The age of the offender and his particular circumstances are also factors that may indicate that a penitentiary term is improper. In *R. v. Marcello*,[20] the Ontario Court of Appeal reduced a sentence of three years' imprisonment upon a charge of trafficking in heroin to one of two years less one day plus probation for two years on a youth only 16 years of age, who had already been a heroin addict for two or three years. The Court was unable to find any error in the length of the sentence imposed, but questioned whether a term served in a setting other than the penitentiary system might not be in the best interests of the appellant and still serve as a protection to society and a deterrent to others. The Court took the view that society would be equally well protected by the new sentence, and the accused better served by it. They further noted that the return of this young man to society without some control or restraint being imposed on him would be fatal to any hope of rehabilitation:

> The sentence which we are imposing is in effect longer than the sentence imposed by the trial Judge. It is true that it is in a different setting and that period in custody may be slightly less but because probation is a restraint on his freedom the supervised control is still there and a breach of probation will undoubtedly lead to a further term of imprisonment.

Similarly, in *R. v. Gilroy and Patrick*,[21] the Ontario Court of Appeal reduced the sentences to take the appellant out of the penitentiary noting that "his parents were divorced when he was young, he has not had the

---

[19] Unreported, June 19, 1974.
[20] (1973), 11 C.C.C. (2d) 302.
[21] (1949), 95 C.C.C. 350.

ordinary opportunities and has had to make his own way. A penitentiary term in his case would probably mean his ruin." Again, in *R. v. Wilson,*[22] noting that the conduct was entirely out of character and unlikely to be repeated, the Court determined that a penitentiary term would be "disastrous" in the circumstances and reduced a sentence of five years for armed robbery of a taxi driver to two years less a day definite and two years less a day indeterminate.

A new policy has been enunciated for youthful first offenders by the Ontario Court of Appeal:[23]

> "Crimes of this nature, in most cases, call for a sentence which protects society and maintains public confidence in the effective enforcement of the criminal law by emphasizing general deterrence to like-minded criminals. Such a sentence will be, almost invariably, a substantial penitentiary term as was imposed here.
>
> "However, in the case of youthful offenders that emphasis must yield to the long term benefit to, and protection of society resulting from, the real possibility of rehabilitation which can seldom be said to be absent in the case of the very young. Rehabilitation for the youthful is unlikely if imprisonment is served in a penitentiary rather than a reformatory."

C. The Intermittent Sentence

Criminal Code, s. 663(1)(c) states:

> 663(1) Where an accused is convicted of an offence the court may, having regard to the age and character of the accused, the nature of the offence and the circumstances surrounding its commission,
>> (c) where it imposes a sentence of imprisonment on the accused, whether in default of payment of a fine or otherwise, that does not exceed ninety days, order that the sentence be served intermittently at such times as are specified in the order and direct that the accused, at all times when he is not in confinement pursuant to such order, comply with the conditions prescribed in a probation order.

Prior to the amendment of the section in 1972, only the Parole Board

---

[22] Unreported, May 8, 1974 (Ont. C.A.).
[23] *R. v. Dunkley* (1976), 3 C.R. (3d) S-51 at p. S-52; see also *R. v. Barnes,* unreported, May 23, 1973 (Ont. C.A.).

had the power to effect an intermittent sentence, and such sentences, when imposed by a trial court, were quashed.[24]

The section is only available for sentences of 90 days or less and this leaves the anomaly that a sentence of "three months" at certain times of the year, because of the vagaries of the Gregorian calendar, could be intermittent, whereas at other times it would not.[25]

The provision has enormous use in preventing the break-up of homes and the loss of employment which is often concomitant with short prison sentences and brings new flexibility into the criminal law. Its primary use is to permit a prisoner to maintain employment,[26] but it can also be used to enable a spouse to care for children,[27] to permit schooling to continue, or simply to prevent one who is imprisoned even for a short period of time from identifying too closely with prisoners serving longer terms.

There is nothing in the legislation that demands that the sentence of intermittent imprisonment should take place at any particular time. There is considerable flexibility in this regard. Accordingly, in *R. v. Dawes*,[28] the accused was an officer in the Canadian Armed Forces and in order to save his career he was given an intermittent sentence that was to be served during time that would otherwise be his leave-time, provided he served a minimum of five days per month.

Though no case decides the point, it is suggested that the intermittent sentence is not available for a period of imprisonment imposed in default of payment of a fine. It would seem that this is because that section assumes continuous imprisonment when the language is examined in its context.

D. Life Imprisonment

Life imprisonment is rare. Except in those offences where this penalty is mandatory the most usual ground for life imprisonment is for cases where there are dangerous psychiatric disturbances together with the commission of an extremely grave offence.

---

[24] *R. v. Kehoe*, [1970] 1 C.C.C. 123 (Ont. C.A.).
[25] *R. v. Ford* (1972), 9 C.C.C. (2d) 515 (B.C. Co. Ct.).
[26] *R. v. Rebertz*, unreported, June 6, 1975 (Ont. C.A.).
[27] *R. v. Jones*, unreported, January 26, 1976 (Ont. C.A.).
[28] (1975), 19 Crim. L.Q. 155 (B.C.).

However, in *R. v. Pion; R. v. McClemens,*[29] the Ontario Court of Appeal, *obiter,* said that where it is demonstrated, without anything further, that the record and evidence before the court discloses a continuing danger to the public from the convicted person, "nothing else need be shown to justify a life sentence and, specifically that mental disease or other abnormality need not be shown."

A life sentence has been imposed for the protection of a particular individual as opposed to the public in general. In *R. v. Costello,*[30] the accused was convicted of wounding one G. with intent to cause grievous bodily harm. G. had seduced the accused's wife and the accused gave evidence "venomously" in the course of which he said "I wanted to put him in hospital for life, killing would be too good for him." A sentence of life imprisonment for the protection of G. was upheld by the Court of Appeal.

Nevertheless the operative general principle usually applies: the maximum penalty is reserved, in the ordinary course of things, for the worst offence and the worst offender.

E. The Length Of The Term Of Imprisonment

The cardinal rule here is that the length of a term must be appropriate to the offence and the offender, must satisfy the requirements of protection of the public, and must satisfy the concept of deterrence to others and to the individual. Nevertheless, this sort of vague text leaves very wide margins and the question remains: On what criteria is the length of imprisonment to be fixed? Even after applying all the general principles and taking into account all the particular circumstances, there are some parameters indicated by the nature of imprisonment itself.

One rule that has been suggested is that for the repetition of a similar offence the term of imprisonment ought to be greater on the second occasion.[31] Although this principle is acted upon from time to time, it has been specifically disapproved by the Ontario Court of Appeal. In *R. v. Weston,*[32] the appellant appealed a maximum sentence of two years

---

[29] (1971), 4 C.C.C. (2d) 224.
[30] (1969), 54 Cr. App. R. 172.
[31] *R. v. Denholm* (1970), 11 C.R.N.S. 380 (Sask. C.A.).
[32] Unreported, March 21, 1972 (Ont. C.A.); *R. v. Gibbings,* [1936] S.R. 36.

imposed upon a charge of being unlawfully at large. She had escaped custody upon a previous occasion and had received at that time the maximum sentence, but the Court stated that "it does not follow that a maximum ought to be applied on this occasion". Bearing in mind some elements of mitigation, the Court imposed a sentence of six months' imprisonment.

In determining the length of imprisonment, subjective factors may be taken into account. In *R. v. Arellano and Sanchez,*[33]

> A further factor which I think it is proper to bear in mind is the fact that the accused are Bolivian nationals and speak little or no English or French. This necessarily means that detention for them in a Canadian penitentiary will be very much more difficult than it would be for a Canadian or even for a foreigner who had a working knowledge of one of the official languages. Also because of the great distances involved, the possibility of either accused receiving visits from or maintaining contacts with family and friends must be regarded as extremely remote. While these facts, of course, do nothing to excuse the accused, I think they do justify some measure of clemency when it comes to pronouncing sentence.

In the case of first offenders, it is submitted that a jail sentence interferes with the possibility of rehabilitation despite the homage our system pays to the notion that rehabilitation occurs in a custodial setting. In some cases, custodial rehabilitation is even theoretically impossible. In *R. v. Belanger and Guay,*[34] the reformatory to which the francophone appellants would have been sentenced operated in English only. The court noted that the trial judge had placed "undue emphasis" upon the value of custodial treatment, and that what value such treatment might have was seriously diminished by reason of the boys' inability to speak English. Accordingly, the sentence of nine months definite and six months indeterminate upon the charge of break, enter and theft was reduced to four months plus two years' probation to be carried out in Montreal where they resided.

Even though the offender had a lengthy criminal record and several terms served in reformatories, the fact that the sentence that was to be imposed had to be served in penitentiary, indicated that it should be as short as possible in the circumstances.[35]

The Ontario Court of Appeal has taken the view that where probation

---

[33] (1975), 30 C.R.N.S. 367 at p. 371 (Que.).
[34] Unreported, June 28, 1973 (Ont. C.A.).
[35] *R. v. Wright,* unreported, August 9, 1978 (Ont. C.A.); *R. v. Michaud,* unreported, August 9, 1978 (Ont. C.A.).

is indicated but a sentence of some incarceration is necessary as well, the two should be properly balanced. A sentence of probation is most effective if it follows a shorter sentence. Accordingly, the Court in *R. v. Reading*[36] reduced a sentence upon a 17-year-old first offender for robbery from 23 months coupled with two years' probation to one year's imprisonment with two years of probation.

The situation where a minor property offence has been committed by one who has a previous record has received judicial consideration. In *Gouchie v. The Queen*,[37] a 17-year-old woman pleaded guilty to theft, possession of marijuana and malicious damage amounting to less than $50. Her previous record included convictions for theft under $50 (three charges), forgery and possession of marijuana. The theft offence under consideration involved stealing from a nurse at a hospital where the accused was undergoing treatment for a narcotic problem. By a majority the court held that a sentence of one year's imprisonment overemphasized deterrence at the expense of rehabilitation and reform. Offences of a minor property nature which did not endanger the victim's safety, and were committed by a young casual offender not committed to a criminal career (although the offender's "lifestyle" may be deplorable) were not properly to be punished by imprisonment.

While in large urban centres lengthy terms of imprisonment are necessary to deter others and uphold respect for law, in a small community a shorter term of imprisonment might have an equal effect "where associations are close, and community, social and religious status is judged more severely." Accordingly in *R. v. Hinch and Salanski*,[38] the British Columbia Court of Appeal upheld a one-month sentence, noting that any conviction and sentence of imprisonment "would be almost totally destructive of these respondents in a small community;" and that considering the impact of a one-month sentence in this context, it was adequate.

Similarly, the time when the sentence is to be served is a factor that may be taken into account. In *R. v. Larre*,[39] the Saskatchewan Court of Appeal held that a trial judge properly exercised his discretion by taking into account his view that a short term of imprisonment that covered the entire Christmas break in a university term was probably more severe

---

[36] Unreported, March 7, 1978 (Ont. C.A.).
[37] (1975), 1 C.R. (3d) S-33 (N.S.C.A.).
[38] [1968] 3 C.C.C. 39.
[39] [1970] 1 C.C.C. 382.

than a longer term imposed at some other time of the year. The trial judge was also convinced that it would not be in the public interest to have imposed a term of imprisonment which would have meant the complete loss of the respondent's university year.

Thoughtful jurists in England are increasingly giving voice to the opinion that lengthy prison sentences are both harmful and ineffective. In *R. v. Sargeant,*[40] the court said:

> Some twenty to twenty-five years ago there was a view abroad, held by many people in executive authority, that short sentences were of little value, because there was not enough time to give in prison the benefit of training. That view is no longer held as firmly as it was. This young man does not want prison training. It is not going to do him any good. It is his memory of the clanging of prison gates which is likely to keep him from crime in the future.

Accordingly, the court imposed a short sentence.

There are a number of cases which put the proposition that: "It is the fact of going to prison which has the deterrent effect: it is not the length of the prison sentence."[41] This reasoning is essentially a reflection of the maxim known as Occam's Razor — that assumptions introduced to explain a thing must not be multiplied beyond necessity. The principle is more often honoured in the breach than the observance, though it has much reason behind it. The view is that a sentence ought not to be longer than is necessary for the punishment of the offender, whether in the hope of deterring others with a lengthy sentence or for other reasons.

In *R. v. Johnson*[42] the Ontario Court of Appeal majority raised a sentence of six years for a very serious manslaughter to a term of ten years because the trial judge did not give sufficient effect to the matter of deterrence to others. Brooke J.A., dissenting, said:

> I do not think it adds materially to the deterrence of other persons in the community — certainly persons such as he was — to increase the sentence to seven, eight or ten years. To concede this is to me to concede that the only real way a deterrent can be achieved is through very large sentences rather than to the fact that a man of previously good character has received a sentence that is to him substantial.
>
> . . .
>
> . . . I do not think it adds materially to the prospect of the protection of society

---

[40] (1974), 60 Cr. App. R. 74; *R. v. King and Ramsden,* [1977] Crim. L. R. 370; *R. v. Wilkins* (1977), 66 Cr. App. R. 49.

[41] *R. v. Anderson* (1972), 56 Cr. App. R. 863; *R. v. Sargeant* (1974), 60 Cr. App. R. 74.

[42] (1971), 4 C.C.C. (2d) 226 at pp. 228-29.

to increase the sentence of this man with his previous good character if the probability is that he can be rehabilitated and to so sentence him is to sacrifice him to the limited hope that the additional two or three years of cost to him will deter them [others] from repeating his act . . .

I agree with the statement in the report of the Canadian Committee on Corrections that unduly harsh sentences not only create a sense of injustice and impair the treatment potential of correctional measures but they also reduce the impact of law in general.

Brooke J.A., speaking for the majority, this time, in *R. v. Fireman*,[43] expressed similar views in the case of a Cree convicted of manslaughter in a remote settlement and sentenced to ten years' imprisonment. Dealing with the factor of deterrence to others, his lordship defined "others" narrowly as the rest of this particular accused's community:

What knowledge would his community have of the reasons of the learned trial Judge in sentencing the appellant or, for that matter of this Court in dealing with his appeal? To ask the question is to answer it.

To the rest of the community the deterrent lies in the fact that this unsophisticated man of previous good character was sent to prison for his crime and surely, it is not dependent on the magnitude of the sentence for its value. I do not think that it adds greatly to the deterrent value of what has taken place that such a severe sentence be imposed. What is important in these circumstances is that to the whole community justice appears to have been done and that there will be respect for the law. This is best accomplished in the case of this first offender if he is returned to his society before time makes him a stranger and impairs his ability to live there with some dignity.

In the result the Ontario Court of Appeal reduced the sentence to two years.

Similarly, again speaking for the majority, in *R. v. Simmons, Allen and Bezzo*,[44] Brooke J.A., noting that three men who were convicted of a gang rape were yet good prospects for rehabilitation, took the view that six years was too long a sentence because:

. . . it is more than is necessary for their punishment and that four years . . . would have been sufficient. Four years is a long time in the life of a man, particularly one who has never been in prison before. We are of the view that if four years is adequate punishment for their crime it would be wrong to justify a sentence of six years on the basis of deterrence and so to sacrifice the appellants for that purpose. It is our opinion that the object of principle of

---

[43] (1971), 4 C.C.C. (2d) 82 at p. 86.
[44] (1973), 13 C.C.C. (2d) 65 at pp. 72-73.

deterrence to others like the appellants lies in the fact that for this crime a penitentiary term will be imposed, the length of which depends upon the circumstances. Finally, we think that the sentence of six years does not give meaningful effect to the principle of rehabilitation but rather to the contrary.

The principle is that if a shorter sentence can adequately emphasize the seriousness of an offence and protect the public, then a shorter sentence ought to be imposed. This has been adopted by implication by Martin J.A., for the Ontario Court of Appeal as a whole in *R. v. Vandale and Maciejewski*.[45] And, in *R. v. Bompas*,[46] Ford C.J.A. said: "Indeed, if 10 years' penal servitude is not a deterrent to a parent from punishing a child so as to endanger the child's life, or amount to cruelty to the child, it would be difficult to decide how long a term would be required to operate as an effective deterrent."

F. Special Provisions For Women In Ontario

Part II of the Prisons and Reformatories Act, which applies to Ontario only, provides that any female convicted of an offence punishable by a term of two months or longer may be sentenced to imprisonment for an indefinite period not exceeding two years in a reformatory for females instead of in a common gaol. The same enactment further provides that any female who is confined in a common gaol may, by a warrant signed by an officer authorized by the Lieutenant Governor of the Province, be transferred from the gaol to the Reformatory for Women or to an Industrial Farm to serve the balance of her sentence. In *R. v. Cameron*,[47] the trial judge sentenced Cameron to a term of imprisonment of two years less one day definite and two years less one day indeterminate. This, of course, is a term that would be served in a common gaol unless there was intervention pursuant to s. 57 of the Prisons and Reformatories Act. The sentence would have been effective in a case of a male person required to serve it in a reformatory. The court noted that if a trial court wished a female prisoner to be assured of serving her sentence in a reformatory, it should impose a sentence for an indefinite period not exceeding two years in a reformatory. The court therefore

---

[45] (1974), 21 C.C.C. (2d) 250.
[46] (1959), 123 C.C.C. 39 at p. 42 (Alta. C.A.).
[47] (1975), 24 C.C.C. (2d) 158 (Ont. C.A.).

varied the sentence to "an indefinite period not exceeding two years in a reformatory" followed by probation for a period of three years. In this connection it is worth noting that s. 659 of the Criminal Code states that "except where otherwise provided" a person who is sentenced to imprisonment for a term of two years or more shall be sentenced to imprisonment in a penitentiary; the Prisons and Reformatories Act does so otherwise provide.

It is hard to imagine a sentence of any substantial length that ought to be served in a common gaol, where there are generally no facilities for exercise or human decencies. In *R. v. Laveille*[48] the Ontario Court of Appeal noted that while it was not mandatory that a female accused be sentenced to the reformatory (as opposed to gaol), and while this was a matter remaining in the discretion of the sentencing court, the appeal court was of the opinion that a sentence of six months definite plus nine months indeterminate upon conviction for two charges of false pretenses would have been an appropriate one to have been served in a women's reformatory. However, noting that the appellant had already served four months in a common gaol, and that serving the balance of the definite sentence in a reformatory would not afford any opportunity for the appellant to gain any benefit from the reformatory program the court varied the sentence to time served.

G. Place Of Incarceration

There would appear to be no principle that a prisoner who has been previously sentenced to a penitentiary term should thereafter be sentenced to a penitentiary term merely for this reason. In *R. v. Ansley,*[49] Dubin J.A. said the issue should be restricted to the question of what under the circumstances would be a proper sentence for the offence committed; in the result, the majority imposed a sentence of one year, reduced from a sentence of three years.

Nevertheless there has been some judicial disquiet about sending persons who have been to penitentiary to reformatory thereafter. In *R. v.*

---

[48] Unreported, November 2, 1971 (Ont. C.A.).
[49] (1974), 22 C.C.C. (2d) 113 (Ont. C.A.).

Burden,[50] the Ontario Court of Appeal reduced a sentence of three years to one of two years, noting:

> We are not changing the sentence to bring him from the penitentiary, where he has been for some months, into a reformatory. He was in a penitentiary on a previous occasion and the disruption of moving a person, who has been incarcerated in a penitentiary for some time, into a reformatory is one that ought to be avoided in most circumstances.

The rationale is not entirely clear. Either the Court is trying to avoid contamination of younger offenders by one who has been hardened by exposure to the penitentiary system, or the Court is uneasy about interrupting a penitentiary term. The rule ought to be given effect only in cases where the crime and its circumstances are serious enough to justify a penitentiary term, without recourse to the notion that a man has previously been in a penitentiary.

Similarly, on appeal the problem becomes one of deciding whether to take a man out of the penitentiary where he has been serving a sentence and put him into a reformatory. While this is done in many cases, there has occasionally been some judicial hesitation. In *R. v. Fireman,*[51] the Ontario Court of Appeal determined that the appropriate sentence would have been two years less one day, or a reformatory term, but having regard to the length of time that had transpired since conviction and sentencing there would "be little benefit to him in the change required by such a sentence" and accordingly the sentence was reduced to two years.

Occasionally the change is made from penitentiary to reformatory because medical treatment[52] is available there which may help the offender with, for example, drug and alcohol problems.

It is not unknown for a court to change the place of incarceration from a penitentiary to a reformatory because of difficulties the prisoner has had or will have in a penitentiary setting. Though no reported cases deal with the problem, this is often done in the case of informers. It is widely believed that there is less chance of an informer being killed or injured in a reformatory than in a penitentiary.

In *R. v. Menkes,*[53] a sentence of seven years was imposed for a number of arson counts and weapons charges. The accused had a lengthy record

---

[50] (1973), 11 C.C.C. (2d) 491 at p. 493; *R. v. Badder* (1976), 18 Crim. L. Q. 293 (Ont. C.A.).

[51] (1971), 4 C.C.C. (2d) 82.

[52] *R. v. Metcalfe,* unreported, January 23, 1976 (Ont. C.A.).

[53] (1977), 19 Crim. L. Q. 278 (Ont. C.A.).

but none relating to violence. Following his arrest he was remanded for psychiatric assessment, which indicated that he suffered from paranoid schizophrenia. He was placed in a maximum security penitentiary. A post-sentence report revealed that the accused suffered exaggerated fears about his safety during imprisonment. Upon appeal, the court held that the penalty had been imposed on his criminal activities without due reference to his psychiatric condition. The court concluded that this condition and the fact of his vulnerability in the prison community were factors to which the court should be sensitive. The court determined that a maximum reformatory term was within the proper range of sentence for the offences and would provide not only the advantage of treatment but would give him less exposure to others who might abuse him.

A court will rarely take a man out of the reformatory system and place him in the penitentiary system, even when a penitentiary term would have been appropriate, unless it is absolutely necessary to do so.[54]

---

[54] *R. v. Bonnell,* unreported, November 1, 1976 (Ont. C.A.); *R. v. Badder* (1976), 18 Crim. L. Q. 293 (Ont. C.A.); *R. v. Michaud,* unreported, August 9, 1978 (Ont. C.A.).

Chapter 14

Consecutive And Concurrent Sentences

Section 645(4) of the Criminal Code sets out certain circumstances wherein the court can impose consecutive sentences.

645(4) Where an accused

(a) is convicted while under sentence for an offence, and a term of imprisonment, whether in default of payment of a fine or otherwise, is imposed;

(b) is convicted of an offence punishable with both fine and imprisonment, and both are imposed with a direction that, in default of payment of the fine, the accused shall be imprisoned for a term certain; or

(c) is convicted of more offences than one before the same court at the same sittings, and

    (i) more than one fine is imposed with a direction in respect of each of them that, in default of payment thereof, the accused shall be imprisoned for a term certain,

    (ii) terms of imprisonment for the respective offences are imposed, or

    (iii) a term of imprisonment is imposed in respect of one offence and a fine is imposed in respect of another offence with a direction that, in default of payment, the accused shall be imprisoned for a term certain,

the court that convicts the accused may direct that the terms of imprisonment shall be served one after the other.

If this is read together with s. 5(1)(b) of the Criminal Code, which provides that where an enactment creates an offence and authorizes punishment to be imposed in respect thereof, a person who is convicted of that offence is not liable to any punishment in respect thereof other than punishment prescribed by this Act or by the enactment that creates the offence,[1] one might conclude that the list of circumstances wherein consecutive sentences may be directed as set out in the Criminal Code was exhaustive. The ordinary rule would be that since Parliament has applied its mind to the problem, one may safely presume that specific mention of some circumstances by implication excludes others, and since *R. v. Doyle and 10 Others*[2] one reads powers into the text of the Criminal Code with great circumspect, if at all. Nevertheless in *R. v. Muise (No. 3),*[3] the majority of the Nova Scotia Court of Appeal took the opposite view. Muise was convicted of having sexual intercourse with a female person under the age of 14 years on May 31, 1974 and was sentenced for that offence June 14, 1974. However, two days before sentence on that offence he was convicted in another town of rape. The Crown appealed from a concurrent sentence given on the rape charge imposed by a trial judge who believed he had no jurisdiction to impose consecutive sentences because when the accused was convicted he was not "under sentence for an offence". MacKeigan C.J.N.S. for the majority took the view that this codification neither removed nor restricted a general power which he found authorized the imposition of consecutive sentences prior to 1867 through and flowing from the Administration of Criminal Justice Act of Nova Scotia. A similar statute existed in the province of Upper Canada, and was almost a word-for-word copy of the English Criminal Law Act, 1827 (7 & 8 Geo. IV), c. 28. The majority took the view that the Parliamentary draughtsmen who removed a similar section from the Criminal Code in the general revision of 1953-54 overlooked the fact that a person is often not sentenced on the same day he is convicted, and that another conviction may, as in the instant case, intervene.

The Chief Justice, obviously keenly aware of a hiatus in the law said:

> . . . my conviction that the law, in conferring the power and imposing the duty on a Judge of sentencing a convicted person to a term of imprisonment, should not be construed as forcing the Judge in any case to make a term of imprisonment on a second offence concurrent with the term imposed by him or some other Judge for another offence. A so-called concurrent sentence does not sentence the convicted person to a term of any imprisonment at all since it does not require him to serve a single day of imprisonment; a person

---

[1] Not so. See *Turcotte v. The Queen; Anderson v. The Queen,* [1970] 5 C.C.C. 245 (S.C.C.).

[2] (1970), 2 C.C.C. (2d) 82 (Alta. C.A.).

[3] (1975), 23 C.C.C. (2d) 440 (N.S.C.A.); see also *R. v. Reddick* (1974), 9 N.S.R. (2d) 425 (C.A.).

cannot serve in jail the same day twice any more than he can be successfully hanged twice. A Judge in imposing a concurrent sentence is therefore not carrying out his duty unless he can find in the *Code* or the general criminal law authority so to do.

Nevertheless, it is suggested that this result is incorrect on general statutory principles, including the view that a penal enactment, even if ambiguous, is to be construed strictly in favour of the liberty of the subject, and in view of the Criminal Code as a whole.

In *Ex parte Risby*,[4] a case decided without reference to *R. v. Muise (No. 3)*, the court took the view that it was restricted to the statutory language of the Criminal Code and that a consecutive sentence imposed outside the terms of that section was illegal. The Crown had conceded the illegality. The same result was reached in *R. v. Putnam*,[5] where a 30-day consecutive sentence was made concurrent because, though he was serving a sentence of imprisonment at the time of sentencing, when the appellant had been convicted of the offence some months earlier he was not then under sentence for an offence. In *R. v. Oakes*[6] the Ontario Court of Appeal considered the cases of *R. v. Reddick; R. v. Muise (No. 3)*, and *Ex parte Risby* in the decision. The Court held that the power of a court in Canada to impose a consecutive sentence in respect of a criminal offence must be found in existing federal legislation and that resort could not be had to pre-Confederation provincial statutes. The Court reached the conclusion that where sentence had been suspended, and then the suspended sentence had been revoked, a trial judge could not impose a consecutive sentence upon that revocation. If the passing of sentence had been suspended pursuant to s. 664(4)(d) no consecutive sentence could have then been imposed (since the accused would not then have been under any sentence to which it could be made consecutive).

If the legislative draughtsman has indeed made an oversight, that can be corrected by the legislature. But the view taken by the Nova Scotia Court of Appeal renders s. 645(4) completely nugatory and meaningless as regards this problem. In addition, the British North America Act, 1867, and the later enactment of Criminal Code s. 645(4) would seem to make resort to such a statute for this purpose constitutionally and legally impermissible.

---

[4] (1975), 24 C.C.C. (2d) 211 (B.C.).
[5] [1967] 3 C.C.C. 37 (B.C.C.A.).
[6] (1977), 37 C.C.C. (2d) 84.

A. Procedure

Because of the wording of s. 645(4), it would appear that a sentence imposed without any direction as to whether it is to be concurrent or consecutive shall be taken to be concurrent. This is in accord with the practice direction on the subject given by the Court of Criminal Appeal in England.[7] That Court expressed the view that "to avoid confusion" an intention to make a sentence concurrent should be expressly stated in the presence of the prisoner and entered upon the indictment.

Even where an order is made that a sentence is to be consecutive, the phrase "consecutive to any term being served" may be inadequate. In *Ex parte McCaud,*[8] just such a phrase had been used. But McCaud had at the time been serving one sentence and had already been sentenced to a further term of ten years, which pursuant to an order of the Court of Appeal had been directed to be served "consecutive to the unexpired portion" of that term. Accordingly the ten-year sentence had not yet begun to run and the phraseology employed had the effect of rendering the sentence concurrent to the ten-year term and consecutive to the term then being served. Mr. Justice Neil Fraser suggested that to avoid such problems where a prisoner already subject to two or more consecutive sentences is being sentenced to yet another term, an apt formula might be "consecutive to the total period of imprisonment to which you are already subject."

The wording of the statute, which speaks of "the terms of imprisonment" as being the "*res*" that may be served one after another, leads to the inference that it is not permissible to make part of a term of imprisonment consecutive to another term. This conclusion was reached by the Criminal Division of the Court of Appeal of England in *R. v. Gregory et al.*[9] The Court noted administrative difficulties that might arise and relied upon the fact that counsel were unable to find any authority for the alternative proposition.

"Practice Direction" (1962), 46 Cr. App. R. 119.
[8] [1970] 1 C.C.C. 293 (Ont.).
[9] [1969] 2 All E.R. 174.

B. The Use Of The Power

Courts have recently begun to articulate guidelines to determine the issue of when a sentence should be consecutive and when it should be concurrent. Granted that there is a discretion in the trial judge, this discretion must be exercised judicially and in accordance with proper sentencing principles.

The older position has been stated by the Ontario Court of Appeal in *R. v. Duguid*.[10] "We think it should be borne in mind that where a man is guilty of several offences the usual rule is not that the sentences should be consecutive. The Court has power to make sentences consecutive but unless the Court exercises that power sentences imposed are served concurrently."

The modern tendency has been to reject this principle and yet it may be supportable on the unusual facts of that case. Duguid was arrested for robbery in 1947 and escaped prison before trial. He lived and worked quietly without resorting to crime until 1953 when, having lost his employment, he was convicted of house-breaking and sentenced to two years. He was then brought back to face the robbery charge for which he was given eight years consecutive. On another robbery charge from 1947 and a prison escape he received seven years and two years respectively, each consecutive, making a total of 19 years. The Court held that where a man seeks deliverance from past crimes which he has committed, "and particularly where he has been living a respectable life for a period of years — it is desirable, if practicable, for one Court to review the whole situation and decide what the total punishment should be in order to permit the accused to resume his life freed from fear of the past."[11] In the result a concurrent sentence of ten years was imposed for all offences.

The modern practice is to impose consecutive sentences for separate offences unless there is a "relationship" between them. Nevertheless, some courts follow another rationale even as regards separate crimes of the same type, reasoning that if sentences were to be concurrent in such cases, that would almost be an inducement to a criminal to continue with crimes of the same sort, or even of different sorts, committed at times closely related to one another. He would reason that if he were caught on the first one, any sentence that he would get on the others would likely be

---

[10] (1954), 17 C.R. 370 at p. 372.
[11] *Ibid.*

concurrent and his liberty not be further restrained because of his committing these other offences.

In imposing consecutive sentences for separate offences upon this ground, it is of course absolutely important that the court should keep in mind the totality principle so as to avoid excessive punishment in the result.

The correct approach to the problem of multiple diverse crimes is illustrated by the Ontario Court of Appeal in *R. v. Haines.*[12] Haines was sentenced to seven years' imprisonment on one charge of fraud and concurrent sentences of one year each were imposed on 16 other charges. The Court held that the charges should have been grouped by subject-matter, and concurrent sentences imposed with respect to each offence in the same category, the sentence for each category to run consecutive to the sentences in other categories, and bearing in mind that the total sentence imposed should not be excessive. Accordingly, charges of fraud, attempted fraud, and obtaining property by false pretenses were placed in one group; charges of unlawful possession were in a second; a charge of theft over $200 was in a third category. Within each category the sentences were made concurrent to each other but consecutive to the sentences in the other categories.

In dealing with the question of consecutive or concurrent sentences, the operation of the totality principle must take priority over the ordinary rule that each sentence must be appropriate to the offence. In *R. v. Robert,*[13] the Ontario Court of Appeal was faced with five charges of assault causing bodily harm committed in an extremely vicious manner by the appellant upon his five children. The maximum penalty of two years was determined to be a proper penalty in this case, and concurrent sentences were not possible because the Court was of the view that the assaults, being in respect of five different children, were not so related as to warrant concurrent sentences. However, the totality of the sentence that resulted from the joint operation of the consecutive sentences was so great that the Court altered the sentence to two years on the first charge and one year on each of the other charges, all sentences to be consecutive, so as to result in a total of six years' imprisonment.

The British Columbia Court of Appeal has a different approach to the problem of how to order consecutive and concurrent sentences and deal with the problem of totality. Their solution is to avoid the problem. In *R.*

---

[12] (1975), 29 C.R.N.S. 239.
[13] (1970), 16 C.R.N.S. 7.

v. Bryce[14] the accused was charged with eight counts of breaking and entering and had been sentenced to four months on each charge, the sentence to run consecutively for a total of 32 months. The Court reduced the sentence to one of two years' imprisonment in each case to run concurrently, saying that in its opinion it would have been better to sentence the appellant to one appropriate term in respect of the worst of these offences, and to make the other sentences concurrent with that. The same Court, however, has adopted the Ontario approach on at least one occasion.[15]

The English cases seem to leave more flexibility in the solution to this problem. In *R. v. Kastercum,*[16] the court acknowledged "the well-known working principle of this court that where several offences are tried together and arise out of the same transaction, it is a good working rule that the sentences imposed for those offences should be made concurrent."

The court justified this course of action by reference to the totality principle. The court went on to state that it was only an ordinary working rule, and a different method could well be appropriate where, for example, a charge of assaulting an officer resulted from a police chase after a robbery. The trial judge could do one of two things: if he thought that the subsidiary charge was really "part and parcel" of the original offence and should be treated as "an aggravation" of it, then he could reflect it in the sentence for the more serious offence. In such a case the subsidiary offence should be the subject of a concurrent sentence. The other alternative would be to have the sentence for the principal offence fixed independently of the subsidiary offence and to deal with the latter with a separate and consecutive sentence. This course was to be followed where it was necessary to emphasize the gravity of the subsidiary offence.

It appears that the Court of Appeal in England does not accept the approach set out in *R. v. Haines* and *R. v. Robert.* In *R. v. Brown,*[17] Brown pleaded guilty to seven counts of larceny as a clerk or servant and seven related counts of falsification of accounts and was sentenced to three months on each count to run consecutively amounting to 42 months in all. The Court stated that it had: "disapproved on more than one occasion in the past of imposing a multiplicity of short sentences which

---

[14] Unreported, March 26, 1976 (B.C.C.A.).
[15] *R. v. Saumer,* [1977] 3 W.W.R. 385.
[16] (1972), 56 Cr. App. R. 298.
[17] (1970), 54 Cr. App. R. 176.

tote up to a substantial sentence in respect to a number of similar offences forming a series of transactions."

The Court concluded, however, in a manner that would undoubtedly meet the approval of Canadian courts: it noted that the falsification of accounts charges really arose out of the thefts, and were committed in order to hide or prevent discovery of the thefts. Regarding them as "paired counts" the court took the view that: ". . . it is the overall picture that really matters, and . . . the duty of the court is to decide what the overall sentence should be . . . A multiplicity of short sentences adding up to a substantial term is always to be deprecated."

In the result, three years' imprisonment concurrent on each of the larceny counts was imposed together with one day concurrent on each of the falsification of accounts charges. This position is very close to that in *R. v. Duguid.*

In at least one case it was held permissible to impose sentences concurrent to an earlier sentence imposed by another judge merely "in an attempt not to frustrate what the previous judge had in mind, namely, placing [the appellant] in a reformatory with a recommendation for psychiatric assessment or treatment." In *R. v. Courtney,* [18] the court held that the offences were "distinct and independent episodes", with the latter committed some 13 months subsequent to the previous offence and that consecutive sentences were demanded. If a general rule, this is insupportable.

However, at least in borderline cases, where the transactions are somewhat related, the need for psychiatric treatment and the hope that this treatment may protect the public in the long run, can lead the court to impose concurrent sentences. In *R. v. Wallace,* [19] some three hours after a robbery, the accused had an argument with his landlord and struck him over the head with the same shotgun that he had used in the robbery. In that case psychiatric evidence indicated that minimum imprisonment was appropriate in order to provide treatment for a mental disorder.

C. Related Offences

The principal problem facing the trial judge is in deciding whether or not

---

[18] (1956), 115 C.C.C. 260 (B.C.C.A.).
[19] (1973), 11 C.C.C. (2d) 95 (Ont. C.A.).

the cases are sufficiently related, whether by time, subject-matter, or pattern to justify a concurrent sentence. In *R. v. White, Dubeau and McCullough,*[20] White and Dubeau raped a 15-year-old girl and McCullough was a party to the offence which took place in the country in an isolated spot. White and Dubeau then drove McCullough home at 11 p.m. and the victim was raped again in a park inside the city shortly after midnight. The court determined that consecutive sentences were justified:

> The commission of the first crime was at an end. There had been (to use rather inappropriate language) "a break in the transaction". The second rape was committed under circumstances quite different from what sometimes happens when an accused person has sexual relations twice with the complainant, but it is all really part of the one criminal offence.

Consistency is, however, in short supply. In *R. v. Robinson,*[21] two incidents of rape, one of indecent assault, and one of attempted rape occurred over a space of 11 days. In each case the accused threatened the complainant with a knife. The court noted that "each of the events followed a comparable pattern". The court imposed a sentence of eight years for each of the offences of rape and attempted rape, and a sentence of five years for indecent assault, all the sentences to run concurrently. And in *R. v. Gillingham*[22] where the accused took two girls aged nine and eight into woods where he had sexual relations with them, the court held that the acts "were not committed at different times, but were under the same impulse", and accordingly imposed concurrent sentences.

In *R. v. Whitney,*[23] three bank robberies, separated in time by some months, characterized as "quite separate and distinct offences" required consecutive sentences. Similarly in *R. v. Bossence,*[24] while on bail on a charge of bank robbery the appellant visited a co-accused at the jail and was found to have strapped to her body a loaded 12-gauge shotgun. The court determined that the sentence on the concealed weapon charge ought to be consecutive.

It is apparent that the cases in this area are in a state of serious conflict.

At one time or another courts have characterized separate crimes as comprising "a series of transactions", "one transaction" or "part of the

---

[20] (1974), 16 C.C.C. (2d) 162 (Ont. C.A.).
[21] (1974), 19 C.C.C. (2d) 193 (Ont. C.A.).
[22] (1955), 112 C.C.C. 78 (Nfld. C.A.).
[23] (1947), 87 C.C.C. 255 (Ont. C.A.).
[24] (1971), 16 C.R.N.S. 6 (Ont. C.A.).

same transaction or endeavour".[25] An example of the latter was *R. v. Courtney,*[26] where consecutive sentences of three months each, imposed for 17 charges of uttering, were altered to 12 months definite and 12 months less one day indeterminate on each count, all to be concurrent. The offences were all committed within a three-day period and arose from the theft by another man of all the cheques. The court was of the view "that the theft, forgery and uttering of the cheques comprised one transaction". In *R. v. Moreau,*[27] the appellant was convicted of assaulting a police officer and being in possession of a weapon for the purpose of danger to the public peace and received consecutive sentences. He had been engaged in a fracas with some acquaintances when a police officer attempted to persuade him to surrender a pair of scissors he was using as a weapon. In the course of this, the appellant made a number of unsuccessful attempts to strike the officer with the scissors. The court determined that the sentences should have been concurrent as they "arose from the same incident". In *R. v. Boudreau,*[28] a charge of theft of a cheque and a subsequent uttering of it, both committed on the same day and relating to the same document, resulted in concurrent sentences.

In *R. v. Turner,*[29] the Ontario Court of Appeal made a sentence for a robbery concurrent to a sentence for rape, both committed at the same time upon the same victim since "the two offences were closely linked together." In *R. v. Benton,*[30] in the English Court of Appeal, consecutive sentences for two assaults upon men stabbed in one single fight were made concurrent (though varied) because "although two people were injured it was in the course really of one attack."

In *R. v. Gabovic,*[31] the accused on two occasions separated by three days broke and entered the same restaurant, and stole approximately $100 on each occasion. The court held that the offences were of the same nature and were committed within a few days of each other and that therefore the sentences should be concurrent.

---

[25] *R. v. Brown* (1970), 54 Cr. App . R. 176; *R. v. Auerswald* (1976), 28 C.C.C. (2d) 177 (Ont. C.A.).

[26] (1956), 115 C.C.C. 260 (B.C.C.A.).

[27] Unreported, Feburary 28, 1972 (Ont. C.A.).

[28] Unreported, November 12, 1974 (Ont. C.A.).

[29] (1970), 1 C.C.C. (2d) 293.

[30] [1966] Crim. L.R. 400; *R. v. McDonald,* unreported, October 24, 1977 (B.C.C.A.).

[31] (1975), 18 Crim. L.Q. 19 (Ont. C.A.); *R. v. Middleton* (1974), 51 Cr. App. R. 366; *R. v. Walsh,* [1965] Crim. L.R. 248.

Concurrent sentences will arise from possession of two unregistered firearms though each one is charged separately.[32]

Generally speaking the English Court of Appeal tends to consider consecutive sentences inappropriate where the accused is found guilty of unlawfully possessing some item and also of an offence consisting of using or dealing with it. One example is that of the offences of housebreaking and possessing instruments for housebreaking on the same occasion: *R. v. McGould;*[33] or wounding and possessing an offensive weapon which was used to commit the offence: *R. v. Southall;*[34] or assault with intent to ravish and having an offensive weapon: *R. v. Turland.*[35]

When two offences are committed on the same occasion, during the same venture, or during the course of a single incident, the consecutive sentences should not exceed the maximum penalty provided for one of these offences. Accordingly, where consecutive sentences were imposed for possession of an offensive weapon, having a firearm in a place other than his dwelling house or place of business without being the holder of a valid permit, and unlawfully having his face covered with a mask, all sentences totalling twelve and one-half years, the court applied *R. v. Turland,*[36] upholding the principle that "the total sentence to be served by appellant should not exceed the maximum for the most serious of the offences committed on this occasion."[37] Accordingly, sentences were made concurrent to effect this result. On the other hand, in *Beaupré v. The Queen*[38] the same court was not faced as it had been in the case above, with a maximum penalty of ten years. In *Beaupré* the offences were robbery and being masked; and a consecutive sentence was imposed for the latter. Noting that "as a general practice" such sentences should be concurrent, the court distinguished *R. v. Valade,*[39] by noting that the maximum penalty here was life imprisonment. The court took the view that the total sentence was justified and that it was not necessary to lay down a general principle demanding without exception concurrent sentences where the judge wishes to emphasize the aggravating feature associated with the wearing of the mask by imposing a consecutive

---

[32] *R. v. Auerswald* (1976), 28 C.C.C. (2d) 177 (Ont. C.A.).
[33] [1965] Crim. L. R. 561.
[34] [1965] Crim. L. R. 616.
[35] [1968] Crim. L. R. 281.
[36] *Ibid.*
[37] *R. v. Valade* (1970), 15 C.R.N.S. 42 (Que. C.A.).
[38] (1973), 21 C.R.N.S. 205 (Que. C.A.).
[39] *Supra,* n. 37.

sentence for it. This is, of course, the adoption of the British view which gives the trial judge a choice; it is the only case which really adopts this position in Canada.

D. The Order Of Offences

In *R. v. Sinnott,*[40] the accused pleaded guilty to robbery and was sentenced to four years' imprisonment. He was later convicted of another robbery which had been committed prior to the robbery for which he received four years' imprisonment, and was sentenced to four years consecutive. The court varied the consecutive sentence to a concurrent one of somewhat greater duration noting that "it was incongruous to give a consecutive sentence for an earlier offence". It may be incongruous but there seems to be no reason in principle why it should not be done.

E. Conspiracy And Substantive Offences

In *R. v. Sommers and Gray,*[41] five substantive charges of giving and accepting bribes were the subject of consecutive sentences and the sentence for conspiracy to commit these offences resulted in a lesser concurrent sentence. The argument of the appellants on appeal was that since the substantive offences of which they were found guilty all arose out of the same conspiracy, the sentences should have been made concurrent and not consecutive. The court varied the sentences so as to make the conspiracy conviction a five-year sentence and the substantive offences one year concurrent each. In *R. v. Hinks,*[42] the Ontario Court of Appeal reduced a sentence of six months consecutive imposed for forgery in the light of a prior sentence of 30 months which had resulted from a charge of conspiracy to utter forged documents. The court allowed the appeal on the basis that the second charge related to overt

---

[40] [1964] Crim. L.R. 483.
[41] (1959), 125 C.C.C. 81 (B.C.C.A.).
[42] Unreported, June 25, 1974 (Ont. C.A.).

acts that constituted part of the conspiracy charge and that there was therefore a duplication in sentences. The sentence appealed from was accordingly made concurrent to the prior sentence. In both cases the courts have treated the conspiracy charge as being primary, and relegated the substantive offences to a lesser role which resulted in concurrent imprisonment. Clearly there must be nexus between the conspiracy and the substantive offence to produce this result, but how close must it be? Would it be sufficient if the conspiracy and the substantive offences formed part of "the same transaction or series of transactions"?

F. The Problem Of Life Imprisonment

There are certain conceptual problems involved in making sentences consecutive to life imprisonment or making life imprisonment consecutive to a limited term of years. In *R. v. Sinclair*,[43] the Ontario Court of Appeal, relying on *R. v. Foy*,[44] held that a sentence imposed after life imprisonment could only be concurrent to it. The English Court of Appeal in *R. v. Jones*,[45] has ruled that a sentence of life imprisonment should not be ordered to begin at the expiration of another sentence. This seems fair.[46]

G. Offences Committed While On Bail

The courts have often invoked the fact that the offence was committed while the accused was on bail as being an important reason for making a sentence consecutive rather than concurrent. The rationale for this thinking has been given by Disbery J. in *R. v. McKinney:*[47]

> It is reasonable to assume that, as a general rule, only hardened criminals

---

[43] (1972), 6 C.C.C. (2d) 523.
[44] (1962), 46 Cr. App. R. 290.
[45] [1961] 3 All E.R. 668.
[46] *Contra: R. v. Lefebvre*, unreported, May 25, 1976 (B.C.).
[47] (1963), 40 C.R. 137 at p. 139 (Sask.).

would be sufficiently defiant of the law to dare to commit further offences while at liberty on bail awaiting their trial for other offences. Such persons, particularly if they reasonably anticipated being convicted, might well come to the conclusion that if they carried out further burglaries while on bail, not only might they possibly escape detection, but even if detected and convicted they might receive sentences to be served concurrently, with the result that they might well suffer little, if any, additional punishment for such further offences. At the same time they would benefit to the extent of the ill-gotten gains they secured from the carrying out of such further thefts. The attractiveness of this possibility to criminals would be greatly diminished, in my opinion, if they also had to weigh the probability that they might have to serve consecutive sentences for offences committed while on bail.

Pursuant to the provisions of s. 137 of the Criminal Code, a judge has discretion to make a sentence for escaping custody either concurrent or consecutive to the unserved portion of the term of imprisonment that was being served at the time of escape. There is also a judicial discretion as to whether or not a sentence of less than two years is to be served in a reformatory or in a penitentiary.

In *R. v. Collins,*[48] the accused surrendered to the police department because his conscience had been bothering him, and it was admitted that, had he not done so, his participation in the offence would not have been discovered. In that case the sentence for breach of recognizance was ordered to be concurrent with the sentence for robbery.

The analysis set out above may in one sense be misleading: it tends toward rigidity. The discretion ultimately does reside with the trial judge and that discretion is often used in cases falling outside the principles in order to relieve hardship, exercise mercy or accommodate unusual circumstances.

H. Jurisdiction On Appeal

In *R. v. McCaud,*[49] the Ontario Court of Appeal made it clear that there is jurisdiction to change a direction given pursuant to s. 645(4) upon an appeal against a sentence, or a motion for *habeas corpus* with *certiorari* in aid thereof.

---

[48] (1959), 124 C.C.C. 173 (Man. C.A.).
[49] (1958), 121 C.C.C. 99.

I. Crimes Committed In Flight Or After Escaping Custody

The Ontario Court of Appeal in *R. v. McCaw et al.,*[50] succinctly stated the principle involved in these situations:

> We think it ought to be said that persons who commit one crime and in the process of flight after the commission of that crime commit another crime should be given the knowledge that the second crime will attract additional punishment, and we accept the submission of the Crown that there should have been consecutive sentences . . .

In that case the two charges were breaking, entering and theft together with a count of discharging a firearm with an intent to endanger life.

Where the other crime is part of the escape itself in the sense that it is a means of facilitating the escape, the British Columbia Court of Appeal has stated that the sentence ought not to be consecutive. In *R. v. Quelle*[51] the accused walked out of a minimum security prison and stole a car and escaped. He was sentenced to nine months for escape and a concurrent sentence of six months on the charge of theft. The opposite point of view, however, has been expressed by the same court. In *R. v. Ewanchuk,*[52] where offences of theft and possession of a narcotic for the purpose of trafficking were committed while the appellant was unlawfully at large, having escaped from prison, the court refused to order the sentences (which were concurrent to each other) for the offences committed while at large be made concurrent with his other sentences, including the sentence for escape. Its opinion was that "somebody who was illegally at large cannot expect to have the sentences imposed for crimes he may commit while he is at large made to run concurrently with sentences for other offences previously committed." It may be that the difference between this rule and that adopted by the English Court of Appeal is one that varies with the seriousness of the offence.

In *R. v. Morris*[53] the accused went into a hotel bedroom at nighttime with intent to steal. One of the occupants awoke and recognized him, having known him formerly. He attacked both occupants with a blunt instrument rendering them unconscious and was charged with attempted murder. An extremely heavy sentence was imposed upon the grounds that it was "obvious" he realized that one of the occupants had roused and realized who he was and had battered him with intent to kill. "Burglars who try to eliminate identifying evidence by attempting to kill

---

[50] (1974), 15 C.C.C. (2d) 321 at p. 323.
[51] Unreported, April 18, 1975 (B.C.C.A.).
[52] Unreported, March 28, 1977 (B.C.C.A.).
[53] [1977] Crim. L.R. 231.

their victims can only expect very severe sentences, even where as here it was a first conviction of violence and he might have acted on the spur of the moment." In *R. v. Lukion and Small,*[54] the court restricted this principle by adding the qualifying phrase "in the absence of special circumstances". It also noted that at the same time consideration must be given to the totality of the sentences and the result so that by virtue of that principle some sentences might be made concurrent which otherwise ought not to be so.

In *R. v. Kastercum,*[55] the court said that it was generally preferable, to emphasize the gravity of assaulting the police as a means of escape, to make the sentence for that assault separate and consecutive to the substantive offence from which escape was sought.

In England, at least for minor offences, the situation is reversed. In *R. v. Hennessey; R. v. Bowers*[56] two offenders escaped custody while serving sentence and thereafter committed a number of offences: theft of an automobile, driving while disqualified, theft of food and camping equipment, and burglary of premises in order to steal supplies. The offences were:

> as one would expect, all offences of a nature which would enable them as absconders to live, stealing foodstuff, a rucksack, blankets, thermos flask and matters of that sort . . . The court has come to the conclusion that in a case such as this of absconders who inevitably commit a certain number of offences, albeit not very serious, in order to live, that it is not right to impose a heavy sentence in respect of those offences although any sentence they receive must as a matter of principle be consecutive.

J. Escape And Related Offences

Criminal Code:

> 137(1) A person convicted for an escape committed while undergoing imprisonment shall be sentenced to serve the term of imprisonment to which he is sentenced for the escape either concurrently with the portion of the term of imprisonment that he was serving at the time of his escape that he had not served or if the court, judge, justice or magistrate by whom he is sentenced for the escape so orders, consecutively and such imprisonment shall be served
>> (*a*) in a penitentiary if the time to be served is two years or more; or

---

[54] (1975), 27 C.C.C. (2d) 11 (Ont. C.A.).
[55] (1972), 56 Cr. App. R. 298.
[56] (1971), 55 Cr. App. R. 148; *R. v. Lukion and Small, supra,* n. 54.

(*b*) if the time to be served is less than two years,
    (i)   in a prison, or
    (ii) notwithstanding the *Parole Act* and section 659, in a penitentiary if the court, judge, justice or magistrate by whom he is sentenced for the escape so orders.

(2) For the purpose of subsection (1), section 14 of the Parole Act applies in determining the term of imprisonment that a person who escapes while undergoing imprisonment was serving at the time of his escape.

(3) For the purposes of subsection (1), "escape" means breaking prison, escaping from lawful custody or, without lawful excuse, being at large before the expiration of a term of imprisonment to which a person has been sentenced.

Parole Act:

14(1) Where, either before, on or after the 25th day of March 1970,
(*a*) a person is sentenced to two or more terms of imprisonment, or
(*b*) an inmate who is in confinement is sentenced to an additional term or terms of imprisonment,
the terms of imprisonment to which he has been sentenced, including in a case described in paragraph (*b*) any term or terms that resulted in his being in confinement, shall, for all purposes of this Act, the *Criminal Code*, the *Penitentiary Act* and the *Prisons and Reformatories Act*, be deemed to constitute one sentence consisting of a term of imprisonment commencing on the earliest day on which any of those sentences of imprisonment commences and ending on the expiration of the last to expire of such terms of imprisonment.

(2) This section does not affect the time at which any sentences that are deemed by subsection (1) to constitute one sentence commence pursuant to subsection 649(1) of the *Criminal Code*.

The provisions in s. 137 of the Criminal Code are new, and considerably change the law in this area. There is no longer any automatic loss of remission on a conviction for escape or a related offence. Any loss of remission will now occur as a result of a finding of guilt in an internal court hearing, usually referred to as "Warden's Court".

The sentencing judge may now direct that the sentence be served concurrently with the sentence which was being served at the time of the escape, if he so wishes. It would appear that, unless he specifically directs otherwise, the sentence should be served consecutively, and the normal rules in s. 649 of the Criminal Code would apply. The sentence for escape is no longer to be served before the remanet of the unserved sentence.

The reference to s. 14 of the Parole Act seems designed to ensure that when a sentence is imposed to run consecutively to a number of existing sentences, the sentence for escape is consecutive to the sum total of all the sentences, not just to the last of them.[57]

K. Use Of A Firearm During Commission Of An Offence

Criminal Code:

83(1)   Every one who uses a firearm

(a)   while committing or attempting to commit an indictable offence, or

(b)   during his flight after committing or attempting to commit an indictable offence,

whether or not he causes or means to cause bodily harm to any person as a result thereof, is guilty of an indictable offence and is liable to imprisonment

(c)   in the case of a first offence under this subsection, except as provided in paragraph (d), for not more than fourteen years and not less than one year; and

(d)   in the case of a second or subsequent offence under this subsection, or in the case of a first such offence committed by a person who, prior to the coming into force of this subsection, was convicted of an indictable offence or an attempt to commit an indictable offence, in the course of which or during his flight after the commission or attempted commission of which he used a firearm, for not more than fourteen years and not less than three years.

(2)   A sentence imposed on a person for an offence under subsection (1) shall be served consecutively to any other punishment imposed on him for an offence arising out of the same event or series of events and to any other sentence to which he is subject at the time the sentence is imposed on him for an offence under subsection (1).

The provisions of s. 83 are new, proclaimed in force January 1, 1978. In effect, this section introduces a minimum sentence of one-year imprisonment, for a first offence, and three years for a second offence, to be served consecutively to any other sentence. In *R. v. Langevin,*[58] the Ontario Court of Appeal held that an accused may be convicted of both this offence and of armed robbery, even where the two charges arise out of the same transaction. Both the wording of s. 83 and the correct nature of the punishment prescribed were thought to show a clear parliamentary intention to multiple convictions in respect of the same delict.

---

[57] *R. v. Deans* (1977), 37 C.C.C. (2d) 221 (Ont. C.A.).
[58] (1979), 47 C.C.C. (2d) 138. See also *R. v. Eby* (1979), 49 C.C.C. (2d) 27 (N.S.C.A.).

Chapter 15

Parole

The advent and use of parole in Canada is a subject that is still being debated. With much reason. The purpose of this chapter is to review the relationship which exists between parole and the sentence. Although this is not the place to debate the proper use of parole, it does appear, with all respect, that regardless of what courts of appeal may say, judges, being practical men, will bear in mind the possibility of parole in assessing sentence. It may be that in practice sentences today are somewhat longer than they might otherwise be because of the assumption that the parole board will interfere at a future date. Nevertheless, it is clear in principle that there must be a sharp distinction between the function of a court in assessing proper sentence and the function of a parole board in determining when it is safe to release a sentenced prisoner. Since many of the same factors are canvassed by both bodies, there has tended to be a blurring of the lines. This assists no one, especially since, though the parole boards have definite advantages in making the decision about the liberty of the subjects, they are subject to political influence and may not provide a fair hearing. In addition, they are not subject to any meaningful review. Taken together these weaknesses tend to make the parole board uniformly arbitrary and autocratic.

In *R. v. Eaton*[1] the English Court of Appeal (Criminal Division) had occasion to explain that in a recent case they had referred to the fact that the appellant's case would no doubt later be reviewed by the parole board. They said: "The court would like to make it plain that they are in no way treating themselves as other than the final court of appeal, and are not, as it were, shirking their task and leaving it to the Parole Board."

---

[1] (1968), 53 Cr. App. R. 118.

The following quote from *R. v. Jarvis; R. v. Smith*[2] is the comment of a five-man bench: "The sentence imposed by the court should be such as the court deems just if carried out to the limit, and should not be pronounced with the idea that it might be made more just by some other authority."

The parole board is not, except within very narrow limits, subject to judicial review; its proceedings are held in secret; it is not possible to know what factors it in fact does consider. The enunciation of a doctrine of "fairness" by the Supreme Court of Canada in *Martineau and Butters v. Matsqui Institution Inmate Disciplinary Board*[3] may well leave room for some judicial review. As well, at the parole suspension hearing stage, proceedings are somewhat fairer in that the prisoner must be given an opportunity to appear personally and present argument. But courts have, by way of delineation between their function and the function of a parole board, mentioned some factors that ought not to be considered by a court but ought to be left to the parole board or the executive.

A. Future Considerations

In *Eaton,* the court expressed the possibility that "in light of matters not now known to this court" the parole board would be able to review the case for the prisoner:

> To take this case, it may well be that in a year's time — the court does not know — those who have this man under observation will be completely satisfied that he is not going to drink again, that he has genuine remorse and that he would no longer be a danger to the public. That would be something that this court today cannot know.

In *R. v. Bezeau,*[4] Porter C.J.O. referred to these future considerations as being the province of the parole board. "If in the course of time, the attitude of the prisoner should change, the executive has the power to exercise clemency upon the altered conditions that may develop." In the same case Schroeder J.A., speaking for the majority said: "If there are circumstances arising later that make it proper to afford relief to the

---

[2] (1925), 44 C.C.C. 97 (Ont. C.A.).
[3] (1977), 33 C.C.C. (2d) 366.
[4] (1958), 28 C.R. 301 (Ont. C.A.).

appellant, that is a matter which can more properly be left for consideration and action by the executive."

Similarly in *R. v. Roberts*,[5] Porter C.J.O., in discussing an earlier case where, upon multiple charges of arson, a total of 24 years was imposed, dismissed the appeal and said that the court was then aware that if the psychiatric treatment available in penitentiaries was successful in removing the causes of the prisoner's dangerous behaviour, the parole board would have an opportunity of taking such action regarding the sentence as the board might deem appropriate. Accordingly, it seems that the principal distinction between a court and a parole board is that the latter is the vehicle which is empowered to deal with those changes in the prisoner's circumstances and attitude which arise after sentence and after appeal.

B. Clemency

In *R. v. Calder*,[6] the court said:

> General public opinion and petitions for clemency are matters for consideration in applying for executive clemency. A Court of Appeal should not consider, in an appeal from sentence, matters which are more properly considered on an application for clemency . . . "An appeal is not intended by the law to give an opportunity to exercise the prerogative of the Crown or the powers of a board of parole, but to correct a failure of justice": *R. v. Townsend* (1925), 29 O.W.N. 296, *per* Magee J.A.

Occasionally, other matters have been considered to be the province of parole boards and outside the jurisdiction of courts. In *R. v. McDonald and Reynolds*,[7] the accused appealed against a sentence of two years in the penitentiary on a charge of robbery. The court dismissed the appeal: "The fact that Reynolds had no previous record is a factor which may well be taken into consideration if an application for parole is made on his behalf, but it is no reason for our reducing his sentence in this case." It is submitted that what the court is really saying is that in such a serious

---

[5] [1963] 1 C.C.C. 27 (Ont. C.A.).

[6] (1956), 114 C.C.C. 155 at p. 162 (Man. C.A.). and *R. v. Bezeau* (1958), 28 C.R. 301 (Ont. C.A.).

[7] (1958), 28 C.R. 197 (N.B.C.A.); see also *R. v. Moncini* (1975), 23 C.C.C. (2d) 452 (B.C.C.A.).

offence a sentence of two years already reflects a sufficient allowance for the fact that he had no criminal record, and that it would be improper for a court, bearing in mind the seriousness of the offence, to make any further reductions, though the parole board might well be persuaded to do so.

On the other hand, Schultz J.A., speaking for himself alone in *R. v. Iwaniw; R. v. Overton*[8] took the view that the parole board rather than the court should take cognizance of such circumstances as deferment of an accused's marriage, his loss of standing in his employment as a result of the offence, or family responsibilities. It is respectfully submitted that though these matters may, in a very grave case, carry more weight with the board of parole than they would with the court they are not matters to be disregarded. This position is, in effect, a negation of the responsibilities of a court.

C. Taking Remission And Parole Into Account On Sentence

1. ENGLAND

The position in England is slightly clearer than the situation in Canada. In *R. v. Maguire and Enos,*[9] the Court of Criminal Appeal had to deal with a sentence set "in order to assure that the prisoner be removed from criminal circulation for four years and eight months, owing to the provision that you automatically receive a reduction of a third of your sentence for good behavior, we have to sentence you to seven years . . .". The Court reaffirmed that its function is to consider what is the proper length of imprisonment to impose for a particular offence and that, as a general rule, courts should not take remission into account. They should impose the sentence which they think the gravity of the case deserves. The sentence was improper because it was equivalent to saying "we think the proper sentence to be passed on you is four years and eight months and not seven years." The Court noted that the prisoner had a prospect and a hope of remission but no right to it and stated that that hope and

---

[8] (1959), 127 C.C.C. 40 (Man. C.A.).
[9] (1956), 40 Cr. App. R. 92; *R. v. Gisbourne,* [1977] Crim. L.R. 490; *R. v. Eaton* (1968), 53 Cr. App. R. 118; *R. v. Cash* (1969), 53 Cr. App. R. 483.

prospect was not to be taken into account when a sentence was being imposed.

The Court acknowledged that in an earlier case it did consider the question of remission regarding a defendant who for no apparent reason went round setting fire to haystacks. The Court in that case said it had to consider what sentence would actually be served because "when [the accused] came out again, he might be a potential danger to the community." The assumption seems to be that punishment may deter or reform ordinary criminals, but those who are mentally disturbed cannot be expected to so respond; and therefore the real question of such offenders becomes one of how long the community needs to be protected by means of his separation from the community. But a separate rule for the mentally disturbed is both dangerous and logically indefensible.

In a later case, *R. v. Turner,*[10] the court had to deal with a tragic case of a shy and lonely boy suffering under a sense of inferiority who was a persistent fire-raiser; and the court once again, bearing in mind that three years of treatment would be required to effect a cure, sentenced him to five years' imprisonment in order to ensure that treatment. The court said, in upholding the sentence:

> It is no doubt true that when one is considering punishment it is quite wrong for the court to take into consideration matters of remission, but it has long been recognized that when one is considering not punishment but considering reform or mental treatment, something which is in the interests of the prisoner, it would be obviously right for this court to take remission into consideration.

The prisoner who finds himself serving a long sentence in the penitentiary as "treatment" instead of as punishment is not likely to readily appreciate this distinction. Moreover, it would be most encouraging if expert opinions on the most efficacious type of reform and the length of treatment necessary to bring about reform were more than occasionally accurate. We still await the day in Canada when courts have the power not only to request "treatment", but to ensure that a prisoner actually gets it.

2. CANADA

The position in Canada is, at best, confused and contradictory. The

---

[10] (1966), 51 Cr. App. R. 72.

British Columbia Court of Appeal, beginning in *R. v. Courtney*,[11] started with the premise that the sentencing judge must exhaust his functions and not simply pass a part of them onto the parole board. They therefore reduced a sentence of six years to one of one year definite and one year indeterminate after the sentencing judge had speculated that the parole board might let the prisoner out after two years. Later, in *R. v. Holden*,[12] the trial judge imposed a "substantial" period of imprisonment in order to benefit the prisoner by way of providing training and education, bearing in mind that he might be eligible for parole at an early stage. The court reduced the sentence, saying that though the trial judge acted in what he sincerely believed to be the interests of the prisoner, he in so doing imposed a sentence far greater than could be justified by the prisoner's record, the nature of the offence and the circumstances in which it was committed. The function of the court was to impose that punishment which the offence merited and to leave it to the parole board to grant parole as it sees fit. But no greater sentence should ever be imposed than the nature of the offence required.

In particular, the Court rejected the position then publicly set forth by the National Parole Board Chairman that persistent offenders should be sentenced, without regard to the circumstances of the particular case, to long terms in jail to protect the public, and to give the authorities an opportunity to rehabilitate the offender, leaving it to the parole board to release the prisoner when it thinks proper to do so. The Court said that such an approach to punishment was quite contrary to the Criminal Code:

> ... the function of the Board is not to determine what is proper punishment — Parliament requires the courts to determine that — but to determine when proper punishment imposed by the courts may be safely alleviated. ...
>
> . . .
>
> Heavier sentences must not be imposed for collateral purposes in the professed interest of society or of the prisoner, either to extend the minimum time the prisoner must serve before obtaining parole, or to keep him in custody until the Parole Board decides he may properly be released.

The same court, differently constituted, later considered both *Holden* and *Courtney* and approved them in a case where the sentencing magistrate considered the parole system:

> ... although it is not clear whether [the magistrate] considered that the

---

[11] (1956), 115 C.C.C. 260.
[12] (1963), 39 C.R. 228 (B.C.C.A.).

sentence should be increased so as to offset any possible reduction by the parole board or that, as advocated by the learned chairman of the board, there should be a long sentence, leaving it to the parole board to release the prisoner when it thinks proper to do so. His considering of either was an error.[13]

This view was adopted by the Manitoba Court of Appeal sitting in a five-man bench.[14] Miller C.J.M., speaking for himself, held that the judge should not be influenced by or take into consideration the provisions for remission or parole:

> . . . to the end that a convicted person after parole would be under the supervision of the Board for a longer period of time to the benefit of the convict and the public. . . . A court cannot properly add to a sentence just to circumvent the statutory reduction nor can the court abrogate to the Parole Board responsibility for sentencing.

On the facts of this case, however, the judges were of the view that the trial judge did not fall into the error of believing that a lighter sentence than the one he imposed would have been proper and then increasing that sentence because of the provisions for remission and parole. The judges were all of the view that the sentence was appropriate to the nature of the offence.

The Newfoundland Court of Appeal also had to deal with a case where the magistrate may have been influenced by the actual length of time the accused would spend in prison. The Court said:

> The duty of any court in imposing sentence is to determine the length of the term of imprisonment without consideration of any reduction due to the grant of parole, or any other reduction . . . In imposing punishment we may not consider the matter of subsequent parole; this is not within our sphere.[15]

Nevertheless, in Ontario, the English view that remission can be taken into account where the object is reform or treatment has found favour. It is submitted that what was meant by the English court by "reform" in this context was psychiatric cure but that is not so in Ontario.

The English position itself was adopted and used in *R. v. Robinson*,[16] where there was a conviction of two counts of rape, one count of indecent assault and one count of attempted rape in respect of which the total sentences were two years less a day definite and two years less a day

---

[13] *R. v. Heck* (1963), 40 C.R. 142 at p. 143 (B.C.C.A.).
[14] *R. v. Richardson* (1963), 40 C.R. 179 at p. 180.
[15] *R. v. Coffey* (1965), 51 M.P.R. 7.
[16] (1974), 19 C.C.C. (2d) 193 (Ont. C.A.).

indeterminate. The court, determining that Robinson's illness produced his conduct, went on to say that the ordinary principles of sentencing could not apply:

> This is a case where it is not really accurate to say that the sentence should be a deterrent because others like him lose touch with reality and . . . this sentence is meaningless to them. Further, the sentence should not proceed on the basis of punishment because the Court should not punish sick people who commit crimes because of mental illness. . . . The emphasis must be on the protection of the public, and . . . this may be first achieved by [Robinson's] cure, and so the sentence must be of sufficient length to ensure full treatment but of course conversely, if that is not successful, that the public must be protected as best as can be accomplished.

The court imposed a term of eight years and "openly stated its reliance" upon the National Parole Board to effect Robinson's release as soon as it was safe for the public that this be done and perhaps to require of him that he continue treatment or observation, if, necessary, for any unexpired portion of his sentence. The court, in imposing this sentence, noted that having regard to all the circumstances they were not imposing a term that exceeded that which would otherwise be fit for the offence.

This case without quite rejecting the earlier cases nevertheless it creates a change of some importance. The new proposition is that within the appropriate range of sentence for an offence a court can increase sentence for the purposes of psychiatric treatment. It should also be mentioned that in *R. v. Robinson* there were recommendations from psychiatrists about the length of treatment necessary and the court could therefore gauge the appropriate sentence in terms of this expert opinion.

The real conflict with the decisions of every other Canadian appellate court that has considered this question arises in two other cases of the Ontario Court of Appeal. In *R. v. Wilmott,*[17] McLennan J.A., speaking for the Court, came to the conclusion that both parole and remission were proper matters for consideration in the determination of sentence "in appropriate cases", although he determined, for reasons that are not immediately apparent, that the weight to be attached to remission is of much less significance than that relating to the possibility of parole. (His decision is to some extent *per incuriam,* for he was not referred to the decisions in *R. v. Coffey* and *R. v. Richardson,* though neither of these decisions were, strictly speaking, binding.) He agreed with the proposition that notwithstanding this point, the duty to impose an

---

[17] [1967] 1 C.C.C. 171.

appropriate sentence cannot be delegated to the parole board. Agreement with both propositions at once may, however, prove difficult.

McLennan J.A. emphasized that the effect of a grant of parole is not to alter the length of a sentence imposed by a court, or to reduce it, but merely to change the place where it is served. He also accepted the proposition that longer sentences than the circumstances of the case warrant should not be imposed merely because of the existence of the parole board; the sentence must still to be appropriate to the offence.

According to this case there are a number of ways in which the Parole Act could properly be taken into consideration.

First, as indicated by *R. v. Holden* itself, when a plea is made that the prisoner has learned his lesson and that a sentence appropriate to the offence need not be imposed, the court should nevertheless impose it, leaving the parole board to grant parole when it is satisfied that the prisoner by his conduct has demonstrated that release is justified.

Secondly, he considered that parole possibilities could be relevant where deterrence to others than the particular offender was an important factor in sentencing. For example, where a particularly harsh sentence is necessary to stem the outbreak of a particular type of crime in the community, the court could impose a severe sentence on the offender: "... with the reasonable assurance that with the availability of parole the particular offender would not be incarcerated for a longer period than appropriate, provided always that he shows the necessary qualifications for release."

This is merely another way of saying that the courts can proceed to sacrifice a prisoner to the demands of deterrence, secure in the belief that the parole board will mitigate any harm done. One rationale for this theory might be that the decisions of courts receive public attention and publicity and thereby deter others of like mind, whereas the decisions of parole boards are not subject to such publicity and early release of an offender would therefore not negate the deterrent aspect of the sentence. But the argument is questionable on two grounds. The release functions of the parole board have been subject to increasing publicity and there is no sign that this will stop. Also, in the community of criminals it is likely that the early release of a prisoner would be known and have an impact quite as great as the heavy sentence originally imposed.

The third situation in which McLennan J.A. thought parole possibilities might be relevant to sentence occurs when it is necessary for the safety of the public to impose a very lengthy sentence to prevent the offender from repeating an offence of a "particularly dangerous kind", such as a dangerous behaviour caused by a mental condition. This is in effect the position taken by the English Court of Appeal (Criminal Division) in *R. v. Eaton* and the Ontario Court of Appeal in *R. v. Robinson*.

So far the decision is reasoned and can be at least understood. However the Court goes on to say that because curative treatment for mental disturbance (and therefore parole) is a proper subject for consideration in the determination of a sentence, it *necessarily* follows that a course of training in some skill in which an offender shows promise and which will serve to rehabilitate and reform him is also a proper matter for consideration:

> It may be necessary, in such a case, to impose a longer sentence than would otherwise be warranted so that the offender may take the course of training. This is subject to the important proviso that the sentence should not be so long as to be out of proportion to the offence and the attendant circumstances.

If this means that within the appropriate range of a sentence the court may increase the term of imprisonment in order that the prisoner may obtain facilities for rehabilitation, then this is a dangerous course upon which to proceed. Unlike psychiatric treatment, where there is a body of expert opinion that at least purports to say that "in so long a time we can effect such and such a cure", for rehabilitation in general no such assurance is possible. Indeed the available evidence indicates that no change of this sort is effected by imprisonment.

The most recent Ontario case to deal with the question is *R. v. Pearce*,[18] where the appellant appealed a sentence of six years following a plea of guilty to a charge of conspiracy to traffic in a controlled drug. There was no suggestion in the evidence that any particular term was needed for rehabilitation or for psychiatric treatment. The court approved the sentence as one which properly gave emphasis to the factor of deterrence to others. But the court went on to say that the trial judge:

> . . . did not fail to take into account the possible rehabilitation of the appellant. In considering the latter aspect of sentencing it is proper to take into account that the appellant need only serve four years and one month of the sentence imposed and that he will be eligible for parole in two years from the time of sentence.

Surely the court is here saying, openly, that it abdicates the rehabilitative

---

[18] (1974), 16 C.C.C. (2d) 369 (Ont. C.A.).

function of sentencing to the parole board in cases where a deterrent sentence is required.

Dubin J.A., dissenting, did not believe that this was an appropriate case to consider either parole or remission. Drawing upon passages from *R. v. Wilmott,* he concluded that where, as in this case, the prospects for rehabilitation were apparent at trial, it is for the court to take them into consideration in determining the appropriate length of the sentence, leaving it to the parole board to deal with cases where the rehabilitative prospects of the accused appeared or improved during the term of imprisonment. This rationale has the virtue of resting upon the principles which distinguish the function of a parole board from that of a sentencing court, and at the same time preserves sufficient flexibility to enable the possibility of parole and remission to be taken into consideration in psychiatric cases where there is some evidence that a particular period of incarceration is needed, and that treatment or rehabilitation is a real likelihood.

Regardless of the merits of the discussion it would certainly be desirable that some measure of uniformity on this issue be attained, as a prisoner serving a lengthy term in Ontario will quite rightfully have a sense of grievance with regard to the consideration given there to his parole possibilities as compared to that of his fellows in other provinces — especially if, as is usually the case, the parole board refuses to grant parole.

D. Revocation Of Parole

In *R. v. Evans,*[19] the prisoner assaulted a waiter, causing him bodily harm, and was sentenced to imprisonment for 18 months, from which he appealed. The majority of the court, bearing in mind all the circumstances, was of the view that a proper sentence would have been one year's imprisonment. However, the accused was on parole at the time of the commission of the offence and would be liable to serve, prior to the commencement of this sentence, the unexpired term of approximately 433 days which remained unexpired at the time his parole was granted. The majority came to the conclusion that the "practical

---

[19] (1975), 11 N.S.R. (2d) 91 (C.A.); *R. v. Marshall* (1977), 20 Crim. L.Q. 146 (N.S.C.A.).

effect" of the conviction was the imposition of two penalties: the sentence imposed for the offence itself and the automatic revocation of parole. The court stated that:

> It is certainly true that the appellant knew, or ought to have known, that if he were convicted while on parole of an indictable offence punishable by a term of imprisonment of two years or more, his parole would be automatically forfeited. In my proposed disposition of this appeal I have kept in mind, and given consideration to, this aspect of the matter.

In the result, the court was of the view that in order that the sentence should be "truly fit" it must to some degree reflect the additional punishment incurred by way of forfeiture of parole, and accordingly the court reduced what would otherwise have been the appropriate sentence of one year by three months, allowing the appeal and varying the sentence to one of nine months' imprisonment. Cooper J.A., dissenting, took the view that to make allowance for the forfeiture of parole was to circumvent the provisions of the Parole Act, and to lessen the sentence which the appellant was serving for his previous offences. He rejected such a course as a "departure from the proper principles of sentencing", relying on *both* the Ontario and British Columbia cases on parole.

In Ontario, however, the Court of Appeal has in effect agreed with the majority that an additional penalty by way of forfeiture remission is a factor to be considered in reducing the sentence, but only in those cases where the period of time forfeited is so great as to result in a sentence that would distort the proper totality of the sentences imposed by the trial judge.[20]

The *Evans* case is supportable upon the totality principle, a consideration that cannot arise when increasing sentence to account for mere possibilities of parole. The crucial distinction between taking into account the forfeiture of parole and taking into account the possibility of parole, is the self-evident feature that forfeiture of parole is certain; it arises purely by operation of statute and is not contingent. Unlike the possibility of parole or remission, it is not "of the future" but of the present.

The converse situation was discussed in *R. v. Murray*,[21] where the court said that a sentence imposed upon a person who has broken parole, for an offence committed during the parole, should not take into

---

[20] *R. v. Edmonds (No.1) and (No.2)*, unreported, May 12, 1976 (Ont. C.A.).
[21] [1956] O.W.N. 168 (C.A.); *R. v. Keeble* (1977), 37 C.C.C. (2d) 387 (P.E.I.C.A.).

consideration the breach of parole. "If it does so there is a danger that the accused may be punished twice for his breach of parole."

In *R. v. McQueen*[22] the Ontario Court of Appeal has canvassed instances where, after sentencing by the trial judge, the Ontario Parole Board revoked a previous parole, resulting in an 11-month remanet from a prior sentence. The Court held if the parole board had acted prior to the time of sentencing it would have been appropriate for the trial judge to take into consideration, in connection with the totality of the sentence he was about to impose, the fact that the appellant was going to have that additional sentence to serve. However, the Court determined that it was not right for it to take it into account on an appeal and therefore refused to consider the totality of sentence viewed from that perspective. This is, at the very least, irrational. If it would have been right for the trial judge to take into account that fact, had it been known to him, then it can hardly make sense for the appeal court to ignore it.

However, in order to cover all possible alternatives on this question, it should be noted that in *R. v. Kissick*[23] the court said: "The fact that these offences were committed while the appellant was on parole evidences a failure on his part to respond to the worthwhile efforts made for his rehabilitation and reformation." This was used, *inter alia,* to justify heavy sentences. One can only comment that most of these cases are in conflict. Since fundamental principles are involved, hopefully we may expect the Supreme Court of Canada to clarify the issues.

The scope for the decisions discussed above may well be significantly reduced because of the revocation of s. 17 of the Parole Act, which provided that parole or mandatory supervision was automatically forfeited by conviction for an indictable offence having a penalty of greater than two years. It is now a matter of discretion in the parole board whether or not to revoke in any individual case.

If the prisoner is on parole or mandatory supervision at the time he is sentenced and revocation takes place, the remanet and the new term are served concurrently unless the sentencing judge directs that the new term is to be served consecutively. However, if the prisoner is on mandatory supervision and is not revoked, then, by virtue of s. 15 (4) of the Parole Act, the period of mandatory supervision is deemed to be interrupted and is resumed when the new term is completed.

Parole eligibility cannot be extended by subsequent amendments to the regulations of the Parole Act, but are determined by the terms of the

---

[22] Unreported, March 2, 1978.
[23] (1969), 70 W.W.R. 365 (Sask. C.A.).

enactment in force on the date of conviction.[24] With respect to sentences other than life imprisonment imposed upon conviction of murder, the period for eligibility for parole depends upon the date the sentence was imposed. If imposed prior to January 4, 1968, one is eligible after seven years; from the period from January 4, 1968 to December 31, 1973, one is eligible after ten years; after January 1, 1974, the period returned again to seven years. It is an interesting anomaly of the criminal process that the calculation of parole eligibility with respect only to life sentences takes into account any time spent in custody between arrest and sentence.

The provisions for fixing non-parole eligibility in the case of second degree murder where the judge may, if he wishes, extend the non-parole period have been the subject of some judicial comment. In *R. v. Leahy*[25] the Ontario Court of Appeal said that a judge before making such an order should have clear reasons and should be able to express them in detail before increasing the non-parole period. A "serious personality disorder" is not by itself sufficient to justify any increase in the non-parole period. Such considerations, in cases where, as in *Leahy,* the accused is a first offender, should be left to the parole authorities.[26]

---

[24] *Ford v. National Parole Board,* [1977] 1 F.C. 359.
[25] (1978), 44 C.C.C. (2d) 479; *R. v. Tait,* unreported, December 11, 1978 (Sask. C.A.).
[26] *R. v. Lahtimer,* unreported, December 20, 1978 (Ont. C.A.).

Chapter 16

Orders

Upon conviction in addition to the usual penalties imposed by the criminal law, certain sections of the Criminal Code provide for the trial judge to make orders. These orders provide much-needed flexibility and serve in many cases to protect the public in a way that the usual penalties cannot. Other orders may be made by virtue of the common law powers of a criminal court.

However, it is clear that part of the problem of authority is the narrow power that exists at common law: there is no general jurisdiction to make orders in a criminal matter. In *Webb v. The Queen*[1] the courts imposed a fine of $50 on a charge of shoplifting and an order that "the accused is also barred from the K-Mart or any other mass-merchandising outlet for a period of one year." On appeal it was conceded that the court was without authority whatever to make such an order against the appellant in such circumstances and in the manner in which it was done. In some circumstances such an order or a similar order could have been incorporated as part of a probation order.

These orders should be distinguished from penalties which arise strictly by operation of law. In such cases there is no jurisdiction in the trial judge to make an order at all. For example in *R. v. Berger*,[2] the trial judge, pursuant to a conviction for having in possession goods unlawfully imported into Canada, purported to penalize the accused by an amount equal to the value of the goods, and to order forfeiture of the goods. The court said that the trial judge had no jurisdiction to make such orders; since these penalties occur by operation of law pursuant to

---

[1] (1975), 39 C.R.N.S. 314 at p. 320 (P.E.I.C.A.).
[2] [1971] 1 O.R. 765 (C.A.).

the terms of the Customs Act they are not part of the sentence imposed by the court. In any event, in the case of the monetary penalty, the Crown had to make a separate application before a competent court. For example, legal disabilities with regard to which no order need or can be made by trial court arise pursuant to s. 682 of the Criminal Code. These include a provision that, when the holder of an office under the Crown or other public employment is convicted of treason or of an indictable offence for which he is sentenced to death or to imprisonment for a term exceeding five years, the office or employment forthwith becomes vacant. Such a person, until the punishment is undergone or a free pardon is received, is incapable of holding any office under the Crown or other public employment, or of being elected or sitting or voting as a member of the Parliament of Canada or of a legislature or of exercising any right of suffrage. Also, any one who is convicted of a fraud upon the government pursuant to s. 110, selling or purchasing an office contrary to s. 113, or selling defective stores to Her Majesty or committing a fraud in connection therewith pursuant to s. 376 of the Criminal Code, thereafter has no capacity to contract with Her Majesty or to receive any benefit under a contract between Her Majesty and any other person, or to hold office under Her Majesty.

Even where no specific penalty is given for disobeying a discretionary order of the court, of the type discussed in this chapter, there is a general power of punishment in the Criminal Code as follows:

> 116(1) Every one who, without lawful excuse, disobeys a lawful order made by a court of justice or by a person or body of persons authorized by any Act to make or give the order, other than an order for the payment of money is, unless some penalty or punishment or other mode of proceeding is expressly provided by law, guilty of an indictable offence and is liable to imprisonment for two years.

This section does not supersede the inherent power of the court to punish summarily for a contempt committed in the face of the court.[3] The key phrase for the operation of this section is "unless some penalty or punishment or other mode of proceeding is expressly provided by law." In *R. v. Sanguigni,*[4] the accused was remanded on bail prior to a preliminary inquiry and he failed to appear on the date set. It was held that the section could not apply to a prosecution based on these facts, because there was doubt as to whether another mode of proceeding was

---

[3] *Re Gerson,* [1946] S.C.R. 547; affirming [1946] S.C.R. 538.
[4] [1972] 1 O.R. 826.

expressly provided by the Criminal Code sections respecting recognizances in Part XXI of the Criminal Code.

A. Mode Of Appeal

Many of the sections of the Criminal Code provide in themselves for an appeal; others have been held in the past, under a different wording of the Criminal Code, to be unappealable. Presently the general right of appeal is set out as follows, upon indictment:

> 601. In this Part
>
>   . . .
>
> "sentence" includes a declaration made under subsection 181(3), an order made under subsection 98(1) or (2), subsection 178.21(1) or 218(6), section 653, 654 or 655 and a disposition made under subsection 234(2), 236(2), 662.1(1), 663(1) or 664(3) or (4);

and upon summary conviction:

> 720(1) In this Part
>
>   . . .
>
> "sentence" includes an order made under subsection 98(1) or (2) or a disposition made under subsection 234(2), 236(2), 662.1(1), 663(1) or 664(3) or (4);

However, under the former reading, in *R. v. Markle,*[5] the Ontario Court of Appeal, upon appeal from sentence, was asked to deal with a prohibition from driving pursuant to then s. 238 of the Criminal Code. There was no provision expressly made anywhere in the Criminal Code for an appeal from this order. It was argued that the Court of Appeal therefore had no jurisdiction to review the question. The Court said:

> It is our opinion that when, consequent upon a conviction the trial Court exercises a discretionary power in imposing one or more of a period of incarceration, a fine, a suspended sentence, a period of probation or prohibits driving as it is empowered to do by s. 238, that action of the Court constitutes a sentence and that all or any part of that sentence, is reviewable by this Court on an appeal for which leave has been granted by the Court.

This interpretation is consistent with the expansive definition of

---

[5] (1973), 11 C.C.C. (2d) 67.

sentence and with the older cases at common law which define sentence. Accordingly, it would appear that all similar orders discussed in this chapter are now appealable as "sentences".

B. The Power To Order Forfeiture

Criminal Code:

443(1) A justice who is satisfied by information upon oath in Form 1, that there is reasonable ground to believe that there is in a building, receptacle or place

(*a*) anything upon or in respect of which any offence against this Act has been or is suspected to have been committed,

(*b*) anything that there is reasonable ground to believe will afford evidence with respect to the commission of an offence against this Act, or

(*c*) anything that there is reasonable ground to believe is intended to be used for the purpose of committing any offence against the person for which a person may be arrested without warrant,

may at any time issue a warrant under his hand authorizing a person named therein or a peace officer to search the building, receptacle or place for any such thing, and to seize and carry it before the justice who issued the warrant or some other justice for the same territorial division to be dealt with by him according to law.

(2) Where the building, receptacle, or place in which anything mentioned in subsection (1) is believed to be is in some other territorial division, the justice may issue his warrant in like form modified according to the circumstances, and the warrant may be executed in the other territorial division after it has been endorsed, in Form 25, by a justice having jurisdiction in that territorial division.

(3) A search warrant issued under this section may be in Form 5.

(4) An endorsement that is made upon a warrant pursuant to subsection (2) is sufficient authority to the peace officers to whom it was originally directed and to all peace officers within the jurisdiction of the justice by whom it is endorsed to execute the warrant and to take the things to which it relates before the justice who issued the warrant or some other justice for the same territorial division.

445. Every person who executes a warrant issued under section 443 may seize, in addition to the things mentioned in the warrant, anything that on reasonable grounds he believes has been obtained by or has been used in the commission of an offence, and carry it before the justice who issued the

warrant or some other justice for the same territorial division, to be dealt with in accordance with section 446.

446(1) Where anything that has been seized under section 445 or under a warrant issued pursuant to section 443 is brought before a justice, he shall, unless the prosecutor otherwise agrees, detain it or order that it be detained, taking reasonable care to ensure that it is preserved until the conclusion of any investigation or until it is required to be produced for the purposes of a preliminary inquiry or trial, but nothing shall be detained under the authority of this section for a period of more than three months after the time of seizure unless, before the expiration of that period,

(*a*) a justice is satisfied on application that, having regard to the nature of the investigation, its further detention for a specified period is warranted and he so orders; or

(*b*) proceedings are instituted in which the thing detained may be required.

(2) When an accused has been committed for trial the justice shall forward anything to which subsection (1) applies to the clerk of the court to which the accused has been committed for trial to be detained by him and disposed of as the court directs.

(3) Where a justice is satisfied that anything that has been seized under section 445 or under a warrant issued pursuant to section 443 will not be required for any purpose mentioned in subsection (1) or (2), he may,

(*a*) if possession of it by the person from whom it was seized is lawful, order it to be returned to that person, or

(*b*) if possession of it by the person from whom it was seized is unlawful,

(i) order it to be returned to the lawful owner or to the person who is entitled to possession of it, or

(ii) order it to be forfeited or otherwise dealt with in accordance with law, where the lawful owner or the person who is entitled to possession of it is not known.

(4) Nothing shall be disposed of under subsection (3) pending any proceeding in which the right of seizure is questioned, or within thirty days after an order is made under that subsection.

(5) Where anything is detained under subsection (1), a judge of a superior court of criminal jurisdiction or of a court of criminal jurisdiction may, on summary application on behalf of a person who has an interest in what is detained, after three clear days notice to the Attorney General, order that the person by or on whose behalf the application is made be permitted to examine anything so detained.

(6) An order that is made under subsection (5) shall be made on such terms as appear to the judge to be necessary or desirable to ensure that anything in respect of which the order is made is safeguarded and preserved for any purpose for which it may subsequently be required.

(7) A person who considers himself aggrieved by an order made under

subsection (3) may appeal from the order to the appeal court, as defined in section 747, and for the purposes of the appeal the provisions of sections 749 to 760 apply, *mutatis mutandis.*

It is important to note that though there is provision for an appeal from an order made under s-s. (3) of s. 446, there is no such provision with regard to s-s. (5).[6] It has been held that the "interest" under s-s. (5) must be one which the law would recognize and protect on legal or equitable principles.[7] But in *Re Canequip Exports Limited and Smith,*[8] "interest" was not confined to a person having a proprietary interest or a connection with contemplated litigation. It extended to commissioners appointed under a provincial statute to carry out an inquiry by reason of which they had a "legal concern" in the documents in question in that case.

Pursuant to s-s. (3) of s. 446, the key phrase is "if possession of it by the person from whom it was seized is lawful", as being the pre-condition for an order that material be returned. In *R. v. Nimbus News Dealers and Distributors Ltd.,*[9] the charge was possession for the purpose of distribution of obscene material and the court ruled that though possession for that purpose might be unlawful, mere possession was permissible. The Court of Appeal therefore exercised its discretion to order the return of the large quantity of magazines involved (except for those few copies needed for the trial), upon the understanding that they would not be distributed in Canada.

Pursuant to s. 446(3), it has been held that where an innocent purchaser of a stolen car improved its value by adding new tires to it, he could retain the tires that he bought; but the vehicle itself must be returned to the owner or the person who is entitled to possession of it. It would be interesting to determine what would happen if the improvements were not so easily severable from the original goods.[10]

1. WEAPONS

Criminal Code:

> 98(1) Where a person is convicted of an indictable offence in the

---

[6] *R. v. Stewart,* [1970] 3 C.C.C. 428 (Sask. C.A.).

[7] *Stewart v. The Queen* (1969), 70 W.W.R. 146 (Sask. Prov. Ct.).

[8] (1972), 8 C.C.C. (2d) 360 (Man.).

[9] (1970), 11 C.R.N.S. 315 (Ont.).

[10] *Re R. and Allison and Glendenning* (1972), 8 C.C.C. (2d) 100 (B.C. Prov. Ct.).

commission of which violence against a person is used, threatened or attempted and for which the offender may be sentenced to imprisonment for ten years or more or of an offence under section 83, the court shall, in addition to any other punishment that may be imposed for that offence, make an order prohibiting him from having in his possession any firearm or any ammunition or explosive substance for any period of time specified in the order that commences on the day the order is made and expires not earlier than

(*a*) in the case of a first conviction for such an offence, five years, and

(*b*) in any other case, ten years,

after the time of his release from imprisonment after conviction for the offence.

(2) Where a person is convicted of an offence involving the use, carriage, possession, handling, shipping or storage of any firearm or ammunition or an offence, other than an offence referred to in subsection (1), in the commission of which violence against a person was used, threatened or attempted, the court, judge, justice or magistrate, as the case may be, may, in addition to any other punishment that may be imposed for that offence, make an order prohibiting him from having in his possession any firearm or any ammunition or explosive substance for any period of time specified in the order that commences on the day the order is made and expires not later than five years after the time of his release from imprisonment after conviction for the offence or, if he is not then imprisoned or subject to imprisonment, after the time of his conviction for that offence.

(3) For the purposes of subsections (1) and (2), "release from imprisonment" means release from confinement by reason of expiration of sentence, commencement of mandatory supervision or grant of parole other than day parole.

(4) Where a peace officer has reasonable grounds to believe that it is not desirable in the interests of the safety of any person that a particular person should possess any firearm or any ammunition or explosive substance, he may apply to a magistrate for an order prohibiting that particular person from having in his possession any firearm or any ammunition or explosive substance.

446.1(1) Where it is determined by a court that a weapon was used in the commission of an offence and that weapon has been seized and detained, the weapon is, subject to subsection (2), forfeited and may be dealt with as the court that makes the determination directs.

(2) If the court by which a determination referred to in subsection (1) is made is satisfied that the lawful owner of a weapon that, but for this subsection, would be forfeited by virtue of the determination, was not a party to the offence and had no reason to believe that the weapon would or might be used in the commission of an offence, the court shall order the weapon

returned to the lawful owner thereof or the proceeds of any sale thereof to be paid to him.

(3) Where any weapon to which this section applies is sold, the proceeds of the sale shall be paid to the Attorney General or, where an order is made under subsection (2), to the person who was, immediately prior to the sale, the lawful owner of the weapon.

There are no reported cases dealing with the sections on weapons, but an example of an order for a five-year prohibition pursuant to s. 95(1) of the Criminal Code can be found in *R. v. Flanagan.*[11]

Another such order was made in *R. v. Auerswald,*[12] where the accused, a supporter of the extreme right-wing Western Guard Party, was convicted of possession of two unregistered handguns. He was also found with Nazi literature and chemicals he kept as a "hobby".

2. EXPLOSIVES

Criminal Code:

447(1) Every person who executes a warrant issued under section 443 may seize any explosive substance that he suspects is intended to be used for an unlawful purpose, and shall, as soon as possible, remove to a place of safety anything that he seizes by virtue of this section and detain it until he is ordered by a judge of a superior court to deliver it to some other person or an order is made pursuant to subsection (2).

(2) Where an accused is convicted of an offence in respect of anything seized by virtue of subsection (1), it is forfeited and shall be dealt with as the court that makes the conviction may direct.

(3) Where anything to which this section applies is sold, the proceeds of the sale shall be paid to the Attorney General.

There are no reported cases under this section.

3. OBSCENE PUBLICATIONS AND CRIME COMICS

Criminal Code:

160(1) A judge who is satisfied by information upon oath that there are reasonable grounds for believing that any publication, copies of which are kept for sale or distribution in premises within the jurisdiction of the court, is obscene or a crime comic, shall issue a warrant under his hand authorizing seizure of the copies.

---

[11] Unreported, September 5, 1974 (Ont. C.A.).
[12] (1976), 28 C.C.C. (2d) 177 (Ont. C.A.).

(2) Within seven days of the issue of the warrant, the judge shall issue a summons to the occupier of the premises requiring him to appear before the court and show cause why the matter seized should not be forfeited to Her Majesty.

(3) The owner and the author of the matter seized and alleged to be obscene or a crime comic may appear and be represented in the proceedings in order to oppose the making of an order for the forfeiture of the said matter.

(4) If the court is satisfied that the publication is obscene or a crime comic, it shall make an order declaring the matter forfeited to Her Majesty in right of the province in which the proceedings take place, for disposal as the Attorney General may direct.

(5) If the court is not satisfied that the publication is obscene or a crime comic, it shall order that the matter be restored to the person from whom it was seized forthwith after the time for final appeal has expired.

(6) An appeal lies from an order made under subsection (4) or (5) by any person who appeared in the proceedings

(a) on any ground of appeal that involves a question of law alone,

(b) on any ground of appeal that involves a question of fact alone, or

(c) on any ground of appeal that involves a question of mixed law and fact,

as if it were an appeal against conviction or against a judgment or verdict of acquittal, as the case may be, on a question of law alone under Part XVIII and sections 601 to 624 apply *mutatis mutandis.*

(7) Where an order has been made under this section by a judge in a province with respect to one or more copies of a publication, no proceedings shall be instituted or continued in that province under section 159 with respect to those or other copies of the same publication without the consent of the Attorney General.

(8) In this section

"court" means

(a) in the Province of Quebec, the provincial court, the court of the sessions of the peace, the municipal court of Montreal and the municipal court of Quebec;

(b) in the Province of Prince Edward Island, the Supreme Court; or

(c) in any other province, a county or district court;

"crime comic" has the same meaning as it has in section 159;

"judge" means a judge of a court.

The right of appeal under s-s. (6) above was discussed briefly in *Brodie v. The Queen.*[13]

---

[13] (1962), 132 C.C.C. 161 (S.C.C.).

4. PRIVACY

Criminal Code:

178.19(1) Where a person is convicted of an offence under section 178.11 or 178.18, any electromagnetic, acoustic, mechanical or other device by means of which the offence was committed or the possession of which constituted the offence, upon such conviction, in addition to any punishment that is imposed, may be ordered forfeited to Her Majesty whereupon it may be disposed of as the Attorney General directs.

(2) No order for forfeiture shall be made under subsection (1) in respect of telephone, telegraph or other communication facilities or equipment owned by a person engaged in providing telephone, telegraph or other communication service to the public or forming part of the telephone, telegraph or other communication service or system of such a person by means of which an offence under section 178.11 has been committed if such person was not a party to the offence.

178.21(1) Subject to subsection (2), a court that convicts an accused of an offence under section 178.11 or 178.2 may, upon the application of a person aggrieved, at the time sentence is imposed, order the accused to pay to that person an amount not exceeding $5,000 as punitive damages.

(2) No amount shall be ordered to be paid under subsection (1) to a person who has commenced an action under Part I.1 of the *Crown Liability Act.*

(3) Where an amount that is ordered to be paid under subsection (1) is not paid forthwith, the applicant may, by filing the order, enter as a judgment, in the superior court of the province in which the trial was held, the amount ordered to be paid, and that judgment is enforceable against the accused in the same manner as if it were a judgment rendered against the accused in that court in civil proceedings.

(4) All or any part of an amount that is ordered to be paid under subsection (1) may be taken out of moneys found in the possession of the accused at the time of his arrest, except where there is a dispute as to ownership of or right of possession to those moneys by claimants other than the accused.

5. GAMING AND BAWDY HOUSES

Criminal Code:

181(1) A justice who receives from a peace officer a report in writing that he has reasonable ground to believe and does believe that an offence under section 185, 186, 187, 189, 190 or 193 is being committed at any place within the jurisdiction of the justice may issue a warrant under his hand authorizing a peace officer to enter and search the place by day or night and seize anything found therein that may be evidence that an offence under section

185, 186, 187, 189, 190 or 193, as the case may be, is being committed at that place, and to take into custody all persons who are found in or at that place and requiring those persons and things to be brought before him or before another justice having jurisdiction, to be dealt with according to law.

(2) A peace officer may, whether or not he is acting under a warrant issued pursuant to this section, take into custody any person whom he finds keeping a common gaming house and any person whom he finds therein, and may seize anything that may be evidence that such an offence is being committed and shall bring those persons and things before a justice having jurisdiction, to be dealt with according to law.

(3) Except where otherwise expressly provided by law, a court, judge, justice or magistrate before whom anything that is seized under this section is brought may declare that the thing is forfeited, in which case it shall be disposed of or dealt with as the Attorney General may direct if no person shows sufficient cause why it should not be forfeited.

(4) No declaration or direction shall be made pursuant to subsection (3) in respect of anything seized under this section until

(*a*) it is no longer required as evidence in any proceedings that are instituted pursuant to the seizure, or

(*b*) the expiration of thirty days from the time of seizure where it is not required as evidence in any proceedings.

(5) The Attorney General may, for the purpose of converting anything forfeited under this section into money, deal with it in all respects as if he were the owner thereof.

(6) Nothing in this section or in section 445 authorizes the seizure, forfeiture or destruction of telephone, telegraph or other communication facilities or equipment that may be evidence of or that may have been used in the commission of an offence under section 185, 186, 187, 189, 190 or 193 and that is owned by a person engaged in providing telephone, telegraph or other communication service to the public or forming part of the telephone, telegraph or other communication service or system of such a person.

(7) Subsection (6) does not apply to prohibit the seizure, for use as evidence, of any facility or equipment described in that subsection that is designed or adapted to record a communication.

193(1) Every one who keeps a common bawdy-house is guilty of an indictable offence and is liable to imprisonment for two years.

(2) Every one who

(*a*) is an inmate of a common bawdy-house,

(*b*) is found, without lawful excuse, in a common bawdy-house, or

(*c*) as owner, landlord, lessor, tenant, occupier, agent or otherwise having charge or control of any place, knowingly permits the place or any part thereof to be let or used for the purposes of a common bawdy-house

is guilty of an offence punishable on summary conviction.

(3) Where a person is convicted of an offence under subsection (1), the court shall cause a notice of the conviction to be served upon the owner, landlord or lessor of the place in respect of which the person is convicted or his agent, and the notice shall contain a statement to the effect that it is being served pursuant to this section.

(4) Where a person upon whom a notice is served under subsection (3) fails forthwith to exercise any right he may have to determine the tenancy or right of occupation of the person so convicted, and thereafter any person is convicted of an offence under subsection (1) in respect of the same premises, the person upon whom the notice was served shall be deemed to have committed an offence under subsection (1) unless he proves that he has taken all reasonable steps to prevent the recurrence of the offence.

Section 181(3), unlike most sections providing for forfeiture, puts an onus on the person opposing the forfeiture to "show sufficient cause". This reverses the usual common law rule that the onus on restoration is on accused.[14]

In *R. v. Owens,*[15] the appellant was charged with gaming house offences. He had been acquitted on two other related charges (keeping a common betting house and registering bets) but pleaded guilty to a charge of agreeing to place a bet on behalf of another person for consideration. An order was made by the trial judge upon sentence that the sum of $806.55, seized under the authority of a search warrant, be forfeited to the Crown. The submission by defence counsel was that the learned trial judge had erred as there was no evidence that this money was used in connection with the operations for which the appellant pleaded guilty, nor was there evidence as to which part of the moneys could be assigned to that illegal operation. Noting that the accused had offered no evidence at trial to show that the moneys seized or a part thereof did not relate to the illegal operation, the court concluded that there was no evidence to suggest that the moneys were not associated with the offence. Accordingly, the order of forfeiture was proper in the circumstances. The court rejected any rule that forfeiture could only be made with respect to moneys that were actually identified with the particular offence of which the accused is guilty. This is consistent with a literal interpretation of the law, but in effect forces the accused into the witness box. In Saskatchewan, moneys that were not connected with the offence of which a person was convicted and which therefore were not

---

[14] *Leitman v. Mackey, Pilkington and Metro Toronto,* [1963] 2 C.C.C. 356 (Ont.).
[15] [1972] 1 O.R. 341 (C.A.).

seized in accordance with s-s. (1) were held not to be subject to forfeiture under s-s. (3).[16]

The right to declare property confiscated is of course dependent upon a valid seizure,[17] but it will be presumed, in the absence of evidence to the contrary, that the seizure is properly made and that the proceedings leading to confiscation are regular.[18] It is important to note that the orders made under this section are not apparently part of the sentence but are orders *in rem:* they do not flow from conviction, but from the seizure. No method of appeal on these sections is expressly provided in the Criminal Code.[19]

6. BOATS AND VESSELS

Criminal Code:

240(7) Where an accused is convicted of an offence under section 203, 204, 219, subsection (1) [dangerous operation of the vessel], (2) [killing a person when no one is keeping watch], (3) [killing a person at night], (4) [operating a vessel while impaired] or (5) [failure to remain after an accident] of this section, section 240.1 [failure to provide sample of breath] or 240.2 [operating a vessel with more than 80 mgs. of alcohol in blood], committed by means of a vessel, the court, judge, justice or magistrate, as the case may be, may, in addition to any other punishment that may be imposed for that offence, make an order prohibiting him from navigating or operating a vessel on or over any of the internal waters of Canada or the territorial sea of Canada at all times or at such times and places as may be specified in the order

(*a*) during any period that the court, judge, justice or magistrate considers proper, if he is liable to imprisonment for life in respect of that offence, or

(*b*) during any period not exceeding three years, if he is not liable to imprisonment for life in respect of that offence.

(8) No order made under subsection (7) shall operate to prevent any person from acting as master, mate or engineer of a vessel that is required to carry officers holding certificates as master, mate or engineer.

(9) Every one who navigates or operates a vessel on or over any of the

---

[16] *R. v. Yee*, [1973] 2 W.W.R. 277 (Sask. Mag. Ct.).

[17] *R. v. Rocco* (1931), 55 C.C.C. 323 (Man. C.A.).

[18] *R. v. Green*, [1935] 1 W.W.R. 526 (Man. C.A.).

[19] *R. v. Louis* (1957), 117 C.C.C. 284 (Sask. C.A.); *R. v. Martin*, [1944] O.W.N. 19 (C.A.); *R. v. Lougheed Drive-In Theatre Ltd.*, [1963] 3 C.C.C. 357 (B.C.C.A.); *R. v. Miles*, [1936] 1 D.L.R. 186 (N.S.C.A.); *R. v. Green, supra,* n. 18.

internal waters of Canada or the territorial sea of Canada while he is prohibited from navigating or operating a vessel by reason of an order made pursuant to subsection (7) is guilty of an offence punishable on summary conviction.

(10) For the purposes of this section and sections 240.1, 240.2 and 295, "vessel" includes a machine designed to derive support in the atmosphere primarily from reactions against the earth's surface of air expelled from the machine.

7. HATE PROPAGANDA

Criminal Code:

281.3(1) A judge who is satisfied by information upon oath that there are reasonable grounds for believing that any publication, copies of which are kept for sale or distribution in premises within the jurisdiction of the court, is hate propaganda, shall issue a warrant under his hand authorizing seizure of the copies.

(2) Within seven days of the issue of the warrant, the judge shall issue a summons to the occupier of the premises requiring him to appear before the court and show cause why the matter seized should not be forfeited to Her Majesty.

(3) The owner and the author of the matter seized and alleged to be hate propaganda may appear and be represented in the proceedings in order to oppose the making of an order for the forfeiture of the said matter.

(4) If the court is satisfied that the publication is hate propaganda, it shall make an order declaring the matter forfeited to Her Majesty in right of the province in which the proceedings take place, for disposal as the Attorney General may direct.

(5) If the court is not satisfied that the publication is hate propaganda, it shall order that the matter be restored to the person from whom it was seized forthwith after the time for final appeal has expired.

(6) An appeal lies from an order made under subsection (4) or (5) by any person who appeared in the proceedings

(*a*) on any ground of appeal that involves a question of law alone,

(*b*) on any ground of appeal that involves a question of fact alone, or

(*c*) on any ground of appeal that involves a question of mixed law and fact,

as if it were an appeal against conviction or against a judgment or verdict of acquittal, as the case may be, on a question of law alone under Part XVIII, and sections 601 to 624 apply *mutatis mutandis.*

(7) No proceeding under this section shall be instituted without the consent of the Attorney General.

(8) In this section

"court" means

(*a*) in the Province of Quebec,
    (i) the court of the sessions of the peace, or
    (ii) where an application has been made to a judge of the provincial court for a warrant under subsection (1), that judge;
(*b*) in the Province of Prince Edward Island, the Supreme Court; or
(*c*) in any province, a county or district court;
"genocide" has the same meaning as it has in section 281.1;
"hate propaganda" means any writing, sign or visible representation that advocates or promotes genocide or the communication of which by any person would constitute an offence under section 281.2;
"judge" means a judge of a court or, in the Province of Quebec, a judge of the provincial court.

8. PRECIOUS METALS OR MINERALS

Criminal Code:

352(2) Where a person is convicted of an offence under this section, the court may order anything by means of or in relation to which the offence was committed, upon such conviction, to be forfeited to Her Majesty in right of the province in which the proceedings take place.

353(1) Where an information in writing is laid under oath before a justice by any person having an interest in a mining claim, that any precious metals or rock, mineral or other substance containing precious metals is unlawfully deposited in any place or held by any person contrary to law, the justice may issue a warrant to search any of the places or persons mentioned in the information.

(2) Where, upon search, anything mentioned in subsection (1) is found, it shall be seized and carried before the justice who shall order

(*a*) that it be detained for the purposes of an inquiry or trial, or
(*b*) if it is not detained for the purposes of an inquiry or trial,
    (i) that it be restored to the owner, or
    (ii) that it be forfeited to Her Majesty in right of the province in which the proceedings take place if the owner cannot be ascertained.

(3) An appeal lies from an order made under paragraph (2)(*b*) in the manner in which an appeal lies in summary conviction proceedings under Part XXIV and the provisions of that Part relating to appeals apply to appeals under this subsection.

9. OBTAINING CARRIAGE BY FALSE BILLING

Criminal Code:

359(1) Every one who, by means of a false or misleading representation, knowingly obtains or attempts to obtain the carriage of anything by any person into a country, province, district or other place, whether or not within Canada, where the importation or transportation of it is, in the circumstances of the case, unlawful is guilty of an offence punishable on summary conviction.

(2) Where a person is convicted of an offence under subsection (1), anything by means of or in relation to which the offence was committed, upon such conviction, in addition to any punishment that is imposed, is forfeited to Her Majesty and shall be disposed of as the court may direct.

10. TRADE MARKS AND PASSING OFF GOODS

Criminal Code:

370(1) Every one who commits an offence under section 365 [forging a trade mark], 366 [passing off wares and services or falsely describing them], 367 [possession of instruments for forging a trade mark], 368 [removing a trade mark], or 369 [failing to disclose reconditioned goods] is guilty of

(a) an indictable offence and is liable to imprisonment for two years, or

(b) an offence punishable on summary conviction.

(2) Anything by means of or in relation to which a person commits an offence under section 365, 366, 367, 368 or 369 is, unless the court otherwise orders, forfeited upon the conviction of that person for that offence.

11. CAUSING UNNECESSARY SUFFERING TO ANIMALS AND BIRDS

Criminal Code:

402(1) Every one commits an offence who

(a) wilfully causes or, being the owner, wilfully permits to be caused unnecessary pain, suffering or injury to an animal or bird,

(b) by wilful neglect causes damage or injury to animals or birds while they are being driven or conveyed,

(c) being the owner or the person having the custody or control of a domestic animal or bird or an animal or bird wild by nature that is in captivity, abandons it in distress or wilfully neglects or fails to provide suitable and adequate food, water, shelter and care for it,

(d) in any manner encourages, aids or assists at the fighting or baiting of animals or birds,

(e) wilfully, without reasonable excuse, administers a poisonous or injurious drug or substance to a domestic animal or bird or an animal or bird wild by nature that is kept in captivity or being the owner of such an animal or bird, wilfully permits a poisonous or injurious drug or substance to be administered to it, (*f*) promotes, arranges, conducts, assists in, receives money for, or takes part in a meeting, competition, exhibition, pastime, practice, display, or event at or in the course of which captive birds are liberated by hand, trap, contrivance or any other means for the purpose of being shot when they are liberated, or

(*g*) being the owner, occupier, or person in charge of any premises, permits the premises or any part thereof to be used for a purpose mentioned in paragraph (*f*).

(2) Every one who commits an offence under subsection (1) is guilty of an offence punishable on summary conviction.

(3) For the purpose of proceedings under paragraph (1)(*a*) or (*b*), evidence that a person failed to exercise reasonable care or supervision of an animal or bird thereby causing it pain, suffering, damage or injury is, in the absence of any evidence to the contrary, proof that such pain, suffering, damage or injury was caused or was permitted to be caused wilfully or was caused by wilful neglect, as the case may be.

(4) For the purpose of proceedings under paragraph (1)(*d*), evidence that an accused was present at the fighting or baiting of animals or birds is, in the absence of any evidence to the contrary, proof that he encouraged, aided or assisted at such fighting or baiting.

(5) Where an accused is convicted of an offence under subsection (1), the court may, in addition to any other sentence that may be imposed for the offence, make an order prohibiting the accused from owning or having the custody or control of an animal or bird during any period not exceeding two years.

(6) Every one who owns or has the custody or control of an animal or bird while he is prohibited from doing so by reason of an order made under subsection (5) is guilty of an offence punishable on summary conviction.

C. Restrictions On Parole Upon Sentence Of Life Imprisonment For Murder

Criminal Code:

669. The sentence to be pronounced against a person who is to be sentenced to imprisonment for life shall be,

(*a*) in respect of a person who has been convicted of high treason or first degree murder, that he be sentenced to imprisonment for life without eligibility for parole until he has served twenty-five years of his sentence;

(*b*) in respect of a person who has been convicted of second degree murder, that he be sentenced to imprisonment for life without eligibility for parole until he has served at least ten years of his sentence or such greater number of years, not being more than twenty-five years, as has been substituted therefor pursuant to section 671; and

(c) in respect of a person who has been convicted of any other offence, that he be sentenced to imprisonment for life with normal eligibility for parole.

671. At the time of the sentencing of an accused under section 669 who is convicted of second degree murder, the judge presiding at the trial of the accused or, if that judge is unable to do so, any judge of the same court may, having regard to the character of the accused, the nature of the offence and the circumstances surrounding its commission, and to any recommendation made pursuant to section 670, by order, substitute for ten years a number of years of imprisonment, (being more than ten but not more than twenty-five) without eligibility for parole, as he deems fit in the circumstances.

672(1) Where a person has served at least fifteen years of his sentence

(a) in the case of a person who has been convicted of high treason or first degree murder, or

(b) in the case of a person convicted of second degree murder who has been sentenced to imprisonment for life without eligibility for parole until he has served more than fifteen years of his sentence, he may apply to the appropriate Chief Justice in the province or territory in which the conviction took place for a reduction in his number of years of imprisonment without eligibility for parole.

(2) Upon receipt of an application under subsection (1), the appropriate Chief Justice shall designate a judge of the superior court of criminal jurisdiction to empanel a jury to hear the application and determine whether the applicant's number of years of imprisonment without eligibility for parole ought to be reduced having regard to the character of the applicant, his conduct while serving his sentence, the nature of the offense for which he was convicted and such other matters as the judge deems relevant in the circumstances and such determination shall be made by no less than two-thirds of such jury.

(3) Where the jury hearing an application under subsection (1) determine that the applicant's number of years of imprisonment without eligibility for parole ought not to be reduced, the jury shall set another time at or after which an application may again be made by the applicant to the appropriate Chief Justice for a reduction in his number of years of imprisonment without eligibility for parole.

(4) Where the jury hearing an application under subsection (1) determine that the applicant's number of years of imprisonment without eligibility for parole ought to be reduced, the jury may, by order,

(a) substitute a lesser number of years of imprisonment without eligibility for parole than that then applicable; or

(b) terminate the ineligibility for parole.

(5) The appropriate Chief Justice in each province or territory may make such rules in respect of applications and hearings under this section as are required for the purposes of this section.

(6) For the purposes of this section, the "appropriate Chief Justice" is

(*a*) in relation to

  (i)   the Provinces of British Columbia and Prince Edward Island, respectively, the Chief Justice of the Supreme Court,

  (ii) the Provinces of Alberta, Nova Scotia and Newfoundland, respectively, the Chief Justice of the Supreme Court, Trial Division,

  (iii) the Provinces of Saskatchewan and Manitoba, respectively, the Chief Justice of the Court of Queen's Bench,

  (iv) the Province of New Brunswick, the Chief Justice of the Supreme Court, Queen's Bench Division,

  (v) the Province of Ontario, the Chief Justice of the High Court of Justice, and

  (vi) the Province of Quebec, the Chief Justice of the Superior Court;

(*b*) in relation to the Yukon Territory, the Chief Justice of the Court of Appeal thereof; and

(*c*) in relation to the Northwest Territories, the Chief Justice of the Court of Appeal thereof.

(7) For the purposes of this section, when the appropriate Chief Justice is designating a judge of the superior court of criminal jurisdiction to empanel a jury to hear an application in respect of a conviction that took place in the Yukon Territory or the Northwest Territories, the appropriate Chief Justice may designate the judge from the Court of Appeal or the Supreme Court of the Yukon Territory or Northwest Territories, as the case may be.

674(1) Unless the Parliament of Canada otherwise provides by an enactment making express reference to this section, no person who has been sentenced to imprisonment for life without eligibility for parole for a specified number of years pursuant to this Act shall be considered for parole or released pursuant to the terms of a grant of parole under the *Parole Act* or any other Act of the Parliament of Canada until the expiration or termination of his specified number of years of imprisonment without eligibility for parole.

(2) Notwithstanding the *Penitentiary Act* and the *Parole Act,* in the case of any person sentenced to imprisonment for life without eligibility for parole for a specified number of years pursuant to this Act, until the expiration of all but three years of his number of years of imprisonment without eligibility for parole, no absence without escort may be authorized under the *Penitentiary Act,* no absence with escort for humanitarian and rehabilitative reasons may be authorized under the *Penitentiary Act* without the approval of the National Parole Board and no day parole may be granted under the *Parole Act.*

Despite the *dicta* in *R. v. McInnis*,[20] to the effect that a conviction includes the ensuing sentence and noting the definition of sentence under s. 601 of the Criminal Code for indictable offenses, in *R. v. Hubbert*,[21] a five-man bench took the view that because of a legislative oversight whereby the then definition of "sentence" omitted all reference to s. 218(6) of the Code at the time that the appeal was launched, it may well be that no appeal lay from such an order.

D. An Order To Keep The Peace And Be Of Good Behaviour

Criminal Code:

745(1) Any person who fears that another person will cause personal injury to him or his wife or child or will damage his property may lay an information before a justice.

(2) A justice who receives an information under subsection (1) shall cause the parties to appear before him or before a summary conviction court having jurisdiction in the same territorial division.

(3) The justice or the summary conviction court before which the parties appear may, if satisfied by the evidence adduced that the informant has reasonable grounds for his fears,

(a) order that the defendant enter into a recognizance, with or without sureties, to keep the peace and be of good behaviour for any period that does not exceed twelve months, and comply with such other reasonable conditions prescribed in the recognizance as the court considers desirable for securing good conduct of the defendant, or

(b) commit the defendant to prison for a term not exceeding twelve months if he fails or refuses to enter into the recognizance.

(4) A recognizance and committal to prison in default of recognizance under subsection (3) may be in Forms 28 and 20 respectively.

(5) The provisions of this Part apply *mutatis mutandis,* to proceedings under this section.

The powers in this section are similar to, and, in at least some provinces, run together with a common law preventive justice power. Pursuant to either this section or the common law power, the court may bind over a man, not because he has committed an offence, but because it is thought from his behaviour that he may himself commit or cause

---

[20] (1973), 13 C.C.C. (2d) 471 (Ont. C.A.).
[21] Unreported, June 17, 1975 (Ont. C.A.).

others to commit offences against the Queen's peace.[22] It is clear that for several centuries justices have bound by recognizance persons whose conduct they consider mischievous or suspicious, but which could not, by any stretch of the imagination, amount to a criminal offence.[23] In *MacKenzie v. Martin*[24] the cause of the order was a number of unsolicited telephone calls to the complainant: "Sometimes he cries. He says he is lonesome. He says he loves me, and he tells me he's going to send someone to kill me. I think he is a madman." The information in this case was that the accused repeatedly called the complainant on the telephone, causing annoyance, loss of sleep, incovenience and worry — all acts tending towards a breach of the public peace, contrary to the common law of England. Similarly, in *R. v. Poffenroth*[25] the subject-matter of an order was conduct which included running after and annoying a woman on a public street which was held to be likely to cause a breach of the peace.

This binding over of a person to keep the peace is not an actual proceeding by way of punishment, but only a precautionary proceeding to prevent a breach of the peace.[26] An order to give security under this section of the Criminal Code is not part of a conviction; and it is not necessary as a condition of requiring a recognizance that any criminal offence should have been committed. In *Lansbury v. Riley*,[27] it was said that an anticipated breach of the peace was sufficient and that it need not be shown that any person was in actual fear. Similarly, in *Wise v. Dunning*,[28] it was said that a person could be bound over though he had not directly incited others to the commission of breaches of the peace, but had used language and intended to use similar language in the future the natural consequence of which was that breaches of the peace would be then committed by others.

---

[22] *MacKenzie v. Martin*, [1954] S.C.R. 361.

[23] *R. v. County of London Q.S.*, [1948] 1 All E.R. 72.

[24] *Supra*, n. 22.

[25] [1942] 2 W.W.R. 362 (Alta.).

[26] *Frey v. Fedoruk*, [1950] S.C.R. 517; *Mann v. Yannacos*, [1977] 16 S.A.S.R. 54.

[27] (1914), 23 Cox C.C. 582.

[28] (1902), 20 Cox C.C. 121; *R. v. Wilkins* (1907), 21 Cox C.C. 443; *R. v. Sandbach*, [1935] 2 K.B. 192; *R. v. Patterson*, [1931] 3 D.L.R. 167 (Ont. C.A.); *Thomas v. Sawkins*, [1935] 2 K.B. 249.

The allegation of a threat must be definite, though it need not be expressed in words and may be inferred from a course of conduct alone.[29]

In *R. v. McCartan*[30] the English Court of Appeal held that the probation order could not be used to send an offender from England back to Ireland and to ensure that he stayed there, because under their statute the offender could not be placed under the supervision of a probation officer in Ireland. Such a problem does not exist within Canada, but in *McCartan* binding the offender over a common law permitted a condition recognizance that he return to Ireland immediately and not return to England for a specified period. Such a measure might well be appropriate in Canada. It is probable that the Canadian Bill of Rights' provisions forbidding arbitrary exile could limit the application of the common law of England though its ambit is restricted to a "law of Canada".

The procedure whereby the binding over is invoked, whether by statute or at common law, must be exercised very carefully. In *R. v. White; Ex p. Chohan*,[31] it was held that a magistrate may either act under s. 745, which requires that he be satisfied "that the informant has reasonable grounds for his belief" of injury or damage, or he may exercise his common law jurisdiction, for which the prerequisite is that "the magistrate (on facts established to his satisfaction), has probable grounds to suspect or be apprehensive that there may be a breach of the peace." These latter grounds are wider than the statutory grounds in s. 745. It was held in *White* that the magistrate, acting under the common law, erred in making an order when he was not in fact satisfied as to the facts and in so doing without giving an opportunity for representations to be made by the persons who were to be subject to the order.

The common law jurisdiction must be exercised pursuant to proof of the facts through evidence. In *Re R. and Shaben*,[32] after convicting an accused person of assult, the magistrate bound over not only the accused but also the three witnesses. The witnesses were not informed of what action the magistrate proposed to take; they were given no opportunity to call evidence, nor to speak on their own behalf, nor to obtain counsel of their choice. It was held that this was a denial of natural justice as well as a denial of a fair hearing contrary to the Canadian Bill of Rights.

---

[29] *R. v. Dunn* (1840), 12 Ad. & El. 599, 113 E.R. 939; *R. v. McCartan* (1958), 42 Cr. App. R. 262.

[30] *Supra*, n. 29.

[31] [1969] 1 C.C.C. 19 (B.C.).

[32] (1972), 8 C.C.C. (2d) 422 (Ont.).

E. Orders Of Restoration Of Property To An Accused Person

Quite often seizures are made by police at or after arrest on the ground that the items are needed for use as evidence. The court is not powerless to prevent an abuse of this power. An application for an order of restoration of exhibits or articles before the court may be made at any time by an accused person. In *R. v. Harris,*[33] the accused was committed for trial upon a charge of murder. Application was made for an order that a sum of money taken by the police from the prisoner on his arrest might be restored to him in order that the prisoner might not be deprived of his only means of defence. The Chief Justice of British Columbia, after inquiring whether the money was required for the purpose of evidence at the trial on the charge upon which the prisoner was committed and being informed it was not and the amount being small, directed that the money should be returned.

In *Ex parte MacMichael,*[34] an application was made to the trial judge for the restoration to the prisoner of a number of items of property valued at about $200. This application was refused. Subsequently a demand was made upon the Chief of Police and it too was refused. Upon application to the Supreme Court of Nova Scotia and upon the prisoner's affidavit showing that these materials were not connected with the offence charged and were not the avails of crime, an order was made directing the Chief Constable for the City of Halifax to deliver the articles to the accused at the county jail — namely, one travelling bag with toilet, one breach-loading rifle, one fishing case and tackle, one portmanteau and one gold chain.

In *Leitman v. Mackey,*[35] the accused was apprehended upon four separate counts relating to betting and keeping a common betting house. When he was arrested at the premises (his residence) the sum of $3,159 was found in his pocket. The money was seized and kept by the police. An application to the presiding judge was refused. Crown counsel argued before the magistrate that there was no evidence before him of the existence of any money and that until the trial judge became seized of the facts he would have no jurisdiction to order anything returned. On appeal it was said:

---

[33] (1883), 1 B.C.R. (Part 1) 255.
[34] (1904), 7 C.C.C. 549 (N.S.).
[35] [1963] 2 C.C.C. 356 (Ont.).

... the rights of a citizen are not totally arrested simply because criminal proceedings are pending and however immaterial may be the relationship between those rights and those proceedings ... One must go beyond and find some relationship between the act complained of and the criminal proceedings; to give an exaggerated example one should not have his watch seized when arrested for speeding and held until the disposition of the case.

It was decided that it is within the jurisdiction of the magistrate at first instance to hear the complaint of any accused person concerning any seized chattels and that his right to possession with personal property must receive the due consideration of that tribunal. The application should be heard summarily. A brief statement by Crown counsel in a given case might be sufficient for him to decide that there is a "close relationship" between the chattel seized and the case at bar. In other cases he might direct that evidence under oath be given by an officer that the chattel seized is required as evidence in the proceedings:

> From the moment he is arraigned, the accused has the right to be heard on a matter incidental to and that arises out of his arrest, if it constitutes in a Magistrate's opinion, an abuse of administrative law. In my opinion the onus that arises ... of establishing that a chattel seized is of evidentiary value in the criminal proceedings is on the Crown and not on the person apprehended.

In the instant case, the Supreme Court Justice held that the amount of money and the denomination which the accused had in his possession at the time of his arrest could easily be given verbally in evidence and the money itself need not be produced.

> To establish the necessity of it being produced, the Crown has to adduce some evidence to continue holding same. An uncontrollable discretionary power in the police officer in that respect could lead to substantial injustice and infringement of the rights of a citizen to his private property. It would, *ipso facto*, revert us to the laws of the fifteenth century when all the chattels and properties of an accused person could be seized on his arrest for any crime.

It has been held in *Re Black and The Queen*,[36] that if items seized illegally under a search warrant pursuant to s. 443 cannot be shown by the Crown to be required as evidence, then the court has an inherent power to order their return.

In *R. v. Percival and McDougall*[37] four sums of money were marked as

---

[36] (1973), 13 C.C.C. (2d) 446 (B.C.); *Re Purdy et al. and The Queen* (1972), 8 C.C.C. (2d) 52 (N.B.C.A.).
[37] (1973), 10 C.C.C. (2d) 566 (B.C.).

exhibits at a preliminary inquiry, but were never used at trial. The accused persons directed in writing that the moneys involved ought to be paid to their defence counsel by an "irrevocable authorization". Some time later, as is the way in these matters, one of them by written document revoked this previous authorization, indicating that all of his moneys were instead to be paid to the co-accused and no one else. Faced with these documents the trial court directed that the exhibits should not be released without a further order of the court. Upon application by the two solicitors, the court held that the four exhibits did not constitute a fund in court, but rather four specific items capable of being possessed, and "as such they are not *choses in action* and not subject to transfer by assignment, and consequently the applicants are unable to show more than an uncompleted gift." On that ground alone the application was refused. However, the learned trial judge went on to examine the transcripts of the preliminary hearing and, with his notes from the trial, he came to the inescapable inference that "the large sum of money was the proceeds of the crime for which the prisoners were arrested and convicted." Citing cases to the effect that it is against public policy to allow a criminal to claim any benefit by virtue of his crime, and holding that his representatives who claimed under him had no wider right, the court indicated that it would not order the delivery of this particular exhibit either to the accused or anyone claiming through or under them.

Chapter 17

The Victim Of Crime

Criminal Code:

655(1) Where an accused is convicted of an indictable offence the court shall order that any property obtained by the commission of the offence shall be restored to the person entitled to it, if at the time of the trial the property is before the court or has been detained so that it can be immediately restored to that person under the order.

(2) Where an accused is tried for an indictable offence but is not convicted, and the court finds that an indictable offence has been committed, the court may order that any property obtained by a commission of the offence shall be restored to the person entitled to it, if at the time of the trial the property is before the court or has been detained, so that it can be immediately restored to that person under the order.

(3) An order shall not be made under this section in respect of

(a) property to which an innocent purchaser for value has acquired lawful title,

(b) a valuable security that has been paid or discharged in good faith by a person who was liable to pay or discharge it,

(c) a negotiable instrument that has, in good faith, been taken or received by transfer or delivery for valuable consideration by a person who had no notice and no reasonable cause to suspect that an indictable offence had been committed, or

(d) property in respect of which there is a dispute as to ownership or right of possession by claimants other than the accused.

(4) An order made under this section shall be executed by the peace officers by whom the process of the court is ordinarily executed.

(5) This section does not apply to proceedings against a trustee, banker, merchant, attorney, factor, broker or other agent entrusted with the possession of goods or documents of title to goods, for an offence under section 290, 291, 292 or 296.

616(1) Where an order for compensation or for the restitution of property is made by the trial court under section 653, 654 or 655, the operation of the order is suspended

(*a*) until the expiration of the period prescribed by rules of court for the giving of notice of appeal or of notice of application for leave to appeal, unless the accused waives an appeal, and

(*b*) until the appeal or application for leave to appeal has been determined, where an appeal is taken or application for leave to appeal is made.

(2) The court of appeal may by order annul or vary an order made by the trial court with respect to compensation or the restitution of property within the limits prescribed by the provision under which the order was made by the trial court, whether or not the conviction is quashed.

663(2) The following conditions shall be deemed to be prescribed in a probation order, namely, that the accused shall keep the peace and be of good behaviour and shall appear before the court when required to do so by the court, and, in addition, the court may prescribe as conditions in a probation order that the accused shall do any one or more of the following things as specified in the order, namely,

. . .

(*e*) make restitution or reparation to any person aggrieved or injured by the commission of the offence for the actual loss or damage sustained by that person as a result thereof;

653(1) A court that convicts an accused of an indictable offence may, upon the application of a person aggrieved, at the time sentence is imposed, order the accused to pay to that person an amount by way of satisfaction or compensation for loss of or damage to property suffered by the applicant as a result of the commission of the offence of which the accused is convicted.

(2) Where an amount that is ordered to be paid under subsection (1) is not paid forthwith the applicant may, by filing the order, enter as a judgment, in the superior court of the province in which the trial was held, the amount ordered to be paid, and that judgment is enforceable against the accused in the same manner as if it were a judgment rendered against the accused in that court in civil proceedings.

(3) All or any part of an amount that is ordered to be paid under subsection (1) may, if the court making the order is satisfied that ownership of or right to possession of those moneys is not disputed by claimants other than the accused and the court so directs, be taken out of moneys found in the possession of the accused at the time of his arrest.

388(1) Every one who wilfully destroys or damages property is, where actual danger to life is not involved, guilty of an offence punishable on summary conviction if the alleged amount of destruction or damage does not exceed fifty dollars.

(2) Where an accused is convicted of an offence under subsection (1) the

summary conviction court may, in addition to any punishment that is imposed, order the accused to pay to a person aggrieved an amount not exceeding fifty dollars that appears to the summary conviction court to be reasonable compensation for the destruction or damage.

(3) The summary conviction court may order that where an amount that is adjudged to be paid as compensation under subsection (2) is not paid forthwith or within the period that the summary conviction court appoints at the time of the conviction, the accused shall be imprisoned for a term not exceeding two months.

(4) The summary conviction court may order that terms of imprisonment that are imposed under this section shall take effect one after the other.

654(1) Where an accused is convicted of an indictable offence and any property obtained as a result of the commission of the offence has been sold to an innocent purchaser, the court may, upon the application of the purchaser after restitution of the property to its owner, order the accused to pay to the purchaser an amount not exceeding the amount paid by the purchaser for the property.

(2) Where an amount that is ordered to be paid under subsection (1) is not paid forthwith the applicant may, by filing the order, enter as a judgment, in the superior court of the province in which the trial was held, the amount ordered to be paid, and that judgment is enforceable against the accused in the same manner as if it were a judgment rendered against the accused in that court in civil proceedings.

(3) All or any part of an amount that is ordered to be paid under subsection (1) may, if the court making the order is satisfied that ownership of or right to possession of those moneys is not disputed by claimants other than the accused and the court so directs, be taken out of moneys found in the possession of the accused at the time of his arrest.

650(1) Where a term of imprisonment is imposed in default of payment of a penalty, the term shall, upon payment of a part of the penalty, whether the payment was made before or after the issue of a warrant of committal, be reduced by the number of days that bears the same proportion to the number of days in the term as the part paid bears to the total penalty.

(2) No amount offered in part payment of a penalty shall be accepted unless it is sufficient to secure reduction of sentence of one day, or some multiple thereof, and where a warrant of committal has been issued, no part payment shall be accepted until any fee that is payable in respect of the warrant or its execution has been paid.

(3) Payment may be made under this section to the person who has lawful custody of the prisoner or to such other person as the Attorney General directs.

(4) A payment under this section shall, unless the order imposing the penalty otherwise provides, be applied to the payment in full of costs and charges, and thereafter to payment in full of compensation or damages that

are included in the penalty, and finally to payment in full of any part of the penalty that remains unpaid.

(5) In this section, "penalty" means all the sums of money, including fines, in default of payment of which a term of imprisonment is imposed and includes the costs and charges of committing the defaulter and of conveying him to prison.

646(3) Where a fine is imposed under this section, a term of imprisonment may be imposed in default of payment of the fine, but no such term shall exceed

(a) two years, where the term of imprisonment that may be imposed for the offence is less than five years, or

(b) five years, where the term of imprisonment that may be imposed for the offence is five years or more.

(12) In this section "fine" includes a pecuniary penalty or other sum of money.

616(1) Where an order for compensation or for the restitution of property is made by the trial court under section 653, 654 or 655, the operation of the order is suspended

(a) until the expiration of the period prescribed by rules of court for the giving of notice of appeal or of notice of application for leave to appeal, unless the accused waives an appeal, and

(b) until the appeal or application for leave to appeal has been determined, where an appeal is taken or application for leave to appeal is made.

(2) The court of appeal may by order annul or vary an order made by the trial court with respect to compensation or the restitution of property within the limits prescribed by the provision under which the order was made by the trial court, whether or not the conviction is quashed.

742. Where several persons join in committing the same offence and upon conviction each is adjudged to pay an amount to a person aggrieved, no more shall be paid to that person than an amount equal to the value of the property destroyed or injured or the amount of the injury done, together with costs, if any, and the residue of the amount adjudged to be paid shall be applied in the manner in which other penalties imposed by the law are directed to be applied.

A. Putting Matters Right

The lawyer who represents the victim of a crime faces a bewildering array of statutory provisions, many of them with conflicting limitations on their invocation and scope. Usually, the terminology used is both inexact and archaic; in many cases, words seem to carry different connotations in different sections of the statute. The Criminal Code is in desperate need of revision in the sections which refer to the victim of the crime. Its inadequacy as a document treating the rights of the victim aside, few ordinary citizens resort to it simply because these provisions are largely unknown. Indeed, it is hard to understand why it is not an obligation of the Crown attorney to inform a victim who has suffered monetary damage of the provisions in the Criminal Code and to explain to him how he can apply for his proper remedy.

Common experience teaches that in the vast majority of cases the question of compensation to a victim or recovery of his property will be simple and clear. In such cases, the Criminal Code is effective and inexpensive. Yet it is often true that the victim of a crime cares more about the restitution of his goods than he does about proper punishment of the offender. Also, there is a danger that if procedures for restitution, restoration and compensation are made too simple the Criminal Code will be resorted to when civil court proceedings, with their attendant safeguards, are more appropriate. It is more important that the grievance find its proper court. The moment of sentencing is hardly a time when the convicted person in a proceeding which is essentially civil in nature can effectively and forcefully assert his or her rights.

B. Interpretation Of The Criminal Code

The language used in the sections of the Criminal Code with which we are now concerned is confusing. O'Driscoll J. has attempted to analyze it.[1]

> An examination of the language of these sections indicates that Parliament viewed the term "restitution" as dealing with the return of identical property obtained as a result of the commission of an offence to its owner, while the term "compensation" covers the making of a financial payment as a replacement for property so taken, or as payment for damage to property as a result of the offence.
>
> "Compensation" is defined in Jowitt's Dictionary of English Law, 2nd ed. (1977), vol. 1, as "satisfying or making amends". The term is sufficiently broad to include damages for personal injuries resulting from an offence.

---

[1] *R. v. Groves* (1977), 39 C.R.N.S. 366 at p. 380 (Ont.).

It is reasonable to suppose that "restitution" has the same meaning in s. 663(2) (*e*) as in the other sections of the Code, i.e., a restoration of property. If this be the case, it seems likely that "reparation" in s. 663(2) (*e*) would have the additional meaning of compensating a victim for loss or damage — both to property and person. This interpretation is consistent with the definition of "reparation" in Jowitt's Dictionary of English Law (1959) as "the making good of a civil wrong by the award of damages". In Webster's New World Dictionary, Second College Edition, "reparation" is defined as the "making of amends, making up for a wrong or injury; or compensation".

It is necessary to justify these sections of the Criminal Code constitutionally as part of the criminal law power of the federal government and not merely to rely on a practical justification from the point of view of the victim. O'Driscoll J. quotes from the Law Reform Commission's paper on "Restitution and Compensation",[2]

"Restitution involves acceptance of the offender as a responsible person with the capacity to undertake constructive and socially approved acts. It challenges the offender to see the conflict in values between himself, the victim, and society. In particular, restitution invites the offender to see his conduct in terms of the damage it has done to the victim's rights and expectations. It contemplates that the offender has the capacity to accept his full or partial responsibility for the alleged offence and that he will in many cases be willing to discharge that responsibility by making amends.

. . .

"To the extent that restitution works towards self-correction, and prevents or at least discourages the offender's committal to a life of crime, the community enjoys a measure of protection, security and savings. Depriving offenders of the fruits of their crimes or ensuring that offenders assist in compensating victims for their losses should assist in discouraging criminal activity . . .

"The offender, too, benefits in a practical way from a sentencing policy that emphasizes restitution. He is treated as a responsible human being; his dignity, personality and capacity to engage in constructive social activity are recognized and encouraged. Rather than being further isolated from social and economic intercourse he is invited to a reconciliation with the community. While he is not permitted to escape responsibility for his crime his positive ties with family, friends and the community are encouraged, as are opportunities for him to do useful work."

It is important that the distinction between these types of orders and the penalty are understood and followed. Otherwise there would be a

---

[2] At pp. 375-76 — "Restitution and Compensation", Working Paper No. 5, Law Reform Commission of Canada (1974).

temptation to reduce the penalty that otherwise would have been imposed by virtue of payment; the purpose of these orders is not "to enable the convicted to buy themselves out of the penalties of the crime."[3]

Although the overall burden on a particular accused must be taken into account in any final disposition, it is best not to think of these orders as part of the sentence for crime at all in the conventional sense. So in *R. v. Stapleton and Lawrie*[4] on charges involving property offences one of the accused received a lower sentence of imprisonment and at the same time was ordered to pay £3,500 compensation. The other two accused appealed because the trial judge's remarks had indicated that his sentence had been reduced because he was able to pay compensation; the others were not. The Court of Appeal lowered all the sentences to the same level thus removing from consideration the ability to pay compensation.

While there is considerable doubt whether all that is claimed for the practice can be substantiated, it is equally beyond doubt that the use of restitution as a sentencing power has considerable advantages over other, more traditional approaches. The individual who has been wronged needs the money far more than does the state; and to the extent that such an order replaces a period of imprisonment, it frees the public from the financial burden associated therewith and relieves the offender from that most striking consequence of imprisonment: the strong likelihood of further imprisonment thereafter.

C. Voluntary Restitution

It is by no means uncommon for persons accused of crime to make restitution prior to trial. Such an act can be taken into account as evidence of remorse and of the probability of rehabilitation. More realistically, it is both an acknowledgment that guilt is likely to be established, and a demonstration of good judgment and a sound ability to deal with reality. Certainly, voluntary restitution suggests that more severe sanctions may not be necessary to deter the accused from future crime.

The English courts have seen problems in a practice which is

---

[3] *R. v. Inwood* (1974), 60 Cr. App. R. 70.
[4] [1977] Crim. L.R. 366.

widespread in Canada, namely, the postponing of sentence after conviction where the prisoner is released from custody to see whether he in fact will make restitution for his wrong.

The rationale for this practice and the analogous practice of release pending sentence to see if the prisoner will take steps to restore stolen property or give some information, again where the prisoner is out of custody, has been commented on by the English Court of Appeal in *R. v. Collins:*[5] "It leads him to think that if he complies with what the court has suggested, he will be put on probation; otherwise he will go to prison; and it is undesirable that an implicit bargain of that sort should be made with the accused."

The practice of keeping someone in custody though postponing sentence for the same purposes has been given limited approval, but only in situations where the eventual sentence will in any event exceed the period kept in custody pending sentence, and only where there is a likelihood of a beneficial result.[6]

In *R. v. West*[7] upon guilty pleas to forgery, uttering a forged document and fraudulent conversion, the court noted that the prisoner was not in a position at the time of his guilty plea to make any reparation to the victim. Upon receiving the information that he could pay up to three pounds per week upon the total sum of approximately £60, sentence was postponed and the prisoner let out of custody for six months. The English Court of Appeal, in this case, said: "If a prisoner is thought fit to be put on probation, let him be put on probation. If it is not a matter of probation let him be sentenced there and then, but it is highly objectionable to postpone sentence, and at the same time to turn the court into a money-collecting agency."

In general, it is better to use the statutory power where that is available, rather than to permit the threat of a harsher sentence to hang over the head of one who is faced with "voluntary" restoration or compensation. Once voluntary compensation to the victim has been seriously attempted the rule must be that the precise amount raised is not to be given much weight in sentence. In *R. v. Crosby and Hayes,*[8] upon a charge of fraud, Crosby raised £3,600 and was sentenced to 12 months' imprisonment suspended for two years; Hayes raised £800 and was sentenced to 18 months' imprisonment. The Court of Appeal indicated

---

[5] (1969), 53 Cr. App. R. 388.
[6] *R. v. Easterling* (1946), 32 Cr. App. R. 5.
[7] (1959), 43 Cr. App. R. 109.
[8] [1975] Crim. L.R. 247.

that they could see no reason for the difference between the sentences, save that Crosby had raised more money than Hayes, which was "not a firm foundation for the difference." Accordingly Hayes' sentence was also suspended for two years. No practice should be permitted that suggests that a more credit-worthy accused can purchase relief from a sentence of imprisonment.

D. Compensation — Section 653

Section 653 of the Criminal Code provides that the application must be made by the "person aggrieved" or his counsel or agent; the Crown cannot act in his stead; an English statute, which contains a similar provision, was referred to in *R. v. Taylor.*[9]

This situation clearly ought to be remedied by legislation; if restitution is legally part of a sentence and imposed for the benefit of the public, then Crown counsel ought to be able to act in this aspect of the sentence as well.

It has been stated that the section applies to indictable offences only. This comment was made by Haines J. in *Re Torek and The Queen*[10] as a part of an argument that this fact protects an accused from deprivation of his right to make full answer and defence because he is entitled to a preliminary hearing on indictment. The ultimate decision is sound insofar as it concludes that the section is *intra vires* the Parliament of Canada. But the argument is weak, because some very common indictable offences remain within the absolute jurisdiction of a magistrate, and because often the likelihood that the preliminary hearing may not be at all concerned with issues that would ordinarily be relevant in a civil trial for damages or possession.[11]

It has been held that the specific wording of s. 653(3), read carefully and literally, does not authorize the court that makes an order for compensation to also order that the compensation shall be paid out of the money found in the possession of the accused at the time of his arrest. It would appear that the compensation ordered can be satisfied by taking these monies pursuant to s. 653(3); there is no power in the court to

---

[9] (1969), 53 Cr. App. R. 357.
[10] (1974), 15 C.C.C. (2d) 296 (Ont.).
[11] *R. v. Groves* (1977), 39 C.R.N.S. 366 (Ont.).

actually order that this be done. The British Columbia Court of Appeal[12] found it not necessary to decide whether the exception to the right to realize the compensation awarded from the monies in question pursuant to s. 653(3) applies to a dispute existing only at the time the orders were made by the court or at any subsequent time before they are actually paid out.

In England it has been held in *R. v. Ferguson,*[13] relying not upon a statute but upon principle to decide the question, that if there is any doubt (the standard mentioned in the case is "proof beyond a reasonable doubt") at all whether the money or the goods in question belong to the third party, a criminal court is not the correct forum at which that issue should be decided.

> To do so in any case of doubt might cause the gravest injustice to a third party because the third party to whom the money may belong has no *locus standi* to appear before a criminal court. Nor is there any appropriate machinery available in the criminal courts for deciding the issue as to who is the true owner. Discovery is sometimes a very important part of the necessary machinery for resolving issues of that sort, and discovery for this purpose can be obtained only in the civil courts. A civil court is the correct forum for deciding matters of this kind.

In England the courts have attempted to set out rules governing all these matters. In *R. v. Miller,*[14] the court noted that when accused persons came up for sentence they were normally anxious to persuade the court that they were willing to make restitution and compensation as soon as possible. There was therefore a temptation to make an order in this regard without full consideration, and the court called for greater care in the assessment of the propriety of making such orders. Among the principles to be followed were: (1) a compensation order was not an alternative to a sentence;[15] (2) an order should only be made where the legal position was quite clear; (3) regard must be had to the defendant's means; (4) the order must be precise — that is it must relate to an offence, specify the amount, and specify the instalments if there was to be payment by instalment; (5) the order must not be oppressive. The court had to bear in mind that a discharged prisoner was often short of money, and he must not be tempted to commit further offences to provide the cash to satisfy an order made under this section. (6) There might,

---

[12] *R. v. Kozack,* [1966] 4 C.C.C. 152.
[13] (1970), 54 Cr. App. R. 410.
[14] [1976] Crim. L.R. 694.
[15] *R. v. Lovett* (1870), 11 Cox C.C. 602.

however, be good moral grounds for making an order, including payment by instalments, to remind the accused of the evil he had done. This might apply particularly when a non-custodial sentence was imposed and the order was not for too great a sum. (7) An order must be realistic. An order for payment by instalments over a long period of time was to be avoided.

An interesting dispute has arisen in the cases in situations where the prisoner has assigned the moneys to a third party after seizure but before sentence, often his lawyer. The cases are canvassed in *R. v. Lebansky; Kushner v. Williams*[16] the question was formerly not free from doubt. In *Lebansky* it was decided that the moment that the money was taken over by the police it became then subject to such compensation order as could thereafter be made, in priority to any disposition which the accused might make of it after his arrest. In any event, such dispute as might have formerly existed is probably laid to rest by the clearer wording in s. 653(3), whereby the earlier requirement that the money should be "his own" is replaced by the broader language "found in the possession of the accused at the time of his arrest."

It is worth noting that the section of the English statute which is comparable (s. 35(1) of the Powers of Criminal Courts Act, 1973), is wider than our own in that it covers compensation for any "personal injury" or "loss" resulting from the offence or any other offence which is taken into consideration by the court in determining sentence. Our legislation covers only "property" damaged or lost as a result of the commission of the offence of which the accused is convicted. Surely out-of-pocket expenses occasioned by personal injury should be included. The restriction of the power in property bespeaks a value system of an earlier age, but not our own.

As will be seen below, the ability of the prisoner to pay compensation must be taken into account. In England orders to pay on instalment over a period of time have been made with frequency; nevertheless long-term instalment orders following a period in custody are generally deplored.[17]

In Canada, the amounts involved in such orders have occasionally been extremely high. In *R. v. Littler*[18] the accused was convicted on a few counts of fraud involving a total of over one million dollars. The money had passed through the accused's hands and was presently in the hands

---

[16] (1938), 70 C.C.C. 260 (Man. C.A.).
[17] *R. v. Bradburn* (1973), 57 Cr. App. R. 948; *R. v. Oddy,* [1974] 2 All E.R. 666; *R. v. Kneeshaw* (1974), 58 Cr. App. R. 439.
[18] (1972), 13 C.C.C. (2d) 530 (Que. Sess. Peace).

of his two sons, about whom the trial judge commented: "They now know the illegal origins of the monies actually in their possession." A sentence of five years' imprisonment was imposed and, upon application by the aggrieved parties, the prisoner was ordered to pay compensation in the amount of $1,078,601.12 with interest.

It is important to note that the order is to be made at the time of sentence,[19] but if the matter of compensation is adjourned to a later date, this is a proper procedure and the order will be valid.[20] Though there is no authority on the point, the wording of the section indicates that the application need not be made at the time the sentence is imposed but may be made at any time prior thereto, especially if the application is made to a court that is seized of the matter.

The section provides that the amount awarded for compensation becomes a judgment debt.

It has been held that there is no power in a magistrate, upon convicting a prisoner on a charge of theft, to order him to make compensation to the victim and in default thereof to be imprisoned.[21] However, in the light of the present language of s. 646(12) such a power now exists.

In *Re Blackhawk Downs Inc. and Arnold et al.,*[22] the prisoner, through funds raised by friends and relatives, had voluntarily paid into court before his sentencing an amount equal to that which he had obtained by his fraud. Before the money had been paid out of court to the persons aggrieved the accused became bankrupt and the trustee in bankruptcy made claim upon that money. It was held that the trustee in bankruptcy did not take priority over the persons aggrieved.

In *R. v. Groves,*[23] the accused was ordered to compensate the victim in the amount of $500, in respect of the pain and suffering sustained by the victim (who was a police officer) when he was assaulted by the accused in an effort to resist arrest. O'Driscoll J. held:

> This power of the court to order "restitution" or "reparation" is restricted to *actual* loss or damage. This qualification must be interpreted in the light of the purpose of probation orders and in light of the procedural safeguards available to an accused in a criminal, as opposed to a civil, action. When so interpreted one is led to the conclusion that the power to award "compensation" in criminal cases is more restricted than in civil actions.

---

[19] *R. v. Gorunuk* (1961), 40 W.W.R. 640 (B.C.C.A.).
[20] *R. v. Scherstabitoff* (1962), 40 W.W.R. 575 (B.C.C.A.).
[21] *R. v. Ramsey,* [1947] 1 D.L.R. 621 (N.B.C.A.).
[22] [1973] 3 O.R. 729.
[23] (1977), 39 C.R.N.S. 366 at pp. 381-83 (Ont.).

In civil actions the general rule is that an aggrieved party should be awarded "that sum of money which will put him in the same position as he would have been had he not sustained the wrong for which he in now getting compensation or reparation": McGregor on Damages, 13th ed. (1972), at p. 10. In civil cases, therefore, damages seek to compensate the victim.

. . .

As Zuber J.A. so aptly stated in *Teno v. Arnold* (1974), 7 O.R. (2d) 276 at 307, 55 D.L.R. (3d) 57:

"As has been so often recognized, setting a dollar figure by way of compensation for personal injuries must be one of the most inexact sciences known to man rather in the category of economic or weather forecasting."

In my view, had Parliament intended to confer upon the criminal courts a remedial power to order an offender to compensate a victim for pain and suffering, it would have set out its intent in clear language. Indeed, it seems to me that the word "actual" as used in the section suggests that Parliament intended to restrict its scope to those damages which are relatively concrete and easily ascertainable and, as such, exclude such vague, amorphous and difficult matters as "pain and suffering." Consequently, I am of the opinion that in order under s. 663(2) (*e*) should be restricted to those damages in the nature of special damages.

. . .

In particular, it is unnecessary for me to determine whether s. 663(2)(*e*) is broad enough to permit orders with respect to damages which may become certain at a future date, for example, medical bills covering the treatment of injuries resulting from the offence but which accounts arise *after* the date of the remedial order. These problems may be settled when they arise . . .

Unlike an order pursuant to ss. 653 or 655, s. 663 operates as part of a probation order; and it must borne in mind that the general purpose of probation orders is to secure the good conduct of the convicted person as opposed to compensating victims of crime.[24] In some cases, the evidence will show that a compensation order will lead to this end; in others, it will not.

In the terms of the statute, there must be evidence before the sentencing judge to show that the amount of restitution or reparation ordered is for actual loss or damage sustained by the person aggrieved or injured.

The Supreme Court of Canada in *R. v. Zelensky*[25] has referred to restitution by approving the passage from Working Paper No. 5 of the Law Reform Commission of Canada:

---

[24] *R. v. Dashner* (1974), 15 C.C.C. (2d) 139 (B.C.C.A.).
[25] (1978), 41 C.C.C. (2d) 97 at p. 105.

"Recognition of the victim's needs underlines at the same time the larger social interest inherent in the individual victim's loss. Thus, social values are reaffirmed through restitution to victim. Society gains from restitution in other ways as well. To the extent that restitution works toward self-correction, and prevents or at least discourages the offender's committal to a life of crime, the community enjoys a measure of protection, security and savings. Depriving offenders of the fruits of their crimes or ensuring that offenders assist in compensating victims for their losses should assist in discouraging criminal activity. Finally, to the extent that restitution encourages society to perceive crime in a more realistic way, as a form of social interaction, it should lead to more productive responses not only by Parliament, the courts, police and correctional officials but also by ordinary citizens and potential victims."

The Supreme Court held in *Zelensky* that in order to justify the restitution provisions as being constitutional it is important not to relax in any way the requirement that the application for compensation be directly associated with the sentence imposed as the public reprobation of the offence. In exercising its discretion as to whether or not to order compensation, the sentencing court should have regard to whether the aggrieved person is invoking these provisions to emphasize the sanctions against the offender as well as to benefit himself. A relevant consideration would be whether civil proceedings have been taken and, if so, whether they are being pursued.

In addition, the Court must look to the means of the offender, and whether the criminal court will be involved in a long process for assessment of the loss, though the provisions do not require exact measurement. A plea of guilty will obviously make the court's task easier when it is asked to make an order of compensation, but there is no reason why an attempt to secure agreement on the amount of loss should not be made where the conviction follows a plea of not guilty. It is not a function of a criminal court to force such an agreement to enable it to make an order for compensation. For all of the above reasons, an order for compensation should only be made with restraint and with caution.

In *Zelensky* itself the Court ruled that an order for compensation should not have been made because the aggrieved company instituted civil proceedings for the recovery of money and merchandise stolen from it a day before the criminal charges were brought against them. It continued with the civil proceedings even while the criminal proceedings were in progress, and even after the offenders had pleaded guilty to theft. The Court went out of its way to make clear that the compensation provision is not to be used *in terrorem* as a substitute for or a reinforcement of civil proceedings.

The process for resolving a dispute as to the quantum of compensation to be ordered is, *ex facie*, summary, but this does not preclude an inquiry by the trial judge to establish the amount of compensation, so long as this can be done expeditiously and without turning the sentencing proceeding into the equivalent of a civil trial or into a reference in a civil proceeding. Therefore, the compensation sections are not the platform upon which to unravel involved commercial transactions in order to provide monetary redress to those entitled thereto as against an accused. An accused may have a proper interest in insisting that civil proceedings be taken against him so that he may avail himself of the procedures for discovery and production of documents, as well as of a proper trial of issues which go to the merit of monetary claims against him.

The criminal court should not act to order compensation if it will be required to interpret written documents in order to arrive at a sum of money sought through an order of compensation. So too, no action should be taken if it is necessary to determine the effect of provincial legislation or to determine what order should be made. Indeed, any serious contest on legal or factual issues, or on whether the person alleging himself to be aggrieved is so in fact, should "signal a denial of recourse" to an order for compensation.

The Court in *Zelensky* left open the question of whether the application for compensation under the Criminal Code is in fact an election against civil proceedings even if the victim is not fully compensated for his loss.

E. Probation Orders — Section 663(2)(e), Restitution

It is a frequent practice for courts to impose, as a condition of probation, a term requiring restitution or reparation to any person aggrieved. It has been said that this provision of the Code provides "a valid object in sentencing to prevent a convicted criminal from profiting from his crime by serving a jail term and then keeping the gains of his illegal venture."[26] The Ontario Court of Appeal, in speaking of this section, has said: "We feel that by requiring the appellants to make a payment towards

---

[26] *Re Torek and The Queen* (1974), 15 C.C.C. (2d) 296 (Ont.).

reparation for the damage they have done, that it will emphasize to them that they must be prepared to take responsibility for their actions."[27]

In *R. v. Lafreniere,*[28] the phrase "for the actual loss or damage sustained . . . as a result thereof" was given a strict interpretation. The court set aside an order for restitution where the accused was convicted only of the offence of possession of a stolen automobile. The loss to the owner of the automobile was suffered as a result of the theft, not the possession.

In many cases the making of an order would be improper. In *R. v. DeKleric,*[29] the court included as a term of probation, the requirement that the accused was to pay to the clerk of the magistrates' courts, a sum of $500 at the rate of $100 per month for the Vancouver Superannuated Police Officers' Association. The British Columbia Court of Appeal held that this was wrong:

> If the circumstances required as a condition of suspended sentence, restitution or reparation to the injured parties within the meaning of the provision of the *Code* which allow such a condition to be imposed as a term of the suspended sentence, then it should have been done that way. This innovation is a most dangerous one. It can lead to the greatest abuses, and for myself I hope it is the last time we see such a condition imposed as a term of any suspended sentence.

The conviction was for possession of marijuana, and it is hard to see that the recipient could be "a party aggrieved". It is also obvious that this was not a "reasonable" condition within the meaning of s. 663, as there was not any "actual loss or damage inflicted".

The form of such orders can raise difficulties as well. In *R. v. Vandale and Maciejewski,*[30] Martin J.A. made an order which, it is submitted, is correct in form, that during the period of two years during which he was to be on probation the accused was to pay a sum of $250 by way of restoration at such times and in such amounts as his probation officer considered that he could reasonably make. Some months earlier that same court, very similarly constituted, *per* Martin J.A. made an order that during the period of probation the accused was to make "such payments by way of restitution from time to time as her probation officer

---

[27] *R. v. Vandale and Maciejewski* (1974), 21 C.C.C. (2d) 250 (Ont. C.A.).
[28] Unreported, October 26, 1976 (B.C.C.A.).
[29] [1969] 2 C.C.C. 367 (B.C.C.A.).
[30] *Supra,* n. 27.

considers that she is reasonably capable of making."[31] It is respectfully submitted that this latter order discloses an improper delegation, as it is for the court to exhaust its function by setting the amount of restitution and wrong to leave that question to the probation officer. Any future inability or unwillingness to pay can later be dealt with in further proceedings for breach of the probation order.

In *R. v. Evans,*[32] the accused was released on an order for probation which was accompanied by an order that he pay compensation under the Criminal Justice Act.[33] Later, the accused was convicted of breach of his probation order and sentenced to imprisonment. The English Court of Appeal held that this sentence did not relieve him of his obligation to pay compensation under the original probation order which remained outstanding. In Canada regard must be had to s. 664(4)(d) and (e) of the Criminal Code, which gives a judge who convicts a person who is bound by a probation order authority either to revoke the order and impose a new sentence or to permit it to stand making such changes as seem advisable. The English result would, of course, follow in the later case, but it would be unlikely to do so in the former.

It is important to note that the "loss or damage" referred to in s. 663(2) is not restricted to loss or damage to property. Accordingly, in *R. v. Gilpin,*[34] upon a charge of assault causing bodily harm, a probation order included the term that a sum of $329 must be paid to the victim by way of restitution to cover the amount of the cost of the surgery resulting from the assault. The payment was to be made in four quarterly instalments.

F. Criminal Code — Section 650

In *R. v. Ramsey,*[35] the court said, *obiter dicta,* that pursuant to the former s. 653 of the Criminal Code, reparation could not be ordered with imprisonment in default. It is doubtful that the precursor of s. 650 was unavailable but it would appear that presently, given the wide definition of "penalty" in this section, a term of imprisonment can be imposed in

---

[31] *R. v. Stein* (1974), 15 C.C.C. (2d) 376 (Ont. C.A.); *R. v. Bates* (1977), 32 C.C.C. (2d) 493 (Ont. C.A.).
[32] (1961), 45 Cr. App. R. 59.
[33] Criminal Justice Act, 1948 (U.K.), c. 58, s. 11.
[34] (1975), 36 C.R.N.S. 363 (Ont. C.A.).
[35] [1947] 1 D.L.R. 621 (N.B.C.A.).

default of payment of a compensation or reparation order. In England there is no power to order a term of imprisonment in default of payment of such an order.[36]

G. Loss Or Damage

In the language of s. 663(2)(e) "restitution or reparation" and "satisfaction or compensation" are restricted to loss or damage. The meaning of this phrase has recently attracted some judicial interest. In *R. v. Cadamarteris,*[37] the English Court of Criminal Appeal had to assess the scope of s. 35 of the Powers of Criminal Courts Act (1973) which has language comparable to our own. This section requires evidence of "loss or damage" as a condition precedent to the making of a compensation order and limits such order to the amount of "loss or damage". In *Cadamarteris* the accused had possessed a stolen motor car which was valued at £ 250. When found in the accused's garage it was partly dismantled (but all the parts were there), some repairs had been done, and it had been repainted; it bore false number plates and the original engine number had been removed. It was suggested by counsel for the accused that the work done on it had enhanced the value of the car. As part of the sentence the Court ordered compensation of £ 250. On appeal, the compensation order was struck upon the ground that the owner of the motor car had not sustained any loss or damage. At the time of the trial she or her insurers were entitled to recover the car, and intended to recover it from the police once the trial was over. Thus there could be no basis for compensation order in the amount of the value of the car as of the day of loss. The Court went on to say that there could be no compensation order based upon an assessment of the difference in value between the car as it was when stolen and in its dismantled condition with the benefit of the work done on it by the accused.

It is not clear whether the Court is accepting that in fact there was no "loss" because the value of the parts was in fact greater than the value of the motor car when stolen. If so, this is a question of fact. However, it would seem to be necessary for the owner to pay an amount she would otherwise not have paid to have the motor car assembled again so that

---

[36] *R. v. Bradburn* (1973), 57 Cr. App. R. 948.
[37] [1977] Crim. L.R. 236.

while there was no "damage" she had been put to a considerable expense. It would not strain the English language to call this a "loss".

H. Ability To Pay[38]

The two Canadian cases which create a non-statutory obligation on the trial judge to determine the ability of the accused to pay before making an order have been confined in their application to s. 663 of the Criminal Code, but it is impossible in principle to restrict the obligation to make such an inquiry to this section only; simple logic requires that it be extended to all similar orders. In *R. v. Stewart,*[39] the court said:

> . . . it is most important that the sanctions of the criminal law and its administration should not be used, or be permitted to appear to be used, for the purpose of enforcing civil obligations. For this reason I think it is essential that careful regard should be given to the ability of an accused to pay when a Court sees fit to exercise the power . . . [or] prescribe as a condition of release that there be restitution and reparation to an aggrieved or injured person. The same considerations apply when it is proposed to change the conditions prescribed for such a purpose. The responsibility for prescribing the conditions is that of the Court which has therefore the duty to form a judicial opinion of the accused's ability to comply. If it were otherwise we might well find that imprisonment for debt has not been truly abolished.

Great care must be taken to see that the respect of the public for the administration of criminal justice does not decrease through using these powers in inappropriate cases. Beyond doubt, a great danger exists. In *R. v. Peel,*[40] the appellant was bound over upon a recognizance that he pay over a period of time a sum of money in respect of which no proceedings had been taken. When he fell into arrears he was sentenced for six months' imprisonment with hard labour. In considering this matter the Court of Criminal Appeal said:

> We have said that we have no doubt at all that the chairman throughout was actuated by the highest motives, and thought that it was the best thing that this man should be helped in that way to pay his debt. But this court

---

[38] See also Chapter 11, "Means".
[39] [1968] 4 C.C.C. 54 at p. 57 (B.C.C.A.); *R. v. Dashner* (1974), 15 C.C.C. (2d) 139 (B.C.C.A.).
[40] [1943] 2 All E.R. 99.

desires it to be understood that it depreciates and strongly disapproves of any criminal court making itself the medium of compelling people to pay their debts. That is not what the criminal courts are for. The Court of Middlesex Quarter Sessions in this case was merely turning itself into a debt-collecting society and helping the [appellant's former employers] to recover money which they might have recovered in the county court, where probably they would have got a very much smaller order than 10s. per week. At all events imprisonment for debt is supposed to be abolished in this country. This man, as we know now, has been sentenced to six months' imprisonment, because he has not paid £4 but apparently has paid £3 out of the £4.

We hope that, if this be a practice, the practice will cease, since it is most undesirable that any criminal court should join in any arrangement about the payment of money week by week. It would have been very much better if in the first instance the chairman had done what obviously it was in his mind to do, namely, to say: "This is a civil matter, this man having undertaken to pay the money which he said that he had lost, and although he has now admitted that he embezzled that money and we must deal with him, we are not going to have anything to do with the attempt by his original masters to force him to pay it upon the threat of criminal proceedings."

It has been suggested that the provisions of s. 305 of the Criminal Code dealing with extortion can provide substantial protection against the possibility under the above: *R. v. Groves*.[41] It is extremely doubtful that this will be the case and the responsibility will rest on the courts to see that abuse does not take place.

The actual nature of the inquiry has not been discussed in Canada, but there is one example that may be of assistance from England. In *R. v. Bradburn*[42] it appeared that the prisoner had "non existent" means in that he was dependent on social security:

Does that mean that no order should be made against him? We think not. We think that as long as a man has his normal physical health and is, therefore, capable of earning something it is perfectly proper to make a compensation order against him although the amount may well be restricted by reason of the probability that his earnings will be comparatively small. It is not right to restrict compensation orders to cases where the defendant can easily pay. There are good moral reasons for making compensation orders which will in a measure hurt the defendant's pocket and act to remind him of what he has done.

---

[41] (1977), 39 C.R.N.S. 366 (Ont.).
[42] (1973), 57 Cr. App. R. 948.

In that case taking into account the defendant's means, the order was for payment of two pounds per week up to a total of one hundred pounds.

Long-term instalment orders following on a period in custody have generally been deplored. The court in England has said: "It is generally much better that these orders should be sharp in their effect rather than protracted . . .".[43] This keeps in mind that a civil remedy for the damage still exists.

The interesting question whether an accused can be compelled through a compensation order to repay more than he actually received as his share of the proceeds from crime has been canvassed in England. In *R. v. Lewis*,[44] the accused's share in an £8,000 robbery was £2,000. Nevertheless, because he had sufficient money to pay, there was an order for compensation to the victim in the amount of £5,445. The court held that liability (which it characterized as civil) to repay the proceeds of the robbery was joint and several as regards all those who took part in it. Because the larger sum had been found in Lewis' possession there was no reason why there should not be a restitution order in respect of all of it, even if he had only received £2,000 from the robbery. However, it was held that there was not sufficient evidence as to his means and financial obligations, apart from the fact that the larger sum had been found in his possession, to justify the order and it was quashed.

I. Restoration — Section 655

The restoration of property obtained by the commission of an offence can only be ordered in the case of indictable offences; there is regrettably no such provision for summary conviction matters. A second requirement is that at the time of trial the property must be before the court and detained in such a fashion that it can immediately be restored.[45]

Similarly there is a requirement that the property in question must be proved or identified as that obtained by the commission of the offence in question, and further that the applicant is entitled to it. In *R. v.*

---

[43] *Ibid.* See also *R. v. Oddy*, [1974] 2 All E.R. 666; *R. v. Kneeshaw* (1974), 58 Cr. App. R. 439.

[44] [1975] Crim. L.R. 353.

[45] *R. v. Ramsey*, [1947] 1 D.L.R. 621 (N.B.C.A.).

Hargraves, McNaughton and Wallden[46] there was no evidence that the money before the court was in fact stolen from the victim of the crime. The principle remains sound although the question would be resolved differently today. In many cases the property is money, which is particularly difficult to identify.[47]

The recent redefinition of "property" in s. 2 of the Criminal Code, includes "any property into or for which it has been converted or exchanged and anything acquired at anytime for such conversion or exchange". In *R. v. Percival and McDougall*,[48] the robbers took the proceeds of their crime and made numerous small purchases in passing the stolen money so that they could avoid detection; seized at the trial was the sum of $2,408.65 which was the change given for the small purchases made. An order was made restoring these moneys to the victim of the robbery.

The precursor of this section was declared *intra vires* as ancillary or necessarily incidental to the proper administration of criminal justice in *Benesiewicz v. Dionne.*[49]

The form of the order is of some importance. In *R. v. Westerland,*[50] an order "that the stolen wire be restored to its rightful owner" was held to be uncertain with regard to both the thing to be restored and the person to whom it was to be restored.

Care must be taken with regard to the operation of ss. 654 and 655. For example, it is important that an innocent third party purchaser should not be deprived both of the goods he purchased and the money which he paid for them. In *R. v. Forbes; Ex parte Selig,*[51] a large quantity of yellow metal was stolen from one Elkin of St. John, New Brunswick. A smaller portion of this metal was sold to Selig for $66 and both the money and the metal were brought into court. After conviction, the trial judge ordered the money and the metal to be delivered to the victim. On appeal, though it was noted that the victim was still "out of pocket" even if he received both money and metal, the court quashed the trial judge's order that the

---

[46] (1959), 124 C.C.C. 167 (B.C.).
[47] *R. v. Haverstock* (1901), 5 C.C.C. 113 (N.S.); *Re Mathews* (1947), 88 C.C.C. 344 (Ont.); *United States v. Tounder* (1914), 23 C.C.C. 76 (N.S.). There is an excellent note on the restitution of stolen property at common law to be found in *Tremecar's, Annotated Criminal Code*, 6th ed., L. J. Ryan, ed., at p. 1199 *et seq.*
[48] (1973), 10 C.C.C. (2d) 566 (B.C.).
[49] [1945] 3 W.W.R. 297 (Alta.).
[50] [1929] 3 W.W.R. 408 (Alta.).
[51] (1910), 17 C.C.C. 70 (N.B.C.A.).

money be given to him so that the third party purchaser should not be injured.

Chapter 18

Appeals

Criminal Code:

613(3) Where a court of appeal dismisses an appeal under subparagraph (1)(*b*)(i), it may substitute the verdict that in its opinion should have been found and affirm the sentence passed by the trial court or impose a sentence that is warranted in law.

(4) Where an appeal is from an acquittal the court of appeal may

(*a*) dismiss the appeal; or

(*b*) allow the appeal, set aside the verdict and

    (i) order a new trial, or

    (ii) except where the verdict is that of a court composed of a judge and jury, enter a verdict of guilty with respect to the offence of which, in its opinion, the accused should have been found guilty but for the error in law, and pass a sentence that is warranted in law.

610(1) For the purposes of an appeal under this Part the court of appeal may, where it considers it in the interests of justice,

(*a*) order the production of any writing, exhibit, or other thing connected with the proceedings;

(*b*) order any witness who would have been a compellable witness at the trial, whether or not he was called at the trial,

    (i) to attend and be examined before the court of appeal, or

    (ii) to be examined in the manner provided by rules of court before a judge of the court of appeal, or before any officer of the court of appeal or justice of the peace or other person appointed by the court of appeal for the purpose;

(*c*) admit, as evidence, an examination that is taken under subparagraph (*b*)(ii);

(*d*) receive the evidence, if tendered, of any witness, including the appellant, who is a competent but not compellable witness;

(*e*) order that any question arising on the appeal that
   (i)   involves prolonged examination of writings or accounts, or scientific or local investigation, and
   (ii) cannot in the opinion of the court of appeal conveniently be inquired into before the court of appeal,
   be referred for inquiry and report, in the manner provided by rules of court, to a special commissioner appointed by the court of appeal; and
(*f*) act upon the report of a commissioner who is appointed under paragraph (*e*) in so far as the court of appeal thinks fit to do so.

(2) In proceedings under this section the parties or their counsel are entitled to examine or cross-examine witnesses and, in an inquiry under paragraph (1) (*e*), are entitled to be present during the inquiry and to adduce evidence and to be heard.

(3) A court of appeal [for a province or a territory] may exercise in relation to proceedings in the court any powers not mentioned in subsection (1) that may be exercised by the court on appeals in civil matters, and may issue any process that is necessary to enforce the orders or sentences of the court but no costs shall be allowed to the appellant or respondent on the hearing and determination of an appeal or any proceedings preliminary or incidental thereto.

(4) Any process that is issued by the court of appeal under this section may be executed anywhere in Canada.

614(1) Where an appeal is taken against sentence the court of appeal shall, unless the sentence is one fixed by law, consider the fitness of the sentence appealed against, and may upon such evidence, if any, as it thinks fit to require or to receive,
(*a*) vary the sentence with the limits prescribed by law for the offence of which the accused was convicted, or
(*b*) dismiss the appeal.

(2) A judgment of a court of appeal that varies the sentence of an accused who was convicted has the same force and effect as if it were a sentence passed by the trial court.

611. A court of appeal or a judge of that court may, at any time, assign counsel to act on behalf of an accused who is a party to an appeal or to proceedings preliminary or incidental to an appeal where, in the opinion of the court or judge, it appears desirable in the interests of justice that the accused should have legal aid and where it appears that the accused has not sufficient means to obtain that aid.

The definition of sentence in s. 601, providing for appeals from indictable offences to the Court of Appeal, specifically includes appeals under ss. 653, 654, 655 and 663. No provision is made for appeal from an order of imprisonment in default of payment of a "fine" which is defined as including "a pecuniary penalty or other sum of money" in s. 646(12).

Since the definition is inclusive, rather than exclusive, it is likely that the scope of a sentence appeal would be broadly construed.

It appears that the relevant time for considering the fitness of sentence may, in a proper case, be the time of the appeal. If matters which should be considered are disclosed for the first time on appeal the sentence may be altered.[1] In *R. v. Vallieres (No. 2),*[2] the Quebec Court of Appeal said: "I do not believe, that in law it is necessary, in view of what follows, to decide at this late date on the fairness of the appealed sentences when they were imposed." The Court looked at material which gave information as to what had transpired after the sentences were imposed.

Since the sentence of the court of appeal has the same force and effect as if it had been a sentence passed by a trial judge, it is clear that any time served pending the appeal must be regarded as time served upon the sentence as varied.[3] It has been said that the power to "vary" a sentence for an indictable offence cannot extend to the quashing of a sentence.[4]

A. The Function Of The Court Of Appeal With Regard To Sentence

The task of an appellate court must be of an appellate nature; it is fundamentally distinct from that of the court of trial. It is clearly not the duty of an appellate judge to decide whether he would have reached the same conclusion had he been the trial judge.[5] It is the trial judge who is charged by statute with the duty of sentencing; the responsibility of a court of appeal is to assess its fitness.

There are two positions taken in the case law with regard to appeal. The first position tends not to interfere unless it can be shown that the trial judge has "gone judicially wrong by any rational test which the appellate courts . . . have come to recognize and apply properly over the years."[6] In *R. v. Gormley*[7] the court said:

---

[1] *R. v. Robinson* (1930), 53 C.C.C. 173 (Ont. C.A.); *Colangelo v. The King* (1941), 76 C.C.C. 334 (Que. C.A.).
[2] (1973), 17 C.C.C. (2d) 361 at p. 375 *per* Brossard J.A.
[3] *R. v. Berger,* [1971] 1 O.R. 765 (C.A.).
[4] *R. v. Noble; Ex p. Ogles,* [1960] 3 C.C.C. 66 (N.B.C.A.).
[5] *R. v. Switlishoff* (1950), 9 C.R. 428 (B.C.C.A.).
[6] *Ibid.*
[7] (1946), 3 C.R. 404 at p. 404 (P.E.I.).

Strong reasons must be shown for the disturbance of a sentence passed in the valid exercise of the convicting court's discretion. Such reasons may appear in the following circumstances:

(a) Where the appellate court is in a better position to determine the appropriate penalty than was the convicting court; *e.g.*, by additional evidence, or more comprehensive view of penalties imposed for similar offences;

(b) Where extenuating circumstances have appeared since the trial;

(c) Where the convicting court proceeded on a wrong principle, or left out of consideration any substantial element;

(d) Where the sentence is clearly excessive or inadequate in relation to the offence proven, or to the record of the accused.

Added to factor (c) should be the comment in *R. v. Nash (No. 2)*[8] where the court noted that "wrong principle" must be taken to include "the matter of the appropriate application of the essential principles."

The second position can be seen in *R. v. Rogers (No. 2)*.[9] The court concluded that if "strong reasons" for interfering are found, then the court of appeal must look at all of the circumstances and then on its own conclude what would be a fit sentence. If a sentence appealed against is a fit sentence, it should be upheld. On the other hand, if the sentence is clearly unfit, it should either be increased or reduced as the circumstances of the case may require.[10]

The two positions differ only in their approach. In the first, one starts with the assumption that the trial judge was correct and seeks to discern an error; then and only then does one consider the question of what the appropriate sentence ought to be. In the more interventionist view, the court decides, after looking at all the facts and the circumstances, what an appropriate or fit sentence would be and measures the sentence imposed by the trial judge against that standard. This latter view has the advantage of fulfilling in an unfettered manner the mandate given by the wording of the statute. It is not a new perspective. In *R. v. Finlay*,[11] Martin J.A. said:

Parliament, by enacting that an appeal may be taken by an accused person against the sentence imposed upon him, must have intended that the accused was entitled to have the opinion of the Court of Appeal after a consideration

---

[8] (1949), 8 C.R. 447 (N.B.C.A.); see also *R. v. Rogers (No. 2)* (1972), 6 C.C.C. (2d) 107 (P.E.I.C.A.).

[9] *Supra,* n. 8.

[10] *R. v. James* (1971), 3 C.C.C. (2d) 1 (P.E.I.C.A.).

[11] [1924] 4 D.L.R. 829 at p. 832 (Sask. C.A.).

of all the circumstances connected with the case; it must have intended that the Court of Appeal should modify such sentence, if, in their opinion, it should be modified.

The dilemma facing courts of appeal in this regard has been put very well by Brooke J.A. speaking for the Ontario Court of Appeal majority in *R. v. Simmons, Allen and Bezzo:*[12]

> Parliament has given the right to the appellant to appeal from the sentence and imposed the duty upon this Court as the final Court of Appeal on such matters to consider "the fitness of the sentence". It has been said the Court should only find the sentence is not fit if it appears that the trial Judge has proceeded upon an error in principle and/or if the sentence is manifestly excessive or inadequate. If it is manifestly excessive or inadequate the trial Judge must have proceeded on an error in principle and the opposite *may* be true. There is no scale other than the scales of justice and it is the duty of this Court to re-examine fact and principle and pass upon the fitness of the sentence imposed. In his able argument Mr. Scullion cautions us we must not interfere simply because had we tried the case we might have imposed a different sentence. On the other hand, one would not interfere if this were not so.

In *R. v. Gunnell,*[13] the Quebec Court of Appeal held that "fitness of sentence" exists when there is, in some way, an equality between the penalty inflicted and the gravity of the offence, as applied to the particular accused whom the judge has before him.

Another function of the court of appeal on sentence is to carry into effect the intention of a trial judge who has by technical error frustrated his purpose.[14]

The position most frequently applied is that the court of appeal will not interfere unless it is shown that the trial judge applied some wrong principle or was influenced by improper considerations or failed to consider all the relevant circumstances.[15] But there are cases where the

---

[12] (1973), 13 C.C.C. (2d) 65 at p. 72; *R. v. Bompas* (1959), 123 C.C.C. 39 (Alta. C.A.). *Cf. R. v. Cormier* (1974), 22 C.C.C. (2d) 235 (N.S.C.A.), which adopts the dissenting judgment in this case.

[13] (1951), 14 C.R. 120.

[14] *R. v. Novak* (1974), 17 C.C.C. (2d) 531 (Ont. C.A.); *R. v. Temple* (1972), 8 C.C.C. (2d) 293 (Ont. C.A.); *R. v. Cameron* (1975), 24 C.C.C. (2d) 158 (Ont. C.A.).

[15] *R. v. Petch,* [1925] 4 D.L.R. 671 (Man. C.A.); *Dristoor v. The King* (1927), 42 Que. K.B. 520; *R. v. Nip Gar* (1930), 53 C.C.C. 321 (B.C.C.A.); *R. v. Awalt* (1936), 66 C.C.C. 132 (N.S.C.A.); *R. v. Lamontagne* (1942), 77 C.C.C. 288 (Sask. C.A.).

court has said that notwithstanding that the learned trial judge made no error in principle in accordance with this rule, the court of appeal would vary the sentence to accord with its own opinion as to the correct sentence.[16] It is not sufficient to show that there was an error in principle. The court does not interfere and revise the sentence unless it decides that the sentence is in fact unfit.[17]

It must also be kept in mind that one of the functions of the court of appeal is to bring about uniformity in sentence.[18]

B. Advantage Of The Trial Judge

The principal reason for caution on the part of courts of appeal in interfering with sentence is the advantage which the trial judge has in setting sentence. In *R. v. Lass*[19] the court said:

> In this Court due regard must be had for the fact that the trial Judge or the Magistrate, as the case may be, has had the opportunity of seeing the prisoner and observing his demeanour, a circumstance which will enable the trial Judge or the Magistrate to form an impression which frequently is valuable in determining the extent of the sentence. This Court has not had that opportunity.

In *R. v. Ayalik*[20] the court in dismissing the appeal of an Eskimo against sentence said:

> However it should be noted that in the present case the learned trial judge had a distinct advantage over the members of the court for with his wide experience in the far-flung areas of the extensive jurisdiction of the trial division of this court he has knowledge of local conditions, ways of life, habits, customs and characteristics of the race of people of which the accused is a member.

Nevertheless there have been cases which take the opposite view. In *R.*

---

[16] *R. v. Hamilton; R. v. Doucette* (1925), 45 C.C.C. 374 (N.S.C.A.); *R. v. Fox; R. v. Sansone* (1925), 4 C.C.C. 262 (Ont. C.A.).
[17] *R. v. James* (1971), 3 C.C.C. (2d) 1 (P.E.I.C.A.).
[18] *R. v. Lee Kim; R. v. Mah Poy* (1930), 53 C.C.C. 252 (B.C.C.A.); *R. v. DeJong* (1970), 1 C.C.C. (2d) 235 (Sask. C.A.).
[19] (1949), 95 C.C.C. 193 at p. 197 (Ont. C.A.).
[20] (1960), 33 W.W.R. 377 at p. 378 (N.W.T.C.A.).

v. Wilson,[21] the court approved an earlier decision of the Manitoba Court of Appeal in *R. v. Venegratsky,*[22] to the effect that where the accused pleads guilty there is no opportunity for the trial judge in any extensive way to see and hear the witnesses and that therefore the appeal court is in as good a position as the trial judge to determine the sentence which should be imposed. The court of appeal may in fact be in a better position than the trial judge in cases where the full circumstances of the offence and the offender are first disclosed to the court of appeal,[23] or where no evidence was taken in the court below.[24]

Occasionally the court says, in justification of the right to interfere:

> In many cases the learned trial Judge is in the best position to form an opinion with respect to the case and the accused but his report to us and his reasons for sentence are intended to place us in as nearly as is possible in the same position and I think the learned trial Judge commendably has achieved this result in this case.[25]

Similarly in *R. v. Morrissette*[26] the court said:

> . . . there must be, in many cases, less emphasis placed upon the advantage enjoyed by the trial Judge in seeing and hearing the prisoner. During recent years there has been a very great increase in appeals from sentence . . . over 90 per cent of these appeals are made by the prisoner in person. As a result, the Appeal Court has every opportunity to enter into direct communication with the appellant.

C. Inherent Power To Reduce Sentence

Even where there is no appeal against sentence or the case comes before the court on appeal against conviction, the court may *proprio motu* reduce the sentence.[27]

---

[21] (1974), 10 N.S.R. (2d) 629 (C.A.); *R. v. Doughty* (1978), 40 C.C.C. (2d) 224 (P.E.I.C.A.).

[22] (1928), 49 C.C.C. 298.

[23] *Stevens v. The King* (1941), 70 Que. K.B. 441 (C.A.).

[24] *Gauthier v. The Queen* (1955), 112 C.C.C. 370 (Que. C.A.).

[25] *R. v. Simmons, Allen and Bezzo* (1973), 13 C.C.C. (2d) 65 at p. 72 (Ont. C.A.).

[26] (1970), 1 C.C.C. (2d) 307 at p. 312 (Sask. C.A.).

[27] *R. v. Musgrave and Reid* (1926), 46 C.C.C. 45 (N.S.C.A.); *R. v. Morscovitch* (1924), 18 Cr. App. R. 37; *R. v. Hervey and Goodwin* (1940), 27 Cr. App. R.

It is unlikely that the power will be widely exercised today; the more usual course is for the court to indicate to counsel that in their view it is a proper case for an appeal against sentence but to advise counsel to apply for leave to extend the time within which an application for leave to appeal against sentence may be brought.

D. Power To Increase Sentence

Just as it has been held that the court may *proprio motu* decrease sentence on an appeal from conviction only, so there has always been a suggestion, as found in *R. v. Christakos,*[28] that there is a power to increase sentence even on an appeal against conviction alone. This proposition was long considered doubtful, because appeals against conviction and sentence are dealt with quite separately by the Criminal Code. The proposition had been explicitly rejected in the case of a summary conviction appeal.[29]

A more pressing but related question is whether the court can, when the accused appeals against sentence, vary that sentence by increasing it. The words of the section would seem to imply that this is proper and various courts of appeal have done so. The Ontario Court of Appeal in *R. v. Willis,*[30] (Laskin J.A. as he then was, dissenting) took the view that this power though it was one that ought to be sparingly exercised, was permitted. A similar course was taken by the Quebec Court of Appeal in *R. v. Valade,*[31] relying upon the majority in *Willis*. In the *Willis* case, counsel for the Crown in his factum had given the accused notice that an increase of sentence would be asked for. The British Columbia Court of Appeal in *R. v. Dashner,*[32] took the position that though the Crown had asked that the sentence should be increased on appeal, because the appellant was not given notice of the intention of the Crown to ask for greater punishment, the request would be refused. This was attributed to the "present practice of the court in that respect" and of the paucity of relevant information.

146; *R. v. MacKay* (1934), 62 C.C.C. 188 (N.S.C.A.); *R. v. McLean,* [1940] 2 D.L.R. 733 (N.B.C.A.).

[28] (1946), 87 C.C.C. 40 (Man. C.A.).

[29] *R. v. Ferencsik,* [1970] 4 C.C.C. 166 (Ont. C.A.).

[30] [1969] 2 C.C.C. 84.

[31] (1970), 15 C.R.N.S. 42.

[32] (1974), 15 C.C.C. (2d) 139.

The issue raised in *Willis,* has now been dealt with by the Supreme Court of Canada. In *Hill v. The Queen,*[33] the practice was sustained. Accordingly, on notice sentence may now be increased upon Crown application but without a Crown sentence appeal.

The question of notice is important because the accused has the right to withdraw his application for leave to appeal from sentence, by giving notice of such withdrawal before the hearing begins. In *R. v. Clifford,*[34] this principle was stated and on the facts of that case, the accused was granted leave to abandon his application for leave to appeal sentence even after the hearing began. But it is clear that notwithstanding this decision, there may be situations where the court will not permit an applicant to withdraw or abandon an application for leave to appeal sentence. In *R. v. Mahon*[35] the court said: "The disposition of an application for leave to appeal against a sentence is in the control of the Court and not of the appellant." In this case the sentence was illegal and therefore the court dismissed the application to abandon and substituted a longer sentence.

E. The Application For Leave To Appeal

Leave of the court of appeal or a judge thereof must be granted before an appeal against sentence can be heard. The practice in many courts of appeal is for the application for leave and the appeal itself to be argued as one matter. Where leave to appeal against sentence is refused, there is, pursuant to s. 613(3), no further appeal to the court of appeal from the refusal to grant leave.

F. Release From Custody Pending Sentence Appeal

Criminal Code:

608(1) A judge of the court of appeal may, in accordance with this

---

[33] (1975), 23 C.C.C. (2d) 321 (S.C.C.); *Hill v. The Queen (No. 2)* (1975), 25 C.C.C. (2d) 6 (S.C.C.); affirming 15 C.C.C. (2d) 145 (Ont. C.A.).
[34] [1969] 2 C.C.C. 363 (Ont. C.A.).
[35] [1969] 2 C.C.C. 179 (B.C.C.A.).

section, release an appellant from custody pending the determination of his appeal if,

(*a*) in the case of an appeal to the court of appeal against conviction, the appellant has given notice of appeal or, where leave is required, notice of his application for leave to appeal pursuant to section 607,

(*b*) in the case of an appeal to the court of appeal against sentence only, the appellant has been granted leave to appeal . . .

(2) Where an appellant applies to a judge of the court of appeal to be released pending the determination of his appeal, he shall give written notice of the application to the prosecutor or to such other person as a judge of the court of appeal directs.

(4) In the case of an appeal referred to in paragraph (1)(*b*), the judge of the court of appeal may order that the appellant be released pending the determination of his appeal or until otherwise ordered by a judge of the court of appeal if the appellant establishes that

(*a*) the appeal has sufficient merit that, in the circumstances, it would cause unnecessary hardship if he were detained in custody,

(*b*) he will surrender himself into custody in accordance with the terms of the order, and

(*c*) his detention is not necessary in the public interest.

(5) Where the judge of the court of appeal does not refuse the application of the appellant, he shall order that the appellant be released

(*a*) upon his giving an undertaking to the judge, without conditions or with such conditions as the judge directs, to surrender himself into custody in accordance with the order,

(*b*) upon his entering into a recognizance without sureties in such amount, with such conditions, if any, and before such justice as the judge directs, but without deposit of money or other valuable security, or

(*c*) upon his entering into a recognizance with or without sureties in such amount, with such conditions, if any and before such justice as the judge directs, and upon his depositing with that justice such sum of money or other valuable security, as the judge directs,

and the person having the custody of the appellant shall, where the appellant complies with the order, forthwith release the appellant.

(6) The provisions of subsections 459(5), (6) and (7) apply *mutatis mutandis* in respect of a person who has been released from custody under subsection (5) of this section.

(9) An undertaking under this section may be in Form 9 and a recognizance under this section may be in Form 28.

(10) A judge of the court of appeal, where upon the application of an appellant he does not make an order under subsection (5) or where he cancels an order previously made under this section, or a judge of the Supreme Court of Canada upon application by an appellant in the case of an appeal to that

Court, may give such directions as he thinks necessary for expediting the hearing of the appellant's appeal or for expediting the new trial or new hearing or the hearing of the reference, as the case may be.

It is important to note that, apparently through a draughtsman's error, if a recognizance with sureties is entered into there may be no jurisdiction to order release without deposit of some "sum of money or other valuable security" however small. Any decision to release or not to release an applicant pending appeal may be reviewed upon the direction of the chief justice or acting chief justice by the court of appeal, which may confirm the decision, vary it, or substitute such other decision as in its opinion should have been made.

Where the appeal is from sentence alone, it is important that the application for leave be made at the same time as the application for release, as the jurisdiction to grant the latter is dependent upon the former.

Because of the necessity to show that the appeal has sufficient merit and that it would cause unnecessary hardship for the appellant to be detained, it is important for counsel to set out in considerable detail the facts supporting both factors on the application for leave. It should be noted that this standard is considerably higher than the standard upon conviction appeals, namely, a showing merely that "the appeal or application for leave to appeal is not frivolous".

As a matter of practice, in appeals from sentence, release is often difficult to obtain. In *R. v. Cavasin*,[36] O'Halloran J.A. noted that in an appeal from sentence only "it must be obvious that the grounds for granting bail must be even more closely restricted" than in an appeal from conviction. In *R. v. Bencardino and DeCarlo*,[37] an application was made for release after a conviction for manslaughter but pending appeal, while the prisoners were on remand for sentence at a later date. Brooke J.A. found that he had jurisdiction to grant release pending appeal even though the proceedings below were incomplete, but because the trial judge's sentence and reasons therefore would be important considerations on the question of release, he declined to grant bail. He concluded that the applicants had failed at this early stage to show that the detention was not necessary in the public interest. The application was dismissed with the right to re-apply after sentence was passed.

---

[36] [1944] 4 D.L.R. 403 (B.C.C.A.).
[37] (1973), 11 C.C.C. (2d) 549 (Ont. C.A.).

G. Suggestions By The Court To Crown Counsel

Occasionally, the court will for one reason or another make suggestions to the Crown as to the course that ought to be followed in a given case for reasons of justice. The court is careful not to interfere with the executive discretion and holds itself to its own powers given by statute; nevertheless such suggestions are common, though rare in the reported cases. In *R. v. Shonias*[38] the court said that "it may be that the Crown will not think any further prosecution necessary" despite the order directing a new trial. In practice, such suggestions are usually followed.

H. Powers Of The Court Of Appeal

The powers of the court of appeal are set out at the beginning of the chapter in ss. 610, 613 and 614. These powers are very wide. In addition, it should be noted that the court of appeal has the general power to make rules pursuant to s. 438 of the Criminal Code. There are few cases reported under that section of the Criminal Code, but in *R. v Ariadne Developments Ltd.,*[39] the court ordered the return of exhibits on an appeal, subject to a direction made regarding their disposition. It is submitted that the disposition of exhibits can be dealt with not only under the rules as above, but also under the general power to make any order that justice requires.[40] Although it was said in *R. v. Kennedy,*[41] that the court is restricted to either varying the sentence or dismissing the appeal and was without power to refer a matter back to the magistrate for sentence, this view has been contradicted. In a later case it was held that in a proper circumstance, where justice requires it, the court may remit a case to the magistrate for sentence.[42]

---

[38] (1974), 21 C.C.C. (2d) 301 (Ont. C.A.).
[39] (1974), 19 C.C.C. (2d) 49 (N.S.C.A.).
[40] *R. v. Marceniuk,* [1923] 3 W.W.R. 758 (Alta. C.A.).
[41] (1956), 23 C.R. 185 (B.C.C.A.).
[42] *R. v. Ashcroft, Toth and King,* [1966] 4 C.C.C. 27 (Ont. C.A.).

I. The Nature Of The Order Made By The Court Of Appeal

It is clear that an order varying sentence pursuant to s. 614(2) has the same force and effect as if it were a sentence passed by the trial court. Accordingly in *Re Keller*,[43] the court of appeal set aside a term of imprisonment and substituted a suspended sentence and probation. The accused was later charged with breach of probation and the trial judge in the lower court declined to act. The Saskatchewan Court of Appeal made clear that the effect of the judgment on appeal was to make the suspended sentences and the probation it had imposed the judgment of the trial court and that the jurisdiction to enforce it lay in that court. Similarly in *Re R. and Ward*,[44] the British Columbia Court of Appeal allowed a sentence appeal and placed the accused on probation. One of the terms required that she reside with her parents in Edmonton. The Crown applied thereafter to have the order transferred to "the Appellate Division, Supreme Court of Alberta". The Attorney-General consented to such a transfer pursuant to s. 665(1) of the Criminal Code. That section permits transfer of the order to "a court in that other territorial division that would, having regard to the mode of trial of the accused, have had jurisdiction to make the order in that other territorial division if the accused had been tried and convicted there." The British Columbia Court of Appeal held that the Appellate Division was not the court referred to in that section and that the order should have been for transfer to the Trial Division of that province.

Once a probation order is varied by the court of appeal it becomes an order of the trial court and can be further varied only by the trial court. An application to the court of appeal to vary a term of probation imposed by that court cannot be brought for lack of jurisdiction.[45]

J. Psychiatric Examination

Criminal Code:

608.2 (1) A judge of the court of appeal may, by order in writing,

---

[43] (1971), 14 C.R.N.S. 234 (Sask.).
[44] (1974), 21 C.C.C. (2d) 443 (B.C.C.A.).
[45] *R. v. Hanson*, unreported, February 8, 1978 (B.C.C.A.).

(a) direct an appellant to attend, at a place or before a person specified in the order and within a time specified therein, for observation, or

(b) remand an appellant to such custody as the judge directs for observation for a period not exceeding thirty days,

where, in his opinion, supported by the evidence or, where the appellant and the respondent consent, by the report in writing, of at least one duly qualified medical practitioner, there is reason to believe that

(c) the appellant may be mentally ill, or

(d) the balance of the mind of the appellant is disturbed, where the appellant is a female person charged with an offence arising out of the death of her newly-born child.

(2) Notwithstanding subsection (1), a judge of the court of appeal may remand an appellant in accordance therewith

(a) for a period not exceeding thirty days without having heard the evidence or considered the report of a duly qualified medical practitioner where compelling circumstances exist for so doing and where a medical practitioner is not readily available to examine the accused and give evidence or submit a report; and

(b) for a period of more than thirty days but not exceeding sixty days where he is satisfied that observation for such a period is required in all the circumstances of the case and his opinion is supported by the evidence or, where the appellant and the respondent consent, by the report in writing, of at least one duly qualified medical practitioner.

An order under former s. 608.2 was made on consent, in *R. v. Fisher*[46] in the course of a Crown appeal, where it was disclosed that the accused had been in mental institutions for approximately 17 years following earlier charges of attempted murder.

K. References

Criminal Code:

617. The Minister of Justice may, upon an application for the mercy of the Crown by or on behalf of a person who has been convicted in proceedings by indictment or who has been sentenced to preventive detention under Part XXI,

. . .

(b) refer the matter at any time to the court of appeal for hearing and determination by that court as if it were an appeal by the convicted

---

[46] Unreported, November 21, 1974 (Ont. C.A.).

person or the person under sentence of preventive detention, as the case may be; or

(c) refer to the court of appeal at any time, for its opinion, any question upon which he desires the assistance of that court, and the court shall furnish its opinion accordingly.

In *R. v. Roberts,*[47] the letter of reference from the Minister of Justice, noted that there was evidence touching on the fitness of the sentence which had not been considered at an earlier appeal. MacKay J.A. who was not contradicted by the other judges on this point, took the view that since there had already been an appeal as to sentence and in the light of the letter of reference, the new hearing on this branch of the case should be limited to the new evidence available. Schroeder J.A. took the view that the court should hear the appeal as if it were an appeal on which leave had been granted to offer further evidence. He said:

> The power conferred upon the Minister of Justice . . . has been sparingly exercised and on those rare occasions when it has been invoked, its application was confined to cases to which the ordinary procedure authorized by the *Criminal Code* did not extend, as *e.g.,* by reason of lapse of time, or of the late discovery of fresh evidence which, if established, might have an important bearing on the question of guilt or innocence or on the matter of sentence. The complete independence of the judiciary in the sphere of the administration of justice civil and criminal is axiomatic in our country, and the line of demarcation between its functions and those of the executive is sharply and distinctly drawn. Accordingly special circumstances must be shown to exist before the Minister of Justice will be prevailed upon to exercise the very exceptional powers conferred upon him . . . When that extraordinary procedure is invoked, it is generally because unusual circumstances of later development imperatively require such action to be taken in order that justice may be done, and it would be erroneous to construe it as reflecting any criticism upon a prior judgment of the Court to which the reference is made. The section is designed, in short, to compensate for some procedural deficiency in the *Criminal Code* and to make available a remedy which might otherwise be beyond the prisoner's reach.

In *R. v. Kehoe*[48] the court said that under a reference to review a sentence "the duty of this Court is to review the sentence with respect to which a complaint has been made as fully and effectually as would be the case in an ordinary appeal to this Court by leave against sentence."

---

[47] [1963] 1 C.C.C. 27 (Ont. C.A.); see also 34 Australian Law Journal 163.
[48] [1970] 1 C.C.C. 123 (Ont. C.A.).

Nevertheless, the court took the view that the legality of the sentence under review was the only point raised in the proceedings: ". . . counsel for the appellant quite properly conceded that in view of the previous appeal and hearing in this Court with respect to sentence, the appropriateness of the sentence as it were was really not an issue."

L. Appeals To The Supreme Court Of Canada

In *Hill v. The Queen,*[49] the Supreme Court of Canada has overruled past decisions purporting to deny a right to appeal pursuant to s. 41(3) of the Supreme Court Act and has held that it will entertain such an appeal, with leave; however, this will be subject to the rule that the court will never entertain an appeal concerning the fitness of a sentence. Thus, appeals are possible on questions of law alone and on questions of jurisdiction.[50] The practice of the Supreme Court is not to grant such leave unless the issue is important to Canada generally.

M. Procedure In The Court Of Appeal

Criminal Code:

611. A court of appeal or a judge of that court may, at any time, assign counsel to act on behalf of an accused who is a party to an appeal or to proceedings preliminary or incidental to an appeal where, in the opinion of the court or judge, it appears desirable in the interests of justice that the accused should have legal aid and where it appears that the accused has not sufficient means to obtain that aid.

615(1) Subject to subsection (2), an appellant who is in custody is entitled, if he desires, to be present at the hearing of the appeal.

(2) An appellant who is in custody and who is represented by counsel is not entitled to be present

(*a*) at the hearing of the appeal, where the appeal is on a ground involving a question of law alone,

---

[49] (1975), 23 C.C.C. (2d) 321; affirmed on rehearing 25 C.C.C. (2d) 6 (S.C.C.).
[50] See *R. v. Bradshaw* (1975), 21 C.C.C. (2d) 69 (S.C.C.); *Lowry and Lepper v. The Queen* (1972), 6 C.C.C. (2d) 531 (S.C.C.); *R. v. Sihler* (1976), 13 O.R. (2d) 285 (C.A.); *R. v. S.S. Kresge Co. Ltd.* (1975), 27 C.C.C. (2d) 420 (P.E.I.C.A.).

(*b*) on an application for leave to appeal, or

(*c*) on any proceedings that are preliminary or incidental to an appeal, unless rules of court provide that he is entitled to be present or the court of appeal or a judge thereof give him leave to be present.

(3) An appellant may present his case on appeal and his argument in writing instead of orally, and the court of appeal shall consider any case of argument so presented.

(4) The power of a court of appeal to impose sentence may be exercised notwithstanding that the appellant is not present.

It would appear that on an appeal against a sentence based on mixed fact and law, despite the fact that the appellant is in custody and is represented by counsel, he has a right if he desires to be present at the hearing of the appeal. Nevertheless, it is not the usual practice for an appellant in custody on a sentence matter to be present in court when his appeal is argued by counsel. But such an appeal cannot proceed in the absence of an appellant who has signified his desire to be present at the hearing of such an appeal.[51]

It has been held that where the court of appeal sets aside an acquittal, enters a conviction and proceeds to sentence the accused, the imposition of sentence should not take place until after the accused has had an opportunity to make his submissions either in person or through counsel before the court of appeal.[52] Where an appellate court sentenced an accused without according him an opportunity to make submissions, the Supreme Court of Canada ordered the appeal remitted to it for that purpose.[53]

The court of appeal may impose sentence notwithstanding the absence of the appellant. The term "appellant" in s. 615(4) is equivalent in the context to "accused". This point arose in the Manitoba Court of Appeal in *R. v. Krawetz,*[54] where the Crown was the appellant and the respondent accused failed to appear. The Court said that "appellant"

... obviously refers to the accused and no one else, for the Court would not be imposing sentence upon the Crown. The section does not in terms deal directly with the case of a Crown appeal. But the principle embodied in the section may be applied by analogy to a Crown appeal. The absence of the accused from the hearing of the appeal, despite due notice to him, is no bar to

---

[51] *Smith v. The Queen,* [1966] 1 C.C.C. 162 (S.C.C.).
[52] *Lowry and Lepper v. The Queen* (1972), 6 C.C.C. (2d) 531 (S.C.C.).
[53] *Dore v. A.-G. Can.* (1974), 15 C.C.C. (2d) 542 (S.C.C.).
[54] (1974), 20 C.C.C. (2d) 173 at p. 174.

the Court imposing sentence, whether the appeal is by the accused or by the Crown.

Nevertheless s. 615(4) is unfortunately worded, for there is nowhere authority for the court to hear the appeal, as distinct from the imposing of sentence, where the appellant or respondent accused fails to appear. However, it seems not to be the practice, generally, to order the arrest of an appellant who does not choose to be present and thus violates conditions of his release pending appeal. The courts of appeal have taken the power to proceed fully in the absence of the accused appellant or respondent. In *Krawetz,* the court of appeal had directed the Crown to notify the accused of the date of the current hearing and efforts to do so were made. In those circumstances and particularly having regard to affidavit proof that the accused had been notified of the time and place of the original hearing of the Crown appeal, leave was given to the Crown to proceed with its submissions in the absence of the accused. In the result, the court proceeded to impose sentence.

Similarly, in *R. v. Shanower,*[55] a Crown appeal, where the accused respondent did not appear, the court, without referring to this section, simply outlined the affidavit evidence which indicated that notice and service of documents had taken place by sending them to the respondent's place of residence in Ohio. By consulting two members of the Bar of Ontario regarding the possibility of retaining them to argue the appeal, the respondent demonstrated that he was aware of the appeal coming on for hearing. In those circumstances the court considered the appeal in his absence and increased the sentence.

The view of the Manitoba Court of Appeal in *Krawetz* was rendered *per incuriam R. v. Ashcroft, Toth and King.*[56] That was an appeal by the Crown from acquittal. The court found that they must set aside the verdict of acquittal and enter a conviction of common assault. The court said, regarding the question as to whether or not they could pass sentence on accused who were neither present nor represented on their appeal:

> Section 594 [now s. 615] does not cover the situation because it deals only with the case where the appellant is an accused and not where the appellant is the Crown. The only provision of the *Criminal Code* that is at all helpful is s. 592(6) [now s. 613] which authorizes this Court, when it exercises *any* of the powers conferred by s. 592(4), to make any order in addition, that justice requires. It seems to us that in exercising our power to enter a conviction for

---

[55] (1972), 8 C.C.C. (2d) 527 (Ont. C.A.).
[56] [1966] 4 C.C.C. 27 at p. 28 (Ont. C.A.).

common assault, we have a discretion to refuse to impose sentence and we may remit the case to the trial Magistrate to do so. This was done by the British Columbia Court of Appeal in *R. v. Lemay (No. 2)* (1951), 100 C.C.C. 365 ... affirmed [1952] 1 S.C.R. 232 ... but there the respondent accused was represented by counsel on the appeal, and it could be envisaged that the trial Judge to whom the matter was remitted for sentence would have the accused before him for that purpose.

The court noted in its judgment that, in *R. v. Lunn,*[57] the court took the view that it had the power to impose a sentence in a similar situation (but where there was representation by counsel), under the provision enabling it to make "such other order as justice requires" and that it could, pursuant to that power, order the accused to appear before the court for sentence. In this case the court was not informed of the whereabouts of the three accused but noted that since they were personally served in Port Arthur and Fort William, localities that are some distance from Toronto, it would be preferable that the case be remitted to the trial magistrate at Port Arthur, or failing him to another magistrate there, to impose sentence after bringing the accused before him for that purpose.

A third situation arose in *R. v. Pion; R. v. McClemens,*[58] where the court proceeded to hear the appeal of the appellant accused, who was represented by counsel, against sentence, despite the fact that at the time of the appeal itself he had escaped custody and was at large. Moreover the court did not take this factor into consideration in assessing the proper sentence.

A different course is occasionally followed where the prisoner escapes custody prior to his own appeal. The court has declined to hear the appeal and dismissed it for non-appearance. Notice of the hearing had been sent by mail and by telephone to the institution from which the prisoner had addressed his notice of appeal.[59]

Procedure in the court can be quite flexible. In *R. v. Watson*[60] the accused filed a notice of appeal and subsequently, following the advice of counsel, he filed notice of abandonment of the appeal. The court acted on the abandonment and dismissed the appeal without hearing the merits. The court declared that it had the power to reopen the appeal because it was not disposed of on its merits; but in the circumstances in this case

---

[57] (1950), 12 C.R. 357 (N.S.C.A.).
[58] (1971), 4 C.C.C. (2d) 224 (Ont. C.A.).
[59] *R. v. Lazenby,* [1969] 4 C.C.C. 221 (Ont. C.A.).
[60] (1975), 23 C.C.C. (2d) 366 (Ont. C.A.).

declined to do so because when he executed his notice of abandonment, the applicant had been advised by a solicitor; as well, there was a delay of almost a year between his abandonment and his application to reopen the appeal. More significantly, the basis for the appeal was further evidence that had not been placed before the trial judge, but it was then in the applicant's possession.

N. Post-Sentence Report

It is often important for the court to know what has happened to the accused since sentence and what effect that sentence has had upon him. One method of producing this information is the obtaining of a post-sentence report.[61] One method of obtaining such a report is a simple request by counsel for the defence to the probation officer to prepare one for use in the Court of Appeal and then offering the report to the court as an affidavit either with or without the consent of counsel for the Crown. A second method is sometimes used, whereby counsel attends, prior to the hearing of the appeal, before a single justice of the court of appeal in chambers and requests an order that such a report be obtained. This latter method is particularly appropriate where no presentence report was obtained by the trial judge.

O. Criminal Code — Section 610(3)

It is important to note that this subsection gives the court the same powers in criminal matters as it has under the relevant provincial statutes in civil matters. This provision has been cited by the Court of Appeal for New Brunswick[62] as foundation for the authority to accept evidence by affidavit upon an appeal. In *R. v. Van Bree*[63] counsel sought to invoke this subsection upon a sentence appeal for the proposition that pursuant to the Ontario Judicature Act he could, without leave and after

---

[61] *R. v. Wooff* (1973), 14 C.C.C. (2d) 396 (Ont. C.A.).
[62] *R. v. Smullin,* [1948] 3 D.L.R. 561; but *cf. R. v. Watson, supra,* n. 60.
[63] (1971), 6 C.C.C. (2d) 187 (Ont. C.A.).

the time for appealing conviction has elapsed, argue the substance of an appeal from conviction. The court took the view that this particular section was not available for that purpose as s. 603 of the Criminal Code and the Criminal Appeal Rules of Ontario made it clear that appeals against conviction and sentence were quite separate matters.

1. CALLING EVIDENCE VIVA VOCE

Section 610(1)(b) and (d) permits the attendance of witnesses and the cross-examination of them before a court of appeal. Though this course is rarely invoked, it was done in *Cavanaugh v. The Queen*,[64] where counsel was given leave to call medical evidence with a view to showing that the present and previous mental conditions of the appellant explained the commission of the offences and disclosed mitigating circumstances that were not before the trial judge.

2. AFFIDAVIT EVIDENCE

The authority for the reception of affidavit evidence rests either with s. 610(3) or with the phrase in s. 614(1) "upon such evidence, if any, as [the court] thinks fit to require or to receive".

It is important to note that the very strict rules regarding fresh evidence admitted in the court of appeal do not seem to be applied by the court on sentence appeals, but seem rather to be confined to appeals against conviction. First, there is undoubtably a wider power in the court on this subject-matter with regard to sentence. The view that s. 614 in its phrasing permits the introduction of further material upon sentence appeals has been sustained in *R. v. Lalonde*.[65] Under this section it has long been the practice upon appeals by accused persons against their sentences to give reasonable opportunity to adduce evidence of relevant facts and circumstances affecting sentence, although in many instances such material may be of an informal nature. The court noted that the very wide discretion conferred upon them as to the nature of the evidence receivable upon matters affecting sentence was set out very clearly in the Criminal Code.

Nevertheless the practice of admitting affidavits can in some cases be

---

[64] (1953), 106 C.C.C. 190 (N.S.C.A.).
[65] (1951), 11 C.R. 71 (Ont. C.A.).

abused and some courts have indicated that the practice is to be regulated. In *R. v. Lockwood,*[66] the affidavits were rejected:

> I should like to emphasize that this Court objects to the practice of counsel introducing or attempting to introduce before it, for the first time, material relating to sentences which was available at the time of the trial. This practice is quite unfair both to the trial Judge and to this Court. Counsel are supposed to prepare and present their cases before going to trial.
>
> In this case, the appellant was examined by various medical persons before trial and, according to one of the affidavits, he was advised by a doctor that it was most important that "he have his lawyer contact me prior to his trial on the charge of breaking and entering". The doctor was not contacted and the only inference that can be drawn is that the appellant did not ask his lawyer to call the doctor. The doctor's evidence is now sought to be adduced before this Court. We think it would be an improper exercise of our discretion to admit this evidence.

In *R. v. Smullin,*[67] the New Brunswick Court of Appeal accepted that affidavits were permissible but sought to restrict their subject-matter. Affidavits were produced from the accused, his father, mother, school-teacher and Sunday school teacher. The Court said: "These, we think, were proper to be heard so far as they deal with character, but not in so far as they state facts in respect of the offence, which facts might have been adduced in the Court below."

The Crown sought to introduce affidavits in contradiction of statements in the affidavit of the accused that he did the victim no harm. These would not have been relevant as a defence on a charge of a sexual offence, as the victim was only nine years old and could not consent to an indecent assault, but were offered in mitigation of sentence. The Court held that these affidavits were not admissible saying: "If the Crown wished the Court to consider such evidence, application should have been made to take the evidence in the presence of the accused."

In a decision of the Court of Appeal of Quebec, *Dore v. The Queen,*[68] such affidavit material was ruled not admissible on the appeal itself. The Court admitted the affidavit material and considered it in relation to the application for leave to appeal sentence, but took the view that the affidavits had no further usefulness at the moment when the application for leave to appeal was granted; from then on they did not form part of the record on which the appeal was based. Noting that the practice had

---

[66] (1972), 5 C.C.C. (2d) 438 at p. 439 (Ont. C.A.).
[67] *Supra,* n. 62; *R. v. McQueen,* unreported, March 2, 1978 (Ont. C.A.).
[68] (1959), 30 C.R. 281.

for some time been widespread of making these affidavits serve the purposes of the appeal itself, or producing new affidavits and asking the court to draw "inspiration from them", the Court proceeded to condemn this practice and declared that it should be abandoned. The Court distinguished *R. v. Smullin,* but the reason for distinguishing it, namely, that that case dealt with a juvenile delinquent who had to be treated according to the provisions of special legislation relating to juvenile delinquents, seems neither cogent nor compelling. The Quebec Court of Appeal took the view that the statutory right to examine or cross-examine witnesses in the presence of the Court of Appeal negated by implication any discretion in the court to take affidavit material as "the rights of the parties to examine or cross-examine will be totally destroyed by a unilateral production of an affidavit."[69] This reasoning may commend itself to some; but the provision of alternate ways of dealing with the same problem is not unusual in the Criminal Code.

The most usual way in which the Ontario Court of Appeal deals with material upon a sentence appeal is by affidavit. In *R. v. Greene and McMann,*[70] the Court permitted evidence on family background and prior history to be filed as a "special indulgence" because the appellants were young, were not represented by counsel at trial and their parents mistakenly believed they could not speak on their behalf. In *R. v. Lalonde,*[71] by reason of an error in the fingerprint section of the R.C.M.P. at Ottawa, a record of the respondent's previous convictions was not available at trial and he was dealt with as a first offender upon two charges of breaking and entering. Counsel for the Crown sought to introduce affidavits to prove the previous convictions admitted by the respondent himself subsequent to the imposition of sentence. Because it appeared that the respondent was advised in writing that he did not have to make any statement whatsoever in connection with his record and that if he did see fit to admit the previous convictions his admission would be used as evidence in the prosecution of the appeal, the court exercised its discretion to permit the introduction of the record and accordingly increased the sentences. In *R. v. Marcon,*[72] the appellant, unrepresented at trial, after pleading guilty gave no explanation for his conduct to the judge when asked to do so. Upon this charge of

---

[69] *Ibid.,* at p. 292.
[70] Unreported, March 22, 1972.
[71] *Supra,* n. 65.
[72] (1974), 18 C.C.C. (2d) 575 (Ont. C.A.); see also *R. v. Mackie* (1942), 81 C.C.C. 338 (B.C.C.A.).

shoplifting, no representations were made either on behalf of the Crown or on behalf of the accused; the judge seemed to have simply imposed the sentence immediately after hearing the statement of the facts. Accordingly, the court gave leave to file an affidavit outlining the background of the appellant.

A further circumstance where affidavit evidence will, it seems, be admitted occurs when post-sentence material is directly relevant to the question of the fitness of sentence. In *R. v. Alfs*,[73] affidavit material was placed before the court which showed that while Alfs was serving his sentence, as a result of information which he gave to the police involving another unrelated offence, he was harassed by inmates, beaten on one occasion and was placed in solitary confinement for four months for his own protection.

3.   PRESENTATION OF OTHER MATERIAL

Though few cases illustrate the practice, it is quite common, with the consent of counsel and in circumstances where the accuracy of the material is not contested, that other material is simply given to the court. In *R. v. Pigeon*,[74] the Quebec Court of Appeal on consent permitted the use of a letter from the John Howard Society. The same Quebec Court of Appeal that took such a rigorous (and isolated) view of affidavit material, permitted the accused appellant to insert in his factum, without prior leave of the court, letters and even a photostat of a newspaper article which came into existence after sentence.[75] The letter was one from his employer setting out the fact of his employment and attesting to the appellant accused's honesty and integrity.

4.   COUNSEL GIVING INFORMATION TO THE COURT

In *Gladu v. The Queen*,[76] the record presented to the court of appeal contained "nothing but the bare essentials" and did not give information

---

[73] (1974), 17 Crim. L.Q. 247 (Ont. C.A.); *R. v. Shaw and Brehn* (1977), 36 C.R.N.S. 358 (Ont. C.A.).

[74] [1970] 2 C.C.C. 177.

[75] *Bédard v. The Queen* (1972), 22 C.R.N.S. 230 (Que. C.A.).

[76] (1960), 35 C.R. 49 (Que. C.A.).

about the circumstances of the case, the nature of the offence, the details of its commission, the social conditions then obtaining nor the identity, history and probable future of the parties involved. There was no report from the trial judge. The court, after critizing the trial judge for permitting this to happen, permitted counsel to explain these matters and then to present facts to the court. On the strength of what they said the court reduced the sentence. Information is also given by counsel in less extreme circumstances. In *R. v. Webster and Martin,*[77] information was given to the court about the circumstances of a third person, not before the court, who was acquitted on the charge under consideration. It appeared that a transcript supporting this material was also filed.

It is common for relatively minor factual matters which are not in the material, to be given orally by counsel. For example in *R. v. Winters, Knox and Palmer,*[78] counsel gave the information that the respondents at the time of the appeal were university students at Fredericton.

Indeed it is hard to imagine how the court could function were they not able to accept the assurance of counsel as to certain facts which enable them to deal with appeals more justly; often the nature of the information is such that neither counsel are able to so closely predict the course of the appeal that they could anticipate that the court would require the information. This is not to say that the court will always permit counsel to supplement the material before the court by oral statements. For example, in *R. v. DeKleric,*[79] the Crown appealed against sentence. The reasons of the trial judge were not before the court of appeal. The court took the view that since this was a Crown appeal, it was the Crown's duty to have before the court all the relevant material which might be required and, in the absence of the reasons for judgment, the court declined to accept counsel's assurance that the magistrate's very extensive report to the court of appeal contained all the information which was involved in the case and that there could be no other information in the reasons for judgment which were not contained in the report.

---

[77] (1958), 28 C.R. 81 (Ont. C.A.).
[78] (1974), 16 C.C.C. (2d) 551 (N.S.C.A.).
[79] [1969] 2 C.C.C. 367 (B.C.C.A.).

P. Trial Judge's Report And Transcript Of Evidence

609(1) Where, under this Part, an appeal is taken or an application for leave to appeal is made, the judge or magistrate who presided at the trial shall, at the request of the court of appeal or a judge thereof, in accordance with rules of court, furnish to it or him a report on the case or on any matter relating to the case that is specified in the request.

(2) A copy or transcript of

(*a*) the evidence taken at the trial,

(*b*) the charge to the jury, if any,

(*c*) the reasons for judgment, if any, and

(*d*) the addresses of the prosecutor and the accused or counsel for the accused by way of summing up, if

(i)   a ground for the appeal is based upon either of the addresses, or

(ii)   the appeal is pursuant to section 604,

shall be furnished to the court of appeal, except in so far as it is dispensed with by order of a judge of that court.

(3) A copy of the charge to the jury, if any, and any objections that were made to it shall, before the copy or transcript is transmitted to the court of appeal pursuant to subsection (2), be submitted to the judge who presided at the trial, and if the judge refuses to certify that the charge and objections accurately set out, he shall immediately certify to the court of appeal

(*a*) the reasons for his refusal, and

(*b*) the charge that was given to the jury, if any, and any objections that were made to it.

(4) A party to an appeal is entitled to receive, upon payment of any charges that are fixed by rules of court, a copy or transcript of any material that is prepared under subsections (1), (2) and (3).

(5) The Minister of Justice is entitled, upon request, to receive a copy or transcript of any material that is prepared under subsections (1), (2) and (3).

It has been held that as the report is not officially part of the record and only for the use of the judges on appeal, its absence will not prevent the appeal court from rendering a decision.[80] Note that where the trial judge furnishes a report to the court of appeal in those provinces or territories where the rules of court require it the accused is entitled as of right to see a copy of it upon payment of any charges that are fixed by the rules of court, despite a comment to the contrary in *Yanovitch v. The Queen.*[81] It has been held that a trial judge should not include, in a report submitted

---

[80] *R. v. Miller* (1926), 30 O.W.N. 318 (C.A.).

[81] (1958), 28 C.R. 220 (Que. C.A.).

under this section, material to supplement the sworn stenographic record of proceedings at the trial and if such material is included, it will be disregarded.[82]

The Prince Edward Island Court of Appeal in *R. v. MacEwen*[83] had before it a case where the trial judge in his reasons for judgment dealt only with the availability of a discharge. In his report to the Court of Appeal, he justified his sentence on the basis of a breach of trust by the accused and the fact that there were two thefts involved on the one charge. The Court held that the trial judge's report should be rejected where it is used by the judge to explain or justify *ex parte* his decision. It is only "in a rare case that such a report is of any use on a sentence appeal since the Court of Appeal has a transcript of proceedings and the pre-sentence report." If the judge has not set out reasons in sentencing (as he did not in this case) his report should be confined to comments on the demeanor or attitude of the accused, any incidents of significance during the trial, and any matter on which the Court of Appeal may want specific comment. Where the report amounts to reasons for judgment, it must be rejected.

In *Ungaro v. The King*,[84] Mr. Justice Locke, dissenting, said:

> It is . . . unfortunate that the section of the Code does not indicate more clearly the nature of the report to be made. . . .
>
> Whatever else may be included in this language, the trial judge may properly . . . state, if he wishes, his findings as to credibility if there are any such issues involved and his other reasons for arriving at his conclusion. . . . The report and such reasons, if any, as have been delivered are to be read together . . . If the report should indicate that the trial judge has proceeded upon a wrong principle, it is manifest that the judgment might properly be set aside, even though reasons given at the time of delivering it indicated no such irregularity.

Where the report of the trial judge was delayed for some months by reason of his illness, a conflict between the reasons for judgment and the report was resolved by disregarding the report.[85] In a case where the conflict could not be resolved, a new trial was ordered.[86]

It is quite clear that in some cases, the court of appeal does consider the

---

[82] *R. v. Hildebrand* (1958), 28 C.R. 136 (B.C.C.A.).

[83] (1978), 39 C.C.C. (2d) 523.

[84] (1950), 9 C.R. 328 at pp. 342-43 (S.C.C.).

[85] *Northey v. The King*, [1948] S.C.R. 135; *R. v. Long*, [1970] 1 C.C.C. 313 (B.C.C.A.).

[86] *R. v. Harris* (1953), 105 C.C.C. 301 (B.C.C.A.).

trial judge's report where it is additional to and explanatory of his reasons for judgment.[87]

Q. Variable Factors Arising On Appeal

Because an appeal occurs after the fact of a trial and sentence, a number of factors can arise only at that stage and can be taken into account in determining sentence. As the court of appeal is charged with assessing the fitness of the sentence, it is quite clear that they are not concerned merely with whether there was an error. The ultimate objective must be to determine whether or not there was "the right result" even if the trial court proceeded for the wrong reasons.[88] Nevertheless several matters arise on a recurrent basis that are relevant to the determination of sentence on appeal.

1.   MISCONCEPTION OF THE EVIDENCE

It is the obligation and responsibility of the court of appeal to assess the evidence for any error that the trial judge may have made in interpreting or understanding it. If, as a result of that error, the sentence is not what it ought to have been or would have been the court will feel free to intervene. In *R. v. Martin*,[89] this principle is shown. The learned trial judge came to the conclusion that the accused was "given to drinking", but there was no evidence of that other than the fact that he had been drinking on the night in question. The learned trial judge, among other errors, also came to the conclusion that the accused was "immorally inclined" and again there was no evidence with regard to that. He misconceived the criminal record of the accused.

---

[87] *R. v. Acker*, [1970] 4 C.C.C. 269 (N.S.C.A.).

[88] *R. v. Murray*, [1956] O.W.N. 168 (C.A.); *contra, cf., R. v. Cusack* (1978), 41 C.C.C. (2d) 289 (N.S.C.A.).

[89] (1947), 3 C.R. 64 (N.B.C.A.).

2. CONDUCT OF THE CROWN AT TRIAL[90]

The conduct of the Crown at trial can be taken into account in a number of ways. The most frequent way is exemplified by *R. v. Gormley,*[91] where there was a cross-appeal by the Crown for an increase of sentence to make consecutive an order for imprisonment in default of payment of a fine. The court noted that the decision to make a sentence consecutive or concurrent is discretionary in the trial judge and that in this particular case that discretion was apparently exercised with the acquiescence of counsel for the Crown. Accordingly, a cross-appeal was not open to the Crown in the light of its conduct at trial.

Where it is shown that a trial has been conducted in a highly informal manner, with the evident understanding that the penalties would not be severe, the Nova Scotia Court of Appeal, in *R. v. Webber,*[92] held that the Court would not increase sentence since the Crown had been a party to the irregularities, though the court was strongly of the view that the sentences were inadequate.

In *R. v. Sinasac,*[93] the Crown unsuccessfully appealed a discharge on a charge of accepting a benefit as a government employee and the crown accepted that the statements of Crown counsel in the court below must be given some weight. At trial Crown counsel had asked for "some small penalty — and certainly I am not suggesting a jail term in this particular case . . .". The court imposed a $1,000 fine, which it referred to as "a very modest one in the circumstances" but a just one having regard to the statement of Crown counsel at trial.

The Saskatchewan Court of Appeal has refused to entertain an appeal where the Crown agreed to a suspended sentence at trial.[94] The Crown cannot be permitted to repudiate upon appeal the position which it took at trial on the question of sentence, claiming at the later date that the sentence it earlier approved was inadequate.[95]

In *R. v. Mighton,*[96] the Crown appeal was dismissed, the court said that the sentence might not have been adequate, "but the Crown seemed to

---

[90] See also Chapter 3, "The Function of Counsel in Sentencing Matters".
[91] (1946), 3 C.R. 404 (P.E.I.).
[92] [1937] 2 D.L.R. 499.
[93] (1977), 35 C.C.C. (2d) 81 (Ont. C.A.).
[94] (1956), 115 C.C.C. 55 (Sask. C.A.).
[95] *R. v. Agozzino,* [1970] 1 C.C.C. 380 (Ont. C.A.); see also Chapter 3, "Plea and Sentence Negotiations".
[96] Unreported, May 16, 1978 (B.C.C.A.).

have conceded that it was appropriate in the lower court and should not be allowed to take a different position on appeal."

In *R. v. Simoneau*,[97] several cases were distinguished, with the comment that different considerations might apply to those cases in which the accused had changed his position as a result of an undertaking by the Crown. The court did note that though it would not, in all cases, necessarily hold the Crown to a position taken at trial, it would certainly consider the earlier stance of the Crown as an important factor to be taken into account. The majority noted that at trial both counsel had joined in a submission that two years less one day would be a proper sentence:

> There are arguable grounds for coming to that conclusion. I do not criticize counsel for his decision although I do not agree with it. But if the Attorney General on further consideration has decided that the trial judge's sentence was an appropriate one, I would not insist that he be precluded from letting the court know of that changed view.

3. CONDUCT OR CIRCUMSTANCES AFTER CONVICTION

It is impossible for a trial judge to predict the future and he must sentence on the basis of the material then available to him. On appeal, however, it is frequently the case that further information is presented to and accepted by the court which puts matters in a different perspective.

In a number of cases the conduct of the accused after sentence has been taken into account. In *R. v. Vallieres (No. 2)*[98] the court took into account that since his sentencing on this and on other earlier charges the accused's conduct during a period when he had been at large was such that he no longer presented himself as a danger to society. The court accordingly held that it was not "in law . . . necessary . . . to decide at this late date on the fairness of . . . sentences when they were imposed" and accordingly reduced the sentence to time served. In *R. v. Laveille*,[99] a trial judge had, probably through error, sentenced a female accused in Ontario to definite terms of imprisonment. Although he had a choice of

---

[97] (1978), 2 C.R. (3d) S-17 (Man. C.A.); *R. v. Agozzino*, [1970] 1 C.C.C. 380 (Ont. C.A.); *R. v. Brown* (1972), 8 C.C.C. (2d) 227 (Ont. C.A.); *A.-G. Can. v. Roy* (1972), 18 C.R.N.S. 89 (Que.).

[98] (1973), 17 C.C.C. (2d) 361 (Que. C.A.).

[99] Unreported, November 2, 1971 (Ont. C.A.).

sending her to reformatory or to jail and the jail authorities in turn had authority to have her transferred to a reformatory, this was not done. The court was of the view that in this particular case (as it would appear to be in most all cases where the statute operates), the sentence was of such a length that it was appropriate to be served in a reformatory. But the court, noting that she had already served four months in jail and that serving the balance of the sentence in a reformatory would not afford her any opportunity to gain a benefit from the reformatory programme, varied the sentence to time served.

In *R. v. Metcalf*,[100] the court took into consideration, in reducing a sentence of eight years for wounding to one of five years, the information that Metcalf was taking a:

> positive attitude in the penitentiary and is well regarded by those in charge of him for the efforts he is making. Although the sentence imposed by the trial judge was not clearly excessive having regard to the offence, this court was of the view, in light of the information before it, that the appeal should be allowed.

In *R. v. Alfs*,[101] the court accepted an affidavit which indicated that while Alfs was serving his sentence, as a result of information which he gave to assist the police in another investigation, he was harassed by inmates, beaten on one occasion, and as a result placed in solitary confinement for his own protection for four months. This factor was relied upon, *inter alia*, in reducing the sentence to one of time served.

Exactly the opposite position has been taken by the English court. *R. v. Davies*[102] notes that the facts that the appellant had testified against his co-accused, offered other assistance to the police following his own conviction, and (as a result of these activities) was placed in solitary confinement for his own protection were relevant. Speaking of this confinement the court said: "That was very hard luck, but it stemmed from the fact that he took part in a robbery." Although the court had sympathy for him and his family it was unwilling to reduce the sentence any further or take into account these factors.

In *Bédard v. The Queen*,[103] the majority took the view that conduct after sentence and before the appeal could be taken into account. They stated that in dealing with appeals from sentence the court was not

---

[100] Unreported, October 29, 1974 (Ont. C.A.).
[101] (1974), 17 Crim. L.Q. 247 (Ont. C.A.).
[102] [1975] Crim. L.R. 596.
[103] [1972], 22 C.R.N.S. 230 (Que. C.A.).

strictly bound by the rules of evidence; finding that the material showed a true indication of rehabilitation and that the appellant was no longer a danger to the society in which he had learned to live, clemency was given. Rinfret J.A. dissented on this point stating that the task of the Court of Appeal was to assess the suitability of a sentence at the time it was imposed; any later material could be of assistance to the Parole Board but not to the court.

If there has been a change of circumstance after the fact of conviction and sentence unknown to the trial judge the court should exercise its discretion and act on it, pursuant to the obligation to assess the fitness of the sentence at the time when the appeal is heard. Assuming the material is properly presented to the court in accordance with established principles as to what will and will not be accepted, there is no statutory authority for limiting the court's inquiry to the time of the original sentence.

So for example in *R. v. Russell,*[104] facts after sentence and before the appeal had indicated that the trial judge's attempt to assist the appellant when imposing sentence had proved fruitless and that the circumstances had changed. It was no longer necessary for the appellant to obtain special psychiatric treatment at Abbotsford Treatment Centre, and accordingly the ten-year sentence that was imposed with this destination in mind no longer made sense. He had not been sent there in any event. The court looked at the situation as it stood at the time of the appeal and substituted a seven-year sentence.

In *R. v. Shaw and Brehn,*[105] upon a Crown appeal, affidavit material was filed showing that the accused, who had been placed on probation, had in fact been carrying out the terms of the order successfully for some four months and had been engaging in volunteer work in the community. The court remarked that no "interests of society would be served by removing both these young men out of the positive environment in which they now are and placing them in custody . . .".

The court determined that, in the end result, the public interest was best served by permitting the sentences originally imposed upon the respondents to stand.

> Although, as I have observed, this was a case in which an appropriate sentence should have included the imposition of a custodial term, in the circumstances which now confront this court general principles of sentencing are not paramount.

---

[104] (1977), 20 Crim. L.Q. 142 (Ont. C.A.).
[105] (1977), 36 C.R.N.S. 358 at p. 362 (Ont. C.A.).

To impose a custodial term now would be a sentence far more crushing than it would have been had it been imposed at the time of trial. The destruction of the positive rehabilitation program presently in progress by the imposition now of a custodial term is apparent.

In *R. v. Miller,*[106] Miller appealed conviction and sentence. West, "an associate and companion in wrong-doing", was tried immediately prior to the appellant and both were convicted of rape. West, having the benefit of counsel, appealed and a new trial was directed. When West was brought before the court for retrial, the Crown reduced the charge from rape to indecent assault whereupon West pleaded guilty and received 18 months' imprisonment. When Miller's appeal was heard, his counsel contended that Miller was entitled to a new trial upon the same grounds as those which were successful in West's case. Counsel for the Crown sought to distinguish the Miller case from the West case, but intimated that, if the court was of opinion that the cases were not distinguishable, the Crown would accede to the request of the accused Miller, made through his counsel, that rather than a new trial he would prefer a reduction of sentence so as to reflect his role in the crime as compared to that of West. The court accepted the view that the principles in the West case demanded a new trial "if pressed for" and also accepted that instead of directing a new trial they might, in these circumstances, reduce the sentence and accordingly did so.

R. Delay In Bringing On The Appeal

There are a number of views across the country on the effect to be given, if any, to the fact of a delay by the Crown which results in a sentence having been served or otherwise completed. In *R. ex rel. Mathieson v. Christopher,*[107] the Crown appealed an illegal sentence of three months in jail imposed pursuant to a statute with a minimum penalty of four months' imprisonment and a $200 fine. By the time the appeal came on for hearing the sentence had been served and the respondent had been released from custody. The court came to the conclusion that "this application has come too late". Arsenault J.A. noted that the statutory power was to review sentence and that in this review ordinarily the court

---

[106] (1926), 30 O.W.N. 318 (C.A.).
[107] (1931), 56 C.C.C. 388 (P.E.I.).

had the power to reverse the judgment either by imposing a greater or lesser penalty or freeing the accused completely. "This discretion has been taken away from this court. The respondent has served his sentence and it is now too late to amend a sentence which has already been paid in full by the respondent."

Since the full range of discretion was no longer open to the court, considerations of fairness therefore required that the appeal not be granted. In *R. v. Chartrand*,[108] the court noted that almost a year had elapsed before hearing of the appeal and it was admitted that during this period the accused attempted to rehabilitate himself, found employment, suffered an accident on the job from which he was recovering and obtained assurance of further employment. The court noted that if the appeal had been heard within a reasonable time, "as could have been the case if the Crown had been truly diligent", they would have been inclined to increase the sentence but declined to do so on the particular facts of that case. In *R. v. Rouleau*,[109] the Quebec Court of Appeal, finding the sentence inadequate in that it did not sufficiently emphasize deterrence, nevertheless noted that the sentences were served and that almost a year had elapsed before the hearing, during which time no further breach of the peace had been committed. They came to the conclusion that to send the accused back to jail at this stage would be "unduly harsh."

Sometimes the formulation of the rationale is different. In *R. v. Vallieres (No. 2)*,[110] the Quebec Court of Appeal felt that it would not "be in the interests of justice" to send the accused back to prison. In *R. v. Buckburrough*,[111] the Ontario Court of Appeal had before it an appeal by the Crown against a suspended sentence and probation imposed upon a conviction for possession of narcotics for the purpose of trafficking. The Court stated that in all such appeals, where convictions involving young men of school age occurred in the few weeks preceding summer vacation, every effort should be made by the Crown to bring the appeal on before the vacation court in August, otherwise by the time the appeal was brought on, the court would be confronted with the circumstance, as here, that in putting his best foot forward the respondent had re-attended school or the like. The Court dismissed the appeal on the ground that it had not been brought on with that dispatch.

---

[108] (1971), 17 C.R.N.S. 233 (Que. C.A.).
[109] (1971), 5 C.C.C. (2d) 34.
[110] (1973), 17 C.C.C. (2d) 361.
[111] Unreported, September 24, 1971.

On the other hand, several courts have refused to follow this line of cases. In particular the clear statement set out in *Christopher*, was not followed in *R. v. Collier*,[112] because no authorities were cited and because no reasons were given (in fact reasons were given); but primarily because it seemed to that county court judge to be contrary to the practice that obtained in the Court of Criminal Appeal in England.

This perception is incorrect. In *R. v. Owen*,[113] the Court of Criminal Appeal had before it a charge where months after the offence was committed the appeal finally reached the court of appeal.

> One of the facts which we have got to bear in mind (and it is unfortunate that we have to) is that justice has been long delayed. It seems to us wrong that after such a long interval as 18 months the appellant should have to go back to prison to serve what would have been a short remnant of his sentence if we had reduced the sentence from nine months to three months . . . In our judgment it would be unduly harsh to make him go back to prison some six months later.

Nevertheless, though there is jurisdiction to increase a sentence when it has already been served, we must distinguish this power from the question of the wisdom of so doing. In *R. v. Deschamps*,[114] the jurisdictional point was raised and the argument made that where a convicted person has endured the punishment he is thereby released from all further or other criminal proceedings for the same cause. This argument was considered by the court to be no longer tenable in view of the right to appeal given by statute in the Criminal Code. In that case, the sentences were in fact increased. Similarly, in *R. v. Tronson*,[115] the British Columbia Court of Appeal had before it a case where a judge of the County Court had held himself barred from proceeding to increase sentence because by the time the appeal reached that court the term of imprisonment had been served. He took the view that the Crown had been dilatory and that by not pressing the appeal sooner had "acquiesced in the punishment". The Court of Appeal of British Columbia rejected this argument upon the simple ground that if it were accepted the object of the statute to secure the imposition of a fit and proper sentence upon appeal could be frustrated; for example, by a magistrate giving a short and trivial sentence of imprisonment that could be completed before it was possible to move to rectify it.

---

[112] (1971), 6 C.C.C. (2d) 438 (N.S. Co. Ct.).
[113] [1976] 3 All E.R. 239; *R. v. Stoneman* (1976), 19 Crim. L.Q. 283 (Ont. C.A.).
[114] (1951), 12 C.R. 378 (Ont. C.A.).
[115] (1956), 25 C.R. 233.

The middle ground, if such indeed it be, is set out in two decisions of the British Columbia Court of Appeal. In *R. v. Hinch and Salanski*[116] the Court said:

> It might be remarked in passing that the sentence of one month has been served and the respondents have been released and have been endeavouring to rehabilitate themselves for some four months. To have them at this time rearrested and returned to the gaol because of what is alleged to have been a mistake on the part of the Magistrate would add unduly to their punishment and would savour of harassment, a result which, with respect, we should not bring about unless we are under compulsion to do because of particularly outrageous circumstances resulting in a clear miscarriage of justice. . . .

Similarly in *R. v. Weber*[117] a more recent case, the Crown appealed against a sentence of three months' imprisonment and the court stated:

> This Court has a disinclination, when a man has served a sentence imposed upon him, to send him back to gaol to serve the remainder of a longer sentence substituted on appeal. But this disinclination cannot be allowed to operate to the detriment of the public when a longer sentence is clearly indicated in order to deter others.

In the result the court increased the sentence to one of nine months. One wonders whether a six-month increase is sufficiently important to justify the exercise of this power.

Even where the delay that has been occasioned in the sentencing process has not been due to any fault on the part of the Crown, as, for example, where further appeals take place to higher courts, it will be taken into account as a mitigating factor — provided it has not been brought about by any fault on the part of the appellant — as having caused him and his family "a long period of great anxiety." [118]

S. The Nature Of The Error Below: An Illegal Sentence

In some cases, the court has taken the nature of the error into account. Where a sentence is illegal, this may produce circumstances in which the effect on the accused ought to be taken into account to ultimately reduce

---

[116] [1968] 3 C.C.C. 39 at pp. 46-47.
[117] (1973), 9 C.C.C. (2d) 49 (B.C.C.A.).
[118] *R. v. Cooper (No. 2)* (1977), 35 C.C.C. (2d) 35 (Ont. C.A.).

the penalty. In *R. v. Giffen*,[119] upon a charge of robbery, the trial court felt that sitting as a Provincial Criminal Court the minimum sentence that it could impose would be one year definite and one year indeterminate. Rather than do so, the court called the prisoner back for sentencing on another day where, sitting as a Judge of the Juvenile and Family Court upon a 17-year-old (which was illegal) the trial judge remanded the case for judgment for two years on condition that the accused enter into a recognizance. He subsequentiy breached the recognizance and was sentenced to 18 months definite and six months indeterminate. The court found the intervening proceedings in the Juvenile Court was a nullity and that the accused had entered into a recognizance which was not authorized by law. The court determined that in view of the seriousness of the crime the sentence ultimately imposed was not unreasonable: "Nevertheless, in view of the irregularities, we came to the conclusion that justice would be done by a reduction of the sentence to the time served by the accused."

In *R. v. Pretty*,[120] the trial judge joined two charges together in one conviction and gave a single sentence to both charges. In addition to this error, the court held that the sentence actually imposed was in excess of jurisdiction. The court took the view (there are others) upon the question whether a probation order is "other punishment" within the meaning of s. 663(1)(b) of the Criminal Code:

> . . . this is not a case where I think the circumstances would warrant any interference by this Court with the assessment of the trial judge. That being so I feel that the sentence to be substituted should not be more severe than the one we are obliged to quash.[121]

T. Penitentiary v. Reformatory

Even where the court does feel they ought to reduce a sentence, it appears that there is a disinclination, in some circumstances, to reduce a penitentiary sentence to a reformatory term. In *R. v. Burden*,[122] upon a

---

[119] (1959), 125 C.C.C. 113 (Ont. C.A.).
[120] (1971), 5 C.C.C. (2d) 332 (P.E.I.C.A.).
[121] *A.-G. Can v. Wong*, [1961] Que. Q.B. 907 (C.A.).
[122] (1973), 11 C.C.C. (2d) 491 (Ont. C.A.). See also Chapter 13, "Place of Incarceration".

charge of robbery the appellant was sentenced to three years' imprisonment. Though there were mitigating factors which justified a reduction in this sentence, the court would not reduce it below two years' imprisonment:

> We are not changing the sentence to bring him from the penitentiary, where he has been for some months, into a reformatory. He was in a penitentiary on a previous occasion and the disruption of moving a person, who has been incarcerated in a penitentiary for some time, into a reformatory is one that ought to be avoided in most circumstances.

Unfortunately the court gives no reasons for this conclusion and the rationale is not readily apparent.

U. Frustration

In *R. v. McLafferty,* [123] the court found that through no fault of his own, McLafferty's appeal documents were misplaced and as a result ultimately he abandoned his appeal with respect to conviction. At the point when the appeal against sentence was heard he had served seven months of a sentence of 12 months definite and three months indeterminate upon a charge of being in possession of stolen property valued at more than $200. On these facts "as the court was of the view that he had struggled long enough against adversity" his sentence was varied to one of time served.

V. Appeals Against Sentences For Summary Offences

Criminal Code:

> 748. Except where otherwise provided by law,
> (*a*) the defendant in proceedings under this Part may appeal to the appeal court
>   (i) from a conviction or order made against him, or
>   (ii) against a sentence passed upon him; and

---

[123] Unreported, May 22, 1975 (Ont. C.A.); *R. v. Willcocks,* [1977] Crim. L.R. 115.

(*b*) the informant, the Attorney General or his agent in proceedings under this Part may appeal to the appeal court

(i)   from an order dismissing an information, or

(ii)   against a sentence passed upon a defendant,

and the Attorney General of Canada or his agent has the same rights of appeal in proceedings instituted at the instance of the Government of Canada and conducted by or on behalf of that government as the Attorney General of a province or his agent has under this paragraph.

750(1)   An appellant who proposes to appeal to the appeal court shall give notice of appeal in such manner and within such period as may be directed by rules of court.

(2)   The appeal court or a judge thereof may at any time extend the time limit within which notice of appeal may be given.

753(1)   A person does not waive his right of appeal under section 748 by reason only that he pays the fine imposed upon conviction, without in any way indicating an intention to appeal or reserving the right to appeal.

(2)   A conviction, order or sentence shall be deemed not to have been appealed against until the contrary is shown.

755(1)   Where an appeal is taken under section 748 in respect of any conviction, acquittal, sentence or order, the provisions of sections 610 to 616, with the exception of subsections 610(3) and 613(5), apply *mutatis mutandis.*

(2)   Where an appeal court orders a new trial, it shall be held before a summary conviction court other than the court that tried the defendant in the first instance, unless the appeal court directs that the new trial be held before the summary conviction court that tried the accused in the first instance.

(3)   Where an appeal court orders a new trial, it may make such order for the release or detention of the appellant pending such trial as may be made by a justice pursuant to section 457 and the order may be enforced in the same manner as if it had been made by a justice under that section and the provisions of Part XIV apply *mutatis mutandis* to the order.

(4)   Notwithstanding subsections (1) to (3), where an appeal is taken under section 748 and where, because of the condition of the record of the trial in the summary conviction court or for any other reason, the appeal court, upon application of the defendant, the informant, the Attorney General or his agent, is of the opinion that the interests of justice would be better served by hearing and determining the appeal by holding a trial *de novo,* the appeal court may order that the appeal shall be heard by way of trial *de novo* in accordance with such rules as may be made under subsection 438 (1.1) and for this purpose the provisions of sections 729 to 744 apply *mutatis mutandis.*

(5)   The appeal court may, for the purpose of hearing and determining an appeal under subsection (4), permit the evidence of any witness taken before

the summary conviction court to be read if that evidence has been authenticated in accordance with section 468 and if

(*a*) the appellant and respondent consent,

(*b*) the appeal court is satisfied that the attendance of the witness cannot reasonably be obtained, or

(*c*) by reason of the formal nature of the evidence or otherwise the court is satisfied that the opposite party will not be prejudiced,

and any evidence that is read under the authority of this subsection has the same force and effect as if the witness had given the evidence before the appeal court.

(6) Where an appeal is taken under subsection (4) against sentence, the appeal court shall, unless the sentence is one fixed by law, consider the fitness of the sentence appealed against and may, upon such evidence, if any, as it thinks fit to require or receive, by order,

(*a*) dismiss the appeal, or

(*b*) vary the sentence within the limits prescribed by law for the offence of which the defendant was convicted;

and in making any order under paragraph (*b*) the appeal court may take into account any time spent in custody by the defendant as a result of the offence.

(7) The following provisions apply in respect of appeals under subsection (4), namely,

(*a*) where an appeal is based on an objection to an information or any process, judgment shall not be given in favour of the appellant

(i)   for any alleged defect therein in substance or in form, or

(ii) for any variance between the information or process and the evidence adduced at the trial,

unless it is shown

(iii) that the objection was taken at the trial, and

(iv) that an adjournment of the trial was refused notwithstanding that the variance referred to in subparagraph (ii) had deceived or misled the appellant; and

(*b*) where an appeal is based on a defect in a conviction or an order, judgment shall not be given in favour of the appellant, but the court shall make an order curing the defect.

Under the former provisions of the Criminal Code it was held that unless an appeal is specifically lodged against a sentence the appeal court had no jurisdiction to deal with it.[124]

In *R. v. Natrall,*[125] all the judges took the view that it was obligatory on an appeal court to "consider the fitness" of the sentence. The majority

---

[124] *R. v. Praisley,* [1965] 1 C.C.C. 316 (B.C.C.A.); *R. v. Ferencsik,* [1970] 4 C.C.C. 166 (Ont. C.A.).

[125] (1973), 9 C.C.C. (2d) 390 (B.C.C.A.).

held that in so doing the judge should consider whether the sentence being appealed was a valid one and whether or not any error of principle was involved in a court below. The majority took the view that the "fitness" of the sentence must be considered at the time it was passed as well as at the time of review in the light of further evidence or information. Branca J.A., dissenting, took the view that the obligation of the Court of Appeal was to consider the fitness of sentence upon the circumstances proved in evidence at appeal quite independently of what had been done in the lower courts.

Any further appeal to the court of appeal for a province can only lie if an error of law is disclosed; there is such an error if the sentence is based upon facts not proved in evidence and wrongly accepted as proved by the trial judge.[126]

Though *Hill v. The Queen*[127] would indicate that quantum of sentence can never be a question of law, *R. v. S.S. Kresge Co. Ltd.*[128] indicates that whether the sentence imposed is "fit" is a question of law. It is submitted that the question needs to be litigated in the Supreme Court of Canada.

In *R. v. Benson*[129] the court stated that "an appeal against conviction and an appeal against sentence are two separate and distinct proceedings". Accordingly, an appeal against conviction can be taken despite the fact that at the time when the appeal was launched sentence had not yet been imposed.

---

[126] *R. v. Sihler* (1976), 13 O.R. (2d) 285 (C.A.).
[127] (1975), 23 C.C.C. (2d) 321 (S.C.C.).
[128] (1975), 27 C.C.C. (2d) 420 (P.E.I.C.A.).
[129] (1978), 40 C.C.C. (2d) 271 (B.C.C.A.).

Chapter 19

Range Of Sentence

In most penal sections of the Criminal Code only the maximum punishment for an offence is set out. Thus the court must judicially arrive at a sentence that may vary in a robbery case, for example, from a suspended sentence with probation to life imprisonment. The maximum or the minimum penalties will not be imposed save under the most unusual circumstances.

In Canada, the appropriate sentence is determined by a weighing of all the relevant principles and the circumstances of the offence and the offender. Regard is also had to other sentences for the same or similar crimes. Thus, partially because of the judicial effort to achieve some uniformity in sentence, certain patterns or ranges of sentence emerge, despite the fact that no single factor or principle is always pre-eminent. The strength of the idea of a range of sentence flows from the fact that criminal statutes apply throughout Canada — though not uniformly.

In England, this indirect approach to uniformity of sentence is not taken. The Court of Appeal (Criminal Division) has approved a "tariff" or normal range of sentence for a particular type of offence. Thus, it seems that one of the operative principles, namely, the sentence customarily imposed for similar offences, has there achieved pre-eminence. Within that range or "tariff", the sentencing court then adjusts upward or downward to accommodate the particular offence and individual offender. For further reading on the "tariff" system and its operation see R. Cross, *The English Sentencing System* at p.15 *et seq.* and D.A. Thomas, *Principles of Sentencing*.

No appellate court in Canada has chosen to adopt this system. It is submitted that though our system permits greater divergence in sentence it retains the undoubted virtue of placing the particular offence and the particular offender first in priority. This helps to keep sentencing human and minimize any tendency to devolve into a mechanical enterprise. It would be wrong, in our sentencing system, to make any single factor more important than the principle that sentence be appropriate to the particular offence and the individual offender. Sensitivity and flexibility in sentencing requires that the approach to be taken should flow from the facts of the case and not from any single rule, however useful or certain that rule may be.

A common failing in this regard is illustrated by *Webb v. The Queen*[1] where the provincial court judge imposed a $50 fine for the offence of shoplifting and in his report to the court commented: "This is the standard penalty which I customarily impose for such an offence." The appeal court held that such a statement was

> ... contrary to all well-recognized principles which should govern a court in considering ... appropriateness ... Each case must be considered separately and upon its own circumstances. Minimum or maximum or "standard" penalties are the exclusive prerogative of Parliament and where no such penalties are prescribed a court is in error in following self-imposed minimum or maximum standards without giving consideration to the individual accused being sentenced.

Nevertheless, for many offences, a range of sentence can be observed after the fact and analyzed. It can be seen from a study of the range that some factors take on more importance than others in particular offences. The information in this chapter must not been seen as a "tariff" against which individual cases are measured; rather, *it reflects individual cases, but does not govern them.*[2] In Canada, what uniformity in sentencing we have or want is achieved through uniform application of principles — not by "fiat" from above. Canada is far more diverse in culture, geography and way of life than the United Kingdom and uniformity of the sort achieved there would in the long run not be helpful here. As long as the Supreme Court of Canada has no jurisdiction over quantum of sentence it is not constitutionally possible to impose a Canada-wide tariff.

The cases analyzed in this book are almost entirely appellate court decisions. This is unfortunate, because no practitioner of criminal law should believe that the quantum of sentence imposed there accurately reflects the system of justice as a whole. Generally, appellate courts tend

---

[1] (1975), 39 C.R.N.S. 314 (P.E.I.C.A.).
[2] *R. v. Brennan and Jensen* (1975), 23 C.C.C. (2d) 403 (N.S.C.A.).

to avoid the extremes of sentence and to impose harsher sentences than the majority of lower courts.

The sample is far from representative; before a case can reach the appellate court, counsel for the Crown or the offender must have decided that the sentence was so extreme that the appellate court would be likely to interfere. Since appeals tend to be expensive, the less serious crimes and penalties rarely reach appeal courts and even more seldom do they find their way into the law reports.

In an effort to avoid giving a misleading impression of quantum of sentence, there are included in the Appendix, tables reproduced and summarized from the Statistics Canada publication "Criminal and Other Offences". These statistics provide the numbers and percentage of persons sentenced by the nature of the indictable offence on the sentence for the years 1962-1973 inclusive. The use of such material has recently been approved by the Ontario Court of Appeal.[3]

A general principle in sentencing is that sentences imposed for the same or similar offences must not be unduly disparate. Courts of appeal have been reluctant to acknowledge any nation-wide character to the principle, but they do have knowledge of matters in their own provincial or territorial jurisdiction. The principle is really an extension of the attempt to prevent unjustifiable disparity of sentence, as applied to persons who are co-accused or were originally linked in the same crime. *A fortiori,* though to a lesser degree, the principle should operate for those who were not connected in any way. There is general agreement that there is no such thing as actual uniformity in sentencing. However, "where there is a marked departure from the sentences customarily imposed in the same jurisdiction . . . the appellate Court . . . should be able to rationalize the reason for such departure."[4]

This approach can be seen in *R. v. Morrissette et al.*[5] wherein the Saskatchewan Court of Appeal stated:

> A provincial Court of Appeal, being the final Court in dealing with appeals in respect of sentences, has a duty to give some guidance to trial Judges in this field. Upon the Court of Appeal, rests the responsibility of stating the principles underlying the imposition of a sentence so that at least uniformity of approach to this problem may be achieved.

In *R. v. Jourdain and Kudyba*[6] the Manitoba Court of Appeal said:

---

[3] *R. v. Richards,* unreported, September 17, 1979 (Ont. C.A.).
[4] *R. v. Baldhead,* [1966] 4 C.C.C. 183 at p. 187 (Sask. C.A.).
[5] (1970), 1 C.C.C. (2d) 307 at p. 311.
[6] (1957), 25 W.W.R. 160 at p. 164.

It is clear that the same punishment should not always be given for a crime called by the same name. That is the reason why a judge is given such large discretion in imposing sentence. There is however another cause for disparity in sentences for crimes called by the same name, and that is the fact that different judges and magistrates inevitably view the same or similar facts differently. That is what leads in some cases to inequality in sentences and, so far as possible, this should be prevented. It is the duty not only of this court but of all the courts of the province and the Crown to do whatever is possible to bring about uniformity and equalization of sentences for crimes of the same or similar gravity.

In this case, the Court of Appeal noted that "over 90 per cent of criminal charges in Canada are disposed of in magistrates' courts . . . Sentences imposed by these Courts, when not appealed, are some indication of what is regarded as fitting."

In *R. v. Jones,*[7] the Prince Edward Island Court of Appeal assigned to the trial judge the error that "no comprehensive view" of penalties imposed for similar offences was taken. The Court of Appeal reviewed cases from across Canada and revised sentence to accord with that information. The same approach was taken by a county court judge who specifically noted the anomaly that "if a man is charged in North Kamloops, and found guilty of impaired driving, for his first offence he goes to jail; if he is found guilty in the city of Kamloops for the same offence, the practice is to fine him about $200. Now, that is an anomaly that should be done away with if possible. . . ."[8] Accordingly, after a survey of penalties for this offence throughout the country he imposed a fine. The principle is that especially where a statute such as the Criminal Code is in force throughout Canada, some measure of uniformity is desirable.[9]

A. Offences Against The Person

1. ATTEMPTED MURDER

The maximum punishment for attempted murder is life imprisonment:

---

[7] (1974), 17 C.C.C. (2d) 31.
[8] *Deal v. The Queen* (1964), 44 C.R. 282 at p. 285 (B.C.).
[9] *R. v. O'Connell,* [1970] 4 C.C.C. 162 (P.E.I.C.A.); see also *R. v. O'Neill* (1973), 13 C.C.C. (2d) 276 (Nfld. C.A.).

Criminal Code, s. 222(a). This is always a serious offence. In *R. v. Faber,*[10] an aggravating factor in the decision to uphold a sentence of nine years' imprisonment was the fact that a senseless attack was made upon a complete stranger. The offence was characterized by serious violence but no evidence of a profit motive. The court was forced to the conclusion that either Faber suffered from a mental condition or he was acting to overcome inner feelings of frustration or inadequacy. In either case, he was a danger and the public had to be protected from him until he overcame his problem.

Where the victim is a police officer, the offence will be more grave. In *R. v. Miller and Kyling*[11] the court upheld sentences of 20 and 15 years respectively for an attack with guns following a high speed chase that ended only with a road block.

In *R. v. Brown,*[12] where the accused had a criminal record which included a conviction for assault and robbery (a purse snatching), he was convicted of attempted murder. A six-year sentence was upheld. The accused, having been ejected from a club, returned shortly thereafter with a 38-calibre revolver which he aimed at the doorman who had ejected him. The doorman pulled the door of the club shut and had not quite hit the floor when the revolver was fired.

In *R. v. Clark*[13] a Crown appeal was allowed and a four-year sentence was raised to one of eight years. The accused, intending to kill one man, had killed another by mistake. He had gone into a room and called for his intended victim by first name and another person with the same first name answered "yes", whereupon Clark fired a pistol through the door, killing the person who answered. Some six days following his arrest, in discussions with the psychiatrist, the accused indicated that he thought he had killed the man he had disliked and that he would do it again. The court was of the view that the respondent was a dangerous man who might well do this kind of thing again.

In *R. v. Letendre* a 14-year sentence was upheld for a charge of attempted murder which occurred during the course of a robbery. A shot was fired and an unarmed victim was killed, the shot passing within an inch of his heart.[14]

Where the purpose of the crime falls outside the usual objects of crime

---

[10] (1973), 16 Crim. L.Q. 16 (Sask. C.A.).
[11] (1971), 13 Crim. L.Q. 431 (Que. C.A.).
[12] Unreported, October 18, 1977 (B.C.C.A.).
[13] Unreported, April 29, 1976 (B.C.C.A.).
[14] (1975), 25 C.C.C. (2d) 180 (Man. C.A.).

and becomes an attempt to defeat the administration of justice, this is a most serious aggravating factor. For example, in *R. v. Mountain,*[15] a Crown appeal was allowed and a sentence raised from eight years to 15 years upon a man with an extensive record who was convicted of attempted murder. He severely beat a female acquaintance with a chain in an alley following a drinking session in a skid row hotel. She had earlier witnessed the injuring of a man who subsequently died; that death was then the subject of a police investigation. The respondent was present at the earlier offence and the court inferred that his intention was that she should neither testify nor give information to the police.

A ten-year sentence was upheld where the facts disclosed that an attempted murder was premeditated, and the attack, extremely brutal — so brutal that the victim (the accused's wife) was rendered helpless for the rest of her life. The defence of insanity was rejected by the jury. The court was of the view that the accused was psychotic when the offence was committed.[16]

2. MANSLAUGHTER

The maximum punishment for manslaughter is life imprisonment: Criminal Code, s. 219.

> As for sentence, manslaughter is . . . a crime which varies very, very greatly in its seriousness. It may sometimes come very close to inadvertence. That is one end of the scale. At the other end of the scale, it may sometimes come very close to murder.[17]

The other end of the scale referred to above is illustrated by *Tremblay v. The Queen.*[18] A rival of the accused's concubine was lured over to the house where the accused hid himself with a loaded rifle. A scuffle followed the victim's arrival, the rifle discharged and the victim was killed. On the charge of murder the accused was convicted of manslaughter. The Court of Appeal termed the crime manslaughter of the worst sort imaginable. Accordingly, it did not disturb a sentence of life imprisonment.

Sentences only comparatively less severe were imposed by the appeal

---

[15] Unreported, January 6, 1978 (B.C.C.A.).
[16] *R. v. Eichman,* unreported, December 10, 1976 (B.C.C.A.).
[17] *R. v. Cascoe* (1970), 57 Cr. App. R. 401 *per* Salmon L.J.
[18] (1969), 7 C.R.N.S. 315 (Que. C.A.).

court in *R. v. Warner, Urquhart, Martin and Mullen,*[19] where four young men had conspired to rob a store; in executing the plan the proprietor was killed. Having regard to the callousness of the preparation for the crime, and the previous record of some of the offenders, the court increased two of the sentences from 20 years and 15 years respectively to 25 years and 20 years respectively. In *R. v. Guthrie et al.,*[20] the accused participated in a break and enter offence during which one of them went berserk and killed the victim. All of them were armed and the sentence of nine years' imprisonment was upheld.

The fact that the victim and the accused did not know each other will affect the court as an indication that the offender is dangerous to society at large. In *R. v. Johnson,*[21] a 22-year-old member of the armed forces became inebriated and viciously beat to death in her bed an elderly woman. Even though the offender had no previous record, the court found that too much attention had been paid to the rehabilitative aspect by the trial judge; a term of ten years' imprisonment was substituted for the original sentence of six years.

Where death occurs as a result of a domestic quarrel involving relatives or friends, the court is inclined to be somewhat more lenient than with the offenders in the cases above.[22]

For example, in *R. v. Soucie,*[23] the accused was drinking heavily after he had found his common-law wife in a sexual encounter in a hotel room with another man, a second man being present. Later on that day he shot her. The court reduced a sentence of ten years to one of eight years citing the background of the accused as well as these mitigating circumstances.

In *R. v. Hardy,*[24] a suspended sentence and period of probation was imposed upon an accused who had, under stress, killed his wife of three years during a period when she was mentally unstable. Other cases where suspended sentences for manslaughter have been imposed are canvassed therein.

A suspended sentence was upheld upon appeal in *R. v. Henry*[25] for

---

[19] [1946] O.R. 808 (C.A.).
[20] (1978), 11 A.R. 177 (C.A.).
[21] (1971), 4 C.C.C. (2d) 226 (Ont. C.A.).
[22] *R. v. Muttart* (1971), 1 Nfld. & P.E.I.R. 404 (P.E.I.C.A.).
[23] Unreported, June 16, 1977 (Ont. C.A.).
[24] (1976), 33 C.R.N.S. 76 (Que.). See also *R. v. Marceau* (1978), 4 C.R. (3d) S-53 (Ont. Prov. Ct.).
[25] (1977), 20 Crim. L.Q. 139 (Que. C.A.).

domestic manslaughter. Problems that had been caused by the removal of the mother from her two small children led to a very lenient result.

This, however, is not the case where the victim is a child. In *R. v. Bezeau,*[26] the accused viciously beat his five-year-old son to death. The court affirmed a sentence of life imprisonment citing the offender's lack of remorse as a sign of low rehabilitative potential. In another case, where a father caused his son's death through cruel disciplinary measures, the Alberta Court of Appeal affirmed a ten-year sentence, although two dissenting judgments would have increased the term to 20 years.[27] The majority in this case asked themselves the question: "If a ten year term is not sufficient to deter parents from beating their children, what term is?" In *R. v. Julian,*[28] 20 years was affirmed upon an accused who, when drunk, set fire to his brother-in-law's home, causing the death of three children.

In *R. v. Antone and Antone*[29] the appellants were convicted of manslaughter of their six-year-old child who had died of malnutrition. Both appellants had personality defects. A sentence of five years was imposed on appeal to give sufficient weight both to the gravity of the crime and society's abhorrence of such conduct, the court stating that had it not been for the mitigating factor of personality defects in the parents the sentence would have attracted a greater penalty.

Consumption of alcohol plays a part in many manslaughter cases, especially in those arising from deaths caused during domestic quarrels or disputes with acquaintances. The court in *R. v. Kennedy*[30] was confronted with an accused who had shot a man in a struggle at a party held in the accused's home. In varying to three and a half years the sentence of two years less a day imposed at trial the court again felt that not enough emphasis was placed on deterrence. In *R. v. Sadowski,*[31] five years' imprisonment followed by two years' probation was imposed on an alcoholic who beat his wife to death. In another example, a husband shot his wife when both parties were intoxicated; the wife had shortly before threatened to deprive the accused of custody of their only child. Three years in penitentiary was deemed appropriate.[32] In *R. v.*

---

[26] (1958), 28 C.R. 301 (Ont. C.A.).
[27] *R. v. Bompas* (1959), 123 C.C.C. 39.
[28] (1973), 24 C.R.N.S. 289 (N.S.C.A.).
[29] (1977), 20 Crim. L.Q. 143 (Ont. C.A.).
[30] (1972), 5 C.C.C. (2d) 373 (Sask. C.A.).
[31] (1968), 3 C.R.N.S. 269 (Ont.).
[32] *R. v. Mikkelson* (1973), 14 C.C.C. (2d) 255 (Sask. C.A.).

Baldhead,[33] the Saskatchewan Court of Appeal substituted a three-year term of imprisonment for the ten years imposed at trial upon an Indian with a long history of drunkenness who shot his wife when he had meant only to frighten her. In *R. v. Zanewich*,[34] a 30-month sentence was affirmed for an accused who stabbed his brother during a drunken argument.

In *R. v. Smith*,[35] the court held that the suspended sentence imposed at trial was too marked a departure from sentences customarily imposed for manslaughter. Accordingly, a three-year sentence was imposed upon an alcoholic husband who beat his wife to death, but rehabilitated himself prior to trial. However in a recent case, a suspended sentence and two years' probation imposed upon a woman convicted of the stabbing death of her common-law husband during a quarrel where both had consumed alcohol was upheld by the Quebec Court of Appeal.[36] The Court appeared particularly concerned about the effect of incarceration on the woman's children.

In *R. v. Kalsta*,[37] a 77-year-old accused who killed under the influence of alcohol, which had a substantial effect on his rigid personality structure, was sentenced to six months' imprisonment, despite evidence that if he drank he might well kill again.

Eighteen months was upheld on appeal in *R. v. Becan*[38] where a fight broke out during a heavy drinking party in a rooming house; all the parties before the court had been drunk.

In *R. v. Cormier*[39] during a quarrel between husband and wife, when both parties were somewhat intoxicated, the husband was killed. There was evidence that the wife had been abused in the past, and she had been beaten that very evening. A suspended sentence and probation was imposed.

In *R. v. MacPhee*[40] the accused appealed her sentence of seven years' imprisonment. She had stabbed the deceased after he had called her derogatory names. Both the accused and the deceased had been drinking heavily. She was 19 years of age and had a previous criminal record of property offences. The appeal was dismissed on the grounds that the

---

[33] [1966] 4 C.C.C. 183 (Sask. C.A.).
[34] (1973), 11 C.C.C. (2d) 374 (Man. C.A.).
[35] (1973), 25 C.R.N.S. 350 (Sask. C.A.).
[36] *R. v. Henry* (1977), 39 C.R.N.S. 45.
[37] (1977), 20 Crim. L.Q. 21 (Ont. C.A.).
[38] Unreported, May 17, 1977 (B.C.C.A.).
[39] (1974), 22 C.C.C. (2d) 235 (N.S.C.A.).
[40] (1977), 20 N.S.R. (2d) 520 (C.A.).

sentence was within the proper range of sentence for this offence and this offender, and that no error in principle was disclosed. But the court did note that had the trial judge imposed a sentence of four to five years it could not have been said that he had erred on the side of leniency.

In *R. v. Russell*[41] a plea to manslaughter was accepted by reason of drunkenness. The accused was an alcoholic but capable of being rehabilitated and had undergone considerable stress in his family life. He was sentenced for killing his common-law wife to seven years' imprisonment on appeal. However, where the evidence indicates that the alcoholism is incurable and that the accused is likely to be violent when drunk, sentence will be increased to protect society from a "continuing danger".[42]

Even though sentences for a death resulting from domestic quarrels fall in the lower end of the range, where the accused has a lengthy criminal record involving violence and there is evidence that the accused has repeatedly assaulted the victim (usually his wife) in the past, a more severe sentence is warranted.[43]

In *R. v. Reno,*[44] where the accused had a lengthy criminal record, including three convictions for assault causing bodily harm, a six-year sentence was upheld. The accused had beaten up a woman in the presence of her children, so severely that she died.

A mitigating factor that has been taken into consideration by the courts is the fact that the accused is a native Canadian. Where the offender would be removed, by going to the penitentiary, from the remote cultural milieu where he had lived all his life with very few contacts with the modern world, the Ontario Court of Appeal reduced to two years an original sentence of ten.[45]

Lastly, there are those situations where death is caused in circumstances approaching inadvertence. In *R. v. O'Neill,*[46] the accused had struck the deceased with his fist, causing no serious injury; the deceased fell to the ground hitting his head on the concrete pavement and fractured his skull. There was evidence that the deceased had been the aggressor and had a long history of violence. Characterizing actions

---

[41] (1977), 20 Crim. L.Q. 142 (Ont. C.A.).

[42] *R. v. Empey* (1978), 4 C.R. (3d) S-59 (Ont. C.A.).

[43] *R. v. MacDonald* (1974), 27 C.R.N.S. 212 (Ont. C.A.), where 15 years' imprisonment was confirmed.

[44] Unreported, May 11, 1977 (B.C.C.A.).

[45] *R. v. Fireman* (1971), 4 C.C.C. (2d) 82 (Ont. C.A.).

[46] (1966), 51 Cr. App. R. 241.

of the accused as akin to self-defence, the court varied to time served a sentence of 18 months imposed at trial upon a plea of guilty.

Where the circumstances of the offence disclose elements of provocation and self-defence the same principles apply: as in *R. v. Muttart,*[47] where a sentence of six months was imposed.

3. CAUSING DEATH BY CRIMINAL NEGLIGENCE

The offence of causing death by criminal negligence may involve an extremely wide variation in circumstances, thus making a range of sentence very difficult to ascertain. However the variation may be illustrated by the cases.

A hunter mistook three men in an aluminum boat for a moose and shot and killed one of them. The accused was a family man with no criminal record and a good reputation in the community. An appeal by the Crown from a sentence of three months' imprisonment imposed at trial was taken; the British Columbia Court of Appeal varied the sentence to nine months' imprisonment.[48]

In *R. v. Batz*[49] the accused was heavily intoxicated and drove his car against the advice of friends. Following an erratic and high speed drive the accused collided with another auto killing both occupants and injuring a pedestrian and an occupant of the accused's car. He appealed his sentence of five years' imprisonment but in light of two previous convictions for dangerous driving the sentence was affirmed.

In *R. v. Gramcaric*[50] a sentence of 18 months was reduced to one of six months' imprisonment. The offender, a man of good background, drove his automobile so negligently that he caused the death of his passenger, his 15-year-old niece, with whom he had a close relationship. This factor had weighed very heavily on his conscience and caused him great remorse. There was no question of alcohol use connected with the accident.

In *R. v. Atkinson,*[51] an 18-year-old girl was struck and killed by a car driven by the appellant who had gone to sleep at the wheel, owing to a

---

[47] (1971), 1 Nfld. & P.E.I.R. 404 (P.E.I.C.A.); *R. v. Dupois,* unreported, March 28, 1977 (Alta.).

[48] *R. v. Weber* (1973), 9 C.C.C. (2d) 49.

[49] (1974), 16 C.C.C. (2d) 156 (Ont. C.A.).

[50] Unreported, January 12, 1976 (Ont. C.A.).

[51] (1977), 20 Crim. L.Q. 141 (N.S.C.A.); *R. v. Walker* (1974), 18 C.C.C. (2d) 179 (N.S.C.A.); *R. v. Devison* (1974), 21 C.C.C. (2d) 225 (N.S.C.A.).

long day away from home and some drinking, to which he was unaccustomed. He left the scene of the accident. The court, noting that there was evidence of excessive speed, increased his six-month sentence to 18 months. It held that the trial judge erred in placing so much emphasis on the absence for any need for reform or personal deterrence. "This offence is one in which the deterrence to others and public denunciation are factors which overwhelmingly dictate a heavy sentence." The court canvassed several other cases where two years' imprisonment had been imposed in Nova Scotia for similar offences.

In *R. v. Porter,*[52] an accused, of previous good character, caused an automobile accident which resulted in the death of three persons in another vehicle. He was speeding and drove through a stop sign at an intersection without slowing down. The weather was clear and the pavement dry. A waitress in a restaurant thought the appellant had had too much to drink and had tried to persuade him not to drive. The court termed it a "flagrant case of criminal negligence", with "no extenuating circumstances" and upheld a sentence of 18 months' imprisonment.

In *R. v. Mellstrom,*[53] three persons were killed and a pedestrian was injured by an accused whose drug intoxication (which was so apparent that friends had cautioned him against driving) caused him to drive at a dangerous speed and resulted in an accident. There had been minor accidents preceding this tragedy which should, the court said, have alerted the respondent to the hazards he was presenting. The accused had a criminal record involving drug use, and on one of those occasions drugs had been found in his car. A sentence of three and one-half years was imposed.

In *R. v. Graham*[54] the accused was driving a motorcycle, and during the pursuit by police reached speeds of 45 miles an hour in a 30 mile per hour residential zone. An accident occurred and the accused's passenger was killed. A six-month sentence, together with 18 months' probation was upheld. Sentences of one year are not unusual.[55]

---

[52] (1976), 15 O.R. (2d) 103 (C.A.).
[53] (1975), 22 C.C.C. (2d) 472 (Alta. C.A.).
[54] Unreported, October 29, 1975 (B.C.C.A.).
[55] *R. v. Lapierre* (1974), 29 C.R.N.S. 353 (Ont. C.A.); *R. v. Simms* (1975), 10 Nfld. & P.E.I.R. 242 (Nfld. Dist. Ct.).

4. WOUNDING

The maximum punishment for wounding is 14 years' imprisonment: Criminal Code, s. 228. The range of sentence for wounding extends from the maximum penalty to a minimum of several months imprisonment. The offence is viewed seriously by the courts because it often brings about grave consequences and has a great potential for danger.

The maximum sentence was given for an unprovoked assault involving the use of a knife upon a young girl. A psychiatric report indicated the offender was a danger both to himself and society and a long period of treatment was recommended.[56]

Another aggravating factor, coupled here with a discouraging psychiatric profile, is an attack on a victim by two or more accused. In *Pye v. The Queen; Young v. The Queen,*[57] two members of a motorcycle gang tortured a member of a rival club in a shocking manner. The court held that in the light of the previous records of the two accused and the facts of the case under consideration, the sentences of eight and five years imposed at trial should not be disturbed.

The seriousness of the harm done to the victim or the lack of it is a mitigating factor. In *R. v. Bouga,*[58] a 74-year-old offender was sentenced to four years on two counts of wounding a child; this was varied on appeal to one and a half years with two years' probation. The court in *Bouga* also considered the appellant's age in mitigation.

The absence of a criminal record and lack of premeditation will also operate in favour of an accused although it will not usually save him from imprisonment: *R. v. Russell,*[59] where an accused who shot and seriously injured another after a scuffle outside a tavern received a sentence of nine months' imprisonment. The court in this offence often attempts to rehabilitate an offender and will take into consideration efforts in this regard made by the accused between the time he is charged and the time of the trial: *Pye v. The Queen,* or between the time of trial and time of the appeal: *R. v. Smith.*[60]

In *R. v. Neale,*[61] the accused had a long record, and was sentenced to three years in prison on a charge that flowed from a dispute between him

---

[56] *R. v. Bradbury* (1973), 14 C.C.C. (2d) 139 (Ont. C.A.).
[57] (1974), 26 C.R.N.S. 175 (N.S.C.A.).
[58] Unreported, June 9, 1971 (Ont. C.A.).
[59] (1974), 26 C.R.N.S. 248 (N.S.C.A.).
[60] (1972), 7 C.C.C. (2d) 174 (Ont. C.A.).
[61] Unreported, March 9, 1976 (B.C. Co. Ct.).

and his neighbor which escalated into a fist fight. The accused stabbed the victim in the stomach with a steak knife with which he had armed himself before leaving his apartment to take up the dispute. The wound was of such consequence that it required six days in hospital for treatment.

Where the offence occurred during the course of a drunken brawl in *R. v. Nichols,*[62] the evidence of self-defence was insufficient to acquit. The court reduced the sentence to one year's imprisonment, noting that the complainant and the accused were "pretty well mated; his record is no more savoury than hers".

A sentence of three years less one day and fine of $2,500 were imposed upon an accused with no record who, after being acquitted of attempted murder, was convicted of wounding. The accused drove a woman home from a beer parlour and made certain amorous advances to her which she resisted. He then grabbed the knife that she had been carrying and stabbed her six times; the court noted that she was fortunate to have survived the wounds: *R. v. Lawley.*[63]

In *R. v. Howard,*[64] a one-year sentence was upheld on appeal together with three years' probation upon an accused who some considerable time earlier had been found guilty of a similar offence. After an altercation in a bar, the accused was told to leave and was escorted out by the manager. He told the manager that he left his coat behind. As the manager turned, the accused struck him with a small penknife inflicting a very serious wound from his shoulder down to his stomach. If he had not had immediate medical attention the manager would have died.

5. ASSAULT CAUSING BODILY HARM AND COMMON ASSAULT

Common assault is punishable by summary conviction with six months' imprisonment, and assault causing bodily harm carries a maximum of five years if indictable, and six months if summary: Criminal Code, s. 245. The range of sentence in the reported cases for assault causing bodily harm lies between a maximum of two years to a minimum of a fine. Where a father viciously assaulted his five children in circumstances amounting to torture, the Ontario Court of Appeal varied

---

[62] Unreported, December 14, 1976 (B.C.C.A.).
[63] Unreported, May 26, 1977 (B.C.).
[64] Unreported, January 13, 1977 (B.C.C.A.).

his sentence to two years on one count and one year on another four counts to run consecutively making a total of six years' imprisonment: *R. v. Robert.*[65] Similarly, see *R. v. Cudmore,*[66] where a father maliciously beat his four-year-old daughter or allowed her to be beaten to the extent that she suffered permanent impairment; he received a term of one year in jail.

An offender with a substantial record of violence tends to get a substantial sentence. In *R. v. Jackson,*[67] Jackson had a past record including manslaughter, robbery with violence, assault causing bodily harm and common assault, and committed the offence in question after being paroled only the week previous to the offence. The court held that 15 months' imprisonment, combined with the seven months unexpired time to be served on revocation of parole, was appropriate. On the other hand, an offender with no previous record will tend to be dealt with lightly. In *R. v. James,*[68] a $500 fine was imposed upon an offender who had no previous record.

In *R. v. Charles,*[69] an absolute discharge was imposed on an accused who was convicted of assault causing bodily harm when, at a party at his home, he broke up a fight between two women. The fight later resumed at which time, he said, "everything went crazy. I just blew up." He struck one of the women in the mouth with his fist, knocking out her tooth. The court of appeal agreed that the force used was excessive, but given all the circumstances a discharge was appropriate, notwithstanding a previous conviction for mischief some three years earlier. In *R. v. St. Croix*[70] a conditional discharge, together with restitution for the loss of teeth of the victim of an assault which occurred during a hockey match, was imposed upon one who, despite a previous record, had taken excellent steps to rehabilitate himself.

The high end of the range for common assault is one year, imposed under previous provisions permitting such penalties. The highest sentences are reserved for offences involving the premeditated beating of the victim. In *Doiron v. The Queen,*[71] the New Brunswick Court of Appeal

---

[65] (1970), 16 C.R.N.S. 7.
[66] (1972), 5 C.C.C. (2d) 536 (Ont. C.A.).
[67] (1975), 23 C.C.C. (2d) 147 (N.S.C.A.).
[68] (1971), 3 C.C.C. (2d) 1 (P.E.I.C.A.).
[69] Unreported, December 15, 1976 (B.C.C.A.).
[70] (1976), 19 Crim. L.Q. 153 (Ont. Dist. Ct.)
[71] (1958), 124 C.C.C. 156 (N.B.C.A.).

approved a sentence of one year's imprisonment for a premeditated assault as opposed to one arising out of the heat of an altercation.

In *R. v. Regan et al.*[72] "savage beatings", using a sawed-off shotgun, pistol, clubs and boots, which arose out of efforts to collect moneys owed in a background of illegal activity, merited a two-year sentence in a penitentiary to offenders with substantial criminal records.

In *R. v. Griffin,*[73] the court cautioned that the amount of harm actually done is not to be given undue weight. Where the assault had not been premeditated, the fact that the victim lost an eye from the attack is not sufficient to indicate that a heavy sentence ought to be imposed. The court said:

> Thus while the appellant was found guilty of an assault [causing bodily harm], from the nature of the act and the circumstances the probability of the drastic results would not have been in the mind of the appellant when the assault took place. On that basis it would appear that the learned trial Judge gave undue weight to the actual results of the assault rather than to the probable results.

In the result an absolute discharge was granted.

In *R. v. Sayer,*[74] the court said "the seriousness of the assault and the punishment which it attracts . . . depend primarily on the nature of the assault itself, rather than upon consequences possibly flowing from it, which it is not shown the accused either intended or contemplated."

In *R. v. Akerman,*[75] following a minor scuffle between the accused and a member of another gang, the latter rode away from the fight but was followed by the accused and his friends. The accused proceeded, to use his own expression, "to carve up" the victim's face, requiring 44 stitches. A razor blade type of knife was used. The court commented that this was about as brutal an attack as it had had the misfortune to see in some considerable time, and upheld a sentence of two years less one day definite and two years less one day indeterminate.

Another aggravating factor occurs when the victim is a visiting dignitary of some importance rather than an ordinary citizen. In *R. v. Matrai,*[76] three months' imprisonment plus two years' probation was the penalty for assaulting the Premier of the Soviet Union.

Prior consumption of alcohol is often but need not be a mitigating

---

[72] (1975), 24 C.C.C. (2d) 225 (Alta. C.A.).
[73] (1975), 23 C.C.C. (2d) 11 (P.E.I.C.A.).
[74] Unreported, February 27, 1976 (Ont. C.A.).
[75] Unreported, April 30, 1975 (B.C.C.A.).
[76] (1972), 6 C.C.C. (2d) 574 (Ont. C.A.).

factor. The court in *Jackson,* quoted Jessup J.A. in *R. v. MacKay, Thompson and Secord*:[77] ". . . a condition of inebriation short of actual intoxication with respect to an assault in a public bar is not a mitigating circumstance, it is quite a usual circumstance."

The amount of harm done to the victim, *i.e.,* whether permanent or temporary, age and sex are factors to be considered. In *Re Shorting*[78] the accused received 30 days for an attack on a supposed rival for his girlfriend's affections.

Finally, the fact that an assault is motivated by inter-racial hostility is an aggravating factor.

B. Sexual Offences

1. RAPE

The maximum punishment for rape is life imprisonment: Criminal Code, s. 144.

This maximum is usually reserved for those offenders who appear to the court to be a real danger to the community, often because of a personality disorder that may approach insanity. The Ontario Court of Appeal in *R. v. Hill,*[79] in a decision apparently inconsistent with one reported three years earlier,[80] varied to life imprisonment a sentence of 12 years imposed at trial on an offender convicted of the very brutal rape of a 14-year-old virgin. The court noted that psychiatric evidence led by the defence disclosed that Hill was potentially dangerous to the community and that no prognosis could be offered as to when, if ever, he could be safely returned to society. The decision as to when to release the offender was left to the Parole Board, which would presumably have the benefit of subsequent psychiatric reports and assessments of Hill.

The court in *Hill* cited Thomas, *Principles of Sentencing,*[81] in noting that its decision was in accord with the policy approved in the English

---

[77] (1972), 16 C.R.N.S. 11 (Ont. C.A.).
[78] Unreported, January 16, 1975 (Ont. C.A.).
[79] (1974), 15 C.C.C. (2d) 145 (Ont. C.A.); affd 23 C.C.C. (2d) 321 (S.C.C.); rehearing of appeal (*Hill v. The Queen (No. 2)*) 25 C.C.C. (2d) 6 (S.C.C.).
[80] *R. v. Jones* (1971), 3 C.C.C. (2d) 153 (Ont. C.A.).
[81] At pp. 272-79.

Court of Appeal, where it has been held[82] that a sentence of life imprisonment is appropriate if the following conditions are present:

i) where the offence or offences are in themselves grave enough to require a very long sentence;

ii) where it appears from the nature of the offences or from the defendant's history that he is a person of unstable character likely to commit such offences in the future; and

iii) where if the offences are committed the consequences to others may be specially injurious, as in the case of sexual offences or crimes of violence.

The offender in *Hill* had no relevant previous record. Where the facts of the rape are "shocking", and the accused has past convictions for rape or other sexual offences and a discouraging psychiatric profile, a sentence of life imprisonment for rape will be more likely.[83]

The court substituted five years' imprisonment and ten straps for a sentence of life imprisonment in *R. v. Willaert.*[84] Factors in mitigation considered by the court were that the accused had no previous record, was a young man in his early twenties and had spent his adolescence in wartime Europe.

In those cases not involving obvious sexual psychopaths, sentences may vary between one and 12 years. The Ontario Court of Appeal approved a sentence of one year's imprisonment for a 17-year-old youth convicted of raping a 14-year-old girl.[85] The accused had injured the complainant, although not seriously. Both parties were well known to each other and this no doubt influenced the court. In *R. v. Shanower,*[86] the court affirmed that there may be cases where, even on a conviction for rape, a suspended sentence would be appropriate. In this instance, however, the court held that where a 29-year-old man raped a 15-year-old babysitter, who was a virgin, a suspended sentence imposed at trial was not suitable. The accused was apparently a model citizen and a good father and husband but the court was of the opinion that the trial judge had not placed the proper emphasis on the deterrent aspect of

---

[82] *R. v. Hodgson* (1967), 52 Cr. App. R. 113.

[83] *Cf. R. v. Head* (1970), 1 C.C.C. (2d) 436 (Sask. C.A.); *R. v. Haig* (1974), 26 C.R.N.S. 247 (Ont. C.A.), *Hill* applied; *R. v. Leech,* [1973] 1 W.W.R. 744 (Alta.).

[84] (1953), 105 C.C.C. 172 (Ont. C.A.).

[85] *R. v. Shonias* (1974), 21 C.C.C. (2d) 301.

[86] (1972), 8 C.C.C. (2d) 527 (Ont. C.A.).

sentencing and consequently substituted a term of three years' imprisonment.

In *R. v. Amero,*[87] a six-year sentence for rape was reduced on appeal to four years. The 18-year-old accused had a prior record for property offences and for breach of probation. Though he had broken a bottle for use as a weapon he did not wound the victim. The court noted that a six-year sentence for rape was reserved for one where, "grave aggravating circumstances" were present.

In *R. v. Oliver,*[88] a 17-year-old was sentenced to 12 years and the sentence was sustained by a court which commented that the rape "characterized by an assault upon the complainant and threats of harm to her" might not merit a sentence of the severity imposed, but the evidence indicated that the accused was a dangerous psychopath who was very apt to cause harm if not death to other persons in the future. Bearing in mind the psychiatric element, this appeal against sentence was rejected. The court noted, in passing, that the circumstances of the rape itself might not merit a sentence of the severity imposed.

In *R. v. Andrejczuk*[89] a 22-year-old male, under the influence of alcohol, obtained access to the complainant's apartment where he assaulted and raped her. The complainant, who was 75 years of age, was struck several times and threatened with death. The accused had no criminal record. A sentence of three years was upheld, the court stating that it was "at the lower range of what might be regarded as appropriate in the circumstances, however, it [was] not so low as to warrant an upward revision."

The character of the complainant is also a factor taken into consideration by the court. Where the victim has low moral standards a lower term than would otherwise have been considered appropriate was imposed, in a case where three men were involved and injury was done to the complainant.[90]

Age is an especially important factor in this crime, and in order to achieve the rehabilitation of the offender the court will be more inclined to leniency where the accused is a young man. In *R. v. Turner,*[91] a 16-year-old, in the company of another youth, had raped a 22-year-old virgin. In the course of the rape the two accused brandished a knife,

---

[87] (1978), 23 N.S.R. (2d) 646 (C.A.).
[88] (1977), 39 C.R.N.S. 345 (Ont. C.A.).
[89] (1976), 19 Crim. L.Q. 152 (Man. C.A.).
[90] *R. v. Simmons, Allen and Bezzo* (1973), 13 C.C.C. (2d) 65 (Ont. C.A.).
[91] (1970), 1 C.C.C. (2d) 293 (Ont. C.A.).

indecently assaulted the victim and robbed her of $160 in cash. The Ontario Court of Appeal was of the opinion that the eight-year sentence for robbery did not pay sufficient regard to the age of the accused or the prospect of his rehabilitation and accordingly substituted a term of six years for the rape and two years concurrent for the robbery. In a similar factual situation where the accused was 24 years of age a sentence of eight years was substituted for 12 years at trial.[92]

Aggravating circumstances in the crime of rape include the fact that two or more men participate;[93] that violence is done to the person of the victim beyond that necessary to effect rape;[94] that the victim is a virgin or of tender years;[95] that the victim was subjected to indecencies or unusual sexual practices;[96] and that the offence was perpetrated through the use of a weapon.[97] Where many of these factors are present, the sentence for the offence will often be in the range of from ten to 12 years.[98] On the other hand, where these circumstances are absent this will be considered in mitigation.[99]

In cases of multiple rape convictions, the court is especially careful not to permit the totality of sentence to lead to too lengthy a term overall. In *R. v. Murphy*,[100] the court had before it three rapes; two of which were committed with the aid of a knife. Despite a good work record, a psychiatric report indicating that the accused was not dangerous to others and was responding well to treatment and a recommendation that a long stay in jail would be harmful, the court could not sustain sentences amounting to two years less a day definite and two years less a day indeterminate. In order to maintain the deterrent aspect of sentencing, the court imposed consecutive terms of two years, three years and one year. It should be noted that the prisoner was on bail for the first two offences when the third offence was committed.

It is submitted that the intention of the court to protect the public can sometimes lead to excessively harsh sentences especially where there is no suggestion that the offender is a member of the class of disordered

---

[92] *R. v. Wilmott*, [1967] 1 C.C.C. 171 (Ont. C.A.).
[93] *R. v. Willaert* (1953), 105 C.C.C. 172 at p. 179 (Ont. C.A.); *R. v. Simmons, Allen and Bezzo, supra,* footnote 90 at p. 71.
[94] *R. v. Willaert, supra,* footnote 93 at p. 179.
[95] *R. v. Wilmott, supra,* footnote 92 at p. 187; *R. v. Turner, supra,* footnote 91.
[96] *Ibid.*
[97] *R. v. Turner, supra,* footnote 91.
[98] *R. v. Bell et al.* (1973), 14 C.C.C. (2d) 225 (N.S.C.A.).
[99] *R. v. Willaert, supra,* footnote 93.
[100] (1972), 15 Crim. L.Q. 13 (Ont. C.A.).

personalities discussed at the beginning of this section. In *R. v. Deschenes*,[101] four young men were sentenced to terms of imprisonment, ranging from 20 to 25 years plus lashes, for the rape of a young married woman even though very minor injuries were suffered by the victim. Such cases are unusual and out of line with the majority of fixed term sentences imposed across Canada.

2. INDECENT ASSAULTS

The range of sentences for indecent assaults is five years' imprisonment in the case of an indecent assault upon a female and ten years for an indecent assault upon a male: Criminal Code, ss. 149(1) and 156. It is not apparent why one offence should be regarded as twice as serious as the other.

However, indecent assault standing by itself is ordinarily not viewed as justifying imprisonment unless aggravating factors are present.[102] The usual course appears to be a suspended sentence and a term of probation for the first offender. Psychiatric assessment plays a large part in the disposition of the case. In *R. v. Allen*,[103] there was medical evidence to the effect that the appellant was not "a true sexual deviate, in that he has not exhibited a pattern of sexually disturbed behaviour." However the court went on to say: "If the report had been to the contrary, or neutral, silent, or doubtful in this respect, or had been effectively challenged in any substantial element, the court would have been confronted with an entirely different situation than it is now." A period of probation, one of the terms being that the appellant seek psychiatric help for his problem, was imposed in lieu of the sentence of two years' imprisonment at trial.

Similarly in *R. v. D.*,[104] a young school teacher voluntarily commenced treatment with a psychiatrist for his pedophiliac tendencies. The court was of the view that pedophiles are not deterred by punishment to others and thus for such offenders the principle of deterrence was "of small moment". Accordingly, the term of imprisonment imposed at trial was reduced to time served together with probation. It was made clear, however, that should the offender be brought before the court again a

---

[101] [1963] 2 C.C.C. 295 (Que. C.A.).
[102] *R. v. Marple* (1973), 6 N.S.R. (2d) 389 (C.A.).
[103] (1954), 20 C.R. 301 (B.C.C.A.); see also *R. v. Pharo* (1970), 12 C.R.N.S. 151 (Ont. Co. Ct.) (alcoholic offender).
[104] (1971), 5 C.C.C. (2d) 366 (Ont. C.A.).

term of imprisonment would than be justified for the protection of society.

There are certain offences for which the penalties are occasionally inexplicably high. In *R. v. Malouf*,[105] there were convictions of indecent assault and attempted buggery. The accused was previously acquainted with his victim and had been smoking marijuana with him. The victim received painful bruises from the incident. Malouf, whose only relevant conviction was for assault causing bodily harm, was sentenced to three years concurrent on each charge.

The protection of the public was a factor which moved the court, in *R. v. Pascoe*,[106] to substitute a custodial sentence (12 months definite, 12 months indefinite) for the suspended sentence imposed at trial. Here the offender was a high grade mental defective with five previous convictions for indecent assault. But even with this record, the court appeared to base its decision upon the fact that Pascoe could receive psychiatric treatment while in custody and not upon the basis of deterring him or others like-minded.

Sentencing for individual deterrence is rare in this class of case but not unknown. In *R. v. Brooke*,[107] where there was a conviction for indecent assault upon the nine-year-old step-daughter of the accused, his criminal record disclosed, *inter alia*, a recent conviction for indecently assaulting the same girl. A sentence of one year definite plus 18 months indeterminate (together with an illegal sentence of two years' probation) was changed on appeal to two years less one day definite and two years less one day indeterminate in order that specific deterrence could be accomplished.

In *R. v. Madill*,[108] alcohol use was a mitigating factor for an accused with an excellent background, who in this instance, had been drinking continually for over seven hours. The willingness of the accused's wife to continue their marital relationship following his conviction was a mitigating factor. The sentence was reduced from 18 months to six months together with two years' probation.

Indecent assault may sometimes be an aggravating factor in a more serious offence such as, for example, breaking and entering. In this case the Crown may wish to proceed with the major offence only and rely upon the circumstance of the indecent assault as a reason to increase the

---

[105] (1976), 19 Crim. L.Q. 153 (Ont. C.A.).
[106] Unreported, October 9, 1974 (Ont. C.A.).
[107] Unreported, November 26, 1976 (Ont. C.A.).
[108] Unreported, May 12, 1976 (Ont. C.A.).

sentence usually imposed for break and enter, upon the theory that the assault is an aggravating factor in the case of the invasion of a private home — a place of security.[109] Care must, however, be taken to see that punishment is not imposed for conduct that has not been the subject of a trial.

3. SEXUAL RELATIONS WITH GIRL — UNDER THE AGE OF FOURTEEN

In *R. v. Skrettas,*[110] the accused pleaded guilty to carnal knowledge of a girl under the age of 14 and was sentenced to three years' imprisonment. The girl had told him she was 17 and she willingly engaged in intercourse. The Ontario Court of Appeal reduced the sentence to three months' imprisonment with probation for two years. It should be noted that this offence is occasionally committed by immigrants from other countries where the cultural standards are different from our own and this fact is taken into consideration in sentencing.

The range of sentence in such cases has been very wide. In *R. v. Taylor,*[111] the English Court of Appeal, Criminal Division, had occasion to discuss the general parameters of sentencing for this type of offence. (The offence in England is one of having sexual intercourse with a girl under 16.)

> At one end of that spectrum is the youth who stands in the dock, maybe 16, 17 or 18 years of age, who has had what started off as a virtuous friendship with a girl under the age of 16. That virtuous friendship has ended with their having sexual intercourse with one another. At the other end of the spectrum is the man in a supervisory capacity, a schoolmaster or social worker, who sets out deliberately to seduce a girl under the age of 16 who was in his charge. . . . Nowadays, most judges would take the view, and rightly take the view, that when there is a virtuous friendship which ends in unlawful sexual intercourse, it is inappropriate to pass sentences of a punitive nature. What is required is a warning to the youth to mend his ways. At the other end, a man in a supervisory capacity who abuses his position of trust for his sexual gratification, ought to get a sentence somewhere near the maximum allowed by law, which is two years' imprisonment. In between there come many degrees of guilt. A common type of offender is a youth who picks up a girl of loose morals at a dance, takes her out into the local park and, behind the

---

[109] *R. v. Brown,* unreported, October 3, 1974 (Ont. C.A.).
[110] (1970), 13 Crim. L.Q. 149 (Ont. C.A.).
[111] [1977] 3 All E.R. 527 at p. 529.

bushes, has sexual intercourse with her. That is the kind of offence which normally is dealt with by a fine. When an older man in his twenties, or older, goes off to a dance and picks up a young girl, he can expect to get a much stiffer fine, and if the girl is under 15 he can expect to go to prison for a short time. A young man who deliberately sets out to seduce a girl under the age of 16 can expect to go to detention. The older man who deliberately so sets out can expect to go to prison. Such is the wide variety of penalties which can be applied in this class of case.

In the case at hand the evidence disclosed "the girl was a wanton. Some of her activities in the way of oral sex show the extent to which she had become debauched almost certainly before she met any of these three applicants . . . the men . . . continue the debauching of the girl, knowing how young she was." Accordingly, short sentences of imprisonment were imposed.

In *R. v. Linda*[112] the victim of the crime was sexually experienced and in fact had been the aggressor. Sentence in this case was accordingly reduced.

In *R. v. Hanuschuk*[113] where the accused was a schoolteacher who had two acts of intercourse with his 13-year-old pupil, a sentence of two years less one day was imposed on appeal.

C. Offences Against Property

1. ROBBERY

The offence of robbery marks the demarcation line between offences against the person and offences against property, since it involves elements of both. As the common law history of this offence discloses, it was the fact that violence had been applied to the person of the victim that made robbery a heinous crime, the amount of money or value of the object taken being of secondary importance: *R. v. Webster and Martin.*[114] Although the maximum punishment for robbery is life imprisonment, Criminal Code, s. 303, the range of sentence appears to have its extreme limits between a 20-year sentence and a suspended sentence.

---

[112] (1924), 42 C.C.C. 110 (Alta.).
[113] Unreported, April 17, 1978 (Man. C.A.).
[114] (1958), 28 C.R. 81 (Ont. C.A.).

Despite the historical origin of the crime, nowadays one important factor in determining sentence is the amount involved. For example, in *R. v. Christie*[115] the two offenders were given terms of six months' imprisonment for a robbery with violence, the fruits of which were $7.

Age, too, is an important factor. In *R. v. Windsor et al.*[116] the two accused, both 16 years old, were convicted of armed robbery. There had been four weeks of pre-trial custody. Both were of previously good character. The court refused a Crown appeal and agreed with the sentence of three months' imprisonment, but added a term of probation.

In *R. v. McKenzie,*[117] an original sentence of two and one-half years was reduced to one year where the amount involved was a few dollars. See also *R. v. MacDonald et al.,*[118] where the court distinguished between "robberies of the serious kind and those of less serious kind." No serious violence was done in the robbery of $280 from a small store, no harm was done to any person, and the amount was termed "not substantial". All but $10 was recovered. Noting co-operation with the police and a guilty plea, together with difficult personal backgrounds, the court reduced the sentences to one year with two years' probation.

Where the offender has a serious criminal record, the sentences will be comparatively more severe, the crime indicating a great danger and the record showing confirmed criminality. In *R. v. Jourdain and Kudyba,*[119] the victim's wallet, watch and one dollar in cash was taken by force. The appropriate sentence was seen by the court to be four years and two years respectively for the offenders. Also in *R. v. McDonald,*[120] the accused robbed a woman of $40; the court refused to interfere with the sentence of eight years where the criminal record was lengthy, even though the offender was 22 years old.

In *R. v. Malcolm,*[121] a sentence of four years was upheld upon a man who mugged another in a parking lot, kicking and punching him and taking his wallet, which contained $90. The appellant had a lengthy record which included previous robbery offences. A sentence of five years was upheld upon an appellant who entered his victim's apartment

---

[115] (1956), 115 C.C.C. 55 (Sask. C.A.).
[116] Unreported, December 30, 1976 (Ont. C.A.).
[117] (1952), 6 W.W.R. 192 (Sask. C.A.).
[118] (1973), 16 Crim. L.Q. 143 (Ont. C.A.).
[119] (1957), 25 W.W.R. 160 (Man. C.A.).
[120] (1969), 12 C.R.N.S. 215 (Ont. C.A.).
[121] Unreported, April 14, 1978 (B.C.C.A.).

and beat and kicked him and then robbed him of $40 and his automobile. His lengthy record included similar convictions: *R. v. Sponsor.*[122]

In *R. v. King,*[123] a sentence of four and a half years was reduced to three years for the robbery of a jug milk store involving $131 taken at knife point by an accused who had obviously been drinking. The 22-year-old accused had a "considerable record", but no previous criminal violence and no previous penitentiary sentence.

A mitigating factor in robbery is that the offence was of a spontaneous nature. In *R. v. Kelly,*[124] the Ontario Court of Appeal substituted a sentence of three months definite and two years' probation for an original sentence of two years less one day, where the accused committed the offence on a busy street while intoxicated. The fresh evidence on appeal made it clear the offence was impulsive and an isolated event in light of the accused's background. This factor operates even in more serious cases of robbery. In *R. v. Dumont and Dumont,*[125] terms were reduced because the crime was not planned or premeditated.

The fact that the method used shows "lack of sophistication" is often a mitigating factor. In *R. v. Johnston,*[126] the accused was not disguised in any way during the bank robbery and stayed in the locality of his crime.

The character of the victim is not a mitigating factor: see *Duval v. The Queen,*[127] where five years was imposed for robbing homosexuals of their jewellery and *R. v. Reid,*[128] where nine months' imprisonment was imposed upon a drug dealer who made off at knife-point with another dealer's purchase money. However the character of the victim may be an aggravating factor: the Manitoba Court of Appeal in *R. v. Iwaniw; R. v. Overton,*[129] considered that a taxi driver's occupation made him more vulnerable to attack and therefor such attacks should be dealt with more severely in sentence. In this case the main actor in the crime had his sentence increased on appeal from 18 months to four years.

Iwaniw may also be cited for the obvious proposition that, in group robberies, the accused who initiated the crime will be punished more severely than the one who merely follows his lead. The follower in

---

[122] Unreported, April 14, 1978 (B.C.C.A.).
[123] Unreported, June 23, 1977 (Ont. C.A.).
[124] Unreported, September 16, 1974.
[125] (1970), 12 Crim. L.Q. 344 (Sask. C.A.).
[126] (1976), 18 Crim. L.Q. 286 (Ont. C.A.).
[127] (1970), 15 C.R.N.S. 140 (Que. C.A.).
[128] (1974), 26 C.R.N.S. 292 (Que. C.A.).
[129] (1959), 127 C.C.C. 40; *R. v. Potts,* unreported, December 13, 1976 (Ont. C.A.).

Iwaniw, although convicted of attempted robbery, received five years on a guilty plea at trial. In considering that his accomplice supplied the gun, suggested the entire scheme, directed the cab driver to an isolated spot and initiated the actual attack, the court substituted a term of two and one-half years. In this regard, see also *R. v. Bailey; R. v. Protheroe,*[130] where equal terms of seven years upon both Bailey and Protheroe for a vicious attack on an elderly couple were approved, even though Bailey had an insignificant record and Protheroe had a lengthy one because it appeared Bailey led Protheroe throughout. The two elements in effect cancelled each other out.

Despite the seriousness of any robbery as such, personal factors are given careful, if limited, consideration. It appears that though a jail sentence is usually warranted, a first sentence of imprisonment (even where there is a criminal record that did not result in a custodial term) should ordinarily be in a reformatory, except for the most serious robberies.[131]

Recently, courts have been taking steps to look beyond the seriousness of the crime itself and take into account individual factors. The most important personal factor that is considered in a robbery case is the age of the offender. A youthful offender will receive a shorter sentence, often in a reformatory. The sentence upon youthful offenders for robbery should not be imposed for the purpose of general deterrence but rather should be directed toward rehabilitation: *R. v. Casey.*[132]

In *R. v. Reading,*[133] a sentence of 23 months and two years' probation for armed robbery of a taxi driver was reduced on appeal to one year and two years' probation. The accused was a 17-year-old first offender and the offence was the result of pressures and alcohol abuse.

In *R. v. LaSorda and Cirella*[134] an eight-year term was lowered to four years for young men aged 21 years. The robbery for which they were convicted included a vicious assault upon a victim of advanced years who was still in hospital at the time of the appeal. Penitentiary sentences

---

[130] [1970] 4 C.C.C. 291 (Ont. C.A.).

[131] *R. v. Ferguson* (1971), 14 Crim. L.Q. 271 (Ont. C.A.); *R. v. Scarrow* (1972), 15 Crim. L.Q. 112 (Ont. C.A.); *R. v. Francis* (1970), 13 Crim. L.Q. 12 (Ont. C.A.); *R. v. Elliot* (1976), 19 Crim. L.Q. 25 (Ont. C.A.); *R. v. Dunkley* (1976), 19 Crim. L.Q. 277 (Ont. C.A.).

[132] (1977), 20 Crim. L. Q. 145 (Ont. C.A.); *R. v. Vandale and Maciejewski* (1974), 21 C.C.C. (2d) 250 (Ont. C.A.).

[133] Unreported, March 7, 1978 (Ont. C.A.).

[134] (1971), 14 Crim. L.Q. 11 (Ont. C.A.).

may be necessary in such cases, but even then they will be shorter than they might otherwise have been.[135]

Bank robbers are regarded by the courts as meriting more severe sentence than robbers of individuals. One reason this is so is that a bank robbery generally involves greater premeditation, planning and audacity. In *R. v. Vigeant* the court said that banks are "particularly exposed to crimes of this nature."[136] There are also higher stakes involved, therefore the principle of deterrence would call for high penalties to discourage those who might be like-minded. One common feature of bank robberies is that they usually involve danger to more than one person, *i.e.,* innocent bystanders and employees and therefore the danger to the public is greater. In *R. v. Farrow*[137] five years was imposed on four counts of bank robbery, one of forgery and one of uttering for a 30-year-old accused with a record. During the robberies threats of violence had been used. The court was of the view that notwithstanding that the accused was not armed, the bank robbery itself might be regarded as a serious offence and cited, as well, the increasing prevalence of this particular crime. Another factor that may account for more severe sentences is that banks are powerful, almost sacred institutions in a society religiously devoted to the protection of property. The greater seriousness accorded to a bank robbery is not however totally understandable, since an individual cannot sustain the loss of valuables as easily as an established financial institution.

Sentences for bank robberies have ranged from 20 years to a suspended sentence. This latter disposition was substituted by the Quebec Court of Appeal for a term of three months in prison imposed at trial on two first offenders who had robbed a credit union with threats of violence.[138] In *R. v. LaPierre,*[139] the accused had a record of break and enter offences prior to the charge of robbery of a credit union; the Quebec Court of Appeal increased the sentence from 15 months to two years. In *R. v. Warren and Kozack,*[140] an offender was sentenced to ten years' imprisonment even though no firearms were involved. The highest end of the scale for robbery is reserved for those offences which parallel the Great Train

---

[135] *R. v. LaSorda* (1972), 14 Crim. L.Q. 11 (Man. C.A.).
[136] (1974), 19 C.C.C. (2d) 512 (Man. C.A.).
[137] Unreported, November 18, 1976 (Ont. C.A.).
[138] *R. v. Dupuis and Presseau,* [1966] 2 C.C.C. 44.
[139] (1972), 17 C.R.N.S. 247.
[140] (1970), 11 C.R.N.S. 217 (Ont. C.A.).

Robbery in scale;[141] the offence was meticulously planned and nearly all the money stolen, over one million dollars, was never recovered.

Whatever the reasons, there is a different range of sentence for robberies of individuals, small stores and financial institutions. The high end of the range for an attack on an individual is seven years, as illustrated by the facts of *Bailey and Protheroe,* where an elderly couple aged 75 and 76 years were extensively beaten in their homes, one of them suffering permanent injuries, by two males 18 and 22. An offender convicted of a robbery and an attempted robbery of an individual, both times using a loaded and cocked revolver, received four years concurrent in each offence: *R. v. Samaras.* [142] A mitigating factor was the absence of any criminal record for the offender. In *R. v. Johnston* [143] where the bank robbery involved relatively little sophistication and despite a criminal record, the sentence was only three years. The low end of the appropriate range for armed robbery, in *R. v. Brennan and Jensen* [144] in Nova Scotia, was stated to be three years' imprisonment in a case where the offenders had good backgrounds. Such a sentence would be "normal" except "in the most exceptional circumstances".

The range for small business or variety store robberies is usually from one year to six years, where little or no violence is involved in the commission of the offence. Where the crime was not premeditated and no weapon was used, the sentence will be at the low end of that range. In *R. v. Smith,* [145] the offender had been drinking all day and later robbed a pizza store by threatening the manager; he had no record and was a family man and these circumstances influenced the Court of Appeal to impose one year's imprisonment plus two years' probation. In *R. v. MacDonald et al.,* [146] no serious violence was used in robbing a variety store and all the accused co-operated with the police. The sentence imposed was one year's imprisonment with two years' probation. Where a weapon is involved, the sentence will be higher. In *R. v. Wallace,* [147] the Ontario Court of Appeal imposed a term of four years for the robbery of a Mac's Milk Store with a shotgun, because of a long record of violence

---

[141] *R. v. Davison, DeRosie and MacArthur* (1974), 20 C.C.C. (2d) 424 (Ont. C.A.).
[142] (1971), 16 C.R.N.S. 1 (Ont. C.A.).
[143] (1976), 18 Crim. L. Q. 286 (Ont. C.A.).
[144] (1975), 23 C.C.C. (2d) 403 (N.S.C.A.)
[145] Unreported, May 7, 1974 (Ont. C.A.).
[146] (1973), 16 Crim. L. Q. 143 (Ont. C.A.).
[147] (1973), 11 C.C.C. (2d) 95.

on the part of the accused. In *R. v. Webster and Martin,*[148] two teenagers who robbed a gas station with a rifle were sentenced to two years less a day when it appeared that the older man who had led them in the robbery had, at a separate trial, been acquitted.

In *R. v. Gugic*[149] the accused used a loaded sawed-off shotgun in a restaurant robbery. It was noted that in a case of an armed robbery where the weapon was loaded, the factor of rehabilitation must be weighed with that of general deterrence.

In *R. v. Chiasson*[150] the accused robbed the pastor of a church while masked and armed; shots were fired. The accused had a record of some substance and had been recommitted to custody on two occasions for parole violations. The court said: "A normal sentence in this Province for such an offence where the accused has no previous criminal record, is one of not less than three years and, where there is a criminal record, a substantially greater sentence." Five years' imprisonment was imposed. The actual firing of a weapon at a victim, even if no injury is caused, will greatly increase the sentence.

In *R. v. Jones; R. v. Zuter; R. v. Snead*[151] one year consecutive sentences were imposed for a series of up to six (in the case of one accused) armed robberies of gas stations and grocery stores. In *R. v. Arthur*[152] a sentence of two years less one day definite and two years less one day indeterminate was imposed on an 18-year-old man who was a first offender and pleaded guilty to five charges of armed robbery.

Where no weapon is used a distinction will be made and the penalties imposed will be lower, as in *R. v. Dumesnil*[153] where an accused robbed a bank without a weapon and had one previous conviction for trafficking in drugs. A sentence of four years was reduced to two years less a day determinate and two years less one day indeterminate.

The fact that the offender used only an imitation weapon (starter's pistol) is a factor that will lead to a lower sentence — two years was imposed in *R. v. Johnston.*[154]

---

[148] (1958), 28 C.R. 81 (Ont. C.A.); see also *R. v. Pigeon,* [1970] 2 C.C.C. 177 (Que. C.A.) and the range of sentences discussed therein.

[149] Unreported, October 21, 1976 (Ont. C.A.).

[150] (1975), 24 C.C.C. (2d) 159 (N.B.C.A.). See also *R. v. Williams* (1976), 3 C.R. (3d) S-50 (Ont. C.A.); but *cf. R. v. Dunkley* (1976), 3 C.R. (3d) S-51 (Ont. C.A.).

[151] (1975), 18 Crim. L. Q. 287 (Ont. C.A.).

[152] Unreported, September 17, 1975 (Ont. C.A.).

[153] Unreported, February 15, 1977 (Ont. C.A.).

[154] (1976), 18 Crim. L.Q. 286 (Ont. C.A.).

Where serious harm is done to the proprietor of the store during the course of the robbery, the sentence will be much more severe. In *R. v. Miller and Couvreur,*[155] two men beat the victim with a crowbar so violently that he was a "human vegetable" at the time the appeal was heard. The majority of the court refused to interfere with sentences of 15 years and ten years respectively.

2. EXTORTION

In *R. v. Pitcher*[156] there was a plea of guilty to both extortion and breaking and entering. A phone call was made saying that the victim's son would die of an overdose of heroin if $10,000 was not delivered to a specific location. With the cooperation of police a "dummy package" was placed pursuant to instructions given. Some children intervened and picked up the package and the attempt was not fruitful. Later that day the accused phoned the victim and identified himself as the original caller and apologized. When apprehended, however, he denied his involvement. While in custody it was discovered his fingerprints matched those found in a garage following a break-in one and a half years earlier. He had a previous record of possession of stolen property. The majority held that the extortion offence was a serious one and that, in the interests of deterrence, and in order to keep the province free of such crimes, a heavy sentence was called for. One year of imprisonment was imposed. Branca J.A., dissented, noting that had the accused not phoned his victim and identified himself it was not likely that he would have been caught or suffered any consequences. The public needed no protection from the accused, he argued, as he had realized the gravity of his act and would not in future repeat it.

3. ARSON

The maximum punishment for the offence of arson is 14 years or five years depending upon the nature of the object set fire to: Criminal Code, s. 389(1) and (2).

Since reported cases for the offence of arson are fortunately rare, it is

---

[155] (1972), 8 C.C.C. (2d) 97 (Man. C.A.).
[156] (1976), 19 Crim. L.Q. 158 (B.C.C.A.).

difficult to determine a range of sentence but four groups of circumstances are discernible:

(A) Where the offender is a pyromaniac or mentally disturbed the total sentence will usually be high — often more than one such offence is before the court. The Ontario Court of Appeal in *R. v. Roberts,*[157] on a reference by the Minister of Justice for a reconsideration of the sentence imposed, reduced a total time on nine counts from 24 years to 12 years upon hearing fresh psychiatric evidence. The individual sentence ranged from four years to two years. The prospects for treatment of this kind of offender often determine the length of sentence he will receive.

But this is not always the case, however. In *R. v. Menkes,*[158] the accused was charged with two arson charges where substantial damage ensued but no one was hurt, together with a charge involving the use of a weapon. He had a lengthy record consisting of 16 convictions but none relating to violence. A psychiatric assessment indicated that he suffered from paranoic schizophrenia at the time of the offences. Other inmates were intolerant of him because of his problems. The court took the sentence that was imposed, namely, seven years, and reduced it to a maximum reformatory term, so that he could have both treatment and less exposure to others who might abuse him, saying that this term was within the proper range of sentence for these offences.

In *R. v. Chamberlain,*[159] the court had to deal with an offender who was described as "near-mentally defective". He had tried to burn down an apartment building containing 450 tenants and caused damage in excess of $25,000. A five-year sentence, though termed "lengthy", was upheld in the interests of public safety and with the hope that psychiatric treatment might benefit him.

The English cases are helpful. In *R. v. Woolland,*[160] five concurrent life sentences were upheld for a psychopathic personality who refused to co-operate in any treatment for his disorder. Where the offender is willing to co-operate, as was the accused in *Roberts,* the English courts will show some leniency and make the sentence appropriate to the prospects for treatment. In *R. v. Cash,*[161] where Cash received seven years on two counts, the court was content to leave the matter of release

---

[157] [1963] 1 C.C.C. 27.
[158] (1977), 19 Crim. L.Q. 278 (Ont. C.A.).
[159] (1970), 13 Crim. L.Q. 434 (Ont. C.A.).
[160] (1967), 51 Cr. App. R. 65.
[161] (1969), 53 Cr. App. R. 483.

to the Parole Board; so also *R. v. Turner,*[162] where a 17-year-old received five years on three counts.

In *R. v. Dudka*[163] where a 17-year-old offender, with a previous conviction for armed robbery, set fire to a friend's car at his request so that he might make a claim on his insurance, the sentence was 18 months' imprisonment together with 18 months' probation.

In *R. v. Sherwood*[164] a sentence of two years in a penitentiary was imposed on appeal for an accused who was convicted of four charges of arson and one of attempted arson. All sentences were concurrent as the offences took place in a single month. The court noted that, with one exception, the fires were started in unused vacated buildings. The accused, who was mentally disturbed, was a member of a volunteer fire department in the area and indeed was president of the association of volunteer fire workers. He set the fires, amongst other reasons, in order to get the satisfaction of extinguishing them. The court would have considered a much more severe sentence were it not for the fact that, with one exception, there was no danger to persons occupying the premises. This case may usefully be contrasted with *R. v. Timms,*[165] where a five-year sentence was reduced to two years upon a man with a serious criminal record and where the evidence of his disturbance was not encouraging. In that case the court noted the fire occurred in occupied premises causing considerable damage and risk of injury to persons who were inhabiting it.

(B) Where the building is set fire to by the beneficiary of an insurance policy on the premises, there is a variation in sentence: in *R. v. Scozzaro*[166] the Crown appealed a sentence of nine months imposed on an accused in this category. Although the court would have imposed a greater sentence if it had dealt with the case at first instance, the accused had an unblemished record and the trial judge had considered all the requisite elements and therefore his original sentence was not disturbed. These cases should be compared with the maximum punishment of 14 years imposed on the prime mover in a conspiracy of apparently professional arsonists who set fires for a commission on the insurance moneys.[167]

A fine of $2000, together with probation, was upheld in circumstances

---

[162] (1966), 51 Cr. App. R. 72.
[163] Unreported, November 14, 1975 (B.C.C.A.).
[164] Unreported, April 7, 1975 (B.C.C.A.).
[165] Unreported, April 1, 1974 (B.C.C.A.).
[166] Unreported, February 19, 1975 (Ont. C.A.).
[167] *R. v. Jarjour,* [1965] Que. Q.B. 639.

similar to *R. v. Scozzaro*[168] where a financially embarrassed accused decided to burn down his own house in order to collect the insurance: *R. v. Sims and Bull.*[169] The court noted that the net result of the crime was that the accused did not receive any insurance money for his act, that he lost the equity in his house and that he still had to pay the mortgage that was on it.

(C) Occasionally, the accused has set fire to an acquaintance's home or property for the purpose of revenge: in *MacLeod v. The Queen,*[170] MacLeod had become intoxicated at a friend's home, quarreled with the occupants and left to return later and burn down his house after the occupants had fled. The court held that three years' imprisonment imposed at trial was not at all excessive.

In *R. v. Boyd,*[171] the accused had arued with her husband and during the argument had ignited his clothing which resulted in their home burning to the ground. No one was hurt. Despite evidence that the particular offence was prevalent in the area, the sentence was reduced to 30 days' imprisonment.

In *R. v. Hockin*[172] a suspended sentence and probation for a period of two years with a condition ensuring psychiatric counselling was imposed on an accused who, without premeditation or any profit motive, in the course of a domestic dispute, set fire to the trailer in which he and his common-law wife were living. He was responding well to treatment at the time of his appeal.

(D) Where the crime is really in the nature of mere vandalism, the sentences will be lower. In *R. v. Losey,*[173] a 17-year-old damaged a school in the amount of $68,000. Upon a charge of wilfully setting a fire, he was sentenced to two years less a day, which was reduced on appeal to one year's imprisonment characterized as a sufficient deterrent to others.

In *R. v. Carr*[174] the conviction of arson of the accused's mobile home was affirmed, but sentence of two and a half-year's imprisonment was reduced to one of nine months, because the 25-year-old accused man had no record for similar offences and had been drinking at the time. Alcohol is a common mitigating factor in these offences.

---

[168] *Supra,* footnote 166.
[169] Unreported, January 9, 1976 (B.C.C.A.).
[170] [1968] 2 C.C.C. 365 (P.E.I.C.A.).
[171] Unreported, November 26, 1976 (Ont. C.A.).
[172] Unreported, December 13, 1976 (B.C.C.A.).
[173] (1972), 15 Crim. L.Q. 16 (Ont. C.A.).
[174] (1978), 23 N.B.R. (2d) 327 (C.A.).

4. BREAK AND ENTER

The maximum sentence for this offence is severe, being life imprisonment if a dwelling-house is broken into and 14 years for other locations: Criminal Code, s. 306. The range appears to vary between a suspended sentence and five years' imprisonment.

Where any of a number of mitigating factors are present, *i.e.,* the accused has no record, a good background and the amount involved is trivial, or only one offence, then a suspended sentence is usual.[175]

Often there are some aggravating factors. A common one is a string of similar offences committed before apprehension. This by cumulative effect may lead to a term of imprisonment. See *R. v. Garcia and Silva,*[176] where three months definite and twelve months indeterminate were imposed for one offence with three other offences "taken into consideration".

Theft is often an element of the charge. The value of the goods stolen either mitigates or aggravates the offence of break and enter. One can compare *R. v. Garcia and Silva* with *R. v. Prieduls,*[177] where a majority of the Ontario Court of Appeal refused to disturb a sentence of nine months determinate and three months indeterminate with probation for two years, upon a young first offender attending university whose carefully planned break-in would, if successful, have cost the merchant victim $20,000. In *R. v. Lemire,*[178] where an adult accused with a lengthy record involving thefts committed a sophisticated and planned break and enter of an auctioneer's premises and stole between $100,000 and $200,000 worth of goods, a four and a half year sentence was approved.

Whether or not the crime was premeditated will also be a factor. In *R. v. Murray,*[179] an intoxicated youth broke a store window and did nominal damage; despite a lengthy previous record, a sentence of three months was imposed in light of the trifling and impulsive nature of the offence.

As in certain other offences, intoxication is generally a mitigating

---

[175] *R. v. Davenport,* unreported, February 17, 1977 (Ont. C.A.).

[176] [1970] 3 C.C.C. 124 (Ont. C.A.); see also *R. v. McLafferty* (1973), 15 Crim. L.Q. 371 (Ont. C.A.); *R. v. Cope* (1973), 15 Crim. L.Q. 371 (Ont. C.A.); *R. v. Atlookan and Atlookan* (1972), 14 Crim. L.Q. 395 (Ont. C.A.); *R. v. Hawley* (1973), 15 Crim. L.Q. 258 (Ont. C.A.); *R. v. Deugo* (1972), 15 Crim. L.Q. 259 (Ont. C.A.).

[177] Unreported, June 6, 1975 (Ont. C.A.).

[178] Unreported, June 8, 1977 (B.C.C.A.).

[179] (1960), 32 W.W.R. 312 (Sask. C.A.).

factor in break and enter offences: *R. v. Ward.*[180] A past record is, as always, an aggravating factor and may lead to imprisonment. In *R. v. Brookes,*[181] an offender with six previous convictions received a suspended sentence at trial, having been of good behaviour from the time of conviction to the time of sentence. The Ontario Court of Appeal substituted one year definite and one year indeterminate.

The commission of these offences by first offenders is common in these cases. Usually, in such circumstances, a suspended sentence and probation is considered appropriate. In *R. v. Caja and Billings,*[182] sentences of 60 and 30 days intermittent were reduced to time served and a term of probation. The accused, who were 18 and 20 years old, stole $3,200 worth of auto parts from a garage. All the property was recovered.

Even in cases where there are multiple charges, which is often the case, imprisonment is avoided. In *R. v. Griffin*[183] the accused pleaded guilty to two charges of break and enter of commercial premises and received three months' imprisonment together with two years' probation. A first offender, he had already spent several days in pre-sentence custody, and had served 16 days of his sentence at the time he was released on bail. The appeal court substituted time served plus probation for the original sentence. The court commented that in the case of youthful first offenders (where the offences are not "numerous") custodial sentences are to be avoided.

Where the previous criminal record discloses that the accused is a "professional burglar", *R. v. Belegratis,*[184] this will justify a very serious penalty; five years' imprisonment was imposed when a previous sentence of incarceration was not sufficient to deter the offender. In *R. v. O'Sullivan*[185] a similar criminal record did not lead to this conclusion, however. The court accepted that the accused's difficulties with the law all stemmed from the fact that he was a heroin addict and that he would do anything to get drugs. Since the addiction itself holds out some hope for his future freedom from the drive to crime a sentence of 18 months definite and 18 months indeterminate was altered to delete the indeterminate portion.

---

[180] (1976), 14 N.S.R. (2d) 96 (C.A.).
[181] [1970] 4 C.C.C. 377 (Ont. C.A.).
[182] (1977), 36 C.C.C. (2d) 401 (Ont. C.A.).
[183] Unreported, June 15, 1977 (Ont. C.A.).
[184] Unreported, November 5, 1975 (B.C.C.A.).
[185] Unreported, June 2, 1975 (B.C.C.A.).

The higher end of the range is for those offences that border on or amount to robbery. In *R. v. Harrell,*[186] the accused broke into a house and stole $70 and a revolver. The householder encountered the accused and was threatened with a gun by the accused in making good his escape. The original sentence of five years imposed at trial was reduced to three years by the Ontario Court of Appeal. The Court noted that a past record for break and enter was "stale", being 11 years old, except for one offence committed three years previously.

A 30-day sentence in *R. v. Brymer*[187] was reduced to time served following conviction of a young first offender for stealing a coat valued at about $180. The court refused to impose a discharge because the offence appeared to have been planned, deliberate and involved a coat of such value.

5. THEFT

The Criminal Code makes a distinction on the basis of the value of the article stolen. For theft of a testamentary instrument or where the value of the thing stolen exceeds $200, ten years is the maximum. For articles under $200 in value, two years is the maximum: Criminal Code, s. 294. These provisions obviously reflect and support the judicial practice of imposing heavier sentences where the value of what is stolen is relatively high compared to those cases involving articles of trifling value.

The latter category is most often found in shoplifting cases. In this area more frequent use is being made of the discharge provisions in the Criminal Code. Thus a 16-year-old girl who had a good scholastic record and committed two petty thefts during a period of family upheaval received a conditional discharge: *R. v. McInnis.*[188] A 37-year-old family man who stole an item worth $1.09 was given an absolute discharge: *R. v. Marcon.*[189] The Ontario Court of Appeal would have given an absolute discharge to a man who stole $10 worth of potato chips for his children had the court then felt that such a disposition was in its power: *R. v. Stafrace.*[190] These cases may be compared with *R. v. Dunton,*[191] where a

---

[186] (1973), 12 C.C.C. (2d) 480 (Ont. C.A.).
[187] Unreported, December 18, 1975 (Ont. C.A.).
[188] (1973), 13 C.C.C. (2d) 471 (Ont. C.A.).
[189] (1974), 18 C.C.C. (2d) 575 (Ont. C.A.).
[190] (1972), 10 C.C.C. (2d) 181 (Ont. C.A.).
[191] (1973), 24 C.R.N.S. 116 (Ont. C.A.).

47-year-old accused of impeccable background had a 30-day jail sentence varied to a suspended sentence for theft of a sum under $50 committed during the course of his employment. The court considered and rejected the suggestion of a discharge on the grounds that "it would be inappropriate in the case of a man of forty-seven with the background this man possesses", a somewhat enigmatic statement which the accused no doubt found enlightening. But the value of the property must bear some rational relationship to the sentence.[192]

This view is not by any means universally held. In *R. v. McGregor*[193] an accused broke and entered school premises while armed with a semi-automatic pistol which was loaded with seven rounds in the clip. He was sentenced to two years' imprisonment for breaking and entering, one year consecutive for possession of a weapon for purposes dangerous to the public peace, and one year concurrent for the possession of an unregistered firearm. The court was of the view that the sentence imposed for breaking and entering was light, and noted that they would have sustained a longer sentence; the Crown had not sought to have the sentence increased. Despite these views, the consecutive sentence regarding the weapon was made concurrent. It is not clear whether the court meant that the use of a weapon was not an aggravating factor or merely that any increase in penalty by reason of this aggravation ought to be reflected in the principal offence. The latter interpretation is unlikely, as on its face it would seem that punishment ought to be for the offence that related to the actual harm involved.

The court in *Dunton* disapproved of the imposition of a fine in cases of theft, stating that this would be the equivalent of a licence fee. Nevertheless, fines for shoplifters are still used very frequently in the lower courts and have been approved by a court of appeal: *R. v. Sanchez-Pino.*[194]

A problem that often faces the court is what to do with those offenders who continually and persistently engage in petty theft, or who do so calculatingly, as opposed to impulsively. It appears that a term of imprisonment should be imposed upon this category of offenders but that this term should not be a lengthy one: *R. v. Pasternak; R. v. McNeil; R. v. Andrews*[195] (three months for "hardened petty offenders").

---

[192] *R. v. Chaplin* (1978), 1 C.R. (3d) S-44 (Ont. C.A.).
[193] Unreported, June 28, 1975 (B.C.C.A.).
[194] (1973), 11 C.C.C. (2d) 53 (Ont. C.A.).
[195] (1961), 36 W.W.R. 423 (B.C.C.A.); see also *R. v. Anderson* (1972), 56 Cr. App. R. 863.

The previously mentioned cases involved the theft of small articles of food or clothing. Where the theft involves a larger item and the offence was premeditated and well planned, the offender with a bad record will not fare as well. In *R. v. Dawdy,*[196] the offender received one and one-half years' imprisonment for a theft of merchandise valued at over $200. The same course was followed for auto thieves with a record of similar offences: *R. v. Pezzo.*[197]

Minor property offences which did not endanger the victim's safety, committed by a young "casual" offender who had a number of previous similar convictions, but who was not committed to a criminal career, were dealt with by a short "exemplary" sentence of imprisonment plus probation: *Gouchie v. The Queen.*[198]

If an accused person, after his apprehension, has been of assistance to the police and has helped them to recover stolen property, this fact is often taken into consideration in imposing sentence. But the mere fact that some of the property has been recovered does not in itself necessarily mitigate the offence: *R. v. Hatfield.*[199]

A different category altogether involves thefts of large amounts by those in a position of trust to the victims. The range for this type of theft appears to be from nine months to nine years.

Since such an accused is usually one of previous good character, the task of the courts is made more difficult. In *R. v. Laroche,*[200] a municipal treasurer who had stolen substantial amounts over a four-year period had her sentence of nine months' imprisonment affirmed on appeal. Apparently a mitigating factor was the offender's poor state of health.

The court in *R. v. Spiller,*[201] focused on the need to deter employees of financial institutions and other large corporations from stealing from their employers; accordingly an original sentence of three years' imprisonment was increased to six years for a bank teller convicted of stealing $492,000.

The theft by a solicitor from his clients of three to four hundred thousand dollars through elaborate schemes was looked upon by the Ontario Court of Appeal as a particularly serious offence: *R. v. Gruson,*[202]

---

[196] (1973), 12 C.C.C. (2d) 477 (Ont. C.A.).
[197] (1972), 9 C.C.C. (2d) 530 (Ont. C.A.).
[198] (1975), 1 C.R. (3d) S-33 (N.S.C.A.).
[199] [1937] O.W.N. 559 (C.A.).
[200] [1965] 2 C.C.C. 29 (Ont. C.A.).
[201] [1969] 4 C.C.C. 211 (B.C.C.A.).
[202] [1963] 1 C.C.C. 240 (Ont. C.A.).

a three-year sentence imposed at trial on 26 counts of theft was increased to nine years.

6. POSSESSION OF STOLEN GOODS

The Criminal Code makes the same distinctions about value in the possession of stolen goods as it does in theft: Criminal Code, s. 313. The penalties are the same as for theft. The same variables reviewed above also operate here.

A discharge is appropriate where the offence amounts to little more than a foolish prank: *R. v. Fallofield,*[203] where a member of the armed forces with no record had been found in possession of small scraps of stolen carpet.

The courts do not consider that the subsequent possessor merits as harsh a punishment as the original thief: *R. v. Roddick,*[204] where a conditional discharge was substituted for a suspended sentence for possession of a stolen auto taken by the co-accused. Though no reported case deals with the problem, it is doubtful if the same distinction between thief and possessor would be made for a professional fence.

For possession over $200 the court is less willing to use the discharge provisions. In *R. v. MacWilliam,*[205] the accused bought a stolen T.V. set although he was apparently a man of means. Even considering the fact the appellant was well respected in the community, the court imposed a 30-day intermittent sentence.

For repeated offenders involved in well-planned schemes imprisonment is inevitable: *R. v. Brookes,*[206] where the offender received one year definite and one year indefinite for possession of goods stolen from a department store.

D. Offences Relating To Currency

The maximum sentence for these offences is 14 years: Criminal Code, ss. 407, 408, and 410.

---

[203] (1973), 13 C.C.C. (2d) 450 (B.C.C.A.).
[204] Unreported, April 11, 1974 (Ont. C.A.).
[205] Unreported, October 4, 1974 (Ont. C.A.).
[206] [1970] 4 C.C.C. 377 (Ont. C.A.).

The courts take a very serious view of charges involving currency. The usual range in reported cases lies between six months and six years, and can be longer.

The one who actually manufactures counterfeit money is treated more severely than those who utter the finished product. In *R. v. Gross,*[207] the Ontario Court of Appeal reduced a sentence of ten years to six years for the instigator of an amateurish scheme of counterfeiting; the accused had no previous record. The inference here is that a professional counterfeiter or one with a record of previous similar offences would suffer a much stiffer penalty. In *R. v. Sonsalla,*[208] circumstances showed that the accused was not likely to be before the courts again. Nevertheless a term of four years' imprisonment was imposed.

The two factors influencing for uttering or possession of counterfeit money are the record of the accused and the amount involved. Where a first offender was found with an appreciable sum in fake bills, six months' imprisonment has been imposed: see *R. v. Zezima,*[209] and *R. v. Jones,*[210] where the cases in this area are canvassed. The English tariff is reviewed in *R. v. Caughie.*[211] In *R. v. Twitchin,*[212] a sentence of one year together with probation for a year was imposed on a first offender found in possession of 24 forged $20 bills.

Where the accused was convicted of conspiracy to possess more than one and a quarter million dollars of American currency and was of good background a sentence of four years was imposed: *R. v. Gallo.*[213]

Shorter sentences have been imposed but in these cases special circumstances applied. In *R. v. Boisvert,*[214] an offender received one week in jail and a $100 fine for an offence involving a single $10 bill. Apparently in *Boisvert,* the Crown appealed the sentence one year after it was passed, making the appeal court reluctant to vary it. Similarly where the Crown had not asked for imprisonment at trial, the Ontario Court of Appeal substituted a one-day jail sentence plus a fine of $2,500 for a two-year suspended sentence at trial: *R. v. Agozzino.*[215]

Lengthy terms have also been imposed where the subject-matter of

---

[207] (1972), 9 C.C.C. (2d) 122 (Ont. C.A.).
[208] (1971), 15 C.R.N.S. 99 (Que. C.A.).
[209] (1970), 13 Crim. L.Q. 153 (Que. C.A.).
[210] (1974), 17 C.C.C. (2d) 31 (P.E.I.C.A.).
[211] (1969), 53 Cr. App. R. 642.
[212] (1970), 13 Crim. L.Q. 295 (Ont. C.A.).
[213] Unreported, June 20, 1977 (B.C.C.A.).
[214] (1970), 13 Crim. L.Q. 153 (Que. C.A.).
[215] [1970] 1 C.C.C. 380 (Ont. C.A.).

the charge was not currency, but cheques and assorted revenue paper and the equipment for manufacturing such items: *R. v. Pilpenko.*[216]

E. Fraud And False Pretences

There are several sections for fraud and false pretences within the Criminal Code and the maximum punishments for these offences range from ten years for the offence of simple fraud to six months for pretending to practice witchcraft.

The difficulty in arriving at a tariff for these offences is that the most common types to come before the courts, for example the "bad cheque artist", are seldom reported. The usual mitigating and aggravating factors found in the theft section may be of some assistance, although it should be remembered that the passing of a bad cheque or other simple fraud involves aspects of premeditation that may well be lacking in shoplifting cases.

The most common fraud cases reported involve schemes either to defraud the public or shareholders in a company. The sentencing for such offences range from a suspended sentence to five years.

The appellant in *R. v. Riordan,*[217] had his sentence reduced from six months to 30 days with probation and a restitution order, for a scheme involving the sale of worthless hearing aids. A suspended sentence might have been imposed had it not been for a previous record.

Since the fraudulent schemes usually involve more than one incident, the possibilities of giving discharges are slight: *R. v. Cano,*[218] where it was held that a discharge was not available to a first offender on 49 instances of fraud (compressed into a single count) but the sentence was varied to time served (25 days).

Those who play secondary roles in a fraudulent operation may expect lighter sentences than the "brains" behind the scheme. In *R. v. Hinch and Salanski,*[219] two contractors were extorted into a scheme to defraud B.C. Hydro initiated by one of its employees. Hinch and Salanski were

---

[216] (1970), 13 Crim. L.Q. 294 (Ont. C.A.).
[217] (1974), 15 C.C.C. (2d) 219 (N.S.C.A.).
[218] Unreported, June 23, 1975 (Ont. C.A.).
[219] [1968] 3 C.C.C. 39 (B.C.C.A.); see also *R. v. Burgess* (1974), 16 Crim. L.Q. 256 (N.S.C.A.).

both family men with unblemished backgrounds. In refusing to disturb a sentence of one month in jail and a $2,000 fine, the court of appeal had regard to the fact that arrangements had been made to repay the corporations the $20,000 illegally obtained.

One would imagine that the type of victim would have some bearing on the sentence. However, despite much verbal indignation expressed prior to sentence, this does not appear to be the case. In *R. v. Major,*[220] the principals in a fraudulent home-repair scheme, whereby elderly people lost their life savings, received sentences of five years and two years respectively, the latter sentence reflecting the lack of a previous record. Those less involved in the scheme received sentences ranging from six months definite and two years less a day indeterminate to a suspended sentence, the latter sentence for a peripheral participant with no significant record. Similarly in *Nantel et al. v. The Queen,*[221] a carefully planned scheme to defraud French speaking people of more than $124,000 on the pretext of advancing the economic future of French Canadians earned the three conspirators sentences of five, four and two years respectively.

Major and *Nantel* should be compared with *R. v. Bellan,*[222] where a bookkeeper defrauded the company she worked for of nearly $64,000. Even though it was her second offence of its kind, her sentence was reduced by the Ontario Court of Appeal from seven years to five years.

In *R. v. Spring,*[223] a sentence of 90 days intermittent was imposed upon a man, with an otherwise good background, who engaged in "a calculated attempt" to defraud the insurer of his motorcycle. He reported it stolen when it had not been stolen; when he became aware that his arrest was imminent he withdrew the claim he lodged with the insurer and was convicted of attempting to defraud. The amount he attempted to obtain was $1,359.

In *R. v. Soble,*[224] the involving of large numbers of innocent people in the fraudulent scheme was an aggravating factor, as it invited innocent members of society to practise fraud for profit. Many thousands of persons were involved in a fraudulent scheme by a pharmacist who submitted false claims to an insurance company using the names and signatures of many innocent adults and children. This factor demanded

---

[220] (1966), 48 C.R. 296 (Ont. C.A.).
[221] (1973), 26 C.R.N.S. 359 (Que. C.A.).
[222] Unreported, December 4, 1973 (Ont. C.A.).
[223] (1977), 35 C.C.C. (2d) 308 (Ont. C.A.).
[224] (1978), 3 C.R. (3d) S-1 (Man. C.A.).

a sentence of imprisonment. For this reason, and because the facts showed a continued premeditated fraud, sentence of 18 months' imprisonment was imposed on the pharmacist.

Where the offender has no previous record, substantial terms of imprisonment are still merited for so called "white collar criminals", who make use of their position in the business community and their knowledge of corporate mechanics to appropriate large sums of money to their own use: *R. v. Foran,*[225] where the sentence imposed was four years for $104,000 fraud; *R. v. Littler,*[226] where five years was imposed for a scheme earning over one million dollars, with compensation ordered for those defrauded; *Curley v. The Queen,*[227] four and a half years imposed for defrauding the Department of Revenue of $40,000. In *R. v. Smith,*[228] the British Columbia Court of Appeal refused to interfere with a four-year sentence for a mining fraud, even though the appellant had no previous record and enjoyed an excellent reputation. The Court was of the view, perhaps shared by the courts in the cases above, that such normally mitigating circumstances aided the offender in defrauding his victims. The element of deterrence has often been stressed in frauds upon employers as in *R. v. Fieldman,*[229] where considerable planning was involved and there was a prior similar offence, suspended sentence was increased to two months definite and eighteen months indeterminate. So too in *R. v. Smerek.*[230] Despite full restitution and an impeccable background a suspended sentence was increased to nine months' imprisonment.

In a relatively rare conviction under s. 110(1) of the Criminal Code, for conferring a benefit on a government employee, the court imposed a 12-month sentence. It was noted that it was a serious offence against the integrity of the public service, and a custodial term was required so that the business community would realize the seriousness of such offences: *R. v. Cooper (No. 2).*[231]

---

[225] [1970] 1 C.C.C. 336 (Ont. C.A.).
[226] (1972), 13 C.C.C. (2d) 530 (Que. Sess. Peace).
[227] (1969), 7 C.R.N.S. 108 (Que. C.A.).
[228] (1962), 38 C.R. 217.
[229] (1970), 13 Crim. L.Q. 14 (Ont. C.A.).
[230] (1977), 20 Crim. L.Q. 148 (Ont. C.A.).
[231] (1977), 35 C.C.C. (2d) 35 (Ont. C.A.).

F. Social Services

A by-product of the modern state is "social services fraud", an offence committed by those citizens receiving governmental benefits to which they are not entitled. Some departments of government have internal administrative machinery that may order an unqualified recipient to repay moneys received: see, for example the Unemployment Insurance Act, R.S.C. 1970, c. U-2, ss. 102 et seq.

Where the criminal process is invoked, the range of sentence for this variety of fraud is from a suspended sentence to a reformatory term. The courts recently have taken a rather severe approach to these offenders, especially where the welfare authorities are defrauded. In R. v. Thurrott,[232] the appellant arrived in Toronto from Nova Scotia with her common-law husband and four children. She immediately went on welfare, despite the fact that her common-law husband found employment, and received $1,700 to which she was not entitled. The Ontario Court of Appeal, in varying her sentence from five months definite to five months indeterminate, noted its duty to discourage those similarly minded. In R. v. Leveille,[233] an unwed mother's sentence of two years' probation was increased to three months' imprisonment plus two years' probation. The court referred to her previous record and the amount involved ($4,720).

In R. v. Fortin,[234] a period of one year's imprisonment with two years' probation on a plea of guilty to conspiracy and fraud in respect of a $64 unemployment insurance cheque was reduced on appeal to 30 days. The accused had a lengthy record and though she was not steadily employed her prospects of rehabilitation were good.

In R. v. Grandmond,[235] a sentence of 45 days intermittent together with three years' probation and restitution was altered by having the custodial time reduced to seven days (time served), based upon the need of the mother to look after her seriously handicapped four-year-old daughter, and by reason of the severe punishment which incarceration in the jail to which she had been directed by the prison authorities would involve.

In R. v. Mill,[236] a sentence of six months plus probation for two years

---

[232] (1972), 5 C.C.C. (2d) 129 (Ont. C.A.).
[233] Unreported, September 17, 1973 (Ont. C.A.).
[234] Unreported, July 18, 1977 (Que. C.A.).
[235] Unreported, November 29, 1976 (Ont. C.A.).
[236] Unreported, January 13, 1976 (Ont. C.A.).

was reduced to an intermittent sentence of 90 days for a charge involving an amount of $1,025. While the accused was committing the offence he was employed by a company that went on strike. Married, with two children, he had recently purchased a house which he was fearful of losing. He had no record and was a steady worker and a good citizen and had made restitution of the amount involved by securing employment as a taxi driver while on bail, pending appeal.

It is submitted that in the older cases, the courts have taken much too severe a view of the offence. Most offenders are women whose illegally obtained gains hardly place them in the lap of luxury but, on the contrary, leave the offenders still attempting to survive on an inadequate income. Where a mother is faced with the problem of raising her children on inadequate funds, the factor of economic duress should be given greater weight by the courts. A term of imprisonment imposed on such an offender will only aggravate an already difficult situation. Few such offenders offend again.

One such example is *R. v. Myles,*[237] where a native Canadian mother on welfare was abused in a common-law relationship and then deserted. As a result of debts incurred in her name by her common-law husband she could not feed, clothe, and house her family and pay her debts. Her basic living expenses plus her debt payment substantially exceeded her income. She offered to make restitution for the fraudulently obtained welfare payments. The court acknowledged that it would not be realistic or right to order restitution. It also found that though the crime was serious, there was no need for society to demand her imprisonment. It would not do her any good, and would not "deter single parents from yielding to temptation in desperate situations where the income is inadequate." Accordingly, the court imposed a sentence of probation together with community service.

Where the recipient was originally entitled to benefits but neglected to inform the government of a change in circumstances that would disqualify him or her from further payments, this fact is considered in mitigation: see *R. v. Bates,*[238] where a one-year suspended sentence was imposed on a woman who voluntarily withdrew from her illegal venture prior to arrest. The amount involved was $487 and restitution was ordered.

Entirely different considerations come into play when a welfare officer

---

[237] (1977), 20 Crim. L.Q. 147 (B.C. Prov. Ct.).
[238] (1972), 9 C.C.C. (2d) 74 (Ont. Co. Ct.); *R. v. Wiggen,* unreported, April 11, 1978 (Ont. C.A.).

diverts to his own use moneys intended for recipients. Where this occurred, the amount involved being around $50,000, the court considered the matter to be a breach of trust comparable to a solicitor stealing money from his clients. In *R. v. Rogers (No. 2)*,[239] an original sentence of one year in jail plus a $5,000 fine was increased to four years' imprisonment plus an order for compensation.

G. Income Tax Evasion

The Income Tax Act, S.C. 1970-71-72, c. 63, provides for both administrative penalties (see ss. 162, 163) and criminal prosecutions (see s. 239). Since the criminal penalties are somewhat more complicated than those found in the Criminal Code, the pertinent provisions for tax evasion are outlined below:

239(1) Every person who has
- (a) made, or participated in, assented to or acquiesced in making of, false or deceptive statements in a return, certificate, statement or answer filed or made as required by or under this Act or a regulation,
- (b) to evade payment of a tax imposed by this Act, destroyed, altered, mutilated, secreted or otherwise disposed of the records or books of account of a taxpayer,
- (c) made, or assented to or acquiesced in the making of, false or deceptive entries, or omitted, or assented to or acquiesced in the omission, to enter a material particular, in records or books of account of a taxpayer,
- (d) wilfully, in any manner, evaded or attempted to evade, compliance with this Act or payment of taxes imposed by this Act, or
- (e) conspired with any person to commit an offence described by paragraphs (a) to (d)

is guilty of an offence and, in addition to any penalty otherwise provided, is liable on summary conviction to
- (f) a fine of not less than 25% and not more than double the amount of the tax that was sought to be evaded, or
- (g) both the fine described in paragraph (f) and imprisonment for a term not exceeding 2 years.

(2) Every person who is charged with an offence described by subsection (1) may, at the election of the Attorney General of Canada, be prosecuted

---

[239] (1972), 6 C.C.C. (2d) 107 (P.E.I.C.A.).

upon indictment and, if convicted, is, in addition to any penalty otherwise provided, liable to imprisonment for a term not exceeding 5 years and not less than 2 months.

(3) Where a person has been convicted under this section of wilfully, in any manner, evading or attempting to evade payment of taxes imposed by Part I, he is not liable to pay a penalty imposed under section 163 for the same evasion or attempt unless he was assessed for that penalty before the information or complaint giving rise to the conviction was laid or made.

The fact that the administrative penalties are to be paid is a mitigating factor: *R. v. Sumarah et al.,*[240] where substantial amounts were involved the accused were given fines of $1,000 and $100. Another factor taken into consideration in this case was that it was not a complicated scheme to defraud, but merely a process of cashing the cheques and not accounting for them.

The amount of the fine appears to increase with the amount involved: *R. v. Kitto,*[241] where a $4,000 fine was imposed for an undeclared sum of $35,000.

Not surprisingly, most offenders are well respected in the community and have no previous record. These facts, unlike in cases of fraud, are taken into consideration as mitigation.

Where the offence has been carefully planned and involves many others in its commission, a term of imprisonment is called for: *R. v. Poynton,*[242] where one year in jail was imposed for concealing an income of $21,000. The moneys were repaid and a penalty of $4,000 was also paid. In *R. v. Novlan,*[243] the accused was an officer of a company that suppressed records of sales in order to avoid paying retail sales tax. Since Novlan was in a position of trust, his sentence on 11 counts was four months concurrent plus a six-month consecutive sentence. The amount of tax involved was $9,600. In *R. v. Kapoor,*[244] a sentence of 18 months' imprisonment was upheld upon taxes that were evaded in the amount of more than $300,000, applying *R. v. Poynton.*[245] The rarity of jail penalties here contrasts remarkably with cases such as "welfare" fraud.

---

[240] [1970] 5 C.C.C. 317 (N.S. Co. Ct.).
[241] (1969), 8 C.R.N.S. 277 (B.C. Prov. Ct.).
[242] (1972), 9 C.C.C. (2d) 32 (Ont. C.A.).
[243] (1971), 9 C.C.C. (2d) 85 (Ont. C.A.).
[244] (1978), 39 C.C.C. (2d) 326 (B.C.C.A.).
[245] (1972), 9 C.C.C. (2d) 32 (Ont. C.A.).

H. Misleading Advertising

The two pertinent provisions in the Combines Investigation Act are: (1) the offence relating to misrepresentations of price and (2) the offence for false statements of fact in the promotion of a business or commercial interest.

The range in sentence is fines from $300 to $10,000. Companies do not go to jail and individuals seem to be rarely charged. This strange pattern of non-prosecution on the part of the Crown is bewildering, and can be explained only by saying that ideology prohibits viewing this crime as "real crime", and so spares businessmen any embarrassing piercing of the corporate veil.

In *R. v. Ben Moss Jewellers Ltd.*,[246] a fine of $350 and the costs was imposed in an offence involving a misrepresentation of price. The court indicated that a serious view is taken of offences where the public relies on the expertise of the seller. In this case a diamond was advertised at a special value at $295 whereas competitive retail prices ran considerably below the one in question.

The lower end of the range for false statements of fact is reserved for those cases where the accused has acted in good faith, as in *R. v. Imperial Optical Co. Ltd.*[247] A $300 fine was deemed appropriate for printing "made in Canada" on boxes of bandages that were actually made in the United States, where it appeared the supplier had switched to an American source unbeknownst to the distributor.

In *R. v. Sinasac*,[248] the accused, a government employee, over a seven-year period, prepared claims for sales tax rebates which were to be given by his branch of government. He was found guilty of six counts of accepting a benefit contrary to s. 110(1) of the Criminal Code. The total amount of the benefit received was in excess of $28,000. An absolute discharge was overturned on appeal and a fine of $1,000 imposed, which the court considered "a very modest one in the circumstances" (which took into account that Crown counsel at trial had asked for a small fine).

Reliance upon a contractor was considered to be no excuse by the Ontario Court of Appeal in *R. v. Hudson's Bay Co.*[249] The company advertised sales of silver bars as a "smart investment in silver bullion".

---

[246] (1972), 8 C.C.C. (2d) 509 (Man. Mag. Ct.).
[247] (1972), 9 C.C.C. (2d) 328 (Ont. Prov. Ct.).
[248] (1977), 35 C.C.C. (2d) 81 (Ont. C.A.).
[249] (1977), 35 C.C.C. (2d) 61 (Ont. C.A.).

The advertisement also said that there was no sales tax on the bars. In fact, the bars could not be treated as bullion, were subject to sales tax and were sold by the respondent at a price considerably higher than could be obtained through a chartered bank. The court noted that the case was not one where there was a policy of the company to flout the law as in *R. v. Browning Arms Co. of Canada Ltd.;*[250] it was more like *R. v. Steinbergs Ltd.*[251] Sound policy was not observed by the Bay's employees. The principles in *Browning Arms* were held nevertheless to be applicable and it was noted that they were used in a similar case, *R. v. Family Tire Centres Ltd.*[252] The fines were increased from $750 to $5,000.

More substantial fines are imposed where the advertisement is promoting curatives of little value; in *R. v. Contour Slim Ltd.,*[253] the corporate offender was fined $1,000 on each of two counts of advertising a slimming compound that had no practical effect. Fines of $2,500 each were imposed on the principals involved in advertising another slimming scheme: *R. v. Gregory, Choquette and Hebert (No. 2);*[254] a factor considered by the court in this case was the anguish and uncertainty a pending fraud charge would have on the accused. The trial judge had studied over one hundred cases in the area and could find none where a term of imprisonment was imposed.

In *R. v. Steinbergs Ltd.,*[255] the court said:

> I recognize the relationship of $10,000 to the volume of sales by a supermarket chain such as the appellant, but when the company is being punished not for deliberately breaking the law, but for failure to ensure that its employees observed it, I think $10,000 per advertisement is too large a fine.

The fines were reduced to $5,000 per charge upon evidence that disclosed that what happened in the store was contrary to the company policy, and the directions from headquarters had not been followed.

---

[250] (1974), 18 C.C.C. (2d) 298 (Ont. C.A.).
[251] (1976), 31 C.C.C. (2d) 30 (Ont. C.A.).
[252] (1975), 28 C.C.C. (2d) 474 (Ont. C.A.).
[253] (1972), 9 C.C.C. (2d) 482 (Ont. Prov. Ct.).
[254] (1974), 20 C.C.C. (2d) 509 (Que. C.A.).
[255] *Supra,* footnote 251 at p. 39.

I. Dangerous Driving

Because of the innumerable variations in circumstances that may give rise to a dangerous driving conviction, a sentencing practice is difficult to determine. The range for the most severe cases and the most marginal cases may be determined by the cases below.

In *R. v. Lafontaine*,[256] a 17-year-old offender with no previous record was sentenced to 30 days with two years' prohibition from driving. The Ontario Court of Appeal was of the view that the offence may have been little more than speeding and accordingly substituted a conditional discharge with probation for six months.

The other end of the range is illustrated by *R. v. Nichol*,[257] where the accused accelerated his car in an effort to shake off a policeman hanging on to a side door. After a struggle in which the car veered all over the road, the accused was subdued. In increasing his sentence to 30 days in jail and one-year probation from a $250 fine imposed at trial, the court was of the view that this was a case of dangerous driving in the most extreme sense.

There is some dispute as to how and to what extent, if any, the fact that a death is caused by the dangerous driving ought to be reflected in the sentence. It would appear that in imposing terms of 18 months, *R. v. McLean*,[258] and six months in *R. v. Huard*,[259] the court reflects this fact in the sentence. Similarly in *R. v. Levesque*,[260] a sentence of one year was imposed by the Ontario Court of Appeal. However, in *R. v. Rance*,[261] a sentence of 21 days was imposed by the county court judge and not appealed; the decision states that "it would be decidedly wrong to permit in law the imposition of punishment governed primarily or predominantly by the extent of the consequences, rather than the degree of culpability in a particular case." It is submitted this is decidedly correct.

There are cases where the facts surrounding the accident aggravate the seriousness of the offence. In *R. v. Reining*,[262] the court imposed a term of

---

[256] Unreported, June 9, 1975 (Ont. C.A.).
[257] [1970] 4 C.C.C. 124 (Ont.).
[258] (1970), 13 Crim. L.Q. 149 (Ont. C.A.).
[259] (1970), 13 Crim. L.Q. 150 (Que. C.A.).
[260] (1971), 13 Crim. L.Q. 433 (Ont. C.A.).
[261] (1972), 14 Crim. L.Q. 393 (Ont. Co. Ct.). See also *R. v. Sayer,* unreported, February 27, 1976 (Ont. C.A.).
[262] Unreported, November 3, 1976 (Ont. C.A.).

18 months' imprisonment together with a five-year prohibition against driving. The accused chose to race down a main street and lost control of his car, killing two people. The accused's very bad driving record was taken into consideration by the court.

J. Leaving The Scene Of An Accident

Leaving the scene of an accident does not usually result in a custodial sentence unless death or a very serious injury results from the accident. It is submitted that this is a charge where the degree of culpability indeed is directly related to the consequences of the criminal conduct. Serious bodily harm has resulted from the actions of the offender and for him or her to flee the scene discloses morally censorable conduct. In *R. v. Leung*,[263] the offender, after finding out he had killed a person, deliberately left the scene.

In some cases there will be aggravating factors that will increase sentence. In *R. v. Jackson*,[264] the accused was a police officer who, while off duty, struck and killed a 15-year-old girl. The court said:

> . . . other crimes . . . [like] the hit and run offence in this category when personal injury or death has occurred, are recognized by Parliament and society as requiring a large measure of imprisonment, even though, almost always, the offender requires no reform from criminal ways and where the horror of the event and trial alone largely deters him from any repetition.

In this case the police officer not only disobeyed the law but added to the offence and further breached his police duty by attempting to conceal his complicity and misleading the investigators. Commenting that "in many ways it is difficult to conceive of a more serious case" the court increased sentence to 12 months' imprisonment.

K. Conspiracy

Section 423 of the Criminal Code outlines the maximum punishments

---

[263] Unreported, December 10, 1975 (B.C.C.A.).
[264] (1977), 20 Crim. L.Q. 22 (N.S.C.A.).

available for conspiracy. The basis for distinction is the object of the conspiracy:

423(1) Except where otherwise expressly provided by law, the following provisions apply in respect of conspiracy, namely,

(*a*) every one who conspires with any one to commit murder or to cause another person to be murdered, whether in Canada or not, is guilty of an indictable offence and is liable to imprisonment for fourteen years;

(*b*) every one who conspires with any one to prosecute a person for an alleged offence, knowing that he did not commit that offence, is guilty of an indictable offence and is liable

    (i)   to imprisonment for ten years, if the alleged offence is one for which, upon conviction, that person would be liable to be sentenced to death or to imprisonment for life or for fourteen years, or

    (ii)   to imprisonment for five years, if the alleged offence is one for which, upon conviction, that person would be liable to imprisonment for less than fourteen years;

(*c*) every one who conspires with any one to induce, by false pretences, false representations or other fraudulent means, a woman to commit adultery or fornication, is guilty of an indictable offence and is liable to imprisonment for two years; and

(*d*) every one who conspires with any one to commit an indictable offence not provided for in paragraph (*a*), (*b*) or (*c*) is guilty of an indictable offence and is liable to the same punishment as that to which an accused who is guilty of that offence would, upon conviction, be liable.

(2) Every one who conspires with any one

(*a*) to effect an unlawful purpose, or

(*b*) to effect a lawful purpose by unlawful means,

is guilty of an indictable offence and is liable to imprisonment for two years.

Thus it can be seen that it depends upon the wording of the information whether the accused is convicted under s. 423(1)(d) or under s. 423(2). This distinction is, strangely enough, relevant to the sentence that may be imposed. In *R. v. Gottselig*,[265] the court reduced the sentence from four years to two years when it appeared that G. was convicted under s. 423(2), even though the unlawful purpose was an indictable offence.

The sentence for conspiring to commit an offence may be more than the maximum permissible for the substantive offence: *Verrier v. Director*

---

[265] (1956), 23 C.R. 361 (Sask. C.A.).

of Public Prosecutions.[266] Leaving aside a conspiracy to commit certain specific offences, s. 423(1) limits the maximum sentence to the maximum allowed for the substantive offence. However, this is not the case in s. 423(2), where the unlawful purpose may be punishable on summary conviction by a maximum of six months' imprisonment, but the conspiracy to effect that same offence carries a maximum of two years.

No attempt is made here to arrive at a tariff for each specific offence of conspiracy because of the innumerable varieties of conspiracy that are possible. However, there are general principles which may affect the sentence.

Common sense dictates that there ought to be different sentences to match the different roles of each conspirator in the scheme. This is not to be confused with *when* an accused joined a conspiracy, but rather what part he played in furthering it: *R. v. Greenfield et al.*[267] In the case of an accused corporation conspiring to restrain competition, regard should be had to the volume of business done and the length of time each was involved in the conspiracy (which is relevant to the benefits received): *R. v. D. E. Adams Coal Ltd.,*[268] where fines ranging from $2,500 to $250 were levied on the corporations involved, the court being unable to find an instance of imprisonment being imposed.

In arriving at the "tariff" for conspiracy, the English Court of Appeal in *R. v. McCann,*[269] considered the sentence should be half of what would be suitable if a substantive offence had actually been committed. On the facts of this case, as reviewed on appeal, the accused may actually have only conspired to commit theft, since an agent provocateur had set a trap to allow the accused to complete his ultimate design. Accordingly, his original sentence of four years for the theft was reduced to two years for the conspiracy. The Nova Scotia Court of Appeal, in *R. v. Guatto et al.,* has held that "slightly lesser" sentences for mere conspiracy as opposed to substantive offences are appropriate.[270]

The practice of charging an offender with the substantive offence and conspiracy as well, using one to bolster the other, was condemned in the judgment of Hyde J. in *Poirier v. The Queen.*[271] However, if convictions

---

[266] [1967] 2 A.C. 195 (H.C.).
[267] (1973), 57 Cr. App. R. 849.
[268] (1957), 27 C.R. 47 (Man.).
[269] (1971), 56 Cr. App. R. 359.
[270] (1977), 21 N.S.R. (2d) 361 (C.A.).
[271] (1961), 37 C.R. 165 (Que. C.A.).

can be upheld on both counts, it is suggested the sentences be concurrent: *R. v. Sommers et al. (No. 11)*.[272]

L. Offences Against The Administration Of Justice

1. ESCAPE

Escape from lawful custody and being unlawfully at large is punishable by a maximum of two years' imprisonment: Criminal Code, s. 133. A term imposed for escape may be ordered to be served consecutively or concurrently to the original sentence: Criminal Code, s. 137(1).

Under the former s. 137(1) an escapee had to serve the sentence for his escape before he served the balance of the original sentence or sentences, and in calculating the original sentence and escape he had to serve a statutory remission time but not his earned remission time ". . . minus any time that he spent in custody between the date on which he was apprehended after his escape and the date on which he was sentenced for that escape." Under the new section the court has the power to direct that the sentence for escape should be served either concurrently with or consecutive to the original sentence: *R. v. Ouellette*.[273]

If total resulting sentence is two years or more, the escapee must be sent to a penitentiary. If the aggregate is less than two years, the sentencing judge still has a discretion to order that the sentence be served in a penitentiary: s. 137(1)(b). It was held in *R. v. Gaddie; R. v. Purdy*:[274] ". . . Parliament, recognizing the custodial conditions prevailing in reformatories, has made an exception in the case of escapees who have been proven to be a custodial risk, giving the Court power in its discretion to sentence such escapees to a penitentiary."

The range appears to be from a fine to a term of imprisonment for one and a half years; however, the usual range of sentence is from three to six months consecutive in the case of escape from a penitentiary.

A fine may be appropriate in a case of flight from a police officer after arrest: see the dissenting judgment of Dubin J.A. in *R. v. Andress*.[275]

---

[272] (1958), 29 W.W.R. 350 (B.C.).
[273] [1978] 2 W.W.R. 378 (B.C.C.A.).
[274] (1956), 22 C.R. 415 at p. 417 (Ont. C.A.).
[275] (1973), 26 C.R.N.S. 61 (Ont. C.A.).

Where there are aggravating circumstances accompanying the flight, such as an attempt to destroy the evidence regarding the original charge, a custodial sentence will be imposed. In *Andress* the accused was stopped for going through a red light and subsequently arrested for impaired driving and having liquor in a place other than his residence. He fled from the police cruiser in which he was placed, taking with him the partially full case of beer which had been discovered in his car. The majority, in approving a sentence of 20 days, noted it was not a frivolous, casual escape but was committed not only to do away with the evidence of the liquor charge, but also to neutralize any breathalyzer test which might have been administered.

Escaping from a penal institution carries a range of imprisonment from three months to 18 months. The British Columbia Court of Appeal has noted that though sentences for this offence vary radically, in recent years they have approved or imposed sentences ranging between three months and ten months: *R. v. Lemire.*[276]

The lower sentences are imposed on escapees from reformatories, where the original sentence was lower to begin with: *Ex parte Boehner,*[277] where three months was imposed on an inmate who had not reported back on a temporary absence pass and had committed offences during the nine-day period he was at large. In *Ex parte Lowe,*[278] where Lowe was at large for two months and committed other minor offences, he was sentenced to three months. Where the accused was awaiting his appeal in the reformatory on a conviction of rape, for which he received four and a half years at trial, his escape warranted a sentence of six months: *R. v. Naskathey.*[279] The escapee who has a bad criminal record will receive a heavier sentence: *R. v. Gaddie; R. v. Purdy,*[280] where Gaddie received one year and Purdy received six months for escape from a reformatory.

Escape from a penitentiary is generally viewed more seriously. In *R. v. Novak,*[281] two inmates escaped from Collins Bay Penitentiary and while at large committed a robbery. For the escape, Novak received one year and his accomplice received 18 months, the latter having a lengthy record.

---

[276] Unreported, October 2, 1976 (B.C.C.A.).
[277] (1973), 11 C.C.C. (2d) 392 (Ont.).
[278] (1972), 7 C.C.C. (2d) 458 (B.C.C.A.).
[279] (1970), 1 C.C.C. (2d) 339 (N.W.T.).
[280] *Supra,* footnote 274.
[281] (1974), 17 C.C.C. (2d) 531 (Ont. C.A.).

Mitigating circumstances were found in *R. v. Weston,*[282] where it appeared Weston was in a state of stress and anxiety as a result of bereavements and contacted the institution from which she had fled to indicate she would return the next day. In these circumstances, the Ontario Court of Appeal reduced her sentence for escape from two years to six months, despite a previous identical offence for which she had received the maximum penalty.

Nevertheless, in *R. v. Ingalls,*[283] where an accused walked away from a minimum security institution, the British Columbia Court of Appeal noted that in some cases such behaviour could be even more serious than a physical breakout from a more secure prison because of the inhibiting effect it has on the continuance and maintenance of open camps for inmates who are put "more or less" on trust. However, in a similar case, a one-day sentence was upheld on a Crown appeal, *inter alia,* because the accused lost his privileges and was sent to a much more unpleasant place of confinement as a result of his breach: *R. v. Hay.*[284]

A mitigating circumstance is the absence of premeditation in the escape as, for example, in a case when the facts disclose that a prisoner takes advantage of a circumstance which develops suddenly: *R. v. Lemire.*[285] On the other hand, the use of any degree of force in an escape is an aggravating factor.

2. PERJURY AND OBSTRUCTING JUSTICE

The punishment for perjury is a maximum of 14 years' imprisonment: Criminal Code, s. 121.

The court looks upon perjury very severely, viewing the offence as an attempt to subvert the judicial system itself. Accordingly, it usually involves a term of imprisonment despite mitigating factors: *R. v. Davies.*[286] In *R. v. Falkenberg,*[287] the accused testified at the preliminary inquiry of a friend that a sum of money had been obtained by fraud, but she changed her testimony at trial; the court stated that it was unusual to send a first offender to jail, but, the offence being quite a serious one, two

---

[282] Unreported, March 21, 1972 (Ont. C.A.).
[283] Unreported, March 3, 1977 (B.C.C.A.).
[284] Unreported, December 13, 1976 (B.C.C.A.).
[285] *Supra,* footnote 276.
[286] (1974), 59 Cr. App. R. 311.
[287] (1973), 13 C.C.C. (2d) 562 (Ont. Co. Ct.); revd 16 C.C.C. (2d) 525 (C.A.).

years less a day was held to be suitable. In *R. v. Simmonds*,[288] the court disregarded a minor criminal record and took into account Simmonds' industry in raising a family, but still imposed an 18-month prison term for perjured testimony in a civil case involving $32. Perjury is an offence that, though it may be committed during a trial for a minor offence, will earn the perjurer a term well above what he would have originally received for the main offence: *R. v. Robertson.*[289] Robertson's sentence of three months for false pretenses was reduced to one month on appeal, but the sentence of nine months for perjury was not disturbed.

The fact that the judge in the court where the perjury occurred had not been influenced by it is of no consequence in assessing sentence: *R. v. Lal.*[290]

In *R. v. Williams*,[291] the accused gave false evidence at a show-cause hearing. He was in fact unemployed but swore that he was employed and that he held two jobs. The court imposed three months for the charge of perjury. The court noted that the offence of perjury in show-cause hearings is difficult to detect and "if it became prevalent would completely undermine the pre-trial release system in force in this Province."

In *R. v. Carmanico*,[292] the accused gave a written statement to the police concerning the trial of another man for conspiracy to commit armed robbery. Carmanico was called as a Crown witness and denied giving the statement; as a result, the accused was acquitted. The Crown appealed a sentence of seven days in jail and a $2,000 fine on this 18-year-old offender — who had a previous conviction for possession of a weapon. The evidence disclosed a genuine fear on Carmanico's part of the other man and a serious attitude towards his offence. The majority of the court determined that the sentence was so low as to amount to an error in principle in that it failed to reflect the seriousness to the administration of justice of the commission of perjury. Had the Crown's appeal been more expeditious the appropriate range of sentence would have been from nine to 12 months, but in the circumstances a period of six months' imprisonment was imposed and the fine deleted. Brooke J.A., dissenting, would have dismissed the Crown appeal:

Prison is not the only, or necessarily the best way to achieve deterrence, if

---

[288] (1969), 53 Cr. App. R. 488.
[289] Unreported, June 28, 1973 (Ont. C.A.).
[290] [1978] Crim. L.R. 52 (C.C.A.).
[291] (1978), 41 C.C.C. (2d) 6 (Ont. C.A.).
[292] (1976), 19 Crim. L.Q. 160 (Ont. C.A.).

other meaningful types of punishment are available, particularly in the case of a youthful first offender. There is nothing to suggest that the fine does not reflect the seriousness of the offence and is a significant deterrent [to the accused] and others like him.

In *R. v. Fitchett,*[293] a sentence of two years less one day was reduced on appeal to three months in order to permit the immediate release of the appellant. A 17-year-old boy was threatened by drug merchants with whom he had been involved and, as a result, he gave false testimony which exculpated an accused. They were, nevertheless, convicted. The court reduced the sentence for perjury on Fitchett because of his age and the pressures under which he had been placed.

3. CONTEMPT

The contempt provisions of the Criminal Code are found in ss. 472, 533, and 636. However, the principle power to punish for contempt is found in the common law, therefore making contempt of court the only common law offence in Canada. Section 636, which deals with the punishment for an absconding witness, fixes the maximum under this section to a $100 fine or 30 days' imprisonment or both. Statutory limits are sometimes found in the statute creating the court *e.g.* the County Courts Act, R.S.O. 1970, c. 94, s. 27 (maximum punishment of $100 fine or six months' imprisonment or both). There is some doubt, however, if the Supreme Court for each province has any limit to the punishment it may impose for contempt, aside from those contempts mentioned in the Code.

The two categories apparent in reported contempt cases are contempt in the face of the court and contempt committed not in the face of the court.

The first category encompasses witnesses refusing to be sworn, impertinent language by the accused and other forms of disruptive behaviour. The range of sentences for witnesses refusing to be sworn was reviewed in *R. v. Lamer*[294] and found to be, for Canada, between a ten-dollar fine and two years' imprisonment. In *Lamer,* a case of refusal to testify, the original sentence of five years imposed on an 18-year-old was reduced to one year, when it appeared his actions had not prevented justice being administered in the case where the accused was a witness.

---

[293] Unreported, November 19, 1976 (B.C.C.A.).
[294] (1973), 17 C.C.C. (2d) 411 (Que. C.A.).

Where there are circumstances in the accused's background, such as a lengthy period of incarceration awaiting trial, that may form a reasonable basis for the accused's perception of injustice, then this will be a mitigating factor: *R. v. Vallieres (No. 2),*[295] where the sentence was reduced to time served (four months). In *R. v. McBain,*[296] a sentence of time served (15 days) was imposed upon an apologetic contemnor who had thrown a steel chair and an obscene remark at the trial judge. Similarly, in *R. v. Ball and Parro,*[297] a 30-day sentence was imposed on appeal as a reduction from 60 days for prisoners who engaged in a fight in the courtroom. For most usual offences, only short terms are upheld, probably out of respect for the unprecedented power and procedure involved in the jurisdiction of the court.

Evidence of contempt not in the face of the court can often be found where trade unions disobey injunctions against picketing or ordering workers back to their jobs. A range of one year's imprisonment to a $500 fine is found in *A.-G. Que. v. Charbonneau,*[298] a case arising from the Common Front of unions in April 1972 in Quebec. The highest sentences in this case were imposed on the trade union presidents, the court holding that the state of turmoil and public emergency was not a mitigating, but rather, an aggravating factor. The 13 union locals involved were fined between $50,000, the maximum under the Code of Civil Procedure of Quebec, and $1,400. A mitigating factor was found in one case where the collective membership of the local voted to obey the court order, but was later swayed by its leader to change its vote. The court was of the opinion that the fines, payable by a levy on each of the members, would remind them of their social duty. Sentences for the leaders of the union locals ranged from six days' imprisonment and a $1,500 fine to a $500 fine. A mitigating factor here was that the local leaders were under external pressures from their union presidents.

The *Charbonneau* case is an extreme one of its kind. A more common situation is found in *Re A.-G. N.S. and Miles,*[299] where union members picketed their employer's premises in defiance of an injunction. Fines were not considered appropriate as they would amount to penalties imposed on the accused's families. Sentences of 30 days and 20 days were imposed on seven accused and six accused respectively, distinction being

---

[295] (1973), 17 C.C.C. (2d) 361 (Que. C.A.).
[296] (1974), 16 Crim. L.Q. 379 (Ont. C.A.).
[297] (1971), 14 C.R.N.S. 238 (Ont. C.A.).
[298] (1972), 13 C.C.C. (2d) 226 (Que. C.A.).
[299] (1970), 1 C.C.C. (2d) 564 (N.S.).

made between those who had ceased picketing upon being served with the notice of the contempt proceedings and those who had continued.

M. Drug Offences

1. POSSESSION OF MARIJUANA OR HASHISH

In the last ten years, drug use has risen rapidly in Canada. As the character and motivations of the user have changed, so too have public attitudes toward drug offenders, especially those involving marijuana and hashish; and this change is now reflected in the approach of the courts to sentencing. Early sentences tended to be harsh. In 1967 a graduate student at university with no previous record was given three months in jail for possession of a small amount of marijuana by the Alberta Court of Appeal: *R. v. Lehrmann.*[300] Similarly, in 1969, possession of 12 marijuana cigarettes was punished by two months in jail, imposed upon an offender with no previous record: *R. v. Joslin,*[301] wherein comparative sentences are reviewed. Such cases should be compared with the more recent case of *R. v. Derksen,*[302] where the Crown prosecutor asked for a ruling on a Crown application that an absolute or conditional discharge should be granted to all first offenders. The ruling was that a discharge should be given only where there were special circumstances and should not be given as a matter of course. The practice of the lower courts in Ontario upon conviction on a guilty plea of possession of a small amount of marijuana or hashish varies from an absolute discharge to $100 fines for first offenders, with higher fines imposed occasionally where it appears that the quantity is very large. For subsequent offences of possession more severe sentences are imposed; a higher fine is given for a second and possibly a third offence and by the fourth offence a short term of imprisonment is usual in some jurisdictions: *R. v. Fairn.*[303]

The role of the accused in the offence is of particular importance. Where the accused is only peripherally involved, in that he acts as "an

---

[300] [1968] 2 C.C.C. 198.
[301] [1970] 3 C.C.C. 50 (P.E.I.C.A.).
[302] (1972), 9 C.C.C. (2d) 97 (B.C. Prov. Ct.).
[303] (1973), 12 C.C.C. (2d) 423 (N.S. Co. Ct.).

introducer" for a monetary reward, a very minimum penalty will be imposed: *R. v. Allison.* [304]

Cultivating marijuana is punishable by seven years' imprisonment, but the maximum has never been reached. It is common, where the number of plants are relatively small, for a suspended sentence or a discharge to be imposed. In *R. v. Haire*, [305] the accused was apprehended transporting some 450 marijuana seedlings which she intended to plant and cultivate on a farm for her personal use. Evidence showed that her personal use would require about three-quarters of a pound annually and that the plants would yield about one pound each annually. She was sentenced to six months. The court of appeal held that the trial judge unduly emphasized the general deterrent aspect of sentencing, particularly "since the offence was more in the nature of an attempt to cultivate or something preparatory to cultivation." The sentence was varied to 90 days intermittent.

2. TRAFFICKING IN MARIJUANA AND HASHISH; POSSESSION FOR THE PURPOSES OF TRAFFICKING

The earlier rule was that where no "exceptional circumstances" are shown, a term of imprisonment should be imposed on an accused convicted of trafficking in drugs even though the accused may be quite young, have no previous record, and come from an excellent background: *R. v. Cuzner.* [306] The exceptional circumstances "should flow from the offence, not the offender." It is not surprising that a rule so harsh and so out of keeping with ordinary sentencing principles should be "neglected" in many instances.

It is also not surprising that there are the beginnings of a jurisprudence which distinguish this general principle. For example, in *R. v. McLay*, [307] the court affirmed a suspended sentence and a two-year probation for a young first offender who sold seven cigarettes at school, each of which contained a drop or two of hashish oil, to an undercover policeman. The court in that case said that where the offence is only technically trafficking rather than substantive or real trafficking, "It is surely not

---

[304] Unreported, June 2, 1977 (B.C.C.A.).
[305] (1976), 19 Crim. L.Q. 282 (Ont. C.A.).
[306] [1970] 5 C.C.C. 187 (Ont. C.A.).
[307] (1976), 17 N.S.R. (2d) 135 (C.A.).

morally or practically more serious than mere possession of marijuana and should be similarly treated." Trafficking on a commercial basis, on the other hand, even on a small scale, requires imprisonment for at least a short term.[308]

The usual sentence in such cases, where the quantity is not extravagantly large, is an intermittent sentence. Occasionally, a short period of imprisonment is coupled with a fine: *R. v. McLaughlin.*[309]

A new and more sensible general principle has recently been enunciated by the British Columbia Court of Appeal. In *R. v. Haskins*[310] a $2,000 fine plus two years' probation were upheld on appeal on an offender with a previous record for the same offence:

> Although this court has laid down the principle that substantial sentences should be imposed in cases of trafficking in marijuana, it has not laid it down that in *every* case a substantial sentence must involve imprisonment . . .
>
> . . .
>
> . . . the very substantial fine imposed and the terms of probation will operate as a deterrent certainly to the respondent and should operate as a considerable deterrent to others who may be inclined to do the same thing. In no other respects do I think that the sentence varies from the principles that have often been laid down.

Where the court is able to conclude from the evidence that the accused was engaged in the trafficking in drugs in a major way, this will be an aggravating factor. For example, in *R. v. Brisson*[311] where the accused had told the police that he could sell marijuana in whatever quantity they required, that he could get M.D.A. and could get it cut with speed, and discussed the prices of M.D.A. in its various forms, the court was led to this conclusion. Particularly, in offences of this kind where persons are *participis criminis* care must be taken to see that balance is preserved between those who are involved in the offence: *R. v. Letinski.*[312]

---

[308] *R. v. MacArthur* (1974), 9 N.S.R. (2d) 353 (C.A.); *R. v. Stuart* (1975), 24 C.C.C. (2d) 370 (N.S.C.A.); *R. v. Eisan* (1975), 12 N.S.R. (2d) 34 (C.A.); *R. v. Dalrymple* (1977), 20 Crim. L.Q. 150 (N.S.C.A.); *R. v. Fifield* (1975), 25 N.S.R. (2d) 407 (C.A.).

[309] (1976), 20 Crim. L.Q. 149 (N.S.C.A.).

[310] (1978), 5 C.R. (3d) S-17 at pp. S-18—S-19.

[311] Unreported, June 4, 1975 (B.C.C.A.).

[312] Unreported, May 28, 1975 (B.C.C.A.).

One such example was in *R. v. Erven*[312a] where the court upheld a sentence of five years' imprisonment in respect of 1,700 pounds of hashish worth three million dollars on the retail market. In *R. v. Shaw and Brehn* [313] the Ontario Court of Appeal singled out the rationale for the rule as, in part, flowing from the "commercial" aspects of the practice.

The particular role in the offence taken by the offender is of extreme relevance. In *R. v. Willis,* [314] where his role in the offence was restricted to allowing the use of his truck for transporting the thirty kilograms of marijuana, a sentence of three years was reduced to one of six months.

Some recent reported cases are reviewed below. Regard should be had to the dates of the cases. It will be seen that a distinct pattern emerges. Sentences for minor offences are getting lower as time passes and use of the intermittent sentencing provisions increases.

(a) Maritimes

1970   Four months was the sentence for the sale of $10 worth of hashish by one acting as "the tool of the actual owners": *R. v. O'Connell.* [315]

An offender who sold drugs to university students, although he was not a student himself, received two years less one day for trafficking in marijuana and LSD. The offender had three previous convictions: *R. v. Robichaud.* [316]

1971   The organizer of systematic arrangements to accommodate customers was sentenced to six months' imprisonment: *R. v. Hemsworth.* [317]

1973   A man who had two prior convictions for fraud was sentenced to 18 months' imprisonment for selling a quarter ounce of hashish: *R. v. Cusack.* [318]

Eighteen months for a 24-year-old who was found with 12 pounds of hashish and $3,000 in cash: *R. v. O'Neill.* [319]

Twelve months was imposed on a 24-year-old student with a previous conviction of possession who knew there was a large quantity of hashish in a house although there was no evidence that he had actually sold it: *R. v. Spencer.* [320]

[312a] (1977), 21 N.S.R. (2d) 653 (C.A.).
[313] (1977), 36 C.R.N.S. 358 (Ont. C.A.).
[314] Unreported, February 28, 1975 (B.C.C.A.).
[315] [1970] 4 C.C.C. 162 (P.E.I.C.A.).
[316] (1970), 2 N.B.R. (2d) 123 (C.A.).
[317] (1971), 2 C.C.C. (2d) 301 (N.S.C.A.).
[318] (1973), 6 N.B.R. (2d) 324 (C.A.).
[319] (1973), 13 C.C.C. (2d) 276 (Nfld. C.A.).
[320] (1973), 16 C.C.C. (2d) 29 (N.S.C.A.).

1974   One month was imposed for a small amount sold to friends where the circumstances disclosed no mercenary motivation: *R. v. Whalen.*[321]

One year imposed for an offender who sold one ounce of marijuana to an undercover agent. The offender had no previous record and there were no aggravating circumstances: *R. v. Sutherland.*[322] The court made it plain in this case that one year is the "usual" sentence in New Brunswick.

Six months' probation was substituted for a fine of $150 on an educated recluse who sold a small amount of marijuana that he had grown himself to pay for his winter supplies: *R. v. Hermann.*[323]

1976   Thirteen ounces of marijuana for an offender of good background produced two months' imprisonment as the "minimum implicitly recognized", without any very unusual or exceptional circumstances being involved: *R. v. Stuart.*[324]

1977   A three-month sentence was imposed on an accused who sold one-half pound of marijuana to an undercover police officer. A good background and other sentences in Canada and across the country were taken into consideration in imposing the sentence: *Paquet v. The Queen.*[325]

(b) Ontario

1970   A 19-year-old with no previous record received six months definite and 12 months indefinite for sales of hashish totalling $111: *R. v. Cuzner.*[326]

Seven years was the penalty for a sophisticated operation involving 150 pounds of marijuana concealed in bongo drums. The accused was a 36-year-old newspaper reporter with no previous record: *R. v. Johnston and Tremayne.*[327]

1971   A joint venture for profit involving $12,000 worth of marijuana earned one of the venturers six months' imprisonment: *R. v. Robert; R. v. Shacher.*[328]

---

[321] (1974), 17 C.C.C. (2d) 162 (Nfld. C.A.).
[322] (1974), 10 N.B.R. (2d) 221 (C.A.).
[323] (1974), 18 C.C.C. (2d) 255 (N.S.C.A.).
[324] (1975), 24 C.C.C. (2d) 370 (N.S.C.A.).
[325] (1977), 3 C.R. (3d) S-11 (P.E.I.C.A.).
[326] [1970] 5 C.C.C. 187 (Ont. C.A.).
[327] [1970] 4 C.C.C. 64 (Ont. C.A.).
[328] (1971), 3 C.C.C. (2d) 149 (Ont. C.A.).

1972   One year definite and six months indeterminate was imposed for possession of hashish worth $1,500. The offender was 21, had no record, but the evidence showed a commercial enterprise: *R. v. Doherty.*[329]

A 22-year-old with no previous record sold $5 worth of marijuana to an undercover agent and received sentence: *R. v. Healey.*[330]

1973   Three months' imprisonment and two years' probation was imposed for possession of ten pounds of hashish for the purposes of trafficking where the offender was in custody prior to his trial and a favourable pre-sentence report was received on him, even though the court discerned a substantial operation involving four other men: *R. v. Wooff.*[331]

1974   Four months' imprisonment and one year's probation was imposed on one who admitted possession of one and one-quarter pounds of marijuana and $700 in cash. Here again there were unspecified mitigating factors: *R. v. Thompson.*[332]

In an offence involving 90 pounds of hashish where the co-accused was armed when discovered, an accused who had been making $2,000 per week out of his activities, and who had committed the offence in question while on bail received six years consecutive to seven and a half years then being served on other drug charges: *R. v. Pelletier.*[333]

Probation for two years was imposed on a trafficker who was attempting to rehabilitate himself and stop using drugs. Since the offender had a record of three breaking and entering offences, this must have been an unusual case indeed: *R. v. Doerr.*[334]

There were unspecified mitigating factors in a sentence of 60 days to be served intermittently where trafficking was carried on by the offender for a lengthy time on a commercial basis: *R. v. Burnett.*[335]

1975   One pound of hashish oil was involved, valued at $4,500. The accused was a first offender whose involvement was in the nature of a wholesaler or broker and he did not play a principal role. The sentence was 90 days intermittent, plus probation for 18 months:

---

[329] (1972), 9 C.C.C. (2d) 115 (Ont. C.A.).
[330] (1972), 7 C.C.C. (2d) 129 (Ont. C.A.).
[331] (1973), 14 C.C.C. (2d) 396 (Ont. C.A.).
[332] Unreported, February 8, 1974 (Ont. C.A.).
[333] (1974), 18 C.C.C. (2d) 516 (Ont. C.A.).
[334] (1974), 20 C.C.C. (2d) 1 (Ont. C.A.).
[335] Unreported, April 3, 1975 (Ont. C.A.).

R. v. Cole.[336] The court distinguished *R. v. Stevens*[337] on the basis that in that case, which involved three and a half pounds of hashish oil, the accused was a person with a previous conviction for a narcotic offence. This decision was taken to the Court of Appeal and upheld.

1976 Seventeen days' imprisonment was imposed by the Ontario Court of Appeal as a reduction from a 60-day sentence for trafficking in marijuana in light of the youthfulness of the offender, the small amount of the drug involved, and the previous good record of the accused: *R. v. Macrae.*[338]

Two years less one day plus probation for two years was imposed upon a 22-year-old man with a previous narcotic conviction who was found with 60 pounds of marijuana on the occasion of his arrest and who admitted to purchasing 40 to 60 pounds of marijuana for distribution on approximately 48 occasions over a four-month period prior to his arrest: *R. v. Badder.*[339]

1978 Upon a charge of possession of marijuana for the purpose of trafficking and simple possession where small quantities were involved, it was said that the sentence would normally be 45 days' imprisonment: *R. v. Fraser.*[340]

(c) Prairie Provinces

1970 An 18-year-old offender with a severe liver ailment, the result of the use of dirty needles in his drug habit, was fined $250 for the sale of two cubes of hashish and eight tablets of LSD: *R. v. Doyle and 10 others.*[341]

A 21-year-old university student who *gave* marijuana cigarettes to his friends received 21 days' imprisonment: *R. v. Larre.*[342]

Where an offender's father was in jail, he was given a suspended sentence to spare him a similar fate: *R. v. Kosh.*[343]

One year was imposed on a 17-year-old from a broken home who

---

[336] (1975), 19 Crim. L.Q. 26 (Ont. Co. Ct.).
[337] (1975), 18 Crim. L.Q. 153 (Ont. C.A.).
[338] Unreported, October 14, 1976 (Ont. C.A.).
[339] (1976), 18 Crim L.Q. 293 (Ont. C.A.).
[340] Unreported, June 11, 1978 (Ont. C.A.).
[341] (1970), 2 C.C.C. (2d) 82 (Alta. C.A.).
[342] [1970] 1 C.C.C. 382 (Sask. C.A.).
[343] (1970), 1 C.C.C. (2d) 290 (Sask. C.A.).

trafficked in two grams of hashish and two tablets of LSD: *R. v. Doyle, supra.*

One year was the penalty for a student with no previous record who aided the police in convicting another. The offence involved $1,300 worth of hashish: *R. v. Doyle, supra.*

Where the hashish was worth $1,300, a 19-year-old with no previous record received one year: *R. v. Doyle, supra.*

Eighteen months' imprisonment plus two years' probation was imposed on a 19-year-old with a previous record who sold hashish to young girls: *R. v. Doyle, supra.*

Where an offender with no previous record was found with 17 ounces of marijuana, he received 18 months' imprisonment: *R. v. Doyle, supra.*

A "brilliant" university student who sold three grams of hashish and seven tablets of LSD was sentenced to 18 months' imprisonment: *R. v. Doyle, supra.*

A 29-year-old "renegade" social worker with a previous record for possession was sentenced to 21 months' imprisonment for trafficking: *R. v. DeJong.*[344]

Two years less one day was imposed on a 19-year-old high school student with no previous record who sold three grams of hashish and two tablets of LSD to other high school students: *R. v. Doyle, supra.*

1971   Twelve months less one day consecutive to other drug sentences was imposed on a 20-year-old "member of the drug culture" who was found with nine ounces of hashish: *R. v. Toth.*[345]

1974   Two years less one day was imposed on two men with previous drug records who were found with six bricks of marijuana; the activities of the offenders disclosed a commercial enterprise: *R. v. Sprague et al.*[346]

1975   A suspended sentence and two years' probation was upheld upon a man who had possession of a quantity of marijuana for another who was to do the actual trafficking. He neither trafficked in the drug nor received any benefits from it (it was seized by the police before anything could be done). He had been led into the activity

---

[344] (1970), 1 C.C.C. (2d) 235 (Sask. C.A.).
[345] (1971), 5 C.C.C. (2d) 358 (Sask. C.A.).
[346] (1974), 19 C.C.C. (2d) 513 (Alta. C.A.).

by another man. These factors were considered exceptional circumstances justifying a suspended sentence: *R. v. Bell, Wand and Marriott.* [347]

The accused M. had a previous conviction for disturbing the peace when he was 17 years of age, and was convicted of trafficking. He had a stable common-law relationship and was employed as a caretaker at the time of the sentencing. There was no "real" evidence that he was in any drug ring. A suspended sentence was upheld upon the grounds that these facts disclosed exceptional circumstances: *R. v. Bell, Wand and Marriott.* [348]

The accused W. was convicted of possession for the purpose of trafficking in marijuana after a trial. The accused came from Montreal where he resided with his widowed mother and had been associated with her in community and church activities. This was the first time he had ever had the drug and he never had the opportunity to traffic in it. A suspended sentence was upheld on the grounds that these constituted exceptional circumstances: *R. v. Bell, Wand and Marriott.* [349]

(d) British Columbia

1969 One year in jail and one year's probation was imposed on an 18-year-old with no criminal record for an offence involving a small amount of marijuana: *R. v. Nickel.* [350]

A 19-year-old boy with no previous record who was convicted of trafficking involving one gram of hashish was sentenced to 18 months definite and one year indeterminate: *R. v. Jenson.* [351]

1972 Three months and a $200 fine plus one year's probation was imposed on an 18-year-old with no previous record and a good background: *R. v. Bruckshaw.* [352]

1974 In an unusual case, one day in jail and a $5,400 fine was imposed on a 27-year-old "courier" with a record of four break and enter

---

[347] (1975), 18 Crim. L.Q. 22 (Sask. C.A.).
[348] *Ibid.*
[349] *Ibid.*
[350] Unreported, December 11, 1969 (B.C.C.A.).
[351] Unreported, May 26, 1969 (B.C.C.A.).
[352] (1972), 9 C.C.C. (2d) 133 (B.C.C.A.).

offences who was found with 450 pounds of marijuana. The offender was very helpful to police: *R. v. Morphy.*[353]

1976   A 24-year-old man with no criminal record was found guilty of possession for the purpose of trafficking relating to approximately $300 worth of marijuana. A suspended sentence and probation order for two years was imposed: *R. v. Stebanuk.*[354]

1977   A 16-year-old offender agreed to sell a small quantity of marijuana to a juvenile and was in the act of doing so when apprehended; a sentence of six months definite and 18 months indeterminate was upheld: *R. v. Coombes.*[355]

All of the above are appellate court judgments. Of the cases reviewed above, most were appeals brought by the Crown and in very few of reported appeals was the Crown unsuccessful. A possible explanation for this phenomena may be found in a report of the Commission of Inquiry into the Non-medical Use of Drugs:[356]

> Judges and magistrates with strong links in the community and some understanding of the social circumstances of drug users arising from personal contacts with street level agencies tend to take a more tolerant view of drug use which is reflected in the sentencing behaviour. This may help to explain the data which show a sharp difference between appeal and trial judges in sentencing philosophy. Most appeal judges tend to support a deterrent philosophy and are somewhat more primitive in their general outlook. . . . It is clear that appeal judges in most provinces have felt it necessary to lay down rather stern sentencing guidelines in drug cases. Appeal judges are much more isolated from the drug offender and social circumstances than lower court judges. Moreover their experience tends to be based on a biased sample of cases coming before the courts. They tend to see the more serious cases.

It may be also noted that western provinces are inclined to more severe penalties than Ontario or the Maritimes. An aggravating factor in any court is the quantity of the drug seized, or any indications of sophisticated organization or large-scale commercialism. A large quantity usually indicates a commercial operation rather a casual distribution to friends and acquaintances. A recurring mitigating factor

---

[353] (1974), 21 C.C.C. (2d) 62 (B.C.C.A.).
[354] Unreported, June 17, 1976 (B.C.C.A.).
[355] (1977), 35 C.C.C. (2d) 85 (B.C.C.A.).
[356] Report on Cannabis (The LeDain Commission) 1972, Ottawa, at p. 247.

in drug cases is co-operation with the police in the apprehension of others.

3. TRAFFICKING IN OTHER NARCOTICS

The reported range of sentence for trafficking in such drugs as morphine, heroin, cocaine, opium, or their derivatives is from a fine to life imprisonment. The appeal courts tend to deal harshly with these drug trafficking offences because they see these drugs as destructive to the life of the purchaser. A distinction is made between these drugs and marijuana or hashish: *R. v. DiGiovanni.*[357]

The lower end of the range of sentences is usually reserved for young offenders who are often addicts themselves. Six months' imprisonment plus two years' probation were imposed on a 19-year-old girl convicted of trafficking in cocaine who subsequent to the offence ceased drug use and was progressing towards rehabilitating herself: *R. v. Catizone.*[358] In *R. v. DiGiovanni,* one year definite and one year indeterminate plus one year's probation was imposed on a 17-year-old from a fine background for selling $80 worth of heroin to undercover agents. A reformatory term is often used in an attempt to rehabilitate the offender. In *R. v. Marcello*[359] two years less a day was imposed on a 16-year-old heroin addict so that he could receive treatment for his habit while being detained.

The role in the offence of the accused will be a serious factor in assessing the appropriate sentence. Where the accused was convicted of two counts of trafficking in cocaine, the first of which was a sample for the second (which involved some $11,000 worth of the drug) a $1,000 fine plus probation for two years was imposed solely upon the ground that the accused was very much on the periphery of the affair and acted "merely as an introducer" of seller to purchaser for a fee of $300: *R. v. Allison.*[360]

Where the amount of the drug involved in the trafficking is "minimal" (five-eights of an ounce of methamphetamine) the sentence must reflect that factor: *R. v. Warmuz.*[361]

It is a common occurrence for a number of different counts of

---

[357] (1973), 10 C.C.C. (2d) 392 (Ont. C.A.), *per* Gale C.J.O.
[358] Unreported, September 14, 1973 (Ont. C.A.).
[359] (1973), 11 C.C.C. (2d) 302 (Ont. C.A.).
[360] Unreported, June 2, 1977 (B.C.C.A.).
[361] Unreported, December 13, 1976 (Ont. C.A.).

trafficking in substances such as heroin, for example, to occur over a separated period of time but all involving the same undercover agent. In these circumstances sentences of three years: *R. v. Wocinski,*[362] and four years, *R. v. Hogan*[363] have been imposed. The differentiation between the two rests on the degree of involvement in trafficking.

In *R. v. Stoneman*[364] a sentence of 90 days intermittent was imposed for possession of phencyclidene for the purpose of trafficking, despite a previous discharge for possession of marijuana. The court upheld the sentence saying it was a lenient one but not disproportionate to the offence and the offender; but it was necessary to require an additional custodial term.

In *R. v. Longeuay,*[365] the accused woman was a heroin user who sold 14 capsules of heroin to an undercover police officer. She was sentenced to five years' imprisonment which was reduced to 12 months' imprisonment together with two years' probation. The majority of the court noted that appeal courts in Ontario and British Columbia had indicated that sentences are from ten years to life imprisonment for heroin trafficking, while sentencing of five or six years had customarily been imposed on relatively large-scale operators who trafficked in other "hard" drugs such as morphine and speed. At a lower level are the "small-time pushers" who peddle heroin on a commercial basis, often to support their own habits. Two years less one day to four years' imprisonment has customarily been imposed across Canada for this class of offence and offender. Still lighter sentences have been imposed (and were reviewed by the court) where the accused was not in the business of trafficking but had sold a small quantity of heroin in an isolated incident. Here, there was no evidence of an intention to traffick on a commercial basis in that Longeuay was not "engaged in the business of trafficking". There was no evidence that she had made any other sales of heroin and there was no evidence pointing towards her being herself an active pusher.

It is a mitigating factor in these offences if the substance sold is not what it was represented to be; that is, if what was sold turned out not to be a "hard" drug. In *R. v. Masters*[366] a 19-year-old with no previous record who sold an innocuous substance represented as heroin was sentenced to

---

[362] Unreported, November 23, 1976 (Ont. C.A.).
[363] Unreported, November 23, 1976 (Ont. C.A.).
[364] (1976), 19 Crim. L.Q. 283 (Ont. C.A.).
[365] (1977), 3 C.R. (3d) S-29 (N.S.C.A.).
[366] (1974), 15 C.C.C. (2d) 142 (Ont. C.A.).

nine months definite and 15 months indeterminate. A 22-year-old who had previous convictions for theft and possession, committed when he was 17, sold aspirin represented as heroin. For this offence he received three and one-half years' imprisonment: *R. v. Lecapoy.*[367]

A similar principle can be seen operating in *R. v. Morris.*[368] The accused, a heroin user, agreed to obtain 25 capsules of heroin for $400 from an undercover officer. He took the $400 but never did deliver the heroin. He testified that he "frequently ripped off" prospective purchasers. The court, reducing 18 months plus one year probation to nine months' imprisonment, stated that the situation was similar to obtaining money by a false pretence. As the appellant had a record for other crimes, the sentence was considered appropriate to that offence.

Where the offender has a previous record this will generally increase the sentence. A 22-year-old who was on probation while he was convicted of trafficking in cocaine was sentenced to four years: *R. v. Bowles.*[369] In *R. v. Salamon,*[370] a 28-year-old male with two prior convictions was sentenced to five years' imprisonment for trafficking in morphine. The evidence showed that the drugs had been sold to young girls. Also see *R. v. Sprague et al.*[371] where seven years' imprisonment was imposed on an offender who was an addict with a long record. Apparently he had spent ten of his last 13 years in jail.

In *R. v. Mearns*[372] the accused had a lengthy record including previous drug offences when he was convicted of possession for the purpose of trafficking in heroin. He was sentenced to three years' imprisonment as a matter of general deterrence.

In *R. v. Haddad*[373] a two-year sentence was imposed for trafficking in cocaine on a 20-year-old offender, the court saying the original sentence imposed, namely, four years, was decidedly on the high side of the range of sentences that are usually imposed in circumstances similar to those that were before the court.

In *R. v. Bell*[374] sentence was six years' imprisonment imposed upon the offender who had possession of 1,750 capsules of heroin with a street value of $35,000 to $40,000. At the time of his arrest the accused was on

[367] (1974), 18 C.C.C. (2d) 496 (Alta. C.A.).
[368] Unreported, March 8, 1978 (B.C.C.A.).
[369] (1974), 16 C.C.C. (2d) 425 (Ont. C.A.).
[370] (1972), 6 C.C.C. (2d) 165 (Ont. C.A.).
[371] (1974), 19 C.C.C. (2d) 513 (Alta. C.A.).
[372] (1975), 22 C.C.C. (2d) 457 (Alta. C.A.).
[373] Unreported, October 17, 1977 (B.C.C.A.).
[374] (1976), 19 Crim. L.Q. 157 (Ont. C.A.).

parole following a conviction for possession for the purposes of trafficking in the same drug. He was not himself a user of heroin.

In *R. v. Kimble*[375] the Crown appeal from a sentence of two years less one day plus two years' probation was allowed, and the sentence increased to three years' imprisonment plus one year's probation. The appellant, who had three previous similar convictions, sold an ounce of heroin to an undercover officer for $3,800. The court found he was obviously trafficking on a regular basis and imposed the sentence despite recent efforts at rehabilitation.

In *R. v. Hogan*[376] a four-year sentence was imposed for trafficking in heroin where the offender had previous convictions for possession of LSD for the purpose of trafficking and possession of a narcotic for the purpose of trafficking on different occasions. He was on probation at the time of the commission of this offence.

In *R. v. Prendergast, Calagoure and Fachira*[377] three young offenders with fair backgrounds and without criminal records sold several thousand dollars' worth of cocaine to an undercover policeman on three separate occasions. Depending upon their involvement, they received sentences of two years less one day, two years less one day definite and one year indeterminate, and one year definite and one year indeterminate. The evidence revealed that because these men were not users of cocaine and there were substantial amounts involved, they were "wholesaling" cocaine. The court would have been inclined to impose a penitentiary term had it not been for the submissions of the Crown at trial, who did not ask for a penitentiary term.

Where there is evidence that a person involved is an addict and is responding to an offer of treatment for addiction, the sentence will be reduced: *R. v. Wright.*[378]

The following further factors will be considered in assessing the quantum of sentence:

Professional connections *R. v. Bowles*[379]

Degree of Planning *R. v. Bosley and Durarte;*[380] *R. v. Hemsworth*[381]

Amount of drugs involved *R. v. Wooff* [382]

---

[375] Unreported, March 20, 1978 (B.C.C.A.).
[376] Unreported, November 23, 1976 (Ont. C.A.).
[377] Unreported, October 14, 1976 (Ont. C.A.).
[378] Unreported, November 23, 1976 (Ont. C.A.).
[379] (1974), 16 C.C.C. (2d) 425 (Ont. C.A.).
[380] [1970] 1 C.C.C. 328 (Ont. C.A.).
[381] (1971), 2 C.C.C. 301 (N.S.C.A.).
[382] (1973), 14 C.C.C. (2d) 396 (Ont. C.A.).

Extent of criminal involvement *R. v. Bosley and Durarte;*[383] *R. v. Morrison.*[384]

The maximum punishment, that of life imprisonment, is reserved for those individuals involved in distributing the drug on a grand scale, and strictly for profit. Life imprisonment has been imposed for trafficking in heroin: *R. v. Richa and Bou-Mourad.*[385]

The British Columbia courts have evolved a sentencing practice quite distinct from that of the rest of the provinces in the case of heroin trafficking. This is no doubt the case because of the severe problem that exists in that province with regard to this drug. An example is *R. v. Ko (No. 2)*[386] where Bouck J. imposed life imprisonment on a 37-year-old first offender who sold a sample of heroin and later a pound of heroin. The court said:

> It is well known in the heroin trade that a necessary cover for selling the drug is to have at least one person who has no criminal record. [The accused was] such an individual. Since [the accused] relied on these qualities to ply [his] disgusting enterprise [he] cannot now use it as an argument for leniency at a sentence hearing . . .
>
> . . .
>
> [S]entences of 15 to 20 years that the courts have fixed for trafficking in heroin [might be described] as brutal. They are certainly severe. Yet they do not seem to have had any noticeable effect. . . .
>
> . . .
>
> [T]he time has come for the law to recognize that the outrage of heroin trafficking involves different principles of sentencing than most other crimes in the Criminal Code . . . and related federal statutes. [The court] speaking particularly of the concept of rehabilitation and the idea that the maximum sentence must only be reserved for those occasions which exemplify the worst possible commission of a particular crime.
>
> [It has] reached the point where it is irrelevant as to whether a heroin trafficker can be rehabilitated. . . .
>
> . . .
>
> Since 15- to 20-year prison terms do not seem to deter heroin traffickers, the next progression is the ultimate penalty allowed by the Narcotic Control

---

[383] *Supra,* n. 380.
[384] [1970] 2 C.C.C. 190 (Ont. C.A.).
[385] (1974), 18 C.C.C. (2d) 63 (Ont. C.A.); see also *R. v. Devlin and Marentette* (1971), 3 C.C.C. (2d) 20 (Ont. C.A.); *R. v. Ponak; R. v. Gunn* (1973), 11 C.C.C. (2d) 346 (B.C.C.A.); *R. v. Zizzo* (1975), 23 C.C.C. (2d) 319 (Ont. C.A.).
[386] [1978] 1 W.W.R. 395 (B.C.C.A.).

Act . . . Never again should anyone trafficking in this amount of heroin be allowed outside of prison walls. . . .

Examples of the 15- to 20-year range, spoken of in the judgment are *R. v. Myhaluk*[387] and *R. v. Puntawang.*[388]

In all these cases the amounts trafficked are extremely substantial. Where the amounts are smaller, sentences range from 18 months for the sale of one capsule of heroin.[389]

Offences related to drugs such as cocaine and morphine are considered by the courts as being more serious than marijuana but not as serious as heroin or the drugs in that category. Where an accused was convicted of trafficking in both cocaine and morphine to an undercover officer in a beer parlour, a sentence of nine months was imposed: *R. v. Fryer.*[390]

4. TRAFFICKING IN RESTRICTED AND CONTROLLED DRUGS

The penalties for these offences are found in the Food and Drugs Act, R.S.C. 1970, c. F-27. For trafficking in restricted or controlled drugs the penalties are the same, *i.e.,* on a summary conviction a maximum of 18 months' imprisonment and on indictment a maximum of ten years. Since both types of drugs have the same penalties for trafficking and the courts have not indicated any differentiation between them it may be assumed that there is no difference in sentencing considerations. Nevertheless, simple possession of a controlled drug is still not an offence. The range of sentence for trafficking in these substances can go as high as ten years' imprisonment.

Two years less one day was imposed on a 27-year-old man with no previous record found with 108 tablets of LSD: *R. v. Sprague et al.*[391] The same sentence was also imposed on a man who had an excellent background and who had been active in the Boy Scouts. He had three recent convictions for possession of marijuana and in the case under consideration he was found with 32 tablets of LSD: *R. v. Sprague et al.* In

---

[387] Unreported, October 31, 1977 (B.C.C.A.).
[388] Unreported, November 10, 1977 (B.C.C.A.).
[389] *R. v. Baragon,* unreported, November 10, 1977 (B.C.C.A.); *R. v. Chisolm,* unreported, November 11, 1977 (B.C.C.A.); *R. v. Crawford,* unreported, September 9, 1977 (B.C.C.A.).
[390] Unreported, January 25, 1977 (B.C.C.A.).
[391] (1974), 19 C.C.C. (2d) 513 (Alta. C.A.).

R. v. Guerriero[392] a term of one year definite and two years' probation was imposed upon an offender with no previous record and a good background who was found in possession of 100 tablets of LSD. An 18-year-old with a previous record and who was involved in drug use and was himself dependent upon drugs received two years less one day for the sale of one tablet of LSD to a police agent: *R. v. Robichaud.*[393] A 20-year-old single man found in possession of 94 tablets of LSD approximately 50 per cent stronger than those normally seen was sentenced to three years' imprisonment. He had a long previous record and had to serve an unexpired term of his parole as a result of this offence: *R. v. Doyle and 10 others.*[394]

In *R. v. Ayre*[395] the accused was found with a bag containing 93 tablets of LSD valued at $250 to $300. He had five unrelated convictions, but a good work record. The court imposed a sentence of six months' imprisonment.

In *R. v. Bell and Neveu*[396] the trial judge heard expert evidence concerning the dangerous nature of the drug phencyclidene and convicted the 23-year-old first offender of possession of this drug for the purpose of trafficking. The value of the drug was $5,000 and a period of 30 months' imprisonment was imposed.

In *R. v. Price*[397] a 20-year-old accused was charged, as a result of the activity of an undercover agent, with trafficking in LSD. Price admitted that on a number of occasions she had been the ultimate distributor of LSD to a number of other persons. She was given a sentence of two months' imprisonment, which the court referred to as "a light sentence".

As noted before, those *entrepreneurs* who traffic in drugs strictly for profit will receive more severe sentences. Six years was imposed on a 23-year-old caught with six pounds of methemphetamine (speed) who admitted that he did not use it himself. The offender had no previous record: *R. v. Pearce.*[398]

In *R. v. McAllister et al.*[399] the accused were charged with trafficking in methamphetamine, the value of which on the "street" was some six million dollars. The leading figure in the trafficking operation was

---

[392] Unreported, April 5, 1974 (Ont. C.A.).
[393] (1970), 2 N.B.R. (2d) 123 (C.A.).
[394] (1970), 2 C.C.C. (2d) 82 (Alta. C.A.).
[395] (1976), 19 Crim. L.Q. 156 (Ont. C.A.).
[396] (1978), 6 Alta. L.R. (2d) 80.
[397] (1970), 12 C.R.N.S. 131 (Ont. C.A.).
[398] (1974), 16 C.C.C. (2d) 369 (Ont. C.A.).
[399] (1976), 1 C.R. (3d) S-46 (Ont. C.A.).

described as a "professional drug trafficker" with a record of five previous convictions, indicating his familiarity with drugs and the risks involved. Invoking the protection of the public, the court imposed the maximum penalty of ten years. A person whose complicity in the operation was at least equal to that of the principal offender had his sentence reduced from nine years to seven, by a majority, because his past did not indicate that he was likely to pursue a career of crime and there was reason to believe he could be rehabilitated. Sentence was reduced from seven years to five years for a third party who had a history of petty theft and a considerably lesser involvement than the two others.

Appendix
Criminal Statistics
1962 – 1973

Table 1(a)

Persons Charged and Sentences of Convicted Persons by Nature of Indictable Offence, Canada, 1962

Indictable offence	Persons charged	Persons convicted	Suspended sentence with/without probation #	%	Fine #	%	Institution* #	%	Death #	%
Abandoning child	21	19	9	47	3	16	7	37	—	0
Abduction and kidnapping	67	46	15	33	1	2	30	65	—	0
Abortion and attempt	27	19	2	11	1	5	16	84	—	0
Assault causing bodily harm	2,486	1,883	463	25	775	41	645	34	—	0
Assault on peace officer and obstructing	1,764	1,633	150	9	1,005	62	478	29	—	0
Bigamy, feigned and unlawful marriage, polygamy	43	41	14	34	3	7	24	59	—	0
Buggery or bestiality, gross indecency	317	291	77	26	107	37	107	37	—	0
Causing bodily harm and danger	198	151	21	14	8	5	122	81	—	0
Common assault	506	459	133	29	201	44	125	27	—	0
Criminal negligence, bodily harm (motor vehicle)	10	5	1	20	1	20	3	60	—	0
Other criminal negligence causing bodily harm	10	8	5	63	1	13	2	25	—	0
Criminal negligence, death (motor manslaughter)	55	33	2	6	2	6	29	88	—	0
Other criminal negligence causing death	56	44	2	5	—	0	42	95	—	0
Criminal negligence in operation of motor vehicle	48	40	3	8	28	70	9	22	—	0
Criminal negligence causing no bodily harm nor death	40	33	2	6	12	36	19	58	—	0
Dangerous driving	50	45	2	4	30	67	13	29	—	0
Duties tending to preservation of life	36	23	11	48	2	9	10	43	—	0
Incest	40	35	2	6	—	0	33	94	—	0
Indecent assault on female	682	550	147	27	106	19	297	54	—	0
Indecent assault on male	93	79	24	30	4	5	51	65	—	0
Infanticide	4	1	—	0	—	0	1	100	—	0
Interfering with transportation facilities	1	1	—	0	1	100	—	0	—	0
Killing unborn child	2	2	—	0	2	100	—	0	—	0
Libel	5	2	1	50	1	50	—	0	—	0
Manslaughter	63	53	3	6	1	2	49	92	—	0
Murder	1	—	—	—	—	—	—	—	—	—
Murder, attempt to commit	21	14	—	0	—	0	14	100	—	0
Murder, capital	25	14	—	0	—	0	1	7	13	93
Murder, non-capital	34	20	—	0	—	0	20	100	—	0
Neglect in childbirth and concealing dead body	7	6	4	67	1	17	1	17	—	0
Procuring	93	74	12	16	2	3	60	81	—	0
Rape	92	54	1	2	2	4	51	94	—	0
Rape, attempt to commit	21	18*	1	*	2	*	15	*	—	0

Offence				%		%		%		
Seduction	2	1	—	0	1	100	—	0	—	0
Sexual intercourse and attempt	133	108	24	22	6	6	78	72	—	0
Other offences against the person	22	22	6	27	12	54	4	18	13	2
Against the person	**7,075**	**5,824**	**1,137**	**19**	**2,318**	**39**	**2,356**	**40**		
Breaking and entering a place	7,311	6,883	2,197	32	141	2	4,545	66		0
Extortion	38	33	12	36	2	6	19	58		0
Forcible entry and detainer	24	14	4	29	4	29	6	43		0
Robbery	828	704	91	13	7	10	606	86		0
Robbery while armed	161	142	3	2	4	3	135	95		0
Against property with violence	**8,362**	**7,776**	**2,307**	**30**	**158**	**2**	**5,311**	**68**		**0**
False pretences	2,299	2,046	637	31	328	16	1,081	53		0
Fraud and corruption	598	504	149	30	58	12	297	59		0
Having in possession	2,261	1,963	634	32	283	14	1,046	53		0
Theft	15,999	14,905	5,495	37	3,679	25	5,731	38		0
Theft by conversion	81	59	26	44	7	12	26	44		0
Theft from mail	36	34	—	0	—	0	34	100		0
Theft of stray cattle	5	3	—	0	3	100	—	0		0
Against property without violence	**21,279**	**19,514**	**6,941**	**36**	**4,358**	**22**	**8,215**	**42**		**0**
Arson and other fires	189	152	43	28	10	7	99	65		0
Other interference with property	812	705	282	40	197	28	226	32		0
Malicious offences against property	**1,001**	**857**	**325**	**38**	**207**	**24**	**325**	**38**		**0**
Forgery and uttering	1,218	1,171	303	26	21	2	847	72		0
Offences relating to currency	105	90	9	10	2	2	79	88		0
Forgery and offences relating to currency	**1,323**	**1,261**	**312**	**25**	**23**	**2**	**926**	**73**		**0**
Attempt to commit and accessories	512	450	124	28	57	13	269	60		0
Bawdy house, keepers	212	183	9	5	111	61	63	34		0
Conspiracy	202	170	32	19	22	13	116	68		0
Gaming, betting and lotteries	606	521	16	3	469	90	36	7		0
Habitual criminal	1	1	—	0	—	0	1	100		0
Motor vehicle										
Driving while ability to drive is impaired	262	251	—	0	235	94	16	6		0
Driving while disqualified	132	132	1	1	86	65	45	34		0
Driving while intoxicated	6	6	—	0	—	0	6	100		0
Failing to stop at scene of accident	68	60	3	5	51	85	6	10		0
Offences tending to corrupt morals	18	16	3	19	10	63	3	19		0
Offensive weapons	517	412	126	31	132	32	154	37		0
Perjury and false statements	82	62	9	15	3	5	50	80		0
Prison breach, escape and rescue	491	479	18	4	33	7	428	89		0
Public mischief	362	325	76	23	183	56	66	20		0
Various other offences	3	2	—	100	—	0	—	—		0
Other	3,474	3,070	419	14	1,392	45	1,259	41		0
Criminal Code	**42,514**	**38,302**	**11,441**	**30**	**8,456**	**22**	**18,392**	**48**	**13**	**0**

*Gaol, reformatory, industrial farm, training school, penitentiary.

Table 1(b)

Persons Charged and Sentences of Convicted Persons by Nature of Indictable Offence, Canada, 1963

Indictable offence	Persons charged	Persons convicted	Sentence							
			Suspended sentence with/without probation		Fine		Institution*		Death	
			#	%	#	%	#	%	#	%
Abandoning child	11	9	5	56	—	0	4	44	—	0
Abducting and kidnapping	50	31	11	35	2	6	18	58	—	0
Abortion and attempt	33	25	5	20	1	4	19	76	—	0
Assault causing bodily harm	2,530	1,942	396	20	812	42	734	38	—	0
Assault on peace officer and obstructing	1,808	1,663	135	8	1,071	64	457	27	—	0
Bigamy, feigned and unlawful marriage, polygamy	38	37	10	27	2	5	25	68	—	0
Buggery or bestiality, gross indecency	388	360	88	24	162	45	110	31	—	0
Causing bodily harm and danger	182	143	16	11	4	3	123	86	—	0
Common assault	516	482	117	24	243	50	122	25	—	0
Criminal negligence, bodily harm (motor vehicle)	11	9	2	22	2	22	5	56	—	0
Other criminal negligence causing bodily harm	23	21	3	14	3	14	15	72	—	0
Criminal negligence, death (motor manslaughter)	71	45	4	9	4	9	37	82	—	0
Other criminal negligence causing death	20	11	1	9	—	0	10	91	—	0
Criminal negligence in operation of motor vehicle	51	43	3	7	19	44	21	49	—	0
Criminal negligence causing no bodily harm nor death	32	28	13	46	5	18	10	36	—	0
Dangerous driving	127	108	2	2	75	69	31	29	—	0
Dangerous operation of vessel	2	2	—	0	2	100	—	0	—	0
Duties tending to preservation of life	24	21	12	57	1	5	8	38	—	0
Incest	61	52	9	17	—	0	43	83	—	0
Indecent assault on female	625	521	140	27	86	17	295	57	—	0
Indecent assault on male	114	104	44	42	7	7	53	51	—	0
Libel	6	4	2	50	2	50	—	0	—	0
Manslaughter	62	50	1	2	—	0	49	98	—	0
Murder, attempt to commit	22	14	3	21	—	0	11	79	—	0
Murder, capital	28	14	—	0	—	0	—	0	11	79
Murder, non-capital	63	31	—	0	—	0	31	100	—	0
Neglect in childbirth and concealing dead body	4	4	2	50	—	0	2	50	—	0
Procuring	78	61	8	13	6	10	47	77	—	0
Rape	127	74	1	1	—	0	73	99	—	0
Rape, attempt to commit	23	19	1	5	3	16	15	79	—	0
Seduction	5	5	1	20	2	40	2	40	—	0
Sexual intercourse and attempt	117	95	14	15	9	9	72	76	—	0
Threatening letters	16	14	9	64	—	0	5	36	—	0
Other offences against the person	28	27	4	15	22	81	1	4	—	0
Against the person	7,296	6,069	1,062	17	2,545	42	2,451	40	11	1

Offence										
Breaking and entering a place	8,081	7,655	2,645	36	177	2	4,833	62	—	0
Extortion	38	32	4	13	1	3	27	84	—	0
Forcible entry and detainer	53	39	12	31	14	36	13	33	—	0
Robbery	870	763	110	14	14	2	639	84	—	0
Robbery while armed	223	212	13	6	—	0	199	94	—	0
Against property with violence	**9,265**	**8,701**	**2,784**	**32**	**206**	**2**	**5,711**	**66**	**—**	**0**
False pretences	2,311	2,088	604	29	331	16	1,153	55	—	0
Fraud and corruption	632	539	156	21	62	12	321	60	—	0
Having in possession	2,674	2,294	703	31	361	16	1,230	54	—	0
Theft	17,814	16,658	6,053	36	4,293	26	6,312	38	—	0
Theft by conversion	89	64	27	42	4	6	33	52	—	0
Theft from mail	41	40	1	2	—	—	39	97	—	0
Theft or stray cattle	3	3	—	0	2	67	1	33	—	0
Against property without violence	**23,564**	**21,686**	**7,544**	**35**	**5,053**	**23**	**9,089**	**42**	**—**	**0**
Arson and other fires	157	134	52	39	13	10	69	51	—	0
Other interference with property	962	853	296	35	285	33	272	32	—	0
Malicious offences against property	**1,119**	**987**	**348**	**35**	**298**	**30**	**341**	**36**	**—**	**0**
Forgery and uttering	1,220	1,172	289	25	29	2	854	73	—	0
Offences relating to currency	84	70	7	10	1	1	62	89	—	0
Forgery and offences relating to currency	**1,304**	**1,242**	**296**	**24**	**30**	**2**	**916**	**74**	**—**	**0**
Attempt to commit and accessories	553	457	137	30	44	10	276	60	—	0
Bawdy house, keepers	238	209	6	3	127	61	76	36	—	0
Conspiracy	224	173	46	27	16	9	111	64	—	0
Counselling or aiding suicide	3	3	3	100	—	0	—	0	—	0
Dangerous sexual offenders	1	—	—	0	—	0	1	100	—	0
Gaming, betting and lotteries	774	681	15	2	624	92	42	6	—	0
Habitual criminal	3	3	—	0	—	0	3	100	—	0
Motor vehicle										
Driving while ability to drive is impaired	686	628	—	0	534	85	94	15	—	0
Driving while disqualified	115	114	2	2	83	73	29	25	—	0
Driving while intoxicated	27	26	—	0	1	4	25	96	—	0
Failing to stop at scene of accident	119	108	3	3	95	88	10	9	—	0
Offences tending to corrupt morals	11	10	—	0	8	80	2	20	—	0
Offensive weapons	608	503	145	29	151	30	207	41	—	0
Perjury and false statements	90	71	20	28	2	3	49	69	—	0
Prison breach, escape and rescue	505	498	19	4	30	6	449	90	—	0
Public mischief	358	330	87	26	177	54	66	20	—	0
Riots	251	—	—	0	—	0	—	0	—	0
Spreading false news	1	1	—	0	—	0	1	100	—	0
Various other offences	5	3	—	0	1	33	2	64	—	0
Other	**4,572**	**3,819**	**483**	**13**	**1,893**	**50**	**1,443**	**38**	**—**	**0**
Criminal Code	**47,120**	**42,504**	**12,517**	**29**	**10,025**	**24**	**19,951**	**47**	**11**	**0**

*Gaol, reformatory, industrial farm, training school, penitentiary.

Table 1(c)

Persons Charged and Sentences of Convicted Persons by Nature of Indictable Offence, Canada, 1964

Indictable offence	Persons charged	Persons convicted	Sentence							
			Suspended sentence with/without probation #	%	Fine #	%	Institution* #	%	Death #	%
Abandoning child	23	16	12	75	1	6	3	19	—	0
Abduction and kidnapping	67	53	18	34	1	2	34	64	—	0
Abortion and attempt	31	24	4	17	1	4	19	79	—	0
Assault causing bodily harm	2,678	2,085	423	20	822	39	840	40	—	0
Assault on peace officer and obstructing	1,959	1,793	190	11	1,163	65	440	26	—	0
Bigamy, feigned and unlawful marriage, polygamy	34	30	11	37	2	7	17	57	—	0
Buggery or bestiality, gross indecency	492	464	82	18	234	50	148	32	—	0
Causing bodily harm and danger	189	146	25	17	6	4	115	79	—	0
Common assault	541	516	134	26	238	46	144	28	—	0
Criminal negligence, bodily harm (motor vehicle)	3	2	—	0	—	0	2	100	—	0
Other criminal negligence, bodily harm	23	17	9	53	2	12	6	35	—	0
Criminal negligence, death (motor manslaughter)	55	30	2	7	1	3	27	90	—	0
Other criminal negligence, death	19	13	—	0	1	8	12	92	—	0
Criminal negligence in operation of motor vehicle	29	27	4	15	16	59	7	26	—	0
Criminal negligence, no bodily harm nor death	23	18	3	17	7	39	8	44	—	0
Dangerous driving	101	92	5	5	49	53	38	41	—	0
Duties tending to preservation of life	20	12	9	75	—	0	3	25	—	0
Incest	47	41	4	10	—	0	37	90	—	0
Indecent assault on female	606	483	146	30	91	19	246	51	—	0
Indecent assault on male	113	98	34	35	9	9	55	56	—	0
Libel	4	1	1	100	—	0	0	0	—	0
Manslaughter	71	56	1	2	—	0	55	98	—	0
Murder, attempt to commit	19	11	—	0	—	0	11	100	—	0
Murder, capital	15	6	—	0	—	0	1	17	5	83
Murder, non-capital	46	32	—	0	—	0	32	100	—	0
Neglect in childbirth and concealing dead body	5	5	5	100	—	0	0	0	—	0
Procuring	62	45	2	4	—	0	43	96	—	0
Rape	126	62	1	2	—	0	61	98	—	0
Rape, attempt to commit	17	16	1	6	1	6	14	88	—	0
Seduction	3	3	1	33	1	33	1	33	—	0
Sexual intercourse and attempt	108	93	13	14	3	3	77	86	—	0
Threatening letters	14	10	6	60	1	10	3	30	—	0
Other offences against the person	19	17	3	18	13	76	1	6	—	0
Against the person	7,562	6,317	1,149	18	2,663	42	2,500	40	5	0

Breaking and entering a place	7,689	7,288	2,555	35	182	2	4,551	62	—	0
Extortion	29	21	9	43	1	4	11	53	—	0
Forcible entry and detainer	35	22	5	23	10	46	7	32	—	0
Robbery	954	824	104	13	7	1	713	87	—	0
Robbery while armed	271	244	23	9	2	1	219	90	—	0
Against property with violence	**8,978**	**8,399**	**2,696**	**32**	**202**	**2**	**5,501**	**65**	—	**0**
False pretences	2,183	1,970	576	29	357	18	1,037	53	—	0
Fraud and corruption	666	545	171	31	65	12	309	57	—	0
Having in possession	2,625	2,279	761	33	317	14	1,201	53	—	0
Theft	17,741	16,550	6,124	37	4,592	28	5,834	35	—	0
Theft by conversion	72	54	17	31	6	11	31	57	—	0
Theft from mail	40	39	1	3	—	0	38	97	—	0
Theft of stray cattle	7	6	—	0	2	33	4	67	—	0
Against property without violence	**23,334**	**21,443**	**7,650**	**36**	**5,339**	**25**	**8,454**	**39**	—	**0**
Arson and other fires	131	104	41	39	6	6	57	55	—	0
Other interference with property	973	865	341	39	303	35	221	26	—	0
Malicious offences against property	**1,104**	**969**	**382**	**39**	**309**	**32**	**278**	**27**	—	**0**
Forgery and uttering	1,269	1,200	330	28	29	2	841	70	—	0
Offences relating to currency	46	38	4	11	—	0	34	89	—	0
Forgery and offences relating to currency	**1,315**	**1,238**	**334**	**27**	**29**	**2**	**875**	**71**	—	**0**
Attempt to commit and accessories	482	420	108	26	55	13	257	61	—	0
Bawdy house, keepers	246	220	11	5	128	58	81	37	—	0
Conspiracy	216	169	58	34	10	6	101	60	—	0
Counselling or aiding suicide	2	2	0	0	—	0	2	100	—	0
Dangerous sexual offenders	3	3	0	0	—	0	3	100	—	0
Gaming, betting and lotteries	690	600	17	3	546	91	37	6	—	0
Habitual criminal	25	25	—	0	—	0	25	100	—	0
Motor vehicle										
Driving while ability to drive is impaired	422	353	1	0	231	65	121	34	—	0
Driving while disqualified	126	123	6	5	83	67	34	28	—	0
Driving while intoxicated	26	22	—	0	—	0	22	100	—	0
Failing to stop at scene of accident	90	79	3	3	66	84	11	13	—	0
Offences tending to corrupt morals	13	11	2	18	8	73	1	9	—	0
Offensive weapons	542	468	165	35	136	29	167	36	—	0
Perjury and false statements	71	54	15	27	4	7	35	65	—	0
Prison breach, escape and rescue	465	453	19	4	53	12	381	84	—	0
Public mischief	374	356	74	21	226	63	56	16	—	0
Riots	5	4	—	0	1	25	3	75	—	0
Trade marks	1	1	—	0	—	0	—	0	—	0
Various other offences	13	12	2	17	2	100	10	83	—	0
Other	3,812	3,375	480	14	1,548	46	1,347	40	—	5
Criminal Code	**46,105**	**41,741**	**12,691**	**30**	**10,090**	**24**	**18,955**	**45**	—	**0**

*Gaol, reformatory, industrial farm, training school, penitentiary.

Table 1(d)

Persons Charged and Sentences of Convicted Persons by Nature of Indictable Offence, Canada, 1965

Indictable offence	Persons charged	Persons convicted	Suspended sentence with/without probation #	%	Fine #	%	Institution* #	%	Death #	%
Abandoning child	22	20	14	70	—	0	6	30	—	0
Abduction and kidnapping	76	51	17	33	7	14	27	53	—	0
Abortion and attempt	28	24	8	33	1	4	15	63	—	0
Assault causing bodily harm	2,739	2,161	390	18	954	44	817	38	—	0
Assault on peace officer and obstructing	2,066	1,896	172	9	1,196	63	528	28	—	0
Bigamy, feigned and unlawful marriage, polygamy	33	30	10	33	1	3	19	63	—	0
Buggery or bestiality, gross indecency	325	299	64	21	142	47	93	31	—	0
Causing bodily harm and danger	233	169	41	24	13	8	115	68	—	0
Common assault	581	522	99	19	287	55	136	26	—	0
Criminal negligence, bodily harm (motor vehicle)	8	6	—	0	3	50	3	50	—	0
Other criminal negligence, bodily harm	21	19	8	42	2	16	8	42	—	0
Criminal negligence, death (motor manslaughter)	43	24	1	4	2	8	21	88	—	0
Other criminal negligence, death	21	12	1	8	—	0	11	92	—	0
Criminal negligence in operation of motor vehicle	41	28	4	14	14	50	10	36	—	0
Criminal negligence, no bodily harm nor death	15	12	2	17	6	50	4	33	—	0
Dangerous driving	107	91	9	10	45	50	37	40	—	0
Dangerous operation of vessel	1	1	—	0	—	0	—	0	—	0
Duties tending to preservation of life	20	16	7	44	—	0	9	56	—	0
Incest	49	37	1	3	—	0	36	97	—	0
Indecent assault on female	632	502	144	29	84	17	274	55	—	0
Indecent assault on male	115	99	3	3	11	11	50	50	—	0
Libel	2	1	—	0	1	100	—	0	—	0
Manslaughter	61	50	—	0	—	0	50	100	—	0
Murder, attempt to commit	16	11	1	9	—	0	10	91	—	0
Murder, capital	31	19	—	0	—	0	—	0	19	100
Murder, non-capital	52	36	—	0	—	0	36	100	—	0
Neglect in childbirth and concealing dead body	4	4	4	100	—	0	—	0	—	0
Procuring	59	48	9	19	1	2	38	79	—	0
Rape	107	54	2	4	—	0	52	96	—	0
Rape, attempt to commit	14	10	—	0	—	0	10	100	—	0
Seduction	12	6	—	0	4	67	2	33	—	0
Sexual intercourse and attempt	113	93	24	26	4	4	65	70	—	0
Threatening letters	22	15	7	47	1	6	7	47	—	0
Other offences against the person	20	20	2	10	15	75	3	15	—	0
Against the person	**7,689**	**6,385**	**1,079**	**17**	**2,795**	**44**	**2,492**	**39**	**19**	**0**

Breaking and entering a place	7,351	6,950	2,629	38	234	3	4,087	59	—	0
Breaking and entering while armed	2	2	1	50		0	1	50	—	0
Extortion	36	31	9	29	—	0	22	71	—	0
Forcible entry and detainer	40	22	7	32	7	32	8	36	—	0
Robbery	941	798	113	14	8	1	677	85	—	0
Robbery while armed	244	224	16	7	—	0	208	93	—	0
Against property with violence	**8,614**	**8,027**	**2,775**	**35**	**249**	**3**	**5,003**	**62**	**—**	**0**
False pretences	2,031	1,837	531	29	371	20	935	51	—	0
Fraud and corruption	718	599	178	30	76	13	345	58	—	0
Fraudulently taking cattle	5	3	1	33	2	67	—	0	—	0
Having in possession	2,607	2,229	738	33	371	17	1,120	50	—	0
Theft	17,862	16,533	5,960	36	5,287	32	5,286	32	—	0
Theft by conversion	77	53	21	40	5	9	27	51	—	0
Theft from mail	28	27		0		0	27	100	—	0
Against property without violence	**23,328**	**21,281**	**7,429**	**35**	**6,112**	**29**	**7,740**	**36**	**—**	**0**
Arson and other fires	134	107	40	37	7	7	60	56	—	0
Other interference with property	1,048	915	314	34	347	38	254	28	—	0
Malicious offences against property	**1,182**	**1,022**	**354**	**35**	**354**	**35**	**314**	**30**	**—**	**0**
Forgery and uttering	1,302	1,238	348	28	41	3	849	69	—	0
Offences relating to currency	87	75	8	11	2	3	65	87	—	0
Forgery and offences relating to currency	**1,389**	**1,313**	**356**	**27**	**43**	**3**	**914**	**70**	**—**	**0**
Attempt to commit and accessories	497	420	133	32	85	20	202	48	—	0
Bawdy house, keepers	212	191	20	10	116	61	55	29	—	0
Conspiracy	248	183	55	30	15	8	113	62	—	0
Counselling or aiding suicide	1					0		0	—	0
Dangerous sexual offenders	4	3		0	3	0	3	100	—	0
Gaming, betting and lotteries	632	560	20	4	489	87	52	8	—	0
Habitual criminal	26	16		0		0	16	100	—	0
Motor vehicle										
Driving while ability to drive is impaired	281	240	2	1	124	52	114	47	—	0
Driving while disqualified	96	92	7	8	72	78	13	14	—	0
Driving while intoxicated	31	28		0	1	4	27	96	—	0
Failing to stop at scene of accident	71	63	5	8	49	78	9	14	—	0
Offences tending to corrupt morals	17	13	1	8	10	77	2	15	—	0
Offensive weapons	671	540	179	33	168	31	193	36	—	0
Perjury and false statements	103	72	30	42	3	4	39	54	—	0
Prison breach, escape and rescue	585	549	36	7	78	14	435	79	—	0
Public mischief	447	420	90	21	248	59	82	20	—	0
Riots	3	3		0	—	0	3	100	—	0
Various other offences	9	8	3	38	1	12	4	50	—	0
Other	**3,934**	**3,401**	**580**	**17**	**1,459**	**43**	**1,362**	**40**	**—**	**0**
Criminal Code	**46,136**	**41,429**	**12,573**	**30**	**11,012**	**27**	**17,825**	**43**	**19**	**0**

*Gaol, reformatory, industrial farm, training school, penitentiary.

Table 1(e)

Persons Charged and Sentences of Convicted Persons by Nature of Indictable Offence, Canada, 1966

Indictable offence	Persons charged	Persons convicted	Suspended sentence with/without probation #	%	Fine #	%	Institution* #	%	Death #	%
Abandoning child	80	71	19	27	24	34	28	39	—	0
Abduction and kidnapping	57	37	16	43	—	0	21	57	—	0
Abortion and attempt	37	27	3	11	—	0	24	89	—	0
Assault causing bodily harm	3,020	2,377	436	18	1,103	46	838	35	—	0
Assault on peace officer and obstructing	2,396	2,192	206	9	1,382	63	604	28	—	0
Bigamy, feigned and unlawful marriage, polygamy	35	30	8	27	4	13	18	60	—	0
Buggery or bestiality, gross indecency	317	283	63	22	148	52	72	25	—	0
Causing bodily harm and danger	241	189	35	19	13	7	141	75	—	0
Common assault	593	528	134	25	279	53	115	22	—	0
Criminal negligence, bodily harm (motor vehicle)	5	5	2	40	2	40	1	20	—	0
Other criminal negligence, bodily harm	30	17	5	29	—	0	12	71	—	0
Criminal negligence, death (motor manslaughter)	25	20	1	5	—	0	19	95	—	0
Other criminal negligence, death	19	10	2	20	3	30	5	50	—	0
Criminal negligence in operation of motor vehicle	39	37	3	8	20	54	14	38	—	0
Criminal negligence, no bodily harm nor death	16	11	4	36	1	9	6	55	—	0
Dangerous driving	109	94	5	5	55	59	34	36	—	0
Dangerous operation of vessel	1	1	—	0	—	0	1	100	—	0
Duties tending to preservation of life	13	9	5	56	3	33	1	11	—	0
Incest	43	34	9	26	—	0	25	74	—	0
Indecent assault on female	669	552	197	36	93	17	262	47	—	0
Indecent assault on male	110	87	35	40	9	10	43	49	—	0
Infanticide	3	2	2	100	—	0	—	0	—	0
Interfering with transportation facilities	2	1	—	0	1	100	—	0	—	0
Libel			—	0	—	0	—	0	—	0
Manslaughter	81	69	2	3	—	0	67	97	—	0
Murder, attempt to commit	24	10	—	0	—	0	10	100	—	0
Murder	1									
Murder, capital	18	9	—	0	—	0	—	0	9	100
Murder, non-capital	54	34	—	0	—	0	34	100	—	0
Neglect in childbirth and concealing dead body	3	2	2	100	—	0	—	0	—	0
Procuring	57	45	7	16	7	16	31	69	—	0
Rape	112	52	—	0	—	0	52	100	—	0
Rape, attempt to commit	16	13	1	8	—	0	12	92	—	0
Seduction	1	1	—	0	—	0	1	100	—	0
Sexual intercourse and attempt	102	77	21	27	5	6	51	66	—	0
Threatening letters	13	5	3	60	—	0	2	40	—	0
Other offences against the person	22	17	1	6	16	94	—	0	—	0

Against the person	8,365	6,948	1,227	18	3,168	46	2,544	37	9	0
Breaking and entering a place	7,404	6,919	2,890	42	160	2	3,869	56	—	0
Extortion	33	23	14	61	—	0	9	39	—	0
Forcible entry and detainer	41	29	9	31	10	34	10	34	—	0
Robbery	1,008	822	137	17	13	2	672	82	—	0
Robbery while armed	190	172	12	7	1	1	159	92	—	0
Against property with violence	8,676	7,965	3,062	38	184	2	4,719	59	—	0
False pretences	2,191	1,968	589	30	371	19	1,008	51	—	0
Fraud and corruption	784	650	176	27	101	16	373	57	—	0
Fraudulently taking cattle	6	—	—	0	2	100	—	0	—	0
Having in possession	2,742	2,384	778	33	419	18	1,187	50	—	0
Theft	20,345	18,831	6,858	36	6,292	33	5,681	30	—	0
Theft by conversion	87	62	25	40	6	10	31	50	—	0
Theft from mail	48	42	1	2	—	0	41	98	—	0
Against property without violence	26,203	23,939	8,427	35	7,191	30	8,321	35	—	0
Arson and other fires	176	139	53	38	12	9	74	53	—	0
Other interference with property	1,252	1,111	395	36	423	38	293	26	—	0
Malicious offences against property	1,428	1,250	448	36	435	35	367	29	—	0
Forgery and uttering	1,155	1,079	361	33	25	2	693	64	—	0
Offences relating to currency	92	72	13	18	—	0	59	82	—	0
Forgery and offences relating to currency	1,247	1,151	374	32	25	2	752	65	—	0
Attempt to commit and accessories	458	383	140	37	77	20	166	43	—	0
Bawdy house, keepers	177	167	24	14	100	60	43	26	—	0
Conspiracy	253	185	57	31	11	6	117	63	—	0
Dangerous sexual offenders	6	6	—	0	6	0	6	100	—	0
Gaming, betting and lotteries	889	836	17	2	767	92	52	6	—	0
Habitual criminal	9	6	—	0	—	0	6	100	—	0
Motor vehicle										
Driving while ability to drive is impaired	368	309	1	0	202	65	106	34	—	0
Driving while disqualified	127	116	4	3	77	66	35	30	—	0
Driving while intoxicated	21	20	—	0	—	0	20	100	—	0
Failing to stop at scene of accident	56	52	4	8	29	56	19	37	—	0
Offences tending to corrupt morals	13	10	3	30	7	70	—	0	—	0
Offensive weapons	749	596	215	36	172	29	209	35	—	0
Perjury and false statements	83	61	19	31	4	7	38	62	—	0
Prison breach, escape and rescue	879	825	66	8	69	8	690	84	—	0
Public mischief	441	404	89	22	231	57	84	21	—	0
Spreading false news	4	4	2	50	1	25	1	25	—	0
Trade marks	1	1	—	0	—	100	—	0	—	0
Various other offences	11	8	3	38	1	13	4	50	—	0
Other	4,545	3,989	644	16	1,749	44	1,596	40	—	0
Criminal Code	50,464	45,242	14,182	31	12,752	28	18,299	40	9	0

*Gaol, reformatory, industrial farm, training school, penitentiary.

Table 1(f)

Persons Charged and Sentences of Convicted Persons by Nature of Indictable Offence, Canada, 1967

Indictable offence	Persons charged	Persons convicted	Suspended sentence with/without probation #	%	Fine #	%	Institution* #	%	Death #	%
Abandoning child	19	17	8	47	—	0	9	53	—	0
Abduction and kidnapping	63	46	19	41	6	13	21	46	—	0
Abortion and attempt	29	22	4	18	3	14	15	68	—	0
Assault causing bodily harm	2,648	2,047	428	21	831	41	788	38	—	0
Assault on peace officer and obstructing	2,248	2,028	188	9	1,313	65	527	26	—	0
Bigamy, feigned and unlawful marriage, polygamy	32	28	10	36	1	4	17	61	—	0
Buggery or bestiality, gross indecency	445	406	59	15	264	65	83	20	—	0
Causing bodily harm and danger	236	176	42	24	13	7	121	69	—	0
Common assault	580	512	163	32	238	46	111	22	—	0
Criminal negligence, bodily harm (motor vehicle)	5	5	1	20	4	80	—	0	—	0
Other criminal negligence, bodily harm	26	21	7	33	1	5	13	62	—	0
Criminal negligence, death (motor manslaughter)	55	35	1	3	5	14	29	83	—	0
Other criminal negligence, death	26	15	2	13	—	0	13	87	—	0
Criminal negligence in operation of motor vehicle	23	22	2	9	11	50	9	41	—	0
Criminal negligence, no bodily harm nor death	17	13	—	0	3	23	10	77	—	0
Dangerous driving	127	100	7	7	61	61	32	32	—	0
Dangerous operation of vessel	1	1	—	0	1	100	—	0	—	0
Duties tending to preservation of life	14	10	6	60	—	0	4	40	—	0
Incest	40	35	4	11	1	3	30	86	—	0
Indecent assault on female	618	484	153	32	84	17	247	51	—	0
Indecent assault on male	121	98	38	39	6	6	54	55	—	0
Infanticide	4	2	2	100	—	0	—	0	—	0
Interfering with transportation facilities	1	1	—	0	—	0	1	100	—	0
Libel	5	4	1	25	1	25	2	50	—	0
Manslaughter	90	75	1	1	—	0	74	99	—	0
Murder, attempt to commit	30	19	2	11	1	5	16	84	—	0
Murder, capital	14	7	—	0	—	0	—	0	7	100
Murder, non-capital	63	36	—	0	—	0	36	100	—	0
Neglect in childbirth and concealing dead body	3	3	2	67	—	0	1	33	—	0
Procuring	70	47	7	15	4	9	36	77	—	0
Rape	127	57	5	9	—	0	52	91	—	0
Rape, attempt to commit	28	18	3	17	1	6	14	78	—	0
Seduction	1	1	—	0	—	0	1	100	—	0
Sexual intercourse and attempt	116	96	21	22	7	7	68	71	—	0
Threatening letters	12	6	4	67	—	0	2	33	—	0
Other offences against the person	20	17	1	6	13	76	3	18	—	0
Against the person	**7,957**	**6,510**	**1,191**	**18**	**2,874**	**44**	**2,438**	**37**	**7**	**0**

Offence										
Breaking and entering a place	7,749	7,165	3,079	43	221	3	3,865	54	—	0
Extortion	37	28	7	25	3	11	18	64	—	0
Forcible entry and detainer	21	16	4	25	8	50	4	25	—	0
Robbery	986	827	145	18	14	2	668	81	—	0
Robbery while armed	162	143	19	13	1	1	123	86	—	0
Against property with violence	8,955	8,179	3,254	40	247	3	4,678	57	—	0
False pretences	2,229	1,996	549	28	374	19	1,063	53	—	0
Fraud and corruption	749	637	182	29	117	18	338	53	—	0
Fraudulently taking cattle	2	2	—	0	2	100	—	0	—	0
Having in possession	3,003	2,596	860	33	460	18	1,276	49	—	0
Theft	20,091	18,550	6,612	36	6,528	35	5,410	29	—	0
Theft by conversion	75	54	26	48	5	9	23	43	—	0
Theft from mail	38	34	1	3	1	3	32	94	—	0
Against property without violence	26,187	23,859	8,230	34	7,487	31	8,142	34	—	0
Arson and other fires	141	115	34	30	3	3	78	68	—	0
Other interference with property	1,253	1,105	375	34	435	39	295	27	—	0
Malicious offences against property	1,394	1,220	409	34	438	36	373	31	—	0
Forgery and uttering	1,204	1,119	338	30	32	3	749	67	—	0
Offences relating to currency	131	107	16	15	5	5	86	80	—	0
Forgery and offences relating to currency	1,335	1,226	354	29	37	3	835	68	—	0
Attempt to commit and accessories	480	417	143	34	69	17	205	49	—	0
Bawdy house, keepers	155	133	15	11	89	67	29	22	—	0
Conspiracy	279	197	44	22	12	6	141	72	—	0
Dangerous sexual offenders	2	2	—	0	—	0	2	100	—	0
Gaming, betting and lotteries	663	629	7	1	565	90	57	9	—	0
Habitual criminal	15	10	—	0	—	0	10	100	—	0
Motor vehicle										
Driving while ability to drive is impaired	210	170	—	0	124	73	46	27	—	0
Driving while disqualified	112	106	4	4	63	59	39	37	—	0
Driving while intoxicated	7	6	—	0	—	0	6	100	—	0
Failing to stop at scene of accident	59	52	5	10	38	73	9	17	—	0
Offences tending to corrupt morals	21	17	4	24	10	59	3	18	—	0
Offensive weapons	850	708	240	34	219	31	249	35	—	0
Perjury and false statements	82	60	13	22	6	10	41	68	—	0
Prison breach, escape and rescue	878	811	60	7	87	11	664	82	—	0
Public mischief	430	398	98	25	225	57	75	19	—	0
Riots	22	22	—	0	5	23	17	77	—	0
Spreading false news	1	1	—	0	1	100	—	0	—	0
Trade marks	2	1	—	0	1	100	—	0	—	0
Various other offences	9	6	1	17	5	83	—	0	—	0
Other	4,277	3,746	634	17	1,519	41	1,593	43	—	0
Criminal Code	50,105	44,740	14,072	31	12,602	28	18,059	40	7	0

*Gaol, reformatory, industrial farm, training school, penitentiary.

Table 1(g)

Persons Charged and Sentences of Convicted Persons by Nature of Indictable Offence, Canada,† 1968

Indictable offence	Persons charged	Persons convicted	Suspended sentence with/without probation #	%	Fine #	%	Institution* #	%	Death #	%
Abandoning child	13	11	8	73	—	0	3	27	—	0
Abduction and kidnapping	62	44	13	30	1	2	30	68	—	0
Abortion and attempt	20	14	8	57	—	0	6	43	—	0
Assault causing bodily harm	2,298	1,776	375	21	724	41	677	38	—	0
Assault on peace officer and obstructing	1,966	1,760	166	9	1,115	63	479	27	—	0
Bigamy, feigned and unlawful marriage, polygamy	19	17	4	24	3	18	10	59	—	0
Buggery or bestiality, gross indecency	258	238	41	17	166	70	31	13	—	0
Causing bodily harm and danger	236	182	34	19	3	2	145	80	—	0
Common assault	494	436	107	25	202	46	127	29	—	0
Criminal negligence, bodily harm (motor vehicle)	2	1	—	0	—	0	1	100	—	0
Other criminal negligence, bodily harm	24	20	5	25	4	20	11	55	—	0
Criminal negligence, death (motor manslaughter)	30	18	—	0	1	6	17	94	—	0
Other criminal negligence, death	20	10	—	0	1	10	9	90	—	0
Criminal negligence in operation of motor vehicle	17	11	1	9	3	27	7	64	—	0
Criminal negligence, no bodily harm nor death	17	12	3	25	6	50	3	25	—	0
Dangerous driving	135	114	11	10	55	48	48	42	—	0
Duties tending to preservation of life	4	3	3	100	—	0	—	0	—	0
Incest	31	26	5	19	—	0	21	81	—	0
Indecent assault on female	540	407	161	40	50	12	196	48	—	0
Indecent assault on male	103	80	36	45	9	11	35	44	—	0
Infanticide	2	2	2	100	—	0	—	0	—	0
Killing unborn child	—	1	—	0	—	0	1	100	—	0
Libel	3	3	2	67	1	33	—	0	—	0
Manslaughter	88	70	2	3	—	0	68	97	—	0
Murder, attempt to commit	8	5	—	0	—	0	5	100	—	0
Murder, capital	1	1	—	0	—	0	—	0	1	100
Murder, non-capital	56	25	—	0	—	0	25	100	—	0
Neglect in childbirth and concealing dead body	1	1	1	100	—	0	—	0	—	0
Procuring	66	41	5	12	4	10	32	78	—	0
Rape	141	68	—	0	—	0	68	100	—	0
Rape, attempt to commit	22	12	—	0	—	0	12	100	—	0
Seduction	1	1	—	0	—	0	1	100	—	0
Sexual intercourse and attempt	74	61	11	18	2	3	48	79	—	0
Threatening letters	13	11	7	64	—	0	4	36	—	0
Other offences against the person	8	5	3	60	2	40	—	0	—	0
Against the person	6,774	5,487	1,014	18	2,352	43	2,120	39	1	0

Breaking and entering a place	6,594	6,001	2,463	41	98	2	3,440	57	—	0
Extortion	18	10	4	40	2	0	6	60	—	0
Forcible entry and detainer	16	7	3	43	2	29	2	29	—	0
Robbery	959	743	63	8	5	1	675	91	—	0
Robbery while armed	77	71	4	6	1	1	66	93	—	0
Against property with violence	**7,664**	**6,832**	**2,537**	**37**	**106**	**2**	**4,189**	**61**	—	**0**
False pretences	2,071	1,860	531	29	331	18	998	54	—	0
Fraud and corruption	619	524	158	30	118	23	248	47	—	0
Fraudulently taking cattle	1	1	1	100		0	—	0	—	0
Having in possession	3,049	2,648	908	34	500	19	1,240	47	—	0
Theft	16,529	15,132	4,822	32	5,865	39	4,445	29	—	0
Theft by conversion	34	27	15	56	2	7	10	37	—	0
Theft from mail	31	27	3	11		0	24	89	—	0
Against property without violence	**22,334**	**20,219**	**6,438**	**32**	**6,816**	**34**	**6,965**	**34**	—	**0**
Arson and other fires	122	98	33	34	5	5	60	61	—	0
Other interference with property	1,018	901	376	42	302	34	223	25	—	0
Malicious offences against property	**1,140**	**999**	**409**	**41**	**307**	**31**	**283**	**28**	—	**0**
Forgery and uttering	1,150	1,077	332	31	23	2	722	67	—	0
Offences relating to currency	68	46	13	28	1	1	32	70	—	0
Forgery and offences relating to currency	**1,218**	**1,123**	**345**	**31**	**24**	**2**	**754**	**67**	—	**0**
Attempt to commit and accessories	344	297	90	30	62	21	145	49	—	0
Bawdy house, keepers	89	71	5	7	53	75	13	18	—	0
Conspiracy	140	97	31	32	2	2	64	66	—	0
Dangerous sexual offenders	1	1	—	0		0	1	100	—	0
Gaming, betting and lotteries	259	229	6	3	203	89	20	9	—	0
Habitual criminal	10	7	—	0		0	7	100	—	0
Motor vehicle	—	—	—				—		—	0
Driving while ability to drive is impaired	105	95	—	0	80	84	15	16	—	0
Driving while disqualified	64	61	2	3	27	44	32	52	—	0
Driving while intoxicated	5	5	—	0		0	5	100	—	0
Failing to stop at scene of accident	42	36	3	8	23	64	10	28	—	0
Offences tending to corrupt morals	4	4	—	0	3	75	1	25	—	0
Offensive weapons	877	668	221	33	189	28	258	39	—	0
Perjury and false statements	69	56	12	21	78	5	41	73	—	0
Prison breach, escape and rescue	714	645	34	5	192	12	533	83	—	0
Public mischief	405	356	88	25		54	76	21	—	0
Various other offences	4	3	1	33		67	—	0	—	0
Other	**3,132**	**2,631**	**493**	**19**	**917**	**35**	**1,221**	**46**	—	**0**
Criminal Code	**42,262**	**37,291**	**11,236**	**30**	**10,522**	**28**	**15,532**	**42**	**1**	**0**

*Gaol, reformatory, industrial farm, training school, penitentiary.

†Excludes Quebec.

Table 1(h)

Persons Charged and Sentences of Convicted Persons by Nature of Indictable Offence, Canada,† 1969

Indictable offence	Persons charged	Persons convicted	Suspended sentence with/without probation #	%	Fine #	%	Institution* #	%	Death #	%
Abandoning child	20	17	10	59	—	0	7	41	—	0
Abduction and kidnapping	39	28	9	32	2	7	17	61	—	0
Abortion and attempt	11	9	5	56	—	0	4	44	—	0
Assault causing bodily harm	2,197	1,670	366	22	723	43	581	35	—	0
Assault on peace officer and obstructing	1,724	1,562	153	10	1,018	65	391	25	—	0
Bigamy, feigned and unlawful marriage, polygamy	15	15	4	27	1	7	10	67	—	0
Buggery or bestiality, gross indecency	270	236	32	14	180	76	24	10	—	0
Causing bodily harm and danger	153	109	22	20	6	6	81	74	—	0
Common assault	519	481	134	28	236	49	111	23	—	0
Other criminal negligence, bodily harm	26	20	8	40	—	0	12	60	—	0
Criminal negligence, death (motor manslaughter)	20	15	1	7	3	20	11	73	—	0
Other criminal negligence, death	20	8	1	13	—	—	7	87	—	0
Criminal negligence in operation of motor vehicle	29	23	2	9	5	22	16	70	—	0
Criminal negligence, no bodily harm nor death	9	8	3	38	2	25	3	38	—	0
Dangerous driving	139	117	9	8	54	46	54	46	—	0
Duties tending to preservation of life	2	1	—	0	—	0	1	100	—	0
Incest	36	27	10	37	—	0	17	63	—	0
Indecent assault on female	554	446	162	36	78	17	206	46	—	0
Indecent assault on male	98	77	45	58	2	3	30	39	—	0
Infanticide	1	—	1	100	—	—	—	0	—	0
Libel	5	2	—	0	2	100	—	0	—	0
Manslaughter	114	98	3	3	—	0	95	97	—	0
Murder, attempt to commit	15	7	—	0	—	0	7	100	—	0
Murder, capital	2	—	—	0	—	0	—	—	—	0
Murder, non-capital	64	22	—	0	—	0	22	100	—	0
Neglect in childbirth and concealing dead body	7	7	7	100	—	0	—	0	—	0
Procuring	56	41	4	10	1	2	36	88	—	0
Rape	144	63	3	5	—	0	60	95	—	0
Rape, attempt to commit	12	—	1	14	—	0	6	86	—	0
Seduction	1	—	—	0	—	0	—	0	—	0
Sexual intercourse and attempt	82	63	11	17	1	2	51	81	—	0
Threatening letters	11	6	3	50	1	17	2	33	—	0
Other offences against the person	13	10	2	20	8	80	—	0	—	0
Against the person	6,408	5,196	1,011	19	2,323	45	1,862	36	—	0

	Charged	Convicted	No.	%	No.	%	No.	%	No.	%
Breaking and entering a place	6,031	5,573	2,310	41	96	2	3,167	57	—	0
Extortion	36	21	12	57	—	0	9	43	—	0
Forcible entry and detainer	16	12	4	33	4	33	4	33	—	0
Robbery	853	689	79	11	2	0	608	88	—	0
Robbery while armed	63	53	5	9	—	0	48	91	—	0
Against property with violence	6,999	6,348	2,410	38	102	2	3,836	60	—	0
False pretences	1,880	1,694	592	35	241	14	861	51	—	0
Fraud and corruption	643	555	168	30	85	15	302	54	—	0
Fraudulently taking cattle	2	2	1	50	—	0	1	50	—	0
Having in possession	3,060	2,699	1,017	38	489	18	1,193	44	—	0
Theft	16,137	14,744	4,827	33	5,961	40	3,956	27	—	0
Theft by conversion	31	24	14	58	—	0	10	42	—	0
Theft from mail	19	18	4	22	2	11	12	67	—	0
Against property without violence	21,772	19,736	6,623	34	6,778	34	6,335	32	—	0
Arson and other fires	151	120	56	47	3	3	61	51	—	0
Other interference with property	1,227	989	346	35	367	37	276	28	—	0
Malicious offences against property	1,378	1,109	402	36	370	33	337	30	—	0
Forgery and uttering	1,023	964	340	35	21	2	603	63	—	0
Offences relating to currency	55	42	8	19	2	5	32	76	—	0
Forgery and offences relating to currency	1,078	1,006	348	35	23	2	635	63	—	0
Attempt to commit and accessories	327	296	82	28	60	20	154	52	—	0
Bawdy house, keepers	136	112	15	13	77	69	20	18	—	0
Conspiracy	124	87	16	18	9	10	62	71	—	0
Dangerous sex offenders	1	1	—	0	—	0	1	100	—	0
Gaming, betting and lotteries	179	140	9	6	123	88	8	6	—	0
Habitual criminal	5	4	—	0	—	0	4	100	—	0
Motor vehicle										
Driving while ability to drive is impaired	167	149	2	1	132	89	15	10	—	0
Driving while disqualified	50	44	—	0	27	61	17	39	—	0
Driving while intoxicated	12	11	—	0	7	64	4	36	—	0
Failing to stop at scene of accident	34	26	—	0	22	85	4	15	—	0
Offences tending to corrupt morals	8	8	7	88	1	13	—	0	—	0
Offensive weapons	885	697	256	37	222	32	219	31	—	0
Perjury and false statements	40	29	4	14	5	17	20	69	—	0
Prison breach, escape and rescue	603	549	28	5	63	11	458	83	—	0
Public mischief	339	307	77	25	188	61	42	14	—	0
Riots	15	13	—	0	10	77	3	23	—	0
Spreading false news	1	1	—	0	—	0	1	100	—	0
Various other offences	7	6	—	0	3	50	3	50	—	0
Other	2,933	2,480	489	20	955	39	1,036	42	—	0
Criminal Code	40,568	35,875	11,283	31	10,551	29	14,041	39	—	0

*Gaol, reformatory, industrial farm, training school, penitentiary.

†Excludes Alberta and Quebec.

Table 1(i)

Persons Charged and Sentences of Convicted Persons by Nature of Indictable Offence, Canada† 1970

Indictable offence	Persons charged	Persons convicted	Suspended sentence with/without probation		Fine		Institution*		Death	
			#	%	#	%	#	%	#	%
Abandoning child	25	22	12	55	3	14	7	32	—	—
Abduction and kidnapping	59	48	22	46	—	—	26	54	—	—
Abortion and attempt	13	10	2	20	—	—	8	80	—	—
Assault causing bodily harm	2474	1848	463	25	727	39	658	36	—	—
Assault on peace officer and obstructing	2082	1862	215	12	1128	61	519	28	—	—
Bigamy, feigned and unlawful marriage, polygamy	22	21	8	38	4	19	9	43	—	—
Buggery or bestiality, gross indecency	311	288	39	14	222	77	27	9	—	—
Causing bodily harm and danger	238	171	38	22	6	4	127	74	—	—
Common assault	810	693	182	26	385	56	126	18	—	—
Criminal negligence, bodily harm (motor vehicle)	3	3	1	33	—	—	2	67	—	—
Other criminal negligence causing bodily harm	14	9	2	22	—	—	6	67	—	—
Criminal negligence, death (motor manslaughter)	20	12	—	—	1	8	11	92	—	—
Other criminal negligence causing death	23	5	1	20	—	—	3	60	—	—
Criminal negligence in operation of motor vehicle	23	21	2	10	10	48	9	43	—	—
Criminal negligence causing no bodily harm nor death	22	21	5	24	4	19	12	57	—	—
Dangerous driving[1]	101	82	12	15	39	48	31	38	—	—
Duties tending to preservation of life	—	—	—	—	—	—	—	—	—	—
Incest	28	26	5	19	—	—	21	81	—	—
Indecent assault on female	498	398	151	38	58	15	189	47	—	—
Indecent assault on male	100	79	40	51	7	9	32	41	—	—
Infanticide	—	—	—	—	—	—	—	—	—	—
Interfering with transportation facilities	—	—	—	—	—	—	—	—	—	—
Killing unborn child	2	2	—	—	—	—	2	100	—	—
Libel	77	65	1	2	—	—	64	98	—	—
Manslaughter	—	—	—	—	—	—	—	—	—	—
Murder[2]	24	5	—	—	—	—	5	100	—	—
Murder, attempt to commit	—	—	—	—	—	—	—	—	—	—
Murder, capital	3	3	—	—	—	—	—	—	3	100
Murder, non-capital	81	37	—	—	—	—	37	100	—	—
Neglect in childbirth and concealing dead body	9	9	8	89	1	11	—	—	—	—
Procuring	54	41	9	22	5	12	27	66	—	—
Rape	118	41	1	2	—	—	40	98	—	—
Rape, attempt to commit	18	10	2	20	—	—	8	80	—	—
Seduction	4	2	1	50	—	—	1	50	—	—
Sexual intercourse and attempt	73	59	19	32	3	5	37	63	—	—
Other offences against the person[3]	26	21	7	33	6	29	8	38	—	—
Against the person	7355	5914	1248	21	2611	44	2052	35	3	—

Breaking and entering a place⁴	6929	6417	2863	45	104	2	3450	54	—
Extortion	30	18	5	28	—	—	13	72	—
Forcible entry and detainer	13	10	5	50	5	50	—	—	—
Robbery	924	717	75	10	5	1	637	89	—
Robbery while armed	87	79	6	8	—	—	73	92	—
Against property with violence	7983	7241	2954	41	114	2	4173	58	—
False pretences	2108	1861	728	39	303	16	830	46	—
Fraud and corruption	917	790	279	35	92	12	419	53	—
Having in possession	3697	3202	1326	41	559	17	1317	41	—
Theft	20789	19094	6170	32	8478	44	4446	23	—
Theft by conversion	42	29	16	55	—	—	13	45	—
Theft from mail	24	22	12	55	—	—	10	45	—
Theft of stray cattle⁵	3	3	3	100	—	—	—	—	—
Against property without violence	27580	25001	8534	34	9432	38	7035	28	—
Arson and other fires	163	137	55	40	5	4	77	56	—
Other interference with property	1231	1072	451	42	324	30	297	28	—
Malicious offences against property	1394	1209	506	42	329	27	374	31	—
Forgery and uttering	1146	1072	406	38	26	2	640	60	—
Offences relating to currency	68	60	13	22	—	—	47	88	—
Forgery and offences relating to currency	1214	1132	419	37	26	2	687	61	—
Attempt to commit and accessories	469	419	163	39	97	23	159	38	—
Bawdy house, keepers	110	93	9	10	70	75	14	15	—
Conspiracy	202	154	39	25	3	2	112	73	—
Gaming, betting and lotteries	185	158	10	6	143	91	6	4	—
Habitual criminal	2	2	—	—	—	—	2	100	—
Motor vehicle	223	200	2	1	186	93	12	6	—
Driving while ability to drive is impaired	47	37	—	—	17	46	20	54	—
Driving while disqualified	—	—	—	—	—	—	—	—	—
Driving while intoxicated	38	26	6	23	18	69	2	8	—
Failing to stop at scene of accident	12	7	—	—	4	57	3	43	—
Offences tending to corrupt morals	1133	939	340	36	267	28	332	35	—
Offensive weapons	62	45	8	18	4	9	33	73	—
Perjury and false statements	737	686	60	9	81	12	545	79	—
Prison breach, escape and rescue	457	414	112	27	227	55	75	18	—
Public mischief	8	8	1	13	3	38	4	50	—
Various other offences⁶	3685	3188	750	24	1120	35	1318	41	—
Other	49211	43685	14411	33	13633	31	15638	36	3
Criminal Code									

*Gaol, reformatory, industrial farm, training school, penitentiary.
†Excludes Alberta and Quebec.

Notes:

¹Does not include "dangerous operation of vessel".

²"Murder" does not appear as an indictable offence in Statistics Canada publications after 1969.

³Includes "threatening letters".

⁴Does not include "breaking and entering while armed".

⁵Treated as "fraudulently taking cattle".

⁶Includes "counselling or aiding suicides", "dangerous sexual offenders", "riots", "spreading false news" and "trade marks".

Table 1(j)

Persons Charged and Sentences of Convicted Persons by Nature of Indictable Offence, Canada† 1971

Indictable offence	Persons charged	Persons convicted	Suspended sentence with/without probation #	%	Fine #	%	Institution* #	%	Death #	%
Abandoning child	15	14	8	57	2	14	4	29	—	—
Abduction and kidnapping	66	47	7	15	7	15	33	70	—	—
Abortion and attempt	6	6	2	33	1	17	3	50	—	—
Assault causing bodily harm	2512	1879	481	26	734	39	664	35	—	—
Assault on peace officer and obstructing	2213	1915	257	13	1156	60	502	26	—	—
Bigamy, feigned and unlawful marriage, polygamy	12	10	6	60	—	—	4	40	—	—
Buggery or bestiality, gross indecency	205	183	39	21	121	66	23	13	—	—
Causing bodily harm and danger	234	162	28	17	6	4	128	79	—	—
Common assault	584	531	153	29	262	49	116	22	—	—
Criminal negligence, bodily harm (motor vehicle)	—	—	—	—	—	—	—	—	—	—
Other criminal negligence causing bodily harm	23	16	3	19	1	6	12	75	—	—
Criminal negligence, death (motor manslaughter)	14	14	—	—	—	—	14	100	—	—
Other criminal negligence causing death	49	27	7	26	2	7	18	67	—	—
Criminal negligence in operation of motor vehicle	35	28	2	7	12	43	14	50	—	—
Criminal negligence causing no bodily harm nor death	21	16	6	38	1	6	9	56	—	—
Dangerous driving¹	109	94	10	11	58	62	26	28	—	—
Duties tending to preservation of life	1	1	—	—	1	100	—	—	—	—
Incest	15	13	4	31	—	—	9	69	—	—
Indecent assault on female	510	405	165	41	67	17	173	43	—	—
Indecent assault on male	81	74	38	51	7	9	29	39	—	—
Infanticide	6	5	3	60	—	—	2	40	—	—
Interfering with transportation facilities	1	1	—	—	1	100	—	—	—	—
Killing unborn child	2	—	—	—	—	—	—	—	—	—
Libel	4	4	3	75	1	25	—	—	—	—
Manslaughter²	87	70	3	4	—	—	67	96	—	—
Murder, attempt to commit	21	11	1	9	—	—	10	91	—	—
Murder, capital	—	—	—	—	—	—	—	—	—	—
Murder, non-capital	60	27	—	—	—	—	27	100	—	—
Neglect in childbirth and concealing dead body	3	3	2	67	1	33	—	—	—	—
Procuring	50	36	5	14	4	11	27	75	—	—
Rape	119	65	1	2	—	—	64	98	—	—
Rape, attempt to commit	18	11	—	—	—	—	11	100	—	—
Seduction	1	—	—	—	—	—	—	—	—	—
Sexual intercourse and attempt	96	76	34	45	5	7	37	49	—	—
Other offences against the person³	37	25	15	60	5	20	5	20	—	—
Against the person	7210	5770	1283	22	2456	43	2031	35	—	—

Breaking and entering a place⁴	—	—	7299	6785	3073	45	125	2	3587	53
Extortion	—	—	59	46	14	30	1	2	31	67
Forcible entry and detainer	—	—	15	10	6	60	3	30	—	10
Robbery	—	—	970	795	94	12	7	1	694	87
Robbery while armed	—	—	55	48	6	13	—	—	42	88
Against property with violence	—	—	8398	7684	3193	42	136	2	4355	57
False pretences	—	—	1855	1649	658	40	259	16	732	44
Fraud and corruption	—	—	1183	1049	411	39	124	12	514	49
Having in possession	—	—	4292	3697	1446	39	709	19	1542	42
Theft	—	—	22030	20238	6120	30	9813	48	4305	21
Theft by conversion	—	—	33	30	17	57	3	10	10	33
Theft from mail	—	—	36	35	15	43	1	3	19	54
Theft of stray cattle⁵	—	—	3	3	—	—	2	67	1	33
Against property without violence	—	—	29432	26701	8667	32	10911	41	7123	27
Arson and other fires	—	—	143	116	36	31	3	3	77	66
Other interference with property	—	—	1431	1264	494	39	403	32	367	29
Malicious offences against property	—	—	1574	1380	530	38	406	29	444	32
Forgery and uttering	—	—	1252	1171	469	40	53	5	649	55
Offences relating to currency	—	—	76	59	16	27	3	1	40	68
Forgery and offences relating to currency	—	—	1328	1230	485	39	56	5	689	56
Attempt to commit and accessories	—	—	381	337	127	38	81	24	129	38
Bawdy house, keepers	—	—	88	78	8	10	55	71	15	19
Conspiracy	—	—	198	119	33	28	7	6	79	66
Gaming, betting and lotteries	—	—	215	177	13	7	155	88	9	5
Habitual criminal	—	—	1	1	—	—	—	—	1	100
Motor vehicle	—	—								
Driving while ability to drive is impaired	—	—	216	191	2	1	172	90	17	9
Driving while disqualified	—	—	84	79	—	—	55	70	24	30
Driving while intoxicated	—	—								
Failing to stop at scene of accident	—	—	53	45	4	9	30	67	11	24
Offences tending to corrupt morals	—	—	18	11	—	—	8	73	3	27
Offensive weapons	—	—	1118	865	337	39	225	26	303	35
Perjury and false statements	—	—	81	66	18	27	5	8	43	65
Prison breach, escape and rescue	—	—	818	735	52	7	92	13	591	80
Public mischief	—	—	491	450	100	22	259	58	91	20
Various other offences⁶	—	—	32	31	3	10	10	32	18	58
Other	—	—	3794	3185	697	22	1154	36	1334	42
Criminal Code	—	—	51736	45950	14855	32	15119	33	15976	35

*Gaol, reformatory, industrial farm, training school, penitentiary.
†Excludes Alberta and Quebec.

Notes:
1 Does not include "dangerous operation of vessel".
2 "Murder" does not appear as an indictable offence in Statistics Canada publications after 1969.
3 Includes "threatening letters".
4 Does not include "breaking and entering while armed".
5 Treated as "fraudulently taking cattle".
6 Includes "counselling or aiding suicides", "dangerous sexual offenders", "riots", "spreading false news" and "trade marks".

Table 1(k)

Persons Charged and Sentences of Convicted Persons by Nature of Indictable Offence, Canada† 1972

Indictable offence	Persons charged	Persons convicted	Suspended sentence with/without probation #	%	Fine #	%	Institution* #	%	Death #	%
Abandoning child	22	17	11	65	1	6	5	29	—	—
Abduction and kidnapping	60	41	20	49	2	5	19	46	—	—
Abortion and attempt	2	2	—	—	1	50	1	50	—	—
Assault causing bodily harm	2276	1599	487	30	519	32	593	37	—	—
Assault on peace officer and obstructing	1884	1632	251	15	989	61	392	24	—	—
Bigamy, feigned and unlawful marriage, polygamy	12	11	2	18	3	27	6	55	—	—
Buggery or bestiality, gross indecency	114	78	26	33	30	38	22	28	—	—
Causing bodily harm and danger	249	179	56	31	9	5	114	64	—	—
Common assault	603	511	152	30	235	46	124	24	—	—
Criminal negligence, bodily harm (motor vehicle)	24	18	9	50	—	—	9	50	—	—
Other criminal negligence causing bodily harm	1	1	—	—	—	—	1	100	—	—
Criminal negligence, death (motor manslaughter)	47	23	6	26	—	—	17	74	—	—
Other criminal negligence causing death	24	21	3	14	7	33	11	52	—	—
Criminal negligence in operation of motor vehicle	28	20	8	40	2	10	10	50	—	—
Criminal negligence causing no bodily harm nor death	73	59	5	8	24	41	30	51	—	—
Dangerous driving¹	2	2	—	—	—	—	2	100	—	—
Duties tending to preservation of life										
Incest	23	21	8	38	1	5	12	57	—	—
Indecent assault on female	447	339	145	43	25	7	169	50	—	—
Indecent assault on male	78	66	34	52	4	6	28	42	—	—
Infanticide	3	2	—	—	—	—	2	100	—	—
Interfering with transportation facilities	2	1	—	—	—	—	1	100	—	—
Killing unborn child	—	—	—	—	—	—	—	—	—	—
Libel										
Manslaughter	99	84	4	5	—	—	80	95	—	—
Murder²	66	43	4	9	3	7	36	84	—	—
Murder, attempt to commit	105	58	—	—	—	—	58	100	—	—
Murder, capital	1	1	—	—	—	—	—	—	1	100
Murder, non-capital	18	15	3	20	2	13	10	67	—	—
Neglect in childbirth and concealing dead body	2	2	—	—	—	—	2	100	—	—
Procuring										
Rape	154	82	3	4	—	—	79	96	—	—
Rape, attempt to commit	16	12	1	8	2	17	9	75	—	—
Seduction										
Sexual intercourse and attempt	61	44	16	36	2	5	26	59	—	—
Other offences against the person³	29	24	10	42	8	33	6	25	—	—
Against the person	6525	5008	1265	25	1870	37	1872	37	1	—

Breaking and entering a place⁴	6691	6031	2774	46	92	2	3165	52	—	—
Extortion	37	28	7	25	—	—	21	75	—	—
Forcible entry and detainer	9	4	2	50	—	—	2	50	—	—
Robbery	944	710	78	11	6	1	626	88	—	—
Robbery while armed	59	54	8	15	—	—	46	85	—	—
Against property with violence	7740	6827	2869	42	98	1	3860	57	—	—
False pretences	2024	1717	661	38	345	20	711	41	—	—
Fraud and corruption	1277	1034	405	39	116	11	513	50	—	—
Having in possession	4389	3523	1436	41	682	19	1405	40	—	—
Theft	21730	18299	5681	31	8926	49	3692	20	—	—
Theft by conversion	25	16	11	69	—	6	4	25	—	—
Theft from mail	31	27	14	52	1	4	12	44	—	—
Theft of stray cattle⁵	7	3	2	67	—	33	—	—	—	—
Against property without violence	29483	24619	8110	33	10072	41	6437	26	—	—
Arson and other fires	175	135	55	41	4	3	76	56	—	—
Other interference with property	1536	1277	542	42	408	32	327	26	—	—
Malicious offences against property	1711	1412	597	42	412	29	403	29	—	—
Forgery and uttering	1221	1099	473	43	47	4	579	53	—	—
Offences relating to currency	52	40	8	20	6	15	26	65	—	—
Forgery and offences relating to currency	1273	1139	481	42	53	5	605	53	—	—
Attempt to commit and accessories	480	383	149	39	87	23	147	38	—	—
Bawdy house, keepers	77	64	15	23	41	64	8	13	—	—
Conspiracy	135	94	21	22	11	12	62	66	—	—
Gaming, betting and lotteries	263	237	19	8	202	85	16	7	—	—
Habitual criminal	3	2	—	—	—	—	2	100	—	—
Motor vehicle										
Driving while ability to drive is impaired	292	193	1	1	177	92	15	8	—	—
Driving while disqualified	91	67	1	1	40	60	26	39	—	—
Driving while intoxicated	—	—	—	—	—	—	—	—	—	—
Failing to stop at scene of accident	36	29	3	11	22	76	6	21	—	—
Offences tending to corrupt morals	27	18	2	11	16	89	—	—	—	—
Offensive weapons	1340	1029	413	40	278	27	338	33	—	—
Perjury and false statements	62	45	15	33	3	7	27	60	—	—
Prison breach, escape and rescue	989	927	49	5	118	13	760	82	—	—
Public mischief	517	444	118	27	262	59	64	14	—	—
Various other offences⁶	44	42	7	17	9	21	26	62	—	—
Other	4356	3573	811	23	1266	35	1496	42	—	—
Criminal Code	51088	42579	14133	33	13771	32	14674	34	—	1

*Gaol, reformatory, industrial farm, training school, penitentiary.

†Excludes Alberta and Quebec.

Notes:

1. Does not include "dangerous operation of vessel".
2. "Murder" does not appear as an indictable offence in Statistics Canada publications after 1969.
3. Includes "threatening letters".
4. Does not include "breaking and entering while armed".
5. Treated as "fraudulently taking cattle".
6. Includes "counselling or aiding suicides", "dangerous sexual offenders", "riots", "spreading false news" and "trade marks".

Table 1(l)

Persons Charged and Sentences of Convicted Persons by Nature of Indictable Offence, Canada[†] 1973

Indictable offence	Persons charged	Persons convicted	Sentence							
			Suspended sentence with/without probation		Fine		Institution[*]		Death	
			#	%	#	%	#	%	#	%
Abandoning child	13	9	5	56	2	22	2	22	—	—
Abduction and kidnapping	69	53	14	26	5	9	34	64	—	—
Abortion and attempt	1	1	1	100	—	—	—	—	—	—
Assault causing bodily harm	2220	1441	394	27	452	31	595	41	—	—
Assault on peace officer and obstructing	1117	939	130	14	554	59	255	27	—	—
Bigamy, feigned and unlawful marriage, polygamy	16	14	7	50	4	29	3	21	—	—
Buggery or bestiality, gross indecency	100	61	25	41	14	23	22	36	—	—
Causing bodily harm and danger	194	144	33	23	5	3	106	74	—	—
Common assault	84	68	12	18	21	31	35	51	—	—
Criminal negligence, bodily harm (motor vehicle)	27	18	8	44	3	17	7	39	—	—
Other criminal negligence causing bodily harm	4	4	—	—	1	25	3	75	—	—
Criminal negligence, death (motor manslaughter)	41	18	4	22	—	—	14	78	—	—
Other criminal negligence causing death	86	72	16	22	24	33	32	44	—	—
Criminal negligence in operation of motor vehicle	15	13	3	23	3	23	7	54	—	—
Criminal negligence causing no bodily harm nor death	45	35	4	11	13	37	18	51	—	—
Dangerous driving[1]	3	2	1	50	—	—	1	50	—	—
Duties tending to preservation of life	28	20	6	30	—	—	14	70	—	—
Incest	408	286	120	42	29	10	137	48	—	—
Indecent assault on female	81	60	26	43	8	13	26	43	—	—
Indecent assault on male	3	2	2	100	—	—	—	—	—	—
Infanticide	—	—	—	—	—	—	—	—	—	—
Interfering with transportation facilities	3	2	—	—	—	—	2	100	—	—
Killing unborn child	1	1	1	100	—	—	—	—	—	—
Libel	—	—	—	—	—	—	—	—	—	—
Manslaughter	101	92	8	7	—	—	84	93	—	—
Murder[2]	—	—	—	—	—	—	—	—	—	—
Murder, attempt to commit	43	27	2	7	—	—	24	89	—	—
Murder, capital	2	1	—	—	—	—	—	—	1	100
Murder, non-capital	95	38	—	—	—	—	38	100	—	—
Neglect in childbirth and concealing dead body	2	2	—	—	—	—	2	100	—	—
Procuring	32	18	4	22	7	39	7	39	—	—
Rape	145	67	2	3	3	4	62	93	—	—
Rape, attempt to commit	12	7	—	—	1	14	6	86	—	—
Seduction	1	1	—	—	—	—	1	100	—	—
Sexual intercourse and attempt	49	36	13	36	2	6	21	58	—	—
Other offences against the person[3]	51	33	18	55	3	9	12	36	—	—
Against the person	**5096**	**3584**	**860**	**24**	**1155**	**32**	**1568**	**44**	**1**	—

Offence											
Breaking and entering a place[4]	6415	5624	2460	44	132	2	—	—	3032	54	—
Extortion	17	7	1	14	—	—	—	—	6	86	—
Forcible entry and detainer	7	3	2	67	1	33	—	—	—	—	—
Robbery	1012	772	90	12	8	1	—	—	674	87	—
Robbery while armed	105	92	12	13	—	—	—	—	80	87	—
Against property with violence	7556	6498	2565	39	141	2	—	—	3792	58	—
False pretences	2045	1572	594	38	351	22	—	—	627	40	—
Fraud and corruption	1134	904	328	36	156	17	—	—	420	46	—
Having in possession	4852	3575	1313	37	805	23	—	—	2177	61	—
Theft	22751	16665	4460	27	8646	52	—	—	3559	21	—
Theft by conversion	23	14	6	43	2	14	—	—	6	43	—
Theft from mail	33	24	14	58	—	—	—	—	10	42	—
Theft of stray cattle[5]	6	2	—	—	—	—	—	—	2	100	—
Against property without violence	30884	22756	6714	30	9961	44	—	—	6081	27	—
Arson and other fires	181	131	54	41	5	4	—	—	72	55	—
Other interference with property	1055	784	299	38	277	35	—	—	208	27	—
Malicious offences against property	1236	915	353	39	282	31	—	—	280	31	—
Forgery and uttering	1052	948	419	44	48	5	—	—	481	51	—
Offences relating to currency	50	43	14	33	1	2	—	—	28	65	—
Forgery and offences relating to currency	1142	991	433	44	49	5	—	—	509	51	—
Attempt to commit and accessories	577	454	181	40	67	15	—	—	206	45	—
Bawdy house, keepers	78	52	12	23	37	71	—	—	3	6	—
Conspiracy	233	146	44	30	10	7	—	—	92	63	—
Gaming, betting and lotteries	444	345	46	13	286	83	—	—	13	4	—
Habitual criminal	2	2	—	—	—	—	—	—	2	100	—
Motor vehicle											
Driving while ability to drive is impaired	128	98	6	6	83	85	—	—	9	9	—
Driving while disqualified	352	326	6	2	277	85	—	—	43	13	—
Driving while intoxicated	16	13	5	38	8	62	—	—	—	—	—
Failing to stop at scene of accident	19	11	2	18	6	55	—	—	3	23	—
Offences tending to corrupt morals											
Offensive weapons	1443	1007	314	31	324	32	—	—	369	37	—
Perjury and false statements	52	39	12	31	9	23	—	—	18	46	—
Prison breach, escape and rescue	798	741	41	6	87	12	—	—	613	83	—
Public mischief	280	222	51	23	145	65	—	—	26	12	—
Various other offences[6]	24	20	3	15	2	10	—	—	15	75	—
Other	4446	3476	750	22	1347	39	—	—	1379	40	—
Criminal Code	50360	38220	11675	31	12935	34	—	—	13609	36	1

*Gaol, reformatory, industrial farm, training school, penitentiary.

†Excludes Alberta and Quebec.

Notes:

[1] Does not include "dangerous operation of vessel".

[2] "Murder" does not appear as an indictable offence in Statistics Canada publications after 1969.

[3] Includes "threatening letters".

[4] Does not include "breaking and entering while armed".

[5] Treated as "fraudulently taking cattle".

[6] Includes "counselling or aiding suicides", "dangerous sexual offenders", "riots", "spreading false news" and "trade marks".

Table 2

Percentage Distribution of Persons Convicted by Indictable Offence and by Nature of Sentence, 1962-1973

Indictable offence	Sentences											
	Suspended (with/without probation)											
	'62	'63	'64	'65	'66	'67	'68	'69	'70	'71	'72	'73
Abandoning child	47	56	75	70	27	47	73	59	55	57	65	56
Abduction and kidnapping	33	35	34	33	43	41	30	32	46	15	49	26
Abortion and attempt	11	20	17	33	11	18	57	56	20	33	—	100
Assault causing bodily harm	25	20	20	18	18	21	21	22	25	26	30	27
Assault on peace officer and obstructing	9	8	11	9	9	9	9	10	12	13	15	14
Bigamy, feigned and unlawful marriage, polygamy	34	27	37	33	27	36	24	27	38	60	18	50
Buggery or bestiality, gross indecency	26	24	18	21	22	15	17	14	14	21	33	41
Causing bodily harm and danger	14	11	17	24	19	24	19	20	22	17	31	23
Common assault	29	24	26	19	25	32	25	28	26	29	30	18
Other criminal negligence, bodily harm[1]	46	17	47	32	32	31	24	40	25	19	50	44
Criminal negligence, death (motor manslaughter)	6	9	7	4	5	3	—	7	—	—	—	—
Other criminal negligence, death	5	9	—	8	20	13	—	13	20	26	26	22
Criminal negligence in operation of motor vehicle	8	7	15	14	8	9	9	9	10	7	14	22
Criminal negligence, no bodily harm nor death	6	46	17	17	36	—	25	38	24	38	40	23
Dangerous driving	4	2	5	10	5	7	10	8	15	11	8	11
Duties tending to preservation of life	48	57	75	44	56	60	100	—	NIL	—	—	50
Incest	6	17	10	3	26	11	19	37	19	31	38	30
Indecent assault on female	27	27	30	29	36	32	40	36	38	41	43	42
Indecent assault on male	30	42	35	3	40	39	45	58	51	51	52	43
Infanticide	—	NIL	NIL	NIL	100	100	100	100	NIL	60	—	100
Libel	50	50	100	—	—	25	67	—	—	75	NIL	100
Manslaughter	6	2	2	—	3	1	3	3	2	4	5	7
Murder, attempt to commit	—	21	—	9	—	11	—	—	—	9	9	7
Murder, capital[2]	—	—	—	—	—	—	—	NIL	—	NIL	—	—
Murder, non-capital	—	—	—	—	—	—	—	—	—	—	—	—
Neglect in childbirth and concealing dead body	67	50	100	100	100	67	100	100	89	67	50	—
Procuring	16	13	4	19	16	15	12	10	22	14	20	22
Rape	2	1	2	4	—	9	—	5	2	2	4	3
Rape, attempt to commit[3]	—	5	6	—	8	17	—	14	20	—	8	—
Seduction	—	20	33	—	—	—	—	NIL	50	NIL	NIL	100
Sexual intercourse and attempt	22	15	14	26	27	22	18	17	32	45	36	36
Threatening letters	—	64	60	47	60	67	64	50	NIL	NIL	NIL	NIL
Other offences against the person	27	15	18	10	6	6	60	20	33	60	42	55
Against the person	19	17	18	17	18	18	18	19	21	22	25	24
Breaking and entering a place	32	36	35	38	42	43	41	41	45	45	46	44
Extortion	36	13	43	29	61	25	40	57	28	30	25	14
Forcible entry and detainer	29	31	23	32	31	25	43	33	50	60	50	67
Robbery	13	14	13	14	17	18	8	11	10	12	11	12
Robbery while armed	2	6	9	7	7	13	6	9	8	13	15	13
Against property with violence	30	32	32	35	38	40	37	38	41	42	42	39
False pretences	31	29	29	29	30	28	29	35	39	40	38	38
Fraud and corruption	30	29	31	30	27	29	30	30	35	39	39	36
Fraudulently taking cattle[4]	—	—	—	33	—	—	100	50	100	—	67	—
Having in possession	32	31	33	33	33	33	34	38	41	39	41	37
Theft	37	36	37	36	36	36	32	33	32	30	31	27
Theft by conversion	44	42	31	40	40	48	56	58	57	57	69	43
Theft from mail	—	3	3	—	2	3	11	22	55	43	52	54
Against property without violence	36	35	36	35	35	34	32	34	34	32	33	30
Arson and other fires	28	39	39	37	38	30	34	47	40	31	41	41
Other interference with property	40	35	39	34	36	34	42	35	42	39	42	38
Malicious offences against property	38	35	39	35	36	34	41	36	42	38	42	39
Forgery and uttering	26	25	28	28	33	30	31	35	38	40	43	44
Offences relating to currency	10	10	11	11	18	15	28	19	22	27	20	33
Forgery and offences relating to currency	25	24	27	27	32	29	31	35	37	39	42	44
Attempt to commit and accessories	28	30	26	32	37	34	30	28	39	38	39	40
Bawdy house, keepers	5	3	5	10	14	11	7	13	10	10	23	23
Conspiracy	19	27	34	30	31	22	32	18	25	28	22	30
Dangerous sexual offenders	—	—	—	—	—	—	—	—	NIL	NIL	NIL	NIL
Gaming, betting and lotteries	3	2	3	4	2	1	3	6	6	7	8	13
Habitual criminal	—	—	—	—	—	—	—	—	—	—	—	—
Motor vehicle												
Driving while ability to drive is impaired	—	—	—	1	—	—	—	1	1	1	1	6
Driving while disqualified	1	2	5	8	3	4	3	—	—	—	1	2
Driving while intoxicated	—	—	—	—	—	—	—	—	NIL	NIL	NIL	NIL
Failing to stop at scene of accident	5	3	3	8	8	10	8	—	23	9	3	15
Offences tending to corrupt morals	19	—	18	8	30	24	—	88	—	—	11	18
Offensive weapons	31	29	35	33	36	34	33	37	36	39	40	31
Perjury and false statements	15	28	27	42	31	22	21	14	18	27	33	31
Prison breach, escape and rescue	4	4	4	7	8	7	5	5	9	7	5	6
Public mischief	23	26	21	21	22	25	25	25	27	22	27	23
Various other offences[5]	100	—	12	27	38	3	33	—	13	10	17	15
Other	14	13	14	17	16	17	19	20	24	22	23	22
Criminal Code	30	29	30	30	31	31	30	31	33	32	33	31

Notes:
[1] 1962-1973 combines criminal negligence causing bodily harm (motor vehicle) and criminal negligence, other causing bodily harm.
[2] The residual % is the death sentence.
[3] Figures are inaccurate for 1962.
[4] Theft of stray cattle.
[5] Includes "riots", "spreading false news", "trade marks".

						Sentences																		
					Fine												Institution*							
'62	'63	'64	'65	'66	'67	'68	'69	'70	'71	'72	'73	'62	'63	'64	'65	'66	'67	'68	'69	'70	'71	'72	'73
16	—	6	—	34	—	—	—	14	14	6	22	37	44	19	30	39	53	27	41	32	29	29	22
2	6	2	14	—	13	2	7	—	15	5	9	65	58	64	53	57	46	68	61	54	70	46	64
5	4	4	4	—	14	—	—	—	17	50	—	84	76	79	63	89	68	43	44	80	50	50	—
41	42	39	44	46	41	41	43	39	39	32	31	34	38	40	38	35	38	38	35	36	35	37	41
62	64	65	63	63	65	63	65	61	60	61	59	29	27	26	28	28	26	27	25	28	26	24	27
7	5	7	3	13	4	18	7	19	—	27	29	59	68	57	63	60	61	59	67	43	40	51	21
38	45	50	47	52	65	70	76	77	66	38	23	38	31	32	31	25	20	13	10	9	13	28	36
5	3	4	8	7	7	2	6	4	4	5	3	81	86	79	68	75	69	80	74	74	79	64	74
44	50	46	55	53	46	46	49	56	49	46	31	27	25	28	26	22	22	29	23	18	22	24	51
15	17	11	24	9	19	19	—	8	6	—	17	36	66	42	44	59	50	57	60	67	75	50	39
6	9	3	8	—	14	6	20	8	—	—	25	88	82	90	88	95	83	94	73	92	100	100	75
—	—	8	—	30	—	10	—	20	7	—	—	95	91	92	92	50	87	90	87	60	67	74	78
70	44	59	50	54	50	27	22	48	43	33	33	22	49	26	36	38	41	64	70	43	50	52	44
36	18	39	50	9	23	50	25	19	6	10	23	58	36	44	33	55	77	25	38	57	56	50	54
67	69	53	50	59	61	48	46	48	62	41	37	29	29	41	40	36	32	42	46	38	28	51	51
9	5	—	—	33	—	—	—	NIL	100	—	—	43	38	25	56	11	40	—	100	NIL	—	100	50
—	—	—	—	—	3	—	—	—	—	5	—	94	83	90	97	74	86	81	63	81	69	57	70
19	17	19	17	17	17	12	17	15	17	7	10	54	57	51	55	47	51	48	46	47	43	50	48
5	7	9	11	10	6	11	3	9	9	6	13	65	51	56	50	49	55	44	39	41	39	42	43
—	NIL	NIL	NIL	—	—	—	NIL	—	—	—	—	100	NIL	NIL	NIL	—	—	—	—	NIL	40	100	—
50	50	—	100	—	25	33	100	—	25	NIL	—	—	—	—	—	—	—	50	—	—	100	—	NIL
2	—	—	—	—	—	—	—	—	—	7	4	92	98	98	100	97	99	97	97	98	96	95	93
—	—	—	—	—	5	—	—	—	—	—	—	100	79	100	91	100	84	100	100	100	—	91	89
—	—	—	—	—	—	NIL	—	NIL	—	—	—	7	21	100	—	—	—	—	—	NIL	—	NIL	—
—	—	—	—	—	—	—	—	—	—	—	—	100	100	100	100	100	100	100	100	100	100	100	100
17	—	—	—	—	33	—	—	11	33	50	—	17	50	—	—	—	—	—	—	—	—	—	100
3	10	—	2	16	9	10	2	12	11	13	39	81	77	96	79	69	77	78	88	66	75	67	39
4	—	—	—	—	—	—	—	—	—	—	4	94	99	98	96	100	91	100	95	98	98	96	93
—	16	6	—	—	6	—	—	—	—	17	14	—	79	88	100	92	78	100	86	80	100	75	86
100	40	33	67	—	—	—	NIL	—	NIL	NIL	—	—	40	33	33	100	100	100	NIL	50	NIL	NIL	—
6	9	3	4	6	7	3	2	5	7	5	6	72	76	86	70	66	71	79	81	63	49	59	58
—	—	10	6	—	—	—	17	NIL	NIL	NIL	NIL	—	36	30	47	40	33	36	33	NIL	NIL	NIL	NIL
54	81	76	75	94	76	40	80	29	20	33	9	18	4	6	15	—	18	—	—	38	20	25	36
39	42	42	44	46	44	43	45	44	43	37	32	40	40	40	39	37	37	39	36	35	35	37	44
2	2	2	3	2	3	2	2	2	2	2	—	66	62	62	59	56	54	57	57	54	53	52	54
6	3	4	—	11	—	—	—	—	2	—	—	58	84	53	71	39	64	60	43	72	67	75	86
29	36	46	32	34	50	29	33	50	30	—	33	43	33	32	36	34	25	29	33	—	10	50	—
10	2	1	1	2	2	1	—	1	1	1	1	86	84	87	85	82	81	91	88	89	87	88	87
3	—	1	1	1	1	—	—	—	—	—	—	95	94	90	93	92	86	93	91	92	88	85	87
2	2	2	3	2	3	2	2	2	2	1	2	68	66	65	62	59	57	61	60	58	57	57	58
16	16	18	20	19	19	18	14	16	16	20	22	53	55	53	51	51	53	54	51	46	44	41	40
12	12	12	13	16	18	23	15	12	12	11	17	59	60	57	58	57	53	47	54	53	49	50	46
100	67	33	67	100	100	—	—	—	67	33	—	—	33	67	—	—	—	—	50	—	33	—	100
14	16	14	17	18	18	19	18	17	19	19	23	53	54	53	50	50	49	47	44	41	42	40	61
25	26	28	32	33	35	39	40	44	48	49	52	38	38	35	32	30	29	29	27	23	21	20	21
12	6	11	9	10	9	7	—	—	10	6	14	44	52	57	51	50	43	37	42	45	33	25	43
—	—	—	—	—	3	—	11	—	3	4	4	100	97	97	100	98	94	89	67	45	54	42	42
22	23	25	29	30	31	34	34	38	41	41	44	42	42	39	36	35	34	34	32	28	27	26	27
7	10	6	7	9	3	5	3	4	3	3	4	65	51	55	56	53	68	61	51	56	66	56	55
28	33	35	38	38	39	34	37	30	32	32	35	32	32	26	28	26	27	25	28	28	29	26	27
24	30	32	35	35	36	31	33	27	29	29	31	38	36	27	30	29	31	28	30	31	32	29	31
2	2	2	3	2	3	2	2	2	5	4	5	72	73	70	69	64	67	67	63	60	55	53	51
2	1	—	3	—	5	2	5	—	1	15	2	88	89	89	87	82	80	70	76	88	68	65	65
2	2	2	3	2	3	2	2	2	5	5	5	73	74	71	70	65	68	67	63	61	56	53	51
13	10	13	20	20	17	21	20	23	24	23	15	60	60	61	48	43	49	49	52	38	38	38	45
61	61	58	61	60	67	75	69	75	71	64	71	34	36	37	29	26	22	18	18	15	19	13	6
13	9	6	8	6	6	2	10	2	6	12	7	68	64	60	62	33	72	66	57	73	66	66	63
—	—	—	—	—	—	—	—	NIL	NIL	NIL	NIL	—	100	100	100	100	100	100	100	NIL	NIL	NIL	NIL
90	92	91	87	92	90	89	88	91	88	85	83	7	6	6	8	6	9	9	6	4	5	7	4
—	—	—	—	—	—	—	—	—	—	—	—	100	100	100	100	100	100	100	100	100	100	100	100
94	85	65	52	65	73	84	89	93	90	92	85	6	15	34	47	34	27	16	10	6	9	8	9
65	73	67	78	66	59	44	61	46	70	60	75	34	25	28	14	30	37	52	39	54	30	39	13
—	4	—	4	—	—	—	64	NIL	NIL	NIL	NIL	100	96	100	96	100	100	100	36	NIL	NIL	NIL	NIL
85	88	84	78	56	73	64	85	69	67	76	62	10	9	13	14	37	17	28	15	8	24	21	23
63	80	73	77	70	59	75	12	57	73	89	82	19	20	9	15	—	18	25	—	43	27	—	—
32	30	29	31	29	31	28	32	28	26	27	32	37	41	36	36	35	35	39	31	35	35	33	37
5	3	7	4	7	10	5	17	9	8	7	23	80	69	65	54	62	68	73	69	73	65	60	46
7	6	12	14	8	11	12	11	12	13	13	12	89	90	84	79	84	82	83	83	79	80	82	83
56	54	63	59	57	54	61	55	58	59	65	20	20	20	16	20	21	19	21	14	18	20	14	12
—	25	12	9	23	40	67	65	38	32	21	10	—	75	76	64	38	57	—	35	50	58	62	75
45	50	46	43	44	41	35	39	35	36	35	39	41	38	40	40	40	43	46	42	41	42	42	40
22	24	24	27	28	28	28	29	31	33	32	34	48	47	45	43	40	40	42	39	36	35	34	36

*Gaol, reformatory, industrial farm, training school, penitentiary

Table 3(a)

Persons Sentenced to Institutions by Indictable Offence and by Length of Sentence for Canada, 1970*

Columns under **Sentence**: *Gaol and Reformatory (Months)[2]* = Under 1 through Indefinite; *Penitentiary (Years)* = Under 2 through Life; plus *Preventive Detention*.

Indictable Offence	Persons Sentenced to Institutions[1]	Under 1	1 to 2	2 to 3	3 to 6	6	6 to 9	9 to 12	12 to 15	15 to 18	18 to 21	21 to 24	Indefinite	Under 2	2 to 5	5 to 10	10 to 14	14 and Over	Life	Preventive Detention
Abandoning child	7	2	1	—	4	—	—	—	—	—	—	—	—	—	—	—	—	—	—	—
Abducting and kidnapping	26	—	1	2	1	—	1	—	4	—	2	3	—	—	5	1	1	1	1	—
Abortion and attempt	8	2	—	—	1	—	—	1	1	—	1	2	1	—	—	—	—	—	—	—
Assault causing bodily harm	658	150	82	58	141	83	6	26	56	3	18	12	1	—	19	—	—	—	—	—
Assault on peace officer and obstructing	519	188	117	42	88	48	8	8	13	1	3	2	—	—	6	—	—	—	—	—
Bigamy, feigned and unlawful marriage, polygamy	9	1	1	—	2	2	—	—	2	—	—	—	—	—	1	—	—	—	—	—
Buggery or bestiality, gross indecency	27	2	3	—	3	2	3	—	2	—	3	—	2	—	7	1	1	—	—	—
Causing bodily harm and danger	127	6	7	2	20	12	6	9	9	7	3	7	—	—	22	1	—	—	—	—
Common assault	126	40	22	8	25	10	8	8	5	2	3	—	—	—	2	1	—	—	—	—
Criminal negligence, bodily harm (motor vehicle)	2	1	—	—	—	—	—	—	1	—	—	—	—	—	—	—	—	—	—	—
Other criminal negligence, bodily harm	6	2	—	—	2	—	—	—	—	—	—	—	—	—	2	—	—	—	—	—
Criminal negligence, death (motor manslaughter)	11	—	1	—	1	—	—	2	2	—	1	1	—	—	3	—	—	—	—	—
Other criminal negligence, death	3	1	—	—	3	—	—	—	—	—	—	—	—	—	—	—	—	—	—	—
Criminal negligence in operation of motor vehicle	9	—	—	—	1	1	2	—	2	—	—	1	—	—	1	—	—	—	—	—
Criminal negligence, no bodily harm or death	12	2	2	—	1	1	—	1	2	—	—	—	—	—	3	1	—	—	—	—
Dangerous driving	31	8	2	3	7	9	—	—	1	—	—	1	—	—	—	—	—	—	—	—
Duties tending to preservation of life	—	—	—	—	—	—	—	—	—	—	—	—	—	—	—	—	—	—	—	—
Incest	21	1	—	—	—	3	—	—	2	—	2	1	—	—	10	1	—	—	—	—
Indecent assault on female	189	10	7	7	25	32	13	25	25	2	8	8	—	—	43	4	—	—	—	—
Indecent assault on male	32	6	2	1	4	3	3	3	3	2	2	1	—	—	5	—	—	—	—	—
Infanticide	—	—	—	—	—	—	—	—	—	—	—	—	—	—	—	—	—	—	—	—
Killing unborn child	—	—	—	—	—	—	—	—	—	—	—	—	—	—	—	—	—	—	—	—
Libel	2	2	—	—	—	2	—	—	—	—	—	—	—	—	—	—	—	—	—	—
Manslaughter	64	—	—	—	2	2	—	—	2	2	4	4	—	—	16	26	6	2	—	2
Murder, attempt to commit	5	—	—	—	—	—	—	—	2	—	—	3	—	—	1	—	1	2	—	—
Murder, capital	—	—	—	—	—	—	—	—	—	—	—	—	—	—	—	—	—	—	—	—
Murder, non-capital	37	—	—	—	—	—	—	—	—	—	—	—	—	—	—	—	—	—	37	—

Offence	Total	2	3	4	5	6	7	8	9	10	11	12	13	14	15	16	17
Neglect in childbirth and concealing dead body	—	—	—	—	—	—	—	—	—	—	—	—	—	—	—	—	—
Procuring	27	—	4	—	9	5	—	—	—	—	3	—	—	1	2	18	—
Rape, attempt to commit	40	1	—	—	—	2	—	—	—	—	—	2	—	4	2	—	—
Seduction	8	—	—	—	—	—	1	—	2	—	—	—	—	2	1	—	—
Sexual intercourse and attempt	1	—	—	—	—	—	—	—	—	—	—	—	—	—	—	—	—
Other offences against the person[3]	37	1	2	—	4	—	—	2	5	3	1	1	3	2	3	6	—
Against the person	2052	428	254	123	337	230	21	74	139	23	59	64	3	162	75	11	2
Breaking and entering a place	3450	382	158	152	530	589	38	285	476	48	125	110	4	510	33	2	2
Extortion	13	1	—	—	4	1	—	—	1	—	1	—	—	4	1	—	—
Forcible entry and detainer	—	—	—	—	—	—	—	—	—	—	—	—	—	—	—	—	—
Robbery	637	17	10	8	46	79	2	27	58	9	35	49	7	177	91	15	—
Robbery while armed	73	—	—	—	2	2	1	1	8	1	6	9	1	23	14	2	—
Against property with violence	4173	401	168	160	582	671	41	313	543	58	167	168	12	714	139	19	2
False pretences	830	176	58	43	157	147	6	39	75	2	17	17	9	83	1	—	—
Fraud and corruption	419	87	30	20	76	47	3	21	38	3	13	15	17	46	3	—	—
Fraudulently taking cattle	—	—	—	—	—	—	—	—	—	—	—	—	—	—	—	—	—
Having in possession	1317	293	89	62	266	193	16	77	121	10	35	33	10	108	3	—	—
Theft	4446	1500	423	227	717	558	40	224	329	14	60	47	13	185	5	—	—
Theft by conversion	13	7	1	1	2	2	—	—	—	—	—	—	—	—	—	—	—
Theft from mail	10	1	1	—	1	—	—	—	2	—	—	—	1	1	—	—	—
Against property without violence	7035	2064	602	353	1219	947	65	363	565	29	126	112	50	423	12	1	—
Arson and other fires	77	7	3	2	5	10	4	7	12	—	5	6	2	19	4	—	—
Other interference with property	297	117	44	25	43	30	—	2	12	—	6	8	3	10	4	—	—
Malicious offences against property	374	124	47	27	48	40	4	9	24	—	11	14	5	29	8	—	—
Forgery and uttering	640	85	36	29	96	99	9	52	80	9	16	10	14	99	6	—	—
Offences relating to currency	47	5	—	—	6	8	2	2	7	1	1	5	3	6	1	—	—
Forgery and offences relating to currency	687	90	36	29	102	107	11	54	87	10	17	15	17	105	7	—	—

*Excludes Alberta and Quebec.

Notes:

[1] Includes persons sentenced to training schools, death and reformatories in Nova Scotia and New Brunswick.

[2] Does not include persons sentenced to reformatories in Nova Scotia and New Brunswick.

[3] Includes "threatening letters".

[4] Includes "counselling or aiding suicides", "dangerous sexual offenders", "riots", "spreading false news", "trade marks".

(Table 3(a) continues on page 530.)

Table 3(a) (continued)

Persons Sentenced to Institutions by Indictable Offence and by Length of Sentence for Canada, 1970*

Indictable Offence	Persons Sentenced to Institutions[1]	Gaol and Reformatory (Months)[2]												Penitentiary (Years)						Preventive Detention
		Under 1	1 to 2	2 to 3	3 to 6	6	6 to 9	9 to 12	12 to 15	15 to 18	18 to 21	21 to 24	Indefinite	Under 2	2 to 5	5 to 10	10 to 14	14 and Over	Life	
Attempt to commit and accessories	159	30	11	12	23	28	—	9	13	1	4	2	1	—	24	1	—	—	—	—
Bawdy house, keepers	14	8	—	1	1	4	—	—	—	—	—	—	—	—	—	—	—	—	—	—
Conspiracy	112	3	3	—	5	13	1	8	20	4	5	3	4	—	33	3	5	2	—	—
Gaming, betting and lotteries	5	3	1	—	1	—	—	—	—	—	—	—	—	—	—	—	—	—	—	—
Habitual criminals	2	—	—	—	—	—	—	—	—	—	—	—	1	—	—	—	—	—	—	1
Motor vehicle: Impaired driving	12	9	—	—	1	1	—	1	—	—	—	—	—	—	—	—	—	—	—	—
Driving while disqualified	20	10	8	1	1	—	—	—	—	—	—	—	—	—	—	—	—	—	—	—
Failing to stop at scene of accident	2	1	—	—	1	—	—	—	—	—	—	—	—	—	—	—	—	—	—	—
Offences tending to corrupt morals	3	1	—	—	2	—	—	—	—	—	—	—	—	—	—	—	—	—	—	—
Offensive weapons	332	75	38	25	79	48	2	8	22	2	5	5	—	—	20	3	—	—	—	—
Perjury and false statements	33	7	4	1	11	4	3	3	2	—	—	—	—	—	1	—	—	—	—	—
Prison breach, escape and rescue	545	103	63	28	95	46	3	26	26	4	7	6	4	84	47	2	—	—	—	—
Public mischief	75	32	6	3	18	8	—	3	1	1	—	1	—	—	2	—	—	—	—	—
Various other offences[4]	4	2	—	—	1	—	—	—	—	—	—	—	—	—	—	—	—	—	—	1
Other	1318	284	134	72	238	152	6	57	84	13	21	17	9	84	127	9	5	2	—	3
Criminal code	15638	3331	1241	764	2526	2147	148	870	1442	133	389	384	94	84	1560	246	36	13	40	5

*Excludes Alberta and Quebec.

Notes:

[1] Includes persons sentenced to training schools, death and reformatories in Nova Scotia and New Brunswick.

[2] Does not include persons sentenced to reformatories in Nova Scotia and New Brunswick.

[3] Includes "threatening letters".

[4] Includes "counselling or aiding suicides", "dangerous sexual offenders", "riots", "spreading false news", "trade marks".

Table 3(b)

Persons Sentenced to Institutions by Indictable Offence and by Length of Sentence for Canada, 1971*

Indictable Offence	Persons Sentenced to Institutions[1]	Gaol and Reformatory (Months)[2]												Penitentiary (Years)						Preventive Detention
		Under 1	1 to 2	2 to 3	3 to 6	6	6 to 9	9 to 12	12 to 15	15 to 18	18 to 21	21 to 24	Indefinite	Under 2	2 to 5	5 to 10	10 to 14	14 and Over	Life	
Abandoning child	4	—	2	—	—	1	—	—	—	—	—	—	1	—	—	—	—	—	—	—
Abducting and kidnapping	33	4	2	4	4	1	—	1	2	—	—	2	—	—	11	—	—	2	—	—
Abortion and attempt	3	—	—	—	—	—	—	—	—	—	—	—	2	—	—	—	—	—	—	—
Assault causing bodily harm	664	147	65	48	176	108	2	27	33	4	9	13	5	—	26	1	—	—	—	—
Assault on peace officer and obstructing	502	242	64	43	85	36	2	4	11	2	3	2	1	—	7	—	—	—	—	—
Bigamy, feigned and unlawful marriage, polygamy	4	2	1	—	—	1	—	—	—	—	—	—	—	—	—	—	—	—	—	—
Buggery or bestiality, gross indecency	23	5	—	—	4	1	1	7	—	—	—	—	—	—	5	—	—	—	—	—
Causing bodily harm and danger	128	4	7	2	11	14	3	7	11	7	7	2	1	—	37	12	3	—	—	—
Common assault	116	40	14	5	16	17	—	3	7	1	3	3	2	—	4	1	—	—	—	—
Criminal negligence, bodily harm (motor vehicle)	—	—	—	—	—	—	—	—	—	—	—	—	—	—	—	—	—	—	—	—
Other criminal negligence, bodily harm	12	3	1	—	1	1	—	1	—	1	—	—	—	—	1	2	—	—	—	—
Criminal negligence, death (motor manslaughter)	14	—	1	—	4	3	—	1	3	1	1	—	—	—	—	—	—	—	—	—
Other criminal negligence, death	18	—	—	—	—	1	1	—	3	1	1	—	—	—	10	1	—	—	—	—
Criminal negligence in operation of motor vehicle	14	1	2	—	5	3	—	—	—	1	—	—	—	—	—	—	—	—	—	—
Criminal negligence, no bodily harm or death	9	2	1	—	—	3	—	—	—	—	1	—	—	2	—	—	—	—	—	—
Dangerous driving	26	6	2	4	5	6	2	—	1	—	—	—	—	—	—	—	—	—	—	—
Duties tending to preservation of life	—	—	—	—	—	—	—	—	—	—	—	—	—	—	—	—	—	—	—	—
Incest	9	—	—	—	—	—	2	1	—	—	—	4	—	—	2	—	—	—	—	—
Indecent assault on female	173	19	4	6	24	25	12	26	—	—	8	16	—	—	29	5	1	—	—	—
Indecent assault on male	29	5	1	—	3	4	1	—	1	—	—	5	—	—	7	1	1	—	—	—
Infanticide	2	—	—	—	1	—	—	—	—	—	—	—	—	—	—	—	—	—	—	1

*Excludes Alberta and Quebec.

Notes:

[1] Includes persons sentenced to training schools, death and reformatories in Nova Scotia and New Brunswick.

[2] Does not include persons sentenced to reformatories in Nova Scotia and New Brunswick. Therefore breakdown of sentences will not in every case total the number of persons sentenced to institutions.

[3] Includes "threatening letters".

[4] Includes "counselling or aiding suicides", "dangerous sexual offenders", "riots", "spreading false news", "trade marks".

(Table 3(b) continues on page 532.)

Table 3(b) (continued)

Persons Sentenced to Institutions by Indictable Offence and by Length of Sentence for Canada, 1971*

Indictable Offence	Persons Sentenced to Institutions[1]	Gaol and Reformatory (Months)[2]												Penitentiary (Years)						Preventive Detention
		Under 1	1 to 2	2 to 3	3 to 6	6	6 to 9	9 to 12	12 to 15	15 to 18	18 to 21	21 to 24	Indefinite	Under 2	2 to 5	5 to 10	10 to 14	14 and Over	Life	
Killing unborn child	—	—	—	—	—	—	—	—	—	—	—	—	—	—	—	—	—	—	—	—
Libel	—	—	—	—	—	—	—	—	—	—	—	—	—	—	—	—	—	—	—	—
Manslaughter	67	—	—	—	—	—	—	1	3	—	1	10	—	—	13	26	7	4	—	—
Murder, attempt to commit	10	—	—	—	—	—	—	—	—	—	—	—	—	—	2	3	1	3	1	—
Murder, capital	—	—	—	—	—	—	—	—	—	—	—	—	—	—	—	—	—	—	—	—
Murder, non-capital	27	—	—	—	—	—	—	—	—	—	—	—	—	—	—	—	—	—	27	—
Neglect in childbirth and concealing dead body	—	—	—	—	—	—	—	—	—	—	—	—	—	—	—	—	—	—	—	—
Procuring	27	4	—	—	6	5	2	2	4	—	—	—	—	—	3	—	—	—	—	—
Rape	64	—	—	—	—	—	—	—	—	2	2	9	—	—	23	19	8	1	—	—
Rape, attempt to commit	11	—	1	—	1	1	—	—	1	—	—	3	—	—	3	1	—	—	—	—
Seduction	—	—	—	—	—	—	—	—	—	—	—	—	—	—	—	—	—	—	—	—
Sexual intercourse and attempt	37	6	—	—	4	4	—	—	5	—	—	—	—	—	9	1	1	—	—	—
Other offences against the person[3]	5	—	—	—	—	—	—	—	—	—	—	1	—	—	2	—	—	—	—	—
Against the person	2031	490	169	112	354	234	11	64	117	16	40	82	12	—	196	73	22	10	28	1
Breaking and entering a place	3587	469	146	119	596	499	54	314	484	59	144	124	5	—	446	25	1	1	—	—
Extortion	31	1	—	—	3	5	—	3	6	—	3	4	—	—	6	—	—	—	—	—
Forcible entry and detainer	1	—	—	—	1	—	—	—	—	—	—	—	—	—	—	—	—	—	—	—
Robbery	694	13	13	8	41	53	5	33	83	12	46	51	3	—	177	114	31	8	—	—
Robbery while armed	42	2	2	—	—	—	—	—	2	—	6	—	1	—	13	9	5	1	—	—
Against property with violence	4355	485	159	127	642	661	59	350	575	71	199	179	9	—	642	148	37	10	—	—
False pretenses	732	200	58	45	126	100	6	40	67	7	10	12	6	—	47	6	—	—	—	—
Fraud and corruption	514	141	33	25	78	59	2	27	45	4	20	10	17	—	46	7	—	—	—	—
Fraudulently taking cattle	1	—	—	—	—	—	—	—	—	—	1	—	—	—	—	—	—	—	—	—
Having in possession	1542	414	97	86	281	218	13	103	158	16	36	24	8	—	86	2	1	—	—	—
Theft	4305	1720	353	208	724	494	34	182	263	28	71	48	15	—	152	8	—	—	—	—
Theft by conversion	10	3	—	—	—	2	—	2	1	—	1	—	—	—	—	—	—	—	—	—

Theft from mail	19	8	1	1	1	—	—	1	3	—	—	—	—	—	4	—	—	—	—
Against property without violence	7123	2486	542	366	1210	873	55	355	537	55	139	94	46	—	335	23	1	—	—
Arson and other fires	77	5	2	1	7	7	2	4	19	2	7	8	—	—	9	3	—	—	—
Other interference with property	367	176	40	25	57	26	3	7	9	1	3	2	2	—	13	—	1	—	—
Malicious offences against property	444	181	42	26	64	33	5	11	28	3	10	10	2	—	22	3	1	—	—
Forgery and uttering	649	129	39	28	87	89	15	48	65	6	29	15	9	—	79	8	1	—	—
Offences relating to currency	40	9	1	—	7	5	1	1	7	—	2	3	—	—	3	1	—	—	—
Forgery and offences relating to currency	689	138	40	28	94	94	16	49	72	6	31	18	9	—	82	9	1	—	—
Attempt to commit and accessories	129	24	7	3	30	19	4	9	13	—	4	3	—	—	12	1	—	—	—
Bawdy house, keepers	15	5	1	2	2	1	—	—	1	—	—	—	—	—	2	—	—	—	—
Conspiracy	79	2	1	1	3	4	—	2	6	1	4	11	2	—	26	12	4	—	—
Gaming, betting and lotteries	9	2	—	2	3	1	—	1	—	—	—	—	—	—	—	—	—	—	—
Habitual criminals	1	—	—	—	—	—	—	—	—	—	—	—	—	—	—	—	—	—	—
Motor vehicle: Impaired driving	17	13	2	—	1	1	—	—	—	—	—	—	—	—	—	—	—	—	—
Driving while disqualified	24	9	7	—	4	2	—	1	—	—	—	1	—	—	2	—	—	—	—
Failing to stop at scene of accident	11	1	—	—	4	1	—	—	3	—	—	—	—	—	—	—	—	—	—
Offences tending to corrupt morals	3	—	1	—	—	—	—	—	2	—	—	—	—	—	2	—	—	—	—
Offensive weapons	303	69	23	20	57	54	2	23	23	—	6	4	3	—	17	2	—	—	—
Perjury and false statements	43	16	4	—	11	1	—	2	4	—	—	2	—	—	3	—	—	—	—
Prison breach, escape and rescue	591	128	65	44	116	60	11	17	22	3	6	—	3	86	29	—	—	—	—
Public mischief	91	51	9	4	16	3	—	2	2	—	1	2	—	—	1	—	—	—	—
Various other offences[4]	18	8	1	1	7	—	—	—	1	—	—	—	—	—	—	—	—	—	—
Other	1334	328	121	77	254	147	17	58	77	4	21	23	8	86	92	15	4	22	28
Criminal code	15976	4108	1073	736	2618	2042	153	887	1406	155	440	406	86	86	1369	271	66	22	28

*Excludes Alberta and Quebec.

Notes:

[1]Includes persons sentenced to training schools, death and reformatories in Nova Scotia and New Brunswick.

[2]Does not include persons sentenced to reformatories in Nova Scotia and New Brunswick.

[3]Includes "threatening letters".

[4]Includes "counselling or aiding suicides", "dangerous sexual offenders", "riots", "spreading false news", "trade marks".

Table 3(c)

Persons Sentenced to Institutions by Indictable Offence and by Length of Sentence for Canada, 1972*

Sentence

Indictable Offence	Persons Sentenced to Institutions[1]	Gaol and Reformatory (Months)[2]											Penitentiary (Years)						
		Under 1	1 to 2	2 to 3	3 to 6	6	6 to 9	9 to 12	12 to 15	15 to 18	18 to 21	21 to 24	Indefinite	Under 2	2 to 5	5 to 10	10 to 14	14 and Over	Life	Preventive Detention
Abandoning child	5	—	—	1	4	—	—	—	—	—	—	—	—	—	—	—	—	—	—	—
Abducting and kidnapping	19	4	—	—	2	1	—	—	3	—	2	1	—	—	2	1	3	—	—	—
Abortion and attempt	1	—	1	—	—	—	—	—	—	—	—	—	—	—	—	—	—	—	—	—
Assault causing bodily harm	593	152	52	53	102	92	17	26	46	3	9	8	4	—	29	—	—	—	—	—
Assault on peace officer and obstructing	392	208	38	23	71	27	2	5	5	3	1	—	1	—	7	1	—	—	—	—
Bigamy, feigned and unlawful marriage, polygamy	6	1	—	1	3	—	—	1	—	—	—	—	—	—	—	—	—	—	—	—
Buggery or bestiality, gross indecency	22	—	1	—	7	—	—	1	—	—	—	—	—	—	2	8	3	—	—	—
Causing bodily harm and danger	114	5	2	4	14	12	—	7	17	4	7	5	1	—	25	8	3	—	—	—
Common assault	124	46	7	9	20	11	3	—	—	—	—	—	—	—	11	8	—	—	—	—
Criminal negligence, bodily harm (motor vehicle)	—	—	—	—	—	—	—	—	—	—	—	—	—	—	—	—	—	—	—	—
Other criminal negligence, bodily harm	9	2	—	—	1	2	—	—	1	—	1	1	1	—	—	—	—	—	—	—
Criminal negligence, death (motor manslaughter)	1	—	—	—	—	—	—	—	—	—	—	—	—	—	1	—	—	—	—	—
Other criminal negligence, death	17	—	—	—	5	—	—	1	1	4	1	1	—	—	3	1	—	—	—	—
Criminal negligence in operation of motor vehicle	11	2	—	1	3	—	1	—	—	2	1	—	1	—	—	—	—	—	—	—
Criminal negligence, no bodily harm or death	10	—	—	5	—	—	—	2	—	—	—	—	—	—	3	—	—	—	—	—
Dangerous driving	30	8	2	5	7	—	1	3	1	1	1	1	—	—	—	—	—	—	—	—
Duties tending to preservation of life	2	—	2	—	—	—	—	—	—	—	—	—	—	—	—	—	—	—	—	—
Incest	12	—	—	—	2	—	—	—	2	—	2	1	—	—	5	—	—	—	—	—
Indecent assault on female	169	13	5	7	30	29	4	19	16	2	2	8	—	—	27	6	—	—	—	1
Indecent assault on male	28	3	—	2	3	4	1	1	2	2	3	—	—	—	4	3	—	—	—	—
Infanticide	2	—	—	—	—	—	—	1	1	—	—	—	—	—	—	—	—	—	—	—
Killing unborn child	—	—	—	—	—	—	—	—	—	—	—	—	—	—	—	—	—	—	—	—
Libel	—	—	—	—	—	—	—	—	—	—	—	—	—	—	—	—	—	—	—	—
Manslaughter	80	—	—	2	—	—	—	—	5	2	—	6	1	—	22	27	10	3	2	—
Murder, attempt to commit	36	1	—	2	—	—	—	—	5	—	—	4	—	—	5	9	8	2	—	—
Murder, capital	—	—	—	—	—	—	—	—	—	—	—	—	—	—	—	—	—	—	—	—
Murder, non-capital	58	—	—	—	—	—	—	—	—	—	—	—	—	—	—	—	—	—	58	—

Neglect in childbirth and concealing dead body	—	—	—	—	—	—	—	—	—	—	—	—	—	—	—	—	—	—	—	—
Procuring	10	2	2	—	2	3	—	—	—	—	1	—	—	—	—	—	—	—	—	—
Rape	79	—	—	—	—	1	—	—	1	—	4	15	—	—	21	31	5	1	—	—
Rape, attempt to commit	9	—	—	—	—	—	—	1	—	—	1	2	—	—	3	2	—	—	—	—
Seduction	—	—	—	—	—	—	—	—	—	—	—	—	—	—	—	—	—	—	—	—
Sexual intercourse and attempt	26	3	1	—	3	4	—	3	2	—	2	1	—	—	7	—	—	—	—	—
Other offences against the person[3]	6	1	—	1	1	3	—	—	—	—	—	—	—	—	—	—	—	—	—	—
Against the person	1871	454	111	110	277	102	31	73	127	10	43	59	9	—	177	89	29	7	62	1
Breaking and entering a place	3165	403	100	126	491	527	64	283	427	46	155	111	10	4	384	32	1	—	—	1
Extortion	21	—	—	—	4	1	—	2	4	1	1	2	—	—	5	2	—	—	—	—
Forcible entry and detainer	2	—	—	—	2	—	—	—	—	—	—	—	—	—	—	—	—	—	—	—
Robbery	626	17	6	8	30	40	8	26	67	15	47	61	6	4	158	93	30	9	1	—
Robbery while armed	46	—	—	—	—	—	—	—	2	—	8	4	—	—	16	11	5	—	—	—
Against property with violence	3860	420	106	134	527	568	72	311	500	62	211	188	16	8	563	138	36	9	1	1
False pretences	711	207	42	38	135	102	11	27	52	4	27	10	9	—	45	—	1	—	—	—
Fraud and corruption	513	129	27	21	94	71	8	14	44	5	20	16	15	1	36	11	1	—	—	—
Fraudulently taking cattle	—	—	—	—	—	—	—	—	—	—	—	—	—	—	—	—	—	—	—	—
Having in possession	1405	376	72	74	297	201	22	90	111	15	44	20	4	2	68	7	—	—	—	—
Theft	3692	1487	272	180	681	489	47	171	227	21	42	22	18	3	123	5	1	—	—	—
Theft by conversion	4	1	1	—	—	2	—	—	—	—	—	—	—	—	—	—	—	—	—	—
Theft from mail	12	5	—	—	4	1	—	—	1	—	—	—	—	—	1	—	—	—	—	—
Against property without violence	6437	2205	414	313	1211	866	88	302	435	45	133	68	46	6	273	23	3	—	—	—
Arson and other fires	76	7	3	—	8	10	1	6	17	1	4	6	1	1	9	2	—	—	—	—
Other interference with property	327	142	36	27	41	37	2	10	9	3	1	—	6	—	9	2	—	—	—	—
Malicious offences against property	403	149	39	27	49	47	3	16	26	4	5	6	7	1	18	4	—	—	—	—
Forgery and uttering	579	121	24	21	101	86	16	46	66	8	13	12	2	—	59	4	—	—	—	—
Offences relating to currency	26	5	—	1	2	2	2	1	7	—	2	—	—	—	3	1	—	—	—	—
Forgery and offences relating to currency	605	126	24	22	103	88	18	47	73	8	15	12	2	—	62	5	—	—	—	—

*Excludes Alberta and Quebec.

Notes:

[1]Includes persons sentenced to training schools, death and reformatories in Nova Scotia and New Brunswick.

[2]Does not include persons sentenced to reformatories in Nova Scotia and New Brunswick.

[3]Includes "threatening letters".

[4]Includes "counselling or aiding suicides", "dangerous sexual offenders", "riots", "spreading false news", "trade marks".

(Table 3(c) continues on page 536.)

Table 3(c) (continued)

Persons Sentenced to Institutions by Indictable Offence and by Length of Sentence for Canada, 1972*

Indictable Offence	Persons Sentenced to Institutions[1]	Gaol and Reformatory (Months)[2]												Penitentiary (Years)						Preventive Detention
		Under 1	1 to 2	2 to 3	3 to 6	6	6 to 9	9 to 12	12 to 15	15 to 18	18 to 21	21 to 24	Inde-finite	Under 2	2 to 5	5 to 10	10 to 14	14 and Over	Life	
Attempt to commit and accessories	147	44	12	7	22	23	2	7	16	—	2	3	1	6	1	1	—	—	—	—
Bawdy house, keepers	8	3	1	—	2	2	—	—	—	—	—	—	—	—	—	—	—	—	—	—
Conspiracy	62	1	1	2	6	7	1	1	8	1	3	4	—	20	6	1	—	—	—	—
Gaming, betting and lotteries	16	11	2	1	2	—	—	—	—	—	—	—	—	—	—	—	—	—	—	—
Habitual criminals	2	—	—	—	—	—	—	—	—	—	—	—	—	—	—	—	—	—	—	2
Motor vehicle:Impaired driving	15	12	1	2	—	—	—	—	—	—	—	—	—	—	—	—	—	—	—	—
Driving while disqualified	26	16	2	1	1	2	1	1	1	—	—	—	—	—	—	—	—	—	—	—
Failing to stop at scene of accident	6	2	2	1	1	—	—	—	—	—	—	—	—	—	—	—	—	—	—	—
Offences tending to corrupt morals	—	—	—	—	—	—	—	—	—	—	—	—	—	—	—	—	—	—	—	—
Offensive weapons	338	73	33	29	69	44	7	14	26	4	7	1	1	29	1	—	—	—	—	—
Perjury and false statements	27	10	2	2	5	3	—	—	3	—	1	1	—	—	—	—	—	—	—	—
Prison breach, escape and rescue	760	156	62	38	176	119	26	52	64	13	23	1	8	19	—	—	—	—	—	—
Public mischief	64	37	6	6	5	4	—	1	4	—	—	—	1	—	—	—	—	—	—	—
Various other offences[4]	26	13	4	3	2	2	—	—	1	—	—	1	—	—	—	—	—	—	—	—
Other	1496	378	126	91	293	205	37	77	125	18	35	10	12	74	8	1	1	1	—	2
Criminal code	14673	3732	820	697	2460	1876	249	826	1286	147	442	343	92	1167	267	*69	17	—	63	4

*Excludes Alberta and Quebec.

Notes:

[1]Includes persons sentenced to training schools, death and reformatories in Nova Scotia and New Brunswick.

[2]Does not include persons sentenced to reformatories in Nova Scotia and New Brunswick.

[3]Includes "threatening letters".

[4]Includes "counselling or aiding suicides", "dangerous sexual offenders", "riots", "spreading false news", "trade marks".

Table 3(d)

Persons Sentenced to Institutions by Indictable Offence and by Length of Sentence for Canada, 1973*

Indictable Offence	Persons Sentenced to Institutions[1]	Gaol and Reformatory (Months)[2]												Penitentiary (Years)						
		Under 1	1 to 2	2 to 3	3 to 6	6	6 to 9	9 to 12	12 to 15	15 to 18	18 to 21	21 to 24	Inde-finite	Under 2	2 to 5	5 to 10	10 to 14	14 and Over	Life	Preventive Detention
Abandoning child	2	—	—	—	1	1	—	—	—	—	—	—	—	—	—	—	—	—	—	—
Abducting and kidnapping	34	3	2	8	2	3	1	2	1	—	2	—	—	—	7	2	—	1	—	—
Abortion and attempt	—	—	—	—	—	—	—	—	—	—	—	—	—	—	—	—	—	—	—	—
Assault causing bodily harm	595	132	57	48	139	72	4	26	45	4	17	7	4	—	31	8	—	—	—	—
Assault on peace officer and obstructing	255	113	33	18	54	23	3	—	2	1	1	1	—	—	6	—	—	—	—	—
Bigamy, feigned and unlawful marriage, polygamy	3	—	1	—	—	2	—	—	—	—	—	—	—	—	—	—	—	—	—	—
Buggery or bestiality, gross indecency	22	6	1	—	6	2	—	2	—	4	—	1	—	—	—	—	—	—	—	—
Causing bodily harm and danger	106	5	1	2	8	12	1	6	3	3	7	5	2	—	25	10	—	1	—	—
Common assault	35	—	8	—	4	6	1	2	1	—	2	—	—	—	1	—	—	—	—	—
Criminal negligence, bodily harm (motor vehicle)	7	1	—	—	—	—	1	1	—	—	1	—	—	—	—	—	—	—	—	—
Other criminal negligence, bodily harm	3	—	—	1	—	—	1	1	—	—	—	—	—	—	—	—	—	—	—	—
Criminal negligence, death (motor manslaughter)	14	1	1	—	3	1	1	—	—	1	1	3	—	—	—	—	—	1	—	—
Other criminal negligence, death	7	1	1	1	3	1	—	—	—	—	—	—	—	—	—	—	—	—	—	—
Criminal negligence in operation of motor vehicle	32	5	3	3	9	1	5	—	2	—	—	1	—	—	2	—	—	—	—	—
Criminal negligence, no bodily harm or death	18	1	—	2	6	2	1	1	2	—	1	—	—	—	2	—	—	—	—	—
Dangerous driving	—	—	—	—	—	—	—	—	—	—	—	—	—	—	—	—	—	—	—	—
Duties tending to preservation of life	1	—	—	—	1	—	—	—	—	—	—	—	—	—	—	—	—	—	—	—
Incest	14	—	—	—	1	1	—	2	1	1	1	—	—	—	3	2	1	—	—	—
Indecent assault on female	137	—	—	—	27	19	8	7	15	1	8	9	—	—	12	2	—	—	—	—
Indecent assault on male	26	13	7	9	4	—	1	1	—	—	2	—	—	—	7	—	—	—	—	—
Infanticide	—	—	—	—	—	—	—	—	—	—	—	—	—	—	—	—	—	—	—	—

*Excludes Alberta and Quebec.

Notes:

[1] Includes persons sentenced to training schools, death and reformatories in Nova Scotia and New Brunswick.

[2] Does not include persons sentenced to reformatories in Nova Scotia and New Brunswick.

[3] Includes "threatening letters".

[4] Includes "counselling or aiding suicides", "riots", "dangerous sexual offenders", "spreading false news", "trade marks".

(Table 3(d) continues on page 538.)

Table 3(d) (continued)

Persons Sentenced to Institutions by Indictable Offence and by Length of Sentence for Canada, 1973*

Column groups: columns "Under 1" through "Inde-finite" = **Sentence — Gaol and Reformatory (Months)[2]**; columns "Under 2" through "Life" = **Penitentiary (Years)**; last column = **Preventive Detention**.

Indictable Offence	Persons Sentenced to Institutions[1]	Under 1	1 to 2	2 to 3	3 to 6	6	6 to 9	9 to 12	12 to 15	15 to 18	18 to 21	21 to 24	Inde-finite	Under 2	2 to 5	5 to 10	10 to 14	14 and Over	Life	Preventive Detention
Killing unborn child	2	1	1	—	—	—	—	—	—	—	—	—	—	—	—	—	—	—	—	—
Libel	—	—	—	—	—	—	—	—	—	—	—	—	—	—	—	—	—	—	—	—
Manslaughter	84	—	—	—	—	—	—	—	—	—	6	3	—	—	26	34	5	5	—	—
Murder, attempt to commit	24	—	—	2	—	—	—	1	1	—	1	—	—	—	6	7	3	2	1	—
Murder, capital	—	—	—	—	—	—	—	—	—	—	—	—	—	—	—	—	—	—	—	—
Murder, non-capital	38	—	—	—	—	—	—	—	—	—	—	—	—	—	—	—	—	—	38	—
Neglect in childbirth and concealing dead body	2	1	1	—	—	—	—	—	—	—	—	—	—	—	—	—	—	—	—	—
Procuring	7	—	1	—	2	—	—	—	—	—	—	—	—	—	—	—	—	—	—	—
Rape	62	—	—	—	—	—	—	—	—	2	1	3	—	—	21	29	3	—	1	—
Rape, attempt to commit	6	—	—	—	2	—	—	—	—	—	—	—	—	—	1	2	—	—	—	—
Seduction	—	—	—	—	—	—	—	—	—	—	—	—	—	—	—	—	—	—	—	—
Sexual intercourse and attempt	21	—	—	—	4	—	1	2	2	1	—	—	—	—	1	1	—	—	—	—
Other offences against the person[3]	12	2	—	—	5	1	2	—	—	—	—	—	—	—	2	—	—	—	—	—
Against the person	1568	286	117	93	283	152	21	59	105	18	60	43	7	—	155	97	12	8	40	—
Breaking and entering a place	3032	374	114	103	457	542	51	286	419	49	142	92	12	—	375	18	1	1	—	—
Extortion	6	—	—	—	1	1	—	—	1	—	—	—	—	—	2	—	—	1	—	—
Forcible entry and detainer	—	—	—	—	—	—	—	—	—	—	—	—	—	—	—	—	—	—	—	—
Robbery	674	15	8	10	39	60	7	35	102	14	34	75	5	—	163	82	19	5	—	—
Robbery while armed	80	—	—	2	3	5	4	2	2	1	3	12	—	—	20	19	7	1	—	—
Against property with violence	3792	391	122	115	499	608	59	326	518	64	179	179	17	—	559	119	27	7	—	—
False pretenses	627	147	50	46	115	89	11	35	47	6	23	13	16	—	28	1	—	—	—	—
Fraud and corruption	420	96	21	21	73	51	6	22	43	5	17	8	17	—	32	7	1	—	—	—
Fraudulently taking cattle	2	1	—	—	—	—	—	—	—	—	1	—	—	—	—	—	—	—	—	—
Having in possession	1457	293	135	84	310	234	18	96	130	17	40	20	10	—	67	3	—	—	—	—
Theft	3559	1159	416	215	624	485	37	192	220	20	44	28	32	—	83	3	1	—	—	—
Theft by conversion	6	1	—	2	—	—	—	—	—	—	—	—	—	—	2	—	1	—	—	—

Theft from mail	10	4	—	1	—	2	—	—	—	—	2	—	—	—	—	—	—	—	—	—
Against property without violence	6081	1701	622	367	1124	861	72	346	440	48	127	69	75	—	213	14	1	2	—	—
Arson and other fires	72	5	—	4	13	9	1	—	9	1	5	7	1	—	13	2	—	—	—	—
Other interference with property	208	50	29	16	52	30	2	8	5	1	1	2	1	—	9	—	—	—	—	—
Malicious offences against property	280	55	29	20	65	39	3	12	14	6	6	9	8	—	22	4	—	—	—	—
Forgery and uttering	481	83	32	16	79	72	11	23	59	—	18	13	8	—	58	2	1	—	—	—
Offences relating to currency	28	2	1	—	2	4	2	2	3	6	—	—	—	—	11	—	1	—	—	—
Forgery and offences relating to currency	509	85	33	16	81	76	13	25	62	6	18	13	8	—	69	2	1	—	—	—
Attempt to commit and accessories	206	40	21	9	32	35	4	11	17	3	7	4	2	—	20	—	1	—	—	—
Bawdy house, keepers	3	—	2	—	—	—	—	—	—	—	1	1	1	—	—	—	—	—	—	—
Conspiracy	92	3	3	3	11	12	—	5	9	—	6	9	2	—	19	7	—	2	—	—
Gaming, betting and lotteries	13	3	2	4	1	—	—	1	—	—	1	—	—	—	1	—	1	—	—	—
Habitual criminals	2	—	—	—	—	—	—	—	—	—	—	—	—	—	—	—	—	—	—	—
Motor vehicle: Impaired driving	9	2	1	2	3	1	—	1	1	—	1	—	—	—	—	—	1	—	—	—
Driving while disqualified	43	25	2	5	6	1	—	—	—	—	—	—	—	—	1	—	—	—	—	—
Failing to stop at scene of accident	3	2	—	—	1	—	—	—	—	—	—	—	—	—	—	—	—	—	—	—
Offences tending to corrupt morals	—	—	—	—	—	—	—	—	—	—	—	—	—	—	—	—	—	—	—	—
Offensive weapons	369	77	26	20	73	57	5	22	22	1	8	9	3	—	13	3	—	—	—	—
Perjury and false statements	18	3	—	1	3	5	3	3	1	—	—	1	—	—	—	—	—	—	—	—
Prison breach, escape and rescue	613	111	71	42	132	106	21	33	44	5	14	1	1	7	25	1	1	—	7	—
Public mischief	26	13	4	5	3	—	—	—	1	—	—	—	—	—	1	—	—	—	—	—
Various other offences⁴	15	4	2	1	—	1	—	—	1	—	—	1	—	—	1	—	—	—	—	1
Other	1379	283	134	92	265	218	30	76	95	9	36	25	10	7	82	10	2	2	2	3
Criminal code	13609	2801	1057	703	2317	1954	198	844	1240	146	426	338	118	7	1100	246	43	17	40	3

*Excludes Alberta and Quebec.

Notes:

¹Includes persons sentenced to training schools, death and reformatories in Nova Scotia and New Brunswick.

²Does not include persons sentenced to reformatories in Nova Scotia and New Brunswick.

³Includes "threatening letters".

⁴Includes "counselling or aiding suicides", "dangerous sexual offenders", "riots", "spreading false news", "trade marks". The remainder are from Nova Scotia and New Brunswick statistics which are not included under sentences.

Index